International Relations

International Relations

Twelfth Edition

Jon C. W. Pevehouse
University of Wisconsin–Madison

Joshua S. Goldstein
American University, Washington, DC
University of Massachusetts Amherst

 Pearson

Executive Portfolio Manager: Jeff Marshall
Content Producer: Mary Donovan
Content Developer: Julie McBurney
Portfolio Manager Assistant: Christina Winterburn
Product Marketer: Candice Madden
Field Marketer: Alexa Macri
Content Producer Manager: Amber Mackey
Content Development Manager: Rebecca Green
Art/Designer: iEnergizer Aptara®, Ltd.
Digital Studio Course Producer: Heather Pagano
Full-Service Project Manager: iEnergizer Aptara®, Ltd.
Compositor: iEnergizer Aptara®, Ltd.
Printer/Binder: LSC Communications, Inc.
Cover Printer: LSC Communications, Inc.
Cover Design: Jill Ort
Cover Credit: ArtisticPhoto/Shutterstock

Library of Congress Cataloging-in-Publication Data

Names: Pevehouse, Jon C., author. | Goldstein, Joshua S., author.
Title: International relations / Jon C.W. Pevehouse, Joshua S. Goldstein.
Description: Twelfth edition. | [Hoboken, New Jersey] : Pearson, [2020] |
    "This twelfth edition was written by Jon C. W. Pevehouse based on
    International Relations, 2013-2014 update by Joshua S. Goldstein and Jon
    C. W. Pevehouse." | Includes bibliographical references and index.
Identifiers: LCCN 2018037571 | ISBN 9780135229255 (Student Edition) |
    ISBN 0135229251 (Student Edition) | ISBN 9780135229552 (Instructor's Review Copy) |
    ISBN 0135229553 (Instructor's Review Copy) | ISBN 9780135247716
    (Loose-leaf Version) | ISBN 0135247713 (Loose-leaf Version)
Subjects: LCSH: International relations.
Classification: LCC JZ1242 .P49 2019 | DDC 327—dc23 LC record available at
    https://lccn.loc.gov/2018037571

Access Code Card
ISBN 10:   0-13-517661-1
ISBN 13: 978-0-13-517661-0

Revel Combo Card
ISBN 10:   0-13-556054-3
ISBN 13: 978-0-13-556054-9

Student Edition
ISBN 10:   0-13-522925-1
ISBN 13: 978-0-13-522925-5

Instructor's Review Copy
ISBN 10:   0-13-522955-3
ISBN 13: 978-0-13-522955-2

Loose-Leaf Edition
ISBN 10:   0-13-524771-3
ISBN 13: 978-0-13-524771-6

1   18

For our children—Solomon and Ruth; Claire, Ava, Carl, and Stephanie

Brief Contents

Contents

START HERE

Preface

We live in an increasingly interconnected world. These connections bring great benefits to our everyday lives: the ability to communicate instantaneously around the world and to share our cultures and beliefs; the possibility of directly helping a person affected by an earthquake through a global network of charities; and the ability to purchase a product made from parts manufactured in a dozen different countries, each using its specialized knowledge to create a better product. There are many potential benefits to an interconnected world. Yet these connections may also worsen existing problems: Terrorist networks use the Internet to coordinate and carry out attacks, global commerce can put undue strain on our natural environment, and millions of people still live with few global connections that are enjoyed by citizens of wealthier countries. In recent years, these interconnections have led some to feel vulnerable and reject these global relationships in favor of local or national interactions.

Despite these increasing connections and their implications for everyday life, many students begin college misinformed about basic facts of international relations (IR), such as the extent of poverty and levels of foreign assistance given to the developing world, and the trend toward fewer wars over the past two decades. An introductory book plays a key role in students' education about international affairs, and we have worked hard to make the twelfth edition of *International Relations* timely, accurate, visually appealing, and intellectually engaging. We hope this book can help a generation develop knowledge and critical thinking so that it can find its voice and place in the changing world.

IR is not only an important topic but also a fascinating one. The rich complexity of international relationships—political, economic, and cultural—provides a puzzle to try to understand. The puzzle is not only intellectually challenging but also emotionally powerful. It contains human-scale stories in which the subject's grand themes, such as war and peace, intergroup conflict and community, integration and division, humans and their environment, poverty and development, play out.

New to the Twelfth Edition

The twelfth edition of *International Relations* includes important revisions throughout to keep the book current in a time of extensive changes and uncertainties in the international system. A theme now developed throughout the book is the growing backlash against globalization and the institutions that have supported its advance. This backlash has resulted in Great Britain's decision to exit from the European Union, the election of an American president challenging the global order, and growing populism and nationalism around the world.

A major new feature in this edition, Public Opinion and International Relations, discusses the status of public opinion on major issues of international relations. In some chapters, the feature examines public opinion within the United States on a current controversy discussed in the chapter. Those "within country" variations examine shifts in opinion over time on topics such as support for NATO or support for foreign aid. In other chapters, the feature takes an "across countries" approach, examining a single point in time across numerous countries to compare what different publics think about issues ranging from the threat of cyberattacks to foreign business relations. Given this edition's theme of rising populism and nationalism, it is important to know the status of public opinion on important issues. The growing availability of reliable public opinion polling data from around the world gives us the opportunity to discover more about trends in public views on international relations. In some cases, you may be surprised at how different countries view the same topic or how opinion in the United States has changed over time. Each feature analyzes the trends within the data, using insights from material presented in that chapter.

In addition, we have moved the popular Careers in International Relations features from the appendix into relevant chapters. For example, the feature on careers in business is now in Chapter 9 in the midst of the discussion of multinational businesses. We have added a new Careers feature, discussing international law, to Chapter 7. We hope these features will give students some guidance and resources concerning jobs in the field of international relations.

Chapter 1:

- Completely updated economic and demographic data
- Reformulation of the levels of analysis discussion
- Updates on Great Britain's planned exit from the European Union, the 2016 U.S. presidential election, and the implications of those events for international relations
- Updates on the status of Middle East conflicts, including those in Syria, Libya, Yemen, and the resulting refugee crises arising from those conflicts
- Updates on China's military efforts in the South China Sea
- Updates on North Korea's nuclear program and relations between the United States and North Korea

Chapter 2:

- Discussion of U.S. tensions with the North Atlantic Treaty Organization (NATO)
- Updates on NATO's mission in Afghanistan
- Discussion of tensions over Russian annexation of Crimea

Chapter 3:

- Updated Policy Perspectives box feature
- Updated discussion of the waning of war
- Updates on violence in the Middle East, especially in Syria and Yemen

Chapter 4:

- Revised Policy Perspectives box feature
- Revised discussion of controversial Iran nuclear deal

Chapter 5:

- Revised listing of wars in the world
- Revised discussion of Islamic groups, including the rise and fall of the Islamic State in Iraq and Syria (ISIS)
- New Policy Perspectives box feature
- Updated discussion of civil wars in Syria and Yemen
- Revised discussion of maritime tensions in East Asia

Chapter 6:

- Completely updated data on military forces worldwide
- New section on evolving technologies, discussing drones and cyberwarfare
- New discussion of North Korean nuclear crisis
- New Policy Perspectives box feature
- Revised Let's Debate the Issue box feature

Chapter 7:

- Completely updated data on and discussion of current UN peacekeeping efforts
- Updated data on status of ratifications of UN human rights treaties
- Updated discussion of International Criminal Court controversies
- Discussion of new UN Treaty on enforced disappearance
- Revised Policy Perspectives box feature

Chapter 8:

- Updated data on and discussion of the recovery from the global economic crisis of 2008–2009
- Discussion of the controversial exit of the United States from the Transatlantic and Trans-Pacific trade agreements
- Updated discussion on the failure of the Doha Round of trade negotiations over new World Trade Organization mandates
- Discussion of the Trump administration's tariffs, including other countries' responses and the growing concerns of a global trade war set off by these tariffs
- New Policy Perspectives box feature

Chapter 9:

- New and updated data on global economic trends in international finance
- Updated discussions of state economic positions in the global economy, including U.S. debt and Russia's troubles
- New Policy Perspectives box feature
- Revised discussion of virtual currencies such as bitcoin

Chapter 10:

- Discussion of Great Britain's decision to exit the EU and the future of the EU without Great Britain
- Discussion of the EU immigration crisis and response
- Revised discussion of the global digital divide, including updated data
- Discussion of state control of the Internet in authoritarian countries

Chapter 11:

- Discussion of the Paris climate treaty and U.S. withdrawal from the treaty by the Trump administration
- Discussion of China's relaxation of the one child policy
- Discussion of South Africa's water crisis
- Revised Seeking the Collective Good box feature
- New Policy Perspectives box feature

Chapter 12:

- Completely updated data on global development
- Discussion of the UN Sustainable Development Goals (SDGs)
- Updated discussion of increase in numbers of global refugees
- Revised Policy Perspectives box feature

Chapter 13:

- Updated discussion on developments in BRIC countries (Brazil, Russia, India, China)
- New Policy Perspectives box feature
- Discussion of the Asian Infrastructure Investment Bank and its role in development
- Revised discussion of foreign assistance

In all chapters, we have updated the tables and figures with the most recent available data. This includes new data on gross domestic product (GDP), military forces, migration and refugees, debt, remittances, foreign aid, the HIV/AIDS epidemic, and UN peacekeeping operations, to name a few.

Finally, this twelfth edition of *International Relations* revises the photo program substantially. Dozens of new photos, many from 2017 and 2018, draw visual attention to current events while reinforcing key concepts in the book.

Structure of the Book

This book aims to present the current state of knowledge in IR in a comprehensive and accessible way—to provide a map of the subject covering its various research communities in a logical order. This map is organized around the subfields of international security and international political economy (IPE). These subfields, although separated physically in this book, are integrated conceptually and overlap in many ways. Common core principles—dominance, reciprocity, and identity—unify the book by showing how theoretical models apply across the range of topics in international security and political economy.

The overall structure of this book follows substantive topics, first in international security and then in international political economy. Chapter 1 introduces the study of IR; explains the collective goods problem and the core principles of dominance, reciprocity, and identity; and provides some geographical and historical context for the subject. The historical perspective places recent trends, especially globalization, in the context of the evolution of the international system over the twentieth century, while the global orientation reflects the diversity of IR experiences for different actors, especially those in the global South. Chapters 2 and 3 lay out the various theoretical approaches to IR: realism, liberal theories, social theories (constructivist, postmodern, and Marxist), peace studies, and gender theories.

Chapter 4 discusses the formulation and implementation of foreign policy, including a discussion of the key institutions involved in that process. Chapter 5 introduces the main sources of international conflict, including ethnic, religious, territorial, and economic conflicts. Chapter 6, on military force and terrorism, discusses the conditions and manner in which such conflicts lead to the use of violence. Chapter 7 shows how international organizations and law, especially the United Nations, have evolved to become major influences in security relations, and how human rights have become increasingly important. The study of international organizations also bridges international security topics with those in international political economy.

The remaining chapters move through the various topics that make up the study of international political economy, beginning with microeconomic principles and national economies through trade and finance; international integration; the environment; and North-South relations, focusing heavily on development. Chapter 8 introduces theoretical concepts in political economy (showing how theories of international security translate into IPE issue areas) and discusses the most important topic in international political economy, namely, trade relations. Chapter 9 describes the politics of global finance and multinational business operations in an era of globalization. Chapter 10 explores the processes of international integration, telecommunications, and cultural exchange on both a regional scale—the European Union—and a global one. Chapter 11 shows how environmental politics and population growth expand international bargaining and interdependence both regionally and globally. Chapter 12 addresses global North-South relations, with particular attention given to poverty in the global South. Chapter 13 then considers alternatives for economic development in the context of international business, debt, and foreign aid. Chapter 14—a brief postscript—reflects on the book's central themes and encourages critical thinking about the future.

Pedagogical Elements

In a subject such as IR, in which knowledge is tentative and empirical developments can overtake theories, critical thinking is a key skill for college students to develop. At various points in the book, conclusions are left open-ended to let students reason their way through an issue, and in addition to the critical thinking questions at the end of each chapter, the boxed features support deeper and more focused critical thinking.

Seeking the Collective Good

These boxes focus on the core organizing concept of the book: the collective goods problem. Each box discusses a collective good and the problems encountered by states in attempting to achieve cooperation to provide the good. In each example, we highlight how one or more of the core principles (dominance, reciprocity, and identity) have been used successfully (or unsuccessfully) in the provision of the good.

Public Opinion and International Relations

This new feature discusses the status of public opinion on major issues of international relations. In some chapters, the feature examines public opinion within the United States, while in other chapters the feature examines opinion across countries. Given this edition's theme of rising populism and nationalism, it is important to know what the status of public opinion is on important global issues. The growing availability of reliable public opinion polling data from around the world gives us the opportunity to discover more about how publics view international relations topics.

Policy Perspectives

This feature in each chapter places students in the decision-making perspective of a national leader. The feature bridges international relations theory to policy problems while demonstrating the trade-offs often present in political decision making and highlighting the interconnectedness of foreign and domestic politics.

Let's Debate the Issue

These boxes help students think through controversial topics. The topic in each chapter is chosen to expand important concepts discussed in that chapter. Thus, this feature deepens the treatment of particular topics while reinforcing the general themes in each chapter.

Careers in International Relations

Finally, the Careers in International Relations feature helps students think about job possibilities in the field. The feature (in appropriate chapters) is devoted to careers in nongovernmental organizations, international law, government and diplomacy, international business, and teaching and research. It responds to the question, "How will this class help me find a job?" and includes books and Web sites to pursue the issue further.

Many people find information—especially abstract concepts—easier to grasp when linked with pictures. Thus, the book uses color photographs extensively to illustrate important points. Photo captions reinforce main themes from each section of the book and link them with the scenes pictured. Many of the photos in this edition are recent, taken in 2017 and 2018.

Students use different learning styles. Students who are visual learners should find not only the photos but also the many color graphics especially useful. The use of quantitative data also encourages critical thinking. Basic data, presented simply and appropriately at a global level, allow students to form their own judgments and to reason through the implications of different policies and theories. The book uses global-level data (showing the whole picture), rounds off numbers to highlight what is important, and conveys information graphically where appropriate.

IR is a large subject that offers many directions for further exploration. The Suggested Readings list additional sources for extra reading on various topics. Unless otherwise noted, they are not traditional source notes. (Also, to save space in the notes, publisher locations are omitted and major university or state names refer to their university presses, although this is not a correct research paper style.)

Jon C. W. Pevehouse
Joshua S. Goldstein

Revel™

Revel is an interactive learning environment that deeply engages students and prepares them for class. Media and assessment integrated directly within the authors' narrative lets students read, explore interactive content, and practice in one continuous learning path. Thanks to the dynamic reading experience in Revel, students come to class prepared to discuss, apply, and learn from instructors and from each other.

Learn more about Revel

www.pearson.com/revel

- Chapter-opening **Current Events Bulletins** feature author-written articles that put breaking news and current events into the context of international relations. Examples include the Paris Climate Agreement, U.S. trade tensions with China, Brexit negotiations, the civil war in Yemen, U.S. negotiations with North Korea, and the rise of virtual currencies.

- **Videos** bring to life chapter contents and key moments in international relations. News footage provides examples from both current and historical events, including tensions in the South China Sea, the conflict in Kashmir, anti-globalization movements, international trade tensions, conflict in Burma, and the military coup in Zimbabwe, among many others.

- **Social Explorer interactive maps and figures** allow frequent updates with the latest data toggles to illustrate movement over time, rollover data that students can explore, and critical thinking questions, increasing students' data literacy and analysis skills.

- **Review the Chapter** interactive summaries tied to the learning objectives and **Key Term Flashcards** allow students to review the chapters and reinforce the content.
- **Assessments** tied to primary chapter sections, as well as full chapter exams, allow instructors and students to track progress and get immediate feedback.
- **Integrated Writing Opportunities**, helping students reason and write more clearly, are offered in two forms of writing prompts in each chapter:
  ○ **Journal prompts** ask students to think critically and apply what they have learned after each special feature.
  ○ **Shared writing prompts** encourage students to consider how to address challenges described in the chapter. Through these prompts, instructors and students can deal with multiple sides of an issue by sharing their own views and responding to each other's viewpoints.
  ○ **Essay prompts** are from Pearson's Writing Space, where instructors can assign both automatically graded and instructor-graded prompts. Writing Space is the best way to develop and assess concept mastery and critical thinking through writing. Writing Space provides a single place within Revel to create, track, and grade writing assignments; access writing resources; and exchange meaningful, personalized feedback quickly and easily to improve results.

Learning Management Systems

Pearson provides Blackboard Learn™, Canvas™, Brightspace by D2L, and Moodle integration, giving institutions, instructors, and students easy access to Revel. Our Revel integration delivers streamlined access to everything your students need for the course in these learning management system (LMS) environments. Single Sign-on: With single sign-on, students are ready on their first day. From your LMS course, students have easy access to an interactive blend of authors' narrative, media, and assessment. Grade Sync: Flexible, on-demand grade synchronization capabilities allow you to control exactly which Revel grades should be transferred to the LMS gradebook.

Revel Combo Card

The Revel Combo Card provides an all-in-one access code and loose-leaf print reference (delivered by mail).

Supplements

Make more time to engage with your students with instructor resources that offer effective learning assessments and classroom engagement. Pearson's partnership with educators does not end with the delivery of course materials; Pearson is there with you on the first day of class and beyond. A dedicated team of local Pearson representatives will work with you to not only choose course materials but also integrate them into your class and assess their effectiveness. Our goal is your goal—to improve instruction with each semester.

Pearson is pleased to offer the following resources to qualified adopters of *International Relations*. Several of these supplements are available for instant download on the Instructor Resource Center (IRC); please visit the IRC at **www.pearsonhighered.com/irc** to register for access.

- **Test Bank**
  Evaluate learning at every level. Reviewed for clarity and accuracy, the Test Bank measures this material's learning objectives with multiple-choice and essay

questions. You can easily customize the assessment to work in any major learning management system and to match what is covered in your course. Word, Black-Board, and WebCT versions are available on the IRC, and Respondus versions are available on request from **www.respondus.com**.

- **Pearson MyTest**
  This powerful assessment generation program includes all of the questions in the Test Bank. Quizzes and exams can be easily authored and saved online, and then printed for classroom use, giving you ultimate flexibility to manage assessments anytime and anywhere. To learn more, visit **www.pearsonhighered.com/mytest**.

- **Instructor's Resource Manual**
  Create a comprehensive road map for teaching classroom, online, or hybrid courses. Designed for new and experienced instructors, the Instructor's Resource Manual includes learning objectives; lecture and discussion suggestions; activities for in or out of class; research activities; participation activities; and suggested readings, series, and films as well as a Revel features section. Available within Revel and on the IRC.

- **PowerPoint Presentation**
  Make lectures more enriching for students. The PowerPoint Presentation includes a full lecture outline and figures from the book and Revel edition. All PowerPoints are ADA compliant. Available within Revel and on the IRC.

- **LiveSlides**
  Social Explorers are data-rich interactive maps and figures that enable students to visually explore demographic data to understand how local trends impact them while improving their data and statistical literacy. LiveSlides are dynamic lecture slides that give you a direct path to all the Social Explorers within your Revel course. Available within Revel and on the IRC.

Acknowledgments

Many scholars, colleagues, and friends have contributed ideas that ultimately influenced the twelve editions of this book. The book owes a special debt to the late Robert C. North, who suggested many years ago that the concepts of bargaining and leverage could be used to integrate IR theory across levels of analysis. For help with military data issues, we thank the late Randall Forsberg. For suggestions, we thank our colleagues and the students in our world politics classes. For help with data research, we thank Sujeong Shim and Micah Dillard. Finally, we appreciate the years of support we received from our late colleague, teacher, and friend Deborah "Misty" Gerner.

The following reviewers made many useful suggestions for the twelfth edition: Todd Allee, University of Maryland; Yury Bosin, University of New Mexico; Caroline Holley, University at Buffalo, SUNY; David Jesuit, Central Michigan University; Johannes Karreth, Ursinus College; Ches Thurber, Northern Illinois University; Daniel Tirone, Louisiana State University; and Raluca Viman Miller, University of North Georgia.

The errors, of course, remain our own responsibility.

About the Authors

Jon C. W. Pevehouse is Vilas Distinguished Achievement Professor of Political Science at the University of Wisconsin–Madison. He is an award-winning teacher and scholar. His research interests focus on international political economy, foreign policy, and international organizations. He is the former editor of the leading professional journal in the field, *International Organization*. He received his BA from the University of Kansas and his Ph.D. from Ohio State University.

Joshua S. Goldstein is Professor Emeritus of International Relations, American University (Washington, DC) and Research Scholar, University of Massachusetts Amherst. He is an award-winning scholar who has written and spoken widely on war and society, including war's effects on gender, economics, and psychological trauma. His book *War and Gender* won the International Studies Association's Book of the Decade award.

To the Student

The topics studied by scholars are like a landscape with many varied locations and terrains. This book is a map that can orient you to the main topics, debates, and issue areas in international relations. Scholars use specialized language to talk about their subjects. This book is a phrase book that can translate such lingo and explain the terms and concepts that scholars use to talk about international relations. However, IR is filled with many voices speaking many tongues. The book translates some of those voices—of presidents and professors, free traders and feminists—to help you sort out the contours of the subject and the state of knowledge about its various topics. In this twelfth edition of *International Relations*, we have especially tried to streamline and clarify this complex subject to help you not just understand but deeply understand international relations. Ultimately, however, the synthesis presented in this book is that of the authors. Both you and your professor may disagree with many points. Thus, this book is only a starting point for conversations and debates.

With a combined map and phrase book in hand, you are ready to explore a fascinating world. The great changes taking place in world politics have made the writing of this book an exciting project. May you enjoy your own explorations of this realm.

J. C. W. P.
J. S. G.

A Note on Nomenclature

In international relations, names are politically sensitive; different actors may call a territory or an event by different names. This book cannot resolve such conflicts; it has adopted the following naming conventions for the sake of consistency. The United Kingdom of Great Britain (England, Scotland, Wales) and Northern Ireland is called Britain. Burma, renamed Myanmar by its military government, is referred to as Burma. The country of Bosnia and Herzegovina is generally shortened to Bosnia (with apologies to Herzegovinians). The former Yugoslav Republic of Macedonia is called Macedonia. The People's Republic of China is referred to as China. The Democratic Republic of the Congo (formerly called the Belgian Congo and then Zaire) is here called Democratic Congo. We refer to Cote D'Ivoire as Ivory Coast. Elsewhere, country names follow common usage, dropping formal designations such as "Republic of." We refer to the Sea of Japan, which some call the East Sea, and to the Persian Gulf, which is also called the Arabian Gulf. The 1991 U.S.-led multinational military campaign that retook Kuwait after Iraq's 1990 invasion is called the Gulf War, and the U.S. war in Iraq after 2003 is called the Iraq War. The war between Iran and Iraq in the 1980s is called the Iran-Iraq War.

[Handwritten annotations:]

Invasion of
Golf War = Iraq's War 1990 - Kuwait
2003 Iraq War \\ Iran-Iraq War 1980s,

Burma [Myanmar]

Bosnia and Herzegovina = [Bosnia]

Yugoslav Republic of Macedonia = [Macedonia]

People's Republic of China is called = [China]

Democratic Rep. of Congo = (formally called the Belgian Congo and the Zaire) = Democratic Congo

Cote D'Ivore = Ivory Coast

Sea of Japan = East Sea = Sea of Japan

Persian Golf = Arabian Golf

Maps

World States and Territories

U.S.A.

BAHAMAS

CUBA

HAITI

DOMINICAN REPUBLIC

PUERTO RICO

VIRGIN ISLANDS

JAMAICA

BARBUDA

MEXICO

BELIZE

ST. KITTS AND NEVIS

ANTIGUA

HONDURAS

DOMINICA

BARBADOS

NICARAGUA

MARTINIQUE

GUATEMALA

NETHERLANDS ANTILLES

ST. VINCENT AND
THE GRENADINES

ST. LUCIA

EL SALVADOR

GRENADA

COSTA RICA

TRINIDAD
AND
TOBAGO

PANAMA

COLOMBIA

VENEZUELA

ARCTIC OCEAN

GREENLAND
(DANISH)

ICELAND

U.S.

CANADA

ATLANTIC OCEAN

PACIFIC OCEAN

UNITED STATES

BERMUDA

TURKEY

CYPRUS

LEBANON

MEXICO

MOROCCO

TUNISIA

ISRAEL

WESTERN SAHARA

ALGERIA

LIBYA

EGYPT

MALI

SENEGAL

MAURITANIA

NIGER

CHAD

SUDAN

NIGER

CAPE VERDE

GAMBIA

MALI

CENTRAL
AFRICAN
REP.

BURKINA
FASO

GUINEA BISSAU

GUINEA

SURINAME

SOUTH
SUDAN

NIGERIA

SIERRA LEONE

FRENCH
GUIANA

CÔTE
D'IVOIRE

LIBERIA

COLOMBIA

UGANDA

RWANDA

BURUNDI

ECUADOR

GUYANA

DEM. CONGO

TAN

TOGO

GHANA

BENIN

CAMEROON

PERU

BRAZIL

ANGOLA

SAO TOME AND PRINCIPE

ZAMBIA

EQUATORIAL GUINEA

GABON

BOLIVIA

CONGO

PARAGUAY

BOTSWANA

CHILE

ATLANTIC OCEAN

DEM. CONGO

NAMIBIA

PACIFIC OCEAN

SOUTH
AFRICA

LE

ANGOLA

ARGENTINA

URUGUAY

NAMIBIA

ARCTIC OCEAN

NORWAY

FINLAND

RUSSIA

SWEDEN

ESTONIA

DENMARK

LATVIA

NETHERLANDS

RUSSIA

LITHUANIA

BELGIUM

BELARUS

POLAND

GERMANY

SLOVAKIA

UKRAINE

IRELAND

CZECH
REPUBLIC

BRITAIN

LUXEMBOURG

LIECHTENSTEIN

AUSTRIA

MOLDOVA

SWITZERLAND

HUNGARY

ROMANIA

FRANCE

SLOVENIA

SAN
MARINO

CROATIA

SERBIA

BULGARIA

MACEDONIA

ANDORRA

ITALY

MONTENEGRO

SPAIN

MONACO

BOSNIA-
HERZEGOVINA

TURKEY

PORTUGAL

ALBANIA

GREECE

MALTA

RUSSIA

UZBEKISTAN

STAN

KAZAKHSTAN

MONGOLIA

NORTH
KOREA

KYRGYZSTAN

SOUTH
KOREA

JAPAN

TAJIKISTAN

C H I N A

RBAIJAN

PACIFIC OCEAN

IT

AFGHANISTAN

NEPAL

BURMA
(MYANMAR)

IRAN

BHUTAN

QATAR

PAKISTAN

LAOS

BANGLADESH

VIETNAM

TAIWAN

BIA

UNITED
ARAB
EMIRATES

INDIA

HONG KONG

OMAN

MACAU

PHILIPPINES

GUAM/MARIANAS

THAILAND

DJIBOUTI

CAMBODIA

BRUNEI

PALAU

MARSHALL
ISLANDS

SRI
LANKA

MALAYSIA

MALDIVES

MICRONESIA

NAURU

SEYCHELLES

SINGAPORE

PAPUA
NEW GUINEA

KIRIBATI

INDIAN OCEAN

SOLOMON
ISLANDS

COMOROS ISLANDS

TUVALU

AMERICAN
SAMOA

EAST TIMOR

MAURITIUS

VANUATU

SAMOA

SCAR

AUSTRALIA

FIJI

TONGA

UE

NEW
ZEALAND

CA

North America

Scale 1:38,700,000

Lambert Conformal Conic Projection,
standard parallels 37° N and 65° N

0   500 Kilometers

0   500 Nautical Miles

Boundary representation is
not necessarily authoritative.

Central America and the Caribbean

North Atlantic Ocean

Tropic of Cancer

North Pacific Ocean

Gulf of Mexico

Caribbean Sea

GREATER ANTILLES

LESSER ANTILLES

Equator

Straits of Florida

UNITED STATES

New Orleans

Miami

THE BAHAMAS

Nassau

Havana

CUBA

Isla de la Juventud

Cayman Islands (U.K.)

George Town

Cancún

Isla Cozumel

Belmopan

BELIZE

MEXICO

GUATEMALA

Guatemala

San Salvador

EL SALVADOR

San Pedro Sula

HONDURAS

Tegucigalpa

Swan Islands (HONDURAS)

NICARAGUA

Managua

Cayos Miskitos (NICARAGUA)

Islas del Maíz (NICARAGUA)

Isla de Providencia (COLOMBIA)

Isla de San Andrés (COLOMBIA)

Puerto Limón

San José

COSTA RICA

Panama Canal

Colón

Panamá

PANAMA

Turks and Caicos Islands (U.K.)

Grand Turk

DOMINICAN REPUBLIC

Santo Domingo

HAITI

Port-au-Prince

Guantánamo Bay (U.S. NAVAL BASE)

Kingston

JAMAICA

Isla del Coco (COSTA RICA)

Galápagos Islands (ECUADOR)

Scale 1:21,500,000

Lambert Conformal Conic Projection, standard parallels 7°N and 19°N

0   300 Kilometers

0   500 Nautical Miles

British Virgin Islands (U.K.)

Anguilla (U.K.)

The Valley

ANTIGUA AND BARBUDA

St. John's

Charlotte Amalie

San Juan

Puerto Rico (U.S.)

Virgin Islands (U.S.)

Road Town

ST. KITTS AND NEVIS

Basseterre

Montserrat (U.K.)

Plymouth

Guadeloupe (FRANCE)

Basse-Terre

DOMINICA

Roseau

Fort-de-France

Martinique (FRANCE)

ST. LUCIA

Castries

BARBADOS

Bridgetown

ST. VINCENT AND THE GRENADINES

Kingstown

GRENADA

St. George's

Leeward Islands

Windward Islands

Netherlands Antilles (NETHERLANDS)

Curaçao

Bonaire

Willemstad

Aruba (NETH.)

Oranjestad

TRINIDAD AND TOBAGO

Port-of-Spain

Caracas

Maracaibo

San Cristóbal

VENEZUELA

Ciudad Guayana

COLOMBIA

Bogotá

Medellín

Cali

Barranquilla

ECUADOR

Orinoco

Río

GUYANA

Georgetown

SURINAME

Paramaribo

French Guiana (FRANCE)

Cayenne

BRAZIL

Boa Vista

Equator

Boundary representation is not necessarily authoritative.

South America

Caribbean Sea

Guadeloupe (FRANCE)
DOMINICA
Martinique (FRANCE)
ST. LUCIA
ST. VINCENT AND THE GRENADINES
BARBADOS
GRENADA

North Atlantic Ocean

HONDURAS
Puerto Lempira
Tegucigalpa
Puerto Cabezas
NICARAGUA
Managua
Liberia
San José
COSTA RICA
David
Colón
Panama
PANAMA

Isla de San Andrés (COLOMBIA)

Barranquilla
Maracaibo
Caracas
Port-of-Spain
TRINIDAD AND TOBAGO

San Cristóbal
Medellín
VENEZUELA
Ciudad Guayana
Georgetown
GUYANA
Paramaribo
French Guiana (FRANCE)
SURINAME
Cayenne

Isla de Malpelo (COLOMBIA)

Bogotá
Cali
COLOMBIA
Boa Vista
Macapá

Mitú

Quito
ECUADOR
Guayaquil
Fonte Boa
Manaus
Santarém
Belém
São Luís

Equator

Iquitos
Rio Negro
Amazon
Rio Tocantins
Fortaleza

Piura
Río Ucayali
Teresina
Natal

Trujillo
Rio Marañón
Rôreto Velho
Rio Branco
B R A Z I L
Recife

Huánuco
PERU
Palmas
Aracaju

South Pacific Ocean

Lima
Ica
Cusco
Salvador

Arequipa
Lago Titicaca
Trinidad
BOLIVIA
Cuiabá
Brasília
Rio São Francisco

Arica
La Paz
Cochabamba
Santa Cruz
Goiânia

Potosí
Sucre
Belo Horizonte

Antofagasta
Vitória

Tropic of Capricorn

Isla San Félix (CHILE)
Isla San Ambrosio (CHILE)

San Miguel de Tucumán
PARAGUAY
Asunción
Rio Paraná
Rio de Janeiro
São Paulo
Curitiba
Florianópolis

Resistencia

CHILE

Archipiélago Juan Fernandez (CHILE)

Córdoba
Rosario
Salto
Pôrto Alegre

Valparaíso
Mendoza
URUGUAY

Santiago
Buenos Aires
Montevideo

Concepción
ARGENTINA

Bahía Blanca
Mar del Plata

South Atlantic Ocean

San Carlos de Bariloche

Puerto Montt

Comodoro Rivadavia

Scale 1:35,000,000

Azimuthal Equal-Area Projection

0   250   500 Kilometers
0   250   500 Nautical Miles

Boundary representation is not necessarily authoritative.

Stanley
Falkland Islands (Islas Malvinas) (administered by U.K., claimed by Argentina)

Strait of Magellan

Punta Arenas
Ushuaia

South Georgia and the South Sandwich Islands (administered by U.K., claimed by Argentina)

Africa

Northern Africa and the Middle East

Europe

Greenland (DENMARK)

Jan Mayen (NORWAY)

Greenland Sea

Barents Sea

Hammerfest

Murmansk

Norwegian Sea

Reykjavik ★ ICELAND

Arctic Circle

Narvik

Kiruna

White Sea

Arkhangel'sk

NORWAY

Oulu

Umeå

FINLAND

Lake Onega

Tórshavn Faroe Islands (DENMARK)

Trondheim

SWEDEN

Tampere

Lake Ladoga

Shetland Islands

Gävle

Helsinki

St. Petersburg

Rockall (U.K.)

Bergen

Oslo

Åland Islands

Gulf of Finland

Hebrides

Orkney Islands

Stockholm

Göteborg

Gotland

ESTONIA

RUSSIA

Aberdeen

North Sea

Skagerrak

Baltic Sea

Riga

LATVIA

Smolensk

North Atlantic Ocean

Edinburgh

Belfast UNITED

Newcastle

DENMARK

Öland

LITHUANIA

Minsk

Dublin

Isle of Man (U.K.)

Copenhagen

Bornholm

Kaliningrad RUSSIA

Vilnius

BELARUS

IRELAND

Liverpool

Gdansk

Irish Sea

KINGDOM

Cardiff

Amsterdam

Rostock

Szczecin

Poznan

Warsaw

Brest

Kiev

Hamburg

Hannover

Berlin

POLAND

London

NETHERLANDS

Brussels

BELGIUM

Berlin

Leipzig

Wroclaw

UKRAINE

Guernsey (U.K.)

Jersey (U.K.)

Le Havre

LUX.

Bonn

Cologne

Prague

Kraków

Seine

Paris

Luxembourg

GERMANY

CZECH REPUBLIC

SLOVAKIA

MOLDOVA

Strasbourg

Stuttgart

Chisinau

Nantes

Loire

Munich

Vienna

Bratislava

Budapest

Odesa

FRANCE

SWITZ.

LIECH

AUSTRIA

HUNGARY

Cluj-Napoca

Bay of Biscay

Geneva

Bern

Graz

ROMANIA

Constanta

Lyon

Ljubljana

Pécs

Bucharest

Turin

Milan

SLOVENIA

Zagreb

Danube

Black Sea

Bordeaux

Po

Venice

CROATIA

Belgrade

Varna

Genoa

BOSNIA AND HERZEGOVINA

Serbia

PORTUGAL

Bilbao

SAN MARINO

Florence

Sarajevo

BULGARIA

Porto

MONACO

Podgorica

Sofia

Marseille

Corsica

ITALY

Adriatic Sea

MONTENEGRO

Skopje

Istanbul

PORTUGAL

SPAIN

ANDORRA

Rome

Tirane

MACEDONIA

Thessaloniki

Madrid

Barcelona

VATICAN CITY

ALB.

TURKEY

Tagus

Valencia

Naples

Ioannina

Aegean Sea

Lisbon

Sardinia

Tyrrhenian Sea

Corfu

GREECE

Athens

Sevilla

Balearic Islands

Ionian Sea

Rhodes

Málaga

Peloponnisos

Mediterranean Sea

Palermo

Sicily

Crete

Strait of Gibraltar

Gibraltar (U.K)

Ceuta (SPAIN)

Algiers

Tunis

Scale 1:19,500,000

Mekila (SPAIN)

Valletta

Rabat ★ MOROCCO

ALGERIA

TUNISIA

MALTA

Lambert Conformal Conic Projection, standard parallels 40°N and 56°N

0 _____ 300 Kilometers

0 _____ 300 Nautical Miles

Asia

Chapter 1
The Globalization of International Relations

NASA

THE MIDDLE EAST AS SEEN FROM THE INTERNATIONAL SPACE STATION, 2010.

 ## Learning Objectives

1.1 Describe the properties of the collective action problem and how each core principle addresses the problem.

1.2 Evaluate whether states are still the key actors in international relations.

1.3 Identify at least three commonalities between states in the global North and states in the global South.

1.4 Explain at least two differences between the Cold War era and the post–Cold War era.

1.1 Globalization, International Relations, and Daily Life

Describe the properties of the collective action problem and how each core principle addresses the problem.

International relations is a fascinating topic because it concerns peoples and cultures throughout the world. The scope and complexity of the interactions among these groups make international relations a challenging subject to master. There is always more to learn. This book is only the beginning of the story.

> **international relations (IR)** The relationships among the world's state governments and the connection of those relationships with other actors (such as the United Nations, multinational corporations, and individuals), with other social relationships (including economics, culture, and domestic politics), and with geographic and historical influences.

Narrowly defined, the field of **international relations (IR)** concerns the relationships among the world's governments. But these relationships cannot be understood in isolation. They are closely connected with other actors (such as international organizations, multinational corporations, and individuals), with other social structures and processes (including economics, culture, and domestic politics), and with geographical and historical influences. These elements together power the central trend in IR today—globalization.

Many events in recent years reflect the ever-growing interconnections of the world. Conflicts in seemingly far-off places like Libya and Syria have brought thousands of refugees to the shores of Europe and the United States. The global economic recession of 2008–2009, which began with a collapse of the U.S. home mortgage market, spread quickly to other nations. Highly integrated global financial markets created a ripple effect across the globe that has influenced nearly every economy in the world. For the United States and many European countries, it has taken nearly a decade to return to employment and economic growth levels seen before the economic crisis.

Globalization brings many positive benefits to our daily lives: Global trade networks allow an individual to order a new phone, have it assembled in one country, shipped through another, to be delivered to that individual's door within a few days. Global connectivity allows instant access to friends, family, and news within seconds nearly anywhere in the world. These interconnections were slower, less common, and very costly even 30 years ago. As technology advances, the world is shrinking year by year. Better communication and transportation capabilities constantly expand the ordinary person's contact with people, products, and ideas from other countries. Globalization is internationalizing us.

It is also true that many individuals around the world have become uneasy with how these interconnections shape their daily lives. The 2016 vote by citizens of Great Britain to leave the European Union (EU), known as Brexit, reflected misgivings of many in that country about their lack of control over policies involving trade and immigration that came with membership in the EU. Many have held that the 2016 election of Donald Trump in the United States demonstrated the American public's concern over globalization, including job losses from trade, concern over immigration, and the desire to prioritize America's interests over global concerns.

Events that seem far off and disconnected can directly influence our daily lives. The prospects for getting jobs after graduation depend on the global economy and international economic competition. Those jobs are also more likely than ever to entail international travel, sales, or communication. And the rules of the world trading system affect the goods that students consume every day, such as electronics, clothes, and gasoline.

In addition to feeling the influence of globalization and international relations on our daily lives, individual citizens can influence the world as well. Often, international relations is portrayed as a distant and abstract ritual conducted by a small group of people such as presidents, generals, and diplomats. Although leaders do play a major role in international affairs, many other people participate. College students and other citizens participate in international relations every time they vote in an election or work on a political campaign, buy a product or service traded on world markets, and watch the news. The choices we make in our daily lives ultimately affect the world we live in. Through those choices, every person makes a unique contribution, however small, to the world of international relations.

The purpose of this book is to introduce the field of IR, to organize what is known and theorized about IR, and to convey the key concepts used by most IR scholars to discuss relations among nations. This first chapter defines IR as a field of study, introduces the actors of interest, and reviews the geographical and historical aspects of globalization within which IR occurs.

[handwritten: chapter 1 purpose]

1.1.1 Core Principles

The field of IR reflects the world's complexity, and IR scholars use many theories, concepts, and buzzwords in trying to describe and explain it. Underneath this complexity, however, lie a few basic principles that shape the field. We will lay out the range of theories and approaches in Chapters 2 through 4, but here we will present the most central ideas as free from jargon as possible (see also the Seeking the Collective Good feature).

IR revolves around one key problem: How can a group—such as two or more countries—serve its *collective* interests when doing so requires its members to forgo their *individual* interests? For example, every country has an interest in stopping global warming, a goal that can be achieved only by many countries acting together. Yet each country also has an individual interest in burning fossil fuels to keep its economy going. Similarly, all members of a military alliance benefit from the strength of the alliance, but each member separately has an interest in minimizing its own contributions

Seeking the Collective Good
Introduction

In explaining how countries behave in IR, a central concept is the "collective goods problem." This recurring problem results when two or more members of a group share an interest in some outcome of value to them all but have conflicting individual interests when it comes to achieving that valued outcome. For example, the world's countries share a desire to avoid global warming, but each one benefits from burning fossil fuels to run its economy. If a few members of a group fail to contribute to a collective good, the others will still provide it and the few can "free ride." But if too many do so, then the collective good will not be provided for anyone. For instance, if too many countries burn too much fossil fuel, then the whole world will suffer the effects of global warming.

Within domestic societies, governments solve collective goods problems by forcing the members of society to contribute to common goals, such as by paying taxes. In international affairs, no such world government exists. Three core principles—dominance, reciprocity, and identity—offer different solutions to the collective goods problem. These principles underlie the actions and outcomes that make up IR.

To help tie together a central topic in a chapter with the core principles used throughout the book, each chapter contains a

Aftermath of Hurricane Maria, Puerto Rico, 2017. Global climate stability is a collective good.

Seeking the Collective Good box feature. Each box will discuss how the world's states deal with an important issue in IR using one (or more) of the core principles. Examples include stopping genocide (Chapter 7), enhancing world trade (Chapter 8), and slowing global warming (Chapter 11).

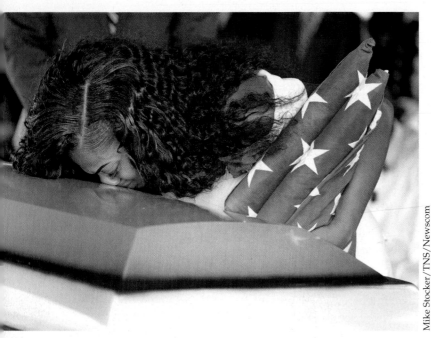

Mike Stocker/TNS/Newscom

TOUCHED BY WAR   IR affects our lives in many ways. Here, a wife kisses her husband's coffin at his memorial service. U.S. Army Sgt. La David Johnson was killed in a military operation in Niger in 2017.

collective goods problem A tangible or intangible good, created by the members of a group, that is available to all group members regardless of their individual contributions; participants can gain by lowering their own contribution to the collective good, yet if too many participants do so, the good cannot be provided.

in troops and money. Individual nations can advance their own short-term interests by seizing territory militarily, cheating on trade agreements, and refusing to contribute to international efforts such as peacekeeping or vaccination campaigns. But if all nations acted this way, they would find themselves worse off, in a chaotic and vicious environment where mutual gains from cooperating on issues of security and trade would disappear.

This problem of shared interests versus conflicting interests among members of a group goes by various names in various contexts—the problem of "collective action," "free riding," "burden sharing," or the "tragedy of the commons." We will refer to the general case as the **collective goods problem**, that is, the problem of how to provide something that benefits all members of a group regardless of what each member contributes to it.

In general, collective goods are easier to provide in small groups than in large ones. In a small group, the cheating (or free riding) of one member is harder to conceal, has a greater impact on the overall collective good, and is easier to punish. The advantage of small groups helps explain the importance of the great power system in international security affairs and of the Group of Twenty (G20) industrialized countries in economic matters.

The collective goods problem occurs in all groups and societies, but it is particularly acute in international affairs because each nation is sovereign, with no central authority such as a world government to enforce on individual nations the necessary measures to provide for the common good. By contrast, in domestic politics *within* countries, a government can force individuals to contribute in ways that do not serve their individual self-interest, such as by paying taxes or paying to install antipollution equipment on vehicles and factories. If individuals do not comply, the government can punish them. Although this solution is far from perfect—cheaters and criminals sometimes are not caught, and governments sometimes abuse their power—it mostly works well enough to keep societies going.

Three basic principles—which we call dominance, reciprocity, and identity—offer possible solutions to the core problem of getting individuals to cooperate for the common good without a central authority to make them do so (see Table 1.1). These three principles are fundamental across the social sciences and recur in other disciplines such as the study of animal societies, child development, social psychology, anthropology, and economics as well as political science. To further explain each principle, we will apply the three principles to a small-scale human example and an IR example.

DOMINANCE   The principle of **dominance** solves the collective goods problem by establishing a power hierarchy in which those at the top control those below—a bit like a government but without an actual government. Instead of fighting constantly over who gets scarce resources, the members of a group can just fight occasionally over position in the "status hierarchy." Then social conflicts such as who gets resources are resolved automatically in favor of the higher-ranking actor. Fights over the dominance position have scripted rules that minimize, to some extent, the harm inflicted on the group members. Symbolic acts of submission and dominance reinforce an ever-present status hierarchy. Staying at the top of a status hierarchy does not depend on strength alone, though it helps. Rather, the top actor may be the one most adept at forming and maintaining alliances among the group's more capable members. Dominance is complex and not just a matter of brute force.

dominance A principle for solving collective goods problems by imposing solutions hierarchically.

In international relations, the principle of dominance underlies the great power system, in which a handful of countries dictate the rules for all the others. Sometimes a so-called *hegemon* or superpower stands atop the great powers as the dominant nation. The UN Security Council, in which the world's five strongest military powers hold a veto, reflects the dominance principle.

The advantage of the dominance solution to the collective goods problem is that, like a government, it forces members of a group to contribute to the common good. It also minimizes open conflict within the group. However, the disadvantage is that this stability comes at a cost of constant oppression of, and resentment by, the lower-ranking members in the status hierarchy. Also, conflicts over position in the hierarchy can occasionally harm the group's stability and well-being, such as when challenges to the top position lead to serious fights. In the case of international relations, the great power system and the hegemony of a superpower can provide relative peace and stability for decades on end but then can break down into costly wars among the great powers.

Ji Haixin/Associated Press

PLENTY OF FISH IN THE SEA? Collective goods, such as healthy global fisheries, depend on group members cooperating to preserve the good. Yet, while members want to protect the collective good, they also have an individual incentive to over-use the good. One of these fishing boats, shown in a Chinese harbor in 2018, might want to catch a few extra fish thinking their few extra will not matter. But if all of these boats adopt that behavior, overfishing will result. Thus, the boats need to cooperate to protect the fish stocks (the collective good). In many issue areas, such as global warming, the international community of nations is similarly interdependent. However, the provision of collective goods presents difficult dilemmas as players seek to maximize their own share of benefits.

RECIPROCITY   The principle of **reciprocity** solves the collective goods problem by rewarding behavior that contributes to the group and punishing behavior that pursues self-interest at the expense of the group. Reciprocity is very easy to understand and can be "enforced" without any central authority, making it a robust way to get individuals to cooperate for the common good.

> **reciprocity** A response in kind to another's actions; a strategy of reciprocity uses positive forms of leverage to promise rewards and negative forms of leverage to threaten punishment.

But reciprocity operates in both the positive realm ("You scratch my back and I'll scratch yours") and the negative ("An eye for an eye, a tooth for a tooth").[1] A disadvantage of reciprocity as a solution to the collective goods problem is that it can lead to a downward spiral as each side punishes what it believes to be negative acts by the other. Psychologically, most people overestimate their own good intentions and underestimate the value of the actions of their opponents or rivals. To avoid tit-for-tat escalations of conflict, one or both parties must act generously to get the relationship moving in a cooperative direction.

In international relations, reciprocity forms the basis of most of the norms (habits, expectations) and institutions in the international system. Many central arrangements in IR, such as World Trade Organization (WTO) agreements, explicitly recognize reciprocity as the linchpin of cooperation. For instance, if one country opens its markets to another's goods, the other opens its markets in return. On the negative side, reciprocity fuels arms races as each side responds to the other's buildup of weapons. But it also allows arms control agreements and other step-by-step conflict-resolution measures, as two sides match each other's actions in backing away the brink of war.

---

[1]Robert Aitkin Bertram(1885). A Homiletic Encyclopaedia of Illustrations in Theology and Morals, 7e. Published by Funk & Wagnalls.

identity A principle for solving collective goods problems by changing participants' preferences based on their shared sense of belonging to a community.

IDENTITY A third potential solution to the collective goods problem lies in the identities of participants as members of a community. Although the dominance and reciprocity principles act on the idea of achieving individual self-interest (by taking what you can, or by mutually beneficial arrangements), the **identity** principle does not rely on self-interest. On the contrary, members of an identity community care about the interests of others in that community enough to sacrifice their own interests to benefit others. The roots of this principle lie in the family, the extended family, and the kinship group. But this potential is not limited to the close family; it can be generalized to any identity community that one feels a part of. As members of a family care about each other, so do members of an ethnic group, a gender group, a nation, or the world's scientists. In each case, individual members accept solutions to collective goods problems that do not give them the best deal as individuals because the benefits are "all in the family," so to speak. A biologist retiring at a rich American university may give away lab equipment to a biologist in a poor country because they share an identity as scientists. A European Jew may give money to Israel because of a shared Jewish identity, or a computer scientist from India may return home to work for lower pay after receiving training in Canada in order to help the community he or she cares about. Millions of people contribute to international disaster relief funds after tsunamis, earthquakes, or hurricanes because of a shared identity as members of the community of human beings.

In international relations, identity communities play important roles in overcoming difficult collective goods problems, including the issue of who contributes to development assistance, world health, and UN peacekeeping missions. The relatively large foreign aid contributions of Scandinavian countries, or the high Canadian participation in peacekeeping, cannot be explained well by self-interest but instead arise from these countries' self-defined identities as members of the international community. Even in military forces and diplomacy (where dominance and reciprocity, respectively, rule the day), the shared identities of military professionals and of diplomats—each with shared traditions and expectations—can take the edge off conflicts. And military alliances also mix identity politics with raw self-interest, as shown by the unusual strength of the U.S.-British alliance, which shared interests alone cannot explain as well as shared identity does.

Nonstate actors, such as nongovernmental organizations or terrorist networks, also rely on identity politics to a great extent. The increasing roles of these actors—feminist organizations, churches, jihadists, and multinational corporations, for example—have brought the identity principle to greater prominence in IR theory in recent years.

AN EVERYDAY EXAMPLE To sum up the three core principles, imagine that you have two good friends who are in a romantic relationship. They love each other and enjoy each other's company, but they come to you for help with a problem: When they go out together, one friend likes to go to the opera, whereas the other friend enjoys going to boxing matches.[2] Because of your training in international relations, you quickly recognize this as a collective goods problem, in which the shared interest is spending time together and the conflicting individual interests are watching opera and watching boxing. (Of course, you know that the behavior of states is more complicated than that of individuals, but put that aside for a moment.) You might approach this problem in any of three ways.

First, you could say, "Well, I know one of you has more money because of a better job, so I think that one should get to decide each time." This would be a dominance solution. It could be a very stable solution, if the less-wealthy friend cares

---

[2]This scenario is adapted from the game theory example "Battle of the Sexes."

more about spending time with their true love than they care about boxing. It would be a simple solution that would settle all future conflicts. It would give one party everything they want, and the other party some of what they want (love, company, a stable relationship). This might be better for both of them than spending all their evenings arguing about where to go out. On the other hand, this solution might leave the less-wealthy friend permanently resentful at the unequal nature of the outcome. They might feel their love diminish over time by a longing for respect and nostalgia for boxing. They might even find another romantic interest who likes boxing.

Second, you could say, "Look, instead of fighting all the time, why don't you establish a pattern and trade off going to boxing one time and opera the next." This would be a reciprocity solution. You could help the couple set up agreements, accounting systems, and shared expectations to govern the implementation of this seemingly simple solution. For example, they could go to boxing on Friday nights and opera on Saturday nights. But what if opera season is shorter than boxing season? Then perhaps they would go to opera more often during its season and boxing more often when opera is out of season. What if one of them is out of town on a Friday night? Does that night count anyway or does it earn a credit for later? Or does the one who is in town go out alone? What if the opera-loving friend *hates* boxing but the boxing-loving friend only mildly dislikes opera? Do you set up a schedule of two operas for each boxing match to keep each side equally happy or unhappy? Clearly, reciprocity solutions can become very complicated (just look at the world trade rules in Chapter 8, for example), and they require constant monitoring to see whether obligations are being met and cheating avoided. Your friends might find it an irritant in their relationship to keep close track of who owes whom a night at the opera or at a boxing match.

Third, you could say, "Who cares about opera or boxing? The point is that you love each other and want to be together. Get past the superficial issues and strengthen the core feelings that brought you together. Then it won't matter where you go or what you're watching." This would be an identity solution. This approach could powerfully resolve your friends' conflict and leave them both much happier. Over time, one partner might actually begin to prefer the other's favorite activity after more exposure—leading to a change in identity. On the other hand, after a while self-interest could creep back in because that loving feeling might seem even happier with a boxing match (or opera) to watch. Indeed, one partner can subtly exploit the other's commitment to get past the superficial conflicts. "What's it matter as long as we're together," they say, "and oh, look, there's a good boxing match tonight!" Sometimes the identity principle operates more powerfully in the short term than the long term: The soldier who volunteers to defend the homeland might begin to feel taken advantage of after months or years on the front line, and the American college student who gives money once to tsunami victims may not want to keep giving year after year to malaria victims.

Table 1.1 Core Principles for Solving Collective Goods Problems

Principle	Advantages	Drawbacks
Dominance	Order, Stability, Predictability	Oppression, Resentment
Reciprocity	Incentives for Mutual Cooperation	Downward Spirals, Complex Accounting
Identity	Sacrifice for Group, Redefine Interests	Demonizing an Out-Group

AN IR EXAMPLE Now consider the problem of nuclear proliferation. All countries share an interest in the collective good of peace and stability, which is hard to achieve in a world where more and more countries make more and more nuclear weapons. If individuals in a particular country acquire dangerous weapons, the government can take them away to keep everyone safe. But in the society of nations, no such central authority exists. For example, North Korea tested its first nuclear bomb in 2006, and has continued to test larger weapons-defying UN resolutions.

One approach to nuclear proliferation legitimizes these weapons' ownership by just the few most powerful countries. The "big five" with the largest nuclear arsenals hold veto power on the UN Security Council. Through agreements like the Non-Proliferation Treaty (NPT) and the Proliferation Security Initiative, the existing nuclear powers actively try to keep their exclusive hold on these weapons and prevent smaller nations from getting them. This is a dominance approach. In 2003, when the United States thought Iraq's Saddam Hussein might have an active nuclear weapons program, as he had a decade earlier, it invaded Iraq and overthrew its government. Similarly, in 1982, when Iraq had begun working toward a nuclear bomb, Israel sent jets to bomb Iraq's nuclear facility, setting back the program by years. One drawback to these dominance solutions is the resentment they create among the smaller countries. Those countries point to an unenforced provision of the NPT stating that existing nuclear powers should get rid of their own bombs as other countries refrain from making new ones. And they ask what gives Israel the right to bomb another country, or the United States the right to invade one. They speak of a double standard for the powerful and the weak.

Reciprocity offers a different avenue for preventing nuclear proliferation. It is the basis of the provision in the NPT about the existing nuclear powers' obligation to disarm in exchange for smaller countries' agreement to stay nonnuclear. Reciprocity also underlies arms control agreements, used extensively in the Cold War to manage the buildup of nuclear bombs by the superpowers and used currently to manage the mutual reduction of their arsenals. Deterrence also relies on reciprocity. The United States has warned North Korea against selling its bombs (an action that would be in North Korea's short-term self-interest), threatening to retaliate against North Korea if any other actor used such a bomb against the United States. And when Libya gave up its nuclear weapons program in 2003, the international community offered it various rewards, including the ending of economic sanctions, in exchange.

The identity principle has proven equally effective, if less newsworthy, against nuclear proliferation. Many nations that have the technical ability to make nuclear weapons have *chosen* not to do so. They have constructed their national identities in ways that shape their self-interests to make nuclear bombs undesirable. Some, like Sweden, do not intend to fight wars. Others, like Germany, belong to alliances in which they come under another nation's nuclear umbrella and do not need their own bombs. South Africa actually developed nuclear weapons in secret but then dismantled the program before apartheid ended, keeping the bomb out of the hands of the new majority-rule government. Nobody forced South Africa to do this (as in dominance), nor did it respond to rewards and punishments (reciprocity). Rather, South Africa's identity shifted. Similarly, Japan's experience of the catastrophic results of militarism, culminating in the destruction of two of its cities by nuclear bombs in 1945, continues generations later to shape Japan's identity as a country that does not want nuclear weapons, even though it has the know-how and even the stockpile of plutonium to make them.

Collective goods problems fascinate social scientists, and especially scholars of IR, precisely because they have no easy solutions. In later chapters, we will see how these three core principles shape the responses of the international community to various collective goods problems across the whole range of IR issues.

1.1.2 IR as a Field of Study

IR is a rather practical discipline. There is a close connection between scholars in colleges, universities, and think tanks and the policy-making community working in the government—especially in the United States. Some professors serve in the government (for instance, political science professor Condoleezza Rice became national security adviser in 2001 and secretary of state in 2005 under President George W. Bush), and sometimes professors publicize their ideas about foreign policy through newspaper columns, blog posts, or TV interviews. Influencing their government's foreign policy gives these scholars a laboratory in which to test their ideas in practice. Diplomats, bureaucrats, and politicians can benefit from the knowledge produced by IR scholars.

Theoretical debates in the field of IR are fundamental but unresolved. It will be up to the next generation of IR scholars—today's college students—to achieve a better understanding of how world politics works. The goal of this book is to lay out the current state of knowledge without exaggerating the successes of the discipline.

As part of political science, IR is about *international politics*—the decisions of governments about foreign actors, especially other governments. To some extent, however, the field is interdisciplinary, relating international politics to economics, history, sociology, and other disciplines. Some universities offer separate degrees or departments for IR. Most, however, teach IR in political science classes, in which the focus is on the *politics* of economic relationships or the *politics* of environmental management, to take two examples. (The domestic politics of foreign countries, although overlapping with IR, generally make up the separate field of *comparative politics*.)

Political relations among nations cover a range of activities—diplomacy, war, trade relations, alliances, cultural exchanges, participation in international organizations, and so forth. Particular activities within one of these spheres make up distinct **issue areas** on which scholars and foreign policy makers focus attention. Examples of issue areas include global trade, the environment, and specific conflicts such as the Arab-Israeli conflict. Within each issue area, and across the range of issues of concern

issue areas Distinct spheres of international activity (such as global trade negotiations) within which policy makers of various states face conflicts and sometimes achieve cooperation.

Policy Perspectives

OVERVIEW International policy makers confront a variety of problems every day. Solving these problems requires difficult decisions and choices. Policy Perspectives is a box feature in each chapter that places you in a particular decision-making perspective (for example, as the prime minister of Great Britain) and asks you to make choices concerning an important international relations issue.

Each box contains four sections. The first, Background, provides information about a political problem faced by the leader. This background information is factual and reflects real situations faced by these decision makers.

The second section, Domestic Considerations, reflects on the implications of the situation for domestic politics within the leader's government and society. How will the lives of ordinary citizens be affected?

The third section, Scenario, suggests a new problem or crisis confronting the leader. Although these crises are hypothetical, all are within the realm of possibility and would require difficult decisions by the leaders and their countries.

The fourth section, Choose Your Policy, asks you to make a choice responding to the Scenario. With each decision, think about the trade-offs between your options. What are the risks and rewards in choosing one policy over another? Do alternative options exist that could address the problem effectively within the given constraints? Does one option pose bigger costs in the short term but fewer in the long term? Can you defend your decision to colleagues, the public, and other world leaders? How will your choice affect your citizens' lives and your own political survival?

As you consider each problem faced by the decision maker, try to reflect on the process and logic by which you have reached the decision. Which factors seem more important and why? Are domestic or international factors more important in shaping your decision? Are the constraints you face based on limited capability (for example, money or military power), or do international law or norms influence your decision as well? How do factors such as lack of time influence your decision?

You will quickly discover that there are often no right answers. At times, it is difficult to choose between two good options; at other times, one has to decide which is the least bad option.

conflict and cooperation The types of actions that states take toward each other through time.

international security A subfield of international relations (IR) that focuses on questions of war and peace.

international political economy (IPE) The study of the politics of trade, monetary, and other economic relations among nations, and their connection to other transnational forces.

state An inhabited territorial entity controlled by a government that exercises sovereignty over its territory.

in any international relationship, policy makers of one nation can behave in a cooperative manner or a conflictual manner—extending either friendly or hostile behavior toward another nation. IR scholars often look at international relations in terms of the mix of **conflict and cooperation** in relationships among nations.

It is also possible to define the scope of the field of IR by the *subfields* it encompasses. Some scholars treat topics such as the chapters in this book (for example, international law or international development) as subfields, but here we will reserve the term for two macro-level topics. Traditionally, the study of IR has focused on questions of war and peace—the subfield of **international security** studies. The movements of armies and of diplomats, the crafting of treaties and alliances, the development and deployment of military capabilities—these are the subjects that dominated the study of IR in the past, especially in the 1950s and 1960s, and they continue to hold a central position in the field. Since the Cold War, regional conflicts and ethnic violence have received more attention, while interdisciplinary peace studies programs and feminist scholarship have sought to broaden concepts of "security" further.

The subfield of **international political economy (IPE)**, a second main subfield of IR, concerns trade and financial relations among nations and focuses on how nations have cooperated politically to create and maintain institutions that regulate the flow of international economic and financial transactions. Although these topics previously centered on relations among the world's richer nations, the widening of globalization and multilateral economic institutions such as the World Trade Organization have pushed IPE scholars to focus on developing states as well. In addition, they pay growing attention to relations between developed and developing nations (often labeled North-South relations), including topics such as economic dependency, debt, foreign aid, and technology transfer. Also newly important are problems of international environmental management and of global telecommunications. The subfield of IPE is expanding accordingly.

The same principles and theories that help us understand international security (discussed in the first half of this book) also help us understand IPE (discussed in the second half). Economics is important in security affairs, and vice versa.

Theoretical knowledge accumulates by a repeated cycle of generalizing and then testing. For a given puzzle, various theories can explain the result (though none perfectly) as a case of a more general principle. Each theory also logically predicts other outcomes, which can be tested empirically. A laboratory science, controlling all but one variable, can test theoretical predictions efficiently. IR does not have this luxury because many variables operate simultaneously. Thus, it is especially important to think critically about IR events and consider several different theoretical explanations before deciding which (if any) provides the best explanation.

1.2 Actors and Influences

Evaluate whether states are still the key actors in international relations.

The principal actors in IR are the world's governments. Scholars of IR traditionally study the decisions and acts of those governments in relation to other governments. The international stage is crowded with actors large and small that are intimately interwoven with the decisions of governments. These actors are individual leaders and citizens. They are bureaucratic agencies in foreign ministries. They are multinational corporations and terrorist groups. But the most important actors in IR are states.

1.2.1 State Actors

A **state** is a territorial entity controlled by a government and inhabited by a population. The locations of the world's states and territories are shown in the reference map at the front of this book. Regional maps with greater detail appear there as well.

A state government answers to no higher authority; it exercises *sovereignty* over its territory—to make and enforce laws, to collect taxes, and so forth. This sovereignty is recognized (acknowledged) by other states through diplomatic relations and usually by membership in the United Nations (UN). The population inhabiting a state forms a *civil society* to the extent that it has developed institutions to participate in political or social life. All or part of the population that shares a group identity may consider itself a *nation* (see Nationalism in Chapter 5). The state's government is a *democracy* to the extent that the members of the population control the government. In political life, and to some extent in IR scholarship, the terms *state, nation,* and *country* are used imprecisely, usually to refer to state governments. (Note that the word *state* in IR does not mean a state in the United States.)

With few exceptions, each state has a capital city—the seat of government from which it administers its territory—and often a single individual who acts in the name of the state. We will refer to this person simply as the "state leader." Often he or she is the *head of government* (such as a prime minister) or the *head of state* (such as a president, or a king or queen). In some countries, such as the United States, the same person is head of state and government. In other countries, the positions of the president or royalty, or even the prime minister, are symbolic. In any case, the most powerful political figures are the ones we mean by "state leaders," and these figures are the key individual actors in IR, regardless of whether these leaders are democratically elected or dictators. The state actor includes the individual leader as well as bureaucratic organizations such as foreign ministries that act in the name of the state. (What the United States calls *departments* are usually called *ministries* elsewhere. U.S. *secretaries* are *ministers* and the State Department corresponds with a *foreign ministry*.)

The **international system** is the set of relationships among the world's states, structured according to certain rules and patterns of interaction. Some such rules are explicit; some are implicit. They include who is considered a member of the system, what rights and responsibilities the members have, and what kinds of actions and responses normally occur between states.

The modern international system has existed for only 500 years. Before then, people were organized into more mixed and overlapping political units such as city-states, empires, and feudal fiefs. In the past 200 years, the idea has spread that *nations*—groups of people who share a sense of national identity, usually including a language and culture—should have their own states. Most large states today are such **nation-states**. But since World War II, the decolonization process in much of Asia and Africa has added many new states, some not at all nation-states. A major source of conflict and war at present is the frequent mismatch between perceived nations and actual state borders. When people identify with a nationality that their state government does not represent, they may fight to form their own state and thus to gain sovereignty over their territory and affairs. This substate nationalism is only one of several trends that undermine the present system of states. Others include the globalization of economic processes, the power of telecommunications, and the proliferation of ballistic missiles.

The independence of former colonies and, more recently, the breakup into smaller states of large multinational states (the Soviet Union, Yugoslavia, and Czechoslovakia) have increased the

international system The set of relationships among the world's states, structured by certain rules and patterns of interaction.

nation-states States whose populations share a sense of national identity, usually including a language and culture.

POWERS THAT BE States are the most important actors in IR. A handful of states are considered great powers and one a "superpower." Here, world leaders of Britain, the United States, China, and Germany pose for a photo at the start of the G20 meetings, 2017.

gross domestic product (GDP) The
size of a state's total annual
economic activity.

number of states in the world. The exact total depends on the status of a number of quasi-state political entities, and it keeps changing as political units split apart or merge. The UN has 193 members in 2018.

The population of the world's states varies dramatically, from China and India with more than 1 billion people each, to microstates such as San Marino with 32,000. With the creation of many small states in recent decades, the majority of states have fewer than 10 million people each, and more than half of the rest have 10 million to 50 million each. But the 16 states with populations of more than 80 million people together contain about two-thirds of the world's population.

States also differ tremendously in the size of their total annual economic activity—**gross domestic product (GDP)**[3]—from the nearly $19 trillion U.S. economy to the economies of tiny states such as the Pacific island of Tuvalu ($37 million). The world economy is dominated by a few states, just as world population is. Figure 1.1 lists the 15 largest countries by population and by economy. Each is an important actor in world affairs, especially the nine in the center that are largest in both population and economy.

A few of these large states possess especially great military and economic strength and influence, and are called *great powers*. They are defined and discussed in Chapter 2. The most powerful of great powers, those with truly global influence, have been called *superpowers*. This term generally meant the United States and the Soviet Union during the Cold War and now refers to the United States alone.

Some other political entities are often referred to as states or countries, although they are not formally recognized as states. Taiwan is the most important of these. It

Figure 1.1 Largest Countries, 2017–2018

Source: World Bank data. GDP estimates for 2017, population for 2018.

Largest Population	Both	Largest Economy
Pakistan	China	Britain
	India	
Nigeria	United States	France
Bangladesh	Indonesia	Italy
Philippines	Brazil	South Korea
	Russia	
Vietnam	Japan	Canada
Ethiopia	Mexico	Spain
	Germany	

Note: Left and center columns listed in population order, right column in GDP order.

[3]GDP is the total of goods and services produced by a nation; it is very similar to the gross national product (GNP). Such data are difficult to compare across nations with different currencies, economic systems, and levels of development. In particular, comparisons of GDP between rich and poor countries should be treated cautiously. GDP data used in this book are mostly from the World Bank. In Chapter 12, we discuss other ways to measure GDP that take into account the relative price of goods purchased in a country. This can be important since the price of goods such as food can vary widely between countries, giving the same economic activity a different value depending on the country. See Feenstra, Robert C., Robert Inklaar, and Marcel P. Timmer. The Next Generation of the Penn World Table. *American Economic Review* 105 (10), 2015: 3150–82. GDP data are for 2017 unless otherwise noted.

operates independently in practice but is claimed by China (a claim recognized formally by outside powers) and is not a UN member. Formal colonies and possessions still exist; their status may change in the future. They include Puerto Rico (U.S.), Bermuda (British), Martinique (French), French Guiana, the Netherlands Antilles (Dutch), the Falkland Islands (British), and Guam (U.S.). Hong Kong reverted from British to Chinese rule in 1997 and retains a somewhat separate identity under China's "one country, two systems" formula. The status of the Vatican (Holy See) in Rome is ambiguous, as is that of Palestine, which in 2012 joined the Vatican to be the UN's two *nonmember observer states*. Including such territorial entities with states brings the world total to about 200 state or quasi-state actors. Other would-be states such as Kurdistan (Iraq), Abkhazia (Georgia), and Somaliland (Somalia) may fully control the territory they claim but are not internationally recognized.

1.2.2 Nonstate Actors

National governments may be the most important actors in IR, but they are strongly influenced by a variety of **nonstate actors** (see Table 1.2). These actors are also called *transnational actors* when they operate across international borders.

First, states often take actions through, within, or in the context of **intergovernmental organizations (IGOs)**—organizations whose members are national governments. IGOs fulfill a variety of functions and vary in size from just a few states to the whole UN membership. The Organization of the Petroleum Exporting Countries (OPEC), the World Trade Organization (WTO), military alliances such as the North Atlantic Treaty Organization (NATO), and political groupings such as the African Union (AU) are all IGOs.

Another type of transnational actor, **nongovernmental organizations (NGOs)**, are private organizations, some of considerable size and resources. Increasingly NGOs are being recognized, in the UN and other forums, as legitimate actors along with states, though not equal to them. Some of these groups have a political purpose, some a humanitarian one, some an economic or technical one. Sometimes NGOs combine efforts through transnational advocacy networks. There is no single pattern to NGOs. Together, IGOs and NGOs are referred to as international organizations (IOs). By one count there are more than 50,000 NGOs and 5,000 IGOs. IOs are discussed in detail in Chapters 7 and 10.

Multinational corporations (MNCs) are companies that span multiple countries. The interests of a large company doing business globally do not correspond with any one state's interests. MNCs often control greater resources, and operate internationally with greater efficiency, than many small states. They may prop up (or even create) friendly foreign governments, as the United Fruit Company did in the "banana republics" of Central America a century ago. But MNCs also provide poor states with much-needed foreign investment and tax revenues. MNCs in turn depend on states to

nonstate actors Actors other than state governments that operate either below the level of the state (that is, within states) or across state borders.

intergovernmental organization (IGO) An organization (such as the United Nations and its agencies) whose members are state governments.

nongovernmental organization (NGO) A transnational group or entity (such as the Catholic Church, Greenpeace, or the International Olympic Committee) that interacts with states, multinational corporations (MNCs), other NGOs, and intergovernmental organizations (IGOs).

Table 1.2 Types of Nonstate Actors

Type		Who Are They?	Examples
IGOs[a]	Intergovernmental Organizations	Members are national governments	United Nations, NATO, Arab League
NGOs[a]	Nongovernmental Organizations	Members are individuals and groups	Amnesty International, Lions Clubs, Red Cross
MNCs	Multinational Corporations	Companies that span borders	ExxonMobil, Toyota, Walmart
Others		Individuals, Cities, Constituencies, etc.	Bono, Iraqi Kurdistan, al Qaeda

[a]*Note:* IGOs and NGOs together make up International Organizations (IOs).

Firat Yurdakul/Anadolu Agency/Getty Images

IN THE ACTION Nonstate actors participate in IR alongside states, although generally in less central roles. Nongovernmental organizations (NGOs) are becoming increasingly active in IR. Here relief workers from a Turkish Islamic charity group distribute clothes and shoes to Rohingya children in a refugee camp in Bangladesh, 2017. The children fled from a violent military crackdown, which many have labeled ethnic cleansing, in their home country of Burma (Myanmar).

provide protection, well-regulated markets, and a stable political environment. MNCs as international actors receive special attention in Chapters 9 and 13.

Various other nonstate actors interact with states, IOs, and MNCs. For example, the terrorist attacks since September 11, 2001, have demonstrated the increasing power that technology gives terrorists as nonstate actors. Just as Greenpeace can travel to a remote location and then beam video of its environmental actions there to the world, so too can the Islamic State place suicide bombers in world cities, coordinate their operations and finances through the Internet and the global banking system, and reach a global audience via social media outlets like YouTube and Twitter. "Global reach," once an exclusive capability of great powers, now is available to many others, for better or worse.

Some nonstate actors are _substate actors_: They exist within one country but either influence that country's foreign policy or operate internationally, or both. For instance, the state of Pennsylvania is entirely a U.S. entity but operates an Office of International Business Development to promote exports and foreign investment, with 15 offices worldwide. The actions of substate economic actors—companies, consumers, workers, investors— help create the context of economic activity against which international political events play out and within which governments must operate.

In this world of globalization, of substate actors and transnational actors, states are still important. But to some extent they are being gradually pushed aside as companies, groups, and individuals deal ever more directly with each other across borders and as the world economy becomes globally integrated. Now more than ever, IR extends beyond the interactions of national governments.

Both state and nonstate actors are strongly affected by the revolution in information technologies now under way. The new information-intensive world promises to reshape international relations profoundly. Technological change dramatically affects actors' relative capabilities and even preferences. Telecommunications and computerization allow economics, politics, and culture alike to operate on a global scale as never before. The ramifications of information technology for various facets of IR will be developed in each chapter of this book.

1.2.3 Levels of Analysis

The many actors involved in IR contribute to the complexity of competing explanations and theories. One way scholars of IR have sorted out this multiplicity of influences, actors, and processes is to categorize them into different _levels of analysis_ (see Table 1.3). A level of analysis is a perspective on IR based on a set of similar actors or processes that suggests possible explanations to "why" questions. IR scholars have proposed various level-of-analysis schemes, most often with three main levels (and sometimes a few sublevels between).

The _individual_ level of analysis concerns the perceptions, choices, and actions of individual human beings. Great leaders influence the course of history, as do individual citizens, thinkers, soldiers, and voters. Without Lenin, it is said, there might well have been no Soviet Union. If a few more college students had voted for Nixon rather than Kennedy in the razor-close 1960 election, the Cuban Missile Crisis might have

Table 1.3 Levels of Analysis

Many influences affect the course of international relations. Levels of analysis provide a framework for categorizing these influences and thus for suggesting various explanations of international events. Examples include:

Systemic Level		
North-South gap	Religious fundamentalism	Information revolution
European imperialism	World environment	Global telecommunications
Norms	Technological change	Worldwide scientific and business communities
Distribution of power	Wars	IGOs
Balance of power	Military alliances	Trade agreements

Domestic Level		
Nationalism	Dictatorship	Gender
Ethnic conflict	Domestic coalitions	Economic sectors and industries
Type of government	Political parties and elections	Military-industrial complex
Democracy	Public opinion	Foreign policy bureaucracies

Individual Level		
Great leaders	Psychology of perception and decision	Citizens' participation (voting, rebelling, going to war, etc.)
Crazy leaders	Learning	
Decision making in crises	Assassinations, accidents of history	

ended differently. The study of foreign policy decision making, discussed in Chapter 3, pays special attention to individual-level explanations of IR outcomes because of the importance of psychological factors in the decision-making process.

The *domestic* (or *state* or *societal*) level of analysis concerns the aggregations of individuals within states that influence state actions in the international arena. Such aggregations include interest groups, political organizations, and government agencies. These groups operate differently (with different international effects) in different kinds of societies and states. For instance, democracies and dictatorships may act differently from one another, and democracies may act differently in an election year from the way they act at other times. The politics of ethnic conflict and nationalism, bubbling up from within states, plays an increasingly important role in the relations among states. Within governments, foreign policy agencies often fight bureaucratic battles over policy decisions.

The *systemic* (or *interstate*) level of analysis concerns the influence of the international system upon outcomes. This level of analysis therefore focuses on the interactions of states themselves, without regard to their internal makeup or the particular individuals who lead them. This level pays attention to states' relative power positions in the international system and the interactions (trade, for example) among them. It has been traditionally the most important of the levels of analysis.

Most scholars also include forces that transcend the interactions of states in the systemic level. The evolution of human technology, of certain worldwide beliefs, and of humans' relationship to the natural environment are all processes at the systemic level that influence international relations. This level includes factors such as the process of transnational integration through worldwide scientific, technical, and business communities (see Chapter 10). Another pervasive systemic influence is the lingering effect of historical European imperialism—Europe's conquest of Latin America, Asia, and Africa (see History of Imperialism, 1500–2000 in Chapter 12).

Levels of analysis offer different sorts of explanations for international events. For example, many possible explanations exist for the 2003 U.S.-led war against Iraq. At the individual level, the war could be attributed to Saddam Hussein's gamble that he could defeat the forces arrayed against him, or to President Bush's desire to remove a leader he personally deemed threatening. At the domestic level, the war could be attributed to the rise of the powerful neoconservative faction that convinced the Bush administration and Americans that Saddam was a threat to U.S. security in a post–September 11 world. At the systemic level, the war might be attributed to the predominance of U.S. power. With no state willing to back Iraq militarily, the United States (as the largest global military power) was free to attack Iraq without fear of a large-scale military response.

Although IR scholars often focus their study mainly on one level of analysis, other levels bear on a problem simultaneously. There is no single correct level for a given "why" question. Rather, levels of analysis help suggest multiple explanations and approaches to consider in explaining an event. They remind scholars and students to look beyond the immediate and superficial aspects of an event to explore the possible influences of more distant causes. Note that the processes at higher levels tend to operate more slowly than those at lower levels. Individuals go in and out of office often; the structure of the international system changes rarely.

1.2.4 Globalization

globalization The increasing integration of the world in terms of communications, culture, and economics; may also refer to changing subjective experiences of space and time accompanying this process.

Globalization encompasses many trends, including expanded international trade, telecommunications, monetary coordination, multinational corporations, technical and scientific cooperation, cultural exchanges of new types and scales, migration and refugee flows, and relations between the world's rich and poor countries. Although globalization clearly is very important, it is also rather vaguely defined and not well explained by any one theory. One popular conception of globalization is "the widening, deepening and speeding up of worldwide interconnectedness in all aspects of contemporary social life. . . ."[4] But at least three conceptions of this process compete.

One view sees globalization as the fruition of liberal economic principles. A global marketplace has brought growth and prosperity (not to all countries but to those most integrated with the global market). This economic process has made traditional states obsolete as economic units. States are thus losing authority to supranational institutions such as the International Monetary Fund (IMF) and the European Union (EU), and to transnational actors such as MNCs and NGOs. The values of technocrats and elite, educated citizens in liberal democracies are becoming global values, reflecting an emerging global civilization. The old North-South division is seen as less important because the global South is moving in divergent directions depending on countries' and regions' integration with world markets.

A second perspective is skeptical of these claims about globalization. Such skeptics note that the world's major economies are no more integrated today than before World War I (when British hegemony provided a common set of expectations and institutions). The skeptics also doubt that regional and geographic distinctions such as the North-South divide are disappearing in favor of a single global market. Rather, they see the North-South gap as increasing with globalization. Also, the economic integration of states may be leading not to a single world free-trade zone but to distinct and rival regional blocs in America, Europe, and

THINK GLOBALLY As the world economy becomes more integrated, markets and production are becoming global in scope. This container port in Shanghai ships goods to and from all over the world, 2013.

Xu Xiaolin/Getty Images

---

[4]Held, David, Anthony McGrew, David Goldblatt, and Jonathan Perraton. *Global Transformations: Politics, Economics and Culture.* Stanford, 1999: 2.

Asia. The supposed emerging world civilization is disproved by the fragmenting of larger units (such as the Soviet Union) into smaller ones along lines of language, religion, and other such cultural factors.

A third school of thought sees globalization as more profound than the skeptics believe, yet more uncertain than the view of supporters of liberal economics. These "transformationalists" see state sovereignty as being eroded by the EU, the WTO, and other new institutions, so that sovereignty is no longer an absolute but just one of a spectrum of bargaining leverages held by states. The bargaining itself increasingly involves nonstate actors. Thus, globalization diffuses authority. State power is not so much strengthened or weakened by globalization but transformed to operate in new contexts with new tools.

While scholars debate these conceptions of globalization, popular debates focus on the growing power of large corporations operating globally, the disruptive costs associated with joining world markets (for example, job loss and environmental impacts), the perception of growing disparities between the rich and the poor, and the collusion of national governments in these wrongs through their participation in IOs such as the WTO and the IMF. Policies to expand free trade are a central focus of antiglobalization protesters (see Chapter 8). Street protests have turned host cities into besieged fortresses in Seattle (1999); Washington, DC (2000 IMF and World Bank meetings); Quebec (2001 summit working toward a Free Trade Area of the Americas); and Genoa, Italy (2001 G8 summit), where protesters engaged police in battles that killed one person. At the 2005 Hong Kong WTO meeting, protesters blocked nearby roads and some even tried to swim across Hong Kong harbor to disrupt the meeting. Although the protests have become less violent, annual WTO meetings are still the targets of antiglobalization protesters from around the globe.

This antiglobalization rhetoric grew in strength in 2016, when British voters rejected membership in the EU and Americans elected a president who criticized global trade agreements, questioned the need for military alliances, and promised to limit immigration from other countries. Within weeks of taking office, President Trump withdrew the United States from a major Asian trade agreement (the Trans-Pacific Partnership [TPP]), demanded military allies do more to pay for the NATO alliance, and attempted to ban immigration from several Muslim-majority countries. Both the British and American political movements behind these phenomena argued that global forces had created dangers to citizens in both countries.

Just as scholars disagree on conceptions of globalization, so do skeptics of globalization disagree on their goals and tactics. Union members from the global North want to stop globalization from shipping their jobs south. But workers in impoverished countries in the global South may desperately want those jobs as a first step toward decent wages and working conditions (relative to other options in their countries). In the United States, many in the Democratic Party (presidential candidate Bernie Sanders) and the Republican Party (President Trump) have expressed skepticism about global trade. Yet, both parties also have numerous members who argue for free trade. And while supporters of Trump and Sanders may agree on trade policy, they likely agree on little else in terms of policy. Thus, neither globalization nor the backlash to it is simple.

Globalization is changing both international security and IPE, as we will see in the coming chapters, but it is changing IPE more quickly and profoundly than security. The coming chapters address a broad range of topics, each affected by globalization. Chapter 4 shows how nonstate actors influence foreign policies of states. Chapter 7 discusses global institutions, international law, and human rights, all of growing importance as globalization continues. Chapters 8 and 9 look at economic globalization in trade, finance, and business, where globalization's influences are most apparent. Chapter 10 considers the information technology side of globalization as the world becomes wired in new ways. Chapter 11 discusses the global environment and examines how increasing interaction through globalization influences our physical environment. Chapters 12 and 13 cover the global North-South divide, which is central to the concept of globalization.

The rest of this chapter takes up two contextual aspects of globalization that shape the issue areas discussed in subsequent chapters—(1) the relations among the world's major regions, especially the rich North and poor South, and (2) the evolution of the international system over the past century.

1.3 Global Geography

Identify at least three commonalities between states in the global North and states in the global South.

To highlight the insights afforded by a global level of analysis, this book divides the world into nine regions. These *world regions* differ from each other in the number of states they contain and in each region's particular mix of cultures, geographical realities, and languages. But each represents a geographical corner of the world, and together they reflect the overall larger divisions of the world.

North-South gap The disparity in resources (income, wealth, and power) between the industrialized, relatively rich countries of the West (and the former East) and the poorer countries of Africa, the Middle East, and much of Asia and Latin America.

The global **North-South gap** between the relatively rich industrialized countries of the North and the relatively poor countries of the South is the most important geographical element at the global level of analysis. The regions used in this book have been drawn to separate (with a few exceptions) the rich countries from the poor ones. The North includes both the West (the rich countries of North America, Europe, and Japan) and the old East, including the former Soviet Union (now Russia) and the *Commonwealth of Independent States (CIS)*, a loose confederation of former Soviet republics excluding the Baltic states.[5] The South includes Latin America, Africa, the Middle East, and much of Asia. The South is often called the *third world* (third after the West and East)—a term that is still widely used despite the second world's collapse. Countries in the South are also referred to as "developing" countries or "less-developed" countries (LDCs), in contrast to the "developed" countries of the North. The world regions are shown in Figure 1.2.

Several criteria beyond income levels help distinguish major geographically contiguous regions. Countries with similar economic levels, cultures, and languages have been kept together where possible. States with a history of interaction, including historical empires or trading zones, are also placed together in a region. Finally, countries that might possibly unify in the future—notably South Korea with North Korea, and China with Taiwan—are kept in the same region. Of course, no scheme works perfectly, and some states, such as Turkey, are pulled toward two regions.

Most of these regions correspond with commonly used geographical names, but a few notes may help. *East Asia* refers to China, Japan, and Korea. *Southeast Asia* refers to countries from Burma through Indonesia and the Philippines. Russia is considered a European state although a large section (Siberia) is in Asia. The *Pacific Rim* usually means East and Southeast Asia, Siberia, and the Pacific coast of North America and Latin America. *South Asia* only sometimes includes parts of Southeast Asia. Narrow definitions of the *Middle East* exclude both North Africa and Turkey. The *Balkans* are the states of southeastern Europe, bounded by Slovenia, Romania, and Greece.

Table 1.4 shows GDP for each of the world's countries, organized by region. Table 1.5 shows the approximate population and economic size (GDP) of each region in relation to the world as a whole. As the table indicates, income levels per capita are, overall, more than five times as high in the North as in the South. *The North contains*

---

[5]Note that geographical designations such as the "West" and the "Middle East" are European-centered. From Korea, for example, China and Russia are to the west, and Japan and the United States are to the east.

Figure 1.2 Nine Regions of the World

Table 1.4 States and Territories with Estimated Total GDP, 2017 *(In billions of 2018 U.S. dollars)*

North America					
United States	19,000	Canada	2,000	Bahamas	10
Europe					
Germany[a]	3,500	Czech Republic[a]	200	Latvia	30
Britain[a]	2,700	Greece[a]	200	Estonia[a]	20
France[a]	2,500	Portugal[a]	200	Cyprus[a]	20
Italy[a]	1,900	Finland[a]	200	Bosnia and Herzegovina	20
Spain[a]	1,200	Romania[a]	200	Iceland	20
Netherlands[a]	800	Hungary[a]	100	Albania	10
Switzerland	700	Slovakia[a]	100	Macedonia	10
Poland[a]	500	Luxembourg	60	Malta[a]	10
Belgium[a]	500	Croatia	50	Montenegro	5
Sweden[a]	500	Slovenia[a]	50	Liechtenstein	4
Norway	400	Bulgaria[a]	50	Andorra	3
Austria[a]	400	Serbia	40	Monaco	1
Denmark[a]	300	Lithuania[a]	40	San Marino	1
Ireland[a]	300				
Japan/Pacific					
Japan	5,000	Fiji	5	Nauru	0
South Korea	1,400	Guam/Marianas[b]	4	Marshall Islands	0
Australia	1,200	Solomon Islands	1	Palau	0
New Zealand	200	Samoa	1	Kiribati	0
North Korea	40	Vanuatu	1	Tuvalu	0
Papua New Guinea	20	Tonga	1	Micronesia	0
Russia/CIS					
Russia	1,500	Belarus	50	Tajikistan	10
Kazakhstan	200	Turkmenistan	40	Kyrgyzstan	10
Ukraine	100	Georgia	20	Moldova	10
Azerbaijan	70	Armenia	10	Mongolia	10
Uzbekistan	70				
China					
China	11,000	Hong Kong[b]	300	Macau[b]	40
Taiwan[b]	500				
Middle East					
Turkey	900	Iraq	200	Lebanon	50
Saudi Arabia	700	Qatar	200	Libya	40
Iran	500	Kuwait	100	Jordan	40
United Arab Emirates	500	Morocco/W. Sahara	100	Bahrain	30
Egypt	300	Oman	70	Yemen	30
Israel/Palestine	300	Tunisia	50	Syria	20
Algeria	200				

Table 1.4 (*Continued*)

Latin America

Brazil	1,800	Panama	60	Suriname	4
Mexico	1,100	Uruguay	50	Guyana	4
Argentina	600	Paraguay	30	Belize	3
Colombia	300	El Salvador	30	Virgin Islands[b]	2
Venezuela	300	Bolivia	30	French Guiana[b]	2
Chile	300	Honduras	20	St. Lucia	2
Peru	200	Trinidad & Tobago	20	Antigua & Barbuda	2
Ecuador	100	Jamaica	10	Grenada	1
Puerto Rico[b]	100	Nicaragua	10	St. Vincent & Grenadines	1
Cuba	90	Haiti	10	St. Kitts & Nevis	1
Dominican Republic	80	Martinique[b]	7	Dominica	1
Guatemala	70	Barbados	5		
Costa Rica	60	Bermuda[b]	5		

South Asia

India	2,300	Vietnam	200	Afghanistan	20
Indonesia	900	Bangladesh	200	Laos	20
Thailand	400	Sri Lanka	90	Maldives	4
Pakistan	300	Burma (Myanmar)	70	Bhutan	3
Malaysia	300	Nepal	30	East Timor	2
Philippines	300	Cambodia	20		
Singapore	300	Brunei	20		

Africa

Nigeria	400	Zimbabwe	20	Swaziland	5
South Africa	300	Mozambique	10	Togo	5
Angola	100	Madagascar	10	Sierra Leone	5
Sudan	100	Mauritius	10	Burundi	4
Ethiopia	80	Burkina Faso	10	Central African Republic	3
Kenya	70	Chad	10	Eritea	3
Ghana	50	Namibia	10	Lesotho	3
Tanzania	50	Equatorial Guinea	10	Djibouti	3
Côte d'Ivoire (Ivory Coast)	40	Congo Republic	10	Reunion[b]	3
Cameroon	30	Niger	10	Gambia	2
Uganda	30	Rwanda	10	Cape Verde	2
Democratic Congo	30	Benin	10	Liberia	2
Botswana	20	Guinea	10	Seychelles	1
Zambia	20	South Sudan	10	Guinea-Bissau	1
Senegal	20	Malawi	6	Comoros Islands	1
Gabon	20	Mauritania	6	São Tomé & Principe	0
Mali	20	Somalia	6		

[a]European Union.
[b]Nonmember of UN.

Note: GDP data are inexact by nature. Estimates for Russia, CIS, China, and other nonmarket or transitional economies are particularly suspect and should be used cautiously. Numbers below 0.5 are listed as 0.

Sources: Data based on World Bank calculations.

Table 1.5 Comparison of World Regions, 2017

Region	Population (Millions)	GDP (Trillion $)	GDP per Capita (Dollars)
The North			
North America	360	$21	$49,000
Europe	550	17	33,000
Japan/Pacific	250	8	31,000
Russia/CIS	290	2	9,000
The South			
China	1,450	12	7,000
Middle East	500	4	7,600
Latin America	650	5	8,300
South Asia	2,500	5	1,800
Africa	1,050	2	1,500
Total North	**1,450 (20%)**	**48 (63%)**	**30,500**
Total South	**6,150 (80%)**	**28 (37%)**	**5,200**
World Total	**7,600**	**$76**	**$10,100**

Note: Data are 2017 GDP figures (in 2018 U.S. dollars) from Table 1.4; those for Russia, CIS, and China should be treated especially cautiously.

Source: Data based on World Bank calculations.

only 20 percent of the world's people but over 60 percent of its goods and services. The other 80 percent of the world's people, in the South, have less than 40 percent of the goods and services.

Within the global North, Russia and the CIS states lag behind in income levels, having suffered declines in the 1990s. In the global South, the Middle East, Latin America, and (more recently) China have achieved somewhat higher income levels than have Africa and South Asia, which remain extremely poor. Even in the somewhat higher-income regions, income is distributed quite unevenly and many people remain very poor. Note that more than half of the world's population lives in the densely populated (and poor) regions of South Asia and China. IR scholars have no single explanation for the huge North-South income gap (see Chapter 12).

1.4 The Evolving International System

Explain at least two differences between the Cold War era and the post–Cold War era.

The basic structures and principles of international relations are deeply rooted in historical developments. Throughout this book, we will review the history that bears on topics such as the great power system (Chapter 2), imperialism (Chapter 12), and nationalism (Chapter 5). Here we will review briefly the key events of the twentieth century and focus in particular on the post–Cold War era since 1990.

1.4.1 The Two World Wars, 1900–1950

World War I (1914–1918) and World War II (1939–1945) occupied only ten years of the twentieth century (see Figure 1.3), but they shaped the character of the century. Nothing like those wars has happened since, and they remain a key reference point for the world in which we live today. With perhaps just two other cases in history—the Thirty Years' War and the Napoleonic Wars—the two world wars were global or hegemonic wars in which almost all major states participated in an all-out struggle over the future of the international system.

For many people, World War I symbolizes the tragic irrationality of war. It fascinates scholars of IR because it was a catastrophic war that seems to have been unnecessary and perhaps even accidental. After a century of relative peace, the great powers marched off to battle for no good reason. There was even a popular feeling that Europe would be uplifted and reinvigorated by a war—that young men could once again prove their manhood on the battlefield in a glorious adventure. Such ideas were soon crushed by the immense pain and evident pointlessness of the war.

The previous major war had been the Franco-Prussian War of 1870–1871, when Germany executed a swift offensive using railroads to rush forces to the front. That war had ended quickly, decisively, and with a clear winner (Germany). People expected that a new war would follow the same pattern. All the great powers made plans for a quick railroad-borne offensive and rapid victory—what has been called the *cult of the offensive*. They believed that the one to strike first would win. Under these doctrines, one country's mobilization for war practically forced its enemies to mobilize as well. Thus, when a Serbian nationalist assassinated Archduke Ferdinand of Austria in 1914 in Sarajevo, a minor crisis escalated and the mobilization plans pushed Europe to all-out war.

Contrary to expectations, the war was neither short nor decisive, and it certainly was not glorious. It bogged down in *trench warfare* along a fixed front. For example, in 1917 at the Battle of Passchendaele (Belgium), the British in three months fired five tons of artillery shells per yard of front line, over an 11-mile-wide front, and then lost 400,000 men in a failed ground attack. The horrific conditions were worsened by chemical weapons and by the attempts of Britain and Germany to starve each other's population into surrender.

Russia was the first state to crumble. Revolution at home removed Russia from the war in 1917 (and led to the founding of the Soviet Union). But the entry of the United States into the war on the anti-German side that year quickly turned the tide. In the *Treaty of Versailles* of 1919, Germany was forced to give up territory, pay reparations, limit its future armaments, and admit guilt for the war. German resentment against the harsh terms of Versailles would contribute to Adolf Hitler's rise to power in the 1930s. After World War I, U.S. president Woodrow Wilson led the effort to create the **League of Nations**, a forerunner of today's United Nations. But the U.S. Senate would not approve U.S. participation, and the League did not prove effective. U.S. isolationism between the world wars, along with declining British power and a Russia crippled by its own revolution, left a power vacuum in world politics.

In the 1930s, Germany and Japan stepped into that vacuum, embarking on aggressive expansionism that ultimately led to World War II. Japan had already occupied Taiwan and Korea after defeating China in 1895 and Russia in 1905. In World War I, Japan gained some German colonies in Asia. In 1931, Japan occupied Manchuria (northeast China) and set up a puppet regime there. In 1937, Japan invaded the rest of China and began a brutal occupation that continues to haunt Chinese-Japanese relations.

Meanwhile, in Europe in the 1930s, Nazi Germany under Hitler had rearmed, intervened to help fascists win the Spanish Civil War, and grabbed territory from its neighbors under the rationale of reuniting ethnic Germans in those territories with their homeland. Hitler was emboldened by the weak response of the international community and the League of Nations to aggression by fascist regimes in Italy and Spain. In an effort to appease German ambitions, Britain and France agreed in the **Munich Agreement** of 1938 to let Germany occupy part of Czechoslovakia (known as the Sudetenland). Appeasement has since had a negative connotation in IR because the Munich Agreement seemed only to encourage Hitler's further conquests.

In 1939, Germany invaded Poland, leading Britain and France to join the war against Germany. Hitler signed a nonaggression pact with his archenemy, Joseph Stalin of the Soviet Union, and threw his full army against France, occupying most of

League of Nations An organization established after World War I and a forerunner of today's United Nations; it achieved certain humanitarian and other successes but was weakened by the absence of U.S. membership and by its own lack of effectiveness in ensuring collective security. See also *collective security*.

Munich Agreement A symbol of the failed policy of appeasement, this agreement, signed in 1938, allowed Nazi Germany to occupy a part of Czechoslovakia. Rather than appease German aspirations, it was followed by further German expansions, which triggered World War II.

Figure 1.3 The Two World Wars, 1900–1950

Source: U.S. Defense Department.

	1900	1910		1920	1930		1940	1950
Europe		mobilization plans developed	**World War I**			Italy invades Ethiopia	**World War II**	
		Balkan crises	Sarajevo	U.S. enters war		Munich Agreement	U.S. enters war	occupied by Allied forces
								D–Day
Germany		naval arms race with Britain →	Defeat	Weimar Republic	Hitler wins power	invasion of Poland	The Holocaust	Defeat
				hyperinflation	rearma-ment	occupation of Austria, Czech.	strategic bombing	
							occupation of Europe	
Russia			Russian Revolution	(civil war)	(industrialization)	pact with Hitler	German invasion	Victory
			USSR formed					
Asia	U.S. in Philippines	Russo-Japanese War	Japan neutral in WW I		Japan occupies Manchuria (China)	Japan invades China	Pearl Harbor	Hiroshima	Occupied by U.S.
							Japan occupies S.E. Asia	island battles
Inter-national Norms & Law		Hague Peace Conferences		Versailles treaty	Japan quits League of Nations			Nuremberg Tribunal
				League of Nations →	U.S. isolationism			United Nations →
				Washington Naval Treaty				
Tech-nology	destroyers		trench warfare		mechanized armor		air war	nuclear weapons
			chemical weapons				radar	
			submarines	tanks				

it quickly. Hitler then double-crossed Stalin and invaded the Soviet Union in 1941. This offensive ultimately bogged down and was turned back after several years. But the Soviet Union took the brunt of the German attack and suffered by far the greatest share of the 60 million deaths caused by World War II. This trauma continues to be a powerful memory that shapes views of IR in Russia and Eastern Europe.

The United States joined World War II against Germany in 1942. The U.S. economy produced critically important weapons and supplies for allied armies. The United States played an important role with Britain in the strategic bombing of German cities—including the firebombing of Dresden in February 1945, which caused 100,000 civilian deaths. In 1944, after crossing the English Channel on June 6 (*D-Day*), British-American forces pushed into Germany from the west while the Soviets pushed from the east. A ruined Germany surrendered and was occupied by the allied powers. At its peak, Nazi Germany and its allies had occupied almost all of Europe except Britain and part of Russia.

While the war in Europe was raging, Japan fought a war over control of Southeast Asia with the United States and its allies. Japan's expansionism in the 1930s had only underscored the dependence on foreign resources that the expansionism was intended to solve: The United States punished Japan by cutting off U.S. oil exports. Japan then destroyed much of the U.S. Navy in a surprise attack at *Pearl Harbor* (Hawaii) in 1941 and seized desired territories (including Indonesia, whose oil replaced that of the United States). The United States, however, built vast new military forces and retook a series of Pacific islands in subsequent years. The strategic bombing of Japanese cities by the United States culminated in the only historical use of nuclear weapons in war— the destruction of the cities of *Hiroshima* and *Nagasaki* in August 1945—which triggered Japan's quick surrender.

The lessons of the two world wars seem contradictory. From the failure of the Munich Agreement in 1938 to appease Hitler, many people have concluded that only a hardline foreign policy with preparedness for war will deter aggression and prevent war. Yet in 1914 it was just such hardline policies that apparently led Europe into a disastrous war, which might have been avoided by more conciliatory policies. Evidently the best policy would be sometimes harsh and at other times conciliatory, but IR scholars have not discovered a simple formula for choosing (see Theories of the Causes of War in Chapter 5).

1.4.2 The Cold War, 1945–1990

The United States and the Soviet Union became the two superpowers of the post–World War II era (see Figure 1.4). Each had its ideological mission (capitalist democracy versus communism), its networks of alliances and clients, and its deadly arsenal of nuclear weapons. Europe was divided, with the massive military forces of the United States and its *NATO* allies on one side and the massive military forces of the Soviet Union and its *Warsaw Pact* allies on the other. Germany itself was split, with three-quarters of the country—and three-quarters of the capital city of Berlin— occupied by the United States, Britain, and France. The remainder, surrounding West Berlin, was occupied by the Soviet Union. Crises in Berlin in 1947–1948 and 1961 led to armed confrontations but not war. In 1961, East Germany built the Berlin Wall separating East from West Berlin. It symbolized the division of Europe by what Winston Churchill had called the "iron curtain."

Despite the hostility of East-West relations during the **Cold War**, a relatively stable framework of relations emerged, and conflicts never escalated to all-out war between the largest states. At a U.S.-Soviet-British meeting at *Yalta* in 1945, when the defeat of Germany was imminent, the Western powers acknowledged the fact of the Soviet army's presence in Eastern Europe, allowing that area to remain under Soviet influence. Although the Soviet bloc did not join Western economic institutions such as

Cold War The hostile relations— punctuated by occasional periods of improvement, or détente—between the two superpowers, the United States and the Soviet Union, from 1945 to 1990.

Figure 1.4 The Cold War, 1945–1990

Sources: Based on Gaddis, John Lewis. *We Now Know: Rethinking Cold War History.* Oxford, 1997. Zubok, Vladislav, and Constantine Pleshakov. *Inside the Kremlin's Cold War: From Stalin to Khrushchev.* Harvard, 1996. Garthoff, Raymond. *Détente and Confrontation: American-Soviet Relations from Nixon to Reagan.* Brookings, 1985. Larson, Deborah Welch. *Anatomy of Mistrust: U.S.–Soviet Relations During the Cold War.* Cornell, 1997. Trachtenberg, Marc. *A Constructed Peace: The Making of the European Settlement, 1945–1963.* Princeton, 1999.

Time axis: 1940 — 1950 — 1960 — 1970 — 1980 — 1990

Soviet Union (leaders): Stalin | Khrushchev | Brezhnev | Andropov | Chernenko | Gorbachev
- A-bomb; Warsaw Pact →
- Sputnik
- nuclear parity with U.S.
- reforms (*perestroika, glasnost*)

United States (leaders): F. D. Roosevelt | Truman | Eisenhower | Kennedy | Johnson | Nixon | Ford | Carter | Reagan | Bush
- (WW II alliance)
- NATO →; containment policy →
- (nuclear superiority over USSR)
- nuclear arms race →
- human rights; (Iran crisis)
- military buildup; "Star Wars" (SDI)
- student protests

China:
- civil war (Nationalists–Communists)
- Sino-Soviet alliance
- People's Republic (Taiwan nationalist) →; Taiwan Straits crises (vs. U.S.)
- Sino-Soviet split; A-bomb
- Cultural Revolution
- Soviet border clashes; joins UN
- U.S.–China rapprochement; death of Mao
- neutral to pro-U.S.

Confrontations:
- Greek civil war
- Berlin crisis
- Korean War
- Soviet invasion of Hungary; U-2 incident
- Berlin Wall; Berlin crisis; Cuban Missile Crisis
- Vietnam War; USSR invades Czechoslovakia

Proxy Wars:
- Cuban revolution
- Suez crisis
- Indonesia
- Arab-Israeli wars
- Chile coup
- Somalia vs. Ethiopia; Cambodia
- Nicaragua →; El Salvador →; Angola →
- U.S. invasion of Grenada
- Afghanistan War

Co-operation:
- Yalta summit
- Geneva summit
- Limited Test Ban Treaty; Non-Proliferation Treaty
- détente; SALT I; SALT II
- START talks
- Paris summit (CFE); INF treaty

the IMF, all the world's major states joined the UN. The UN (unlike the ill-fated League of Nations) managed to maintain almost universal membership and adherence to basic structures and rules throughout the Cold War era.

The central concern of the West during the Cold War was that the Soviet Union might gain control of Western Europe—either through outright invasion or through communists taking power in war-weary and impoverished countries of Western Europe. This could have put the entire industrial base of the Eurasian landmass (from Europe to Siberia) under one state. The *Marshall Plan*—U.S. financial aid to rebuild European economies—responded to these fears, as did the creation of the NATO alliance. Half of the entire world's military spending was devoted to the European standoff. Much spending was also devoted to a superpower nuclear arms race, in which each superpower produced tens of thousands of nuclear weapons (see Chapter 6).

Through the policy of **containment**, adopted in the late 1940s, the United States sought to halt the expansion of Soviet influence globally on several levels at once— military, political, ideological, and economic. The United States maintained an extensive network of military bases and alliances worldwide. Almost all of U.S. foreign policy in subsequent decades, from foreign aid and technology transfer to military intervention and diplomacy, came to serve the goal of containment.

containment A policy adopted in the late 1940s by which the United States sought to halt the global expansion of Soviet influence on several levels—military, political, ideological, and economic.

The *Chinese communist revolution* in 1949 led to a Sino-Soviet alliance (*Sino* means "Chinese"). But China became fiercely independent in the 1960s following the **Sino-Soviet split**, when China opposed Soviet moves toward *peaceful coexistence* with the United States. In the late 1960s, young radicals, opposed to both superpowers, ran China during the chaotic and destructive *Cultural Revolution*. But feeling threatened by Soviet power, China's leaders developed a growing affiliation with the United States during the 1970s, starting with a dramatic visit to China by U.S. president Richard Nixon in 1972. This visit led to U.S.-Chinese diplomatic relations in 1979. During the Cold War, China generally tried to play a balancing role against whichever superpower seemed most threatening at the time.

Sino-Soviet split A rift in the 1960s between the communist powers of the Soviet Union and China, fueled by China's opposition to Soviet moves toward peaceful coexistence with the United States.

In 1950, the *Korean War* broke out when communist North Korea attacked and overran most of U.S.-allied South Korea. The United States and its allies (under UN authority obtained after the Soviets walked out of the Security Council in protest) counterattacked and overran most of North Korea. China sent masses of "volunteers" to help North Korea, and the war bogged down near the original border until a 1953 truce ended the fighting. The Korean War hardened U.S. attitudes toward communism and set a negative tone for future East-West relations, especially for U.S.-Chinese relations in the 1950s.

The Cold War thawed temporarily after Stalin died in 1953. The first **summit meeting** between superpower leaders took place in Geneva in 1955. This thaw in relations led both sides to agree to reconstitute Austria, which had been split into four pieces like Germany. But the Soviet Union sent tanks to crush a popular uprising in Hungary in 1956 (an action it repeated in 1968 in Czechoslovakia), and the Soviet missile program that orbited *Sputnik* in 1957 alarmed the United States. The shooting down of a U.S. spy plane (the *U-2*) over the Soviet Union in 1960 scuttled a summit meeting between superpower leaders Nikita Khrushchev and Dwight D. Eisenhower. Meanwhile in Cuba, after Fidel Castro's communist revolution in 1959, the United States attempted a counterrevolution in the botched 1961 *Bay of Pigs* invasion.

summit meeting A meeting between heads of state, often referring to leaders of great powers, as in the Cold War superpower summits between the United States and the Soviet Union or today's meetings of the Group of Twenty (G20) on economic coordination.

These hostilities culminated in the **Cuban Missile Crisis** of 1962, when the Soviet Union installed medium-range nuclear missiles in Cuba. The Soviet aims were to reduce the Soviet Union's strategic nuclear inferiority, to counter the deployment of U.S. missiles on Soviet borders in Turkey, and to deter another U.S. invasion of Cuba. U.S. leaders, however, considered the missiles threatening and provocative. As historical documents revealed years later, nuclear war at that time was quite possible. Some U.S. policy makers favored military strikes before the missiles became operational when in fact some nuclear weapons in Cuba were already operational and commanders were authorized to use

Cuban Missile Crisis (1962) A superpower crisis, sparked by the Soviet Union's installation of medium-range nuclear missiles in Cuba, that marks the moment when the United States and the Soviet Union came closest to nuclear war.

Bettmann/Getty Images

IRON CURTAIN During the Cold War, the U.S. and Soviet sides sought spheres of influence. Europe was divided, and Germany itself was split, with its capital, Berlin, also divided. In 1961 the communist side built the Berlin Wall, seen here in 1962, to keep its population from leaving. It was dismantled as the Cold War ended in 1989.

proxy wars Wars in the third world—often civil wars—in which the United States and the Soviet Union jockeyed for position by supplying and advising opposing factions.

them in the event of a U.S. attack. Instead, President John F. Kennedy imposed a naval blockade to force their removal. The Soviet Union backed down on the missiles, and the United States promised not to invade Cuba in the future. Leaders on both sides were shaken, however, by the possibility of nuclear war. They signed the *Limited Test Ban Treaty* in 1963, prohibiting atmospheric nuclear tests, and began to cooperate in cultural exchanges, space exploration, aviation, and other areas.

The two superpowers often jockeyed for position in the global South, supporting **proxy wars** in which they typically supplied and advised opposing factions in civil wars. The alignments were often arbitrary. For instance, the United States backed the Ethiopian government and the Soviets backed next-door rival Somalia in the 1970s; however, when an Ethiopian revolution caused the new government to seek Soviet help, the United States switched its support to Somalia instead.

One flaw of U.S. policy in the Cold War period was to see all regional conflicts through an East-West lens. Its preoccupation with communism led the United States to support unpopular pro-Western governments in a number of poor countries, nowhere more disastrously than during the *Vietnam War* in the 1960s. The war in Vietnam divided U.S. citizens and ultimately failed to prevent a communist takeover. The fall of South Vietnam in 1975 appeared to signal U.S. weakness, especially combined with U.S. setbacks in the Middle East—the 1973 Arab oil embargo against the United States and the 1979 overthrow of the U.S.-backed shah of Iran by Islamic fundamentalists.

During this period of apparent U.S. weakness, the Soviet Union invaded Afghanistan in 1979. But, like the United States in Vietnam, the Soviet Union could not suppress rebel armies supplied by the opposing superpower. The Soviets ultimately withdrew after almost a decade of war that considerably weakened the Soviet Union. Meanwhile, President Ronald Reagan built up U.S. military forces to record levels and supported rebel armies in the Soviet-allied states of Nicaragua and Angola (and one faction in Cambodia) as well as Afghanistan. Superpower relations slowly improved after Mikhail Gorbachev, a reformer, took power in the Soviet Union in 1985. But some of the battlegrounds of the global South (notably Afghanistan and Angola) continued to suffer from brutal civil wars (fought with leftover Cold War arms) into the new century.

In retrospect, it seems that both superpowers exaggerated Soviet strength. In the early years of the nuclear arms race, U.S. military superiority was absolute, especially in nuclear weapons. The Soviets managed to match the United States over time, from A-bombs to H-bombs to multiple-warhead missiles. By the 1970s, the Soviets had achieved strategic parity, meaning that neither side could prevent its own destruction in a nuclear war. But behind this military parity lay a Soviet Union lagging far behind the West in everything else—wealth, technology, infrastructure, and citizen/worker motivation.

In June 1989, massive pro-democracy demonstrations in China's capital of Beijing (Tiananmen Square) were put down violently by the communist government. Hundreds were shot dead in the streets. Later that year, as the Soviet Union stood by, one Eastern European country after another replaced its communist government under pressure of mass demonstrations. The toppling of the Berlin Wall in late 1989 symbolized the end of the Cold War division of Europe. Germany formally reunified in 1990. The Soviet leader, Gorbachev, allowed these losses of external power (and more) in hopes of concentrating on Soviet domestic restructuring under his policies of *perestroika* (economic reform) and *glasnost* (openness in political discussion). China remained a communist, authoritarian government but liberalized its economy and avoided military conflicts. In contrast to the Cold War era, China developed close ties with both the United States and Russia and joined the world's liberal trading regime.

Scholars do not agree on the important question of why the Cold War ended. One view is that U.S. military strength under President Reagan forced the Soviet Union into bankruptcy as it tried to keep up in the arms race. A different position is that the Soviet Union suffered from internal stagnation over decades and ultimately imploded because of weaknesses that had little to do with external pressure. Indeed, some scholars think the Soviet Union might have fallen apart earlier without the United States as a foreign enemy to bolster the Soviet government's legitimacy with its own people.

1.4.3 The Post–Cold War Era, 1990–2018

The post–Cold War era began with a bang while the Soviet Union was still disintegrating. In 1990, perhaps believing that the end of the Cold War had left a power vacuum in its region, Iraq occupied its neighbor Kuwait in an aggressive grab for control of Middle East oil. Western powers were alarmed—both about the example that unpunished aggression could set in a new era and about the direct threat to energy supplies for the world economy. The United States mobilized a coalition of the world's major countries (with almost no opposition) to counter Iraq. Working through the UN, the U.S.-led coalition applied escalating sanctions against Iraq.

When Iraq did not withdraw from Kuwait by the UN's deadline, the United States and its allies easily smashed Iraq's military and evicted its army from Kuwait in the *Gulf War*. But the coalition did not occupy Iraq or overthrow its government. The costs of the Gulf War were shared among the participants in the coalition, with Britain and France making military commitments while Japan and Germany made substantial financial contributions. The pass-the-hat financing for this war was an innovation, one that worked fairly well.

The final collapse of the Soviet Union followed only months after the Gulf War. The 15 republics of the Soviet Union—of which Russia was just one—had begun taking power from a weakened central government, declaring themselves sovereign states. This process raised complex problems ranging from issues of national self-determination to the reallocation of property. Russia and the other former republics struggled throughout the 1990s against economic and financial collapse, inflation, corruption, war, and military weakness, although they remained political democracies. A failed Russian military coup attempt in 1991—and the prominent role of Russian president Boris Yeltsin in opposing it—accelerated the collapse of the Soviet Union. Soon both capitalism and democracy were adopted as the basis of the economies and political systems of the former Soviet states. The republics became independent states and formed the CIS. Of the former Soviet republics, only the three small Baltic states and Georgia are nonmembers.

Western relations with Russia and the other republics have been highly varied since the 1990s. Because of their own economic problems, and because of a sense that Russia needed internal reform more than external aid, Western countries provided only limited aid for the region's harsh economic transition, which had drastically reduced living standards. Russia's brutal suppression of its secessionist province of Chechnya in 1995 and 1999 provoked Western fears of an expansionist, aggressive Russian nationalism. Russian leaders feared NATO expansion into Eastern Europe that placed threatening Western military forces on Russia's borders. Tensions with Western states have increased since Russia's annexation of Crimea in 2014 and

Russian support of rebels fighting against Ukraine's government in the eastern part of that country. Moreover, revelations that Russia has attempted to directly influence democratic elections in several Western states in the 2010s have led to increasing distrust of Russian motives and behavior.

Despite these problems, compared to the Cold War, the post–Cold War era has seen more cooperation between the great powers. Russia and the United States agreed to major reductions in their nuclear weapons and carried them out in the 1990s. Military tensions between the great powers, even with diplomatic disputes and economic sanctions levied against Russia, are relatively low by historical standards.

Just after the Gulf War in 1991, the former Yugoslavia broke apart, with several of its republics declaring independence. Ethnic Serbs, who were minorities in Croatia and Bosnia, seized territory to form a "Greater Serbia." With help from Serbia, which controlled the Yugoslav army, they killed hundreds of thousands of non-Serb Bosnians and Croatians and expelled millions more to create an ethnically pure state.

The international community recognized the independence of Croatia and Bosnia, admitting them to the UN and passing dozens of Security Council resolutions to protect their territorial integrity and their civilian populations. But in contrast to the Gulf War, the great powers showed no willingness to bear major costs to protect Bosnia. Instead they tried to contain the conflict by assuming a neutral role as peacekeeper and intermediary. In 1995, Serbian forces overran two UN-designated "safe areas" in eastern Bosnia, expelling the women and slaughtering thousands of the men. Finally, two weeks of NATO airstrikes (the alliance's first-ever military engagement), along with losses to Croatia on the ground, induced Serbian forces to come to terms. The treaty to end the war (authored by U.S. negotiators) formally held Bosnia together but granted Serbian forces autonomy on half of their territory. Meanwhile, Serbian strongman Slobodan Milosevic was indicted for war crimes by the UN tribunal for the former Yugoslavia, was delivered to the tribunal in 2001, and died in 2006 near the end of a lengthy trial.

In contrast to their indecision early in the Bosnian crisis, the Western powers acted decisively in 1999 when Serbian forces carried out "ethnic cleansing" in the Serbian province of Kosovo, predominantly populated by ethnic Albanians. NATO launched an air war that escalated over ten weeks. NATO came under criticism from Russia and China for acting without explicit UN authorization and for interfering in Serbia's internal affairs. (The international community and the UN considered Kosovo, unlike Bosnia, to be part of Serbia.) In the end, Serbian forces withdrew from Kosovo and NATO has controlled the province ever since. In 2008, with the UN Security Council still deadlocked over its status, Kosovo declared independence, bringing protests from Serbia and its allies. In 2010, the World Court declared Kosovo's *declaration* of independence legal, although its substantive status remains in dispute as of 2018.

Other Western military intervention decisions since 1990 were less effective. In Somalia, a U.S.-led coalition sent tens of thousands of troops to suppress factional fighting and deliver relief supplies to a large population that was starving. However, when those forces were drawn into the fighting and sustained casualties, the United States abruptly pulled out. In Rwanda in 1994, the genocide of more than half a million civilians in a matter of weeks was practically ignored by the international community. The great powers, burned by failures in Somalia and Bosnia, decided that their vital interests were not at stake. In 1996, the U.S. military did intervene closer to home, in Haiti, to restore the elected president, but Haiti remains mired in poverty. In 1997, the Rwanda conflict spilled into neighboring Zaire (now Democratic Congo), where rebels overthrew a corrupt dictator. Neighboring countries were drawn into the fighting, but the international community steered clear even as millions of civilians died of hunger and disease.

A major shift occurred in global politics when the United States was attacked by terrorists on September 11, 2001. The four coordinated attacks destroyed the World Trade Center in New York and a wing of the Pentagon in Washington, DC, while one flight crashed in Somerset County, Pennsylvania, after its passengers attempted to overtake the terrorists. Thousands of Americans and citizens of about 60 other countries were killed. The attacks mobilized support for the United States by a very broad coalition of states. President Bush declared a "war on terrorism" that lasted for years and spanned continents, employing both conventional and unconventional means. In late 2001, U.S. and British forces and their Afghan allies ousted the Taliban regime in Afghanistan, which had harbored the al Qaeda network (led by Osama bin Laden).

The great power divisions reappeared, however, as the United States and Britain tried to assemble a coalition to oust Iraq's Saddam Hussein by force in early 2003. France and Germany (along with Russia and China) bitterly opposed the war, as did millions of protesters around the world. The dispute disrupted the Atlantic alliance for several years and weakened the UN's role as the U.S.-led coalition went forward despite its failure to win Security Council authorization for war.

The invasion itself was brief and decisive. A U.S. military force of 250,000 troops with advanced technology overpowered the Iraqi army in three weeks. Many Iraqis welcomed the end of a dictatorial regime, as had most Afghans in late 2001, but the war inflamed anti-American sentiment, especially in Muslim countries. Insurgent forces in Iraq gained strength as the U.S. occupation stretched on for years, and within several years U.S. public opinion had turned against the protracted war. After a U.S. troop surge in 2007 and the arming of Sunni communities fed up with foreign Islamist radicals, violence in Iraq fell. U.S. forces withdrew from Iraq between 2009 and 2011. Estimates of Iraqi deaths caused by the war range from tens of thousands to more than 600,000. Elections in 2010 and 2014 were relatively peaceful, but both left the country divided along ethnic lines. Sporadic violence and unrest continued through 2011–2013 until conflict in neighboring Syria spilled into Iraq in 2014. A powerful Islamist group known as ISIS (the Islamic State in Iraq and Syria) began capturing large cities in central and northern Iraq. Iraq's prime minister resigned and traditional enemies Iran and the United States began assisting Iraq (separately) in confronting ISIS forces. By the fall of 2017, Iraq declared victory over ISIS and had regained control over all territory claimed by the Islamic State.

In Afghanistan, fighting worsened beginning in 2007 as the Taliban ran an insurgency campaign from bases in Pakistan. Disputed elections, corruption, and "insider" attacks by members of Afghan security forces on NATO troops all made the foreigners' jobs difficult. NATO sent in tens of thousands of additional troops in 2009 but then began a withdrawal that has left around 11,000 troops in 2018. NATO forces now serve mostly in a training and advising role for Afghanistan's own security forces, which still struggle to counter the Taliban. One goal of the Afghan intervention was accomplished in 2011, when U.S. special forces killed Osama bin Laden in Pakistan. U.S. drone attacks on other militants inside Pakistan and elsewhere weakened al Qaeda but raised thorny legal and political issues. As of 2018, Taliban forces continue to hold territory and carry out attacks against Afghanistan military and civilian targets. Several attempts at peace talks have been unsuccessful and in 2018, the United States stopped $900 million in security aid to Pakistan as a punishment for harboring Taliban leaders.

Meanwhile, nuclear weapons programs in North Korea and Iran have raised alarms. North Korea has produced several nuclear bombs and conducted six tests since 2006. In 2012, it successfully tested an advanced long-range missile in defiance of a UN Security Council ban. In 2017, it tested what it described as an intercontinental ballistic missile (ICBM), which had the potential to reach portions of the United States. Its sixth nuclear test, also in 2017, was possibly a hydrogen bomb, with a more powerful yield than past bombs (see Chapter 6). In response to these tests, the United States imposed further sanctions with the help of the United Nations. The United States also significantly increased its military presence near the Korean peninsula as a threat to North Korea.

Starting in 2004, Iran made and broke several agreements to suspend the enrichment of uranium that could be used to build nuclear weapons. In response, the UN

Security Council passed a series of sanctions against Iran, demanding that it stop its enrichment program. In 2010, centrifuges key to its enrichment program began mysteriously destroying themselves, and investigation pinned the problem on a sophisticated computer virus, evidently a creation of Israeli and American defense scientists. It set back Iran's program by a year or more. In the summer of 2015, the major powers and Iran agreed to a deal to reduce Iran's nuclear program. The agreement was hailed by some as a victory in significantly slowing Iran's progress, while others were critical, noting that the agreement still allowed for the possibility that Iran could eventually build a nuclear weapon. President Trump withdrew the United States from the agreement in 2018. European states then began negotiating with Iran to continue the agreement. Meanwhile, protests against the Iranian government broke out in 2018 in Iran, possibly threatening political stability.

The Arab Spring uprisings began in 2011 with nonviolent protests in Tunisia and Egypt, both resulting in the overthrow of dictators and the holding of free elections. Egypt elected a leader of the long-banned Muslim Brotherhood as president, only to have the military overthrow him in 2013. In Libya and Syria, violent repression against protesters sparked violent uprisings, leading to the bloody overthrow of Libya's dictator with NATO air support, and a prolonged and agonizing civil war in Syria with a divided international community unable to respond effectively. Eventually, the Syrian war spilled into neighboring Iraq, destabilizing Iraq's government. The use of chemical weapons in Syria brought worldwide condemnation of the Syrian government on multiple occasions. Russia intervened with airstrikes in Syria (attacking antigovernment rebels and ISIS) to prop up its only military ally in the Middle East, while the United States and Western allies tried to assist rebels and Kurdish fighters (an ethnic minority in Syria and Iraq) against ISIS and ISIS-affiliated groups. Meanwhile violence in Libya continued into 2018.

Yemen had its own revolution—a mix of peaceful protest, violent repression, ethnic conflict, and political compromise leading to a transitional government. The transitional government (aided by Saudi Arabia and Western allies) fought a bloody war against rebel groups (some aided by Iran, others by al Qaeda). By 2017, the war had escalated as rebel groups controlled significant parts of the country, a naval blockade threatened to worsen a famine, and fighters from around the region converged on Yemen to take up arms both for and against the government. And far away in Burma, after a long-standing military regime finally made a slow, concerted move toward democracy, the regime committed what many have described as "ethnic cleansing" against a minority group in 2017, creating a humanitarian disaster.

The post–Cold War era may seem a conflict-prone period in which deadly violence flares up with unexpected intensity around the world, in places such as Rwanda and Syria—even New York City. Yet *the post–Cold War era has been more peaceful than the Cold War* (see Chapter 5). Old wars have ended faster than new ones have begun. Latin America and parts of Africa have nearly extinguished wars in their regions, joining a zone of peace already encompassing North America, Europe, Japan and the Pacific, and China.

Warfare is diminishing even in the arc of conflict from Africa through the Middle East to South Asia. Since 1990, long, bloody wars have ended in South Africa, Mozambique, Angola, southern Sudan, and Ethiopia-Eritrea, as did the various conflicts in Central America and the civil war in Sri Lanka. Wars in West Africa, Rwanda, and Indonesia have also wound down. After the Cold War, world order did not spiral out of control with rampant aggression and war.

However, the Israeli-Palestinian conflict, which saw rising expectations of peace in the 1990s, worsened after a proposed deal fell through in 2000. With the 2006 Palestinian election victory of the militant Islamist party Hamas, responsible for many violent attacks on Israel, hopes for a durable peace faded. In 2006, Israel fought a brief but intense war with Hezbollah guerrillas in southern Lebanon, while violent clashes between Israel and Hamas continued from 2009 to 2014. Israel deployed a new "Iron Dome" missile defense system against Hamas missiles in 2012 and 2014 clashes. By 2018, Israelis continued to propose and build more settlements on disputed land, while Palestinians continued to press for international recognition as an independent state. Each side's moves brought denouncements from the opposing side, further diminishing hopes for peace. In the fall of 2017, the United States declared it would move the U.S. embassy to Jerusalem (from Tel Aviv), further aggravating tensions in the region.

In international economic relations, the post–Cold War era is one of globalization. New hubs of economic growth are emerging, notably in parts of Asia with remarkable economic growth. Yet, globalization has brought difficulties as well. In 2007–2008, a major economic recession crippled the developed economies of the United States, Europe, and Asia—leading to widespread unemployment, a large decline in international trade, and tremendous economic anxiety. Although the Great Recession technically ended, it took

PREPARING FOR THE WORST Peaceful trends mark the post–Cold War era, though war and terrorism continue. The most likely possibility of interstate conflict is around the Korean peninsula, where North and South Korea remain enemies 65 years after the end of their war. North Korea's development of nuclear weapons and ballistic missiles is the key source of tension between it and the rest of the world, especially neighbors like South Korea and Japan. Here, Japanese schoolchildren practice emergency drills in response to a simulation of a North Korean missile launch, 2017.

many economies years to recover. For example, employment levels in many Organisation for Economic Co-operation and Development (OECD) states did not return to pre-2007 levels until 2016.

In Europe, the Great Recession brought not only an economic but also a political crisis. During the recession, several southern European countries (Spain, Portugal, Italy, and Greece) struggled to maintain economic targets needed to support membership in the European Union's common currency (the euro). Greece then admitted to having lied about its economic position to the European Union (EU), leading investors to flee investments in Greece, which further deepened the recession there. The EU, led by Germany, chose to bail out Greece in order to keep it in the euro (see Chapter 10). The economic crisis led to a rise in anti-EU sentiment in parts of Europe. This political tension worsened in 2015 when tens of thousands of refugees, fleeing violence in Libya and Syria, made their way to Europe. Still on the road to recovery from the economic recession, European citizens were divided as to whether to allow the refugees to stay. Some argued for acceptance of the refugees on moral and humanitarian grounds, while others raised economic and security concerns.

In addition, globalization has created backlashes among people who are adversely affected or who believe their identities are threatened by foreign influences. The resurgence of nationalism and ethnic-religious conflict—occasionally in brutal form—results partly from that backlash. So does the significant protest movement against capitalist-led globalization. This backlash was important in two elections in 2016: the American presidential election and the British referendum on membership in the European Union. In both elections, prevalent themes included the dangers of open borders and of rising international trade. The backlash included calls to return to country-first policies that were more consistent with nationalist foreign policies than globalist foreign policies (see the Public Opinion and International Relations feature).

With increasing globalization, transnational concerns such as environmental degradation and disease have become more prominent as well. Global warming looms as

Public Opinion and International Relations

In each chapter, this feature will discuss the public's view about a key issue in international relations. As the past few years have shown, global publics are increasingly vocal about international relations issues ranging from human rights, to immigration, to terrorism, to trade. On some of these issues, public opinion is increasingly divided, creating political tensions within societies.

Each feature will focus either on the United States or on multiple countries where public opinion data are available and reliable. If the data pertain only to the United States, we will discuss how that opinion has changed over time. If the data pertain to a larger sample of countries, we will discuss how opinion varies among those states.

In the first feature, we examine public opinion in the United States on the question of whether America should be active in global affairs or mind its own business. Public opinion polls in the United States have asked a version of this question for many years, although at irregular intervals. Figure 1.5 graphs these polls. Three trends emerge when examining the data.

First, at the height of the Cold War, in the 1950s and 1960s, the American public overwhelmingly believed that the United States should be active in international affairs. This was driven by competition with the Soviet Union, which most Americans believed posed a threat to the United States. The public thought that the only way to deal with that threat was to confront it with an active foreign policy. Second, the 1970s brought an increase in what we might call isolationist sentiment in the United States. Some of the decline in the belief about an active role in global affairs was owed to the war in Vietnam, which became unpopular in the United States and symbolized to many Americans the excesses of the active foreign policy during the Cold War. Some of the decline was also due to economic troubles in the United States during the early 1970s, which included leaving the gold standard and an oil embargo.

Third, a new isolationist sentiment has emerged more recently. As discussed elsewhere in this chapter, this represents a growing backlash against the forces of globalization such as global trade and increasing immigration. Indeed, for the first time in many years, the average of these polls is nearly split between those who suggest the United States should be active in global affairs and those who believe the United States should mind its own business.

Does public opinion matter to leaders who make foreign policy? We discuss this issue more in Chapter 4, but the prevailing belief among scholars is that in democracies, the public at least serves as a constraint on leaders' behavior: A president or prime minister is unlikely to choose a policy he or she is sure will be unpopular. Scholars are less sure how much political leaders actively think about public opinion on specific policies (e.g., economic sanctions, immigration, free trade).

Finally, it is worth considering that public opinion could be an effect as well as a cause. It could be that public opinion reflects what leaders are saying about international affairs. During the Cold War, for example, in the United States, both political parties strongly supported activity in global affairs. This was a constant message delivered by U.S. presidents and other leaders: An active foreign policy helps the United States. It is perhaps not surprising then that most Americans supported an active global role for the United States.

Will isolationist sentiment continue to grow or will American public opinion become more supportive of an active foreign policy? While we cannot predict the future with much certainty, it is likely that the answer to that question will be shaped both by international events and by U.S. leaders' positions on global issues.

Figure 1.5 United States Public Opinion on Global Engagement

Source: Data from Roper Center for Public Opinion Research, 2017.

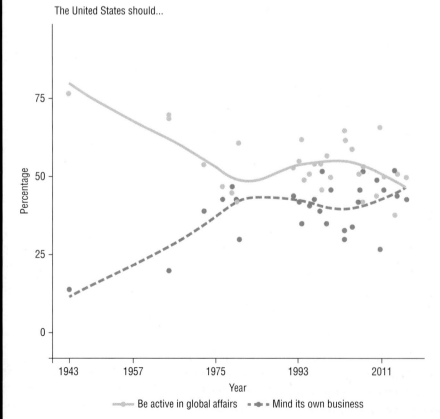

The United States should...

Be active in global affairs   Mind its own business

an ever-increasing danger that is underscored by the accelerating melting of arctic ice and increasing coastal flooding around the world. In 2014 and 2015, a virus known as Ebola killed thousands in western Africa and threatened to spread worldwide, triggering efforts to control the virus through quarantines. Major oil spills in the Gulf of Mexico and China in 2010 refocused international attention on the issue of pollution and the environment, especially in the context of the global race for natural resources.

China is becoming more central to world politics as the twenty-first century begins. Its size and rapid growth make China a rising power—a situation that some scholars liken to Germany's rise a century earlier. Historically, such shifts in power relations have caused instability in the international system. China is the only great power that is not a democracy. Its poor record on human rights makes it a frequent target of Western criticism from both governments and NGOs.

China holds (but seldom uses) veto power in the UN Security Council, and it has a credible nuclear arsenal. China adjoins several regional conflict areas and affects the global proliferation of missiles and nuclear weapons. It claims disputed territory in the resource-rich South China Sea and challenges ownership of islands by Japan in the East China Sea, but it has not fought a military battle in 25 years. With the transfer of Hong Kong from Britain in 1997, China acquired a valuable asset and turned to hopes of someday reintegrating Taiwan as well, under the Hong Kong formula of "one country, two systems." China is the only great power from the global South. Its population size and rapid industrialization from a low starting point make China a big factor in the future of global environmental trends such as global warming. All these elements make China an important actor in the coming decades.

It remains to be seen whether the international system can provide China with appropriate status and respect to reflect its rising power and historical importance, and whether China in turn can begin to conform to international rules and norms. In recent years, China has attempted a strategy that both conforms with and challenges the international system. For example, in 2015, China founded a new international organization—the Asian Infrastructure Investment Bank (AIIB)—that attempts to provide loans for development to states in the global South. On one hand, the bank clearly mimics the operation of the World Bank; on the other, it has fewer standards relating to the environment and labor rights than other development banks. China has thus set up a new international development organization to challenge the way existing development organizations operate.

The transition into the post–Cold War era has been a turbulent time, full of changes and new possibilities both good and bad. It is likely, however, that the basic rules and principles of IR—those that scholars have long struggled to understand—will continue to apply, though their contexts and outcomes may change. Most central to those rules and principles is the concept of power, to which we now turn.

Chapter Review

Summary

- IR affects daily life profoundly; we all participate in IR.
- IR is a field of political science concerned mainly with explaining political outcomes in international security affairs and in the international political economy.
- Theories complement descriptive narratives in explaining international events and outcomes, and although scholars do not agree on a single set of theories or methods, the three core principles (i.e., dominance,

• environment
• disease.

reciprocity, and identity) shape various solutions to collective goods problems in IR.

- States are the most important actors in IR; the international system is based on the sovereignty of about 200 independent territorial states of varying size.

- Nonstate actors such as intergovernmental organizations (IGOs), nongovernmental organizations (NGOs), and multinational corporations (MNCs) exert a growing influence on international relations.

- Three levels of analysis—individual, domestic, systemic—suggest multiple explanations (operating simultaneously) for outcomes in IR.

- Globalization, though conceived of differently by various scholars, generally refers to the growing scope, speed, and intensity of connectedness worldwide. The process may be weakening, strengthening, or transforming the power of states. Antiglobalization activists oppose growing corporate power but disagree on goals and tactics.

- World Wars I and II dominated the twentieth century, yet they seem to offer contradictory lessons about the utility of hardline or conciliatory foreign policies.

- For nearly 50 years after World War II, world politics revolved around the East-West rivalry of the Cold War. This bipolar standoff created stability and avoided great power wars, including nuclear war, but turned states in the global South into proxy battlegrounds.

- The post–Cold War era holds hope of growing peace and great-power cooperation despite the appearance of new ethnic and regional conflicts.

- The U.S. military campaign in Iraq overthrew a dictator, but it divided the great powers, heightened anti-Americanism worldwide, and led to years of insurgency and sectarian violence.

- The NATO campaign in Afghanistan against Taliban influence ended in 2014, although some NATO troops remain. In 2011, U.S. special forces killed Osama bin Laden in Pakistan, where drone attacks targeted other militants.

- The Arab Spring uprisings, which began in 2011, overthrew governments in Tunisia, Egypt, Libya, and Yemen, and sparked a brutal civil war in Syria.

- Two events highlight the existence of a backlash to globalization: the Brexit vote and the election of Donald Trump. Both showed that themes of national over global concerns resonate with many citizens.

Key Terms

international relations (IR) 2
collective goods problem 4
dominance 4
reciprocity 5
identity 6
issue areas 9
conflict and cooperation 10
international security 10
international political economy (IPE) 10
state 10
international system 11
nation-states 11
gross domestic product (GDP) 12
nonstate actors 13
intergovernmental organization (IGO) 13
nongovernmental organization (NGO) 13
globalization 16
North-South gap 18
League of Nations 23
Munich Agreement 23
Cold War 25
containment 27
Sino-Soviet split 27
summit meeting 27
Cuban Missile Crisis 27
proxy wars 28

Critical Thinking Questions

1. Pick a current area in which interesting international events are taking place. Can you think of possible explanations for those events from each of the three levels of analysis? (See Table 1.3.) Do explanations from different levels provide insights into different aspects of the events?

2. The Cold War is long over, but its influences linger. Can you think of three examples in which the Cold War experience continues to shape the foreign policies of today's states?

3. In what ways does international economics affect our daily lives? Is this true for all people in all places? Or

do economic processes such as globalization affect some regions more than others?

4. Given the contradictory lessons of World Wars I and II, can you think of situations in today's world in which appeasement (a conciliatory policy) would be the best course? Situations in which hardline containment policies would be best? Why?

5. What do you expect will be the character of the twenty-first century? Peaceful? War-prone? Orderly? Chaotic? Why do you have the expectations you do, and what clues from the unfolding of world events might tell you whether your guesses are correct?

Suggested Readings

Booth, Ken, ed. *Critical Security Studies and World Politics.* Rienner, 2005.

Cohen, Benjamin J. *International Political Economy: An Intellectual History.* Princeton, 2008.

Doyle, Michael W. *Ways of War and Peace: Realism, Liberalism, and Socialism.* Norton, 1997.

Drezner, Daniel W. *All Politics Is Global.* Princeton, 2008.

Gilpin, Robert. *Global Political Economy: Understanding the International Economic Order.* Princeton, 2001.

Held, David, and Anthony McGrew. *Globalization/Anti-Globalization: Beyond the Great Divide.* Polity, 2007.

Neack, Laura. *Elusive Security: States First, People Last.* Rowman & Littlefield, 2007.

Rodrik, Dani. *The Globalization Paradox: Democracy and the Future of the World Economy.* Norton, 2012.

Rudra, Nita. *Globalization and the Race to the Bottom in Developing Countries: Who Really Gets Hurt?* Cambridge, 2008.

Let's Debate the Issue

Globalization: Vanishing State Power?

Overview

For over 300 years, the nation-state has been the main organizing principle in the world. State governments fight wars, protect their citizens, collect taxes, and provide services for everyday life (from running transit systems to collecting garbage). The idea of the state as a key organizing principle dates back hundreds of years. Political philosophers such as Thomas Hobbes saw governments as providing individuals protection from the state of nature (where life without the state was "nasty, brutish, and short") and from other groups of individuals.

The idea of a nation-state was European in origin. Prior to colonization, large portions of Africa, Asia, and Latin America were organized in different ways: either by families, clans, or other group units. Yet as Europeans spread throughout the world in efforts to colonize and settle new lands, they brought the idea of a nation-state with them. In a relatively short period of time, the world was organized as a set of states interacting on the world stage. States became the central actors providing services to individuals and came into conflict or cooperated with one another.

Yet in the era of globalization, the power of the state is being challenged. With globalization has come the rise of technology, nonstate actors, fluid state borders, and intergovernmental organizations, all of which are eroding the state's ability to control what goes on within and across its borders. Could we be seeing the beginning of the end of the nation-state as an organizing principle in international relations?

ARGUMENT 1

State Power Is on the Decline

Nonstate actors are now as important as the state. Whether they are nongovernmental organizations (NGOs) or multinational corporations (MNCs), nonstate actors play an increasingly important part in world politics. NGOs pressure governments to change human rights practices, MNCs compel states to adapt laws to suit their businesses, and terrorist groups undermine state security. These challenges to state power have grown in the past decade and will continue to grow as globalization allows citizens more access to one another.

States are no longer the key economic actors. Except for the economically largest states such as the United States and Japan, MNCs and private investors control more

resources and capital than many nation-states. Add to this list the powerful IGOs such as the World Bank, the World Trade Organization, and the International Monetary Fund, and states are but one category of player in the global economic game.

Many substitutes for nationalism have emerged. While nationalism was a powerful force supporting the state in the past, other ideas have emerged to challenge it. Religion has replaced allegiance to the state for some, and strong ethnic ties also challenge loyalty to the state. If more individuals' primary loyalty is to something besides their nation-state, state power will continue to decline.

ARGUMENT 2

States Are Down, but Not Out

States have always been challenged, but they have always persevered. States have been under threat for centuries. Whether the threat was from nonstate actors (pirates), from NGOs (the antislavery movement), or from MNCs (the British East India Tea Company), the state has emerged as the central power in international relations. No successful replacement for the state has yet arisen.

States still perform functions that cannot be handed off to other actors. Despite the rise of nonstate actors, certain functions will always fall to states, such as collecting taxes, making laws, and protecting citizens from external threats. States will always need help to perform these duties, and no other entity can perform them outright.

Nationalism will remain a powerful ideological force for the foreseeable future. While alternatives to nationalism exist, none are as widely accepted. Individuals still have strong allegiances to their countries. Witness the number of separatist groups that still try to achieve their independence as a state. If the state did not still have distinct advantages, why would people go to such lengths to achieve statehood?

Why?

Questions

- How has globalization played a role in challenging the power of the state? In other words, which of the challenges are attributable to globalization and which are attributable to forces that may run counter to globalization, such as religion?

- Is there an alternative to the nation-state? Are there more natural ways to organize politics? Think about alternatives that are smaller (ethnic groups, tribes, regions) and larger (multistate coalitions like the European Union or world government).

- One way to think about the European Union is as a natural progression into larger political units. Centuries ago, Europe was a series of city-states, then slightly larger kingdoms, then larger principalities, then nation-states, and now a larger union. Can you foresee a similar evolution in any other geographic region, such as Latin America or Africa?

For Further Reading

Bhagwati, Jagdish. *In Defense of Globalization.* Oxford, 2007.

Cameron, David. *Globalization and Self-Determination: Is the Nation-State under Siege?* Routledge, 2006.

Fukuyama, Francis. *Political Order and Political Decay: From the Industrial Revolution to the Globalization of Democracy.* Farrar, Straus and Giroux, 2014.

Stiglitz, Joseph E. *Globalization and Its Discontents.* Norton, 2003

Chapter 2
Realist Theories

Kyodo/AP Images

LIVE FIRE DRILLS NEAR DMZ, SOUTH KOREA, 2017.

 Learning Objectives

2.1 Identify at least three assumptions of the theory of realism.

2.2 Describe two different ways to conceptualize and measure power.

2.3 Define anarchy and explain its importance in preventing international cooperation.

2.4 Explain the purpose of the North Atlantic Treaty Organization (NATO) alliance and how the purpose has changed over the history of the alliance.

2.5 Describe the Prisoner's Dilemma game, and explain how it is an analogy for the international system.

this approach ---

2.1 Realism

Identify at least three assumptions of the theory of realism.

No single theory reliably explains the wide range of international interactions, but one theoretical framework has historically held a central position in the study of IR. This approach, called **realism**, is favored by some IR scholars and vigorously contested by others, but almost all take it into account.

Modern realist theory developed in reaction to a liberal tradition that realists called **idealism** (of course, idealists themselves do not consider their approach unrealistic). Idealism emphasizes international law, morality, and international organizations, rather than power alone, as key influences on international events. Idealists think that human nature is basically good. They see the international system as one based on a community of states that have the potential to work together to overcome mutual problems (see Chapter 3). For idealists, the principles of IR must flow from morality. Idealists were particularly active between World War I and World War II, following the painful experience of World War I. U.S. president Woodrow Wilson and other idealists placed their hopes for peace in the League of Nations as a formal structure for the community of nations.

Those hopes were dashed when that structure proved helpless to stop German, Italian, and Japanese aggression in the 1930s. Since World War II, realists have blamed idealists for looking too much at how the world *ought* to be instead of how it *really* is. Sobered by the experiences of World War II, realists set out to understand the principles of power politics without succumbing to wishful thinking. Realism provided a theoretical foundation for the Cold War policy of containment and the determination of U.S. policy makers not to appease the Soviet Union and China as the West had appeased Hitler at Munich in 1938.

Realists ground themselves in a long tradition. The Chinese strategist *Sun Tzu*, who lived 2,000 years ago, advised the rulers of states how to survive in an era when war had become a systematic instrument of power for the first time (the "warring states" period). Sun Tzu argued that moral reasoning was not very useful to the state rulers of the day, faced with armed and dangerous neighbors. He showed rulers how to use power to advance their interests and protect their survival.

At roughly the same time, in Greece, *Thucydides* wrote an account of the Peloponnesian War (431–404 B.C.) focusing on relative power among the Greek city-states. He stated that "the strong do what they have the power to do and the weak accept what they have to accept."[1] Much later, in Renaissance Italy (around 1500), *Niccolò Machiavelli* urged princes to concentrate on expedient actions to stay in power, including the manipulation of the public and military alliances. Today the adjective *Machiavellian* refers to excessively manipulative power maneuvers.

The English philosopher *Thomas Hobbes* in the seventeenth century discussed the free-for-all that exists when government is absent and people seek their own self-interests. He called it the "state of nature" or "state of war"—what we would now call the "law of the jungle" in contrast to the rule of law. Hobbes favored a strong monarchy (which he labeled a *Leviathan*) to tame this condition—essentially advocating a dominance approach to solve the collective goods problem in domestic societies. Realists see in these historical figures evidence that the importance of power politics is timeless and cross-cultural.

After World War II, scholar *Hans Morgenthau* argued that international politics is governed by objective, universal laws based on national interests defined in terms of power (not psychological motives of decision makers). He reasoned that no nation has "God on its side" (a universal morality) and that all nations have to base their actions

realism A broad intellectual tradition that explains international relations mainly in terms of power. See also *idealism* and *neorealism*.

idealism An approach that emphasizes international law, morality, and international organizations, rather than power alone, as key influences on international relations. See also *realism*.

- State of Nature.
- State of War.
- Strong Monarchy
- Leviathan
Dominance approach to solve the collective goods problems in domestic societies

1600s

Power Politics

---

[1] Thucydides. *History of the Peloponnesian War.* Translated by Rex Warner, With an Introd. and Notes by M.I. Finley. 1972, p. 402.

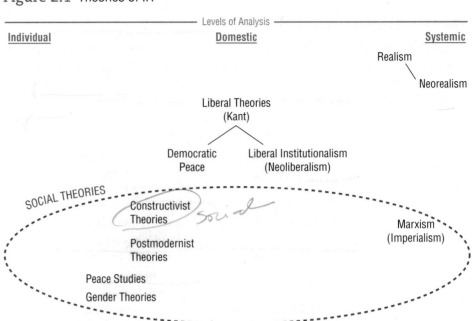

Figure 2.1 Theories of IR

on prudence and practicality. He opposed the Vietnam War, arguing in 1965 that a communist Vietnam would not harm U.S. national interests.

Similarly, in 2002, before the U.S. invasion of Iraq, leading realists figured prominently among the 33 international relations (IR) scholars signing a *New York Times* advertisement warning that "war with Iraq is *not* in America's national interest." Thus, realists do not always favor using military power, although they recognize the necessity of doing so at times. The target of the IR scholars' ad was the group of foreign policy makers in the Bush administration known as *neoconservatives*, who advocated more energetic use of American power, especially military force, to accomplish ambitious and moralistic goals such as democratizing the Middle East.

Thus, realism's foundation is the principle of dominance; alternatives based on reciprocity and identity will be reviewed in Chapter 3. Figure 2.1 lays out the various theoretical approaches to the study of IR we discuss here and in Chapter 3.

Realists tend to treat political power as separate from, and predominant over, morality, ideology, and other social and economic aspects of life. For realists, ideologies do not matter much, nor do religions or other cultural factors with which states may justify their actions. Realists see states with very different religions, ideologies, or economic systems as quite similar in their actions with regard to national power. Thus, realists assume that IR can be best (although not exclusively) explained by the choices of states operating as autonomous actors rationally pursuing their own interests in an international system of sovereign states without a central authority.

Table 2.1 summarizes some major differences between the assumptions of realism and idealism.

Table 2.1 Assumptions of Realism and Idealism

Issue	Realism	Idealism
Human Nature	Selfish	Altruistic
Most Important Actors	States	States and others including individuals
Causes of State Behavior	Rational pursuit of self-interest	Psychological motives of decision makers
Nature of International System	Anarchy	Community

2.2 Power

Describe two different ways to conceptualize and measure power.

Power is a central concept in international relations—the central one for realists—but it is surprisingly difficult to define or measure.

2.2.1 Defining Power

Power is often defined as the ability to get another actor to do what it would not otherwise have done (or not to do what it would have done). A variation on this idea is that actors are powerful to the extent that they affect others more than others affect them. These definitions treat power as influence. For actors to get their way a lot, they must be powerful.

One problem with this definition is that we seldom know what a second actor would have done in the absence of the first actor's power. There is a danger of circular logic: Power explains influence, and influence measures power.

Power is not influence itself, however,

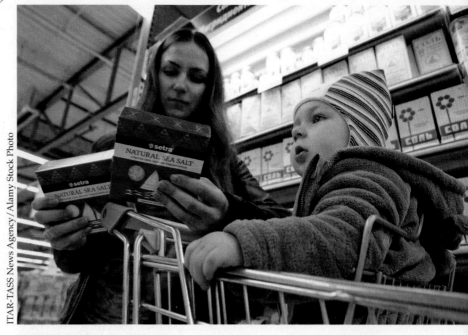

PUTTING SALT IN THE WOUND Power is the ability to influence the behavior of others. Military force and economic sanctions are among the various means that states and nonstate actors use to try to influence each other. The European Union (EU) and the United States have levied several rounds of sanctions against Russia in the past five years to influence its policy toward Ukraine and to deter Russia from meddling in Western elections. In response, Russia has banned the import of goods from Europe and the United States, including salt. Here, a Russian shopper stocks up on salt before the ban goes into effect, 2017.

but the ability or potential to influence others. Many IR scholars believe that such potential is based on specific (tangible and intangible) characteristics or possessions of states—such as their sizes, levels of income, and armed forces. This is power as *capability*. Capabilities are easier to measure than influence and are less circular in logic.

Measuring capabilities to explain how one state influences another is not simple, however. It requires summing up various kinds of potentials. States possess varying amounts of population, territory, military forces, and so forth. *The best single indicator of a state's power may be its total gross domestic product (GDP)*, which combines overall size, technological level, and wealth. But even GDP is at best a rough indicator, and economists do not even agree how to measure it. For example, most GDP figures in this book use traditional methods of computing GDP, but an alternative method gives GDP estimates that are, on average, about 50 percent lower for countries in the global North and about 50 percent higher for those in the global South, including China (see footnote 2 in Chapter 1). So GDP is a useful estimator of material capabilities but not a precise one.

Power also depends on nonmaterial elements. Capabilities give a state the potential to influence others only to the extent that political leaders can mobilize and deploy these capabilities effectively and strategically. This depends on national will, diplomatic skill, popular support for the government (its legitimacy), and so forth. Some scholars emphasize the *power of ideas*—the ability to maximize the influence of capabilities through a psychological process. This process includes the domestic mobilization of capabilities—often through religion, ideology, or (especially) nationalism. International influence is also gained by forming the rules of behavior to change how others see their own national interests. If a state's own values become widely shared among other states, it will easily influence others. This has been called *soft power*. For example, the United States has influenced many other states to accept the value of free markets and free trade.

power The ability or potential to influence others' behavior, as measured by the possession of certain tangible and intangible characteristics.

Thus, dominance is not the only way to exert power (influence others). The core principles of reciprocity and (in the case of soft power) identity can also work. For example, a father who wants his toddler to stop screaming in a supermarket might threaten or actually administer a spanking (dominance), he might promise a candy bar at the checkout as a reward for good behavior (reciprocity), or he could invoke such themes as "Be a big boy/girl" or "You want to help Daddy, don't you?" (identity). Although realists emphasize dominance approaches, they acknowledge that states often achieve their interests in other ways. Furthermore, even realists recognize that power provides only a general understanding of outcomes. Real-world outcomes depend on many other elements, including accidents or luck.

Because power is a relational concept, a state can have power only relative to other states' power. *Relative power* is the ratio of the power that two states can bring to bear against each other. What matters to realists is not whether a state's capabilities are rising or declining in absolute terms, but only whether a state is falling behind or overtaking the capabilities of rival states. For example, India may be growing its military power quickly, but if rival China is expanding its military power at a faster rate, India may still find itself disadvantaged.

2.2.2 Estimating Power

The logic of power suggests that, in wars, the more powerful state will generally prevail. Thus, estimates of the relative power of the two antagonists should help explain outcomes. These estimates could take into account the nations' relative military capabilities and the popular support for each one's government, among other factors. But most important is the total size of each nation's economy—the GDP—which reflects both population size and income per person. With a healthy enough economy, a state can buy a large army, popular support (by providing consumer goods), and even allies.

For example, the Libyan revolutionaries fighting against dictator Muammar Gaddafi in 2011 had passion and determination but could not defeat the government with its heavy weaponry. Then, with the government poised to crush the rebels with tanks, the United States and NATO allies began an air campaign that decisively turned the tide. The rebels made gains and, several months later, claimed victory. The power disparity was striking. In GDP, NATO held an advantage of about 300:1, and NATO forces were much more capable technologically. They also enjoyed the legitimacy conferred by the UN Security Council. In the end, Gaddafi lay dead, his supporters routed, and NATO had not suffered a single casualty.

Despite the decisive outcome of this lopsided conflict, the exercise of power always carries risks of unintended consequences. In 2012, ethnic fighters and Islamic militants who had fought for Gaddafi took large quantities of weapons and crossed the desert to northern Mali, where they seized control of half the country. In early 2013, France had to intervene militarily in Mali to stop them, and the Islamist militants crossed into Algeria, where they seized hundreds of foreign hostages at a gas facility and killed dozens of them when the Algerian army attacked. Moreover, the situation in Libya itself remained unstable. By 2018, competing groups claimed to rule Libya from different cities. Thus, a big GDP may help a country win a war, but it does not eliminate the elements of complexity and luck as situations evolve over the longer term.

2.2.3 Elements of Power

State power is a mix of many ingredients. Elements that an actor can draw on over the *long term* include total GDP, population, territory, geography, and natural resources. These attributes change only slowly. Less tangible long-term power resources include political culture, patriotism, education of the population, and strength of the scientific and technological base. The credibility of its commitments (reputation for keeping its word) is also a long-term power base for a state. So is the ability of one state's culture and values to shape the thinking of other states consistently (the power of ideas).

The importance of long-term power resources was illustrated after the Japanese surprise attack on the U.S. fleet at Pearl Harbor in 1941, which decimated U.S. naval capabilities in the Pacific. In the short term, Japan had superior military power and was able to occupy territories in Southeast Asia while driving U.S. forces from the region. In the longer term, the United States had greater power resources due to its underlying economic potential. It built up military capabilities over the next few years that gradually matched and then overwhelmed those of Japan.

THE ECONOMICS OF POWER Military power such as tanks rests on economic strength, roughly measured by GDP. The large U.S. economy supports U.S. military predominance. In the 2003 U.S. invasion of Iraq, the United States could afford to send a large and technologically advanced military force to the Middle East. Here, U.S. forces enter Iraq, March 2003.

Other capabilities allow actors to exercise influence in the short term. Military forces are such a capability—perhaps the most important kind. The size, composition, and preparedness of two states' military forces matter more in a short-term military confrontation than their respective economies or natural resources. Another capability is the military-industrial capacity to produce weapons quickly. The quality of a state's bureaucracy is another type of capability, allowing the state to gather information, regulate international trade, or participate in international conferences. Less tangibly, the *support* and *legitimacy* that an actor commands in the short term from constituents and allies are capabilities that the actor can use to gain influence. So is the *loyalty* of a nation's army and politicians to their leader.

Given the limited resources that any actor commands, trade-offs among possible capabilities always exist. Building up military forces diverts resources that might be put into foreign aid, for instance. Or buying a population's loyalty with consumer goods reduces resources available for building up military capabilities. To the extent that one element of power can be converted into another, it is *fungible*. Generally, money is the most fungible capability because it can buy other capabilities.

Realists tend to see *military force* as the most important element of national power in the short term, and other elements such as economic strength, diplomatic skill, or moral legitimacy as being important to the extent that they are fungible into military power. Yet, depending on the nature of the conflict in question, military power may be only one of many elements of power. Robert Gates, as U.S. secretary of defense under President Barack Obama, called for a "dramatic increase" in spending on diplomacy and economic aid, noting that, despite very high military spending, these "other elements of national power" have lagged behind in an era of asymmetric warfare (for example, counterterrorism) in which conflicts are "fundamentally political in nature" and not simply military. Secretary Gates went on to point out that the United States had more members of military marching bands than foreign service officers. In 2013, General Jim Mattis, later to become the U.S. secretary of defense under President Donald Trump, argued that "If you don't fund the state department fully, then I need to buy more ammunition ultimately."[2] Consistent with this thinking, U.S. spending on foreign aid increased dramatically (along with military spending) after the attacks of 9/11 (see Chapter 13). Morality can contribute to power by increasing the will to use power and by attracting allies. States have long clothed their actions, however aggressive, in rhetoric about their peaceful and defensive intentions. For instance, the 1989 U.S. invasion of Panama was named "Operation

[2] Sanger, David. A Handpicked Team for a Sweeping Shift in Foreign Policy. *New York Times,* December 1, 2008. Lamothe, Dan. Retired Generals Cite Past Comments from Mattis Opposing Trump's Proposed Foreign Aid Cuts. *Washington Post,* February 27, 2017: A9.

geopolitics The use of geography as an element of power, and the ideas about it held by political leaders and scholars.

Just Cause." Of course, if a state uses moralistic rhetoric to cloak self-interest too often, it loses credibility even with its own population.

The use of geography as an element of power is called **geopolitics**. It is often tied to the logistical requirements of military forces. In geopolitics, as in real estate, the three most important considerations are location, location, location. States increase their power to the extent that they can use geography to enhance their military capabilities, such as by securing allies and bases close to a rival power or along strategic trade routes, or by controlling key natural resources. Today, control of oil pipeline routes, especially in Central Asia, is a major geopolitical issue. Military strategists have also pointed out that the melting of the continental ice shelf (see Chapter 11) has opened new shipping routes for military purposes, creating a new geopolitical issue for Russia and the United States.

2.3 The International System

Define anarchy and explain its importance in preventing international cooperation.

States interact within a set of long-established "rules of the game" governing what is considered a state and how states treat each other. Together, these rules shape the international system.

2.3.1 Anarchy and Sovereignty

anarchy In IR theory, a term that implies not complete chaos but the lack of a central government that can enforce rules.

Realists believe that the international system exists in a state of **anarchy**—a term that implies not complete chaos or absence of structure and rules but rather the lack of a central government that can enforce rules. In domestic society within states, governments can enforce contracts, deter citizens from breaking rules, and use their monopoly on legally sanctioned violence to enforce a system of law. Both democracies and dictatorships provide central government enforcement of a system of rules. Realists contend that no such central authority exists in the international system to enforce rules and ensure compliance with norms of conduct. This makes collective goods problems especially acute in IR. The power of one state is countered only by the power of other states. States must therefore rely on *self-help*, which they supplement with allies and the (sometimes) constraining power of international norms.

Some people think that only a world government can solve this problem. Others think that adequate order, short of world government, can be provided by international organizations and agreements (see Chapter 7). But most realists think that IR cannot escape from a state of anarchy and will continue to be dangerous as a result. In this anarchic world, realists emphasize prudence as a great virtue in foreign policy. Thus, states should pay attention not to the *intentions* of other states but rather to their *capabilities*.

norms The shared expectations about what behavior is considered proper.

Despite its anarchy, the international system is far from chaotic. The great majority of state interactions adhere closely to **norms** of behavior—shared expectations about what behavior is considered proper. Norms change over time, slowly, but the most basic norms of the international system have changed little in recent centuries.

sovereignty A state's right, at least in principle, to do whatever it wants within its own territory; traditionally, sovereignty is the most important international norm.

Sovereignty—traditionally the most important norm—means that a government has the right, in principle, to do whatever it wants in its own territory. States are separate and autonomous and answer to no higher authority. In principle, all states are equal in status, if not in power. Sovereignty also means that states are not supposed to interfere in the internal affairs of other states. Although states do try to influence each other (exert power) on matters of trade, alliances, war, and so on, they are not supposed to meddle in the internal politics and decision processes of other states. More controversially, some states claim that sovereignty gives them the right to treat their own people in any fashion, including behavior that other states call genocide.

The lack of a "world police" to punish states if they break an agreement makes enforcement of international agreements difficult. For example, in the 1990s, North Korea announced it would no longer allow inspections of its nuclear facilities by other states, which put it in violation of the Non-Proliferation Treaty (NPT). The international community used a mix of positive incentives and threats to persuade North Korea to stop producing nuclear material. But in 2002, North Korea withdrew from the NPT and built perhaps a half dozen nuclear bombs, one of which it exploded in 2006 (the world's first nuclear test in a decade). After reaching an agreement with the United States to stop producing nuclear weapons in 2008, North Korea refused to allow physical inspection of some of its nuclear facilities, noting that "it is an act of infringing upon sovereignty."[3] North Korea continued to work on its nuclear program and missile delivery systems in the years following, conducting more tests of both in 2016 and 2017. These examples show the difficulty of enforcing international norms in the sovereignty-based international system.

PASSPORT PLEASE Sovereignty and territorial integrity are central norms governing the behavior of states. Terrorism and secessionist movements present two challenges to these norms, but the world's mostly stable borders uphold them. Every day, millions of people cross international borders, mostly legally and peacefully, respecting states' territorial integrity. Here, hundreds of Ukrainians line up to enter Poland on the first day that a visa requirement for travel between Ukraine and the EU was eliminated, 2017.

In practice, most states have a harder and harder time warding off interference in their affairs. "Internal" matters such as human rights or self-determination are increasingly concerns for the international community. For example, election monitors often watch internal elections for fraud, while international organizations monitor ethnic conflicts for genocide. Also, the integration of global economic markets and telecommunications (such as the Internet) makes it easier than ever for ideas to penetrate state borders.

States are based on territory. Respect for the territorial integrity of all states, within recognized borders, is an important principle of IR. Many of today's borders are the result of past wars (in which winners took territory from losers) or were imposed arbitrarily by colonizers.

The territorial nature of the interstate system developed long ago when agrarian societies relied on agriculture to generate wealth. In today's world, in which trade and technology rather than land create wealth, the territorial state may be less important. Information-based economies are linked across borders instantly, and the idea that the state has a hard shell seems archaic. The accelerating revolution in information technologies may dramatically affect the territorial state system in the coming years.

States have developed norms of diplomacy to facilitate their interactions. An embassy is treated as though it were the territory of the home state, not the country where it is located (see Chapter 4). For instance, in 2012, when Ecuador's embassy in Britain harbored the founder of WikiLeaks, who had been ordered extradited to Sweden, British authorities did not simply come in and take him away. To do so would have violated Ecuador's territorial integrity. Yet in 1979, Iranian students took over the U.S. embassy in Iran, holding many of its diplomats hostage for 444 days—an episode that has soured U.S.-Iranian relations ever since.

---

[3] *BBC News Online.* (November 12, 2008). N Korea rejects nuclear sampling.

Diplomatic norms recognize that states try to spy on each other. Each state is responsible for keeping other states from spying on it. In 2002, China discovered that its new presidential aircraft—a Boeing 767 refurbished in Texas—was riddled with sophisticated listening devices. But China did not make an issue of it (the plane had not gone into service), and a U.S.-China summit the next month went forward. In the post–Cold War era, spying continues, even between friendly states.

Realists acknowledge that the rules of IR often create a **security dilemma**—a situation in which states' actions taken to ensure their own security (such as deploying more military forces) threaten the security of other states. The responses of those other states (such as deploying more of their own military forces) in turn threaten the states that first took action. The dilemma is a prime cause of arms races in which states spend large sums of money on mutually threatening weapons that do not ultimately provide security.

The security dilemma is a negative consequence of anarchy in the international system. If a world government could reliably detect and punish aggressors who arm themselves, states would not need to guard against this possibility. Yet the self-help system requires that states prepare for the worst. Realists tend to see the dilemma as unsolvable, whereas liberals think it can be solved through the development of institutions (see Chapters 3 and 7).

As we shall see in later chapters, changes in technology and in norms are undermining the traditional principles of territorial integrity and state autonomy in IR. Some IR scholars find states practically obsolete as the main actors in world politics, as some states integrate into larger entities and others fragment into smaller units. Other scholars find the international system quite enduring in its structure and state units. One of its most enduring features is the balance of power.

security dilemma A situation in which actions that states take to ensure their own security (such as deploying more military forces) are perceived as threats to the security of other states.

2.3.2 Balance of Power

In the anarchy of the international system, the most reliable brake on the power of one state is the power of other states. The term **balance of power** refers to the general concept of the power of one or more states being used to balance that of another state or group of states. Balance of power can refer to any ratio of power capabilities between states or alliances, or it can mean only a relatively equal ratio. Alternatively, balance of power can refer to the *process* by which counterbalancing coalitions have repeatedly formed in history to prevent one state from conquering an entire region.

The theory of balance of power argues that such counterbalancing occurs regularly and maintains the stability of the international system. The system is stable in that its rules and principles stay the same: State sovereignty does not collapse into a universal empire. This stability does not imply peace, however; it is rather a stability maintained by means of recurring wars that adjust power relations.

Alliances (to be discussed shortly) play a key role in the balance of power. Building up one's own capabilities against a rival is a form of power balancing, but forming an alliance against a threatening state is often quicker, cheaper, and more effective. In the Cold War, the United States encircled the Soviet Union with military and political alliances to prevent Soviet territorial expansion. Sometimes a particular state deliberately becomes a balancer (in its region or the world), shifting its support to oppose whatever state or alliance is strongest at the moment. Britain played this role on the European continent for centuries, and China played it during the Cold War.

balance of power The general concept of the power of one or more states being used to balance that of another state or group of states. The term can refer to (1) any ratio of power capabilities between states or alliances, (2) a relatively equal ratio, or (3) the process by which counterbalancing coalitions have repeatedly formed to prevent one state from conquering an entire region.

But states do not always balance against the strongest actor. Sometimes smaller states "jump on the bandwagon" of the most powerful state; this has been called *bandwagoning* as opposed to balancing. For instance, after World War II, a broad coalition did not form to contain U.S. power; rather, most major states joined the U.S. bloc. States may seek to balance threats rather than raw power. For example, U.S. power was greater than Soviet power but was less threatening to Europe and Japan (and later to China as well). Furthermore, small states create variations on power-balancing themes when they play rival great powers against each other. For instance, Cuba during the Cold War received massive Soviet subsidies by putting itself in the middle of the U.S.-Soviet rivalry. Other small states may, for domestic reasons, fail to mobilize to balance against threats.

In the post–Cold War era of U.S. dominance, balance-of-power theory would predict closer relations among Russia, China, and even Europe to balance U.S. power. And indeed, Russian-Chinese relations improved dramatically in areas such as arms trade and demilitarization of the border. French leaders have even criticized U.S. "hyperpower." But in recent years, with U.S. power seemingly stretched thin in Afghanistan and Iraq, its economy weak, and Chinese power on the rise, more countries are balancing against China and fewer against the United States. In 2012–2013, Japan struck military agreements with former enemies South Korea and the Philippines and reaffirmed its U.S. ties, all in response to China's growing power.

World public opinion also reflects shifts in the balance of power. As the 2003 Iraq War began, widespread anti-American sentiment revealed itself in Muslim countries. In Indonesia, Pakistan, Turkey, and Nigeria—containing half of the world's Muslims—more than 70 percent worried that the United States could become a threat to their own countries, a worry shared by 71 percent of Russians. A survey of 38,000 people in 44 nations showed a dramatic drop in support for the United States from 2002 to 2003. As Figure 2.2 illustrates, this decline in favorable views of the United States worldwide continued through 2007. Then after 2008, with the United States seeking to exit its wars and exert its power less forcefully around the world, opinions turned upward. More recently, views of the United States have moved wildly in some states (Russia) but have started to decline since 2016 in states traditionally friendly to the United States. These shifts in public opinion can be both a cause and an effect in international politics. Public opinion can make the governments in those countries more or less likely to cooperate with the United States on the world stage, and public opinion in these countries can change based on whether there is cooperation (or hostility) with the United States.

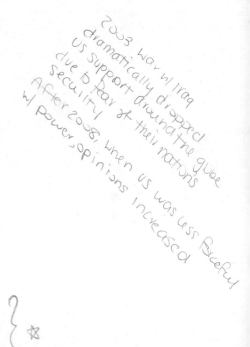

[handwritten margin note: 2003 war w/ Iraq dramatically dropped US support around the globe due to fear of their nations security. After 2008, when US was less Forceful w/ power, opinions increased]

Figure 2.2 Views of the United States in Six Countries, 2002–2017
(Percent favorable view in public opinion polls)

Source: Pew Global Attitudes Project. 2000 data from State Department surveys.

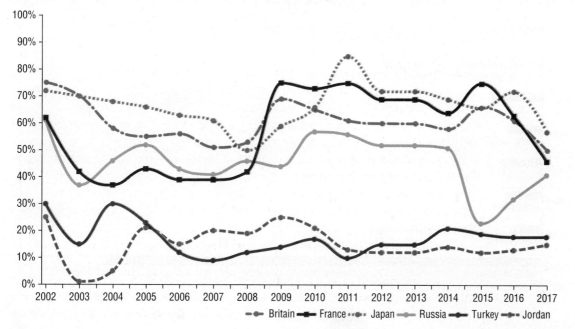

2.3.3 Great Powers and Middle Powers

The most powerful states in the world exert most of the influence on international events and therefore get the most attention from IR scholars. Although there is no firm dividing line, **great powers** are generally considered the half dozen or so most powerful states. Until the past century, the great power club was exclusively European. Sometimes great power status is formally recognized in an international structure such as the nineteenth-century Concert of Europe or today's UN Security Council. In general, great powers are often defined as states that can be defeated militarily only by another great power. Great powers also tend to share a global outlook based on national interests far from their home territories.

The great powers generally have the world's strongest military forces—and the strongest economies to pay for them—and other power capabilities. These large economies in turn rest on some combination of large populations, plentiful natural resources, advanced technology, and educated labor forces. Because power is based on these underlying resources, membership in the great power system changes slowly. Only rarely does a great power—even one defeated in a massive war—lose its status as a great power because its size and long-term economic potential change slowly. Thus, Germany and Japan, decimated in World War II, are powerful today, and Russia, after gaining and then losing the rest of the Soviet Union, is still considered a great power.

What states are great powers today? Although definitions vary, seven states appear to meet the criteria: the United States, China, Russia, Japan, Germany, France, and Britain. Together they account for more than half of the world's total GDP and two-thirds of its military spending (see Figure 2.3). They include the five permanent members of the UN Security Council, which are also the members of the "club" openly possessing large nuclear weapons arsenals.

Notable on this list are the United States and China. The United States is considered the world's only superpower because of its historical role of world leadership (especially in and after World War II) and its predominant military might. China has the world's largest population; rapid economic growth (averaging 8–10 percent annually over 30 years); and a large and modernizing military, including a credible nuclear arsenal. China is poised to have a profound effect on the world over the next

great powers Generally, the half dozen or so most powerful states; the great power club was exclusively European until the twentieth century. See also *middle powers*.

Figure 2.3 Great Power Shares of World GDP, 2017, and Military Expenditures, 2016

Data Sources: World Bank Development Indicators, 2017; *SIPRI Yearbook*, 2016.

20 years—perhaps more than any other state, Japan and Germany are economically great powers, but both countries have played constrained roles in international security affairs since World War II. Nonetheless, both have large and capable military forces, which they have begun to deploy abroad, especially in peacekeeping operations. Russia, France, and Britain were winners in World War II and have been active military powers since then. Although much reduced in stature from their colonial heydays, they still qualify as great powers.

Middle powers rank somewhat below the great powers in terms of their influence on world affairs. Some are large but not highly industrialized; others have specialized capabilities but are small. Some aspire to regional dominance, and many have considerable influence in their regions.

A list of middle powers (not everyone would agree on it) might include midsized countries of the global North such as Canada, Italy, Spain, the Netherlands, Poland, Ukraine, South Korea, and Australia. It could also include large or influential countries in the global South such as India, Indonesia, Brazil, Argentina, Mexico, Nigeria, South Africa, Israel, Turkey, Iran, and Pakistan. Middle powers have not received as much attention in IR as have great powers.

> **middle powers** States that rank somewhat below the great powers in terms of their influence on world affairs (for example, Brazil and India). See also *great powers*.

2.3.4 Power Distribution

With each state's power balanced by that of other states, the most important characteristic of the international system in the view of some realists is the *distribution* of power among states. Power distribution as a concept can apply to all the states in the world or just the states in one region, but most often it refers to the great power system.

Neorealism, sometimes called *structural realism*, is a 1980s adaptation of realism. It explains patterns of international events in terms of the system structure—the international distribution of power—rather than in terms of the internal makeup of individual states. Compared to traditional realism, neorealism is more "scientific" in the sense of proposing general laws to explain events, but neorealism has lost some of the richness of traditional realism, which took account of many complex elements (geography, political will, diplomacy, etc.). Recently, *neoclassical realists* have sought to restore some of these lost aspects.

> **neorealism** A version of realist theory that emphasizes the influence on state behavior of the system's structure, especially the international distribution of power. See also *realism*.

The *polarity* of an international power distribution (world or regional) refers to the number of independent power centers in the system. This concept encompasses both the underlying power of various participants and their alliance groupings. Figure 2.4 illustrates several potential configurations of great powers.

A **multipolar system** typically has five or six centers of power that are not grouped into alliances. Each state participates independently and on relatively equal terms with the others. In the classical multipolar balance of power, the great power system itself was stable but wars occurred frequently to adjust power relations.

> **multipolar system** An international system with typically five or six centers of power that are not grouped into alliances.

Tripolar systems, with three great centers of power, are fairly rare because of the tendency for a two-against-one alliance to form. Aspects of tripolarity colored the "strategic triangle" of the United States, the Soviet Union, and China during the 1960s and 1970s. Some scholars imagine a future tripolar world with rival power centers in North America, Europe, and East Asia. A *bipolar* system has two predominant states or two great rival alliance blocs. IR scholars do not agree about whether bipolar systems are relatively peaceful or warlike. The U.S.-Soviet standoff seemed to provide stability and peace to great power relations, but rival blocs in Europe before World War I did not. At the far extreme, a *unipolar* system has a single center of power around which all others revolve. This is called *hegemony*, and we will discuss it shortly.

Some might argue that peace is best preserved by a relatively equal power distribution (multipolarity) because then no country has an opportunity to win easily. The empirical evidence for this theory, however, is not strong. In fact, the opposite

Figure 2.4 Power Distribution in the International System

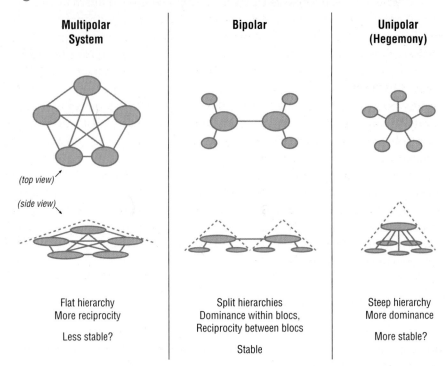

| Multipolar System | Bipolar | Unipolar (Hegemony) |

(top view)

(side view)

Flat hierarchy
More reciprocity

Less stable?

Split hierarchies
Dominance within blocs,
Reciprocity between blocs

Stable

Steep hierarchy
More dominance

More stable?

power transition theory A theory that the largest wars result from challenges to the top position in the status hierarchy, when a rising power is surpassing (or threatening to surpass) the most powerful state.

proposition has more support: Peace is best preserved by hegemony (unipolarity), and it is preserved next best by bipolarity.

Power transition theory holds that the largest wars result from challenges to the top position in the status hierarchy, when a rising power is surpassing (or threatening to surpass) the most powerful state. At such times, power is relatively equally distributed, and these are the most dangerous times for major wars. Status quo powers that are doing well under the old rules will try to maintain them, whereas challengers that feel locked out by the old rules may try to change them. If a challenger does not start a war to displace the top power, the latter may provoke a "preventive" war to stop the rise of the challenger before it becomes too great a threat.

When a rising power's status (formal position in the hierarchy) diverges from its actual power, the rising power may suffer from relative deprivation: Its people may feel they are not doing as well as others or as they deserve, even though their position may be improving in absolute terms. Germany's rise in the nineteenth century gave it great power capabilities even though it was left out of colonial territories and other signs of status; this tension may have contributed to the two world wars.

It is possible China and the United States may face a similar dynamic in the future. China may increasingly bristle at international rules and norms that it feels serve the interests of the United States. For its part, the United States may fear that growing Chinese economic and military power will be used to challenge U.S. power. In 2010, the U.S. military's strategic review questioned China's "long-term intentions," raising new questions about future power transitions (see Let's Debate the Issue at the end of this chapter).

According to power transition theory, then, peace among great powers results when one state is firmly in the top position and the positions of the others in the hierarchy are clearly defined and correspond with their actual underlying power.

2.3.5 Hegemony

hegemony The holding by one state of a preponderance of power in the international system so that it can single-handedly dominate the rules and arrangements by which international political and economic relations are conducted. See also *hegemonic stability theory*.

Hegemony is one state's holding a preponderance of power in the international system, allowing it to single-handedly dominate the rules and arrangements by which international political and economic relations are conducted. Such a state is called a *hegemon*. (Usually, *hegemony* means domination of the world, but sometimes it refers to regional domination.) The Italian Marxist theorist Antonio Gramsci used the term *hegemony* to refer to the complex of *ideas* that rulers use to gain consent for their legitimacy and keep subjects in line, reducing the need to use force to accomplish the same goal. By extension, such a meaning in IR refers to the hegemony of ideas such as democracy and capitalism, and to the global predominance of the United States.)

Most studies of hegemony point to two examples: Britain in the nineteenth century and the United States after World War II. Britain's predominance followed the defeat of its archrival France in the Napoleonic Wars. Both world trade and naval capabilities were firmly in British hands, as "Britannia ruled the waves." U.S. predominance followed the defeat of Germany and Japan (and the exhaustion of the Soviet Union, France, Britain, and China in the effort). In the late 1940s, the U.S. GDP was more than half the world's total, U.S. vessels carried the majority of the world's shipping, the U.S. military could single-handedly defeat any other state or combination of states, and only the United States had nuclear weapons. U.S. industry led the world in technology and productivity, and U.S. citizens enjoyed the world's highest standard of living.

Jun Nakayama/Yomiuri Shimbun/AP Images

CHINA RISING Realists emphasize relative power as an explanation of war and peace. The modernization of China's military—in conjunction with China's rapidly growing economy—will increase China's power over the coming decades. Some observers fear instability in Asia if the overall balance of power among states in the region shifts rapidly. Here, Chinese citizens celebrate China's second aircraft carrier, 2017.

As the extreme power disparities resulting from major wars slowly diminish (states rebuild over years and decades), hegemonic decline may occur, particularly when hegemons have overextended themselves with costly military commitments. IR scholars do not agree about how far or fast U.S. hegemonic decline has proceeded, if at all, and whether international instability will result from such a decline.

Hegemonic stability theory holds that hegemony provides some order similar to a central government in the international system: reducing anarchy, deterring aggression, promoting free trade, and providing a hard currency that can be used as a world standard. Hegemons can help resolve or at least keep in check conflicts among middle powers or small states. When one state's power dominates the world, that state can enforce rules and norms unilaterally, avoiding the collective goods problem. In particular, hegemons can maintain global free trade and promote world economic growth, in this view.

hegemonic stability theory The argument that regimes are most effective when power in the international system is most concentrated. See also *hegemony*.

This theory attributes the peace and prosperity of the decades after World War II to U.S. hegemony, which created and maintained a global framework of economic relations supporting relatively stable and free international trade, as well as a security framework that prevented great power wars. By contrast, the Great Depression of the 1930s and the outbreak of World War II have been attributed to the power vacuum in the international system at that time—Britain was no longer able to act as hegemon, and the United States was unwilling to begin doing so.

Why should a hegemon care about enforcing rules for the international economy that are for the common good? According to hegemonic stability theory, hegemons as the largest international traders have an inherent interest in the promotion of integrated world markets (where the hegemons will tend to dominate). As the most advanced state in productivity and technology, a hegemon does not fear competition from industries in other states; it fears only that its own superior goods will be excluded from competing in other states. Thus, hegemons use their power to achieve free trade and the political stability that supports free trade. Hegemony, then, offers both the ability and the motivation to provide a stable political framework for free international trade, according to hegemonic stability theory. Yet not all IR scholars accept this theory.

From the perspective of less powerful states, of course, hegemony may seem an infringement of state sovereignty, and the order it creates may seem unjust or illegitimate. For instance, China chafed under U.S.-imposed economic sanctions for 20 years after 1949, at the height of U.S. power, when China was encircled by U.S. military bases and hostile alliances led by the United States. To this day, Chinese leaders use the term *hegemony* as an insult, and the theory of hegemonic stability does not impress them.

Even in the United States there is considerable ambivalence about U.S. hegemony. U.S. foreign policy has historically alternated between *internationalist* and *isolationist* moods. It was founded as a breakaway from the European-based international system, and its growth in the nineteenth century was based on industrialization and expansion within North America. The United States acquired overseas colonies in the Philippines and Puerto Rico but did not relish a role as an imperial power. In World War I, the country waited three years to weigh in and refused to join the League of Nations afterward. U.S. isolationism peaked in the late 1930s when polls showed 95 percent of the public was opposed to participation in a future European war, and about 70 percent was against joining the League of Nations or joining with other nations to stop aggression.

Internationalists, such as Presidents Theodore Roosevelt and Woodrow Wilson, favored U.S. leadership and activism in world affairs. These views seemed vindicated by the failure of isolationism to prevent or avoid World War II. U.S. leaders after that war feared Soviet (and then Chinese) communism and pushed U.S. public opinion toward a strong internationalism during the Cold War. The United States became an activist, global superpower. In the post–Cold War era, U.S. internationalism was tempered by a new cost consciousness, and by the emergence of a new isolationist camp born in reaction to the displacements caused by globalization and free trade. However, the terrorist attacks of September 2001 renewed public support for U.S. interventionism in distant conflicts that no longer seemed so distant. Recently, though, opposition to the Iraq War, a protracted conflict in Afghanistan, and difficult economic times at home have spurred a new isolationist trend in the United States. This trend culminated in the election of President Donald Trump, who promised to prioritize American interests at the expense of adversaries and allies alike.

A second area of U.S. ambivalence is *unilateralism* versus *multilateralism* when the United States does engage internationally. Multilateral approaches—working through international institutions—augment U.S. power and reduce costs, but they limit U.S. freedom of action. For example, the United States cannot always get

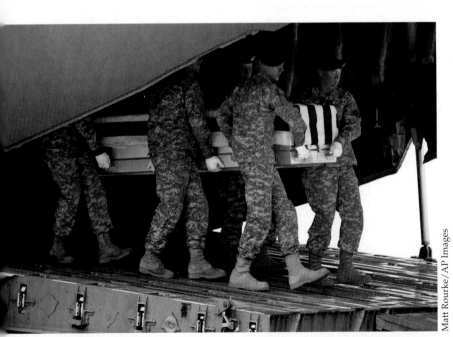

PRICE OF HEGEMONY The United States is the world's most powerful single actor. Its ability and willingness to resume a role as hegemon—as after World War II—are important factors that will shape world order, but the U.S. role is still uncertain. America's willingness to absorb casualties will affect its role. Here, soldiers return from Afghanistan, 2009.

Matt Rourke/AP Images

the UN to do what it wants. Polls show that a majority of U.S. citizens support working through the UN and other multilateral institutions. In the 1990s, the United States slipped more than $1 billion behind in its dues to the UN, and it declined to participate in international efforts such as a treaty on global warming (Chapter 11), a conference on racism, and an International Criminal Court (see Chapter 7). The 2003 U.S.-led war in Iraq, with few allies and no UN stamp of approval, was a strong expression of U.S. unilateralism.

This changed in the late 2000s, however, as the Barack Obama administration emphasized multilateral approaches to international conflicts such as those in Libya, Syria, and Iran. The NATO alliance assumed new importance in Afghanistan and in the 2011 Libya campaign, and UN dues were repaid. However, members of the U.S. Congress (in growing numbers since the 1990s) and the Donald Trump administration have consistently expressed skepticism about the UN and about international agencies, generally favoring a more unilateralist approach. In fact, the Trump administration quickly implemented more unilateralist policies once in office, withdrawing the United States from a global climate treaty (see Chapter 11), leaving a recently negotiated preferential trade agreement (the Trans-Pacific Partnership), withdrawing the United States from a major UN body (UNESCO), threatening friends and allies with trade tariffs, and criticizing NATO allies for paying too little for American military protection (see the Public Opinion and International Relations feature).

2.3.6 The Great Power System, 1500–2000

To illustrate how concepts such as the balance of power, power transition, and hegemony have operated historically, we briefly review the origins of the modern international system. Noted by the presence of great powers, sovereignty, balance of power, and periods of hegemony, the modern great power system is often dated from the *Treaty of Westphalia* in 1648, which established the principles of independent, sovereign states that continue to shape the international system today (see Figure 2.5). These rules of state relations did not originate at Westphalia, however; they took form in Europe in the sixteenth century. Key to this system was the ability of one state, or a coalition, to balance the power of another state so that it could not gobble up smaller units and create a universal empire.

This power-balancing system placed special importance on the handful of great powers with strong military capabilities, global interests and outlooks, and intense interactions with each other. (Great powers are defined and discussed in Chapter 1.) A system of great power relations has existed since around A.D. 1500, and the structure and rules of that system have remained fairly stable through time, although the particular members have changed. The structure is a balance of power among the six or so most powerful states, which form and break alliances, fight wars, and make peace, letting no single state conquer the others.

The most powerful states in sixteenth-century Europe were Britain (England), France, Austria-Hungary, and Spain. The Ottoman Empire (Turkey) recurrently fought with the European powers, especially with Austria-Hungary. Today, that historic conflict between the (Islamic) Ottoman Empire and (Christian) Austria-Hungary is a source of ethnic conflict in the former Yugoslavia (the edge of the old Ottoman Empire).

Within Europe, Austria-Hungary and Spain were allied under the control of the Hapsburg family, which also owned the territory of the Netherlands. The Hapsburg countries (which were Catholic) were defeated by mostly Protestant countries in northern Europe—France, Britain, Sweden, and the newly independent Netherlands—in the *Thirty Years' War* of 1618–1648. The 1648 Treaty of Westphalia established the basic rules that have defined the international system ever since—the sovereignty and territorial integrity of states as equal and independent members of an international system. Since then, states defeated in war might have been stripped of some territories

Figure 2.5 The Great Power System, 1500–2000

Category	1500	1600	1700	1800	1900	2000
Wars		Spain conquers Portugal / Spanish Armada / 30 Years' War	War of the Spanish Succession / 7 Years' War	Napoleonic Wars	Franco-Prussian War / World War I / World War II	Cold War
Major Alliances	Turkey (Muslim) vs. Europe (Christian)	Hapsburgs (Austria-Spain) vs. France, Britain, Netherlands, Sweden	France vs. Britain, Spain	France vs. Britain, Netherlands	Germany (& Japan) vs. Britain, France, Russia, United States, China	Russia vs. U.S., W. Eur., Japan
Rules & Norms	Nation-states (France, Austria)	Dutch independence / Treaty of Westphalia 1648 / Grotius on int'l law	Treaty of Utrecht 1713	Kant on peace / Congress of Vienna 1815 / Concert of Europe	League of Nations / Geneva conventions / Communism	UN Security Council 1945- / Human rights
Rising Powers	Britain, France	Netherlands	Russia	Prussia	United States, Germany, Japan, Italy	China
(hegemony)			Netherlands hegemony		British hegemony	U.S. hegemony
Declining Powers	Venice		Spain / Netherlands / Sweden / Ottoman Empire		Britain, France, Austria, Italy	Russia

but were generally allowed to continue as independent states rather than being subsumed into the victorious state.

In the eighteenth century, the power of Britain increased as it industrialized, and Britain's great rival was France. Sweden, the Netherlands, and the Ottoman Empire all declined in power, but Russia and later Prussia (the forerunner of modern Germany) emerged as major players. In the *Napoleonic Wars* (1803–1815), which followed the French Revolution, France was defeated by a coalition of Britain, the Netherlands, Austria-Hungary, Spain, Russia, and Prussia. The *Congress of Vienna* (1815) ending that war reasserted the principles of state sovereignty in reaction to the challenges of the French Revolution and Napoleon's empire. In the *Concert of Europe* that dominated the following decades, the five most powerful states tried, with some success, to cooperate on major issues to prevent war—a possible precedent for today's UN Security Council. During this period, Britain became a balancer, joining alliances against whatever state emerged as the most powerful in Europe.

By the outset of the twentieth century, three new rising powers had appeared on the scene: the United States (which had become the world's largest economy), Japan, and Italy. The great power system became globalized instead of European. Powerful states were industrializing, extending the scope of their world activities and the might of their militaries. After Prussia defeated Austria and France in wars, a larger Germany emerged to challenge Britain's position. In *World War I* (1914–1918), Germany, Austria-Hungary, and the Ottoman Empire were defeated by a coalition that included Britain, France, Russia, Italy, and the United States. After a 20-year lull, Germany, Italy, and Japan were defeated in *World War II* (1939–1945) by a coalition of the United States, Britain, France, Russia (the Soviet Union), and China. Those five winners of World War II make up the permanent membership of today's UN Security Council.

After World War II, the United States and the Soviet Union, which had been allies in the war against Germany, became adversaries for 40 years in the Cold War. Europe was split into rival blocs—East and West—with Germany divided into two states. The rest of the world became contested terrain where each bloc tried to gain allies or influence, often by sponsoring opposing sides in regional and civil wars. The end of the Cold War around 1990, when the Soviet Union collapsed, returned the international system to a more cooperative arrangement of the great powers somewhat similar to the Concert of Europe in the nineteenth century.

2.4 Alliances

Explain the purpose of the North Atlantic Treaty Organization (NATO) alliance and how the purpose has changed over the history of the alliance.

An *alliance* is a coalition of states that coordinate their actions to accomplish some end. Most alliances are formalized in written treaties, concern a common threat and related issues of international security, and endure across a range of issues and a period of time. Shorter-term arrangements, such as the U.S.-led forces in Iraq, may be called a *coalition.* But these terms are somewhat ambiguous. Two countries may have a formal alliance and yet be bitter enemies, such as the Soviet Union and China in the 1960s or NATO members Greece and Turkey today. Or two countries may create the practical equivalent of an alliance without a formal treaty.

2.4.1 Purposes of Alliances

Alliances generally have the purpose of augmenting their members' power by pooling capabilities. For smaller states, alliances can be their most important power element, and for great powers the structure of alliances shapes the configuration of power in the system. Of all the elements of power, none can change as quickly and

MARRIAGE OF CONVENIENCE Alliances generally result from a convergence of practical interests, not sentimental or ideological reasons. Here, a U.S. general gets rival Afghan warlords to patch up relations, 2002.

Chris Hondros/Getty Images

decisively as alliances. Most alliances form in response to a perceived threat. When a state's power grows and threatens that of its rivals, the latter often form an alliance to limit that power. This happened to Iraq when it invaded Kuwait in 1990, as it had to Hitler's Germany in the 1940s and to Napoleon's France in the 1800s.

Realists emphasize the fluidity of alliances. They are not marriages of love but marriages of convenience. Alliances are based on national interests and can shift as national interests change. This fluidity helps the balance-of-power process operate effectively. Still, it is not simple or costless to break an alliance: One's reputation may suffer, and future alliances may be harder to establish. So states often adhere to alliance terms even when it is not in their short-term interest to do so. Nonetheless, because of the nature of international anarchy, the possibility of turning against a friend is always present. Realists would agree with the British statesman Lord Palmerston, who told Parliament in 1848, "We have no eternal allies and we have no perpetual enemies. Our interests are perpetual and eternal and those interests it is our duty to follow."[4]

Examples of fluid alliances are many. Anticommunist Richard Nixon could cooperate with communist Mao Zedong in 1972. Joseph Stalin could sign a nonaggression pact with a fascist, Adolf Hitler, and then cooperate with the capitalist West against Hitler. The United States could back Islamic militants in Afghanistan against the Soviet Union in the 1980s, then attack them in 2001. Every time history brings another such reversal in international alignments, many people are surprised. Realists are not so surprised.

The fluidity of alliances deepens the security dilemma. If there were only two states, each could match capabilities to have adequate defense but an inability to attack successfully. But if a third state is free to ally with either side, then each state has to build adequate defenses against the potential alliance of its enemy with the third state. The threat is greater and the security dilemma is harder to escape.

alliance cohesion The ease with which the members hold together an alliance; it tends to be high when national interests converge and when cooperation among allies becomes institutionalized.

Alliance cohesion is the ease with which the members hold together an alliance. Cohesion tends to be high when national interests converge and when cooperation within the alliance becomes institutionalized and habitual. When states with divergent interests form an alliance against a common enemy, the alliance may come apart if the threat subsides (as with the U.S.-Soviet alliance in World War II, for instance). Even when alliance cohesion is high, as in NATO during the Cold War, conflicts may arise over who bears the costs of the alliance (**burden sharing**).

burden sharing The distribution of the costs of an alliance among members; the term also refers to the conflicts that may arise over such distribution.

Great powers often form alliances (or less formal commitments) with smaller states, sometimes called client states. *Extended deterrence* refers to a strong state's use of threats to deter attacks on weaker clients—such as the U.S. threat to attack the Soviet Union if it invaded Western Europe. Great powers face a real danger of being dragged into wars with each other over relatively unimportant regional issues if their respective clients go to war. If the great powers do not come to their clients' aid, they may lose credibility with other clients, but if they do, they may end up fighting a costly war. The Soviet Union worried that its commitments to China in the 1950s, to Cuba in

---

[4] Remarks in the House of Commons, March 1, 1848.

the 1960s, and to Syria and Egypt in the 1970s (among others) could result in a disastrous war with the United States.

2.4.2 NATO

At present, two important formal alliances dominate the international security scene. By far the more powerful is the **North Atlantic Treaty Organization (NATO)**, which encompasses Western Europe and North America. (The second is the U.S.-Japanese alliance.) Using GDP as a measure of power, the 29 NATO members possess nearly half the world total. Members are the United States, Canada, Britain, France, Germany, Italy, Belgium, the Netherlands, Luxembourg, Denmark, Norway, Iceland, Spain, Portugal, Greece, Turkey, Poland, the Czech Republic, Hungary, Lithuania, Estonia, Latvia, Slovenia, Slovakia, Bulgaria, Romania, Albania, Croatia, and Montenegro. At NATO headquarters in Brussels, Belgium, military staff members from the member countries coordinate plans and periodically direct exercises in the field. The NATO *allied supreme commander* has always been a U.S. general. In NATO, each state contributes its own military units—with its own national culture, language, and equipment specifications.

NATO was founded in 1949 to oppose and deter Soviet power in Europe. Its counterpart in Eastern Europe during the Cold War, the Soviet-led **Warsaw Pact**, was founded in 1955 and disbanded in 1991. During the Cold War, the United States maintained more than 300,000 troops in Europe, with advanced planes, tanks, and other equipment. After the Cold War ended, these forces were cut to about 100,000. But NATO stayed together because its members believed that NATO provided useful stability even though its mission was unclear. Article V, considered the heart of NATO, asks members to come to the defense of a fellow member under attack. It was envisioned as a U.S. commitment to help defend Western Europe against the Soviet Union, but instead was invoked for the first time when Europe came to the defense of the United States after the terrorist attacks in 2001.

The first actual use of force by NATO was in Bosnia in 1994, in support of the UN mission there. A "dual key" arrangement gave the UN control of NATO's actions in Bosnia, and the UN feared retaliation against its lightly armed peacekeepers should NATO attack the Serbian forces to protect Bosnian civilians. As a result, NATO made threats, underlined by symbolic airstrikes, but then backed down after UN qualms; this waffling undermined NATO's credibility. Later, NATO actions in the Balkans (the air war for Kosovo in 1999 and peacekeeping in Macedonia in 2001) went more smoothly in terms of alliance cohesion.

NATO's intervention in Libya in 2011 also proved effective when air power turned the tide of the rebel war that overthrew Libya's dictator. With UN Security Council and Arab League backing for a no-fly zone, and European countries providing most of the combat planes, NATO rated the operation a great success.

Currently, NATO troops from a number of member countries are fighting Taliban forces in Afghanistan. From 2003 to 2014, these forces, known as the International Security Assistance Forces (ISAF), were under NATO leadership. At its height (between 2010 and 2012), over 100,000 troops served in the ISAF, with NATO states providing the bulk of the forces. Non-NATO states, such as Australia, New Zealand, and Jordan, have also contributed troops to ISAF. In 2015, the ISAF mission formally ended and the Resolute Support mission replaced it. The charge of this new mission was to provide support for Afghanistan's own military forces, and the number of troops fell to around 13,000, with most troops again provided by NATO countries (see the Seeking the Collective Good box).

The European Union has formed its own rapid deployment force, outside NATO. The decision grew in part from European military weaknesses demonstrated in the 1999 Kosovo war, in which the United States contributed the most power by far.

North Atlantic Treaty Organization (NATO) A U.S.-led military alliance, formed in 1949 with mainly Western European members, to oppose and deter Soviet power in Europe. It is currently expanding into the former Soviet bloc. See also *Warsaw Pact*.

Warsaw Pact A Soviet-led Eastern European military alliance founded in 1955 and disbanded in 1991. It opposed the NATO alliance. See also *North Atlantic Treaty Organization (NATO)*.

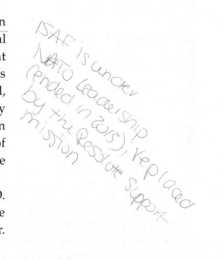

Public Opinion and International Relations
U.S. Public Opinion and NATO

For nearly 70 years, the North Atlantic Treaty Organization has served as a military alliance protecting the interests and security of countries in Western Europe and North America. During most of the Cold War, public support for NATO was strong. With the end of the Cold War, however, some began to question the value of the alliance, especially its cost to the United States. President Donald Trump has called for greater contributions from alliance partners to support NATO and, as a presidential candidate, described the alliance as "obsolete."

Yet, despite these doubts about NATO's future, the alliance remains very popular among the public in the United States. When asked their opinions about NATO, a clear majority describe their view of the alliance as "somewhat positive" or "very positive." This number has remained around or above 60 percent throughout the post–Cold War period. And while NATO's popularity was higher immediately at the end of the Cold War, there is very little variance in the American public's view of the alliance. Indeed, in only one poll have less than 50 percent of Americans viewed the alliance in a positive light.

Of course, while Americans may have a favorable view of NATO, they may still want allies to contribute more in terms of troops and money. As is often the case in public opinion polls, respondents may favor a policy until they are asked how much the policy costs. Unfortunately, very few polls have been taken to gauge Americans' views on the cost of military spending in alliances.

We do know, however, that public opinion in other NATO countries is very supportive of the alliance.[5] A 2017 Pew survey of public opinion among several NATO members found that in most countries, as in the United States, NATO remains a popular alliance. A strong majority in each country favors the alliance, except in Spain, where only a plurality (45 percent to 40 percent) holds a favorable versus an unfavorable view.

Finally, as shown in Figure 2.6, it appears as though the increasing criticism of NATO is causing the public to value it more highly. A 2017 poll by Gallup found the highest percentage of Americans had a favorable view of NATO since Gallup had begun asking the question in 1989.[6] Moreover, since 2011, the number of Americans holding a negative view of NATO has been declining steadily. It is possible that growing discussions about NATO are increasing support for the Western-based alliance.

Figure 2.6 United States Public Opinion Toward NATO

Source: Roper Center for Public Opinion Research.

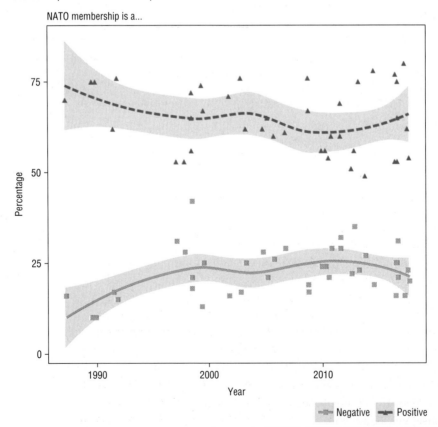

[5]Pew Research Center. NATO's Image Improves on Both Sides of the Atlantic. May 23, 2017. http://www.pewglobal.org/2017/05/23/natos-image-improves-on-both-sides-of-atlantic/.

[6]Gallup.com. Most Americans Support NATO Alliance. February 17, 2017.

Seeking the Collective Good
NATO in Afghanistan

COLLECTIVE GOOD: Defeating the Taliban in Afghanistan

BACKGROUND: After the terrorist attacks in 2001, NATO member states pledged their assistance in fighting the forces of al Qaeda and its Taliban protectors in Afghanistan. Countries formed the multinational International Security Assistance Forces (ISAF), made up of mostly NATO troops deployed in Afghanistan. The forces' goals were to provide security for the fledgling Afghan government, train a new military, and build political institutions to prevent the Taliban from retaking power. Although the ISAF formally came to an end in 2015, Operation Resolute Support replaced it. Like that of the ISAF, the goal of Resolute Support is to help provide support and security in Afghanistan.

Getting an adequate force to prevail in Afghanistan is a collective good. Providing troops and equipment for Resolute Support is voluntary on the part of NATO members. Regardless of how many troops the different countries send, they share equally the benefit of a stable Afghanistan. But if too many countries are too stingy in contributing, the overall force will be too small and the goal will not be achieved, potentially leading to the reemergence of the Taliban or other extremist groups.

CHALLENGE: After more than 15 years, the war in Afghanistan is still active, but NATO forces remain, even if in smaller numbers. The war became a controversial political issue in nearly every country contributing troops to ISAF. Pro-Taliban forces have continued to carry out widespread attacks and threaten to undermine the progress made to date.

At the height of the conflict, NATO members became stingy in committing troops. Both the Bush and Obama administrations pressured allies to send more troops and money, but with limited results. In the 2010 "surge," America added 30,000 troops and other NATO members only 10,000. The allies faced limits because of the war's eventual unpopularity, budget pressures because of the global recession, and uncertain prospects

Rui Vieira / AP Images

Funeral of a British soldier killed in Afghanistan, 2013.

for victory. Most notably, in 2010, the sitting Dutch government lost an election when it tried to keep troops in Afghanistan.

SOLUTION: In theory, NATO operates on reciprocity—its members are equals with all contributing to the common good. The members also share an identity as Western democracies fighting violent religious terrorists. But in the hard currency of boots on the ground and flag-draped coffins coming home, not enough NATO members found these reasons compelling.

The solution to the collective goods problem in this case was for the dominant power to provide the good. NATO is not really a club of equals but a hierarchy, with one member having more military might than the others combined. Being on top of a dominance hierarchy does not just mean ordering around underlings. Often the actors best able to stay on top of a hierarchy are those who form alliances well and use power and wealth to keep other members loyal.

Although this Eurocorps generally works with NATO, it also gives Europe more independence from the United States. In 2003, the European Union sent military forces as peacekeepers to Democratic Congo—the first multinational European military operation to occur outside NATO. In 2004, NATO and U.S. forces withdrew from Bosnia after nine years, turning over peacekeeping there to the European Union (as they had in Macedonia). But NATO forces including U.S. soldiers remain next door in Kosovo.

The biggest issue for NATO is its recent eastward expansion, beyond the East-West Cold War dividing line (see Figure 2.7). In 1999, former Soviet bloc countries Poland, the Czech Republic, and Hungary joined the alliance. Joining in 2004 were Estonia, Latvia, Lithuania, Slovakia, Slovenia, Romania, and Bulgaria. In 2009, Albania and Croatia accepted membership in NATO, and in 2017, Montenegro became the twenty-ninth state to join. Georgia, Bosnia, and Macedonia all aspire to join NATO in the future. Making the new members' militaries compatible with NATO is a major undertaking, requiring increased military spending by existing and new NATO members. NATO expansion was justified both as a way to solidify new democracies and as

National Archives and Records Administration

ALLIANCE OF THE STRONG The NATO alliance has been the world's strongest military force since 1949; its mission in the post–Cold War era is somewhat uncertain. Here, President Kennedy reviews U.S. forces in Germany, 1963.

protection against possible future Russian aggression. Yet the 2003 Iraq War bypassed and divided NATO members. Longtime members France and Germany strongly opposed the war, and Turkey refused to let U.S. ground forces cross into Iraq. At the same time, U.S. leaders began shifting some operations (and money) to new members in Eastern Europe such as Romania—with lower prices and a location closer to the Middle East—while drawing down forces based in Germany.

Russian leaders oppose NATO's expansion into Eastern Europe as aggressive and anti-Russian. They view NATO expansion as reasserting dividing lines on the map of Europe but pushed closer to Russia's borders. These fears strengthen nationalist and anti-Western political forces in Russia. To mitigate the problems, NATO created a category of symbolic membership—the Partnership for Peace—which almost all Eastern European and former Soviet states including Russia joined. However, the 1999 NATO bombing of Serbia heightened Russian fears regarding NATO's eastward expansion. More recently, NATO cooperation with Ukraine and Georgia, the latter of which fought a short war against Russia in 2008, has also angered Russia. Tensions between Russia and NATO have run high since Russia's 2014 annexation of Crimea and its support of rebels in eastern Ukraine. In response to NATO expansion, Russia has expanded its own military cooperation with states such as Venezuela, a government critical of U.S. foreign policy, and China, with whom it conducts joint military exercises, including near the Baltic states and near North Korea in 2017. In 2016, Russia moved quickly to protect the Syrian government, a longtime ally and home to the only Russian military base in the Middle East.

2.4.3 Other Alliances

U.S.-Japanese Security Treaty A bilateral alliance between the United States and Japan, created in 1951 against the potential Soviet threat to Japan. The United States maintains troops in Japan and is committed to defend Japan if that nation is attacked, and Japan pays the United States to offset about half the cost of maintaining the troops.

The second most important alliance is the **U.S.-Japanese Security Treaty**, a bilateral alliance. Under this alliance, the United States maintains nearly 50,000 troops in Japan (with weapons, equipment, and logistical support). Japan pays the United States several billion dollars annually to offset about half the cost of maintaining these troops. The alliance was created in 1951 (during the Korean War) against the potential Soviet threat to Japan.

Because of its roots in the U.S. military occupation of Japan after World War II, the alliance is very asymmetrical. The United States is committed to defend Japan if it is attacked, but Japan is not similarly obligated to defend the United States. The United States maintains troops in Japan, but not vice versa. The United States belongs to several other alliances, but Japan's only major alliance is with the United States. The U.S. share of the total military power in this alliance is also far greater than its share in NATO.

Japan's constitution (written by U.S. General Douglas MacArthur after World War II) renounces the right to make war and maintain military forces, although interpretation has loosened this prohibition over time. For example, in 2015, Japan's parliament approved a new law allowing the use of military force overseas. Japan maintains military forces, called the Self-Defense Forces, strong enough for territorial defense but not for aggression. It is a powerful army by world standards but much smaller

Figure 2.7 NATO Expansion

Sources: U.S. Department of Defense.

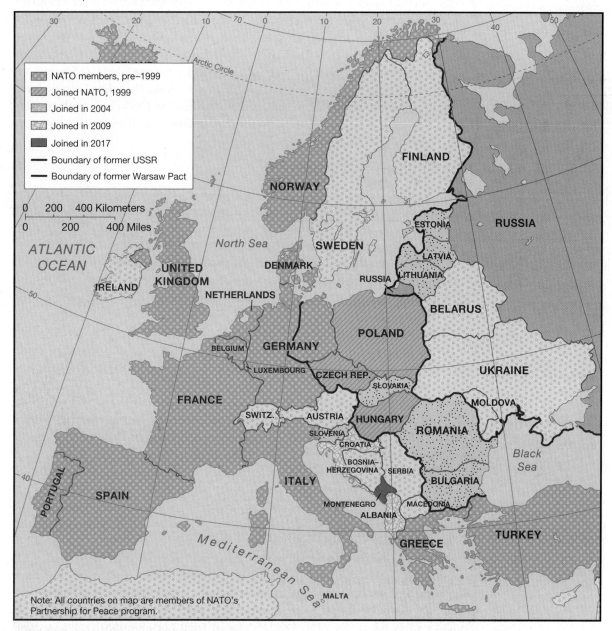

Note: All countries on map are members of NATO's Partnership for Peace program.

than Japan's economic strength could support. Japanese public opinion restrains militarism in general and precludes the development of nuclear weapons in particular after Japanese cities were destroyed by nuclear weapons in World War II. Nonetheless, some Japanese leaders believe that Japan's formal security role should expand commensurate with its economic power. Japanese troops participated in Afghanistan in 2001 and Iraq in 2004 (though not in combat roles), and Japan seeks a permanent seat on the UN Security Council. The UN in turn is pressing Japan to participate fully in peacekeeping missions.

For its part, the United States has used the alliance with Japan as a base to project U.S. power in Asia, especially during the wars in Korea (1950–1953) and Vietnam (1964–1975), when Japan was a key staging area. The continued U.S. military presence in Japan (as in Europe) symbolizes the U.S. commitment to remain engaged in Asian security affairs.

Parallel with the U.S.-Japan treaty, the United States maintains military alliances with several other states, including Australia and South Korea, where 35,000 military personnel are stationed under a bilateral alliance dating to the Korean War. Close U.S. collaboration with militaries in other states such as Israel make them de facto U.S. allies.

The nine full members of the *Commonwealth of Independent States* (*CIS*) comprise the former Soviet republics except the Baltic states (Estonia, Latvia, and Lithuania). Russia, the official successor state to the Soviet Union, is the leading member and Ukraine the second largest. Although some military coordination takes place through the CIS, initial plans for a joint military force did not succeed. Among the largest CIS members, Kazakhstan and Belarus are the most closely aligned with Russia, while Ukraine is the most independent (and in fact never officially ratified the CIS agreement). In 2009, Georgia withdrew from the CIS because of its 2008 military conflict with Russia.

2.4.4 Regional Alignments

Beyond the alliances just discussed and the regional intergovernmental organizations (IGOs), most international alignments and coalitions are not formalized in alliances. Among the great powers, a close relationship has developed, but with China and Russia somewhat independent.

nonaligned movement A movement of third world states, led by India and Yugoslavia, that attempted to stand apart from the U.S.-Soviet rivalry during the Cold War.

In the global South, many states joined a **nonaligned movement** during the Cold War, standing apart from the U.S.-Soviet rivalry. This movement, led by India and Yugoslavia, was undermined by the membership of states such as Cuba that were clearly clients of one of the superpowers.

At the turn of the century, the 53-member Organisation of African Unity, an IGO with few powers, re-formed as the African Union (AU), a stronger organization with a continent-wide parliament, central bank, and court. The African Union's first real test came with allegations of genocide in the Darfur region of Sudan in 2004. In response, the AU deployed 3,000 troops, joined by a much larger force of UN peacekeepers. The AU has also deployed forces, mostly Ugandan, in Somalia, where they routed Islamist militants from most of the country. Those forces were withdrawn at the end of 2017 after the AU and the UN Security Council agreed to return security responsibilities to the Somali army.

In Asia, China has long been loosely aligned with Pakistan in opposition to India (which was aligned with the Soviet Union). The United States tended to favor the Pakistani side as well, but both U.S.-Indian and U.S.-Chinese relations have improved since the Cold War ended. China also has a loose alliance with North Korea, whom it values as a counterweight to South Korea. Yet China maintains concerns about the North's political and economic stability.

Long-standing U.S. friends in Asia include Japan, South Korea, the Philippines (where joint antiterrorist operations began in 2002), the Chinese Nationalists on Taiwan (only informally since the 1970s), Singapore, and Thailand.

In the Middle East, the Arab-Israeli conflict created a general anti-Israel alignment of the Arab countries for decades, but that alignment broke down as Egypt in 1978 and then Jordan in 1994 made peace with Israel. As the Israeli-Palestinian peace process moves forward and backward year by year, Arab countries continue to express varying degrees of solidarity with each other and opposition to Israel. Troughs in Israeli-Arab relations came in 2006, when Israel fought a month-long war with Hezbollah guerrillas in southern Lebanon, and in 2008 and 2012, when it fought Hamas militants in Gaza. Meanwhile, Israel and Turkey formed a close military relationship that amplified Israeli power, but relations deteriorated after Israel killed Turkish protesters on a ship trying to break the blockade of Gaza in 2009. Despite improved relations by 2016, in 2018 Turkey's president called Israel a "terrorist state," leading to a renewal of tensions. Israeli-Palestinian relations have been in a deep freeze since 2011. The main conflict dynamic in the Middle East became the opposition of Shi'ite and Sunni countries, centered on Iran and Saudi Arabia. The civil war in Syria that spread to neighboring Iraq embodies that split, as does the civil war in Yemen, with Iran and Saudi Arabia fighting a proxy war using opposing groups.

Figure 2.8 Current Alignment of Great and Middle Powers

Source: U.S. Department of Defense.

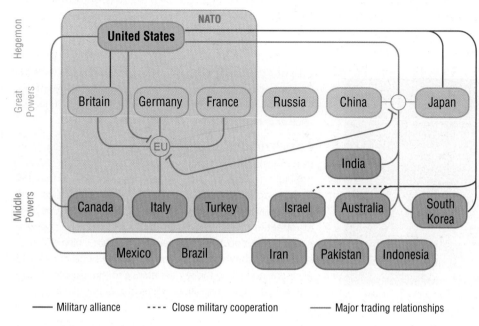

—— Military alliance   - - - - Close military cooperation   —— Major trading relationships

The United States has close relations with Egypt (since 1978) and cooperates closely with Turkey (a NATO member), Kuwait, Saudi Arabia, and Morocco. U.S.-Iranian relations remain chilled 30 years after the 1979 revolution. But, oddly, Iran, with its Shi'ite population, has close ties with Iraq's new U.S.-backed government, which is dominated by Shi'ite religious parties. Indeed, Iran and the United States provided support (although not coordinated) to Iraqi forces fighting to retake control of territory lost to the Islamic State (ISIS) in 2016–2017.

It is unclear what new international alignments may emerge in the years to come. The fluidity of alliances makes them a wild card for scholars to understand and for policy makers to anticipate. For the present, international alignments—both military alliances and trade relationships—center on the United States (see Figure 2.8). Although several independent-minded states such as China and Russia keep U.S. hegemony in check, little evidence exists of a coherent or formal rival power alignment emerging to challenge the United States.

2.5 Strategy

Describe the Prisoner's Dilemma game, and explain how it is an analogy for the international system.

Actors use *strategy* to pursue good outcomes in bargaining with one or more other actors. States deploy power capabilities as leverage to influence each other's actions. Bargaining is interactive and requires an actor to take account of other actors' interests even while pursuing its own.

2.5.1 Statecraft

Classical realists emphasize *statecraft*—the art of managing state affairs and effectively maneuvering in a world of power politics among sovereign states. Power strategies are plans actors use to develop and deploy power capabilities to achieve their goals.

A key aspect of strategy is choosing the kinds of capabilities to develop, given limited resources, in order to maximize international influence. This requires foresight

Policy Perspectives
Prime Minister of India, Narendra Modi

PROBLEM   *How do you confront a fluid security environment by managing current and formal rivals?*

Dinodia Photos / Alamy Stock Photo

BACKGROUND   As the world's largest democracy, your country faces many challenges both at home and abroad. In particular, in the past 60 years, you have fought wars against your two largest neighbors, China and Pakistan. Both states possess nuclear weapons, as do you. China and Pakistan have cooperated with each other in the past, including on sales of high technology military goods such as missiles.

Your generally hostile relationship with Pakistan grows from a territorial dispute over half of the region of Kashmir, which both of you claim but India maintains control over. The territory is coveted not only by your respective governments but by the publics in each country as well. While there has been some cooperation between each country, tensions still run high over Kashmir. In the aftermath of the November 2008 terrorist attacks in Mumbai, many in your country blamed Pakistan because it is home to Islamic militant groups.

Your hostilities with China have cooled over the years, but China remains a major rival in the region and you still maintain competing claims over territory. Like your own country, China is large economically as well as militarily, and it attempts to exert

strong leadership in your region. In the past eight years, however, your country has increased ties with China. You visited China in 2015, after China's leader visited India to sign trade and investment agreements. Your armies (the two largest in the world) have held joint training exercises yet also accuse one another of border violations.

DOMESTIC CONSIDERATIONS   Within your country, neither Pakistan nor China is a popular choice for an ally. Your population is still angered by the Chinese victory in the 1962 Sino-Indian war and the disputed border territory that gave rise to the conflict. Yet your largely Hindu population is also angry at repeated attempts by Muslim Pakistan to gain control of Kashmir. Your advisers also remind you that China still has a healthy relationship with Pakistan, selling large numbers of weapons and giving military assistance to that country. Indeed the main political opposition parties argue that you have been too "soft" on both Pakistan and China. Any public backlash against your foreign policy on these issues could be widespread and bring calls for new elections that could unseat your government.

SCENARIO   Imagine the government of Pakistan begins to suffer from large-scale instability. Islamist militants are close to overthrowing the government there, giving them control of Pakistan's nuclear weapons. They are also calling for Muslims in Kashmir to rise up against Indian control, promising openly to assist a rebellion in that province by providing weapons and intelligence. Your own intelligence service considers the collapse of the current Pakistani government "likely."

CHOOSE YOUR POLICY   Do you push for closer relations with China as a result of instability in Pakistan? Can you trust China to support you in a dispute with Pakistan, given those countries' close relationship? Do you ask China to help mediate between your government and Pakistan in the event of hostilities? Or do you continue your course as independently as possible, not trusting Chinese intentions toward your country?

because the capabilities required to manage a situation may need to be developed years before that situation presents itself. Yet the capabilities chosen often will not be fungible in the short term. Central to this dilemma is deciding what kind of standing military forces to maintain in peacetime—enough to prevent a quick defeat if war breaks out, but not so much as to overburden one's economy (see Chapter 6).

Strategies also shape policies for when a state is willing to use its power capabilities. The *will* of a nation or leader is hard to estimate. Even if leaders make explicit their intention to fight over an issue, they may be bluffing.

The strategic actions of China in recent years exemplify the concept of strategy as rational deployment of power capabilities. China's central foreign policy goal is to prevent the independence of Taiwan, which China considers an integral part of its territory (as does the United Nations and, at least in theory, the United States). Taiwan's government was set up to represent all of China in 1949, when the nationalists took refuge there after losing to the communists in China's civil war. Since the international community's recognition of the Beijing government as "China," however, Taiwan has attempted to operate more and more independently, with many Taiwanese favoring independence. China may not have the military power to invade Taiwan successfully, but it has declared repeatedly that it will go to war if Taiwan declares independence. So far, even though such a war might be irrational on China's part, the threat has deterred Taiwan from formally declaring independence. China might lose such a war, but it would certainly inflict immense damage on Taiwan. In 1996, China held war games near Taiwan, firing missiles over the sea. The United States sent two aircraft carriers to signal to China that its exercises must not go too far.

Not risking war by declaring independence, Taiwan instead has engaged in diplomacy to gain influence in the world. It lobbies the U.S. Congress, asks for admission to the UN and other world organizations, and grants foreign aid to countries that recognize Taiwan's government (17 mostly small, poor countries worldwide as of 2018).

China has used its own diplomacy to counter these moves. It breaks diplomatic relations with countries that recognize Taiwan, and it punishes any moves in the direction of Taiwanese independence. Half the countries that recognize Taiwan are in the Caribbean and Central America, leading to a competition for influence in the region. China has tried to counter Taiwanese ties with those countries by manipulating various positive and negative leverages. For example, in Panama, where China is a major user of the Panama Canal (which reverted to Panama from U.S. ownership in 1999), Taiwan has cultivated close relations, invested in a container port, and suggested hiring guest workers from Panama in Taiwan. But China has implicitly threatened to restrict Panama's access to Hong Kong or to reregister China's many Panamanian-registered ships in the Bahamas instead. (The Bahamas broke with Taiwan in 1997 after a Hong Kong conglomerate, now part of China, promised to invest in a Bahamian container port.) Similarly, when the Pacific microstate of Kiribati recognized Taiwan in late 2003 to gain Taiwanese aid, China broke off relations and removed a Chinese satellite-tracking station from Kiribati. Because the tracking station played a vital role in China's military reconnaissance and growing space program—which had recently launched its first astronaut—its dismantling underscored China's determination to give Taiwan priority even at a cost to other key national goals.

Two of the eleven vetoes China has used in the UN Security Council were to block peacekeeping forces in countries that extended recognition to Taiwan. These vetoes demonstrate that if China believes its Taiwan interests are threatened, it can play a spoiler role on the Security Council. When the former Yugoslav republic of Macedonia recognized Taiwan in 1999 (in exchange for $1 billion in aid), China vetoed a UN peacekeeping mission there at a time of great instability in next-door Kosovo (by 2001, Macedonia had switched its diplomatic recognition to China). By contrast, when its Taiwan interests are secure, China cooperates on issues of world order. For example, although China opposed the 1991 Gulf War, it did not veto the UN resolution authorizing it.

These Chinese strategies mobilize various capabilities, including missiles, diplomats, and industrial conglomerates, in a coherent effort to influence the outcome of China's most important international issue. Strategy thus amplifies China's power.

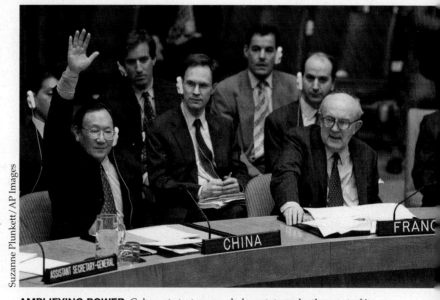

Suzanne Plunkett/AP Images

AMPLIFYING POWER Coherent strategy can help a state make the most of its power. China's foreign policy is generally directed toward its most important regional interests, above all preventing Taiwan's formal independence. Despite conflicts with a number of its neighbors, China has had no military engagements for 40 years. Here, China uses its veto in the UN Security Council for only the fifth time ever, to end a peacekeeping mission in Macedonia, which had just established ties with Taiwan, 1999.

deterrence The threat to punish another actor if it takes a certain negative action (especially attacking one's own state or one's allies). See also *mutually assured destruction (MAD)*.

potential threat

compellence The threat of force to make another actor take some action (rather than, as in deterrence, refrain from taking an action).

arms race A reciprocal process in which two or more states build up military capabilities in response to each other.

rational actors Actors conceived of as single entities that can "think" about their actions coherently, make choices, identify their interests, and rank the interests in terms of priority.

The strategy of **deterrence** uses a threat to punish another actor if it takes a certain negative action (especially attacking one's own state or one's allies). If deterrence works, its effects are almost invisible; its success is measured in attacks that did not occur.

Generally, advocates of deterrence believe that conflicts are more likely to escalate into war when one party to the conflict is weak. In this view, building up military capabilities usually convinces the stronger party that a resort to military leverage would not succeed, so conflicts are less likely to escalate into violence. A strategy of **compellence**, sometimes used after deterrence fails, refers to the threat of force to make another actor take some action (rather than refrain from taking an action). Generally, it is harder to get another state to change course (the purpose of compellence) than it is to get it to refrain from changing course (the purpose of deterrence).

One strategy used to try to compel compliance by another state is *escalation*—a series of negative sanctions of increasing severity applied in order to induce another actor to take some action. In theory, the less severe actions establish credibility—showing the first actor's willingness to exert its power on the issue—and the pattern of escalation establishes the high costs of future sanctions if the second actor does not cooperate. These actions should induce the second actor to comply, assuming that it finds the potential costs of the escalating punishments greater than the costs of compliance. But escalation can be quite dangerous. During the Cold War, many IR scholars worried that a conventional war could lead to nuclear war if the superpowers tried to apply escalation strategies.

An **arms race** is a reciprocal process in which two (or more) states build up military capabilities in response to each other. Because each wants to act prudently against a threat, the attempt to reciprocate leads to a runaway production of weapons by both sides. The mutual escalation of threats erodes confidence, reduces cooperation, and makes it more likely that a crisis (or accident) could cause one side to strike first and start a war rather than wait for the other side to strike. The arms race process was illustrated vividly in the U.S.-Soviet nuclear arms race, which created arsenals of tens of thousands of nuclear weapons on each side.

2.5.2 Rationality in International Relations

Most realists (and many nonrealists) assume that those who wield power while engaging in statecraft behave as **rational actors** in their efforts to influence others. This view has two implications for IR.

First, the assumption of rationality implies that states and other international actors can identify their interests and put priorities on various interests: A state's actions seek to advance its interests. Many realists assume that the actor (usually a state) exercising power is a single entity that can "think" about its actions coherently and make choices. This is called the *unitary* actor assumption, or sometimes the *strong leader* assumption. The assumption is a simplification because the interests of particular politicians, parties, economic sectors, or regions

INTERNAL DIVISIONS The unitary actor assumption holds that states make important decisions as though they were single individuals able to act in the national interest. In truth, factions and organizations with differing interests put conflicting pressures on state leaders. Iraq is deeply divided between Shi'ite, Sunni, and Kurdish groups, making governing difficult. Here, a member of a Kurdish military battalion casts a vote in the Kurdish independence election in 2017. Kurds have long desired an independent state, but the Iraqi government refused to recognize the vote as valid.

SAFIN HAMED/AFP/Getty Images

of a country often conflict. Yet realists assume that the exercise of power attempts to advance the **national interest**—the interests of the state itself.

But what are the interests of a state? Are they the interests of a particular agency within the government? Are they the interests of domestic groups? The need to prevail in conflicts with other states (see Chapter 5)? The ability to cooperate with the international community for mutual benefit (see Chapter 7)? There is no simple answer. Some realists simply define the national interest as maximizing material power—a debatable assumption. Others compare power in IR with money in economics—a universal measure. In this view, just as firms compete for money in economic markets, states compete for power in the international system.

Second, rationality implies that actors are able to perform a **cost-benefit analysis**—calculating the costs to be incurred by a possible action and the benefits that action is likely to bring. Applying power incurs costs and should produce commensurate gains. As in the problem of estimating power, one has to add up different dimensions in such a calculation. For instance, states presumably do not initiate wars that they expect to lose except when they stand to gain political benefits, domestic or international, that outweigh the costs of losing the war. But it is not easy to tally intangible political benefits against the tangible costs of a war. Even victory in a war may not be worth the costs paid. Rational actors can miscalculate costs and benefits, especially when using faulty information (although this does not mean they are irrational). Finally, human behavior and luck can be unpredictable.

These assumptions about rationality and the actors in IR are simplifications that not all IR scholars accept. But realists consider these simplifications useful because they allow scholars to explain in a general way the actions of diverse actors.

2.5.3 The Prisoner's Dilemma

Game theory is a branch of mathematics concerned with predicting bargaining outcomes. A game is a setting in which two or more players choose among alternative moves, either once or repeatedly. Each combination of moves (by all players) results in a set of payoffs (utility) to each player. The payoffs can be tangible items such as money or any intangible items of value. Game theory aims to deduce likely outcomes (what moves players will make), given the players' preferences and the possible moves open to them. Games are sometimes called formal models.

Scholars first used game theory extensively in IR in the 1950s and 1960s to try to understand U.S.-Soviet nuclear war contingencies. Moves were decisions to use nuclear weapons in certain ways, and payoffs were outcomes of the war. The use of game theory to study international interactions has become more extensive among IR scholars in recent years, especially among realists, who accept the assumptions about rationality. To analyze a game mathematically, one assumes that each player chooses a move rationally, to maximize its payoff.

Different kinds of situations are represented by different classes of games, as defined by the number of players and the structure of the payoffs. One basic distinction is between **zero-sum games**, in which one player's gain is by definition equal to the other's loss, and *non-zero-sum games*, in which it is possible for both players to gain (or lose). In a zero-sum game, there is no point in communication or cooperation between the players because their interests are diametrically opposed. But in a non-zero-sum game, coordination of moves can maximize the total payoff to the players, although each may still maneuver to gain a greater share of that total payoff.

The game called **Prisoner's Dilemma (PD)** captures the kind of collective goods problem common to IR. In this situation, rational players choose moves that produce an outcome in which all players are worse off than under a different set of moves. They all could do better, but as individual rational actors, they are unable to achieve this outcome. How can this be?

national interest The interests of a state overall (as opposed to particular parties or factions within the state).

cost-benefit analysis A calculation of the costs to be incurred by a possible action and the benefits it is likely to bring.

game theory A branch of mathematics concerned with predicting bargaining outcomes. Games such as Prisoner's Dilemma and Chicken have been used to analyze various sorts of international interactions.

zero-sum games Situations in which one actor's gain is by definition equal to the other's loss, as opposed to a non-zero-sum game, in which it is possible for both actors to gain (or lose).

Prisoner's Dilemma (PD) A situation modeled by game theory in which rational actors pursuing their individual interests all achieve worse outcomes than they could have by working together.

The original story tells of two prisoners questioned separately by a prosecutor. The prosecutor knows they committed a bank robbery but has only enough evidence to convict them of illegal possession of a gun unless one of them confesses. The prosecutor tells each prisoner that if he confesses and his partner doesn't confess, he will go free. If his partner confesses and he doesn't, he will get a long prison term for bank robbery (while the partner goes free). If both confess, they will get a somewhat reduced term. If neither confesses, they will be convicted on the gun charge and serve a short sentence. The story assumes that neither prisoner will have a chance to retaliate later, that only the immediate outcomes matter, and that each prisoner cares only about himself.

This game has a single solution: Both prisoners will confess. Each will reason as follows: "If my partner is going to confess, then I should confess too because I will get a slightly shorter sentence that way. If my partner is not going to confess, then I should still confess because I will go free that way instead of serving a short sentence." The other prisoner follows the same reasoning. The dilemma is that, by following their individually rational choices, both prisoners end up serving a fairly long sentence—when they could have both served a short one by cooperating (keeping their mouths shut).

PD-type situations occur frequently in IR. One good example is an arms race. Consider the decisions of India and Pakistan about whether to build sizable nuclear weapons arsenals. Both have the ability to do so. Neither side can know whether the other is secretly building up an arsenal unless they reach an arms control agreement with strict verification provisions. To analyze the game, we assign values to each possible outcome—often called a *preference ordering*—for each player. This is not simple: If we misjudge the value a player puts on a particular outcome, we may draw wrong conclusions from the game.

The following preferences regarding possible outcomes are plausible: The best outcome would be for one player to develop a nuclear arsenal while the other player did not (the expense of building nuclear weapons would be worth it because one could then use them as leverage); second best would be for neither to go nuclear (no leverage, but no expense); third best would be for both to develop nuclear arsenals (a major expense without gaining leverage); worst would be to forgo nuclear weapons oneself while the other player developed them (and thus be subject to blackmail).

The game can be summarized in a *payoff matrix* (see Figure 2.9). The first number in each cell is India's payoff, and the second number is Pakistan's. To keep things simple, 4 indicates the highest payoff, and 1 the lowest. As is conventional, a decision to refrain from building nuclear weapons is called *cooperation*, and a decision to proceed with nuclear weapons is called *defection*. The dilemma here parallels that of the prisoners—each state's leader reasons: "If they go nuclear, we must; if they don't, we'd be crazy not to." The model seems to predict an inevitable Indian-Pakistani nuclear arms race, although both states would do better to avoid one.

In 1998, India detonated underground nuclear explosions to test weapons designs, and Pakistan promptly followed suit. In 2002, the two states nearly went to war, with

Figure 2.9 Payoff Matrix in India-Pakistan PD Game

		Pakistan	
		Cooperate	Defect
India	Cooperate	(3,3)	(1,4)
	Defect	(4,1)	(2,2)

Note: First number in each group is India's payoff, second is Pakistan's. The number 4 is highest payoff, a 1 lowest.

projected war deaths of up to 12 million. A costly and dangerous arms race continues, and each side now has dozens of nuclear missiles, and counting. Avoiding an arms race would benefit both sides as a collective good, but the IR system, without strong central authority, does not allow them to realize this potential benefit. This example illustrates why realists tend to be pessimistic about cooperative solutions to collective goods problems such as the one that the PD game embodies.

IR scholars have analyzed many other games beyond PD. For example, *Chicken* represents two male teenagers speeding toward a head-on collision. The first to swerve is "chicken." Each reasons: "If he doesn't swerve, I must; but if he swerves, I won't." The player who first commits irrevocably not to swerve (for example, by throwing away the steering wheel or putting on a blindfold while behind the wheel) will win. Similarly, in the 1962 Cuban Missile Crisis, some scholars argued that President John F. Kennedy "won" by seeming ready to risk nuclear war if Soviet Premier Nikita Khrushchev did not back down and remove Soviet missiles from Cuba. (There are alternative explanations, however, of the outcome of the crisis.)

Chicken sheds light on the concept of *deterrence*. Deterrence involves convincing another actor not to undertake an action it otherwise would. Just as in the game of Chicken, when one driver commits to not swerving, state leaders attempt to convince others that they will respond harshly if they (or an ally) are attacked. But because not swerving risks disaster for both sides, it is difficult for one side to convince the other that he or she will risk crashing (fighting a war) if the other side decides not to swerve. Game theory often studies *interdependent decisions*—the outcome for each player depends on the actions of the other.

This chapter has focused on the concerns of realists—the interests of states, distribution of power among states, bargaining between states, and alliances of states. The chapter has treated states as unitary actors, much as one would analyze the interactions of individual people. The actions of state leaders have been treated as concerned with maximizing power through pursuing definable interests through coherent bargaining strategies. But realism is not the only way to frame the major issues of international relations. Chapter 3 reexamines these themes critically, relying less on the core principle of dominance and more on reciprocity and identity.

Chapter Review

Summary

- Realism explains international relations in terms of power.

- Realists and idealists differ in their assumptions about human nature, international order, and the potential for peace.

- Power can be conceptualized as influence or as capabilities that can create influence.

- The most important single indicator of a state's power is its GDP.

- Short-term power capabilities depend on long-term resources, both tangible and intangible.

- Realists consider military force the most important power capability.

- International anarchy—the absence of world government—means that each state is a sovereign and autonomous actor pursuing its own national interests.

- The international system traditionally places great emphasis on the sovereignty of states, their right to control affairs in their own territory, and their responsibility to respect internationally recognized borders.

- Seven great powers account for half of the world's GDP as well as the great majority of military forces and other power capabilities.

- Power transition theory states that wars often result from shifts in relative power distribution in the international system.

- Hegemony—the predominance of one state in the international system—can help provide stability and peace in international relations, but with some drawbacks.

- The great power system is made up of about half a dozen states (with membership changing over time as state power rises and falls).

- States form alliances to increase their effective power relative to that of another state or alliance.

- Alliances can shift rapidly, with major effects on power relations.

- The world's main alliances, including NATO and the U.S.-Japanese alliance, face uncertain roles in a changing world order.

- International affairs can be seen as a series of bargaining interactions in which states use their power capabilities as leverage to influence the outcomes. But bargaining outcomes also depend on strategies and luck.

- Rational-actor approaches treat states as though they were individuals acting to maximize their own interests. These simplifications are debatable but allow realists to develop concise and general models and explanations.

- Game theory draws insights from simplified models of bargaining situations. The Prisoner's Dilemma game embodies a difficult collective goods problem.

Key Terms

realism 41
idealism 41
power 43
geopolitics 46
anarchy 46
norms 46
sovereignty 46
security dilemma 48
balance of power 48
great powers 50
middle powers 51

neorealism 51
multipolar system 51
power transition theory 52
hegemony 52
hegemonic stability theory 53
alliance cohesion 58
burden sharing 58
North Atlantic Treaty
   Organization (NATO) 59
Warsaw Pact 59
U.S.-Japanese Security Treaty 62

nonaligned movement 64
deterrence 68
compellence 68
arms race 68
rational actors 68
national interest 69
cost-benefit analysis 69
game theory 69
zero-sum games 69
Prisoner's Dilemma (PD) 69

Critical Thinking Questions

1. Using Table 1.4 (with GDP as a measure of power) and the maps at the front of the book, pick a state and speculate about what coalition of nearby states might form with sufficient power to oppose the state if it were to become aggressive.

2. Choose a recent international event and list the power capabilities that participants used as leverage in the episode. Which capabilities were effective, and which were not? Why?

3. The modern international system came into being at a time when agrarian societies relied primarily on farmland to create wealth. Now that most wealth is no longer created through farming, is the territorial nature of states obsolete? How might the diminishing economic value of territory change the ways in which states interact?

4. If you were the leader of a small state in Africa, bargaining with a great power about an issue where your interests diverged, what leverage and strategies could you bring into play to improve the outcome for your state?

5. Given the distinction between zero-sum and non-zero-sum games, can you think of a current international situation that is a zero-sum conflict? One that is non-zero-sum?

Suggested Readings

Barnett, Michael, and Raymond Duvall, eds. *Power in Global Governance.* Cambridge, 2005.

Brooks, Stephen G., and William Wohlforth. *World Out of Balance: International Relations and the Challenge of American Primacy.* Princeton, 2008.

Johnston, Seth A. *How NATO Adapts: Strategy and Organization in the Atlantic Alliance Since 1950.* Johns Hopkins, 2016.

Kreps, Sarah. *Coalitions of Convenience: United States Military Interventions After the Cold War.* Oxford, 2011.

Kydd, Andrew. *International Relations Theory: The Game Theoretic Approach.* Cambridge, 2015.

Mearsheimer, John J. *The Tragedy of Great Power Politics.* Norton, 2003.

Narang, Vipin. *Nuclear Strategy in the Modern Era: Regional Powers and International Conflict.* Princeton, 2014.

Schelling, Thomas C. *The Strategy of Conflict.* Harvard, 1960.

Walt, Stephen M. *Taming American Power: The Global Response to U.S. Primacy.* Norton, 2005.

Waltz, Kenneth. *Theory of International Politics.* Addison-Wesley, 1979.

Let's Debate the Issue
Can the United States and China Coexist Peacefully?

Overview

In this chapter, we noted that realists emphasize the idea of the balance of power—states may ally with one another to prevent another state from becoming too dominant. Yet in the current system, the United States is clearly unparalleled in military and economic power. Some scholars argue that China will be the state that challenges the leadership position of the United States in the future.

Historically, the relationship between China and the United States has been rocky. During the Cold War, after the United States opened the relationship with China, the two great powers cooperated against a common enemy, the Soviet Union. After the Cold War, that cooperation has varied significantly as China has expanded economically and militarily, filling the global power vacuum left by the collapse of the Soviet Union.

Although China is still smaller economically and less powerful militarily than the United States, if current growth continues, it will eventually surpass the United States in economic might. Armed with such a large economy, it will not take long for China to then catch the United States militarily. These changes are referred to as power transitions (see this chapter). While sometimes these transitions between powerful states are peaceful (the United States replacing Great Britain, for example), often they are not (Germany's attempts to overtake Great Britain in World Wars I and II). Should China grow to challenge the United States, what does the future hold for these two great powers? Will their relationship be one of peace or hostility?

ARGUMENT 1

The United States and China Will Find It Difficult to Coexist Peacefully

U.S. and Chinese allies create conflicts between them. China's ties to North Korea, Iran, and Sudan have strengthened in the past ten years. The United States considers each of these states to be hostile, while China has courted each for economic or strategic reasons. On the U.S. side, although there is no formal alliance, American friendliness to Taiwan, which China regards as a renegade province, also creates tensions.

China already promotes its interests in conflict with the United States. China currently pegs its currency to keep its goods cheap in the United States. Despite many protests against this policy, China persists in pegging its currency, which harms domestic manufacturers in the United States.

China is already attempting to compete with the United States as a global superpower. China has expanded foreign aid to Africa (even to states sanctioned by the United States). China has increased weapons sales around the world. China is also courting states with hostile relationships to the United States such as Venezuela and Iran. All signs point to China attempting to compete with the United States for global supremacy.

ARGUMENT 2

The United States and China Can Coexist Peacefully

The United States and China agree on many important issues. On issues such as terrorism and nuclear proliferation, China sees eye to eye with the United States. As with the United States and the Soviet Union during the Cold War, there is room for agreement on issues of strategic importance that will allow for cooperation between the two great powers. In addition, China's "peaceful rise" strategy has avoided direct military conflict with the United States for over 60 years.

Nuclear deterrence will keep relations stable. Each state has a large, credible nuclear force that can deter the opponent from attacking. While this may not rule out proxy wars (as in the Cold War), it does suggest that relations will remain civil and stable between the United States and China.

Economic interdependence will keep relations peaceful. The United States and China depend on one another economically. America depends on Chinese goods flowing in at reasonable prices, while China depends on the U.S. market for its export-led growth strategy. This situation of mutual dependence will keep relations warm because hostility would threaten to undermine these trade relationships.

Questions

- Is conflict inevitable between the United States and China? If China were to become a democracy, would conflict be more or less likely?

- If conflicts occur in the future, are there ways to discourage them? Or are these conflicts just part of global politics between great powers? Can international organizations (such as the United Nations) help to ameliorate the potential for great power conflict?

- Taiwan is an important source of friction between the United States and China. Although the United States does not formally recognize Taiwan, it has signed a friendship treaty with the island. Should the United States risk its relationship with China over honoring its commitments to Taiwan? If China were to force the United States to choose between Taiwan and lower tensions, which should the United States choose?

For Further Reading

Allison, Graham. *Destined for War: Can America and China Escape Thucydides's Trap?* Houghton Mifflin Harcourt, 2017.

Hachigian, Nina. *Debating China: The U.S.–China Relationship in Ten Conversations.* Oxford, 2014.

Mearsheimer, John J. *The Tragedy of Great Power Politics.* Norton, 2003.

Shirk, Susan L. *China: Fragile Superpower.* Oxford, 2008.

Chapter 3
Liberal and Social Theories

ANTINUCLEAR PROTESTERS IN GERMANY, 2017.

Adam Berry/Getty Images

 ## Learning Objectives

3.1 Compare two explanations for the trend toward less warfare in the past century.

3.2 Distinguish between two different theories to explain why democracies do not wage war on one another.

3.3 Illustrate how social theories could explain two countries moving from rivalry to alliance.

3.4 Distinguish Marx's domestic theory of class struggle from Lenin's theory of imperialism.

3.5 Describe the ways in which mediation can be used to resolve conflict in international relations.

3.6 Identify two global issues in international relations where gender is an important factor in understanding or solving the problems.

3.1 The Waning of War

Compare two explanations for the trend toward less warfare in the past century.

In recent years, a strong trend toward fewer and smaller wars has become evident. To many, the world seems more war-prone and violent than ever because images of violence from around the world appear on their televisions and phones very frequently. Yet for the world as a whole, the current period is one of the least warlike ever.

First consider the long-term trend. In the first half of the twentieth century, world wars killed tens of millions and left whole continents in ruin. In the second half of that century, during the Cold War, proxy wars killed millions, and the world feared that a nuclear war could wipe out our species. Now, in the early twenty-first century, wars like those in Afghanistan and Syria kill tens or even hundreds of thousands. We fear terrorist attacks that could destroy a city, but not life on the planet. Generation by generation, the world has moved forward, unevenly but inexorably, from tens of millions killed, to millions, to hundreds of thousands. This is still a large number and the impacts of war are still catastrophic. Perhaps most important, if we could understand and sustain this trend, major wars might fade away altogether, although minor wars and terrorist attacks might continue to kill thousands of people.

Events in the post–Cold War era continued this long-term trend toward smaller wars. The late 1990s and early twenty-first century saw the termination of lingering Cold War–era conflicts such as in Angola, Northern Ireland, Guatemala, and southern Sudan (following South Africa and Mozambique earlier in the 1990s). Most of the wars that flared up after the Cold War ended—such as in Bosnia, Kosovo, Algeria, Rwanda, Burundi, and Uganda—have also come to an end. This waning of war continues in recent years. Liberia and Ivory Coast established power-sharing governments and brought in international peacekeepers—following in the path of Sierra Leone (which in 2003 held democratic elections). In 2005, the Irish Republican Army finished permanently dismantling its weaponry. In 2015, Colombia and the largest rebel group in that country agreed to a peace deal that was approved by its parliament in 2017.

Today's most serious conflicts consist mainly of skirmishing rather than all-out, large-scale battles. The last battles between heavily armed forces on both sides (with, for example, artillery, tanks, and airplanes) were the 2003 invasion of Iraq and the 2008 Russian-Georgian war, both short and one-sided affairs. The last sustained interstate war, between Ethiopia and Eritrea, ended in 2000. The last great power war (with great powers fighting each other) ended more than 60 years ago.

In 2018, the world's most destructive war was in Syria, where a rebellion and the government's brutal suppression of it have cost 200,000 lives over seven years. The war spread into neighboring Iraq where Islamic militants captured significant territory, then lost it to a government offensive and Kurdish fighters. Military forces from several countries, including the United States and Russia, attacked the Islamic militants extensively from 2015 to 2017. In Yemen, estimates are that over 10,000 have been killed in what has developed into a proxy war between Iran and Saudi Arabia. A deadly civil conflict continues in Ukraine, where its military fights pro-Russian separatists (supported by Russia), and threatens political relations between Europe and Russia. In Afghanistan, the long war dragged on (but with fewer international troops), and fighting continues in Somalia. Nigerian troops have moved against Islamist militants in the northern part of that country. By historical standards, these are all small wars.

Deaths caused by all types of war, including actions such as shelling, car bombs, and airstrikes (but not including indirect deaths from disease), have fallen quite dramatically over the past 70 years. Figure 3.1 charts the decline in war-related fatalities since the end of World War II. While some years record higher or lower battle-related deaths than others, there is a consistent trend downward in this graph over recent decades, suggesting an overall movement toward less war in the international system.

Figure 3.1 Battle-Related Deaths in War, 1946–2016

Sources: Human Security Report Project. Human Security Brief 2012. Vancouver: HSRP, 2012, and Uppsala University Conflict Data Program.

Although the past six years have seen an increase in casualties due mostly to the conflicts in Syria and Yemen, we are still in a period of relative peace.

3.2 Liberal Theories

Distinguish between two different theories to explain why democracies do not wage war on one another.

If realism offers mostly dominance solutions to the collective goods problems of international relations (IR), several alternative theoretical approaches discussed in this chapter draw mostly on the reciprocity and identity principles (recall Figure 2.1 in Chapter 2). Among other common elements, these approaches generally are more optimistic than realism about the prospects for peace.

Although realists see the laws of power politics as relatively timeless and unchanging, liberal theorists generally see the rules of IR as slowly, incrementally evolving through time and becoming more and more peaceful. This evolution results primarily from the gradual buildup of international organizations and mutual cooperation (reciprocity) and secondarily from changes in norms and public opinion (identity). The main theories discussed in this and the following chapter all hold that we are not doomed to a world of recurring war but can achieve a more peaceful world. In addition, Chapter 4 will review liberal theories of domestic politics and foreign policy making that, unlike realism, place importance on the domestic and individual levels of analysis in explaining state behavior.

3.2.1 Kant and Peace

Liberal theories of IR try to explain how peace and cooperation are possible. The German philosopher Immanuel Kant over 200 years ago gave three answers. The first answer, based on the reciprocity principle, was that states could develop the organizations and rules to facilitate cooperation, specifically by forming a world federation resembling today's United Nations (UN). This answer forms the foundation of present-day liberal institutionalism, discussed shortly.

Kant's second answer, operating at a lower level of analysis, was that peace depends on the internal character of governments. He reasoned that republics, with a legislative branch that can hold the monarch in check, will be more peaceful than autocracies. This answer, along with Kant's related point that citizens of any country deserve hospitality in any other country, is consistent with the reciprocity principle but also relies on the identity principle. Like the social theories discussed later in this chapter, it explains states' preferences based on the social interactions within the state. A variation on Kant's answer, namely, that democracies do not fight each other, is the basis of present democratic peace theory, also discussed later in this chapter. (Kant himself distrusted democracies as subjecting policy to mob rule rather than rationality, a view influenced by witnessing the French Revolution.)

Kant's third answer, that trade promotes peace, relies on the presumption that trade increases wealth, cooperation, and global well-being—all while making conflict less likely in the long term because governments will not want to disrupt any process that adds to the wealth of their state. Moreover, as trade between states increases, they will find that they become mutually dependent on one other for goods. This mutual dependence between states is referred to as economic **interdependence**. Scholars often differentiate situations of *sensitivity*, where one state relies on another to provide an important good but can find alternate suppliers, with those of *vulnerability*, where there are few or no alternative suppliers.

NASA TV/AP Images

HAPPY FAMILY Liberal theories emphasize the potential for rivalries to evolve into cooperative relationships as states recognize that achieving mutual benefits is most cost effective in the long run. For example, the U.S. and Soviet/Russian space programs began cooperating in the 1960s and continue today, with other countries. Here, astronauts from the United States, Russia, Germany, and Sweden share the International Space Station, 2006.

interdependence A political and economic situation in which two states are simultaneously dependent on each other for their well-being. The degree of interdependence is sometimes designated in terms of "sensitivity" or "vulnerability."

Realists are skeptical of the peace-promotes-trade argument, however, arguing that one state's reliance on another creates *more* tensions in the short term because states are nervous that another actor has an important source of leverage over them. In particular, states worry about their reliance on other states for strategic minerals needed for military purposes, such as special minerals or alloys for aircraft production and uranium for atomic weapons. Leaders worry about vulnerability in giving other countries leverage over them in instances of conflict. Realists point to the fact that arguments about interdependence and peace were common prior to World War I, yet war occurred anyway.

3.2.2 Liberal Institutionalism

Now let us return to Kant's first answer to the question of how peace can evolve, namely, the ability of states to develop and follow mutually advantageous rules, with international institutions to monitor and enforce them. Liberal theories treat rational actors as capable of forgoing short-term individual interests in order to further the long-term well-being of a community to which they belong—and hence indirectly their own well-being. The core principle of reciprocity lies at the heart of this approach because international institutions operate by reciprocal contributions and concessions among formally equal members (peers). Indeed, in several important institutions, such as the World Trade Organization (WTO) and the European Union (EU), decisions require *consensus* among all members, making them all equal in governance.

neoliberal Shorthand for "neoliberal institutionalism," an approach that stresses the importance of international institutions in reducing the inherent conflict that realists assume in an international system; the reasoning is based on the core liberal idea that seeking long-term mutual gains is often more rational than maximizing individual short-term gains. See also *economic liberalism*.

Kant argued that states, although autonomous, could join a worldwide federation like today's UN and respect its principles even at the cost of forgoing certain short-term individual gains. To Kant, international cooperation was a more rational option for states than resorting to war. Thus, in realist conceptions of rationality, war and violence appear rational (because they often advance short-term state interests), but in liberal theories, war and violence appear as irrational deviations that result from defective reasoning and that harm the (collective, long-term) interests of warring states.

The **neoliberal** approach differs from earlier liberal approaches in that it concedes to realism several important assumptions—among them, that states are unitary actors rationally pursuing their self-interests in a system of anarchy. Neoliberals say to realists, "Even if we grant your assumptions about the nature of states and their motives, your pessimistic conclusions do not follow." States achieve cooperation fairly often because it is in their interest to do so, and they can learn to use institutions to ease the pursuit of mutual gains and the reduction of possibilities for cheating or taking advantage of another state.

Despite the many sources of conflict in IR, states cooperate most of the time. Neoliberal scholars try to show that even in a world of unitary rational states, the neorealists' pessimism about international cooperation is not valid. States can create mutual rules, expectations, and institutions to promote behavior that enhances cooperation.

In particular, reciprocity in IR helps international cooperation emerge despite the absence of central authority. Through reciprocity, not a world government, norms and rules are enforced. In international security, reciprocity underlies the gradual improvement of relations sought by arms control agreements and peacekeeping missions. In international political economy (IPE), in which cooperation can create great benefits through trade, the threat to restrict trade in retaliation for unfair practices is a strong incentive to comply with rules and norms. The WTO and its predecessor, the General Agreement on Tariffs and Trade (GATT), function on this principle—states that defect on their obligations by increasing tariffs must suffer punishment by allowing other states to place tariffs on their goods.

Neoliberals argue that reciprocity can be an effective strategy for achieving cooperation in a situation of conflicting interests. If one side expresses willingness to cooperate and promises to reciprocate the other's cooperative and conflictual actions, the other side has an incentive to work out a cooperative bargain. Because reciprocity is relatively easy to interpret, the vow of future reciprocity often need not be stated explicitly. For example, in 1969, China's relations with the United States had been on ice for 20 years. A U.S. economic embargo against China was holding back the latter's economic development. China's support of North Vietnam was costing American lives. The two states were not on speaking terms. President Nixon (and his adviser Henry Kissinger) decided to relax slightly the U.S. trade embargo against China. Three days later, China released three U.S. citizens whose boat had earlier drifted into Chinese waters. China reciprocated other U.S. initiatives, and in 1972, Nixon visited China in a spirit of rapprochement.

Similarly, in 2009, the Obama administration announced it would stop building a missile defense system in Europe that Russia considered provocative. Some saw this as a move to gain Russian support for sanctions against Iran for its nuclear program. And indeed, in the spring of 2010, the UN Security Council approved tighter sanctions on Iran, with the Russians voting in favor.

Neoliberals use the *Prisoner's Dilemma* (PD) game (see Chapter 2) to illustrate their argument that cooperation is possible. Each actor can gain by individually defecting, but both lose when both defect. Similarly, in IR, states often have a mix of conflicting and mutual interests. The dilemma can be resolved if the game is played over and over again—an accurate model of IR in which states deal with each other in repeated interactions. In that case, a strategy of strict reciprocity after an initial cooperative move (nicknamed *tit-for-tat*) can bring about mutual cooperation in a repeated PD

Figure 3.2 Reciprocity in Israeli-Palestinian Conflict and Cooperation, 1979–1997

game because the other player must conclude that any defection will merely provoke a like defection in response.

But side by side with the potential for eliciting cooperation, reciprocity contains a danger of runaway hostility. When two sides both reciprocate but never manage to put relations on a cooperative footing, the result can be a drawn-out, nasty, tit-for-tat exchange of punishments. This characterizes Israeli relations with Palestinian militants over the years, for instance. Figure 3.2 charts data tracking the interactions between Israeli and Palestinian actors over an 18-year period. Note that as one actor exhibits conflictual behavior (negative values on the graph), the other matches with negative responses. Likewise, cooperative behavior (positive values on the graph) brings reciprocated cooperation in the immediate time period. Over time, however, this reciprocity has done little to keep cooperation high—periods of agreement, even those reciprocated by each side, eventually give way to reciprocated conflict.

Building on the reciprocity principle, many norms mediate states' interactions. For example, diplomatic practices and participation in international organizations (IOs) are both strongly governed by shared expectations about the rules of correct behavior. As collective goods problems crop up in IR, states rely on a context of rules, norms, habits, and institutions that make it rational for all sides to avoid the self-defeating outcomes that would result from pursuing narrow, short-term self-interest. Neoliberals study historical and contemporary cases in IR to see how institutions and norms affect the possibilities for overcoming dilemmas and achieving international cooperation. (As we will soon see, some constructivists emphasize that these norms eventually function without states thinking about self-interest at all.) Thus, for neoliberals the emergence of international institutions is key to understanding how states achieve a superior rational outcome that includes long-term self-interest and not just immediate self-interest.

3.2.3 International Regimes

Achieving good outcomes is not simple, though. Because of the contradictory interpretations that parties to a conflict usually have, it is difficult to resolve conflicts without a third party to arbitrate or an overall framework to set common expectations for all parties. These considerations underlie the creation of IOs.

international regime A set of rules, norms, and procedures around which the expectations of actors converge in a certain international issue area (such as oceans or monetary policy).

An **international regime** is a set of rules, norms, and procedures around which the expectations of actors converge in a certain issue area (whether arms control, international trade, or Antarctic exploration). The convergence of expectations means that participants in the international system have similar ideas about what rules will govern their mutual participation: Each expects to play by the same rules. (This meaning of the word *regime* is not the same as that referring to the domestic governments of states, especially governments considered illegitimate, as in *regime change*.)

Regimes can help solve collective goods problems by increasing transparency—because everyone knows what everyone else is doing, cheating is riskier. The current revolution in information technologies is strengthening regimes particularly in this aspect. Also, with better international communication, states can identify conflicts and negotiate solutions through regimes more effectively.

The most common conception of regimes combines elements of realism and liberalism. States are seen as autonomous units maximizing their own interests in an anarchic context. Regimes do not play a role in issues in which states can realize their interests directly through unilateral applications of leverage. Rather, regimes come into existence to overcome collective goods dilemmas by coordinating the behaviors of individual states. Although states continue to seek their own interests, they create frameworks to coordinate their actions with those of other states if and when such coordination is necessary to realize self-interest (that is, in collective goods dilemmas).

Regimes do not substitute for the basic calculations of costs and benefits by states; they just open up new possibilities with more favorable cost-benefit ratios. Regimes do not constrain states, except in a very narrow and short-term sense. Rather, they facilitate and empower national governments faced with issues in which collective goods or coordination problems would otherwise prevent these governments from achieving their ends. Regimes can be seen as *intervening variables* between the basic causal forces at work in IR—for realists, the relative power of state actors—and the outcomes such as international cooperation (or lack thereof). For realists in particular, regimes do not negate the effects of power; more often, they codify and normalize existing power relations in accordance with the dominance principle. For example, the nuclear nonproliferation regime protects the status quo in which only a few states have nuclear weapons.

Because regimes depend on state power for their enforcement, some IR scholars argue that regimes are most effective when power in the international system is most concentrated—when there is a hegemon to keep order (see Hegemony in Chapter 2). Yet regimes do not always decline with the power of hegemons that created them. Rather, they may take on a life of their own. Although hegemony may be crucial in *establishing* regimes, it is not necessary for *maintaining* them. Once actors' expectations converge around the rules embodied in a regime, the actors realize that the regime serves their own interests. Working through the regime becomes a habit, and national leaders may not seriously consider breaking out of the established rules. This persistence of regimes was demonstrated in the 1970s, when U.S. power declined following the decades of U.S. hegemony since 1945. The international economic regimes adjusted somewhat and survived.

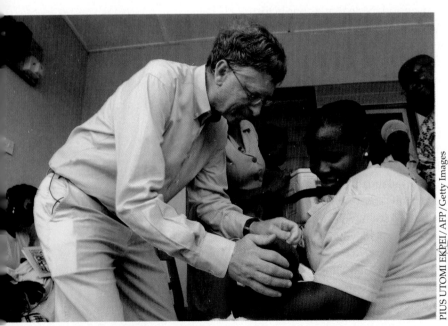

HEALTHY REGIME International regimes are sets of rules, norms, and procedures, not always codified into institutions, that govern the behavior of actors in IR. The world health regime includes states, IGOs such as the World Health Organization (WHO), nonprofit organizations such as the Gates Foundation, and others, all working with common expectations about activities to improve health and stem epidemics. Here, Bill Gates, former chairman of Microsoft and co-chair of the Gates Foundation, gives a child a rotavirus vaccine to protect against diarrhea in Ghana, 2013.

PIUS UTOMI EKPEI/AFP/Getty Images

In part, the survival of regimes rests on their becoming embedded in permanent *institutions* such as the UN, NATO, and the International Monetary Fund (IMF). These institutions become the tangible manifestation of shared expectations as well as the machinery for coordinating international actions based on those expectations. In international security affairs, the UN and other IOs provide a stable framework for resolving disputes (Chapter 7). IPE is even more institutionalized, again because of the heavier volume of activity and the wealth that can be realized from cooperation.

Institutions gain greater stability and weight than do noninstitutionalized regimes. With a staff and headquarters, an international institution can actively promote adherence to the rules in its area of political or economic life. These bureaucracies, however, can also promote policies not intended by the states that created the institutions.

Discussions of important institutions in international security and IPE are in Chapters 7 and 8, respectively. Liberal institutionalism also places high value on international law, discussed in Chapter 7. The culmination of liberal institutionalism to date is the EU, discussed in depth in Chapter 10. After centuries of devastating wars, European states now enjoy a stable peace among themselves with strong international institutions to bind them.

3.2.4 Collective Security

The concept of **collective security**, which grows out of liberal institutionalism, refers to the formation of a broad alliance of most major actors in an international system for the purpose of jointly opposing aggression by any actor. Kant laid out the rationale for this approach. Because past treaties ending great power wars had never brought permanent, lasting peace, Kant suggested a federation (league) of the world's states. Through such a federation, Kant proposed, the majority of states could unite to punish any one state that committed aggression, safeguarding the collective interests of all the nations while protecting the self-determination of small nations that all too easily became pawns in great power games.

After the horrors of World War I, the *League of Nations* was formed to promote collective security. But it was flawed in two ways. Its membership did not include all the great powers (including the most powerful one, the United States), and its members proved unwilling to bear the costs of collective action to oppose aggression when it did occur in the 1930s, starting with Japan and Italy. After World War II, the United Nations was created as the League's successor to promote collective security (see Chapter 7 and the Seeking the Collective Good box). Several regional IGOs also currently perform collective security functions (deterring aggression) as well as economic and cultural ones—the *Organization of American States (OAS)*, the *Arab League*, and the *African Union (AU)*.

The success of collective security depends on two points. First, the members must keep their alliance commitments to the group (that is, members must not free-ride on the efforts of other members). When a powerful state commits aggression against a weaker one, it often is not in the immediate interest of other powerful states to go to war over the issue. Suppressing a determined aggressor can be very costly.

A second requisite for collective security is that enough members must agree on what constitutes aggression. The UN Security Council is structured so that its definition of aggression is what all five permanent members, in addition to at least four of the other ten members, can agree on (see The Security Council in Chapter 7). This collective security system does not work against aggression by a great power. When the Soviet Union invaded Afghanistan, or the United States mined the harbors of Nicaragua, or France blew up the Greenpeace ship *Rainbow Warrior*, the UN could do nothing—because those states can veto Security Council resolutions.

collective security The formation of a broad alliance of most major actors in an international system for the purpose of jointly opposing aggression by any actor; sometimes seen as presupposing the existence of a universal organization (such as the United Nations) to which both the aggressor and its opponents belong. See also *League of Nations*.

Seeking the Collective Good
Great Nations Pay Their Bills
COLLECTIVE GOOD: The UN Budget

BACKGROUND: Since its founding at the end of World War II, the United Nations has performed many valuable services for its members, the countries of the world. Countries use the UN for diplomacy, peacekeeping, and humanitarian assistance, among other things. These services are a collective good for the world's countries because each country enjoys them whether or not it pays more or less of the UN budget. The organization sets dues for its members, and each is supposed to pay on time, but not infrequently, members pay late, or later and later.

CHALLENGE: In the 1980s, the United States got into a series of conflicts with the UN about how much the U.S. dues should be. By the mid-1990s, the UN members owed billions of dollars in back dues, with the United States alone owing more than a billion dollars and Russia about half a billion. Diplomats met in chilled rooms, as the UN could not afford to heat its headquarters building in New York City during the winter. U.S. domestic politics contributed to the problem because the Republican Congress did not approve of President Clinton's budget requests for the UN, which they saw as toothless and ineffective at best, corrupt and anti-American at worst.

SOLUTION: Reciprocity governs UN dues in principle because all countries contribute according to a formula based on each individual economy's size, but in practice, countries defected from that formula to promote their own short-term interests. The dominance principle is of little use because the UN cannot use military force to make a country pay its dues.

The UN Foundation, founded in 1998 with a large contribution by media mogul Ted Turner, started a campaign to use the identity principle to solve the problem of U.S. nonpayment of dues. The campaign's slogan, "Great nations pay their bills,"[i] subtly portrayed the delinquent United States as a deadbeat dad

The UN headquarters in New York.

who had failed to make his child support payments! This appeal to Americans' concept of their nation as great changed the tone of debate about the UN dues. The United States began to catch up on arrears, and in 2009, it paid up the last of its back obligations. In 2017, however, the United States again threatened to withhold money from the UN over a disagreement concerning policy in the Middle East. Once again, domestic politics in the United States will play a key role in the UN budget (see the Public Opinion and International Relations box). And whether the identity principle will lead to a solution remains to be seen.

---

[i] Testimony of Sen. Timothy E. Wirth, President of the United Nations Foundation and the Better World Fund, House Foreign Affairs Committee's Subcommittee on International Organizations. In (June 13, 2007) Wirth: "Great Nations Pay Their Bills". United Nations Foundation Press Release

Collective security worked in 1990–1991 to reverse Iraq's conquest of Kuwait because the aggression brought all the great powers together and because they were willing to bear the costs of confronting Iraq. It was the first time since the founding of the UN that one member state had invaded, occupied, and annexed another—attempting to erase it as a sovereign state. The invasion was so blatant a violation of Kuwaiti sovereignty and territorial integrity that the Security Council had little trouble labeling it aggression and authorizing the use of force by a multinational coalition. The threat Iraq posed to the world's oil supplies provided additional incentive for coalition members to contribute money or troops to solve the problem.

In 2002–2003, by contrast, the Security Council repeatedly debated Iraq's failure to keep the agreements it had made at the end of the Gulf War, in particular the promise to disclose and destroy all its weapons of mass destruction. But the great powers split, and a proposed U.S.-British resolution authorizing military force was withdrawn after France promised to veto it; Germany, Russia, and China had all strongly opposed it and the war. Public opinion around the world, especially in predominantly Muslim

Public Opinion and International Relations
The United States and the United Nations

The institution that embodies collective security and efforts to keep global peace is the United Nations. Even though the United States was instrumental in creating the UN and serves as the host of the UN headquarters, American public opinion toward the United Nations has always been divided. Although the particulars of the argument change over time, one core frustration with the UN for some Americans is that it does not always promote the interests of the United States. If the United States is going to host the institution and pay extensive dues, goes the argument, the UN should support American foreign policy goals and those of American allies.

Those in the United States who are more supportive of the UN argue that it is an independent institution, meant to serve the interests of all countries, not just those of the United States. And while the UN does sometimes act in ways that do not favor the United States, say its supporters, it is equally likely to challenge China or Russia or France.

How has public opinion changed in the United States regarding the UN? Interestingly, while there have been changes in opinion over the past 30 years, none of these changes are particularly large. The data in Figure 3.3 divide up survey respondents among those who hold a very unfavorable, somewhat unfavorable, somewhat favorable, or very favorable view of the UN. Since the mid-1980s, by far the most common opinion in the United States has been somewhat favorable. This has declined slightly over time, from about 55 percent to 45 percent on average. Over that same period, those who view the UN as very favorable has risen from around 12 percent to nearly 20 percent on average.

Those who view the UN as somewhat unfavorable has grown over this period, from around 8 percent to 17 percent—a growth of nearly 10 percent. Yet, those who view the UN as very unfavorable has fallen—from around 18 percent to around 12 percent. Taken together, this suggests a clear majority of Americans view the UN in a favorable light. In sum, around 65 percent have a favorable view while roughly 30 percent hold an unfavorable view.

We can draw a couple of conclusions from these data. First, opinion about the UN has not changed very much over time: There are no cases of massive shifts in how people view the UN despite continued debates in the United States over the role of the UN in American foreign policy. Second, it appears that while U.S. citizens do share some frustrations with the UN, on balance, they are still supportive of the institution and its mission.

Figure 3.3 United States Public Opinion of the United Nations

Source: Roper Center for Public Opinion Research, 2017.

countries, also opposed the war. When the UN did not act, the United States, Britain, and Australia sent military forces and overthrew Saddam Hussein by force, comparing the UN to the ineffective League of Nations. However, the United States discovered no weapons of mass destruction in Iraq, and then found itself in a prolonged counterinsurgency war, which became very unpopular with the public. In retrospect, although the world's collective security system is creaky and not always effective, bypassing it to take military action also holds dangers.

The concept of collective security has broadened in recent years. For example, failed states have very weak control of their territory, making them potential havens for drug trafficking, money laundering, and terrorist bases. Essentially, domestic politics looks rather like international anarchy. Currently, Somalia is such a case. It has an extremely weak government that cannot control large parts of its territory, and it has become a home to terrorist organizations (see Chapter 5) and pirates (see Chapter 6). In these cases, the international community has a duty to intervene, according to some approaches, to restore law and order.

3.2.5 The Democratic Peace

Kant argued that lasting peace would depend on states' becoming republics, with legislatures to check the power of monarchs (or presidents) to make war. He thought that checks and balances in government would act as a brake on the use of military force—compared to autocratic governments in which a single individual (or small ruling group) could make war without regard for the effects on the population.

Somewhat similarly, IR scholars have linked democracy with a kind of foreign policy fundamentally different from that of authoritarianism. One theory they considered was that democracies are generally *more peaceful* than authoritarian governments (fighting fewer, or smaller, wars). This turned out not to be true. Democracies fight as many wars as do authoritarian states. Indeed, the three most war-prone states of the past two centuries (according to political scientists who count wars) were France, Russia, and Britain. Britain was a democracy throughout, France for part of the period, and Russia not at all.

What *is* true about democracies is that, although they fight wars against authoritarian states, *democracies almost never fight each other*. No major historical cases contradict this generalization, which is known as the **democratic peace**. Why this is so is not entirely clear. As there have not been many democracies for very long, the generalization could be just a coincidence, though this seems unlikely. It may be that democracies do not tend to have severe conflicts with each other because they are usually capitalist states whose trade relations create strong interdependence (war would be costly because it would disrupt trade). Or citizens of democratic societies (whose support is necessary for wars to be waged) may simply not see the citizens of other democracies as enemies. By contrast, authoritarian governments of other states *can* be seen as enemies. Note that the peace among democracies gives empirical support to a long-standing liberal claim that, because the democratic peace is rooted in the domestic level of analysis, it contradicts realism's claim that the most important explanations are at the systemic level.

Over the past two centuries, democracy has become more widespread as a form of government, and this trend has changed the nature of the foreign policy process worldwide. In recent decades the trend has accelerated in several ways. New democracies emerged in several (though not all) states of the old Soviet bloc. Military governments gave way to democratically elected civilian ones throughout most of Latin America as well as in several African and Asian countries. South Africa, the last white-ruled African country, adopted majority rule in 1994. In the late 1990s,

democratic peace The proposition, strongly supported by empirical evidence, that democracies almost never fight wars against each other (although they do fight against authoritarian states).

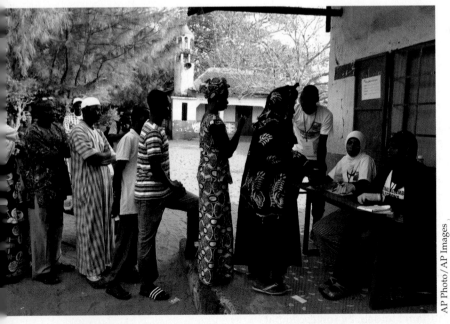

DEMOCRATIC TIDE Upsurges of democratic movements throughout the world in recent years testify to the power of the idea of democracy. Because democracies rarely fight each other, worldwide democratization might lead to lasting peace. Here, Gambians vote in a parliamentary election after a transition to democracy, 2017.

AP Photo/ AP Images

democracy replaced long-standing dictatorships in Indonesia and Nigeria, both regional giants. In 2004–2005, pro-democracy forces won victories in Ukraine, Afghanistan, Iraq, and Kyrgyzstan. In 2008, Pakistan's military-run government stepped down to make way for a democratically elected regime. In 2012, Burma began a transition toward democracy after decades of harsh military rule.

In 2011–2013, the Arab Spring revolutions catalyzed regime transitions in Tunisia, Egypt, Libya, and Yemen. Yet, only Tunisia has fared well on its path to democracy; the other states have experienced significant difficulties in establishing democratic rule. Military coups took place in Guinea-Bissau and Mali in 2012, Egypt in 2013, Thailand in 2014, and Zimbabwe in 2017. Iran rigged an election in 2009 and brutally cracked down on those protesting it. In addition, many states do not yet have democratic governments (the most important of these is China).

It is also important to note that the current backlash against globalization has raised concerns that democracy is at risk in countries ranging from Turkey to the Philippines to Russia, where political opposition has been silenced. It remains to be seen how these changes, potentially undermining democracy, will influence foreign policy. If Kant is correct, the reversal of the growth of democracy could lead to more international conflicts.

Although mature democracies almost never fight each other, a period of *transition* to democracy may be more prone to war compared to either a stable democracy or a stable authoritarian government. Therefore, the process of democratization does not necessarily bode well for peace in the short term. This theory gained support in early 2006, when Iraqi elections were followed by a rise in sectarian violence, and then Palestinian elections brought to power the militant faction Hamas, which rejects Israel's right to exist. In 2017, the recently elected government of Burma unleashed a violent response against an ethnic minority in that country, which some have labeled genocide.

Finally, it is important to note that, while democracy is often associated with peace and cooperation, democratic institutions can make cooperation more difficult. For example, pressures for raising trade tariffs often arise from democratically elected legislatures. Some democratic countries may fail to join international organizations because of domestic opposition, as was the case with the United States and the League of Nations after World War I (see Chapter 1). Public opposition can also lead states to end cooperation with existing international organizations, as when the British voted to withdraw from the European Union (see Chapter 10). Thus, while liberal scholars often extol the virtues of democracy, these same domestic institutions can complicate the process of international cooperation.

Liberal theories thus provide a host of alternatives to power-based realist theories. Nearly all liberal theories focus on solving the collective goods problem using the reciprocity principle. Whether because of international or domestic institutions, states come to expect reciprocal behavior regarding cooperation from other states. In this way, their calculations of interests move from short-term concerns to long-term considerations. Next, we review another set of alternatives to realism that focus on the identity principle.

3.3 Social Theories

Illustrate how social theories could explain two countries moving from rivalry to alliance.

Several distinct approaches in IR theory may be grouped together as *social theories*, meaning that they rely on social interaction to explain individuals' and states' preferences. These theories contrast with the assumption of fixed, timeless preferences in most theories based on realism (states want more power) and liberalism (states, interest groups, and individuals want peace and prosperity).

constructivism A movement in IR theory that examines how changing international norms and actors' identities help shape the content of state interests.

Constructivism, a fast-growing approach in IR, asks how states construct their interest through their interactions with one another. It is best described as an approach rather than a theory because, when stripped to its core, it mentions nothing about IR per se. However, its lessons about the nature of norms, identity, and social interactions can provide powerful insights into the world of IR. In fact, most constructivist explanations draw heavily on the identity principle to explain international behavior.

3.3.1 Identities and Ideas Matter

Constructivism is interested in how actors define their national interests, threats to those national interests, and their interests' relationships to one another. Realists (and neoliberals) tend to take state interests simply as given. Thus, constructivism puts IR in the context of broader social relations. States decide what they want based not only on material needs but also on "social" interaction. Just as shoppers may decide to buy a particular smartwatch because they perceive it as cool (that is, more socially acceptable), so states may choose policies based on what they perceive will be "popular" with other states. Yet, just as shoppers may have limits placed on which smartwatch they can afford to buy (limited resources), constructivists also recognize that power is not absent from international relations.

Constructivist research has many strands. One prominent line examines how states' interests and identities are intertwined, as well as how those identities are shaped by interactions with other states. For example, why is the United States concerned when North Korea builds nuclear weapons, but not when Great Britain does? Realists would quickly answer that North Korea poses a bigger threat, but from a pure military power perspective, Great Britain is a *far* superior military force to North

Korea. Yet no one would argue that Great Britain is a threat to the United States no matter how many nuclear weapons it builds and no matter how deep their disagreements about foreign policy become. Constructivist scholars would point out the shared history, shared alliances, and shared norms that tell Americans and the British they are not a threat to each other, although they are very powerful militarily.

The identity of the potential adversary matters, not just its military capabilities and interests. This is a rejection of the realist assumption that states always want more, rather than less, power and wealth as well as the assumption that state interests exist independently of a context of interactions among states. Constructivists hold that these state identities are complex and changing, and arise from interactions with other states—often through a process of *socialization*. Some constructivist scholars contend that over time, states can conceptualize one another so that there is no danger of a security dilemma, arms races, or the other effects of anarchy. They point to Europe as an example—a continent that was the center of two military conflicts in the first half of the twentieth century that killed millions. By the end of that century, war had become unthinkable. European identities are now intertwined with the EU, not

CONSTRUCTING AND CHANGING IDENTITIES Constructivist approaches, based on the core principle of identity, see actors' preferences as constructed by the actors rather than given "objectively." These approaches may do better than realist or liberal approaches in explaining major changes in a state's foreign policy goals and image in the world that arise from internal changes and new self-concepts rather than external constraints or opportunities. Saudi Arabia's foreign policy is heavily influenced by its identity as a conservative, predominantly Muslim state. Yet, constructivists emphasize that norms and identities can change over time. Here, Saudi women shop for cars in Jeddah after the Saudi government ended the ban on women driving cars in 2017. Saudi Arabia had been the only state to have banned women from driving.

with the violent nationalism that led to two world wars. For constructivists, power politics, anarchy, and military force cannot explain this change. They see institutions, regimes, norms, and changes in identity as better explanations.

Societies as a whole also change over time in what they consider to be threatening. Two hundred years ago, pirates were the scourge of the high seas. These nonstate actors invaded ports, pillaged goods, committed murder, and flaunted all international authority. It would not be hard to consider such behavior as terrorism, even though the pirates had no political goals in their violence. Even if not terrorism, no one would doubt the costs associated with piracy. Many states, including the United States, used their navies in attempts to eradicate pirates. Despite the danger and harm historically caused by these actors, today we celebrate pirates by making them sports mascots, naming amusement rides after them, and glorifying them in movies.

Of course, one could argue that pirates are no longer a threat—even though numerous acts of piracy still occur on the high seas. Even apart from the high-profile pirate hijackings near Somalia in 2008–2009, the threat from piracy has remained high for many years. Yet we find it acceptable to play down the piracy threat by incorporating it into popular culture. No doubt someone from two centuries ago would find such acceptance odd.

How odd? Imagine in 200 years your great-great-grandchildren riding a terrorist-themed ride at Disneyland or watching the latest *Terrorists of the Persian Gulf* movie. Constructivists are quick to point out that what societies or states consider dangerous is not universal or timeless. Social norms and conventions change, and these changes can have tremendous implications for foreign policy.

States may also come to value and covet something like status or reputation, which are social, not material, concepts. Switzerland, for example, values its role as a neutral, nonaligned state (it belongs to neither the EU nor NATO, and joined the UN only in 2002). This status as a neutral state gives Switzerland prestige and power—not a material power like money or guns—but a normative power to intervene diplomatically in important international affairs. Similarly, Canada's foreign policy contains its own identity-driven imperatives usually revolving around peacekeeping and humanitarian operations.

These identity-based theories can help to explain the behavior of great powers as well. In 1993, the UN Security Council established a war crimes tribunal for the former Yugoslavia. Its effectiveness was limited in its first years by inadequacy of funding necessary to hire investigators and translators, rent offices and phone lines, and so forth. The contributions of the great powers to support the tribunal varied, with the United States providing the most support (though still not adequate to the need) and Great Britain providing very little.

Liberal theorists would quickly recognize a collective goods problem in paying for the tribunal. The world community benefits from the work of the tribunal (inasmuch as it deters future aggression and genocide), but each individual state gains this benefit—however beneficial it ends up being—regardless of its own contribution. By this logic, Britain was being rational to free-ride because the United States and others were willing to pick up enough of the tab to make the tribunal at least minimally effective.

Realists might well question this explanation. They might see Britain's lack of support as more straightforward: British leaders may not have wanted the tribunal to succeed because Britain tacitly sided with Serbia (a traditional ally), and Serbia was not cooperating with a tribunal that had indicted the Bosnian Serb leaders as war criminals. The same geopolitical factors that led Britain in the past to side with Serbia (and Russia and France) against Croatia (and Germany, Austria, and Turkey) were still operating. War crimes come and go, by this reasoning, but great power interests remain fairly constant.

Both theories seem to have merit, but sometimes history provides "experiments" that, even though we do not control them, help sort out competing explanations. In this case, in 1997, a liberal government headed by Prime Minister Tony Blair replaced the conservative government of John Major. This change did not affect the explanatory "variables" of either theory—the nature of the collective goods problem inherent in the tribunal, and the nature of Britain's strategic and historical interests and alliances in the Balkans. But in fact, Blair's government shifted its Bosnia policy dramatically, leading a raid to arrest two war crimes suspects and contributing substantial funds for the tribunal to construct a second courtroom. The fact that a change in political leadership changed British behavior suggests that identity-based explanations do play some role: Blair's idea of Britain's place in the international community drove the outcome of the case.

Another field of constructivist research also relies heavily on international norms and their power to constrain state action. Although realists (and neoliberals) contend that states make decisions based on a *logic of consequences* ("What will happen to me if I behave a certain way?"), constructivist scholars note that there is a powerful *logic of appropriateness* ("How should I behave in this situation?"). For example, some cases of humanitarian intervention—military intervention by a state or states to protect citizens or subjects of another state—seem difficult to explain in realist or liberal terms. Why, for example, did the United States in 1992 send troops to Somalia—a country of minimal strategic and economic importance to the United States—as Somalia descended into political chaos and faced the possibility of mass starvation? A constructivist explanation might point to changing norms about which kinds of people are worthy of protection. In the nineteenth century, European powers occasionally intervened to protect Christian subjects of the Ottoman Empire from massacres but generally ignored non-Christian victims. However, as decolonization enshrined the principle of self-determination and as human rights became widely valued, the scope of humanitarian intervention expanded. Although the international community does not always respond effectively to humanitarian crises, it is no longer acceptable to view only Christians as deserving protection. The United States in this example tried to act in an appropriate fashion rather than according to the dictates of cost-benefit calculations.

Examples of this identity approach can be found in the developing world as well. Some constructivists have argued that countries in Latin America, Africa, and the Middle East have adopted or changed policies in response to international norms—not because it provided large benefits but because doing so was perceived as the appropriate course of action. For example, many developing states have raced to create science bureaucracies and/or begin technological modernization of their militaries. Constructivists point out that the reason developing states choose to spend their limited resources on such projects is their desire to be perceived as "modern" by the international system. "Modern" states have science bureaucracies and advanced militaries. Ironically, many states that build science bureaucracies have few scientists, while many states that build advanced militaries have few enemies. Thus, constructivists emphasize that identities and norms must be used to explain this seemingly puzzling behavior.

How are these international norms spread around the world? In an age of global communication and relative ease of transportation, many possibilities exist. Constructivists emphasize different sets of actors who spread norms. Some contend that individuals, labeled *norm entrepreneurs*, through travel, writing, and meeting with elites, change ideas and encourage certain types of norms. Some point to broad-based social movements and nongovernmental organizations (NGOs), such as the anti-apartheid movement encouraging the development of a global norm of racial equality. Others show how international organizations (such as the UN and NATO) can diffuse norms of what is appropriate and inappropriate behavior. In each case, however, new ideas and norms, rather than power and self-interest, drive state behavior.

Policy Perspectives
President of Georgia, Giorgi Margvelashvili

PROBLEM *How do you achieve security cooperation with international institutions in the face of pressure from a powerful neighbor?*

Mindaugas Kulbis/AP Images

BACKGROUND Since 2003, your country has attempted to gain membership in NATO. In 2008, NATO leaders promised that Georgia would eventually become a member of the alliance.

As of 2018, NATO members have not offered you a Membership Action Plan—the agreement that begins the process of joining the alliance. They have offered you increased military support and military aid, while continuing to promise your eventual membership in the alliance, as recently as 2017.

Your powerful neighbor to the north, Russia, openly opposes your membership in NATO. In 2008, you fought a war with Russia over two provinces in your country where many ethnic Russians live. During that war, Russia deployed troops to the two provinces and bombed your capital. Russian troops still occupy those provinces and the EU recognizes this area as "occupied territory."

DOMESTIC CONSIDERATIONS Historically, most of your population supports NATO membership. A referendum in 2008 showed that 77 percent of the public favored joining NATO. A 2014 public opinion poll showed similar numbers—78 percent in favor of NATO membership. A 2017 poll revealed that only 20 percent oppose NATO membership. Nearly all political parties in Georgia support NATO membership.

The public, while supporting NATO membership, is also fearful of Russia. The same 2014 public opinion poll showed 76 percent of your population believing that Russia is a significant threat. Moreover, Georgians are very nervous about the political and economic future, with 55 percent saying the country is moving in the "wrong direction." This could spell trouble for your party coalition.

SCENARIO Imagine that NATO offers a Membership Action Plan for Georgia. Russia responds by threatening to break the cease-fire over the disputed provinces within Georgia. Russia is demanding that you lessen your cooperation with NATO and abandon the goal of membership. European and American leaders have denounced Russian threats and support your membership in NATO. The same leaders, however, have also issued ambiguous statements as to whether they would go to war with Russia to protect your country.

CHOOSE YOUR POLICY Do you continue to strengthen ties with NATO, even though Russia has threatened you over joining the alliance? Do you give in to Russia and abandon this cooperation? Do you change your own position on NATO in response to Russia's bullying and push for full NATO membership as soon as possible? Can you continue to cooperate with NATO while keeping a fragile peace with Russia?

Research in the constructivist tradition has expanded rapidly in recent years. Scholars have examined the role of the EU in socializing elites in new member states as well as the role of the United Nations in conferring legitimacy on the use of force as a source of its power. Others have investigated how international organizations gain authority through their expertise (for example, the IMF on international financial issues) to make decisions that run counter to what their member states desire. Finally, constructivist scholars have begun to investigate how notions of identity and symbolism are important for understanding terrorist movements and counterterrorism policy. Of course, like any approach or theory of IR, constructivism has its share of critics. Realists suggest that norms are simply covers for state (or personal) interests. Liberals argue that some constructivist scholars pay too little attention to the formal institutions and the politics within them. Moreover, both realists and liberals point out that it is difficult to tell when a person's identity is genuine or is adopted for strategic reasons to bring material benefits (such as more aid, trade, or membership into an exclusive organization). Despite these criticisms, constructivist thinking and its emphasis on the identity principle will continue to be at the core of IR research for years to come.

3.3.2 Postmodernism

postmodernism An approach that denies the existence of a single fixed reality and pays special attention to texts and to discourses—that is, to how people talk and write about a subject.

Postmodernism is a broad approach to scholarship that has left its mark on various academic disciplines, especially the study of literature. Because of their literary roots, postmodernists pay special attention to *texts* and to *discourses*—how people talk and write about their subject (IR). Postmodern critiques of realism thus center on analyzing realists' words and arguments. A central idea of postmodernism is that there is no single, objective reality but a multiplicity of experiences and perspectives that defy easy categorization. For this reason, postmodernism itself is difficult to present in a simple or categorical way. Postmodern scholarship in IR preceded, set the stage for, and has largely been supplanted by constructivism.

From a postmodern perspective, realism cannot justify its claim that states are the central actors in IR and that states operate as unitary actors with coherent sets of objective interests (which they pursue through international power politics). Postmodern critics of realism see nothing objective about state interests, and certainly nothing universal (in that one set of values or interests applies to all states).

More fundamentally, postmodernism calls into question the whole notion of states as actors. States have no tangible reality; they are "fictions" that we (as scholars and citizens) construct to make sense of the actions of large numbers of individuals. For postmodernists, the stories told about the actions and policies of states are just that—stories. From this perspective, an arbitrary distinction leads bookstores to put spy novels on the fiction shelf whereas biographies and histories go on the non-fiction shelf. None of these is an objective reality, and all are filtered through an interpretive process that distorts the actual experiences of those involved. Contrary to realism's claim that states are unitary actors, postmodernists see multiple realities and experiences lurking below the surface of the fictional entities that realists construct (states). For example, realists treated the Soviet Union as a single actor with a single set of objective interests. Indeed, it was considered the second most important actor in the world. Realists were amazed when the Soviet Union split into 15 pieces, each containing its own fractious groups and elements. It became clear that the "unitary state" called the Soviet Union had masked (and let realists ignore) the divergent experiences of constituent republics, ethnic groups, and individuals.

Postmodernists seek to "deconstruct" concepts such as states, the international system, and the associated stories and arguments (texts and discourses) with which realists portray the nature of international relations. To *deconstruct* a text—a term borrowed from literary criticism—means to tease apart the words in order to reveal hidden meanings, looking for what might have been omitted or included only implicitly. The hidden meanings not explicitly addressed in the text are often called the **subtext**.

subtext Meanings that are implicit or hidden in a text rather than explicitly addressed. See also *postmodernism*.

Omissions are an aspect of subtext, for example, when realist theories of IR omit women and gender. In its emphasis on states, realism omits the roles of individuals, domestic politics, economic classes, multinational corporations (MNCs), and other nonstate actors. In its focus on the great powers, realism omits the experiences of poor countries. In its attention to military forms of leverage, it omits the roles of various nonmilitary forms of leverage.

Realism focuses so narrowly because its aim is to reduce IR to a simple, coherent model. The model is claimed to be objective, universal, and accurate. To postmodernists, the realist model is none of these things; it is a biased model that creates a narrow and one-sided story for the purpose of promoting the interests of powerful actors. Postmodernists seek to destroy this model along with any other model (including neoliberalism) that tries to represent IR in simple objective categories. Postmodernists instead want to celebrate the diversity of experiences that make up IR without needing to make sense of them by simplifying and categorizing.

3.4 Marxism

Distinguish Marx's domestic theory of class struggle from Lenin's theory of imperialism.

Historically most important among social theories, Marxist approaches to IR hold that both IR and domestic politics arise from unequal relationships between **economic classes**. This emphasis on classes—implying that the domestic and economic attributes of societies shape external relations with other states—contrasts with the realist approach to IR, with its separation of domestic and international politics. We will discuss Marxist theories of IR in Chapter 12, as they primarily concern the global divisions of North and South arising from the history of imperialism. Here we will show, briefly, how Marxist theories as social theories contrast with the realist paradigm.

Marxism is a branch of socialism, a theory that holds that the more powerful classes oppress and exploit the less powerful by denying them their fair share of the surplus they create. The oppressed classes try to gain power in order to seize more of the wealth for themselves. This process, called *class struggle*, is one way of looking at the political relationships between richer and poorer people, and ultimately between richer and poorer world regions.

RICH AND POOR Disparity of wealth is a central aspect of global North-South relations. Marxists see international relations and domestic politics alike as being shaped by a class struggle between the rich and the poor. In São Paulo, Brazil, rich and poor neighborhoods sit side by side.

economic classes A categorization of individuals based on economic status.

Marxism A branch of socialism that emphasizes exploitation and class struggle and includes both communism and other approaches.

Marxism includes both communism and other approaches. In the mid-nineteenth century, *Karl Marx* emphasized labor as the source of economic surplus. At that time, the Industrial Revolution was accompanied by particular hardship among industrial workers (including children) in Europe. Marxists still believe that the surplus created by labor should be recaptured by workers through political struggle. Today, Marxism is most influential in countries of the global South, where capital is scarce and labor conditions are wretched.

One important class in revolutions during the past century (contrary to Marx's expectations) has been *peasants*. Marxists traditionally consider peasants backward, ignorant, individualistic, and politically passive compared to the better-educated and class-conscious proletariat. But in practice, the successful third world revolutions have been peasant rebellions (often led by Marxists talking about the proletariat). The largest was the Chinese revolution in the 1930s and 1940s.

Marx's theories of class struggle were oriented toward *domestic* society in the industrializing countries of his time, not toward poor countries or international relations. Traditional Marxists looked to the advanced industrialized countries for revolution and socialism, which would grow out of capitalism. In their view, the third world would have to develop through its own stages of accumulation from feudalism to capitalism before taking the revolutionary step to socialism. What actually happened was the opposite. Proletarian workers in industrialized countries enjoyed rising standards of living and did not make revolutions. Meanwhile, in the backward third world countries, oppressed workers and peasants staged a series of revolutions, some successful and others failed.

Why did revolutions occur in backward rather than advanced countries? The answer largely shapes how one sees North-South relations today. Marxists have mostly (but not exclusively) followed a line of argument developed by *V. I. Lenin*, founder of the Soviet Union, before the Russian Revolution of 1917. Russia was then a relatively backward state, as the global South is today, and most Marxists considered a revolution there unlikely (looking instead to Germany).

Lenin's theory of imperialism argued that European capitalists were investing in colonies where they could earn big profits and then using part of these profits to *buy off* the working class at home. But Lenin saw that, after the scramble for colonies in the 1890s, few areas of the world remained to be colonized. Imperialist expansion could occur only at the expense of other imperialist states, leading to interimperialist competition and wars such as World War I. Seizing on Russia's weakness during that war, Lenin led the first successful communist revolution there in 1917.

Lenin's general idea still shapes a major approach to North-South relations—the idea that industrialized states exploit poor countries (through both formal and informal colonization) and buy off their own working classes with the profits. Through this *globalization of class relations*, world accumulation concentrates surplus toward the rich parts of the world and away from the poor ones. Revolutions, then, would be expected in poor regions.

Many third world revolutionaries sought to break loose from exploitation by the European colonizers. After European colonization ended, the United States, as the world's richest country (with large investments in the global South and a global military presence), became the target of revolutionaries agitating against exploitation in poor countries. In a number of countries, imperialists were thrown out (often violently, sometimes not) and revolutionary nationalists took power.

One of the most important such revolutions was in China, where Mao Zedong's communists took power in 1949 on a Leninist platform adapted to the largely peasant-based movement they led. Mao declared that China had stood up on its own feet, throwing off foreign domination and foreign exploitation. In India at the same time, the movement led by Gandhi used a different means (nonviolence) to achieve similar ends—national independence from colonialism. Indonesia threw out the Dutch. Lebanon threw out the French. Cuba threw out the Americans. This pattern was repeated, with variations, in dozens of countries.

According to the revolutionaries in these countries, exploitation of third world countries by rich countries takes away the economic surplus of the global South and concentrates the accumulation of wealth toward the rich parts of the world. By breaking free of such exploitation, third world states can then retain their own surplus and begin to accumulate their own wealth. Eventually they can generate their own self-sustaining cycles of accumulation and lift themselves out of poverty. However, such an approach has not worked well. A policy of self-reliance does not foster growth (see Autarky in Chapter 8). And within a single poor country, trade-offs arise between concentrating or distributing wealth. For former colonies, the realities of economic development after independence have been complex. These realities are discussed in Chapter 12.

Not all Marxist approaches favor a policy of self-reliance after revolution. Leon *Trotsky*, a Russian revolutionary, believed that, after the 1917 revolution, Russia would never be able to build socialism alone and should make its top priority the spreading of revolution to other countries to build a worldwide alliance. Trotsky's archrival Stalin wanted to build "socialism in one country," and he prevailed (and had Trotsky killed).[1] Most third world revolutions since then, including China's, have had a strongly nationalist flavor.

Marxist theories in IR entered a low-visibility phase after the collapse of the Soviet Union and China's turn toward capitalism—events that seemed to discredit Marxist theories. However, in the past few years, Marxists and former Marxists have taken power in a number of Latin American countries. Venezuela and Bolivia, as a result, have become active allies of Cuba, forming an anti-American coalition (although

---

[1] Mandel, Ernest. *From Stalinism to Eurocommunism: The Bitter Fruits of "Socialism in One Country."* Translated by Jon Rothschild. N. L. B., 1978.

America's normalization with Cuba in 2015 could bring tensions to this coalition). In Nicaragua, the former communist leader whom U.S.-organized rebels fought in the 1980s won election as president in 2006. These events, along with China's continuing formal adherence to Marxism, suggest that Marxist theories of IR have ongoing importance in the post–Cold War era.

3.5 Peace Studies

Describe the ways in which mediation can be used to resolve conflict in international relations.

Peace studies challenges fundamental concepts behind both realism and neoliberalism. In particular, peace studies seeks to shift the focus of IR away from the systemic level of analysis and toward a broad conception of social relations at the individual and domestic levels of analysis. Peace studies connects war and peace with individual responsibility, economic inequality, gender relations, cross-cultural understanding, and other aspects of social relationships. Peace studies also seeks peace not in the transactions of state leaders but in the transformation of entire societies (through social revolution) and in transnational communities (bypassing states and ignoring borders to connect people and groups globally). Another way in which peace studies seeks to broaden the focus of inquiry is to reject the supposed objectivity of traditional (realist and liberal) approaches. Most scholars in peace studies think that a good way to gain knowledge is to participate in action—not just to observe objectively. This lack of objectivity has been criticized as *normative bias* because scholars impose their personal norms and values on the subject. Scholars in peace studies respond, however, that realism itself has normative biases and makes policy prescriptions.

The development and implementation of peaceful strategies for settling conflicts—using alternatives to violent forms of leverage—are known by the general term **conflict resolution**. These methods are at work, competing with violent methods, in almost all international conflicts. Recently, the use of conflict resolution has been increasing, becoming more sophisticated, and succeeding more often. Most conflict resolution uses a third party whose role is **mediation** between two conflicting parties. Most of today's international conflicts have one or more mediating parties working regularly to resolve the conflict short of violence. No hard-and-fast rule states what kinds of third parties mediate what kinds of conflicts. The UN is the most important mediator on the world scene. Some regional conflicts are mediated through regional organizations, single states, or even private individuals.

The involvement of the mediator can vary. Some mediation is strictly *technical*—a mediator may take an active but strictly neutral role in channeling communication between two states that lack other channels of communication. For example, Pakistan secretly passed messages between China and the United States before the breakthrough in U.S.-Chinese relations in 1971. Such a role is sometimes referred to as offering the mediator's *good offices* to a negotiating process. In facilitating communication, a mediator listens to each side's ideas and presents them in a way the other side can hear. The mediator works to change each side's view of difficult issues. In these roles, the mediator is like the translator between the two sides, or a therapist helping them work out psychological problems in their relationship. Travel and discussion by private individuals and groups can serve as *citizen diplomacy* to ease tensions as well.

If both sides agree in advance to abide by a solution devised by a mediator, the process is called *arbitration*. In that case, both sides present their arguments to the arbitrator, who decides on a "fair" solution. For example, when Serbian and Bosnian negotiators could not agree on who should get the city of Brcko, they turned the issue over to arbitration rather than hold up the entire 1995 Dayton Agreement. Arbitration often uses a panel of three people, one chosen by each side unilaterally and a third on whom both sides agree.

conflict resolution The development and implementation of peaceful strategies for settling conflicts.

mediation The use of a third party (or parties) in conflict resolution.

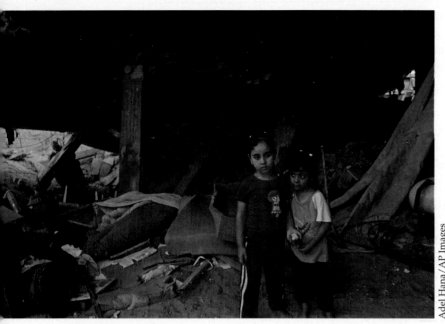

SHADOW OF WAR Militarism in a culture, or the lack thereof, can influence foreign policy. In societies at war, children's psychological trauma contributes to intergroup conflicts decades later. Generations of Palestinians have grown up in a society affected by violent conflict. These Palestinian girls, standing by their home in Gaza City, raided by Israeli forces in 2014, have lived around violent conflict their whole lives, as have their parents and grandparents.

Adel Hana / AP Images

militarism The glorification of war, military force, and violence.

positive peace A peace that resolves the underlying reasons for war; not just a cease-fire but a transformation of relationships, including elimination or reduction of economic exploitation and political oppression.

Conflicting parties (and mediators) can also use *confidence-building* measures to gradually increase trust. By contrast, *linkage* lumps together diverse issues so that compromises on one can be traded off against another in a grand deal. This was the case, for instance, in the Yalta negotiations of 1945 among the United States, Britain, and the Soviet Union. On the table simultaneously were matters such as the terms of occupation of Germany, the Soviet presence in Eastern Europe, the strategy for defeating Japan, and the creation of the UN.

Peace studies scholars argue that war is not just a natural expression of power but one closely tied to militarism in (some) cultures. **Militarism** is the glorification of war, military force, and violence through TV, films, books, political speeches, toys, games, sports, and other such avenues. Militarism also refers to the structuring of society around war—for example, the dominant role of a military-industrial complex in a national economy, or the dominance of national security issues in domestic politics. Militarism may underlie the propensity of political leaders to use military force. Historically, militarism has had a profound influence on the evolution of societies. War has often been glorified as a "manly" enterprise that ennobles the human spirit (especially before World War I, which then changed that perspective). Not only evil acts but also exemplary acts of humanity are brought forth by war—sacrifice, honor, courage, altruism on behalf of loved ones, and bonding with a community larger than oneself.

Examples of less militarized cultures show that realism's emphasis on military force is not universal or necessary. Costa Rica has had no army for 70 years (just lightly armed forces), even during the 1980s when wars occurred in neighboring Nicaragua and Panama. Japanese culture since World War II has developed strong norms against war and violence even in the shadow of threats from China and North Korea.

Anthropologists have tried to connect the domestic characteristics of hunter-gatherer societies with their external propensity to engage in warfare. Some evidence shows that war occurs more frequently in societies with internal (especially gender) inequalities, with harsh child-rearing practices, and with fathers who are absent from child rearing. By contrast, relatively peaceful societies are more likely to have open decision-making processes, relative gender equality, and permissive and affectionate child rearing. But all these societal attributes could as well be *effects* of war as causes. And because all kinds of societies seem to have the potential for warfare under some conditions (see Chapter 5), distinctions such as "warlike" are only relative.

Just as war is seen in peace studies as a pervasive aspect of society as a whole, so can peace be reconceptualized in a broader way. Because realism assumes the normalcy of military conflicts, it recognizes only a negative kind of peace—the temporary absence of war. By contrast, **positive peace** refers to a peace that resolves the underlying reasons for war—peace that is not just a cease-fire but a transformation of relationships. Under positive peace, not only do state armies stop fighting each other, they stop arming, stop forming death squads against internal protest, and reverse the economic exploitation and political oppression that scholars in peace studies believe are responsible for social conflicts that lead to war.

Proponents of this approach see broad social and economic issues—assumed by realists to be relatively unimportant—as inextricably linked with positive peace. Some scholars define poverty, hunger, and oppression as forms of violence—which they call *structural violence* because it is caused by the structure of social relations rather than by direct actions such as shooting people. Structural violence in this definition kills and harms many more people each year than do war and other forms of direct political violence. Positive peace is usually defined to include the elimination of structural violence.

Advocates of positive peace also criticize militaristic culture. The social construction of war—a complex system of rules and relations that ultimately supports the existence of war—touches our lives in many ways: from children's war toys to patriotic rituals in schools, from teenagers' gender roles to military training for young men, from the taxes we pay to the sports we play. The positive peace approach seeks to change the whole system, not just one piece of it.

Associated Press

GIVE PEACE A CHANCE Peace demonstrators play a role in many conflicts. Here, demonstrators in London respond to U.S. president Donald Trump's promise to build more nuclear weapons and his threats against North Korea, 2017.

Positive peace encompasses a variety of approaches to social change. These include alternative mechanisms for conflict resolution to take the place of war; popular pressure on governments through peace movements and political activism; the strengthening of norms against the use of violence (including the philosophy of nonviolence); the development of international or global identity transcending national, ethnic, and religious divisions; and egalitarian relations within societies in the economic, social, and political realms (including changes in gender roles).

The creation of a **world government** has long been debated by scholars and pursued by activists. Some scholars believe progress is being made (through the UN) toward the eventual emergence of a world government. Others think the idea is impractical or even undesirable (merely adding another layer of centralized control, when peace demands decentralization and freedom).

world government A centralized world governing body with strong enforcement powers.

Scholars in peace studies also study how to achieve the conditions for positive peace. Most peace studies scholars share a skepticism that state leaders left to themselves would ever achieve positive peace. Rather, they believe the practice of IR will change only as a result of pressures from individuals and groups. The most commonly studied method of exerting such pressure is through **peace movements**—people taking to the streets in protest against war and militarism. As U.S. president Dwight Eisenhower once said, "People want peace so much that one of these days governments had better get out of their way and let them have it."[2]

peace movements Movements against specific wars or against war and militarism in general, usually involving large numbers of people and forms of direct action such as street protests.

The philosophy of *nonviolence* is based on a unilateral commitment to refrain from using any violent forms of leverage in bargaining. No state today follows such a strategy, but substate actors do. *Mahatma Gandhi*, who led India's struggle for independence from the British Empire before 1948, emphasized that nonviolence must be *active* in seeking to prevent violence, to resolve conflicts without violence, and especially to stand up against injustice enforced violently. Gandhi organized Indians to resist the British colonial occupation without resorting to violence, even when British troops shot down unarmed Indian protesters.

[2] Eisenhower, Dwight D. *Ike's Letters to a Friend, 1941–1958.* Edited by Robert Griffith. Kansas, 1984.

Proponents of nonviolence emphasize the practical side of nonviolence in addition to its morality. As a tool of the powerless standing up against injustices by the powerful, nonviolence is often the most cost-effective approach—because the costs of violent resistance would be prohibitive. In the United States, the philosophy of nonviolence spread widely in the 1960s in the civil rights movement, especially through the work of Martin Luther King, Jr. Protesters in the Arab Spring movements in 2011 followed Dr. King's example as well as specific strategies recommended by an American, Gene Sharp, whose ideas were taught to young Arab activists at earlier workshops in Europe. These nonviolent approaches worked in Tunisia and Egypt; were swept aside by a violent rebellion in Libya; and gave way to wars in Syria, which claimed over 200,000 lives in 2011–2018, and in Yemen, where war and rebellion claimed over 10,000 lives during that same period.

The dilemma of nonviolence is how to respond to violence. Gandhi believed that there is always a third alternative to passivity or response in kind. Nonviolence does not always succeed when faced with violence, but then neither does violent response. However, political leaders may believe they have done their duty if they respond violently without success, but not if they respond nonviolently without success.

3.6 Gender Theories

Identify two global issues in international relations where gender is an important factor in understanding or solving the problems.

Scholarship on gender has cut a broad swath across academic disciplines, from literature to psychology to history. In recent years, it has made inroads in international relations, once considered one of the fields most resistant to gendered arguments.

3.6.1 Why Gender Matters

Gender scholarship encompasses a variety of strands of work, but all have in common the insight that gender matters in understanding how IR works—especially in issues relating to war and international security. *Feminist scholarship* in various disciplines seeks to uncover hidden assumptions about gender in how we study a subject. What scholars traditionally claim to be universal often turns out to be true only of males. Some feminist IR scholars argue that the core assumptions of realism—especially of anarchy and sovereignty—reflect the ways in which males tend to interact and to see the world. In this view, the realist approach simply assumes male participants when discussing foreign policy decision making, state sovereignty, or the use of military force.

This critique is somewhat complex. Because the vast majority of heads of state, diplomats, and soldiers *are* male, it may be realistic to study them as males. What the feminist critics then ask is that scholars explicitly recognize the gendered nature of their subject (rather than implicitly assuming all actors are male). In this view, our understanding of male actors in IR can be increased by considering how their gender identity affects their views and decision processes. And females also influence IR (more often through nonstate channels than males do)—influences often ignored by realism. Some feel that women scholars tend to be more interested in these roles and effects than are

A GUY THING Feminists from various theoretical traditions agree that the gender makeup of international summits and national governments matters. Here, China's new ruling group marks the transition of power, 2017.

Kyodo/AP Images

their male colleagues, who largely ignore gender topics. One list of "fifty key thinkers" in IR includes four women, three of whom it lists as gender scholars, while none of the 46 males are listed as gender scholars. And when a survey in 2014 listed the 20 most influential IR scholars, only three were women.

Beyond revealing the hidden assumptions about gender in a field of scholarship, feminist scholars often *challenge traditional concepts of gender* as well. In IR, these traditional concepts revolve around the assumptions that males fight wars and run states, whereas females are basically irrelevant to IR. Such gender roles are based in the broader construction of masculinity as suitable to *public* and political spaces, whereas femininity is associated with the sphere of the *private* and domestic.

Like realists (see Chapter 2), gender theorists follow a long line of tradition.[3] Not long before Thucydides, the ancient Greek woman poet Sappho wrote love poems to women on the island of Lesbos. Just before Machiavelli, the Italian-born writer Christine de Pisan praised women's abilities to make peace. A century after Hobbes, Mary Wollstonecraft in Britain argued for equal rights for women. And a century before Morgenthau founded American realism, the American Susan B. Anthony worked tirelessly for pacifism, abolitionism, and suffrage.

Beyond a basic agreement that gender is important, there is no such thing as "the feminist approach" to IR but several such approaches—*strands* of scholarship and theory. Although they are interwoven (all paying attention to gender and to the status of women), they often run in different directions. On some core issues, the different strands of feminism have conflicting views, creating interesting debates *within* feminism.

One strand, **difference feminism**, focuses on valorizing the feminine—that is, valuing the unique contributions of women *as* women. Difference feminists do not think women do all things as well as men, or vice versa. Because of their greater experience with nurturing and human relations, women are seen as potentially more effective than men (on average) in conflict resolution as well as in group decision making. Difference feminists believe there are real differences between the genders that are not just social constructions and cultural indoctrination (although these contribute to gender roles, too). Some difference feminists believe there is a core biological essence to being male or female (sometimes called *essentialism*), but most think women's difference is more culturally than biologically determined. In either case, feminine perspectives create a *standpoint* from which to observe, analyze, and criticize the traditional perspectives on IR. Another strand, **liberal feminism**, rejects these claims as being based on stereotyped gender roles. Liberal feminists see the "essential" differences in men's and women's abilities or perspectives as trivial or nonexistent—men and women are equal. They deplore the exclusion of women from positions of power in IR but do not believe that including women would change the nature of the international system. Liberal feminists seek to include women more often as subjects of study—such as women state leaders, women soldiers, and other women operating outside the traditional gender roles in IR.

A third approach combines feminism with postmodernism, discussed later in this chapter. **Postmodern feminism** tends to reject the assumptions about gender made by both difference and liberal feminists. Where difference feminists consider gender differences important and fixed, and liberal feminists consider those differences trivial, postmodern feminists find them important but arbitrary and flexible.

difference feminism A strand of feminism that believes gender differences are not just socially constructed and that views women as inherently less warlike than men (on average).

liberal feminism A strand of feminism that emphasizes gender equality and views the "essential" differences in men's and women's abilities or perspectives as trivial or nonexistent.

postmodern feminism An effort to combine feminist and postmodernist perspectives with the aim of uncovering the hidden influences of gender in IR and showing how arbitrary the construction of gender roles is.

3.6.2 The Masculinity of Realism

Difference feminism provides a perspective from which to reexamine the core assumptions of realism—especially the assumption of autonomy, from which flow the key realist concepts of sovereignty and anarchy. To realists, the international system consists of autonomous actors (states) that control their own territory and have no right to

---

[3] Thanks to Francine D'Amico for these comparisons.

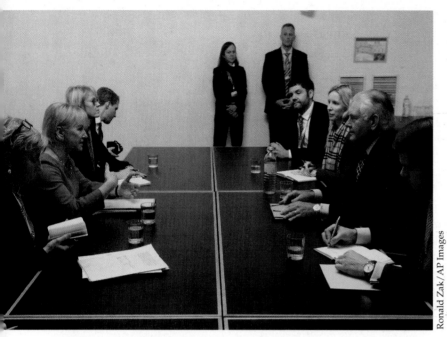

Ronald Zak / AP Images

A SEAT AT THE TABLE Feminist scholars emphasize the importance of gender roles in IR, especially the traditional distinction between males in the political-military roles and females in the domestic-family roles. Changing this division could change IR, they think. Here, Sweden's foreign minister, Margot Wallstrom, negotiates with former U.S. secretary of state, Rex Tillerson, at the Organization for Security and Cooperation in Europe (OSCE) meetings, 2017.

infringe on another's territory. Some difference feminists have argued that realism emphasizes autonomy and separation because men find separation easier to deal with than interconnection.

This view rests on a psychological theory that boys and girls grow up from a young age with different views of separateness and connection. In this theory, because a child's primary caretaker is almost always female in the early years, girls form their gender identity around the perception of *similarity* with their caretaker (and by extension the environment in which they live), but boys perceive their *difference* from the caretaker. From this experience, boys develop social relations based on individual *autonomy*, but girls' relations are based on *connection*. As a result, women are held to be more likely than men to fear abandonment, whereas men are more likely to fear intimacy.

In *moral* reasoning, according to this theory, boys tend to apply abstract rules and stress individual rights, but girls pay more attention to the concrete contexts of different situations and to the responsibility of group members for each other. In playing *games*, boys resolve disputes through arguments about the rules and then keep playing, but girls are more likely to abandon a game rather than argue over the rules and risk the social cohesion of their group. In *social relations*, boys form and dissolve friendships more readily than do girls, who are more likely to stick loyally with friends. (The empirical evidence in psychological research for these theorized gender differences is mixed at best.)

Realism, of course, rests on the concept of states as separate, autonomous actors that make and break alliances freely while pursuing their own interests (but not interfering in each other's internal affairs). Such a conception of autonomy parallels the masculine psyche just described. Thus, some feminist scholars find in realism a hidden assumption of masculinity. Furthermore, the sharp distinction that realists draw between international politics (anarchic) and domestic politics (ordered) parallels the distinction in gender roles between the public (masculine) and private (feminine) spheres. Thus, realism constructs IR as a man's world.

By contrast, an international system based on *feminine* principles might give greater importance to the interdependence of states than to their autonomy, stressing the responsibility of people to care for each other with less regard for states and borders. In the struggle between the principles of human rights and of sovereignty (noninterference in internal affairs), human rights would receive priority. In the choice of forms of leverage when conflicts arise between states, violence might be less prevalent.

The realist preoccupation with the systemic level of analysis presumes that the logic of war itself is autonomous and can be separated from other social relationships such as economics, domestic politics, sexism, and racism. Difference feminism, however, reveals the *connections* of these phenomena with war. It suggests new avenues for understanding war at the domestic and individual levels of analysis—underlying causes that realists largely ignore.

From this difference-feminist perspective, neoliberalism has gone backward from traditional liberalism, by accepting the realist assumption of separate unitary states as the important actors and downplaying substate and transnational actors, including women. Neoliberalism's conception of cooperation as rule-based interactions among autonomous actors also reflects masculinist assumptions.

3.6.3 Gender in War and Peace

In addition to its emphasis on autonomy and anarchy, realism stresses military force as the key form of leverage in IR. Here, too, many difference feminists see in realism a hidden assumption of masculinity. They see war as not only a male occupation but also the quintessentially male occupation. According to this view, men are inherently the more warlike gender, and women the more peaceful. Although realism may accurately portray the importance of war and military force in IR as we now know it, this merely reflects the male domination of the international sphere to date—not a necessary, eternal, or inescapable logic of relations among states.

Difference feminists find much evidence to support the idea of war as a masculine pursuit. Anthropologists have found that in all known cultures, males are the primary (and usually the only) combatants in warfare, despite the enormous diversity of those cultures in so many other ways. (Of course, voting and political leadership were also male domains for most of history, yet feminist scholars would hardly call those activities essentially masculine.)

One supposed link between war and masculinity is the male sex hormone testosterone (along with related hormones), which some biologists have connected with aggressive behavior in animals. However, testosterone does not *cause* aggression. Rather, social interactions "feed back" to affect testosterone levels (winners' testosterone levels rise while losers' levels fall). Thus, testosterone is a link in a complex system of relationships between the organism and the social environment. Complex behaviors such as aggression and war cannot be said to be biologically *driven* or predetermined because humanity's most striking biological capability is flexibility. Even some feminist scholars who see gender differences as strictly cultural, and not biological at all, view war as a masculine construction.

Both biologically and anthropologically, no firm evidence connects women's caregiving functions (pregnancy and nursing) with any particular kinds of behavior such as reconciliation or nonviolence—although females have been studied less than males. The role of women varies considerably from one society to another. Although they rarely take part in combat, women sometimes provide logistical support to male warriors and sometimes help drive the men into a war frenzy by dancing, shaming nonparticipating males, and other activities supportive of war. Yet in other cultures, women restrain the men from war or play special roles as mediators in bringing wars to an end.

The idea of women as peacemakers has a long history. In ancient Athens, the (male) playwright Aristophanes speculated about how women might end the unpopular Peloponnesian War with Sparta, then in progress. (His play *Lysistrata* was read in 1,000 locations in 56 countries on March 3, 2003, to protest the coming Iraq War.) In the play, a young woman named Lysistrata organizes the Athenian and Spartan women to withhold sex from the men until the latter stop the war (the women also make off with the war treasury). In short order, the men come to their senses and make peace. Women have formed their own organizations to work for peace on many occasions. In 1852, *Sisterly Voices* was published as a newsletter for women's peace societies. Bertha von Suttner in 1892 persuaded

Rune Hellestad/Getty Images

WOMAN POWER Difference feminists see women as inherently less warlike than men and more adept at making peace because of their potential and actual experiences as mothers. In this view, women play distinct roles in politics and also have distinct needs. During the rule of the Taliban in Afghanistan and parts of Pakistan, girls were barred from attending schools. Malala Yousafzai advocated for human rights, especially the education of women, in Pakistan. She survived an assassination attempt in 2012 and went on to become the youngest person to win the Nobel Peace Prize in 2014.

Alfred Nobel to create the Nobel Peace Prize (which Suttner won in 1905). During World War I, in 1915, Jane Addams and other feminists convened an international women's peace conference at The Hague. They founded the Women's Peace Party (now called the Women's International League for Peace and Freedom). After World War I, the *suffrage* movement won the right for women to vote. Difference feminists thought that women would vote for peace and against war, changing the nature of foreign policy, but women generally voted as their husbands did. Similarly, decades later when women participated in liberation struggles against colonialism in the global South, some feminists thought such participation would change foreign policies in the newly independent countries, but in general such changes did not materialize (partly because women were often pushed aside from political power after the revolutions).

Nonetheless, U.S. public opinion on foreign policy issues since the 1930s partially vindicates difference feminists. A **gender gap** in polls shows that women are about ten percentage points lower than men on average in their support for military actions. This gender gap shrinks, however, when broad consensus on a military action exists, as when U.S. forces attacked terrorist supporters in Afghanistan in late 2001.

Meanwhile, feminists in recent decades have continued to organize women's peace organizations. In the 1980s, Women's Action for Nuclear Disarmament (WAND) opposed the nuclear arms buildup, and women encamped for years at Britain's Greenham Common air base. In 1995, the UN-sponsored Beijing conference on women brought together women activists from around the world and helped deepen feminists' engagement with global issues such as North-South inequality.

In 2000, the UN Security Council passed Resolution 1325, mandating greater inclusion of women and attention to gender in UN peacekeeping and reconstruction. But in several locations, UN peacekeepers participated in local prostitution, rape, and even sex trafficking. In 2004, Secretary General Annan called "shameful" the reported behavior of UN troops from several countries serving in Democratic Congo. Investigators there found hundreds of cases of sexual crimes committed by UN personnel (see also Chapter 7).

As a result of Resolution 1325, "gender advisers" have begun to accompany international peacekeeping and relief operations to provide practical advice on more effective operations in the context of local cultures' gender relations. For example, the head of a group of Swedish men sent to build a bridge in Sri Lanka initially said, "Our task is to build a bridge, we don't need to worry about gender issues." When asked how it would be used, he replied, "By car mostly," but when asked, "The women too?" he said, "No, they'll probably walk." As a result of this gender perspective, the bridge was redesigned to include a pedestrian walkway. [4]

Through these various actions, difference feminists began developing a feminist practice of international relations that could provide an alternative to the masculine practice of realism. The motto of UNESCO is, "Since war begins in the minds of men, it is in the minds of men that the foundations for peace should be sought." For difference feminists, war does indeed begin in the minds of men, but the foundations for peace would better be sought in the minds of women.

gender gap Refers to polls showing women lower than men on average in their support for military actions, as well as for various other issues and candidates.

3.6.4 Women in IR

Liberal feminists are skeptical of difference-feminist critiques of realism. They believe that when women are allowed to participate in IR, they play the game basically the same way men do, with similar results. They think that women can practice realism—based on autonomy, sovereignty, anarchy, territory, military force, and all the rest—just as well as men can. Liberal feminists therefore tend to reject the critique of realism as masculine. (In practice, many feminist scholars draw on both difference feminists' and liberal feminists' views in various proportions.)

---

[4] Margot Wallström (October 16, 2008). Women's Forum Global Meeting. Deauville, France. In "Women and European politics: time for change", European Commission Press Release [http://europa.eu/rapid/press-release_SPEECH-08-536_en.htm]

Liberal feminism focuses on the integration of women into the overwhelmingly male preserves of foreign policy making and the military. In most states, these occupations are typically at least 90 percent male. For instance, in 2016, the heads of the world's diplomatic delegations to the UN General Assembly were 80 percent male. Of the 71 General Assembly sessions held at the UN, only three have been led by women. The U.S. military, with one of the highest proportions of women anywhere in the world or in history, is still 85 percent male. For liberal feminists, the main effect of this gender imbalance on the nature of IR—that is, apart from effects on the status of women—is to waste talent. Liberal feminists think that women have the same capabilities as men, so the inclusion of women in traditionally male occupations (from state leader to foot soldier) would bring additional capable individuals into those areas. Gender equality would thus increase national capabilities by giving the state a better overall pool of diplomats, generals, soldiers, and politicians.

In support of their argument that, on average, women handle power just as men do, liberal feminists point to the many examples of women who have served in such positions. No distinctly feminine feature of their behavior in office distinguishes these leaders from their male counterparts. Rather, they have been diverse in character and policy. Of course, women in traditionally male roles may have been selected (or self-selected) on the basis of their suitability to such roles: They may not act the way "average" women would act. Still, they do show that individuals cannot be judged accurately using group characteristics alone.

Female state leaders do not appear to be any more peaceful, or any less committed to state sovereignty and territorial integrity, than are male leaders (see Table 3.1). Some have even suggested that women in power tend to be more warlike to

Table 3.1 Notable Women State Leaders of Recent Decades

Leader	Country	Record in Office	Time Frame
Indira Gandhi	India	Led war against Pakistan in 1971; assassinated in 1984	1966–1977; 1980–1984
Golda Meir	Israel	Led war against Egypt and Syria in 1973	1969–1974
Margaret Thatcher	Britain	First woman to lead a great power in a century; went to war to recover Falkland Islands from Argentina in 1982	1979–1990
Corazon Aquino	Philippines	Struggled to control own military	1986–1992
Benazir Bhutto	Pakistan	Struggled to control own military; assassinated 2007	1988–1990; 1993–1996
Violetta Chamorro	Nicaragua	Kept the peace between factions after civil war	1990–1997
Tansu Çiller	Turkey	Led a harsh war to suppress Kurdish rebels	1993–1996
Chandrika Kumaratunga	Sri Lanka	Tried to make peace with separatists, but returned to war	1994–2005
Megawati Sukarnoputri	Indonesia	Struggled to keep country calm; lost reelection bid	2001–2004
Angela Merkel	Germany	Put limits on German troops with NATO forces in Afghanistan	2005–
Ellen Johnson-Sirleaf	Liberia	First woman president in Africa; kept country calm after civil war	2006–2018
Sheikh Hasina Wazed	Bangladesh	Attempting to consolidate democratic transition	2008–
Rosa Otunbayeya	Kyrgyz Republic	First woman president of former communist Central Asian state; calmed ethnic tensions	2010–2011
Julia Gillard	Australia	Arranged to host U.S. Marine base	2010–2013
Yingluck Shinawatra	Thailand	Tensions with military; secessionist war	2011–2014
Park Geun-hye	S. Korea	Dealt with N. Korean conflict	2013–2017
Tsai Ing-wen	Taiwan	Tensions with China	2016–
Aung San Suu Kyi	Burma	Ruled as prime minister beside military; criticized for nonresponse to ethnic cleansing	2016–
Theresa May	Great Britain	Negotiating exit from the European Union	2017–

Note: Other states, such as Finland, Norway, Latvia, Chile, New Zealand, Denmark, Brazil, Thailand, and Iceland, have had women leaders when war and peace were not major political issues in those countries.

Sources: Based on D'Amico, Francine, and Peter R. Beckman, eds. Women in World Politics: An Introduction. Bergin & Garvey, 1995. Nelson, Barbara J., and Najma Chowdhury, eds. Women and Politics Worldwide. Yale, 1994. Genovese, Michael A., ed. Women as National Leaders: The Political Performance of Women as Heads of Government. Sage, 1993. McGlen, Nancy E., and Meredith Reid Sarkees. Women in Foreign Policy: The Insiders. Routledge, 1993.

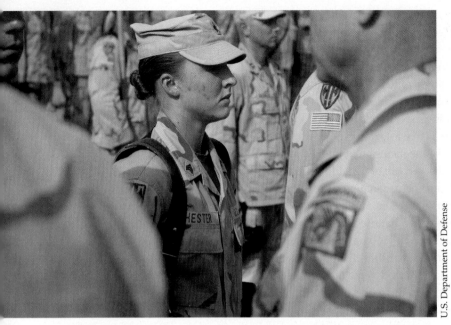

U.S. Department of Defense

COMBAT HERO Women soldiers have performed as well as men in military tasks, as predicted by liberal feminists. But in state armies, women are barred from virtually all infantry combat units worldwide. Guerrilla forces more often include women, and female U.S. military police in Iraq often participate in fighting. Here, in 2005, a sergeant from the Kentucky National Guard receives the Silver Star for heroism in combat after fighting off an ambush in Iraq.

compensate for being females in traditionally male roles. Overall, women state leaders, like men, seem capable of leading in war or in peace as circumstances demand.

In the U.S. Congress, it is hard to compare men's and women's voting records on foreign policy issues because there have been so few women. The U.S. Senate, which approves treaties and foreign policy appointments, was 98–99 percent male until 1992 (but dropped to 80 percent male in 2013; there were 22 female senators in 2018). Women had never chaired the key foreign policy committees (Armed Services and Foreign Relations/International Relations) in the Senate or House until 2011—although Representative Nancy Pelosi was the first woman Speaker of the House, third in line to the presidency, in 2007–2010.

Globally, the number of women serving in legislatures is increasing. A 2017 report from the Inter-Parliamentary Union found that women comprised over 24 percent of members of parliaments across the world, up from 7 percent in 1995. As of 2018, nine women served as head of state and eight served as head of government. Some nations set aside a certain number of seats for females in parliament. Yet female candidates often capture more seats than are set aside. In Rwanda, for example, women make up over 60 percent of the lower house of parliament, even though the law requires only 30 percent female representation.

Liberal feminists also believe that women soldiers, like women politicians, have a range of skills and abilities comparable to men's. Again, the main effect of including more women would be to improve the overall quality of military forces. About 200,000 women soldiers serve in the U.S. military (a little under 15 percent of the total) and nearly 2 million women are veterans. Women perform well in a variety of military roles, including logistical and medical support, training, and command. In 2015, the first two women graduated from the U.S. Army's elite Ranger School. Women have also had success in other countries that have allowed them into the military (or, in a few cases, drafted them).

Although women have served with distinction in military forces, most of those forces have excluded them from combat roles. In some countries, military women are limited to traditional female roles such as nurses and typists. Even when women may hold nontraditional positions such as mechanics and pilots (as in the United States), most women remain in the traditional roles. This is beginning to change. In 2013, the U.S. military lifted the ban on women serving in combat units.

Those cases of serving with distinction include historical examples of individual women who served in combat (sometimes disguised as men, sometimes not). In the fifteenth century, Joan of Arc rallied French soldiers to defeat England, turning the tide of the Hundred Years' War. (The English burned her at the stake as a witch after capturing her.) Women have often participated in combat in rebel forces fighting guerrilla wars in Vietnam, Nicaragua, and elsewhere, as well as in terrorist or paramilitary units in countries such as Peru, Germany, Italy, and Palestine. Women in Eritrea's guerrilla forces became part of that country's regular army after independence and then served in frontline combat units during Eritrea and Ethiopia's trench warfare in the late 1990s.

In recent years, U.S. women soldiers have found themselves in combat (today's mobile tactics and fluid front lines make it hard to separate combat from support roles). During the 1991 Gulf War, tens of thousands of U.S. women served, 13 were killed, and 2 were captured as prisoners of war. In the late 1990s, women began serving on some U.S. combat ships and airplanes but not in ground combat units. In the 2003 Iraq War, women flew all types of airplanes and helicopters, and one woman was in the first group of U.S. prisoners of war (POWs) captured early in the war. During the subsequent years of war in Iraq, U.S. women military police have acquitted themselves well in numerous firefights. All these cases suggest that (at least some) women are able to hold their own in combat.

The main reason that military forces exclude women from combat seems to be fear about what effect their presence might have on the male soldiers, whose discipline and loyalty have traditionally been thought to depend on male bonding and single-minded focus. Liberal feminists reject such arguments and contend that group bonding in military units does not depend on gender segregation. (After all, similar rationales were once given for racial segregation in U.S. military forces.) The effect of war on noncombatant women has also received growing attention. Attacks on women in Algeria, Rwanda, Bosnia, Afghanistan, Democratic Congo, and Sudan pointed to a possible new trend toward women as military targets. Systematic rape was used as a terror tactic in Bosnia and Rwanda, and the Japanese army in World War II operated an international network of sex slaves known as "comfort women." Rape has long been treated as a normal if regrettable by-product of war, but recently certain instances of rape were declared war crimes (see Chapter 7).

In sum, liberal feminists reject the argument that women bring uniquely feminine assets or liabilities to foreign and military affairs. They do not critique realism as essentially masculine in nature but do criticize state practices that exclude women from participation in international politics and war.

3.6.5 Difference Feminism Versus Liberal Feminism?

The arguments of difference feminists and liberal feminists may seem totally at odds. Difference feminists argue that realism reflects a masculine perception of social relations, whereas liberal feminists think that women can be just as realist as men. Liberal feminists believe that female participation in foreign policy and the military will enhance state capabilities, but difference feminists think women's unique abilities can be put to better use in transforming (feminizing) the entire system of international relations rather than in trying to play men's games.

The evidence in favor of both positions can be reconciled to some extent by bearing in mind that the character and ability of an individual are not the same as that of his or her group. Rather, the qualities of individuals follow a bell curve distribution, with many people clustered in the middle and fewer people very high or low on a given capability.

Gender differences posited by difference feminists mean that one bell curve is shifted from the other, even though the two may still overlap quite a bit (see Figure 3.4). To take a simple example, a few women are physically larger than almost all men, and a few men are smaller than almost all women. But on average, men are somewhat larger than women. On various dimensions of capability, the women's curve is above or below the men's on average, but there is still much overlap.

Liberal feminist arguments emphasize the overlap of the two bell curves. They say that individual women—*most* women on most relevant dimensions—are well within the male curve and thus can perform equally with the men. Indeed, women in nontraditional gender roles may well perform better than their male counterparts because presumably women who self-select into such roles (such as joining the military) are near the high end of the female bell curve, whereas the men are closer to the

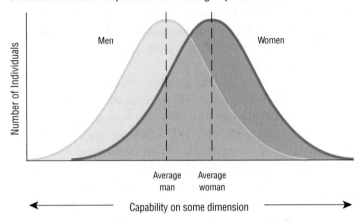

Figure 3.4 Overlapping Bell Curves

Bell curves show that individuals differ in capabilities such as physical strength or peacemaking ability. Although the genders differ on average, for most individuals (in the area of overlap) such differences do not come into play. Liberal feminists emphasize the area where the curves overlap; difference feminists emphasize the overall group differences.

middle of the male curve (because more of them join). Similarly, women who become state leaders are presumably more adept at foreign policy making than most women (or men) because political processes tend to select women at the high end of the curve in terms of their affinity for realism.

Difference feminists are more interested in the shift in the two bell curves, not their overlap. On average, according to this perspective, women tend to see international relations in a somewhat different way than men do. So although *individuals* selected to participate in foreign policy and the military may not differ from their male counterparts, women as a group differ. Women voters display different concerns regarding IR than men (as shown by the gender gap in opinion polls and voting patterns).

By this logic, then, profound differences in IR—and a shift away from the utility of realism in explaining state behavior—would occur only if many women participated in key foreign policy positions. That is, a *few* women politicians or women soldiers do not change the masculine foundations of IR. Women foreign policy makers today are surrounded by males (advisers, military officers, political leaders, and foreign state leaders). But a world in which *most* politicians or soldiers were female might be a different story. Then, instead of the selection of women for their ability to fit into men's games, the rules of the game might themselves change to reflect the fact that "average" women would be the main actors in the traditionally important IR roles. Of course, these theories of difference feminists have never been tested because women have never attained predominance in foreign policy making in any country—much less in the international system as a whole.

In addition to the liberal and difference strands of feminism, the third strand, postmodern feminism, is connected with the rise of postmodernism in the social sciences.

3.6.6 Postmodern Feminism

One line of criticism directed at realism combines feminism and postmodernism. *Postmodern feminism* seeks to deconstruct realism with the specific aim of uncovering the pervasive hidden influences of gender in IR while showing how arbitrary the construction of gender roles is. Feminist postmodernists agree with difference feminists that realism carries hidden meanings about gender roles but deny that there is any fixed inherent meaning in either male or female gender. Rather, feminist postmodernists look at the interplay of gender and power in a more open-ended way. Postmodern feminists criticize liberal feminists for trying merely to integrate women into traditional structures of war and foreign policy. They criticize difference feminists as well, for glorifying traditional feminine virtues.

In studying war, postmodern feminists have challenged the archetypes of the (male) "just warrior" and the (female) "beautiful soul." They argue that women are not just passive bystanders or victims in war but active participants in a system of warfare tied to both genders. Women act not only as nurses and journalists at the "front" but also as mothers, wives, and girlfriends on the "home front." These scholars believe that stories of military forces should not omit the roles of prostitutes at military bases, nor should stories of diplomacy omit the roles of diplomats' wives.

Postmodern feminists reject not only realism but also some of the alternative approaches that emphasize the protection of women and other noncombatants. Just-war doctrine (see Chapter 7) is considered too abstract—a set of concepts and rules that does not do justice to the richness of each historical context and the varied roles of individual men and women within it.

Postmodern feminists have tried to deconstruct the language of realism, especially when it reflects influences of gender and sex. For instance, the first atomic bombs had male gender (they were named "Fat Man" and "Little Boy"); the coded telegram informing Washington, DC, that the first hydrogen bomb had worked said simply, "It's a boy" (presumably, being born a girl would have indicated a failure). The plane that dropped the atomic bomb on Hiroshima (the *Enola Gay*) had female gender; it was named after the pilot's mother. Likewise the French atom-bomb test sites in the South Pacific were all given women's names. Similarly, pilots have pasted pinup photos of nude women onto conventional bombs before dropping them. In all these cases, postmodern feminists would note that the feminine gender of vehicles, targets, or decorations amplifies the masculinity of the weapon itself.

These efforts find sex and gender throughout the subtext of realism. For example, the terms *power* and *potency* refer to both state capability and male virility. Military force depends on phallic objects—weapons designed to shoot projectiles, penetrate targets, and explode. For many years, in basic training, men would chant: "This is my rifle [holding up rifle], this is my gun [pointing to crotch]; one's for killing, the other's for fun."[5] Nuclear weapons are also repeatedly spoken of in sexual terms, perhaps due to their great "potency." Female models are hired to market tanks, helicopter missiles, and other "potent" weapons to male procurement officers at international military trade shows. The phallic character of weapons has seemingly persisted even as technology has evolved from spears to guns to missiles.

All three strands of feminist theories provide explanations that often differ from both realist and liberal theories. In the case of response to aggression, feminists might call attention to the importance of gender roles such as the need for state leaders to prove their manhood by standing up to the bad guys. This is connected with the male role as protector of the orderly domestic sphere (home, family, country) against the dangerous and anarchic outside world. Since 2001, gender roles have become increasingly visible on both sides of the "war on terror," with both women's positions in society and men's concepts of masculinity becoming contested territory between the West and armed Islamic groups. Traditional theories of IR that ignore these issues may lack explanatory power as a result.

Whether states' interests reflect fixed assumptions about power and well-being or states and substate actors construct them based on ideas and social interactions, such interests do sometimes conflict with those of other states. Theories about how substate actors shape foreign policy is the subject of the next chapter.

[5] Dyer, Gwynne. *War*. Crown, 1985.

Chapter Review

Summary

- The central claims of realism—regarding anarchy, state actors, rationality, and the utility of military force—have been challenged on a variety of grounds.

- Liberals dispute the realist notion that narrow self-interest is more rational than mutually beneficial cooperation.

- Reciprocity can be an effective strategy for reaching cooperation in ongoing relationships but carries a danger of turning into runaway hostility or arms races.

- Neoliberalism argues that even in an anarchic system of autonomous rational states, cooperation can emerge through the building of norms, regimes, and institutions.

- Collective goods are benefits received by all members of a group regardless of their individual contributions. Shared norms and rules are important in getting members to pay for collective goods.

- International regimes—convergent expectations of state leaders about the rules for issue areas in IR—help provide stability in the absence of a world government.

- Hegemonic stability theory suggests that the holding of predominant power by one state lends stability to international relations and helps create regimes.

- In a collective security arrangement, a group of states agrees to respond together to aggression by any participating state; the UN and other IGOs perform this function.

- Democracies have historically fought as many wars as authoritarian states, but democracies have almost never fought wars against other democracies. This is called the democratic peace.

- Constructivists reject realist assumptions about state interests, tracing those interests in part to social interactions and norms.

- Postmodern critics reject the entire framework and language of realism, with its unitary state actors. Postmodernists argue that no simple categories can capture the multiple realities experienced by participants in IR.

- Marxists view international relations, including global North-South relations, in terms of a struggle between economic classes (especially workers and owners) that have different roles in society and different access to power.

- Peace studies programs are interdisciplinary and seek to broaden the study of international security to include social and economic factors ignored by realism.

- For scholars in peace studies, militarism in many cultures contributes to states' propensity to resort to force in international bargaining.

- Feminist scholars of IR agree that gender is important in understanding IR but diverge into several strands regarding their conception of the role of gender.

- Difference feminists argue that men are more warlike on average than women. They believe that although individual women participants (such as state leaders) may not reflect this difference, the participation of large numbers of women would make the international system more peaceful.

- Liberal feminists disagree that women have substantially different capabilities or tendencies as participants in IR. They argue that women are equivalent to men in almost all IR roles. As evidence, liberal feminists point to historical and present-day women leaders and women soldiers.

- Postmodern feminists seek to uncover gender-related subtexts implicit in realist discourse, including sexual themes connected with the concept of power.

Key Terms

interdependence 79
neoliberal 80
international regime 82
collective security 83
democratic peace 86
constructivism 88
postmodernism 92

subtext 92
economic classes 93
Marxism 93
conflict resolution 95
mediation 95
militarism 96
positive peace 96

world government 97
peace movements 97
difference feminism 99
liberal feminism 99
postmodern feminism 99
gender gap 102

Critical Thinking Questions

1. U.S.-Canadian relations seem better explained by liberal institutionalism than by realism. What other (one or more) interstate relationships have this quality? Show how the contrasting tenets of realism and liberal institutionalism apply to the relationship(s).

2. Inasmuch as democracies almost never fight wars against each other, do existing democracies have a national security interest in seeing democratization spread to China and other authoritarian states? If so, how can that interest be reconciled with the long-standing norm of noninterference in the internal affairs of other sovereign states?

3. Can you think of a case in which a state's actions clearly followed a constructed identity rather than objective national interests? Where did the key ideas in that identity originate and how did they come to influence the state's actions?

4. Would IR operate differently if most leaders of states were women? What would the differences be? What evidence (beyond gender stereotypes) supports your answer?

5. In what ways do the explanations of IR events change if women are considered primary players rather than peripheral ones? Which women, in which roles, would you consider important?

Suggested Readings

Bacevich, Andrew J. *The New American Militarism: How Americans Are Seduced by War.* Oxford, 2005.

Barnett, Michael, and Martha Finnemore. *Rules for the World.* Cornell, 2004.

Elshtain, Jean Bethke. *Women and War.* 2nd ed. Chicago, 1995.

Goldstein, Joshua S. *War and Gender: How Gender Shapes the War System and Vice Versa.* Cambridge, 2001.

Keck, Margaret, and Kathryn Sikkink. *Activists Beyond Borders: Advocacy Networks in International Politics.* Cornell, 1998.

Keohane, Robert O., and Joseph S. Nye. *Power and Interdependence.* 3rd ed. Pearson, 2001.

Mansfield, Edward D., and Jack Snyder. *Electing to Fight: Why Emerging Democracies Go to War.* MIT, 2005.

McDonald, Patrick. *The Invisible Hand of Peace.* Cambridge, 2009.

Runyon, Anne Sisson, and V. Spike Peterson. *Global Gender Issues in the New Millennium.* Routledge, 2013.

Tickner, J. Ann. *Gendering World Politics: Issues and Approaches in the Post–Cold War Era.* Columbia, 2001.

Let's Debate the Issue

Legislative Quotas for Women: An Effective Tool for Equality?

Overview

Many countries now use gender quotas when electing legislatures. This is especially true of new democracies in the developing world. As of 2013, 34 countries legally require women to hold some number of seats in at least one house of the national legislature, and 60 countries require women to be listed on party candidate lists for parliamentary election. The requirements for number of seats range from a low of 2 percent of seats in Bangladesh (which also elected a woman to be prime minister in 2009), to nearly 30 percent of seats of the lower house in Rwanda.

These quotas vary not only by the number of seats reserved for women but also by their implementation. Some countries have amended their constitutions to require more equal representation. Other countries pass laws (which are easier to change at a later time than a constitution) to carve out a minimum number of legislative seats for women, while still other countries place the burden on political parties. In these latter cases, parties must nominate a certain percentage of women to run in elections. This method does not guarantee seats to women (because they could lose the election), but it does guarantee an opportunity to hold a seat.

Western states (especially Europe) and human rights organizations have often encouraged this growing phenomenon of gender quotas. Should the Western states that assist with democratization encourage (or even require) these quotas? Do these quotas help or hurt the goal of female equality in the developing world?

ARGUMENT 1

Legislative Quotas Are Important for Equality and Development

Equal representation is important for democratic government. Women make up half the population of most countries. They should thus have an equal say in the political process. A healthy democracy demands that all citizens feel invested in the political process.

Women will face discrimination and slower political acceptance without quotas. In the United States and Europe, despite having the vote, it took years for women to be represented in significant numbers in legislatures. There is no reason to expect the developing world to be different. Quotas will speed the acceptance of women in the political world, giving them more of a say on matters of public policy.

Women's political empowerment will help economic development. Studies have shown that the empowerment of women can accelerate economic growth in the developing world (see Chapter 12). Quotas can accelerate the pace of that empowerment. Moreover, the costs of economic reform often fall disproportionately on women. Giving women more of a say in how that reform takes places is important.

ARGUMENT 2

Legislative Quotas Will Not Help Equality and Are Undemocratic

Quotas could create animosity toward women. Reserving seats for women in legislatures risks a backlash against women's rights. Other groups (ethnic, religious, etc.) may push for quotas as well, creating a hostile political environment. The result could be political instability as various groups press their case for legally protected seats in the legislature.

Quotas are undemocratic. The ideal of democracy is to allow anyone to serve as a representative regardless of race, gender, ethnicity, or any other personal quality. By their very nature, gender-based quotas violate this idea, reserving certain seats for one group based on a personal quality that is irrelevant to that person's qualifications.

Quotas achieve a gender equality that is Western-oriented in nature. The idea of individual rights is a Western-oriented concept of human rights. Rather than encouraging gender quotas, other policies should be promoted that are more compatible with local political culture.

Questions

- Should developing countries be encouraged to use gender quotas to bring more women into the political process? Does this practice violate the idea of democratic representation? Would a legislature made up of predominantly men also violate the idea of democratic representation?

- Do you expect similar or different policies coming from a legislature with significant female representation? Recall the views of liberal and difference feminism. What would proponents of those theories predict?

- What might be other ways to encourage female participation in the political process aside from legislative quotas? Are such steps necessary only in countries with no history of democracy or in older established democracies as well?

For Further Reading

Goetz, Anne Marie. *Governing Women: Women's Political Effectiveness in Contexts of Democratization and Governance Reform*. Routledge, 2008.

Hartmann, Heidi. *Gendering Politics and Policy: Recent Developments in Europe, Latin America, and the United States*. Routledge, 2006.

Irving, Helen. *Gender and the Constitution: Equity and Agency in Comparative Constitutional Design*. Cambridge, 2008.

Tremblay, Manon. *Women and Legislative Representation: Electoral Systems, Political Parties, and Sex Quotas*. Palgrave, 2008.

Chapter 4
Foreign Policy

NATIONAL SECURITY BRIEFING, 2017.

The White House/AP Images

 Learning Objectives

4.1 Explain three factors that can hamper individual decision making in an international crisis.

4.2 Compare the influence of public opinion and interest groups on the foreign policy process.

4.1 Making Foreign Policy

Explain three factors that can hamper individual decision making in an international crisis.

This chapter will examine how states make foreign policy. Foreign policy is the study of how leaders and states make decisions about how they will behave toward other international actors, whether states, intergovernmental organizations (IGOs), nongovernmental organizations (NGOs), or multinational corporations (MNCs). Nearly all theories of foreign policy emphasize the individual and domestic levels of analysis, the latter being the groups or institutions within a country that make decisions about its policies. These policies are meant to influence the country's relationships with international actors in many different ways. Yet what foreign policy analysts emphasize is that the many actors within a country making foreign policy decisions are sometimes at odds with one another. These internal politics can have significant consequences for a state's behavior internationally.

4.1.1 Models of Decision Making

The foreign policy process is a process of *decision making*. States take actions because people in governments—*decision makers*—choose those actions. Decision making is a *steering* process in which adjustments are made as a result of feedback from the outside world. Decisions are carried out by actions taken to change the world, and then information from the world is monitored to evaluate the effects of these actions. These evaluations—along with information about other independent changes in the environment—go into the next round of decisions (see Figure 4.1).

A common starting point for studying the decision-making process is the **rational model.** In this model, decision makers set goals, evaluate the relative importance of those goals, calculate the costs and benefits of each possible course of action, then choose the one with the highest benefits and lowest costs (see Figure 4.2).

The choice may be complicated by *uncertainty* about the costs and benefits of various actions. In such cases, decision makers must attach probabilities to each possible outcome of an action. For example, will pressuring a rival state to give ground in peace talks work or backfire? Some decision makers are relatively *accepting of risk,* whereas others are *averse to risk*. These factors affect the importance that decision makers place on various alternative outcomes that could result from an action.

Of course, one may believe decision makers are rational but not accept the realist assumption that states may be treated as unitary actors. Governments are made up of individuals, who may rationally pursue their goals. Yet the goals of different individuals involved in making a decision may diverge, as may the goals of different state agencies. For example, the U.S. secretary of state may have a different goal than the secretary of defense, just as the Central Intelligence Agency (CIA) may view a situation differently

rational model A model in which decision makers calculate the costs and benefits of each possible course of action, then choose the one with the highest benefits and lowest costs.

Figure 4.1 Decision Making as Steering

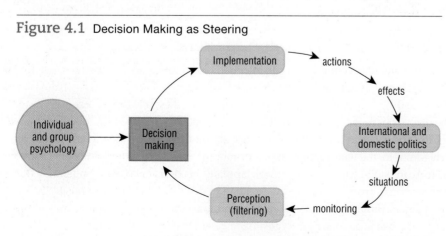

Figure 4.2 Rational Model of Decision Making

Clarify Your Goals in the situation

↓

Order Them by importance

↓

List the Alternatives for achieving your goals

↓

Investigate the Consequences of each alternative

↓

Choose the alternative that best achieves your goals

than the National Security Council does. The rational model of decision making is somewhat complicated by uncertainty and the multiple goals of decision makers. Thus, the rational model may imply that decision making is simpler than is actually the case.

An alternative to the rational model of decision making is the **organizational process model**. In this model, foreign policy decision makers generally skip the labor-intensive process of identifying goals and alternative actions, relying instead for most decisions on standardized responses or *standard operating procedures*. For example, every day the U.S. State Department receives more than a thousand reports or inquiries from its embassies around the world and sends out more than a thousand instructions or responses to those embassies. Most of those cables are never seen by the top decision makers (the secretary of state or the president); instead, they are handled by low-level decision makers who apply general principles—or who simply try to make the least controversial, most standardized decisions. These low-level decisions may not even reflect the high-level policies adopted by top leaders but rather have a life of their own. The organizational process model implies that much of foreign policy results from "management by muddling through."

Another alternative to the rational model is the **government bargaining model** (also known as the bureaucratic politics model), in which foreign policy decisions result from the bargaining process among various government agencies with somewhat divergent interests in the outcome. In 1992, the Japanese government had to decide whether to allow sushi from California to be imported—a weakening of Japan's traditional ban on importing rice (to maintain self-sufficiency in its staple food). The Japanese Agriculture Ministry, with an interest in the well-being of Japanese farmers, opposed the imports. The Foreign Ministry, with an interest in smooth relations with the United States, wanted to allow the imports. The final decision to allow imported sushi resulted from the tug-of-war between the ministries. Thus, according to the government bargaining model, foreign policy decisions reflect (a mix of) the interests of state agencies.

organizational process model
A decision-making model in which policy makers or lower-level officials rely largely on standardized responses or standard operating procedures.

government bargaining model
A model that sees foreign policy decisions as flowing from a bargaining process among various government agencies that have somewhat divergent interests in the outcome ("where you stand depends on where you sit"). Also called *bureaucratic politics model*.

4.1.2 Individual Decision Makers

Every international event is the result, intended or unintended, of decisions made by individuals. International relations (IR) does not just happen. President Harry Truman, who decided to drop U.S. nuclear bombs on two Japanese cities in 1945, had a sign on his desk: "The buck stops here." As leader of the world's greatest power, he had nobody to pass the buck to. If he chose to use the bomb (as he did), more than 100,000 civilians would die. If he chose not to, the war might drag on for months with tens of thousands of U.S. casualties. Truman had to choose. Some people applaud his decision; others condemn it. But for better or worse, Truman as an individual had to decide and to take responsibility for the consequences. Similarly, the decisions of individual citizens, although they may not seem important when taken one by one, create the great forces of world history.

The study of individual decision making revolves around the question of rationality. To what extent are national leaders (or citizens) able to make rational decisions in the national interest—if indeed it is possible to define such an interest—and thus to conform to a realist view of IR? Individual rationality is not equivalent to state rationality. States might filter individuals' irrational decisions to arrive at rational choices, or states might distort individual rational decisions and end up with irrational state choices. But realists tend to assume that both states and individuals are rational and that the goals or interests of states correlate with those of leaders.

The most simplified rational-actor models assume that interests are the same from one actor to another. If this were so, individuals could be substituted for each other in various roles without changing history very much. And states would all behave similarly to each other (or rather, the differences between them would reflect different resources and geography, not differences in the nature of national interests). This assumption is at best a great oversimplification; individual decisions reflect the *values* and *beliefs* of the decision maker.

FIRE AWAY Foreign policies often deviate from rationality as a result of the misperceptions and biases of decision makers and populations. Here, in 2017, North Korea's dictator Kim Jong-Un watches a test of an intermediate range ballistic missile with his military staff. His country's nuclear weapons program and its delivery vehicles are a significant concern in the West. These weapons will pose a much greater threat if Kim, who took over in 2011, is an irrational madman than if he turns out to be a shrewdly rational actor.

Individual decision makers not only have differing values and beliefs but also have unique personalities—their personal experiences, intellectual capabilities, and personal styles of making decisions. Some IR scholars study individual psychology to understand how personality affects decision making. Psychoanalytic approaches hold that personalities reflect the subconscious influences of childhood experiences. For instance, Bill Clinton drew much criticism in his early years as president for a foreign policy that seemed to zigzag. A notable Clinton personality trait was his readiness to compromise. Clinton himself has noted that his experience of growing up with a violent, alcoholic stepfather shaped him into a "peacemaker, always trying to minimize the disruption."[1]

Beyond individual *idiosyncrasies* in goals or decision-making processes, individual decision making diverges from the rational model in at least three *systematic* ways. First, decision makers suffer from **misperceptions and selective perceptions** (taking in only some kinds of information) when they compile information on the likely consequences of their choices. Decision-making processes must reduce and filter the incoming information on which a decision is based; the problem is that such filtration is often biased. **Information screens** are subconscious filters through which people put the information coming in about the world around them. Often they simply ignore any information that does not fit their expectations. Information is also screened out as it passes from one person to another in the decision-making process. For example, prior to the September 2001 terrorist attacks, U.S. intelligence agencies failed to interpret available evidence adequately because too few analysts were fluent in Arabic. Similarly, Soviet leaders in 1941 and Israeli leaders in 1973 ignored evidence of pending invasions of their countries.

Misperceptions can affect the implementation of policy by low-level officials as well as its formulation by high-level officials. For example, in 1988, officers on a U.S. warship in the Persian Gulf shot down a civilian Iranian jet that they believed to be a military jet attacking them. The officers were trying to carry out policies established by national leaders, but because of misperceptions, their actions instead damaged their state's interests.

misperceptions and selective perceptions The mistaken processing of the available information about a decision; one of several ways—along with affective and cognitive bias—in which individual decision making diverges from the rational model. See also *information screens*.

information screens The subconscious or unconscious filters through which people put the information coming in about the world around them. See also *misperceptions and selective perceptions*.

---

[1] Collins, Nancy. A Legacy of Strength and Love [interview with President Clinton]. *Good Housekeeping* 221 (5), 1995: 113–15.

Second, the rationality of individual cost-benefit calculations is undermined by emotions that decision makers feel while thinking about the consequences of their actions—an effect referred to as *affective bias*. (*Positive* and *negative affect* refer to feelings of liking or disliking someone.) As hard as a decision maker tries to be rational in making a decision, the decision-making process is bound to be influenced by strong feelings held about the person or state toward which a decision is directed. (Affective biases also contribute to information screening, as positive information about disliked people or negative information about liked people is screened out.)

Third, *cognitive biases* are systematic distortions of rational calculations based not on emotional feelings but simply on the limitations of the human brain in making choices. The most important of these distortions seems to be the attempt to produce *cognitive balance*—or to reduce *cognitive dissonance*. These terms refer to the tendency people have to try to maintain mental models of the world that are logically consistent (this seldom succeeds entirely).

One implication of cognitive balance is that decision makers place greater value on goals that they have put much effort into achieving—the *justification of effort*. This is especially true in a democracy, in which politicians must face their citizens' judgment at the polls and so do not want to admit failures. The Vietnam War trapped U.S. decision makers in this way in the 1960s. After sending half a million troops halfway around the world, U.S. leaders found it difficult to admit to themselves that the costs of the war were greater than the benefits.

Decision makers also achieve cognitive balance through *wishful thinking*—an overestimate of the probability of a desired outcome. A variation of wishful thinking is to assume that an event with a *low probability* of occurring will *not* occur. This could be a dangerous way to think about catastrophic events such as accidental nuclear war or a terrorist attack.

Cognitive balance often leads decision makers to maintain a hardened image of an *enemy* and to interpret all of the enemy's actions in a negative light (because the idea of bad people doing good things would create cognitive dissonance). A *mirror image* refers to two sides in a conflict maintaining very similar enemy images of each other ("We are defensive, they are aggressive," etc.). A decision maker may also experience psychological *projection* of his or her own feelings onto another actor. For instance, if (hypothetically) Indian leaders wanted to gain nuclear superiority over Pakistan but found that goal inconsistent with their image of themselves as peaceful and defensive, the resulting cognitive dissonance might be resolved by believing that Pakistan was trying to gain nuclear superiority (the example works as well with the states reversed).

Another form of cognitive bias, related to cognitive balance, is the use of *historical analogies* to structure one's thinking about a decision. This can be quite useful or quite misleading, depending on whether the analogy is appropriate. Each historical situation is unique in some way, and when a decision maker latches onto an analogy and uses it as a shortcut to a decision, the rational calculation of costs and benefits may be cut short as well. In particular, decision makers often assume that a solution that worked in the past will work again—without fully examining whether the situations really are similar. For example, U.S. leaders used the analogy of Munich in 1938 to convince themselves that appeasement in the Vietnam War would lead to increased communist aggression in Asia. In retrospect, the differences between North Vietnam and Nazi Germany made this a poor analogy (largely because of the civil war nature of the Vietnam conflict). Vietnam itself then became a potent analogy that helped persuade U.S. leaders to avoid involvement in certain overseas conflicts, such as in Bosnia; this was called the "Vietnam syndrome" in U.S. foreign policy.

 All of these psychological processes—misperception, affective biases, and cognitive biases—interfere with the rational assessment of costs and benefits in making a decision. Two specific modifications to the rational model of decision making have been proposed to accommodate psychological realities.

First, the model of *bounded rationality* takes into account the costs of seeking and processing information. Nobody thinks about every single possible course of action when making a decision. Instead of **optimizing**, or picking the very best option, people usually work on the problem until they come up with a "good enough" option that meets some minimal criteria; this is called **satisficing**, or finding a satisfactory solution. The time constraints faced by top decision makers in IR—who are constantly besieged with crises requiring their attention—generally preclude their finding the very best response to a situation. U.S. Secretary of Defense William Cohen in 1997 described these time constraints: "The unrelenting flow of information, the need to digest it on a minute-by-minute basis, is quite different from anything I've experienced before … . There's little time for contemplation; most of it is action."[2]

Second, **prospect theory** provides an alternative explanation (rather than simple rational optimization) of decisions made under risk or uncertainty. According to this theory, decision makers go through two phases. In the *editing phase*, they frame the options available and the probabilities of various outcomes associated with each option. Then, in the *evaluation phase*, they assess the options and choose one. Prospect theory holds that evaluations take place by comparison with a *reference point*, which is often the status quo but might be some past or expected situation. The decision maker asks whether he or she can do better than that reference point, but the value placed on outcomes depends on how far from the reference point the outcomes are.

Individual decision making thus follows an imperfect and partial kind of rationality at best. Not only do the goals of different individuals vary, but decision makers face a series of obstacles in receiving correct information, constructing accurate models of the world, and reaching decisions that further their own goals. The rational model is only a simplification at best and must be supplemented by an understanding of individual psychological processes that affect decision making.

optimizing Picking the very best option; contrasts with satisficing, or finding a satisfactory but less than best solution to a problem. The model of "bounded rationality" postulates that decision makers generally "satisfice" rather than optimize.

satisficing The act of finding a satisfactory or "good enough" solution to a problem.

prospect theory A decision-making theory that holds that options are assessed by comparison to a reference point, which is often the status quo but might be some past or expected situation. The model also holds that decision makers fear losses more than they value gains.

groupthink The tendency of groups to validate wrong decisions by becoming overconfident and underestimating risks.

4.1.3 Group Psychology

What are the implications of group psychology for foreign policy decision making? In one respect, groups promote rationality by balancing out the blind spots and biases of any individual. Advisers or legislative committees may force a state leader to reconsider a rash decision. And the interactions of different individuals in a group may result in the formulation of goals that more closely reflect state interests rather than individual idiosyncrasies. However, group dynamics also introduce new sources of irrationality into the decision-making process.

Groupthink refers to the tendency for groups to reach decisions without accurately assessing their consequences because individual members tend to go along with ideas they think the others support. The basic phenomenon is illustrated by a simple psychology experiment. A person asks a group of six people to compare the lengths of two lines projected onto a screen. When five of the people are secretly instructed to say that line A is longer—even though anyone can see that line B is actually longer—the sixth person is likely to agree with the group rather than believe his or her own eyes.

Unlike individuals, groups tend to be overly optimistic about the chances of success and are

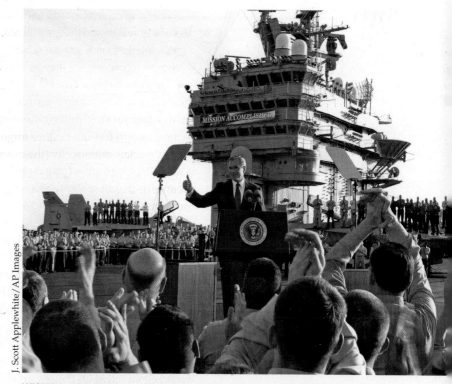

J. Scott Applewhite/AP Images

WISHFUL THINKING Both individual misperception and group psychology encourage overconfidence and excessive optimism among decision makers. This general tendency in every government especially marked the period of the U.S. invasion of Iraq. Here, President Bush declares victory on an aircraft carrier, May 2003.

[2] Bradley Graham, March 5, 1997. On First Trip as Pentagon Chief, Cohen Discusses Bosnia Endgame. *Washington Post*, A22.

Figure 4.3 Some Psychological Pitfalls of Decision Making

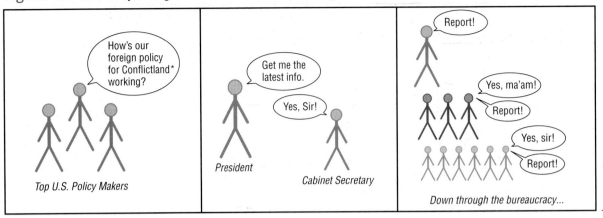

Note: Conflictland could be Vietnam in 1968, Bosnia in 1994, or Iraq in 2006.

thus more willing to take risks. Participants suppress their doubts about dubious undertakings because everyone else seems to think an idea will work. Also, because the group diffuses responsibility from individuals, nobody feels accountable for actions.

In a spectacular case of groupthink, President Ronald Reagan's close friend and director of the CIA bypassed his own agency and ran covert operations spanning three continents using the National Security Council (NSC) staff in the White House basement. The NSC sold weapons to Iran in exchange for the freedom of U.S. hostages held in Lebanon, and then it used the Iranian payments to fund Nicaraguan Contra rebels illegally. The *Iran-Contra scandal* resulted when these operations, managed by an obscure NSC aide named Oliver North, became public.

The U.S. war in Iraq may also provide cautionary examples to future generations about the risks of misinformation, misperception, wishful thinking, and groupthink in managing a major foreign policy initiative. Some of the problems of individual and group psychology in the policy process—be they in Vietnam, Bosnia, or Iraq—are illustrated in Figure 4.3.

The *structure of a decision-making process*—the rules for who is involved in making the decision, how voting is conducted, and so forth—can affect the outcome, especially when no single alternative appeals to a majority of participants. Experienced participants in foreign policy formation are familiar with the techniques for manipulating decision-making processes to favor outcomes they prefer. A common technique is to control a group's formal *decision rules*. These rules include the items of business the group discusses and the order in which proposals are considered (especially important when participants are satisficing). Probably most important is the ability to *control the agenda* and thereby structure the terms of debate.

State leaders often rely on an inner circle of advisers in making foreign policy decisions. The composition and operation of the inner circle vary across governments. For instance, President Lyndon Johnson had "Tuesday lunches" to discuss national security policy with top national security officials. Some groups depend heavily on *informal* consultations in addition to formal meetings. Some leaders create a "kitchen cabinet"—a trusted group of friends who discuss policy issues with the leader even though they have no formal positions in government. For instance, Israel's Golda Meir held many such discussions at her home, sometimes literally in the kitchen. Russian president Boris Yeltsin relied on the advice of his bodyguard, who was a trusted friend.

4.1.4 Crisis Management

The difficulties in reaching rational decisions, both for individuals and for groups, are heightened during a crisis. *Crises* are foreign policy situations in which outcomes are very important and time frames are compressed. Crisis decision making is harder to understand and predict than is normal foreign policy making.

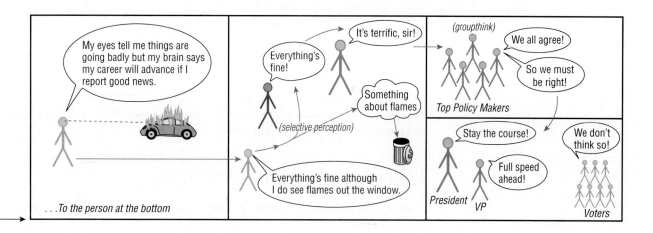

In a crisis, decision makers operate under tremendous time constraints. The normal checks on unwise decisions may not operate. Communications become shorter and more stereotyped, and information that does not fit a decision maker's expectations is more likely to be discarded simply because there is no time to consider it. In framing options, decision makers tend to restrict the choices, again to save time, and tend to overlook creative options while focusing on the most obvious ones. (In the United States, shifting time constraints are measurable in a doubling or tripling of pizza deliveries to government agencies as decision makers work through mealtimes.)

Groupthink occurs easily during crises. During the 1962 Cuban Missile Crisis, President John F. Kennedy created a small, closed group of advisers who worked together intensively for days on end, cut off from outside contact and discussion. Even the president's communication with Soviet leader Nikita Khrushchev was rerouted through Kennedy's brother Robert and the Soviet ambassador, cutting out the State Department. Recognizing the danger of groupthink, Kennedy left the room from time to time—removing the authority figure from the group—to encourage free discussion. Through this and other means, the group managed to identify an option (a naval blockade) between its first two choices (bombing the missile sites or doing nothing). Sometimes leaders purposefully designate someone in the group (known as a *devil's advocate*) to object to ideas.

Participants in crisis decision making not only are rushed but also experience severe psychological *stress*, amplifying the biases just discussed. Decision makers tend to overestimate the hostility of adversaries and to underestimate their own hostility toward those adversaries. Dislike easily turns to hatred, and anxiety to fear. More and more information is screened out in order to come to terms with decisions being made and to restore cognitive balance. Crisis decision making also leads to physical exhaustion. *Sleep deprivation* sets in within days as decision makers use every hour to stay on top of the crisis. Unless decision makers are careful about getting enough sleep, they may make vital foreign policy decisions under shifting perceptual and mood changes.

Because of the importance of sound decision making during crises, voters pay great attention to the

Alexandra Avakian/Contact Press Images Inc.

WORKING UNDER STRESS Crisis management takes a high toll psychologically and physiologically. President Eduard Shevardnadze of Georgia seemed to show this strain in 1992—just the beginning of years of civil war and perpetual crisis in that country. Shevardnadze, formerly a Soviet foreign minister, had returned to lead his native Georgia when the Soviet Union dissolved. He left office in 2003 after a popular uprising against corruption.

psychological stability of their leaders. Before Israeli Prime Minister Yitzhak Rabin won election in 1992, he faced charges that he had suffered a one-day nervous breakdown when he headed the armed forces just before the 1967 war. Not so, he responded; he was just smart enough to realize that the crisis had caused him both exhaustion and acute nicotine poisoning, and he needed to rest up for a day in order to go on and make good decisions.

Whether in crisis mode or normal routines, individual decision makers do not operate alone. The government and society in which they work shape their decisions. And substate actors such as government agencies, political interest groups, and industries constrain and shape foreign policy.

4.2 Domestic Influences

Compare the influence of public opinion and interest groups on the foreign policy process.

The remainder of this chapter considers other liberal theoretical approaches that, like the democratic peace, operate at the domestic level of analysis. These approaches, in contrast to realism, see international outcomes as the result of processes within states rather than just those among states. The actions of a state in the international arena result from individual human choices—by citizenry, political leaders, diplomats, and bureaucrats—aggregated through the state's internal structures. We will look at the state from the inside out, trying to understand the processes and structures *within* states that make them behave as they do.

4.2.1 Bureaucracies

Of the many substate actors that influence states' actions in the international arena, those closest to the action are the bureaucratic agencies that states maintain for developing and carrying out foreign policy. Different states maintain different foreign policy bureaucracies, but these bureaucracies share some common elements.

DIPLOMATS Almost all states maintain a *foreign service* of diplomats working in *embassies* in foreign capitals (and in *consulates* located in noncapital foreign cities), as well as diplomats who remain at home to help coordinate foreign policy. States appoint *ambassadors* as their official representatives to other states and to international organizations. Diplomatic activities are organized through a *foreign ministry* or the equivalent (for example, the U.S. State Department).

In many democracies, some diplomats are *political appointees* who come and go with changes in government leaders (often as patronage for past political support). Others are *career diplomats* who come up through the ranks of the foreign service and tend to outlast changes in administration.

Diplomats provide much of the information that goes into making foreign policies, but their main role is to carry out rather than create policies. Nonetheless, foreign ministry bureaucrats often make foreign relations so routine that top leaders and political appointees can come and go without greatly altering the country's relations. The national interest is served, the bureaucrats believe, by the stability of overall national goals and positions in international affairs.

Tension is common between state leaders and foreign policy bureaucrats. Career diplomats try to orient new leaders and their appointees, and to control the flow of information they receive (creating information screens). Politicians struggle to exercise power over the formal bureaucratic agencies because the latter can be too "bureaucratic" (cumbersome, routinized, conservative) to control easily. Also, these agencies are often staffed (at lower levels) mostly by career officials who may not owe loyalty to political leaders.

Size alone does not guarantee power for a bureaucracy. For example, the National Security Council (NSC) has a staff approaching 400 people, compared with 5,000 people with responsibilities for similar matters in the Commerce and State departments. The power of these agencies is their proximity to the U.S. president. The NSC chief traditionally briefs the president every morning on international security issues.

Sometimes state leaders appoint a close friend or key adviser to manage the foreign policy bureaucracy. President George W. Bush did this in his second term with his former NSC chief and confidante, Condoleezza Rice. Chinese leader Mao Zedong put his loyal ally Zhou Enlai in charge of foreign policy. At other times, state leaders may appoint rivals with differing views of foreign policy—as President Barack Obama did with his former political rival Hillary Clinton.

At times, frustration with the bureaucracy leads politicians to bypass normal channels of diplomacy. For example, during the 1962 Cuban Missile Crisis, President Kennedy demanded to be put in direct contact with military personnel in the Caribbean overseeing the blockade of Cuba, bypassing the secretary of defense and high-ranking officers.

INTERAGENCY TENSIONS *Interagency* tensions also affect the formulation of foreign policy. Certain agencies traditionally clash, and an endless tug-of-war shapes the foreign policies that emerge. In an extreme example of interagency rivalry, the U.S. State Department and the CIA backed opposite sides in a civil war in Laos in 1960. In the United States and the Soviet Union during the Cold War, the defense ministry was usually more hawkish (favoring military strength) and the foreign ministry or State Department more dovish (favoring diplomacy), with the president or premier holding the balance.

In general, bureaucracies promote policies under which their own capabilities will be effective and their power will increase. There is a saying that "where you stand" on an issue "depends on where you sit" (in the bureaucratic structure). One can often predict just from the job titles of participants how they will argue on a policy issue. The government bargaining model pays special attention to the interagency negotiations that result from conflicts of interest between agencies of the same government. For example, after Americans were taken hostage in Iran in 1979, military and CIA officials pushed President Carter to attempt a military rescue, while the State Department vehemently opposed such a mission. After days of debate, the president decided to go ahead with the rescue mission (which proved disastrous), but he did not invite the secretary of state to the meeting where the final decisions were made.

Although representatives of bureaucratic agencies usually promote the interests of their own bureaucracies, sometimes heads of agencies try to appear loyal to the state leader by forgoing the interests of their own agencies. Also, it is not always possible to predict the preferences of leaders of bureaucratic agencies, given the goals of their institutions. For example, during the Cuban Missile Crisis, defense officials were hesitant to commit to a military solution to the crisis, while some diplomatic officials favored a preemptive military strike.

Units within agencies have similar tensions. In many countries, the different military services (army, navy, air force) pull in somewhat different directions, even if they ultimately unite in a single voice to debate with their colleagues in the foreign ministry. Bureaucrats working in particular units or projects become attached to them. Officials responsible for a new weapon system lose bureaucratic turf, and perhaps their jobs, if the weapon's development is canceled.

Of special concern in many poor states is the institutional interest that military officers have in maintaining a strong military. If civilian state leaders allow officers' salaries to fall or the size of the military forces to be cut, they may well face institutional resistance from the military—in the extreme case, a military takeover of the government (see Chapter 6). These issues were important factors (among several) in military coups in Niger, Honduras, and Egypt in the last decade.

In general, bureaucratic rivalry as an influence on foreign policy challenges the notion of states as unitary actors in the international system. Such rivalries suggest that a state does not have any single set of goals—a national interest—but that its actions may result from the bargaining of subunits, each with its own set of goals. Furthermore, such a perspective extends far beyond bureaucratic agencies because other substate actors have their own goals, which they seek to advance by influencing foreign policy.

4.2.2 Interest Groups

Foreign policy makers operate not in a political vacuum but in the context of the political debates in their society. In all states, societal pressures influence foreign policy, although these are aggregated and made effective through different channels in different societies. In pluralistic democracies, interested parties influence foreign policy through interest groups and political parties. In dictatorships, similar influences occur but less visibly. Thus foreign policies adopted by states generally reflect some kind of process of domestic coalition formation. Of course, international factors also have strong effects on domestic politics.

Interest groups are coalitions of people who share a common interest in the outcome of some political issue and who organize themselves to try to influence the outcome. For instance, French farmers have a big stake in international negotiations in the European Community (which subsidizes agriculture) and in world trade talks (which set agricultural tariffs). The farmers exert political pressure on the French government through long-established and politically sophisticated associations and organizations. They lobby for desired legislation and contribute to politicians' campaigns. More dramatically, when their interests have been threatened—as during a U.S.-European trade dispute in 1992—French farmers have turned out in large numbers to block roads, stage violent street demonstrations, and threaten to grind the national economy to a halt unless the government adopts their position. Similarly (but often less dramatically), interest groups form around businesses, labor unions, churches, veterans, senior citizens, members of an occupation, or citizens concerned about an issue such as the environment.

Lobbying is the process of talking with legislators or officials to influence their decisions on some set of issues. Three important elements that go into successful lobbying are the ability to gain a hearing with busy officials, the ability to present cogent arguments for one's case, and the ability to trade favors in return for positive action on an issue. These favors—legal and illegal—range from campaign contributions to dinners at nice restaurants, trips to golf resorts, securing illicit sexual liaisons, and paying bribes. In many states, corruption is a major problem in governmental decision making (see Chapter 13), and interest groups may induce government officials by illegal means to take certain actions.

Ethnic groups within one state often become interest groups concerned about their ancestral nation outside that state. Many members of ethnic groups feel strong emotional ties to their relatives in other countries; because the rest of the population generally does not care about such issues one way or the other, even a small ethnic group can have considerable influence on policy toward a particular country. Such ethnic ties are emerging as a powerful foreign policy influence in various ethnic conflicts in poor regions. The effect is especially strong in the United States, which is ethnically

interest groups Coalitions of people who share a common interest in the outcome of some political issue and who organize themselves to try to influence the outcome.

A HOUSE DIVIDED Foreign policies are affected by the pulling and tugging of various domestic actors. Legislatures respond to these groups, constituencies, lobbyists, and media. Here, Israeli Prime Minister Benjamin Netanyahu gives a controversial address to a joint session of Congress in 2015. Netanyahu was not invited by President Obama but by Congressional Republicans, causing tensions between the United States and Israel (see also the Seeking the Collective Good box).

Seeking the Collective Good
Israeli-Palestinian Peace Talks
COLLECTIVE GOOD: An End to 70 Years of Violent Conflict

BACKGROUND: Since the founding of Israel in 1948, in the wake of World War II, Jews and Arab Palestinians have been fighting over the land. After several destructive wars, Israel and its main neighbors, Egypt and Jordan, arrived at a durable (though cold) peace. The Israelis and Palestinians, however, have yet to reach a peace agreement based on a Palestinian state in lands occupied by Israel in the 1967 war—the West Bank and the Gaza Strip—and Palestinian recognition of Israel's right to exist.

In many rounds of negotiations over the years, the two sides have gotten closer. At the end of 2000, negotiators nearly reached agreement on the parameters for a Palestinian state side by side with Israel. The effort fell short, however; new governments took power in both Israel and the United States, and a new wave of violence ensued. Israeli-Palestinian peace is a collective good that would benefit each side regardless of which side made the concessions that led to an agreement.

CHALLENGE: The United States has led many rounds of fruitless peace talks. These talks have always faced great challenges as a result of the domestic politics on each side. In Israel, the parliamentary ruling coalition usually includes parties opposed to concessions toward Palestine, so the Israeli government lacks maneuvering room to make concessions even if it wanted to. In Palestine, the militant armed group Hamas controls Gaza, leaving the Israelis negotiating with a Palestinian Authority that does not fully control the territory it hoped to claim as a state. In these ways, foreign policy processes even in democracies can constrain each side's ability to make peace.

SOLUTION: Reciprocity, a strong norm in Israeli-Palestinian relations over the decades, is basic to the negotiation of peace agreements. Yet it has not sufficed, in part because domestic

Israeli prime minister and Palestinian president, 2016.

constraints make it harder for governments to have cooperation based on reciprocity.

To get around these domestic constraints, the dominance principle helps. Most analysts agree that the peace talks can succeed only if the United States applies strong leadership (including pressure and inducements) to get the two parties to make concessions. Opponents on each side can then blame the United States rather than their own leaders, who thus gain maneuvering room to compromise. If an Israeli-Palestinian peace agreement is ever to occur, American leadership of the process will likely play a key role in reaching it.

mixed and has a pluralistic form of democracy. For example, Cuban Americans organize to influence U.S. policy toward Cuba, as do Greek Americans on Greece, Jewish Americans on Israel, and African Americans on Africa. In a 1996 U.S. Senate election in South Dakota, one candidate raised large contributions from the Pakistani-American community and the other candidate from the rival Indian-American community. But whether or not a foreign country has a large constituency of ethnic nationals within another country, it can lobby that country's government.

Clearly, interest groups have goals and interests that may or may not coincide with the national interest as a whole (if indeed such an interest can be identified). As with bureaucratic agencies, some question the view of the state as a unitary actor. Defenders of interest-group politics argue that various interest groups tend to push and pull in different directions, with the ultimate decisions generally reflecting the interests of society as a whole. But according to *Marxist* theories of international relations, the key domestic influences on foreign policy in capitalist countries are rich owners of big businesses. For instance, European imperialism benefited banks and big business, which made huge profits from exploiting cheap labor and resources in overseas colonies. This is the official view (if not always the operative one) of the

Chinese government toward Western industrialized states. During the Cold War, Marxists argued that Western foreign policies were driven by the profit motive of arms manufacturers.

4.2.3 The Military-Industrial Complex

military-industrial complex A huge interlocking network of governmental agencies, industrial corporations, and research institutes, all working together to promote and benefit from military spending.

A **military-industrial complex** refers to a huge interlocking network of governmental agencies, industrial corporations, and research institutes, working together to supply a nation's military forces. The military-industrial complex was a response to the growing importance of technology (nuclear weapons, electronics, and others) and of logistics in Cold War military planning. Because of the domestic political clout of these actors, the complex was a powerful influence on foreign policy in both the United States and the Soviet Union during the Cold War.

States at war have long harnessed their economic and technological might for the war effort. But during the Cold War, military procurement occurred on a massive scale in "peacetime," as the superpowers raced to develop new high-technology weapons. This race created a special role for scientists and engineers in addition to the more traditional role of industries that produce war materials. In response to the launch of the Soviet satellite *Sputnik* in 1957, the United States increased spending on research and development and created new science education programs. By 1961, President Dwight Eisenhower warned in his farewell speech that the military-industrial complex (a term he coined) was gaining "unwarranted influence" in U.S. society and that militarization could erode democracy in the United States. The size of the complex gave it more political clout than ordinary citizens could muster. Yet its interest in the arms race conflicted with the interest of ordinary citizens in peace.

The complex encompasses a variety of constituencies, each of which has an interest in military spending. *Corporations* that produce goods for the military profit from government contracts. So do military *officers* whose careers advance by building bureaucratic empires around new weapons systems. And so do universities and scientific institutes that receive military research contracts—a major source of funding for scientists in Russia and the United States.

Subcontractors and parts suppliers for big U.S. weapons projects are usually spread around many states and congressional districts so that local citizens and politicians join the list of constituents benefiting from military spending. Early funding for the Strategic Defense Initiative (or Star Wars) was given to each military service branch, the Department of Energy, NASA, and hundreds of private contractors. Recently, a similar phenomenon has emerged in the European Community (EC), where weapons development programs have been parceled out to several European states. A new fighter jet is less likely to be canceled if one country gets the contract for the wings, another for the engines, and so forth.

Executives in military industries, who best understand their industries, are often appointed as government officials responsible for military procurement decisions and then return to their companies again—a practice called the *revolving door*. In democracies, military industries also influence public opinion through advertising that ties their products to patriotic themes. U.S. military industries also give generous campaign contributions to national politicians who vote on military budgets, and these industries sometimes offer bribes to Pentagon officials as well.

4.2.4 Public Opinion

public opinion In IR, the range of views on foreign policy issues held by the citizens of a state.

Many domestic actors seek to influence **public opinion**—the range of views on foreign policy issues held by the citizens of a state (see the Public Opinion and International Relations box). Public opinion has greater influence on foreign policy in democracies than in authoritarian governments. But even dictators must pay attention to what citizens think. No government can rule by force alone. It needs

Public Opinion and International Relations
The National Interest and Foreign Policy

As we discuss in this chapter, public opinion can play a key role in shaping foreign policy. One of the fundamental questions for publics in any country is how much to sacrifice a country's own interests for the sake of advancing international goals, such as the interests of allies. Of course, in some circumstances, a country's own interests will be synonymous with those of its allies. For example, all NATO members had a strong national and collective interest in deterring Soviet aggression in Europe.

But at other times, foreign policy choices mean trade-offs between a country's own priorities and the interests of others. Recall our discussion of collective goods: Free riding would benefit one's own well-being (the national interest) at a cost to the group (allies' interests). For example, NATO asked member states to contribute military forces to the conflict in Afghanistan, but some did not, while others withdrew their troops due to political pressures (see Chapter 2).

In 2016, a Pew public opinion poll asked citizens of several countries whether their leaders should make foreign policy by only considering the national interest or by also considering the interests of their allies. The results showed considerable variation across the populations of the countries (see Figure 4.4 for a comparison of answers across countries).

As discussed in Chapter 1, part of the recent backlash against globalization has included a return to nationalism. One interesting trend in the data is that states who have experienced some recent pressures of globalization—the financial crisis (Greece, Italy, and Spain) or increased migration from conflicts in Syria or Libya (Britain, France, Italy, and Hungary)—have a larger portion of their population wanting to consider only the national interest. Yet, there are exceptions to this. German citizens, affected by both the financial crisis and migration pressures, overwhelmingly believe the interests of allies should play a role in foreign policy.

A second observation from the data is that, with the exception of Germany, Greece, and India, the population of the countries are quite evenly split on the question—almost never more than 10 percentage points apart. This suggests divisions within these countries on how much national interests versus allies' interests should govern foreign policy. Given the British vote to leave the EU; the anti-EU sentiment in Greece; the rise of nationalist parties in France, Poland, and Hungary; and the election of Donald Trump as president of the United States, these findings should not be terribly surprising. Across the globe, publics are increasingly turning inward to focus on issues at home rather than abroad.

Figure 4.4 Defining the National Interest Across Twelve Countries

Source: Pew Research Center.

legitimacy to survive. It must persuade people to accept (if not to like) its policies because, in the end, policies are carried out by ordinary people—soldiers, workers, and bureaucrats.

Because of the need for public support, even authoritarian governments spend great effort on *propaganda*—the public promotion of their official line—to win support for foreign policies. States use television, newspapers, and other information media in this effort. In many countries, the state owns or controls major mass media such as television and newspapers, mediating the flow of information to its citizens; however, new information technologies with multiple channels make this harder to do.

Journalists serve as the gatekeepers of information passing from foreign policy elites to the public. The media and government often conflict because of the traditional role of the press as a watchdog and critic of government actions and powers. The media try to uncover and publicize what the government wants to hide. Foreign policy decision makers also rely on the media for information about foreign affairs.

Yet the media also depend on government for information; the size and resources of the foreign policy bureaucracies dwarf those of the press. These advantages give the government great power to *manipulate* journalists by feeding them information in order to shape the news and influence public opinion. Government decision makers can create dramatic stories in foreign relations—through summit meetings, crises, actions, and so forth. Bureaucrats can also *leak* secret information to the press in order to support their own point of view and win bureaucratic battles. Finally, the military and the press have a running battle about journalists' access to military operations, but both sides gained from the open access given to journalists "embedded" with U.S. forces in Iraq in 2003.

In democracies, where governments must stand for election, an unpopular war can force a leader or party from office, as happened to U.S. president Lyndon Johnson in 1968 during the Vietnam War. Or a popular war can help secure a government's mandate to continue in power, as happened to Margaret Thatcher in Britain after the 1982 Falkland Islands War. A key influence on public opinion is the content of scenes appearing on television: U.S. soldiers were sent to Somalia to assist in relief efforts in 1992 after TV news showed the heartrending results of civil war and famine there. But after TV news showed an American soldier's body being dragged through the streets by members of a Somali faction after a deadly firefight that killed 18 U.S. soldiers, public opinion shifted quickly against the Somalia operation. During the war in Bosnia, officials in the U.S. State Department said privately that the main goal of U.S. policy was often just to keep the conflict there off the front pages of U.S. newspapers (an elusive goal, as it turned out).

Occasionally a foreign policy issue is decided directly by a referendum of the entire citizenry (the United States lacks such a tradition, which is strong in Switzerland and Denmark, for example). In 2016, Great Britain held a referendum to decide whether it would leave the European Union (EU). Despite Britain's prime minister campaigning to remain in the EU, voters, by a small majority, decided to leave the EU. This surprised experts and led to some short-term economic instability as businesses attempted to figure out how to adjust to the new reality of a Britain outside the EU.

Even in the most open democracies, states do not merely *respond* to public opinion. Decision makers enjoy some autonomy to make their own choices, and they are pulled in various directions by bureaucracies and interest groups, whose views often conflict with the direction favored by public opinion at large. Furthermore, public opinion is seldom unified on any policy, and sophisticated polling can show that particular segments of the population (regions of the country, genders, income groups, races, etc.) often differ in their perceptions of foreign policy issues. So a politician may respond to the opinion of one constituency rather than that of the whole population. Public opinion varies considerably over time on many foreign policy issues. States use propaganda (in dictatorships) or try to manipulate the media (in democracies) to keep public opinion from diverging too much from state policies.

In democracies, public opinion generally has less effect on foreign policy than on domestic policy. National leaders traditionally have additional latitude to make decisions in the international realm. This derives from the special need of states to act in a unified way to function effectively in the international system, as well as from the traditions of secrecy and diplomacy that remove IR from the realm of ordinary domestic politics. However, in the case of Japan, public opinion is a major political force restraining the military spending of the government, its commitment of military forces beyond Japan's borders, and especially the development of nuclear weapons (which is within Japan's technical abilities). The ruling party—under pressure from the United States to share the burden of defense and to shoulder its responsibilities as a great power—has slowly but steadily pushed to increase Japan's military spending and allow Japanese military forces to expand their role modestly (in the 1980s, to patrol Asian sea lanes vital to Japanese trade; in the 1990s, to participate in UN peacekeeping operations). Repeatedly, strong public opinion against the military has slowed or rebuffed these efforts. In Japan, people remember the horrible consequences of militarism in the 1930s and World War II,

can affect foreign policy

Policy Perspectives
Prime Minister of Japan, Shinzo Abe

PROBLEM *How do you decide what foreign policy tools best balance domestic and international concerns?*

Takehiko Kobayashi/AP Images

BACKGROUND Imagine that you are the prime minister of Japan. Since the end of the Korean War in 1953, relations with your neighbor to the west, North Korea, have been tense. Military tensions have persisted as North Korea has made and then broken several agreements regarding its nuclear program. North Korea has tested nuclear weapons six times since 2006, most recently in 2017. It has also test-fired short-range ballistic missiles directly over Japan in an effort to intimidate your country. In 2017, it tested a new long-range rocket in defiance of international warnings. You won election in 2012 on a hawkish platform, calling for large increases in defense spending and the deployment of antimissile weapons to protect your country from a North Korean launch.

Talks to remove the threat of North Korean nuclear weapons and missiles have not progressed. Escalating tensions fueled by a war of words between North Korean leader Kim Jong-Un and U.S. president Donald Trump caused you to purchase antimissile defense systems from the United States to deploy against the North Korean threat. Peace talks between Kim Jong-Un and Donald Trump in 2018 eased tensions temporarily.

In 1967, Japan adopted the Three Non-Nuclear Principles, promising not to develop, possess, or hold nuclear weapons. The result of this policy has been that, although your country has the technology to build its own nuclear weapons, you have refrained from doing so. Moreover, Japan has refused to station American nuclear weapons on its territory as a result of the Three Principles. Yet, with the rising threat of North Korea, some military leaders in Japan have called for abandoning the Three Principles in favor of nuclear weapons development.

DOMESTIC CONSIDERATIONS Public opinion in Japan is very sensitive to relations with North Korea. Not only are many Japanese worried about the North Korean nuclear threat, but in 2002, North Korea admitted to having secretly abducted Japanese citizens in the 1970s and 1980s, transporting them to North Korea, and using them to train North Korean spies. Your country has demanded that North Korea return the bodies of those abducted. And while these abductions are a sensitive issue in Japanese public opinion, so are nuclear weapons. The majority of Japanese citizens do not support developing or holding nuclear weapons at this time.

SCENARIO Now imagine that North Korea continues to develop its nuclear program, building more high-powered weapons. It also continues to develop missiles, including firing test missiles over your island. The United States has asked whether you would consider stationing its nuclear weapons on your territory to deter North Korea from its aggressive policies in the region. Japan would not own these weapons and the decision to fire them would be up the United States, although American military officials have promised to consult you on their usage.

CHOOSE YOUR POLICY How do you respond to U.S. pressure to place its nuclear weapons on your territory? Do you risk a backlash from your citizens, who mostly support a nonnuclear Japan? Do you resist pressure from the United States, your most important ally, and refuse the weapons? Do you fear that North Korea could become more aggressive if you were to hold the weapons? Or will the weapons enhance deterrence against the potentially aggressive regime? How do you balance domestic public opinion with a pressure from allies and an international security threat?

culminating in the nuclear bombings of 1945. They are thus suspicious of any increase in the size or role of military forces and are set against Japan's having nuclear weapons. In this case, public opinion constrains the state's conduct of foreign policy and has slowed the pace of change.

The *attentive public* in a democracy is the minority of the population that stays informed about international issues. This segment varies somewhat from one issue to another, but there is also a core of people who care in general about foreign affairs and follow many issues closely. The most active members of the attentive public on foreign affairs constitute a foreign policy *elite*—people with power and influence who affect foreign policy. This elite includes people within governments as well as outsiders such as businesspeople, journalists, lobbyists, and professors of political science. Public opinion polls show that elite opinions sometimes (but not always) differ considerably from those of the general population and sometimes from those of the government as well.

Governments sometimes adopt foreign policies for the specific purpose of generating public approval and hence gaining domestic legitimacy. This is the case when a government undertakes a war or foreign military intervention at a time of domestic difficulty, to distract attention and gain public support—taking advantage of the **"rally 'round the flag" syndrome** (the public's increased support for government leaders during wartime, at least in the short term). Citizens who would readily criticize their government's policies on education or health care often refrain from criticism when the government is at war and the lives of the nation's soldiers are on the line. Policies of this sort are often labeled **diversionary foreign policy**. Unfortunately, it is always difficult to tell whether a state adopts a foreign policy to distract the public because leaders would never admit to trying to divert public attention.

However, wars that go on too long or are not successful can turn public opinion against the government and even lead to a popular uprising to overthrow the government. In Argentina, the military government in 1982 led the country into war with Britain over the Falkland Islands. At first Argentineans rallied around the flag, but after losing the war they rallied around the cause of getting rid of the military government, and they replaced it with a new civilian government that prosecuted the former leaders. In 2006, President Bush's popularity, which had soared early in the Iraq War, deflated as the war dragged on (see Figure 4.5), and voters threw his party out of power in Congress. By the 2008 elections, his party had lost control of the Senate, House, and presidency—all of which the Republicans had held at the beginning of the Iraq War in 2003.

"rally 'round the flag" syndrome The public's increased support for government leaders during wartime, at least in the short term.

diversionary foreign policy Foreign policies adopted to distract the public from domestic political problems.

Figure 4.5 The "Rally 'Round the Flag" Syndrome

President Bush's approval rating demonstrates the "rally 'round the flag" syndrome, in which war triggers a short-term boost in public approval.

Source: Gallup Poll.

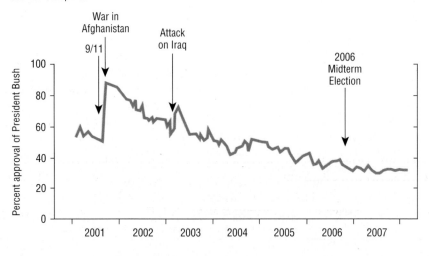

4.2.5 Legislatures

One conduit through which interest groups and public opinion may wield influence is legislatures. Some democracies, such as the United States, have presidential systems, in which legislative bodies are elected apart from the president (also referred to as an *executive*). In these systems, legislatures play a direct role in making foreign policy by passing budgets, regulating bureaucratic rules, creating trade law, and even controlling immigration policy. Although executives may attend summits and talks, any agreement they sign must be approved by their domestic legislature.

Although few would argue that legislatures in presidential democracies do not influence foreign policy generally, different rules may apply to the use of military force. Some contend that legislatures, like public opinion, rally around the flag during times of international crises. For example, three days after the September 11, 2001, attacks, the U.S. Congress voted to give President Bush full authority to prosecute a war in Afghanistan. In October 2002, Congress passed a resolution authorizing the use of force in Iraq. Thus, legislatures rarely if ever challenge an executive on important military matters. An important exception to this occurred in 2015 when the Republican legislators in the U.S. Congress demanded that the Obama administration allow Congress to review the nuclear weapons deal signed with Iran. Congress tried to stop the nuclear deal, but Obama used his veto power to preserve it.

Others point to a different dynamic in which legislatures do stand up to executive power regarding military force. For example, because legislatures hold the "purse strings" (the ability to approve or reject new spending), they have the ability to stop a war in its tracks. In the United States, the War Powers Act, enacted during the close of the Vietnam War, requires the president to notify Congress when U.S. troops are deployed for combat. After this notification, the president has 60 days (plus a possible 30-day extension) to recall the troops unless Congress explicitly approves the military action.

During the 2011 Libya air campaign, the Obama administration claimed that the War Powers Act did not apply because the action was not a war. However, during the American military campaign against ISIS forces in Iraq in 2014–2015, the Obama administration sought congressional approval for the use of force. The Bush, Obama, and Trump administrations have also claimed a 2001 act passed by Congress three days after the September 11 attacks, the Authorization for Use of Military Force (AUMF), gives the president the right to use military force against any threat linked to terrorism. Finally, some historical evidence from the United States suggests that presidents are more likely to use military force when their own political party is in power in Congress, suggesting that politics does not stop at the water's edge.

In parliamentary systems, such as Great Britain, executives (for example, prime ministers) are chosen by the political parties that hold a dominant position in the legislative bodies. Often parliamentary executives do not need to submit treaties or policies for formal approval by the legislature. Yet legislatures in parliamentary systems still hold power regarding foreign policy. In Great Britain, for example, Parliament is not required to vote on international agreements negotiated by the prime minister, but it must approve any change to British laws that such agreements entail. Because most international agreements do involve these types of changes, Parliament effectively exercises a right of ratification over international agreements.

In many parliamentary systems, if a policy is controversial, parties that do not have a majority in the legislature can attempt to call elections—meaning that the country votes again on which parties will hold seats in the legislature. If different parties win a majority of seats, a new executive is appointed. Thus, in parliamentary systems, legislatures play a key role in designing and implementing foreign policy.

4.2.6 Making Foreign Policy

Foreign policies are the strategies that governments use to guide their actions in the international arena. Foreign policies spell out the objectives state leaders have decided to pursue in a given relationship or situation. But in general, IR scholars are less interested in specific policies than in the **foreign policy process**—how policies are arrived at and implemented.

foreign policy process The process by which foreign policies are arrived at and implemented.

States establish various organizational structures and functional relationships to create and carry out foreign policies. IR scholars are especially interested in exploring whether certain kinds of policy processes lead to certain kinds of decisions—whether certain processes produce better outcomes (for the state's self-defined interests) than do others.

Comparative foreign policy is the study of foreign policy in various states in order to discover whether similar types of societies or governments consistently have similar types of foreign policies (comparing across states or across different time periods for a single state). Such studies have focused on three characteristics: size, wealth, and extent of democratic participation in government. Unfortunately, no simple rule has been found to predict a state's warlike tendencies based on these attributes. States vary greatly from one to the next and even within a single state over time. For example, both capitalist and communist states have proven capable of naked aggression or peaceful behavior, depending on circumstances.

Some political scientists have tried to interpret particular states' foreign policies in terms of each one's *political culture and history*. For example, the Soviet Union (Russia) experienced repeated, devastating land invasions over the centuries (culminating in World War II), while the United States experienced two centuries of safety behind great oceans. Thus the military might of the Soviet Union, and its control of buffer states in Eastern Europe, seemed defensive in nature to Soviet leaders but appeared aggressive to U.S. leaders.

Foreign policy outcomes result from multiple forces at various levels of analysis. The outcomes depend on individual decision makers, on the type of society and government they are working within, and on the international and global context of their actions. The study of foreign policy processes runs counter to realism's assumption of a unitary state actor. Because the study of foreign policy concentrates on forces within the state, its main emphasis is on the individual and domestic levels of analysis.

The differences in the foreign policy process from one state to another are also influenced by a state's type of government, such as military dictatorship, communist party rule, one-party (noncommunist) rule, and various forms of multiparty democracy. Relatively democratic states tend to share values and interests and hence tend to get along better with each other than with nondemocracies (see The Democratic Peace in Chapter 3). In practice, most states lie along a spectrum with some mix of democratic and authoritarian elements.

The attempt to explain foreign policy in a general and *theoretical* way has met only limited success. This is one reason why

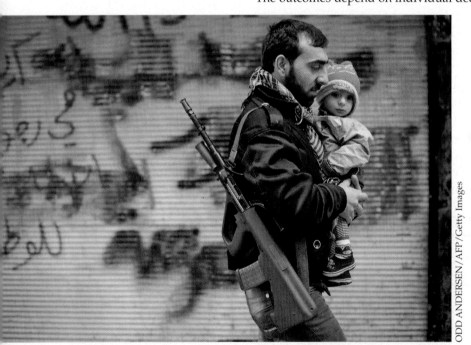

ODD ANDERSEN/AFP/Getty Images

INDIVIDUAL CHOICE Foreign policy outcomes result from processes at several levels of analysis, including the roles of individuals. All these levels were in play in 2011–2013 as Syria went from protest to civil war. In 2012, this father chose, like many other individuals, to take up arms and join rebel fighters. The country's future will be decided in no small part by the aggregation of many such individual decisions.

realists continue to find simple unitary-actor models of the state useful, the domestic and individual elements of the foreign policy process add much complexity and unpredictability. One area of foreign policy in which knowledge stands on a somewhat firmer basis is the *descriptive* effort to understand how particular mechanisms of foreign policy formation operate in various states. Such approaches belong to the field of comparative politics.

To summarize, foreign policy is a complex outcome of a complex process. It results from the struggle of competing themes, competing domestic interests, and competing government agencies. No single individual, agency, or guiding principle determines the outcome. Yet foreign policy does achieve a certain overall coherence. States form foreign policy on an issue or toward a region; it is not just an incoherent collection of decisions and actions taken from time to time. Out of the turbulent internal processes of foreign policy formation come relatively coherent interests and policies that states pursue.

Careers in International Relations: Government and Diplomacy

Summary

Jobs in government and diplomacy offer team players the chance to affect policy, but these jobs require patience with large bureaucracies.

BENEFITS AND COSTS Both governments and intergovernmental organizations (IGOs) play key roles in international relations (IR) and employ millions of people with interests and training in IR.

Despite differences between careers in governments and in IGOs, there are numerous similarities. Both are hierarchical organizations, with competitive and highly regulated working environments. Whether in the U.S. State Department or the UN, entrance into and promotion in these organizations are regulated by exams, performance evaluations, and tenure with the organization.

Another similarity lies in the challenges of being pulled in many directions concerning policies. Governments face competing pressures of public opinion, constituencies, and interest groups—each with distinct policy opinions. IGOs also deal with interest groups such as nongovernmental organizations (NGOs), but an IGO's constituents are states, which in many cases disagree among themselves.

Many employees of governments or IGOs thrive on making decisions that influence policies. Both work environments also attract coworkers with deep interests in international affairs, and the resulting networks of contacts can bring professional and intellectual rewards. Finally, jobs in governments or IGOs may involve travel or living abroad, which many enjoy.

However, promotion can be slow and frustrating. Usually, only individuals with advanced degrees or technical specializations achieve non–entry level positions. It can take years to climb within the organization and the process may involve working in departments far from an individual's original interests. In addition, both governments and IGOs are bureaucracies with formal rules and procedures, requiring great patience. Employees often express frustration that initiative and "thinking outside the box" are not rewarded.

SKILLS TO HONE The key to working in governments or IGOs is to get your foot in the door. Be flexible and willing to take entry level positions that are not exactly in your area of interest. For example, the State Department is only one of many parts of the U.S.

government that deal with IR. Do not assume that you must be a diplomat to work in foreign affairs.

Foreign language training is also important, especially for work in large IGOs with many field offices. The ability to work well in groups and to network within and across organizations is a vital asset. People who can strengthen lines of communication can gain support from many places in an organization.

Finally, strong analytical and writing abilities are extremely helpful. Both governments and IGOs deal with massive amounts of information daily. The ability to analyze information (even including mathematical or computational analysis) and to write clear, concise interpretations will make one invaluable.

Resources

Dorman, Shawn. *Inside a U.S. Embassy: Diplomacy at Work*. 3rd ed. Potomac, 2011.

Fasulo, Linda. *An Insider's Guide to the UN*. 3rd ed. Yale, 2015.

http://jobs.un.org

http://careers.state.gov

http://www.usajobs.gov

Chapter Review

Summary

- Foreign policies are strategies that governments use to guide their actions toward other states. The foreign policy process is the set of procedures and structures that states use to arrive at foreign policy decisions and to implement them.

- In the rational model of decision making, officials choose the action whose consequences best help meet the state's established goals. By contrast, in the organizational process model, decisions result from routine administrative procedures; in the government bargaining (or bureaucratic politics) model, decisions result from negotiations among governmental agencies with different interests in the outcome.

- The actions of individual decision makers are influenced by their personalities, values, and beliefs as well as by common psychological factors that diverge from rationality. These factors include misperception, selective perception, emotional biases, and cognitive biases (including the effort to reduce cognitive dissonance).

- Foreign policy decisions are also influenced by the psychology of groups (including groupthink), the procedures used to reach decisions, and the roles of participants. During crises, the potentials for misperception and error are amplified.

- Struggles over the direction of foreign policy are common between professional bureaucrats and politicians, as well as between different government agencies.

- Domestic constituencies (interest groups) have distinct interests in foreign policies and often organize politically to promote those interests.

- Prominent among domestic constituencies—especially in the United States and Russia, and especially during the Cold War—have been military-industrial complexes consisting of military industries and others with an interest in high military spending.

- Public opinion influences governments' foreign policy decisions (more so in democracies than in authoritarian states), but governments also manipulate public opinion.

- Legislatures can provide a conduit for public opinion and interest groups to influence foreign policy. Executives and legislators may differ on how best to achieve a state's national interest.

Key Terms

rational model 113
organizational process model 114
government bargaining model 114
misperceptions and selective
   perceptions 115
information screens 115

optimizing 117
satisficing 117
prospect theory 117
groupthink 117
interest groups 122
military-industrial complex 124

public opinion 124
"rally 'round the flag" syndrome 128
diversionary foreign policy 128
foreign policy process 130

Critical Thinking Questions

1. Uncertainty about costs and benefits of an action can complicate foreign policy decision making. What are the sources of uncertainty in IR? Can decision makers take steps to reduce that uncertainty?

2. Consider an event in IR that you are familiar with. Think about the actors involved in making a decision concerning that event. How would the rational-actor model explain that event? Might it be better explained by considering standard operating procedures or bureaucratic politics?

3. Sometimes aggressive international actions are attributed to a "madman" such as Iraq's Saddam Hussein or Nazi Germany's Adolf Hitler. Do you agree that such leaders (each of whose actions severely damaged

his state's well-being) must be "mad"? What other factors could account for their actions? How do you think such people achieve and maintain national leadership?

4. India and Pakistan are neighbors and enemies. Given the problems of misperception and bias in foreign policy decision making, what steps could you propose that each government adopt to keep these problems from interfering in the rational pursuit of national interests?

5. Traditionally, foreign policy elites have faced only sporadic pressure from mass public opinion. Is the role of television and the Internet changing this relationship? If you were a top foreign policy maker, what steps could you take to keep TV news and online blogs from shaping the foreign policy agenda before you could define your own goals and directions?

Suggested Readings

Allison, Graham T., and Philip Zelikow. *Essence of Decision: Explaining the Cuban Missile Crisis.* 2nd ed. Longman, 1999.

Beasley, Ryan K., et al., eds. *Foreign Policy in Comparative Perspective: Domestic and International Influences on State Behavior.* CQ Press, 2002.

Holsti, Ole R. *Public Opinion and American Foreign Policy.* Rev. ed. Michigan, 2004.

Milner, Helen V., and Dustin Tingley. *Sailing the Water's Edge: The Domestic Politics of American Foreign Policy.* Princeton, 2015.

Neustadt, Richard E., and Ernest R. May. *Thinking in Time: The Uses of History for Decision Makers.* Free Press, 1986.

Page, Benjamin I., and Marshall M. Bouton. *The Foreign Policy Disconnect.* Chicago, 2006.

Smith, Tony. *Foreign Attachments: The Power of Ethnic Groups in the Making of American Foreign Policy.* Harvard, 2000.

Let's Debate the Issue
Should Legislatures Play a Role in Deciding Whether to Use Military Force?

Overview

In nearly all democracies, there are debates about the best way to conduct foreign policy. One particularly controversial issue involves using military force—for example, initiating a war. Executives (presidents or prime ministers) usually claim the right to initiate the use of force as commanders of their militaries. Yet legislatures (Congress or parliaments) may object that they should have a say in whether a country goes to war.

In the United States, the president is the commander in chief of the military and thus has the power to order the deployment of American military forces. Yet Congress has the exclusive power to declare war. This has led to extensive debates in the United States about who has the ultimate authority to undertake military action. While the president has extensive advantages in terms of military intelligence and analysis (because the foreign policy bureaucracy reports to the president, not Congress), Congress must authorize funds to pay for military action. And although American presidents often seek congressional approval before taking military action, there have been important exceptions (for example, the U.S. invasion of Panama in 1989).

What is the proper relationship between a legislature and the executive regarding the use of military force? Should initiating military force be invested only in the executive, or should legislatures also have a say in when and where a country's military is put in harm's way?

ARGUMENT 1

Legislatures Should Not Play a Role in Deciding Whether to Use Military Force

Legislatures are slow to act in times of crisis.
Because legislatures are made up of hundreds of members, it is difficult to get agreement among all members on what constitutes a threat to national security. Discussions over whether to use military force can thus be long, drawn-out affairs, which can limit the ability of a country to respond to dangers. Executives also have faster access to information at their disposal.

Internal debates can show division to enemies.
Debates over the appropriateness of military force show open divisions within a country that can encourage adversaries to remain stubborn in bargaining. If an adversary feels a country is too divided to use military force against it, it will not treat threats to use force as credible.

Most legislators know little about foreign affairs.
Most legislators are elected to serve the interests of local constituencies rather than invest their time and energy in foreign affairs. Legislators have little incentive to become highly knowledgeable about foreign affairs, thus making their decisions about whether to engage in military force less informed.

ARGUMENT 2

Legislatures Should Play a Role in Deciding Whether to Use Military Force

More input regarding military force leads to more careful policy. Having an effective legislative debate over the potential use of military force can lead to better policy, avoiding some of the psychological pitfalls associated with small-group decision making such as groupthink.

Legislators are more directly accountable to constituents. Because a state's citizens will bear the brunt of the costs of war, it is appropriate that their representative bodies have a say in whether the country's men and women should be sent to fight. Open debates in a legislature better allow the public's voice to be heard.

Executives need checks and balances, especially with regard to decisions about war. Because of the weight of a decision to initiate military conflict, it is important to have a checks and balances system to stop hasty wars. In the United States, the Constitution specifically grants Congress the power to declare war for this reason.

Questions

- Should legislatures play a role in the decision to use military force? Are there some circumstances in which it is better or worse for a society to have open debates about potential military action?

- Short of military action, should legislatures play a significant role in other foreign policy areas such as economic sanctions, immigration, or military alliances? How are these foreign policy issues similar to or different from questions of using military force?

- Do you think potential adversaries pay attention to debates within a country contemplating military force? Do potential adversaries use this information to their advantage? Should this be a concern for a country contemplating the use of military force?

For Further Reading

Feaver, Peter D., and Christopher Gelpi. *Choosing Your Battles: American Civil-Military Relations and the Use of Force.* Princeton, 2003.

Fisher, Louis. *Presidential War Power.* 3rd ed. Rev. Kansas, 2013.

Howell, William G., and Jon C. Pevehouse. *While Dangers Gather: Congressional Checks on Presidential War Powers.* Princeton, 2007.

Thurber, James A., and Jordan Tama. *A Creative Tension: The Foreign Policy Roles of the President and Congress.* Rowman & Littlefield, 2017.

Chapter 5
International Conflict

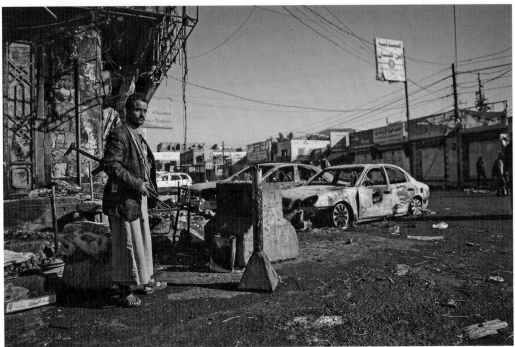

HUTHI REBEL IN YEMEN, 2017.

Hani Al-Ansi/picture-alliance/dpa/AP Images

⌄ Learning Objectives

5.1 Distinguish between two different theories of causes of war at two different levels of analysis.

5.2 Identify at least four different international conflicts where religion plays a role in creating or exacerbating the conflict.

5.3 Summarize two different international territorial disputes and evaluate the prospects for their peaceful settlement.

5.1 The Wars of the World

Distinguish between two different theories of causes of war at two different levels of analysis.

Chapter 3 (in the The Waning of War section) discussed the decreasing number and size of wars in the world. This chapter will focus on the remaining wars and historical cases to explain the causes of international conflicts.

Figure 5.1 shows the 14 wars in progress in May 2018. The largest are in Syria, Afghanistan, and Iraq. Of the 14 wars, 13 wars are in the global South. All but Ukraine and the Philippines are in a zone of active fighting (outlined on the map) spanning parts of Africa, the Middle East, and South Asia.

In four smaller zones (dotted lines on the map), dozens of wars of recent decades have ended. Some of the countries in these zones still face difficult postwar years with the possibility of sliding back into violence. In Sierra Leone, for example, a ten-year civil war ended in 2002, but occasional political instability has threatened to reignite that conflict. Colombia's largest rebel group began to disarm in 2016, but some fear elections there could bring to power a government that opposes the recent peace agreement. And while conflict in the Philippines has escalated in the past four years, most of Southeast Asia remains at peace. Indeed, most peace agreements in the world's postwar zones are holding up (for example, see the Seeking the Collective Good box).

5.1.1 Types of War

Many different activities are covered by the general term *war*. Consequently, it is not easy to say how many wars are going on in the world at the moment. But most lists of wars set some minimum criteria—for instance, a minimum of a thousand battle deaths—to distinguish war from lower-level violence such as violent strikes or riots.

Wars are very diverse. Wars arise from different situations and play different roles in bargaining over conflicts. Starting from the largest wars, we may distinguish the following main categories.

Hegemonic war is a war over control of the entire *world order*—the rules of the international system as a whole, including the role of world hegemony (see Hegemony in Chapter 2). This class of wars (with variations in definition and conception) is also known as *world war*, *global war*, *general war*, or *systemic war*. The last hegemonic war was World War II. Largely because of the power of modern weaponry, this kind of war probably cannot occur any longer without destroying civilization.

Total war is warfare by one state waged to conquer and occupy another. The goal is to reach the capital city and force the surrender of the government, which can then be replaced with one of the victor's choosing. Total war began with the massively destructive Napoleonic Wars, which introduced large-scale conscription and geared the entire French national economy toward the war effort. The practice of total war evolved with industrialization, which further integrated all of society and economy into the practice of war. The last total war between great powers was World War II.

In total war, with the entire society mobilized for the struggle, the entire society of the enemy is considered a legitimate target. For instance, in World War II, Germany attacked British civilians with V-2 rockets, while British and U.S. strategic bombing killed 600,000 German civilians and hundreds of thousands of Japanese.

Limited war includes military actions carried out to gain some objective short of the surrender and occupation of the enemy. For instance, the U.S.-led war against Iraq in 1991 retook the territory of Kuwait but did not go on to Baghdad to topple Saddam Hussein's government. Many border wars have this character. After occupying the land it wants, a state may stop short and defend its gains, as Russia did after expelling Georgian troops from disputed Georgian provinces in 2008, for example.

hegemonic war War for control of the entire world order—the rules of the international system as a whole. Also called *world war*, *global war*, *general war*, or *systemic war*.

total war Warfare by one state waged to conquer and occupy another; modern total war originated in the Napoleonic Wars, which relied on conscription on a mass scale.

limited war Military actions that seek objectives short of the surrender and occupation of the enemy.

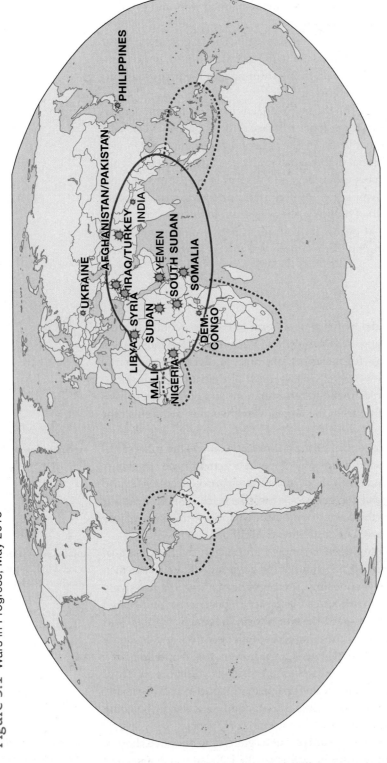

Figure 5.1 Wars in Progress, May 2018

❀ Estimated deaths over 1,000 per year
❀ Estimated deaths under 1,000 per year
— Zone of active wars
⋯ Zones of transition from wars in recent decades

PHILIPPINES
AFGHANISTAN/PAKISTAN
UKRAINE
INDIA
IRAQ/TURKEY
SYRIA
YEMEN
SOUTH SUDAN
SOMALIA
LIBYA
SUDAN
DEM. CONGO
MALI
NIGERIA

Raids are limited wars that consist of a single action—a bombing run or a quick incursion by land. In 2007, Israeli warplanes bombed a facility in Syria that Israel believed to be a nuclear research facility in order to stop Syria from making progress on nuclear weapons. Raids fall into the gray area between wars and nonwars because the destruction they cause is limited and they are over quickly. Raiding that is repeated or fuels a cycle of retaliation usually becomes a limited war or what is sometimes called *low-intensity conflict*.

Civil war refers to war between factions within a state trying to create, or prevent, a new government for the entire state or some territorial part of it. (The aim may be to change the entire system of government, merely to replace the people in it, or to split a region off as a new state.) The U.S. Civil War of the 1860s is a good example of a secessionist civil war, as is the war of Eritrea province in Ethiopia (now the internationally recognized state of Eritrea) in the 1980s. The war in El Salvador in the 1980s is an example of a civil war for control of the entire state (not secessionist). Civil wars often seem to be among the most brutal wars. People fighting their fellow citizens act no less cruelly than those fighting people from another state. The 50,000 or more deaths in the civil war in El Salvador, including many from massacres and death squads, were not based on ethnic differences. Of course, many of today's civil wars emerge from ethnic or clan conflicts as well. In Chad, for example, a rebel group composed of rival clans to the president's nearly overthrew the government in 2007. Sustaining a civil war usually requires a source of support for rebels from neighboring states, diaspora ethnic communities, or revenue from natural resources or illegal drugs.

Guerrilla war, which includes certain kinds of civil wars, is warfare without front lines. Irregular forces operate in the midst of, and often hidden or protected by, civilian populations. The purpose is not to confront an enemy army directly but rather to harass and punish it and thus gradually limit its operation and effectively liberate territory from its control. Rebels in most civil wars use such methods. U.S. military forces in South Vietnam fought against Vietcong guerrillas in the 1960s and 1970s, with rising frustration. Efforts to combat a guerrilla army—counterinsurgency—are discussed in Chapter 6. In guerrilla war, without a fixed front line, there is much territory that neither side controls; both sides thus exert military leverage over the same places at the same time. Often the government controls a town by day and the guerrillas do so by night. Thus, guerrilla wars are extremely painful for civilians, who suffer most when no military force firmly controls a location, opening the door to banditry, personal vendettas, sexual violence, and other such lawless behavior. The situation is doubly painful because conventional armies fighting against guerrillas often cannot distinguish them from civilians and punish both together. In one famous case in South Vietnam, a U.S. officer who had ordered an entire village burned to deny its use as a sanctuary by the Vietcong commented, "We had to destroy the village to save it."[1] Warfare increasingly is irregular and guerrilla-style; it is less and less often an open, conventional clash of large state armies, although the latter still occurs occasionally.

In all types of war, the abstractions and theories of international relations (IR) scholars hardly capture the horrors experienced by those on the scene, both soldiers and civilians. War suspends basic norms of behavior and, especially over time, traumatizes participants and bystanders. Soldiers see their best friends blown apart before their eyes, and they must kill and maim their fellow human beings; some experience lifelong psychological traumatic stress as a result. Civilians experience terror, violence, and rape; they lose loved ones and homes; they too often live with trauma afterward. The violence of war does not resemble that of war movies but instead creates a nearly psychotic experience of overwhelming confusion, noise, terror, and adrenaline. Soldiers in professional armies train to keep functioning in these conditions—but still have an incredibly difficult job—whereas those in irregular forces and civilian populations caught in civil wars

civil war A war between factions within a state trying to create, or prevent, a new government for the entire state or some territorial part of it.

guerrilla war Warfare without front lines and with irregular forces operating in the midst of, and often hidden or protected by, civilian populations.

---

[1] "Major Describes Move." *New York Times*, February 08, 1968.

Kaveh Kazemi/Getty Images.

GIVING UP THE GUNS Once armed groups stop shooting, a long process of postwar transition ensues. Disarming and demobilizing militias is not only the most critical aspect of this transition, but also the most difficult because it leaves disarmed groups vulnerable. Here, a member of the main rebel group in Colombia turns in her weapon to a demobilization camp, 2016.

have little hope of coping. The horrors of all wars are magnified in cases of genocide and massacre, of child soldiers, and of brutal warfare that continues over years.

Scholars and policy makers have been paying more attention in recent years to the difficult transitions from war to peace around the world—postwar reconciliation, conflict resolution, transitional governments representing opposing factions, economic reconstruction, and so forth. These efforts often address collective goods problems among the parties, as when Somali clan elders in 2007 agreed that all would be better off by giving up their guns to the new central government but none wanted to go first. After the shooting stops, international peacekeepers and nongovernmental organizations (NGOs) focus on Security Sector Reform (SSR) to create professional military and police forces instead of warlord militias. The process of Disarmament, Demobilization, and Reintegration (DDR) deals with the common problem of what to do with irregular forces after civil wars end.

truth commissions Governmental bodies established in several countries after internal wars to hear honest testimony and bring to light what really happened during these wars, and in exchange to offer most of the participants asylum from punishment.

In several countries where long internal wars in the 1990s had led to dehumanization and atrocities—notably in South Africa—new governments used **truth commissions** to help the society heal and move forward. The commission's role was to hear honest testimony from the period, to bring to light what really happened during these wars, and in exchange to offer most of the participants asylum from punishment. Sometimes international NGOs helped facilitate the process. However, human rights groups objected to a settlement in Sierra Leone in 1999 that brought into the government a faction that had routinely cut off civilians' fingers as a terror tactic. (Hostilities did end, however, in 2001.) In 2006, Colombian right-wing militia leaders called from jail for the creation of a truth commission before which they could confess their role in a long civil war, but also forced the government to admit to harming civilians during the war. As a part of the Colombian peace settlement of 2017, a truth commission began operation in December of that year. Thus, after brutal ethnic conflicts give way to complex political settlements, most governments try to balance the need for justice and truth with the need to keep all groups on board.

Experts have debated how much truth and reconciliation are necessary after long conflicts. Some now argue that in certain circumstances, tribunals and government-sponsored panels to investigate past crimes could lead to political instability in transitional states. Other experts disagree, noting that the work of such panels can be essential to building trust, which is important for democracy.

5.1.2 Theories of the Causes of War

The Roman writer Seneca said nearly 2,000 years ago: "Of war men ask the outcome, not the cause."[2] This is not true of political scientists. They want to know why countries fight.

conflict A difference in preferred outcomes in a bargaining situation.

The term **conflict** in IR generally refers to armed conflict. Conflict itself is ever present in the international system—the condition against which bargaining takes place. In conflict bargaining, states develop capabilities that give them leverage to obtain more favorable outcomes than they otherwise would achieve. Whether fair or unfair, the ultimate outcome of the bargaining process is a settlement of the particular conflict. Rarely do conflicts lead to violence, however.

[2] Seneca, Hercules Furens. *In Seneca's Tragedies*. Vol. 1. Translated by Frank Justus Miller. Heinemann, 1917.

Seeking the Collective Good
Peace in Latin America

COLLECTIVE GOOD: Peaceful Relations Among Latin American States

BACKGROUND: Of all the world regions, Latin America is one of the most peaceful. Some scholars have gone so far as to describe Latin America as a security community given the very low incidence of interstate war in the region for the past 100 years. This is despite civil wars and numerous border disagreements between states in the region. The stable peace is a collective good enjoyed by all countries in the region, even though countries that violate it might gain territory or wealth by using military force.

CHALLENGE: Despite years of relatively peaceful interstate relations in the region, persistent conflicts still exist between some states. In 1995, Peru and Ecuador fought a border skirmish. Since 2000, other disputes have escalated. Bolivia wants to reclaim a corridor to the sea that it lost to Chile more than 100 years ago. Colombia and Venezuela trade accusations over Venezuela's support of rebels fighting in Colombia. Rival countries have linguistic differences, ideological differences, territorial disputes, economic competition, and a range of other conflicts. With the countries having sizable armies and navies at the ready, the potential for war is always present.

SOLUTION: How has Latin America avoided more large-scale interstate war? The solution can be found in both the reciprocity and identity principles. All states are members of the Organization of American States (OAS), which promotes reciprocity and negotiation when political disputes arise. Even when some fighting occurs, conflicts do not escalate and become long,

South American leaders discuss trade, not war, in Argentina, 2017.

large-scale military conflicts. This negotiation process has succeeded in settling many of the existing disputes, even the Peru-Ecuador dispute, three years after their border war.

The identity principle is also at work. Latin America has developed a shared norm of conflict resolution. A dispute between any two states is perceived as a threat to all states in the region. Each state thinks broadly about its own interests to include the continuation of peace in the region. In this way, threats to peace are actively dealt with by the community as a whole.

The question of when conflict becomes violent can be approached in different ways. Descriptive approaches, favored by historians, tend to focus narrowly on specific direct causes of the outbreak of war, which vary from one war to another. For example, one could say that the assassination of Archduke Franz Ferdinand in 1914 "caused" World War I. More theoretical approaches, favored by many political scientists, tend to focus on the search for general explanations, applicable to a variety of contexts, about why wars break out. For example, one can see World War I as caused by shifts in the balance of power among European states, with the assassination having been only a catalyst.

One way to organize the many theories offered by political scientists to explain why wars begin is to use the levels of analysis concept from Chapter 1. Using this framework reminds us that most important events in IR have multiple causes at different levels of analysis.

THE INDIVIDUAL LEVEL On the *individual* level of analysis, theories about war center on rationality. One theory, consistent with realism, holds that the use of war and other violent means of leverage in international conflicts is normal and reflects *rational* decisions of national leaders. "Wars begin with conscious and reasoned decisions based on the calculation, made by *both* parties, that they can achieve more by going to war than by remaining at peace."[3]

---

[3] Howard, Michael. *The Causes of Wars, and Other Essays*. Harvard, 1983, p. 22. Emphasis in original. For a related argument, see Fearon, James. Rationalist Explanations for War. *International Organization* 49 (3), 1995: 379–414.

An opposite theory holds that conflicts often escalate to war because of *deviations* from rationality in the individual decision-making processes of national leaders. These potentials, discussed in Chapter 4, are information screens, cognitive biases, group-think, and so forth. A related theory holds that the education and mentality of whole populations of individuals determine whether conflicts become violent. In this view, public nationalism or ethnic hatred—or even an innate tendency toward violence in human nature—may pressure leaders to solve conflicts violently.

Unfortunately, none of these theories holds up very well. Some wars clearly reflect rational calculations of national leaders, whereas others clearly were mistakes and cannot be considered rational. Certainly some individual leaders seem prone to turn to military force to try to settle conflicts on favorable terms. But a maker of war can become a maker of peace, as did Egypt's Anwar Sadat, for example. Individuals of many cultural backgrounds and religions lead their states into war, as do both male and female leaders. Research in international relations often finds that a combination of individual-level and contextual factors is needed to explain when leaders choose war or peace in a particular situation.

THE DOMESTIC LEVEL The *domestic* level of analysis draws attention to the characteristics of states or societies that may make them more or less prone to use violence in resolving conflicts. During the Cold War, Marxists frequently said that the aggressive and greedy *capitalist* states were prone to using violence in international conflicts, whereas Western leaders claimed that the expansionist, ideological, and totalitarian nature of *communist* states made them especially prone to using violence. In truth, both types of society fought wars regularly.

Likewise, rich industrialized states and poor agrarian ones both use war at times. In fact, anthropologists have found that a wide range of *preagricultural* hunter-gatherer societies were much more prone to warfare than are today's societies. Thus, the potential for warfare seems to be universal across cultures, types of society, and time periods—although the importance and frequency of war vary greatly from case to case.

Some argue that domestic political factors shape a state's outlook on war and peace. For example, the democratic peace suggests that democracies almost never fight other democracies (see Chapter 3), although both democracies and authoritarian states fight wars. Recent work by political science scholars argues that some authoritarian states (for example, those ruled by single parties) may also be relatively peaceful, compared to other types of authoritarian states (for example, those ruled by individual dictators). Others claim that domestic political parties, interest groups, and legislatures play an important role in whether international conflicts become international wars.

Few useful generalizations can tell us which societies are more prone or less prone to war. The same society may change greatly over time. For example, Japan was prone to using violence in international conflicts before World War II, but it has been averse to such violence since then. The !Kung bush people in Angola and Namibia—a hunter-gatherer society—were observed by anthropologists in the 1960s to be extremely peaceful. Yet anthropologists in the 1920s

WHY WAR? Political scientists do not agree on a theory of why great wars like World War II occur and cannot predict whether they could happen again. The city of Stalingrad (Volgograd) was decimated during Germany's invasion of the Soviet Union, 1943.

SPUTNIK/Alamy Stock Photo

[handwritten margin note: Capitalist & communist states fought wars regularly]

had observed them engaging in murderous intergroup violence. If there are general principles to explain why some societies at some times are more peaceful than others and why they change, political scientists have not yet identified them.

THE SYSTEMIC LEVEL Theories at the *systemic* level explain wars in terms of power relations among major actors in the international system. Some of these theories are discussed in Chapter 2. For example, power transition theory holds that conflicts generate large wars at times when power is relatively equally distributed and a rising power is threatening to overtake a declining hegemon in overall position. At this level, too, competing theories exist that seem incompatible. Deterrence, as we have seen, is supposed to stop wars by building up power and threatening its use. But the theory of arms races holds that wars are caused, not prevented, by such actions. No one has discovered a general formula to identify in what circumstances each of these principles holds true. Several theories argue that major warfare in the international system is *cyclical.* One approach links large wars with *long economic waves* (also called *Kondratieff cycles*) in the world economy, of about 50 years' duration. Another approach links the largest wars with a 100-year cycle based on the creation and decay of world orders (see Hegemony in Chapter 2). These **cycle theories** can explain at best only general tendencies toward war in the international system over time.

An opposite approach in some ways is the theory of linear long-term change—that war as an outcome of conflict is becoming less likely over time due to the worldwide development of both technology and international norms. Some IR scholars argue that war and military force are becoming *obsolete* as leverage in international conflicts because these means of influence are not very effective in today's highly complex, interdependent world. A parallel line of argument holds that today's military technology is too powerful to use in most conflicts; this is especially applicable to nuclear weapons. Advocates of these theories make historical analogies to the decline of the practices of slavery, dueling, and cannibalism—once considered normal but now obsolete. These approaches have a strong empirical basis (see The Waning of War in Chapter 3), but no consensus has emerged regarding the best explanation for this trend.

Some political scientists study war from a statistical perspective, analyzing data on types of wars and the circumstances under which they occurred. Current research focuses on the effects of democracy, government structure, trade, international organizations, and related factors in explaining the escalation or settlement of military disputes between states.

Thus, on all three levels of analysis, competing theories offer different explanations for why some conflicts become violent and others do not. For these reasons, political scientists cannot yet predict with any confidence which of the world's many international conflicts will lead to war. We can gain insight, however, by studying various types of conflicts to understand better what states are fighting about.

cycle theories An effort to explain tendencies toward war in the international system as cyclical, for example, by linking wars with long waves in the world economy (Kondratieff cycles).

5.2 Conflicts of Ideas

Identify at least four different international conflicts where religion plays a role in creating or exacerbating the conflict.

The following sections discuss six types of international conflict: ethnic, religious, ideological, territorial, governmental, and economic. The first three are conflicts over ideas; the last three are conflicts over interests. These six types of conflict are not mutually exclusive, and they overlap considerably in practice. For example, the conflicts between Russia and Ukraine after the 1991 Soviet breakup were complex. *Ethnic* Russians living in Ukraine, and ethnic Ukrainians in Russia, experienced conflict. There are also *religious* differences between Ukrainian and Russian forms of Christianity. In addition, the two new states had a *territorial* dispute over the Crimean peninsula, which Soviet leader Nikita Khrushchev had transferred to Ukraine in the 1950s.

The two states also had *economic* conflicts over trade and money after the Soviet breakup, which created new borders and currencies. These multiple conflicts did not lead to the use of military force, however, until 2014. After protesters forced the resignation of Ukraine's pro-Russian president, Russia annexed Crimea. Russia also supported a rebellion in the eastern portion of Ukraine, where many ethnic Russians lived. As of 2018, that conflict is ongoing, with many failed attempts at cease-fires. So the types of conflict discussed here come into play in combination rather than separately.

We will look first at the most difficult types of conflict, in which intangible elements such as ethnic hatred, religious fervor, or ideology come into play—conflicts of ideas. These identity-based sources of international conflict today have been shaped historically by nationalism as the link between identity and internationally recognized statehood. Therefore, we will briefly review the development of nationalism before examining the three types of conflicts of ideas.

5.2.1 Nationalism

nationalism Identification with and devotion to the interests of one's nation. It usually involves a large group of people who share a national identity and often a language, culture, or ancestry.

Nationalism—devotion to the interests of one's own nation over the interests of other states—may be the most important force in world politics in the past two centuries. A nation is a population that shares an identity, usually including a language and culture. But nationality is a difficult concept to define precisely. To some degree, the extension of political control over large territories such as France created the commonality necessary for nationhood—states created nations. At the same time, however, the perceived existence of a nation has often led to the creation of a corresponding state as a people win sovereignty over their own affairs—nations created states.

Around A.D. 1500, countries such as France and Austria began to bring entire nations together into single states. These new nation-states were very large and powerful and overran smaller neighbors. Over time, they conquered and incorporated many small territorial units. Eventually the idea of nationalism itself became a powerful force and ultimately contributed to the disintegration of large multinational states such as Austria-Hungary (in World War I), the Soviet Union, and Yugoslavia.

The principle of *self-determination* implies that people who identify as a nation should have the right to form a state and exercise sovereignty over their affairs. Self-determination is a widely praised principle in international affairs today (although not historically). But it is generally secondary to the principles of sovereignty (noninterference in other states' internal affairs) and territorial integrity, with which it frequently conflicts. Self-determination does not give groups the right to change international borders, even those imposed arbitrarily by colonialism, in order to unify a group with a common national identity. Generally, though not always, self-determination has been achieved by violence. When the borders of (perceived) nations do not match those of states, conflicts almost inevitably arise. Today such conflicts are widespread—in Chechnya, Quebec, Israel-Palestine, India-Pakistan, Sri Lanka, Tibet, and many other places.

The Netherlands helped establish the principle of self-determination when it broke free of Spanish ownership around 1600 and set up a self-governing Dutch republic. The struggle over control of the Netherlands was a leading cause of the Thirty Years' War (1618–1648), and in that war, states mobilized their populations for war in new ways. For instance, Sweden drafted one man out of ten for long-term military service, while the Netherlands used the wealth derived from global trade to finance a standing professional army.

This process of popular mobilization intensified greatly in the French Revolution and the subsequent Napoleonic Wars, when France instituted a universal draft and a centrally run "command" economy. Its motivated citizen armies, composed for the first time of Frenchmen rather than mercenaries, marched longer and faster. People participated in part because they were patriotic. Their nation-state embodied their aspirations and brought them together in a common national identity.

The United States meanwhile had followed the example of the Netherlands by declaring independence from Britain in 1776. Latin American states gained independence early in the nineteenth century, and Germany and Italy unified their nations out of multiple political units (through war) later in that century.

Before World War I, socialist workers from different European countries had banded together as workers to fight for workers' rights. In that war, however, most abandoned such solidarity and instead fought for their respective nations; nationalism thus proved a stronger force than socialism. Before World War II, nationalism helped Germany, Italy, and Japan build political orders based on *fascism*—an extreme authoritarianism girded by national chauvinism. And in World War II, it was nationalism and patriotism (not communism) that rallied the Soviet people in order to sacrifice by the millions to turn back Germany's invasion.

In the past 70 years, nations by the dozens have gained independence and statehood. Jews worked persistently in the first half of the twentieth century to create the state of Israel, and Palestinians aspired in the second half to create a Palestinian state. While multinational states such as the Soviet Union and Yugoslavia have fragmented in recent years, ethnic and territorial units such as Ukraine, Slovenia, and East Timor have established themselves as independent nation-states. Others, such as Kosovo and Kurdistan, seek to do so and already run their own affairs. The continuing influence of nationalism in today's world is evident. It affects several of the main types of conflict that occupy the rest of this chapter.

5.2.2 Ethnic Conflict

ethnic groups Large groups of people who share ancestral, language, cultural, or religious ties and a common identity.

Ethnic conflict is quite possibly the most important source of conflict in the numerous wars now occurring throughout the world. **Ethnic groups** are large groups of people who share ancestral, language, cultural, and/or religious ties and a common *identity* (individuals identify with the group). Although conflicts between ethnic groups often have material aspects—notably over territory and government control—ethnic conflict itself stems from a dislike or hatred that members of one ethnic group systematically feel toward another ethnic group. Ethnic conflict is thus not based on tangible causes (what someone does) but on intangible ones (who someone is).

Ethnic groups often form the basis for nationalist sentiments. Not all ethnic groups identify as nations; for instance, within the United States, various ethnic groups coexist (sometimes uneasily) with a common *national* identity as Americans. But in locations where millions of members of a single ethnic group live as the majority population in their ancestors' land, they usually think of themselves as a nation. In most such cases, they aspire to have their own state with its formal international status and territorial boundaries.

Territorial control is closely tied to the aspirations of ethnic groups for statehood. Any state's borders deviate to some extent (sometimes substantially) from the actual location of ethnic communities. Members of

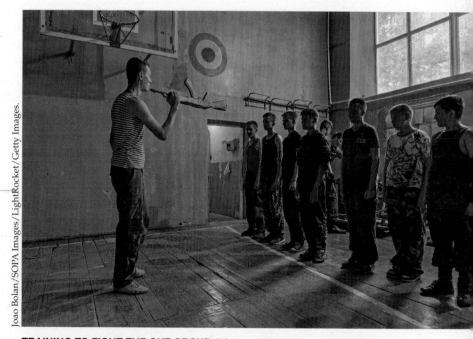

Joao Bolan/SOPA Images/LightRocket/Getty Images.

TRAINING TO FIGHT THE OUT-GROUP Ethnic conflicts play a role in many international conflicts. Ethnocentrism based on an in-group bias can promote intolerance and ultimately dehumanization of an out-group, as in genocides in Darfur (Sudan), Rwanda, and Bosnia; South African apartheid; the persecution of Jews and other minorities in Nazi Germany; and slavery in the United States. In 2014, Ukraine erupted in violence, pitting pro-European forces in western Ukraine against pro-Russian forces in eastern Ukraine. Here, children in a pro-Russian city attend an after-school military tactics club to train for combat, 2017.

Figure 5.2 Kurdish Areas
Ethnic populations often span international borders. The shaded region shows the approximate area of Kurdish settlements.

the ethnic group are left outside its state's borders, and members of other ethnic groups are located within the state's borders. The resulting situation can be dangerous, with part of an ethnic group controlling a state and another part living as a minority within another state controlled by a rival ethnic group. Frequently the minority group members suffer discrimination in the other state, and the "home" state tries to rescue or avenge them.

Other ethnic groups lack any home state. Kurds share a culture, and many of them aspire to create a state of Kurdistan. But Kurds reside in four states—Turkey, Iraq, Iran, and Syria—all of which strongly oppose giving up control of part of their own territory to create a Kurdish state (see Figure 5.2). In the 1990s, rival Kurdish guerrilla armies fought both Iraqi and Turkish military forces and each other. Repeatedly in the late 1990s, Turkey sent large military forces into northern Iraq to attack Kurdish guerrilla bases. Kurds enjoyed autonomy in part of northern Iraq under U.S. protection in the 1990s and maintained a quasi-autonomous status in post-Saddam Iraq. The Kurds' success in the 2010 Iraqi elections gave them a strong position to retain this status. In the Syrian civil war that began in 2011, Kurdish areas gained considerable autonomy while straddling the fence politically between the government and the rebels. Kurdish fighters (known as Peshmerga) also received significant international military support in fighting Islamic State in Iraq and Syria (ISIS) militants who at one point controlled significant territory in northern Iraq and Syria. For several years, the United States assisted Kurdish Peshmerga in ousting ISIS forces, especially in northern Iraq. Yet by late 2017, Turkey was undertaking significant military operations against both the Kurds and ISIS militants. This included airstrikes against Kurdish groups that were supported by the United States. Whether the Kurds will be able to further their aims of establishing an independent territory in the region remains to be seen.

Ethnic conflicts often create pressures to redraw borders by force. When ethnic populations are minorities in territories controlled by rival ethnic groups, they may even be driven from their land or (in rare cases) systematically exterminated. By driving out the minority ethnic group, a majority group can assemble a more unified, more contiguous, and larger territory for its nation-state, as ethnic Serbs tried to do through *ethnic cleansing* (a term they invented) after the breakup of Yugoslavia in the 1990s. Similarly, ethnic conflict between majority Kyrgyz and minority Uzbeks in 2010 in Kyrgyzstan (Central Asia) displaced hundreds of thousands of people, another example of the potency of such identity conflicts.

Outside states often worry about the fate of "their people" living as minorities in neighboring states. For instance, Albania is concerned about ethnic Albanians who are the majority population in the Serbian province of Kosovo (but a minority of the population in Serbia). But as Kosovo moved toward independence from Serbia, Serbia worried about the minority of ethnic Serbs living in Kosovo. Similar problems have fueled wars between Armenia and Azerbaijan and between India and Pakistan. The dangerous combination of ethnic conflict and territorial disputes could lead to more wars in the future.

CAUSES OF ETHNIC HOSTILITY Why do ethnic groups frequently dislike each other? Often there are long-standing historical conflicts over specific territories or natural resources, or over one ethnic group's economic exploitation or political domination of another. They become driven not by tangible grievances (though these may well persist as irritants) but by the kinds of processes described by social psychology that are set in motion when one group of people has a prolonged conflict with another and experiences violence at the hands of the other group. The ethnic group is a kind of extended *kinship* group—a group of related individuals sharing some ancestors. Even when kinship relations are not very close, a *group identity* makes a person act as though the other members of the ethnic group were family. For instance, African American men who call each other "brother" express group identity as kinship. Likewise, Jews around the world treat each other as family, even though each community has intermarried over time and shares more ancestors with local non-Jews than with distant Jews. Perhaps as technology allows far-flung groups to congregate in cyberspace, there will be less psychological pressure to collect ethnic groups physically in a territorial nation-state. Or tools such as social media may link individuals previously unknown to each other and encourage them to reunite physically to be with kinship groups.

Ethnocentrism, or *in-group bias*, is the tendency to see one's own group in favorable terms and an *out-group* in unfavorable terms. Some scholars believe that ethnocentrism has roots in a biological propensity to protect closely related individuals, though this idea is controversial. More often, in-group bias is understood in terms of social psychology. In either case, the ties that bind ethnic groups together, and divide them from other groups, are based on the identity principle (see Chapter 1). Just as the reciprocity principle has its negative side (see Chapter 1), so does the identity principle. The same forces that allow sacrifice for a group identity, as in the European Union (EU), also allow the formation of in-group bias.

No *minimum criterion* of similarity or kin relationship is needed to evoke the group identity process, including in-group bias. In psychological experiments, even trivial differentiations can evoke these processes. If people are assigned to groups based on a known but unimportant characteristic (such as preferring, say, circles to triangles), before long the people in each group show in-group bias and find they don't much care for the other group's members.

In-group biases are far stronger when the other group looks different, speaks a different language, or worships in a different way (or all three). All too easily, an out-group can be dehumanized and stripped of all human rights. This **dehumanization** includes the common use of animal names—pigs, dogs, and so forth—for members of the out-group. U.S. propaganda in World War II depicted Japanese people as apes. Especially in wartime, dehumanization can be extreme. The restraints on war that have evolved in regular interstate warfare, such as not massacring civilians (see war crimes in Chapter 7), are easily discarded in interethnic warfare.

Experience in Western Europe shows that over time, education can overcome ethnic animosities between traditionally hostile nations, such as France and Germany. After World War II, these states' governments rewrote the textbooks that a new generation would use to learn its people's histories. Previously, each state's textbooks had glorified its own past deeds, played down its misdeeds, and portrayed its traditional enemies in unflattering terms. In a continent-wide project, new textbooks that gave a more objective and fair rendition were created. By contrast, present-day Japanese textbooks that gloss over Japan's crimes in World War II continue to inflame its relations with both China and Korea.

The existence of a threat from an out-group promotes the cohesion of an in-group, thereby creating a somewhat self-reinforcing process of ethnic division. However, ethnocentrism also often causes members of a group to view themselves as disunited (because they see their own divisions up close) and the out-group as monolithic (because they see it only from the outside). This usually reflects a group's sense of vulnerability. In the Arab-Israeli conflict, Israelis tend to see themselves as fragmented into dozens of political parties and diverse immigrant communities pulling in different directions, while they see "the Arabs" as a monolithic bloc united against them. Meanwhile, Arab Palestinians see themselves as fragmented into factions and weakened by divisions among the Arab states, while "the Israelis" appear monolithic to them.

Ethnic groups are only one point along a spectrum of kinship relations—from nuclear families through extended families, villages, provinces, and nations, up to the entire human race. Loyalties fall at different points along the spectrum. Again, there is no minimum criterion for in-group identity. For instance, experts said that of all the African countries, Somalia was surely immune from ethnic conflicts because Somalis

ethnocentrism The tendency to see one's own group (in-group) in favorable terms and an out-group in unfavorable terms.

dehumanization Stigmatization of enemies as subhuman or nonhuman, leading frequently to widespread violence. See also *crimes against humanity* and *genocide*.

Policy Perspectives
Prime Minister of Bangladesh, Sheikh Hasina Wazed

PROBLEM *How do you prevent civil conflict while providing humanitarian assistance?*

Open Government Licence sourced by / Alamy Stock Photo

BACKGROUND Imagine you are the prime minister of Bangladesh. You are in your third term as prime minister of this populous South Asian country. You are a popular leader and are considered one of the most powerful women in the world.

In 2017, however, a significant challenge appeared: Due to violence in the Rakhine state of neighboring Burma, hundreds of thousands of refugees fled into Bangladesh. The refugees, known as the Rohingya, were fleeing ethnic violence that many observers have described as ethnic cleansing. Your government quickly organized refugee camps to contain this potential humanitarian disaster. The international community has assisted with money and food to help sustain the Burmese refugees in your country. Yet, the task is monumental—by one estimate, well over 500,000 now live in refugee camps in your border regions.

DOMESTIC CONSIDERATIONS While Bangladesh is a stable, peaceful country, it is quite poor. Around 15 percent of your population lives in extreme poverty. Your infrastructure system is weak and your capital city, Dhaka, is considered to be very overcrowded. Recently, however, your economy has begun to grow—posting its highest growth rate in several decades in 2016. Unemployment and poverty have both fallen in the last decade. Politically, you have a vocal opposition party. Its members point out (frequently) that your previous election was a violation of Bangladesh's constitution since prime ministers are supposed to serve only two terms.

SCENARIO Now imagine that the international community, through the UN High Commissioner for Refugees (UNHCR), asks you to continue to keep the Rohingya in your territory for a much longer period of time. The UNHCR will not allow you to forcibly repatriate the Rohingya since they still face significant threats to their security should they return to Burma.

Your economic advisers are nervous. Supporting an extra half million people in your territory is becoming costly. They are concerned the cost will threaten the economic growth your country has enjoyed the past few years. And while the international community—both international organizations (IOs) and nongovernmental organizations (NGOs)—have helped bear the cost, the aid you receive is far short of what you need to support the camps. Moreover, many of the refugee camps are located in agricultural areas, where their presence has either ruined crops or made the harvest impossible.

The conflict in Burma continues. It is still not safe for the Rohingya to return there without facing the threat of genocide. There are also no prospects for international intervention to stop the violence in Burma.

CHOOSE YOUR POLICY How do you handle the refugee situation? Do you ask for more assistance from the international community? What if that assistance falls short? Do you risk your recent economic success by allowing the refugees to stay and take up resources that would otherwise go to your own population? Do you force the Rohingya to return to Burma to face certain political violence? How can you best confront this crucial humanitarian situation while keeping an eye on your own country's political and economic stability?

were all from the same ethnic group, spoke the same language, and shared the same religion. Then in 1991–1992, a ruinous civil war erupted between members of different clans (based on extended families), leading to mass starvation, the intervention of foreign military forces, and two decades of near-anarchy and nonstop violence.

It is unclear why people identify most strongly at one level of group identity. In Somalia, loyalties are to clans; in Serbia, they are to the ethnic group; in the United States and elsewhere, multiethnic nations command people's primary loyalty. States reinforce their citizens' identification with the state through flags, anthems, pledges of allegiance, patriotic speeches, and so forth. Perhaps someday people will shift loyalties even further, developing a *global identity* as humans first and members of states and ethnic groups second.

5.2.3 Genocide

In extreme cases, governments use **genocide**—systematic extermination of ethnic or religious groups in whole or in part—to try to destroy scapegoated groups or political rivals. Under its fanatical policies of racial purity, Nazi Germany exterminated 6 million Jews and millions of others, including homosexuals, Roma, and communists. The mass murders, now known as the Holocaust, along with the sheer scale of war unleashed by Nazi aggression, are considered among the greatest *crimes against humanity* in history. Responsible German officials faced justice in the *Nuremberg Tribunal* after World War II (see Chapter 1). The pledges of world leaders after that experience to "never again" allow genocide have been found wanting as genocide recurred in the 1990s in Bosnia and Rwanda, and most recently in Darfur, Sudan.

In 1994, in Rwanda, where the Hutu group is the majority and the Tutsi group the minority, a Hutu-nationalist government carried out the most deadly genocide of recent decades. The minority Tutsis had earlier held power over the Hutus, and Belgian colonialism had exploited local rivalries. In 1994, ethnic Hutu extremists in the government gave orders throughout the country to kill ethnic Tutsis and those Hutus who had opposed the government. In short order, an estimated 800,000 men, women, and children were massacred, mostly by machete, and their bodies dumped into rivers; thousands at a time washed up on lakeshores in neighboring Uganda.

It might be tempting to view Hutu-Tutsi hatred as part of a pattern of age-old ethnic hatreds that cropped up in the post–Cold War era, especially in "backward" areas such as Africa. (Western politicians often articulated this age-old-hatreds theory in the Bosnia case, portraying the Balkans, like Africa, as "backward" and conflict-prone.) If killings based on age-old hatreds are inevitable, then inaction by the rest of the world might be justifiable. However, explaining genocide as a result of backwardness does not work well because one of the world's most civilized, "advanced" states, Germany, exterminated its Jews even more efficiently than Rwanda did its Tutsis—the difference being that the "advanced" society could kill with industrial chemicals instead of at knifepoint.

Social psychology theories treat the Rwandan genocide as pathological—a deviation from both rationality and social norms. In-group biases based on fairly arbitrary group characteristics become amplified by a perceived threat from an out-group, and exaggerated by history, myth, and propaganda (including schooling). Such feelings can be whipped up by politicians pursuing their own power. A key threshold is crossed when the out-group is dehumanized; norms of social interaction, such as not slitting children's throats, can then be disregarded.

As the genocide in Rwanda unfolded, the international community stood by. A weak UN force there had to withdraw, although its commander later estimated that with 5,000 more troops he could have changed the outcome. The weak international response to this atrocity reveals how frail international norms of human rights are compared to norms of noninterference in other states' internal affairs—at least when no strategic interests are at stake. The Hutu ultranationalists quickly lost power when Tutsi rebels defeated the government militarily, but the war spread into Democratic Congo, where the ultranationalists took refuge and where sporadic fighting continues over 20 years later. Top U.S. officials, including President Clinton, later apologized for their inadequate response, but the damage had been done. Worse yet, renewed vows of "never again" proved wanting once more in the next case, Darfur.

In Sudan, the warring sides (largely northern Muslims versus southern Christians) in a decades-long civil war signed a peace agreement in 2003, ending a war that had

genocide An intentional and systematic attempt to destroy a national, ethnic, racial, or religious group, in whole or in part. It was confirmed as a crime under international law by the UN Genocide Convention (1948). See also *crimes against humanity* and *dehumanization*.

killed more than a million people. The agreement called for withdrawing government forces from the south of the country, establishing a power-sharing transitional government and army, and holding a referendum in the rebel areas in six years. These processes led to the successful independence of South Sudan in 2011. But following this peace agreement, rebels in the western Darfur region began to protest their exclusion from the peace agreement. In response, the government helped Arab (Muslim) militias raid black African (also Muslim) Darfur villages, wantonly killing, raping, and burning. In late 2004, the government and some of the Darfur rebels reached a tentative peace agreement, and the African Union (AU) and United Nations (UN) sent in a joint peacekeeping mission in 2007. After years of Sudanese government delays and other frustrations, the force had 23,000 uniformed personnel on the ground by 2011 and much of that force remains there as of 2018. The international community's ineffective response to the mass murders in Darfur, like that in Rwanda in 1994, shows the limited reach of international norms in today's state-based international system.

In cases of both genocide and less extreme scapegoating, ethnic hatreds do not merely bubble up naturally. Rather, politicians provoke and channel hatred to strengthen their own power. Often, in ethnically divided countries, political parties form along ethnic lines, and party leaders consolidate their positions in their own populations by exaggerating the dangers from the other side.

The Cold War, with its tight system of alliances and authoritarian communist governments, seems to have helped keep ethnic conflicts in check. In the Soviet Union and Yugoslavia—multinational states—the existence of a single strong state (willing to oppress local communities) kept the lid on ethnic tensions and enforced peace between neighboring communities. The breakup of these states allowed ethnic and regional conflicts to take center stage, sometimes bringing violence and war. These cases may indicate a dilemma where freedom comes at the expense of order, and vice versa. Of course, not all ethnic groups get along so poorly. After the fall of communism, most of the numerous ethnic rivalries in the former Soviet Union did not lead to warfare, and in Czechoslovakia and elsewhere, ethnic relations were relatively peaceful after the fall of communism.

5.2.4 Religious Conflict

One reason ethnic conflicts often transcend material grievances is that they find expression as *religious* conflicts. Because religion is the core of a community's value system in much of the world, people whose religious practices differ are easily disdained and treated as unworthy or even inhuman. When overlaid on ethnic and territorial conflicts, religion often surfaces as the central and most visible division between groups. For instance, most people in Azerbaijan are Muslims; most Armenians are Christians. This is a very common pattern in ethnic conflicts.

Nothing inherent in religion mandates conflicts—in many places, members of different religious groups coexist peacefully. But religious differences hold the potential to make existing conflicts more intractable because religions involve core values, which are held as absolute truth.

This is increasingly true as *fundamentalist* movements have gained strength in recent decades. (The reasons for fundamentalism are disputed, but it is clearly a global-level phenomenon.) Members of these movements organize their lives and communities around their religious beliefs; many are willing to sacrifice, kill, and die for those beliefs. Fundamentalist movements have become larger and more powerful in recent decades in Christianity, Islam, Judaism, Hinduism, and other religions. In India, for example, Hindu fundamentalists have provoked violent clashes and massacres that have reverberated internationally. In 2002, a frenzy of burning, torturing, and raping by Hindu nationalist extremists killed nearly a thousand Muslims in India's Gujarat state, where the Hindu nationalist party controls the state government. In

Israel, Jewish fundamentalists have used violence, including the assassination of Israel's own prime minister in 1995, to derail Palestinian-Israeli peace negotiations.

Fundamentalist movements challenge the values and practices of **secular** political organizations—those created apart from religious establishments. The secular practices threatened by fundamentalist movements include the rules of the international system, which treat states as formally equal and sovereign whether they are "believers" or "infidels." As transnational belief systems, religions are often taken as a higher law than state laws and international treaties. Iranian Islamist fundamentalists train and support militias in other states such as Iraq and Lebanon. Jewish fundamentalists build settlements in Israeli-occupied territories and vow to cling to the land even if their government evacuates it. Christian fundamentalists in the United States persuaded their government to withdraw from the UN Population Fund (UNFPA) because of that organization's views on family planning and abortion. Each of these actions runs counter to the norms of the international system and to the assumptions of realism.

Some have suggested that international conflicts in the coming years may be generated by a "clash of civilizations"—based on the differences among the world's major cultural groupings, which overlap quite a bit with religious communities. Others have criticized the idea for being overly general and for assuming that cultural differences naturally create conflict. In fact, although religious and ethnic conflicts receive tremendous attention in the media, *most* ethnic and religious groups living together in states do not fight.

ISLAMIST MOVEMENTS   Currently, violent conflicts are being prosecuted in the name of all the world's major religions. But special attention is due to conflicts involving Islamic groups and states. Islamist actors are active participants in 12 of the world's 14 wars in progress. In addition, the U.S. "war on terror" is directed against a network of Islamic terror groups. However, most Islamist movements are not violent.

Islam, the religion practiced by **Muslims**, is broad and diverse. Its divergent populations include Sunni Muslims (the majority), Shi'ite Muslims (concentrated in Iran, southern Iraq, southern Lebanon, and Bahrain), and many smaller branches and sects. Most countries with mainly Muslim populations belong to the Islamic Conference, an intergovernmental organization (IGO). The world's predominantly Islamic countries stretch from Nigeria to Indonesia, centered historically in the Middle East (see Figure 5.3) but with the largest populations in South and Southeast Asia. Many international conflicts around this zone involve Muslims on one side and non-Muslims on the other, as a result of geographical and historical circumstances including colonialism and oil.

Islamist groups advocate basing government and society on Islamic law. These groups vary greatly in the means they employ to pursue this goal. Most are nonviolent—charities and political parties. Some are violent—militias and terrorist networks. In the 1990s, Islamic parties gained ground in Turkey—a secular state in which the military has intervened repeatedly to prevent religious politics—and a former Islamist leader has been prime minister since 2003, making Turkey an

secular Created apart from religious establishments and in which there is a high degree of separation between religious and political organizations.

Islam A broad and diverse world religion whose divergent populations include Sunni Muslims, Shi'ite Muslims, and many smaller branches and sects from Nigeria to Indonesia, centered in the Middle East and South Asia.

Muslims See *Islam*.

Islamist Describing a political ideology based on instituting Islamic principles and laws in government. A broad range of groups using diverse methods come under this category.

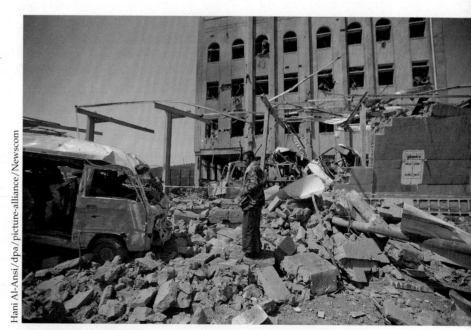

Hani Al-Ansi / dpa / picture-alliance / Newscom

RELIGIOUS DIFFERENCES Religious intolerance can exacerbate tensions between groups, sometimes increasing violence, with international implications. The most salient religious conflict today is between Shi'ite and Sunni branches of Islam, centered in Iran and Saudi Arabia. The split, played out in devastating violence in Iraq after 2007, helps fuel the Syrian civil war and more recently the Yemeni civil war (here, 2018).

Figure 5.3 Members of the Islamic Conference and Areas of Conflict

Shaded countries are members of the conference; numbered regions are areas of conflict between Muslims and non-Muslims or secular authorities.

1 Europe	10 Tajikistan	19 Somalia
2 Bosnia-Herzegovina	11 Western China	20 Israel/Palestine
3 Serbia/Kosovo	12 Philippines	21 Egypt
4 Turkey	13 Indonesia	22 Algeria/Tunisia
5 Cyprus	14 Burma/Bangladesh	23 Sudan
6 Georgia	15 India	24 Central African Republic
7 Southern Russia/Chechnya	16 Pakistan	25 Nigeria/Mali
8 Armenia/Azerbaijan	17 Lebanon	
9 Afghanistan	18 Syria	

important model of moderate Islam in the region. Islamist parties have also played leading roles in Iraq's government since 2003 and played central roles in the Arab Spring countries, initially winning elections in Tunisia and Egypt. Armed Islamist factions became key players in the Syrian civil war in 2013. By 2014, one group, ISIS, had become the strongest of these groups and captured significant territory in Syria and neighboring Iraq. Its rapid expansion in both countries triggered military action against it by several North Atlantic Treaty Organization (NATO) states, Russia, and regional powers.

If Islamist movements seek changes primarily in domestic policies, why do they matter for IR? Islamist politics may lead to different foreign policies, but the more important answer is that some Islamist movements have become a transnational force shaping world order and global North-South relations in important ways.

In several countries, Islamists reject Western-oriented secular states in favor of governments more explicitly oriented to Islamic values. These movements reflect long-standing *anti-Western* sentiment in these countries—against the old European colonizers who were Christian—and are in some ways *nationalist* movements expressed through religious channels. In some Middle Eastern countries with authoritarian governments, religious institutions (mosques) have been the only available avenue for political opposition. Religion has therefore become a means to express opposition to the status quo in politics and culture. These anti-Western feelings in Islamic countries came to a boil in 2006 after a Danish newspaper published offensive cartoons depicting the prophet Muhammad. Across the world, Muslims protested, set fire to several Danish embassies, rioted (with dozens of deaths resulting), and boycotted Danish goods. In 2015, Islamic militants attacked a Paris-based satirical newspaper, *Charlie Hebdo*, for publishing similar cartoons.

Public opinion in both Muslim and non-Muslim countries shows some misconceptions and differences in opinion (see Figure 5.4). Support for Islamist radicals varies greatly among countries. A 2011 poll recalls "mirror image" perceptions (see Chapter 4). In Western non-Muslim-majority countries, 58 percent thought Muslims were "fanatical," and around 20 percent thought they were respectful of women. But in a survey of seven Muslim-majority countries, 53 percent thought non-Muslims were "fanatical," and 42 percent felt non-Muslims were respectful of women.

The more radical Islamist movements not only threaten some existing governments—especially those tied to the West—but also undermine traditional norms of state sovereignty. They reject Western political conceptions of the state (based on individual autonomy) in favor of a more traditional Islamic orientation based on community. Some aspire to create a single political state encompassing most of the

Figure 5.4 Public Opinion in Muslim and Non-Muslim Countries

Source: Based on Pew Global Attitudes Survey, 2005, 2010 and 2014.

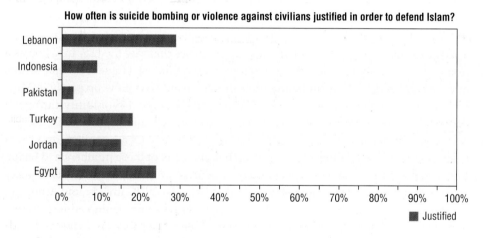

How often is suicide bombing or violence against civilians justified in order to defend Islam?

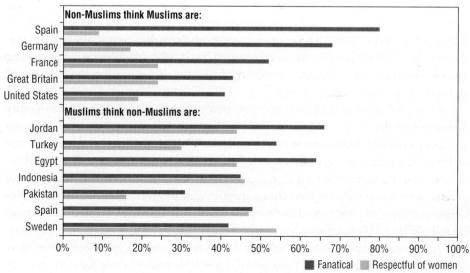

Middle East, as existed in the *caliphate* of A.D. 600–1200. Such a development would create a profound challenge to the present international system—particularly to its current status quo powers—and therefore the world's most powerful states would oppose it at every turn.

Islamists in Middle Eastern countries, like revolutionaries elsewhere, derive their main base of strength from championing the cause of the poor masses against rich elites. Like other revolutionaries throughout the global South, Islamist movements in countries such as Turkey, Egypt, and Lebanon draw their base of support from poor slums, where the Islamists sometimes provide basic services unmet by the government.

In a public opinion poll in 2010 in Morocco and Saudi Arabia, a plurality of respondents identified primarily as Muslims, more than identified primarily as citizens of their states or as Arabs. But in Jordan, Lebanon, Egypt, and the United Arab Emirates, the pattern was reversed, with large majorities identifying primarily as citizens of their states. Islamist movements tap into the public's identification with issues that may not materially affect them but affect their identities as Muslims, across national borders—especially the Arab-Israeli conflict. The public in Muslim countries also cared about wars in the 1990s in Bosnia, Azerbaijan, and Chechnya, where Christian armed forces attacked Muslim civilians. Islamists see all these conflicts as part of a broad regional (or even global) struggle of Islam against Western, Christian imperialism—a struggle dating back to the Crusades almost a thousand years ago. From the perspective of some outsiders, the religious conflicts boiling and simmering at the edges of the Islamic world look like an expansionist threat to be contained. The view from within looks more like being surrounded and repressed from several directions (see the Public Opinion and International Relations box).

The 2003 Iraq War inflamed anti-American feeling and helped radicalize politics across the Muslim world, especially in Arab countries that saw the U.S. invasion as a humiliation to Arab dignity. Initially, the presidency of Barack Hussein Obama, whose middle name reflects Muslim family roots in Kenya and who grew up partly in Muslim Indonesia, began to alter this anti-American dynamic. Favorability ratings of America climbed in the region, in part due to President Obama's speech on America's relations with Muslim states in Cairo in June 2009, where Obama called for a "new beginning" to those relationships. By 2010, though, many of those numbers had begun to fall again as the Arab world began to express frustration in the Middle East peace process and the U.S. decision to stay in Afghanistan. By 2018, already low American favorability ratings in the Arab world fell even lower when the Trump administration announced the relocation of the U.S. embassy in Israel from Tel Aviv to Jerusalem—a move criticized by all Arab states.

ARMED ISLAMIST GROUPS Anti-American and anti-Western sentiments in predominantly Islamic countries have accelerated the growth of violent Islamist groups as well. Although they are in the minority, they have disproportionate effects on IR and receive the most public attention.

Armed Islamist groups vary tremendously, and in some cases they violently disagree with each other (see Table 5.1). In particular, divisions between the Sunni and Shi'ite wings of Islam have led to violence. This split played out prominently in Iraq, where Saddam Hussein was a Sunni ruling over a Shi'ite majority (brutally repressing their rebellion after the 1991 Gulf War) and earlier fighting a long deadly war against Shi'ite Iran. After the U.S.-led overthrow of Saddam in 2003, Shi'ite parties took power and Shi'ite militias exacted revenge, while some Sunnis waged a relentless insurgency that turned into deadly waves of sectarian violence. The violence in Iraq has since diminished, but the Sunni-Shi'ite relationship there remains unsettled.

Public Opinion and International Relations
Islamic Extremism

Several Islamist groups have carried out or supported attacks in numerous countries. Islamist groups such as al Qaeda and the Islamic State have threatened to further attack civilian targets around the world. These threats, of course, are meant to cause fear and force targeted states to change their policies, usually toward long-standing conflicts in the Middle East.

Interestingly, different populations perceive these threats very differently. Figure 5.5 presents data on the perceived threat of Islamic extremism from surveys in 23 countries. The surveys asked respondents how concerned they were about Islamic extremism. Several trends are evident in the data.

First, majorities in all 23 countries express some concern (somewhat or very) about Islamic extremism. This is true regardless of the geographic location of the country. Second, the two countries with the lowest level of concern (adding together somewhat and very concerned) are Muslim-majority countries: Indonesia and Turkey. Yet, in other Muslim-majority states, such as Lebanon and Pakistan, these concerns loom large. Thus, it is clearly not the case that Muslims feel immune

to the threat of this violence. Given our discussion of the Shi'ite and Sunni split, this is perhaps not surprising.

Finally, there are only five countries where a sizable segment of those polled (greater than 10 percent) feel that the threat of Islamic extremism is of no concern at all. Those five countries are Canada, Indonesia, Senegal, Tunisia, and Turkey. Two of these countries (Canada and Senegal) have had little experience with violence from Islamic extremist groups. The other states have had significant experience with this type of violence.

The big question is whether these concerns then influence how these individuals live their daily lives. Given that the goal of terrorism (see Chapter 6) is to disrupt daily lives and force changes in politics, it would be interesting to know what these concerns translate into. Similarly, we can also wonder whether these concerns influence voting in those countries that hold democratic elections. Extremist attacks and terrorism could influence election outcomes, which in some cases may lead to policy changes desired by extremist groups. Ironically, however, concerns about extremism can also lead to the election of parties and leaders that do much more to crack down on extremist groups.

Figure 5.5 Views of Islamic Extremism in 23 Countries

Source: Pew Research Center.

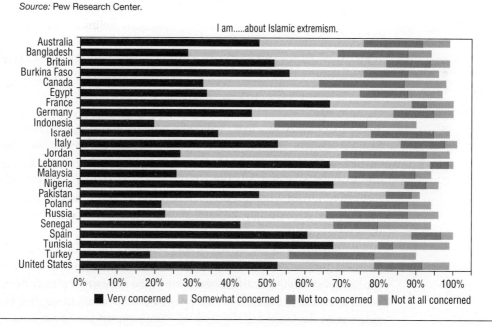

Since 2011, the Sunni-Shi'ite divide has centered on Syria, where the ruling family is Alawite (an offshoot of Shi'ism) and the majority of the population is Sunni. The civil war there has also taken on sectarian overtones, reinforced by outside backers—Shi'ite Iran for the government along with the Shi'ite Lebanese militia Hezbollah, and Sunni Turkey and Arab Gulf states for the rebels.

By 2014, Islamist rebels that had emerged in Syria united with Sunnis from Iraq to form ISIS. This group quickly gained adherents and achieved quick military victories, especially in Sunni-populated areas of Iraq. The group gained global attention as it released videos showing the beheadings of its hostages. Its quick military advances and videos led to a significant military effort to reestablish Iraqi government control

Table 5.1 Major Armed Islamist Groups

Group	Country	Branch of Islam	Actions
Islamic Republic of Iran	Iran	Shi'ite	Only Islamic revolution to successfully control a state (since 1979); held off secular Iraq in 1980s war; now attempting to build nuclear weapons
Hezbollah	Lebanon	Shi'ite	Fought Israeli army in 2006; part of ruling coalition in Lebanon
Mahdi Army/ Peace Brigades	Iraq	Shi'ite	Clashed with U.S. forces in Iraq; faction in Iraqi government; fought ISIS to retake territory in Iraq
Al-Nusra Front	Syria	Sunni	Leading rebel militia in civil war
Ansar Dine	Mali	Sunni	Controlled north of country in 2012; took hostages in Algeria in 2013
Hamas	Palestine (Gaza)	Sunni	Forces have killed hundreds of Israeli civilians and fought a war against Israel in 2008 and 2014; won Palestinian elections in 2006; controls Gaza Strip
al Shabab	Somalia	Sunni	Controlled most of country in 2007–2012; allied with al Qaeda; ousted by African Union in 2012; continued attacks in Somalia in 2017
Moro Islamic Liberation Front	Philippines	Sunni	Forces have fought for independence of certain regions in the Muslim-populated southern Philippine Islands
al Qaeda	World (Pakistan?)	Sunni	9/11 attacks and European bombings; weakened by deaths of top leaders
Taliban	Afghanistan	Sunni	Major insurgent group fighting foreign forces; controlled country in 1996–2001
The Islamic State (ISIS/ISIL/ Daesh)	Syria/Iraq	Sunni	Emerged from Sunni militant groups in Iraq; reemerged as key actor in Syrian civil war; targeted by international airstrikes in 2014–2017
Houthis	Yemen	Shi'ite	Took control of much of Yemen in 2014; supported by Iran; attacked by Saudi Arabia
Boko Haram	Nigeria	Sunni	Has killed or displaced millions in northern Nigeria since 2009; high-profile kidnappings and bombings
Islamist guerrilla fighters/terrorists are also active in Chechnya (Russia), Kashmir (India), Central Asia, Libya, Mali, Indonesia, and Europe.			

Source: U.S. Department of Defense.

and defeat ISIS. Actors that included Kurdish guerrillas, Iran, Jordan, and the United States worked to undermine ISIS. By 2015, Islamist groups in Libya, Yemen, and Egypt carried out terrorist attacks claiming ties to ISIS. In 2017, both the Iraqi government and Russian president Vladimir Putin declared victory over ISIS in Iraq and Syria, respectively. And while the amount of territory controlled by ISIS in those countries has declined dramatically, ISIS still attempts to coordinate terrorist attacks in the Middle East and Western Europe.

Regionally, Iran and Saudi Arabia represent the split, facing each other over the Persian Gulf (also known as the Arabian Gulf) and engaged in a major arms race, with the Saudis stocking jets and missiles while the Iranians export arms to their allies and could be racing to build a nuclear weapon. Russia tends to support the Iranian-Shi'ite side, while the United States and its allies support the Saudi-Sunni side. However, neither side gets along with Israel, lending a triangular aspect to the conflict.

In Iran, a popular uprising in 1979 overthrew the U.S.-backed shah and installed an Islamic government in which the top religious leaders (ayatollahs) can overturn the laws passed by the parliament. The rejection of international norms by some Islamists was dramatically illustrated when Iran refused to protect U.S. diplomats (in Iran) in 1979. Defying the UN Security Council, Iran is currently developing nuclear technology that could produce nuclear weapons within a few years. In 2009, a disputed presidential election led to the harsh repression of protesters. In 2012, Iran's currency lost half its value as harsh international sanctions hurt the economy, and Israel has threatened military attack if necessary to stop Iran's nuclear ambitions. And despite a lifting of many international sanctions in 2016, protests over the state of Iran's economy in 2017 led to violent street protests.

Iran strongly supports—with money, arms, and training—the Hezbollah militia in Lebanon and the government in Syria. Hezbollah runs hundreds of schools, hospitals, and other charities, but it is also included on the U.S. list of terrorist organizations. Hezbollah fought Israel for years, winning popular support throughout the Arab world, even among Sunnis. Hezbollah took a leading role in Lebanon's government in 2011, despite a UN tribunal's indictment of its members for the 2005 assassination of Lebanon's prime minister.

On the Sunni side, the major militant Islamist groups, as well as some less violent ones, are Salafis. They adhere to some version of Wahhabism, a fundamentalist interpretation of Islamic law with roots in Saudi Arabia. The most important center of this fundamentalist movement is currently in Afghanistan and the next-door tribal areas of western Pakistan. Militants following the same philosophy were also active across northern Africa in 2018, notably in Nigeria, Mali, Libya, and Somalia.

In Afghanistan, an Islamic government was established in 1992 after a civil war (and following a decade of ill-fated Soviet occupation). Rival Islamic factions then continued the war with even greater intensity for several years. By 1997, a faction called the Taliban had taken control of most of Afghanistan and imposed an extreme interpretation of Islamic law. With beatings and executions, the regime forced women to wear head-to-toe coverings, girls to stay out of school, and men to grow beards, among other repressive policies.

The incendiary mixture in Afghanistan in the 1990s—unending war, grinding poverty, Islamic fundamentalism, and an ideologically driven government—allowed Afghanistan to become a base for worldwide terrorist operations, culminating in the September 11, 2001, attacks. In response, the United States exerted its power to remove the Taliban from power in Afghanistan and disrupt the al Qaeda terrorist network headquartered there. Despite U.S. and NATO successes, the Taliban continues to attack NATO forces. Attacks on civilians also continue in Afghanistan.

The Taliban's defeat in Afghanistan in 2001 led its members, with like-minded Pakistani militants, to establish bases in the lawless "tribal areas" of western Pakistan, a much larger neighbor with nuclear weapons. Pakistan's intelligence service is widely believed to use Islamist militants to exert influence both in Afghanistan and in Kashmir, a territory disputed by Pakistan and India. In late 2008, Pakistan-based terrorists attacked Mumbai, India, and killed about 150 civilians there. Pro-democracy forces ousted Pakistan's military ruler and installed an elected government in 2008, though not until after the movement's leader, Benazir Bhutto, had been assassinated.

The war in Afghanistan has strained relations between Pakistan and the United States and its NATO allies. These strains worsened in 2011 when U.S. forces found and killed Osama bin Laden in a Pakistani

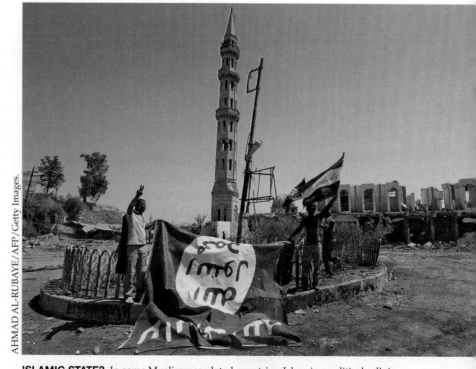

AHMAD AL-RUBAYE/AFP/Getty Images.

ISLAMIC STATE? In some Muslim-populated countries, Islam is a political rallying point—especially in authoritarian countries in which the mosque is a rare permitted gathering point. Some Islamist politicians are developing new models of government, mixing democracy and Islamic tradition, especially in the countries most affected by the Arab Spring protests. Other Islamist groups, such as the Islamic State in Iraq and Syria (ISIS), fight violently for a state founded on Islamic law. Until late 2017, ISIS controlled significant pieces of territory in Iraq and Syria. Here, fighters supporting Iraq's army in its battle against the Islamic State remove the ISIS flag from a city retaken by government forces, 2017.

city. Pakistanis objected to the intrusion that violated their sovereignty, while Americans wondered whether the Pakistani military had colluded in hiding bin Laden.

Al Qaeda is a transnational group—more a network or movement than a central organization in recent years—that recruits fighters from various countries, encourages and sometimes trains them, and helps them fight in foreign conflicts (such as in Afghanistan in the 1980s, Iraq after 2003, or Syria and Yemen today).

Although al Qaeda as a "brand" has picked up followers in northern Africa in recent years, it has lost steam in Asia and Europe, where the years after 2001 saw various terror bombings from Bali, Indonesia, to Morocco, Saudi Arabia, Russia, the Philippines, Indonesia, Iraq, and Turkey. In 2004, bombings of trains in Madrid killed hundreds and apparently tipped an election against the pro-American Spanish government—thus inducing Spain to pull its troops out of Iraq. The next year, the London subway was the target.

In Saudi Arabia—home to the world's largest oil reserves, Islam's holiest sites, and the roots of Wahhabism—al Qaeda has long hoped to overthrow the monarchy.

Saudi Arabia's neighbor to the south, Yemen, has an active branch of al Qaeda–affiliated fighters. These fighters have tried several times to bomb U.S.-bound aircraft and seized territory in the south of the country in 2011–2012, while the government was paralyzed by political unrest in the capital (part of the Arab Spring). Yemen is the poorest country in the Middle East and has suffered from decades of civil conflict. Since 2010, the United States has operated a campaign of drone attacks to combat the Yemeni militants. By 2015, Yemen was in full-scale civil war, with several groups fighting each other. One minority group known as the Houthis (allied with Iran but opposed to al Qaeda) fought to take control of the government and captured Yemen's capital in 2017. In response, Saudi Arabia (Iran's rival) attacked the Houthi rebels (mostly with airstrikes) to restore control to the government. In the midst of this chaos, new Islamic fighters claiming allegiance to ISIS began carrying out suicide bombings. By 2018, the Houthis remained in control of the capital, occasionally attacking Saudi Arabia with rockets, while war raged throughout most of the country.

Somalia's al Shabab fighters, affiliated with al Qaeda, were ousted from most cities and towns in 2012 by an African Union (AU) force, but not before taking revenge on Ethiopia and Uganda, which had contributed troops to support the Somali government. Al Shabab carried out deadly bombings in Uganda during the 2010 World Cup finals. Although the AU force in Somalia pushed al Shabab out of the capital, a terrible famine in 2011, caused by drought and war, gripped the al Shabab–held areas of the country and forced refugees into Kenya. In response, Kenya also sent military forces into Somalia to attack al Shabab. These invasions have weakened al Shabab, but it continues to attack targets within Somalia.

In Libya, the overthrow of dictator Muammar Gaddafi in 2011 (with NATO assistance) empowered armed Islamist groups that had formerly been repressed. They killed the U.S. ambassador in 2012, and they joined ethnic rebels from Mali, who had been fighting as mercenaries for Gaddafi, to seize northern Mali, using large quantities of weapons they had brought from Libya. The Islamists swept aside the ethnic rebels and took power for themselves, but by 2013, a military intervention by France and neighboring African countries ousted them to return control to the government of Mali.

In the West African country of Nigeria, an Islamist group known as Boko Haram has attacked government officials and civilians since 2009. Most notably, the group attacked several girls' schools in 2014, taking young girls hostages in each attack. The Nigerian government has declared a state of emergency and has deployed thousands of troops to the northern provinces, where the group is strongest.

In Palestine, the radical Islamist faction Hamas is another important Sunni Islamist militia, although it is not connected with al Qaeda or the Taliban. Centered in the Gaza Strip, Hamas sent suicide bombers who killed hundreds of Israelis after 2000, then won free parliamentary elections in 2006 because it was seen as less corrupt than the dominant party. Palestine remains divided, however, with the Palestinian Authority controlling the West Bank and Hamas controlling Gaza.

The two great powers to face Islamist violence within their borders are Russia in its far south and China in its far west. The predominantly Sunni Muslim republic of Chechnya, a Russian province, tried to split away from Russia in the early 1990s after the Soviet Union collapsed. After destructive wars in 1994–1995 and 1999–2000, the threat abated, although Chechen guerrillas then turned to airline hijackings, hostage taking, and suicide bombings. In 2004, hundreds of children died after Chechen terrorists took over a school and held them hostage. In 2005, Russian forces killed the Chechen separatist leader they held responsible, and political violence in Chechnya has since been sporadic.

Overall, conflicts involving Islamist movements are more complex than simply religious conflicts; they concern power, economic relations, ethnic chauvinism, and the effects of historical empires as well.

5.2.5 Ideological Conflict

To a large extent, ideology is like religion: It symbolizes and intensifies conflicts between groups and states more than it causes them. Ideologies have a somewhat weaker hold on core values and absolute truth than religions do, so they pose somewhat fewer problems for the international system.

For realists, ideological differences among states do not matter much because all members of the international system pursue their national interests in the context of relatively fluid alliances. For example, the Cold War was a global ideological struggle between capitalist democracy and communism. But the alliances and military competitions in that struggle were fairly detached from ideological factors. The two communist giants—the Soviet Union and China—did not stay together very long. India, a democracy and capitalist country, chose not to ally with the United States. And even the two great rival superpowers managed to live within the rules of the international system for the most part (for example, both remained UN members).

Over the long run, even countries that experience revolutions based on strong ideologies tend to lose their ideological fervor—be it Iran's Islamic fundamentalism in 1979, China's Maoist communism in 1949, Russia's Leninist communism in 1917, or even U.S. democracy in 1776. In each case, the revolutionaries expected that their assumption of power would dramatically alter their state's foreign policy because in each case their ideology had profound international implications. Yet within a few decades, each of these revolutionary governments turned to the pursuit of national interests above ideological ones.

Sometimes even self-proclaimed ideological struggles are not really ideological. In Angola in the 1980s, the United States backed a rebel army called UNITA against a Soviet-aligned government—supposedly a struggle of democracy against Marxism. In truth, the ideological differences were quite arbitrary. The government mouthed Marxist rhetoric to get the Soviet Union to give it aid

Mark Ralston/AFP/Getty Images

IDEOLOGICAL SPLIT Ideology plays only a limited role in most international conflicts. After revolutions, ideologies such as Marxism may affect foreign policy, but over the following decades, countries such as China or the Soviet Union typically revert to a foreign policy based more on national interests than ideology. Nonetheless, ideological clashes still occur, as between the freedom-loving United States and authoritarian North Korea. Here, the different styles of the two countries are on display as the New York Philharmonic performs a rare concert in North Korea, 2008.

(a policy it reversed as soon as Soviet aid dried up). The rebels who used democratic rhetoric to get U.S. support had earlier received Chinese support and mouthed Maoist rhetoric. When the government won UN-sponsored elections, the "democratic" UNITA refused to accept the results and resumed fighting. This conflict, which finally ended in 2002, really had nothing to do with ideology. It was a power struggle between two armed, ethnically based factions fighting to control Angola's oil, diamonds, and other wealth.

In the short term, revolutions *do* change international relations—they make wars more likely—but not because of ideology. Rather, the sudden change of governments can alter alliances and change the balance of power. With calculations of power being revised by all parties, it is easy to miscalculate or to exaggerate threats on both sides. But ideology itself plays little role in this postrevolutionary propensity for wars. Revolutions are seldom exported to other states.

5.3 Conflicts of Interest

Summarize two different international territorial disputes and evaluate the prospects for their peaceful settlement.

If conflicts of ideas can be intractable because of psychological and emotional factors, conflicts about material interests are somewhat easier to settle based on the reciprocity principle. In theory, given enough positive leverage—a payment in some form—any state should agree to another state's terms on a disputed issue.

5.3.1 Territorial Disputes

Among the international conflicts that concern tangible "goods," those about territory have special importance because of the territorial nature of the state (see Anarchy and Sovereignty in Chapter 2). Conflicts over control of territory are really of two varieties: territorial disputes (about where borders are drawn) and conflicts over control of entire states within existing borders (discussed next under Control of Governments). Consider first differences over where borders between two states should be drawn— that is, who controls a disputed piece of land.

Because states value home territory with an almost fanatical devotion, border disputes tend to be among the most intractable in IR. States seldom yield territory in exchange for money or any other positive reward. Nor do states quickly forget territory that they have lost involuntarily. For example, in 2002, Bolivian public opinion opposed a gas export pipeline through Chile to the sea because Chile had seized the coastline from Bolivia in 1879. The goal of regaining territory lost to another state is called **irredentism**. This form of nationalism often leads directly to serious interstate conflicts. Because of their association with the integrity of states, territories are valued far beyond any inherent economic or strategic value they hold. For example, after Israel and Egypt made peace in 1978, it took them a decade to settle a border dispute at Taba, a tiny plot of beachfront on which Israeli developers had built a hotel just slightly across the old border. The two states finally submitted the issue for binding arbitration, and Egypt ended up in possession. For Egypt, regaining every inch of territory was a matter of national honor and a symbol of the sovereignty and territorial integrity that defined Egyptian statehood.

The value states place on home territory seems undiminished despite the apparent reduction in the inherent value of territory as technology has developed. Historically, territory was the basis of economic production—agriculture and the extraction of raw materials. Winning and losing wars meant gaining or losing territory, which meant increasing or decreasing wealth. Today, however, much more wealth derives from trade and technology than from agriculture. The costs of most territorial disputes

irredentism A form of nationalism whose goal is to regain territory lost to another state; it can lead directly to violent interstate conflicts.

appear to outweigh any economic benefits that the territory in question could provide. Exceptions exist, however, such as the capture of diamond-mining areas in several African countries by rebels who use the diamond revenues to finance war. In 2002, 40 states created a program of UN certification for legitimate diamonds, trying to keep the "conflict diamonds" off the international market. Today, more than 80 countries participate in that program known as the Kimberley Process.

SECESSION   Efforts by a province or region to secede from an existing state are a special type of conflict over borders—not the borders of two existing states but the efforts to draw international borders around a new state. Dozens of secession movements exist around the world, of varying sizes and political effectiveness, but they succeed in seceding only rarely. The existing state almost always tries to hold on to the area in question. For example, in the 1990s, the predominantly Albanian population of the Serbian province of Kosovo fought a war to secede from Serbia. NATO intervention, including sustained bombing of Serbia (not approved by the UN), led to the withdrawal of Serbia's army from Kosovo and its replacement with European and American peacekeeping troops who have been there ever since. Most of the Kosovo population wants to secede and become an internationally recognized state, but Serbians argue that Kosovo is historically and presently under Serbian sovereignty. While the UN and the great powers negotiated over the future of Kosovo, with Russia insisting there be no promise of independence, Kosovars took matters into their own hands. In 2008, Kosovo declared independence without UN approval. Several countries, including the United States and the largest EU states, recognized Kosovo's independence, angering Serbia, Russia, and China. In 2011, South Sudan successfully gained independence, with UN membership and the support of Sudan.

Wars of secession can be large and deadly, and they can easily spill over international borders or draw in other countries. This spillover is particularly likely if members of an ethnic or a religious group span two sides of a border, constituting the majority group in one state and a majority in a nearby region of another state, but a minority in the other state as a whole. In the Kosovo case, Albanian Muslims are the majority in Albania and in Kosovo but the minority in Serbia. The same pattern occurs in Bosnia-Serbia, Moldova-Russia, and India-Pakistan. In some cases, secessionists want to merge their territories with the neighboring state, which amounts to redrawing the international border. International norms frown on such an outcome.

The strong international norms of sovereignty and territorial integrity treat secession movements as domestic problems of little concern to other states. The general principle seems to be this: "We existing states all have our own domestic problems and disaffected groups or regions, so we must stick together behind sovereignty and territorial integrity." Thus, Russia and China opposed the secession of Kosovo from Serbia because of its implications for Chechnya and Taiwan, respectively.

This principle does have limits, however. In August 2008, after fighting broke out

SHOULD I STAY OR SHOULD I GO? Efforts by a region to secede from a state are a frequent source of international conflict, but international norms generally treat such conflicts as internal matters unless they spill over borders. Here, pro-independence advocates hold a rally in Barcelona in the Catalonia region of Spain, which voted to become independent in a 2017 referendum. Spain has refused to acknowledge Catalonian claims of independence, declaring the referendum illegal.

Davide Bonaldo / Alamy Stock Photo

between the Georgian military and the Georgian province of South Ossetia, Russia intervened militarily on behalf of South Ossetia and Abkhazia, resulting in a brief war between Russia and Georgia. Russia then recognized both Georgian provinces as independent, a move denounced by the United States and the EU and not accepted by the UN.

Messy border problems can result when multinational states break up into pieces. In such cases, borders that had been internal become international; because these borders are new, they may be more vulnerable to challenge. In the former Yugoslavia, ethnic groups had intermingled and intermarried, leaving mixed populations in most of the Yugoslav republics. When Yugoslavia broke up in 1991–1992, several republics declared their independence as separate states. Two of these, Croatia and Bosnia, contained minority populations of ethnic Serbs. Serbia seized effective control of significant areas of Croatia and Bosnia that contained Serbian communities or linked such populations geographically. Non-Serbian populations in these areas were driven out or massacred—euphemistically called **ethnic cleansing**. Then, when Croatia reconquered most of its territory in 1995, Serbian populations in turn fled. Ethnic nationalism, whipped up by opportunistic politicians, proved stronger than multiethnic tolerance in both Serbia and Croatia.

The breakup of a state need not lead to violence, however. Serbia split peacefully from Montenegro (another of the former Yugoslav republics) in 2006. Czechoslovakia split into the Czech Republic and Slovakia in a cooperative manner. And the breakup of the Soviet Union did not lead to violent territorial disputes between republics in *most* cases, even when ethnic groups spanned new international borders.

The norm against forceful redrawing of borders does not apply to cases of decolonization. International norms protect only the territorial integrity of existing, recognized states. Colonies and other territorial possessions historically had value only as property to be won, lost, sold, or traded in political deals and wars. The transfer of Hong Kong from British to Chinese control in 1997 also illustrates how colonial territory is dispensable (Britain's perspective) while home territory is nearly sacred (China's perspective). The views of the inhabitants do not carry much weight from either perspective.

Increasingly, autonomy for a region has become a realistic compromise between secession and full control by a central government. In 2005, spurred partly by the devastating tsunami a year earlier, separatists in the Aceh province of Indonesia disbanded, giving up on independence and instead participating in regional elections in 2006. The Indonesian government withdrew its 24,000 troops from Aceh and offered the province limited self-rule along with 70 percent of the oil, gas, and mineral wealth earned there.

INTERSTATE BORDERS   Border disputes between existing states are taken more seriously by the international community but are less common than secessionist conflicts. Because of the norm of territorial integrity, few important border conflicts remain among long-established states. At one time, huge chunks of territory passed between states at the stroke of a pen (on a peace treaty or marriage contract). However, this kind of wholesale redrawing of borders has not occurred among established states for 70 years. Since the end of World War II, only a minuscule amount of territory has changed hands between established states through force (this does not apply to the formation of new states and the fragmenting of old ones). Such efforts have been made but have failed. For instance, when Iraq attacked Iran in 1980, one objective was to control the Shatt al Arab waterway (with access to the Persian Gulf) because of its commercial and strategic value. But ten years and a million deaths later, the Iran-Iraq border was back where it had started.

Furthermore, when territorial disputes do occur between established states, they *can* be settled peacefully, especially when the disputed territory is small compared with the states disputing it. In 1994, a panel of Latin American judges settled a century-long border dispute between Argentina and Chile over some mountainous terrain that both claimed. The 3-to-2 ruling, after the countries submitted the dispute for judicial arbitration, awarded the territory to Argentina and provoked howls of protest from Chile—and even a hair-pulling fight between the Chilean and Argentine contestants in the Miss World beauty contest two months later. But despite the strong

ethnic cleansing Euphemism for forced displacement of an ethnic group or groups from a territory, accompanied by massacres and other human rights violations; it has occurred after the breakup of multinational states, notably in the former Yugoslavia.

feelings evoked by the loss of territory, Argentina and Chile settled 22 of 24 remaining border disputes peacefully after nearly going to war in 1978 over disputed islands.

The possibility of peaceful resolution of territorial disputes was highlighted in 2006 with the withdrawal of Nigerian troops from the potentially oil-rich Bakassi Peninsula, which Nigeria ceded to Cameroon's sovereignty. The resolution of the dispute, dating from colonial times, followed more than a decade of painstaking progress through the World Court, the personal mediation of the UN Secretary General when Nigeria initially rejected the Court's decision, and the promise of outside powers to monitor implementation of the agreement. Why would Nigeria—a country with nine times Cameroon's population, more than triple its gross domestic product (GDP), and a much stronger military—voluntarily cede territory? Doing so would seem to run counter to the predictions of realism in particular and the dominance principle in general. Liberal theories would do better at explaining this outcome: Nigeria acted in its own self-interest because turning the dispute over to the World Court and bringing in the UN to assist with implementation brought the kind of stability needed for foreign investment to develop Nigeria's own resources, primarily oil.

LINGERING DISPUTES   Today, the few remaining interstate border disputes generate important international conflicts. Among the most difficult are the borders of *Israel*. The 1948 cease-fire lines resulting from Israel's war of independence expanded in the 1967 war. Israel returned the Sinai Peninsula to Egypt, but the remaining territories occupied in 1967—the *West Bank* near Jordan, the *Gaza Strip* near Egypt, and the *Golan Heights* of Syria—are central to the Arab-Israeli conflict. In particular, Israel's ongoing construction of Jewish settlements in the West Bank, bitterly opposed by Palestinians and considered illegal by most international actors, remains a contentious sticking point. Israeli-Palestinian agreements since 1993 tried to move toward Palestinian autonomy in parts of the West Bank and Gaza, and negotiations seemed headed toward creation of a state of Palestine there. However, that effort completely stalled in the twenty-first century, notwithstanding the 2012 upgrading of Palestine's UN status to nonmember "state," a symbolic gesture.

Another serious border dispute is in the *Kashmir* area where India, Pakistan, and China intersect. The Indian-held part of Kashmir is predominantly inhabited by Muslims, a group that is the majority in Pakistan but a minority in India. A *Line of Control* divides the disputed province. Pakistan accuses India of oppressing Kashmiris and thwarting an international agreement to decide Kashmir's future by a popular referendum. India accuses Pakistan of aiding and infiltrating Islamic radicals who carry out attacks in Indian-occupied Kashmir. The two countries went to war twice over the issue, and nearly did so again in 2002—that time armed with nuclear-armed missiles. A cease-fire took hold in 2003 and stopped most of the incessant low-level fighting along the Line of Control, although violent skirmishes continue, with some of the worst fighting in years occurring since 2014.

Many of the world's other remaining interstate territorial disputes—and often the most serious ones—concern the control of small islands, which often provide strategic advantages, natural resources (such as offshore oil), or fishing rights. International law now gives an island's owner fishing and mineral rights in surrounding seas for 200 miles in each direction. The tiny disputed *Spratly Islands* in the South China Sea, whose surrounding waters may hold substantial oil reserves, are claimed in part or in full by China, Taiwan, Vietnam, the Philippines, Malaysia, and Brunei (see Figure 5.6). All of those states except Brunei have resorted to military actions at times to stake their claims. About half of the

Figure 5.6 Disputed Islands

The Spratly Islands exemplify contemporary conflicts over territory and natural resources around islands. All or part of the Spratlys are claimed by China, Vietnam, Malaysia, Brunei, the Philippines, and Taiwan.

Bullit Marquez / AP Images

UP FROM THE DEPTHS The Spratly Island chain in the South China Sea is the source of significant political and military tension in Asia. Recently, China has begun to build larger islands on smaller reefs in order to place military forces on those islands. Here, a photo of human-made Subi Reef, taken in 2017, shows a significant Chinese military presence, including an airstrip.

world's trade tonnage passes through the South China Sea, including Persian Gulf oil and other key resources headed for Japan, China, South Korea, and Taiwan.

Recently, China has undertaken a significant buildup of military forces on several small islands and reefs in the Spratly Islands. It has also dredged up material to make the islands larger, which allows the Chinese military to build large airstrips and bases. Nearby states protest this construction since the ownership of some of these islands and reefs is still a point of contention. The U.S. Navy frequently sails near these islands to protest Chinese activity, which China claims is a violation of its sovereignty.

Japan and China also dispute tiny islands elsewhere, as do Japan and South Korea. These disputes involve low economic stakes, but they have become a focus of nationalist sentiments on both sides, fueled partly by memories of World War II, when Japan occupied China and Korea. The most serious is over small islands in the East China Sea that Japan controls but China claims and would give Chinese submarines a clear route to the Pacific. The two navies and air forces have confronted each other there repeatedly, though without violence. In 2015, Japan deployed its largest naval vessel (a helicopter carrier) since World War II to patrol the area. In 2017, China sailed naval vessels very close to the disputed islands—bringing protests and threats from Japan.

A number of smaller island conflicts exist around the globe. In the Middle East, Iran and the United Arab Emirates dispute ownership of small islands near the mouth of the Persian Gulf. In 2002, Spain sent soldiers to oust a handful of Moroccan troops from islands off Morocco's coast. In South America, Argentina and Britain still dispute control of the *Falkland Islands* (*Islas Malvinas*), over which they fought a war in 1982. And the major bone of contention in Russian-Japanese relations is the ownership of the strategically located *Kuril Islands*, occupied by the Soviet Union in 1945. With islands now bringing control of surrounding economic zones, international conflicts over islands will undoubtedly continue in the coming years.

territorial waters The waters near states' shores generally treated as part of national territory. The UN Convention on the Law of the Sea provides for a 12-mile territorial sea (exclusive national jurisdiction over shipping and navigation) and a 200-mile exclusive economic zone (EEZ; covering exclusive fishing and mineral rights but allowing for free navigation by all). See also *high seas* and *UN Convention on the Law of the Sea* (*UNCLOS*).

TERRITORIAL WATERS States treat **territorial waters** near their shores as part of their national territory. Definitions of such waters are not universally agreed upon, but norms have developed in recent years, especially since the *UN Convention on the Law of the Sea* (*UNCLOS*) (see Chapter 11). Waters within three miles of shore have traditionally been recognized as territorial, but beyond that there are disputes about how far out national sovereignty extends and for what purposes. UNCLOS generally allows a 12-mile limit for shipping and a 200-mile *exclusive economic zone* (*EEZ*) covering fishing and mineral rights (but allowing for free navigation by all). The EEZs together cover a third of the world's oceans. In 2010, Russia and Norway agreed to divide portions of the Arctic Ocean into EEZs for the purposes of oil and gas extraction, ending a 40-year dispute between those states.

Because of the EEZs, sovereignty over a single tiny island can now bring with it rights to as much as 100,000 square miles of surrounding ocean. But these zones overlap greatly, and shorelines do not run in straight lines; thus numerous questions of interpretation arise about how to delineate territorial and economic waters. For example, Libya claims ownership of the entire Gulf of Sidra, treating it as a bay; the United States treats it as a curvature in the shoreline and insists that most of it is international waters. In 1986, the United States sent warships into the Gulf of Sidra to make its point. U.S. planes shot down two Libyan jets that challenged the U.S. maneuvers.

Canada in 1994–1995 sent its navy to harass Spanish fishing boats just *beyond* the 200-mile zone (but affecting fish stocks within the zone). In the Sea of Okhotsk, which is a little more than 400 miles across, Russia's EEZ includes all but a small "doughnut hole" of international waters in the middle. Non-Russian boats have fished intensively in the "hole," which of course depletes fish stocks in Russia's EEZ.

A dangerous maritime dispute flared in 2010 when a South Korean warship sank in disputed waters in the Yellow Sea. International investigators concluded that a North Korean torpedo sank the vessel, although North Korea denied involvement. South Korea continues to conduct military operations in the disputed waters, while North Korea continues to fire artillery shells in the area, including an attack that killed several civilians in 2010. The two countries have never formally ended the Korean War by signing a peace treaty.

AIRSPACE **Airspace** above a state is considered the territory of the state. To fly over a state's territory, an airplane must have that state's permission. For example, in a 1986 raid on Libya, U.S. bombers based in Britain had to fly a long detour over the Atlantic Ocean because France (between Britain and Libya) would not grant permission for U.S. planes to use its airspace during the mission.

Outer space, by contrast, is considered international territory like the oceans. International law does not define exactly where airspace ends and outer space begins. However, orbiting satellites fly higher than airplanes, move very fast, and cannot easily change direction to avoid overflying a country. Also, very few states can shoot down satellites. Because satellites have become useful to all the great powers as intelligence-gathering tools, and because all satellites are extremely vulnerable to attack, a norm of demilitarization of outer space has developed. No state has ever attacked the satellite of another. In 2007, however, China rattled nerves by successfully destroying one of its own satellites with an anti-satellite missile, strewing high-speed debris around orbital space.

Masanori Genko/AP Images

LOCATION, LOCATION, LOCATION Control of islands, and of the large exclusive economic zone (EEZ) that surrounds them under the law of the sea, has created a number of complicated interstate conflicts. Japan claims Okinotori, shown here in 2014, as an island with an EEZ, but China calls it merely a "rock" without surrounding economic rights.

airspace The space above a state that is considered its territory, in contrast to outer space, which is considered international territory.

5.3.2 Control of Governments

Despite the many minor border disputes that continue to plague the world, most struggles to control territory do not involve changing borders. Rather, they are conflicts over which governments will control entire states.

In theory, states do not interfere in each other's governance because of the norm of sovereignty. In practice, however, states often have strong interests in the governments of other states and use a variety of means of leverage to influence who holds power in those states. These conflicts over governments take many forms, some mild and some severe, some deeply entwined with third parties, and some more or less bilateral. Sometimes a state merely exerts subtle influences on another state's elections; at other times, a state supports rebel elements seeking to overthrow the second state's government.

During the Cold War, both superpowers actively promoted changes of government in countries of the global South through covert operations and support of rebel armies. The civil wars in Angola, Afghanistan, and Nicaragua are good examples. Both superpowers poured in weapons, money, military advisers, and so forth—all in hopes of influencing who controlled the country's government.

In 2004–2005, shadows of these old Cold War rivalries fell over Ukraine, as Russia and the West backed opposite sides in a disputed election. The election divided the largely Russian-speaking, Eastern Orthodox part of Ukraine to the east from the Ukrainian-speaking, Catholic western part of the country. The pro-Russian incumbent carried the eastern region and was declared the winner after an election that international monitors declared unsound. Russian president Vladimir Putin had personally campaigned with the incumbent and strongly opposed letting Ukraine—a former part of the Soviet Union—come under the influence of the West. Meanwhile, the pro-Western candidate was poisoned during the campaign but survived. His supporters took to the streets in late 2004 demanding new elections, which the top Ukrainian court eventually ordered and which the opposition won.

A more serious and deadly dispute erupted in 2013–2014, when Ukraine's then pro-Russian president cracked down on pro-Western protesters. Opposition forces succeeded in forcing the president to resign, but his supporters in eastern Ukraine, aided by Russia, took up arms against the new pro-Western government. Meanwhile, Russia annexed the Crimean peninsula, which it said desired to reunite with Russia. By 2018, although there were no major battles taking place between Russian-aided rebels and the Ukrainian military, multiple cease-fires had failed, and there is no end to the violence in sight.

Occasionally, one state invades another in order to change its government. The Soviet Union did this in Czechoslovakia in 1968; the United States did so in Iraq in 2003. People generally resent having foreigners choose their government for them—even if they did not like the old government—and the international community frowns on such overt violations of national sovereignty.

International conflicts over the control of governments—along with territorial disputes—are likely to lead to the use of violence. They involve core issues of the status and integrity of states, the stakes tend to be high, and the interests of involved actors are often diametrically opposed. By contrast, economic conflicts among states are more common but far less likely to lead to violence.

5.3.3 Economic Conflict

Economic competition is the most pervasive form of conflict in international relations because economic transactions are pervasive. Every sale made and every deal reached across international borders entails a resolution of conflicting interests. Costa Rica wants the price of coffee, which it exports, to go up; Canada, which imports coffee, wants the price to go down. Angola wants foreign producers of Angolan oil to receive fewer profits from oil sales; those companies' home states want them to take home more profits. In a global capitalist market, all economic exchanges involve some conflict of interest.

However, such economic transactions also contain a strong element of mutual economic gain in addition to the element of conflicting interests (see Chapters 3 and 8). These mutual gains provide the most useful leverage in bargaining over economic exchanges: States and companies enter into economic transactions because they profit from doing so. The use of violence would, for the most part, interrupt and diminish such profit by more than could be gained as a result of the use of violence. Thus, economic conflicts do not usually lead to military force and war.

Economic conflicts seldom lead to violence today because military forms of leverage are no longer very effective in resolving them. With the tight integration of the world economy and the high cost of military actions, the use of force is seldom justified to solve an economic issue. Even if an agreement is not ideal for one side in an economic conflict, rarely is what can be gained by military force worth the cost of war. Thus, most economic conflicts are not issues of international security; they are discussed in Chapters 8 through 13 (on international political economy). But economic conflicts do still bear on international security in some ways.

First, many states' foreign policies are influenced by *mercantilism*—a practice of centuries past in which trade and foreign economic policies were manipulated to build up a monetary surplus that could be used to finance war (see Liberalism and Mercantilism in Chapter 8). Because a trade surplus confers an advantage in international security affairs over the long run, trade conflicts have implications for international security relations.

(2) Second, the theory of *lateral pressure* also connects economic competition with security concerns. This theory holds that the economic growth of states leads to geographic expansion as they seek natural resources beyond their borders (by various means, peaceful and violent). As great powers expand their economic activities outward, their competition with other states leads to conflicts and sometimes to war. Scholars have used the theory to help explain both World War I and the expansion of Japan prior to World War II.

Another kind of economic conflict that affects international security concerns *military industry*—the capacity to produce military equipment, especially high-technology weapons such as fighter aircraft or missiles. There is a world trade in such items, but national governments try (not always successfully) to keep control of such production—to try to ensure that national interests take priority over those of manufacturers and that the state is militarily self-sufficient in case of war. Economic competition (over who profits from such sales) is interwoven with security concerns (over who gets access to the weapons). In 2009, proponents of a bailout for the U.S. automobile industry argued that the industry could provide vital production capacity in a time of war, as it had during World War II. The transfer of knowledge about high-tech weaponry and military technologies to potentially hostile states is a related concern.

A different kind of economic conflict revolves around the distribution of wealth within and among states. As discussed in Chapter 12, the tremendous disparities in wealth in our world create a variety of international security problems with the potential for violence—including terrorist attacks on rich countries by groups in poor countries. Revolutions in poor countries are often fueled by disparities of wealth within the country as well as its poverty relative to that of other countries. These revolutions in turn frequently draw in other states as supporters of one side or the other in a civil war.

Marxist approaches to international relations, discussed in Chapters 4 and 12, treat class struggle between rich and poor people as the basis of interstate relations. According to these approaches, capitalist states adopt foreign policies that serve the interests of the rich owners of companies. Conflicts and wars between the global North and South—rich states versus poor states—are seen as reflections of the domination and exploitation of the poor by the rich—imperialism in direct or indirect form. For example, most Marxists saw the Vietnam War as a U.S. effort to suppress revolution in order to secure continued U.S. access to cheap labor and raw materials in Southeast Asia. Many Marxists portray conflicts among capitalist states as competition over the right to exploit poor areas. Soviet founder V. I. Lenin portrayed World War I as a fight over the imperialists' division of the world.

DRUG TRAFFICKING As a form of illegal trade across international borders, drug trafficking is smuggling, which deprives states of revenue and violates states' legal control of their borders. But smuggling in general is an economic issue rather than a security one (see illicit trade in Chapter 8). Unlike other smuggling operations, however, drug trafficking supplies illegal products that are treated as a security threat because of their effect on national (and military) morale and efficiency. Drug trafficking also has become linked with security concerns because military forces participate regularly in operations against the

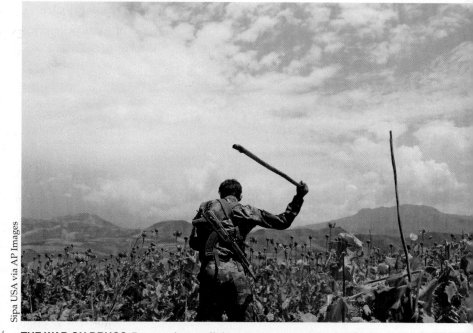

THE WAR ON DRUGS Because drug trafficking crosses national borders and involves lots of guns and money, it is a source of interstate conflict. Afghanistan supplies most of the opium used to make heroin worldwide, and this illicit trade funds the Taliban in its fight against NATO and the Afghan government. Here, Afghan police destroy a poppy field, 2017.

heavily armed drug traffickers. Conflicts over drugs generally concern states on one side and nonstate actors on the other. But other states can be drawn in because the activities in question cross national borders and may involve corrupt state officials.

These international ramifications are evident in the efforts of the U.S. government to prevent *cocaine cartels* based in Colombia from supplying cocaine to U.S. cities. Such cocaine derives mostly from coca plants grown by peasants in mountainous areas of Peru, Bolivia, and Colombia itself. Processed in simple laboratories in the jungle, the cocaine moves from Colombia through other countries such as Panama before arriving in the United States. In each of these countries (even the United States), the drug smugglers have bribed some corrupt officials, including military or police officers, to stay clear. But other state officials in each country are working with U.S. law enforcement agencies and the U.S. military to crack down on the cocaine trade. In 2005, Bolivians elected as president an anti-American former coca farmer who supports farming coca though not the production of cocaine.

Segments of the populations in several of these countries, especially in cocaine-producing regions, benefit substantially from the drug trade. For poor peasants, the cocaine trade may be their only access to a decent income. More important for international security, rebel armies can fund their operations primarily through control of the trade in illicit drugs. Afghanistan, the central front in the West's struggle against Islamist extremism (specifically the Taliban), supplies most of the raw material for heroin in the world. In Mexico, a major supplier of illegal drugs to the next-door United States, deadly violence among drug gangs has spiraled out of control in the past decades, claiming tens of thousands of lives.

In Latin America, the long history of U.S. military intervention makes state cooperation with U.S. military forces a sensitive political issue. In some countries, governments have faced popular criticism for allowing the "Yankees" to "invade" in the drug war. In one case, the U.S. military literally invaded. In 1989, U.S. forces invaded Panama; arrested its leader, dictator Manuel Noriega; and convicted him in U.S. courts of complicity in drug trafficking through Panama.

Just as there are many possible outcomes of conflict, many types of war, and varied propensities for violence among different states, so too is there great diversity in how force is used if conflict leads to violence. States develop a wide array of military forces, which vary tremendously in their purposes and capabilities. These military forces are the focus of the next chapter.

Chapter Review

Summary

- When violent means are used as leverage in international conflicts, a variety of types of war results. These vary greatly in size and character, from guerrilla wars and raids to hegemonic war for leadership of the international system. Along this spectrum of uses of violence, the exact definition of war is uncertain.

- Many theories have been offered as general explanations about when such forms of leverage come into play—the causes of war. Contradictory theories have been proposed at each level of analysis and, with two exceptions, none has strong empirical support. Thus, political scientists cannot reliably predict the outbreak of war.

- Nationalism strongly influences IR; conflict often results from the perception of nationhood, leading to demands for statehood or for the adjustment of state borders.

- Ethnic conflicts, especially when linked with territorial disputes, are very difficult to resolve because of psychological biases. It is hard to explain why people's loyalties are sometimes to their ethnic group and sometimes to a multiethnic nation.

- Fundamentalist religious movements pose a broad challenge to the rules of the international system in general and to state sovereignty in particular.

- Ideologies do not matter very much in international relations, with the possible exception of democracy as an ideology. State leaders can use ideologies to justify whatever actions are in their interests.

- Territorial disputes are among the most serious international conflicts because states place great value on territorial integrity. With a few exceptions, however, almost all the world's borders are now firmly fixed and internationally recognized.

- Conflicts over the control of entire states (through control of governments) are also serious and are relatively likely to lead to the use of force.

- Economic conflicts lead to violence much less often because positive gains from economic activities are more effective inducements than negative threats of violence.

Key Terms

hegemonic war   137
total war   137
limited war   137
civil war   139
guerrilla war   139
truth commissions   140
conflict   140

cycle theories   143
nationalism   144
ethnic groups   145
ethnocentrism   147
dehumanization   147
genocide   149
secular   151

Islam/Muslims   151
Islamist   151
irredentism   160
ethnic cleansing   162
territorial waters   164
airspace   165

Critical Thinking Questions

1. Given the definitions of war provided at the beginning of the chapter, name two current international situations that clearly fit the definition of war and two that are ambiguous "quasi-wars" (almost but not quite fitting the definition). Which do you think are more serious, the wars or the quasi-wars? Do they involve different types of actors? Different kinds of conflicts? Different capabilities?

2. European textbooks were revised after World War II to reduce ethnic and national stereotypes and to give a fairer portrayal of Europe's various nations. What about the textbooks you used to learn your country's history? Did they give an accurate picture, or did they overstate the virtues of your own ethnic group or nation at the expense of others? How?

3. The rise of fundamentalism among the world's major religions challenges traditional notions of state sovereignty. How might this trend strengthen, or weaken, the United Nations and other attempts to create supranational authority (which also challenges state sovereignty)?

4. Suppose that you were the mediator in negotiations between two states, each claiming the same piece of land. What principles could you follow in developing a mutually acceptable plan for ownership of the territory? What means could you use to persuade the two states to accept your plan?

5. How many of the six types of international conflicts discussed in this chapter can you connect with the phenomenon of *nationalism*, as it is defined in this chapter? What are the connections in each case?

Suggested Readings

Horowitz, Donald L. *Ethnic Groups in Conflict*. 2nd ed. California, 2000.

Kalyvas, Stathis N. *The Logic of Violence in Civil War*. Cambridge, 2006.

Saunders, Elizabeth. *Leaders at War: How Presidents Shape Military Interventions*. Cornell, 2014.

Straus, Scott. *Making and Unmaking Nations: War, Leadership, and Genocide in Modern Africa*. Cornell, 2015.

Van Evera, Stephen. *Causes of War: Power and the Roots of Conflict*. Cornell, 1999.

Waltz, Kenneth N. *Man, the State, and War: A Theoretical Analysis*. Columbia, 2001.

Weeks, Jessica L. P. *Dictators at War and Peace*. Cornell, 2014.

Let's Debate the Issue

The United States and Russia: A New Cold War?

Overview

When the Cold War ended (a process starting in 1989 and ending in 1991), observers hoped for a new age of U.S.-Russian cooperation. Initially, all signs pointed to a healthy relationship between these superpowers: They worked together to secure Russian nuclear weapons, cooperated to stabilize the Russian economy, and reached an understanding to allow NATO expansion to some former Warsaw Pact members.

Lately, however, relations have taken a turn for the worse. As NATO has enlarged, Russia has objected to further expansion. The United States has arrested several high-profile spies who were continuing to operate in America long after the end of the Cold War. American withdrawal from the Anti-Ballistic Missile Treaty in 2001 spurred Russian fears that the United States would engage in another arms race. During the lead-up to the 2003 Iraq War, Russia consistently opposed American efforts to gain UN Security Council approval, threatening to veto any resolution proposed by the United States. In 2008, Russia fought a war against Georgia, a U.S. ally. In 2014, Russia annexed the Crimea from Ukraine, then supported rebel groups fighting against the government in eastern Ukraine. In response, the United States placed significant sanctions against Russia. Russia has also been accused of attempting to meddle in the 2016 U.S. presidential election. Needless to say, the friendship has cooled considerably. Although no one believes Russia and the United States will engage in war with each other, many do wonder whether a new Cold War will emerge between these former rivals. What are the prospects for a new Cold War emerging between these great powers?

ARGUMENT 1

A New Cold War Will Emerge Between the United States and Russia

Russia and the United States have major differences in key policy areas. On several important issues, Russia and the United States do not see eye to eye. In particular, the United States is committed to NATO expansion, which Russia considers a direct threat to its security. In addition, the United States is committed to deploying antiballistic missiles in Europe, which Russia opposes.

Russian democracy is weak. Democracy in Russia is imperfect at best, creating additional tensions with the United States. Opposition leaders are jailed or shot, corruption is extensive, and the press is threatened when it investigates wrongdoing. The United States now spends significant resources funding pro-democracy programs in Russia's neighbors, which angers Russian leaders.

Russia reaches out to U.S. enemies and confronts U.S. allies. Russia has recently conducted joint military exercises with Venezuela and has a cordial relationship with Iran. Russia has gone to war with Georgia over disputed territory, and annexed portions of Ukraine while aiding rebels there. Both Georgia and Ukraine are strong American allies.

ARGUMENT 2

No New Cold War Will Emerge Between the United States and Russia

Russia depends on Western acceptance. Russia greatly values its membership in key IGOs such as the World Bank and the International Monetary Fund (IMF). It also covets membership in the World Trade Organization (WTO), which it hopes to join. Russia will not pursue policies that threaten these relationships.

There are no major ideological differences between the United States and Russia. Unlike during the Cold War, there are no major ideological divides between these two great powers. While Russian democracy may be imperfect, Russia is unlikely to embrace communism anew or abandon its experiment with capitalism. Where their interests converge, as in the war against Islamic extremists in Afghanistan, U.S.-Russian cooperation works smoothly.

Europe will help keep tensions low. During the Cold War, Europe was divided into two camps, each supported by one of the superpowers. Now, Europe is united and can serve as a mediator between the United States and Russia. Europe has strong economic and political interests in continued cooperation with both sides and will work to ensure that tensions do not spiral out of control.

Questions

- Are Russia and the United States headed for a second Cold War? What issues are likely to continue to exacerbate tensions between these two states? Are there issues of common interest that may unite them?

- Would steps to better relations with Russia, such as ending efforts to deploy a missile shield, make relations with some European allies (for example, Poland or Ukraine) more difficult? Will the United States have to choose between improving relations with Russia and honoring its promises to European allies?

- How important is it for Russia to remain democratic to keep tensions low between it and the United States? How would the different IR theories answer this question? Do Russia's attempts at democracy explain differences in American perceptions of the danger from Russia as opposed to the danger from China?

For Further Reading

Gessen, Masha. *The Future Is History: How Totalitarianism Reclaimed Russia.* Penguin, 2017.

Goldman, Marshall I. *Petrostate: Putin, Power, and the New Russia.* Oxford, 2008.

Levgold, Robert. *Return to Cold War.* Polity, 2016.

Lucas, Edward. *The New Cold War: Putin's Russia and the Threat to the West.* 3rd ed. St. Martin's, 2014.

Chapter 6
Military Force and Terrorism

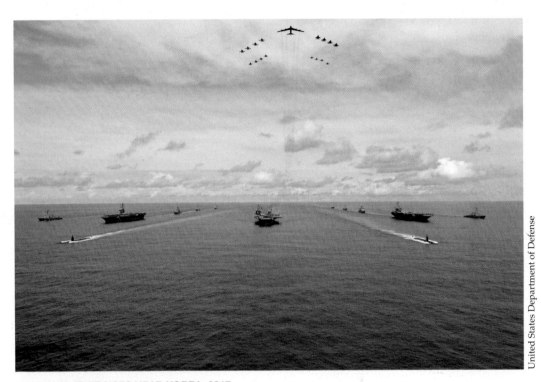

U.S. NAVAL EXERCISES NEAR KOREA, 2017.

⌄ Learning Objectives

6.1 Compare the trade-offs in the use of different instruments of leverage.

6.2 Evaluate the importance of new technologies in transforming the nature of war.

6.3 Assess potential advantages and disadvantages to two different approaches to counterterrorism.

6.4 Contrast the effectiveness of the global regime to prevent the spread of nuclear weapons with that of the global regime to prevent the spread of chemical weapons.

6.5 Explain how tensions in civil-military relations can undermine military operations and even threaten political stability.

6.1 Conventional Forces

Compare the trade-offs in the use of different instruments of leverage.

A state leader in a conflict can apply various kinds of leverage to influence the outcome of that conflict (see Figure 6.1). One set of levers represents nonviolent means of influencing other states, such as foreign aid, economic sanctions, and personal diplomacy (less tangible means include the use of norms, morality, and other ideas). A second set of levers—the subject of this chapter—represents violent actions. These levers set armies marching, suicide bombers blowing up, or missiles flying. They tend to be costly to both the attacker and the attacked. Military force tends to be a last resort. Evidence also shows that the utility of military force relative to nonmilitary means is slowly declining over time.

Yet most states still devote vast resources to military capabilities compared to other means of influence. For example, the United States has about 20,000 diplomatic personnel but roughly 1.3 million active-duty soldiers; it spends about $50 billion a year on foreign aid but about $600 billion on military forces and war (see the Public Opinion and International Relations feature). Because of the security dilemma (see Chapter 2), states believe they must devote large resources to military capabilities if other states are doing so.

Beyond defending their territories, states develop military capabilities for several other purposes. They often hope to *deter* attack by having the means to retaliate. They may also hope to *compel* other states to behave in certain ways, by threatening an attack if another state does not comply. States also use military forces for humanitarian assistance after disasters, for peacekeeping, for surveillance of drug trafficking, and for repression of domestic political dissent, among other missions. The sizes and types of military forces reflect these missions.

Great powers continue to dominate the makeup of world military forces. Table 6.1 summarizes the most important forces of the great powers. Together, they account for about 65 percent of world military spending, 30 percent of the world's soldiers, nearly 50 percent of conventional weapons, 97 percent of nuclear weapons, and 90 percent of arms exports. (The table also indicates the sizable military forces maintained by Germany and Japan despite their nontraditional roles in international security since World War II.)

Figure 6.1 Military and Nonmilitary Means of Leverage

Conventional armed force is the most commonly used military form of leverage.

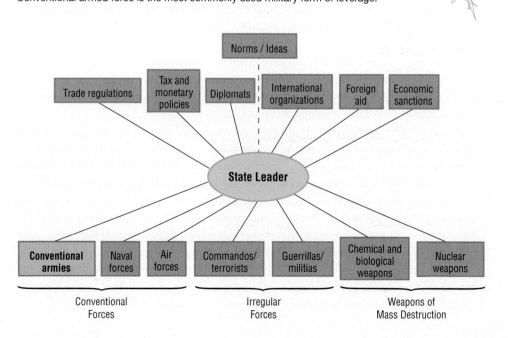

Table 6.1 Estimated Great Power Military Capabilities, 2017

| | Military Expenditures[a] (Billions of US $) | Active Duty Soldiers[b] (Millions) | Heavy Weapons[b] | | | Nuclear Weapons[c] | Arms Exported[a] (Billions of US $) |
			Tanks	Carriers/ Warships/ Submarines	Combat Airplanes / Heavy Drones		
United States	610	1.3	2,800	10 / 93 / 14	3,500 / 640	6,600	10
Russia	70	1.0	2,950	1 / 32 / 13	1,050 / 0	6,800	6
China	215	2.2	6,700	1 / 78 / 4	1,900 / 4	270	2
France	55	0.2	200	1 / 23 / 4	275 / 7	300	2
Britain	50	0.2	225	0 / 19 / 4	200 / 10	215	2
Germany	40	0.2	400	0 / 15 / 0	120 / 0	0	3
Japan	50	0.2	700	0 / 47 / 0	400 / 0	0	0
Approximate % of world total	65%	30%	70%	93 / 70 / 50%	40 / 90%	97%	90%

Problematic data: Russian and Chinese military expenditure estimates vary. U.S. and Russian nuclear warheads include deployed strategic weapons (1,800 U.S., 1,710 Russian) with the remainder held in reserve or retired (awaiting destruction).

Data on soldiers exclude reserves. Tanks include only post-1980 modern main battle tanks. Warships are cruisers, destroyers, and frigates. Submarines include ballistic-missile nuclear-powered units only. Airplanes are tactical fighters. Nuclear warheads include both strategic and tactical weapons. Arms exports are for orders placed, 2016.

Sources: Author's estimates based on data provided by the following sources:

[a]2017 data from Stockholm International Peace Research Institute.

[b]2017 data from International Institute for Strategic Studies. *The Military Balance 2017.*

[c]Federation of American Scientists data: for 2/1/2018.

Military capabilities divide into three types: conventional forces, irregular forces (terrorism, militias), and weapons of mass destruction (nuclear, chemical, and biological weapons).

6.1.1 Land Forces: Controlling Territory

Whatever their ultimate causes and objectives, most wars involve a struggle to *control territory.* Territory holds a central place in warfare because of its importance in the international system, and vice versa. Borders define where a state's own military forces and rival states' military forces are free to move. Military logistics makes territoriality all the more important because of the need to control territories connecting military forces with each other. An army's supplies must flow from home territory along *supply lines* to the field. Thus, the most fundamental purpose of conventional forces is to take, hold, or defend territory.

Armies are adapted to this purpose. Military forces with armed foot soldiers can *occupy* a territory militarily. Although inhabitants may make the soldiers' lives unhappy through violent or nonviolent resistance, generally only another organized, armed military force can displace occupiers.

Foot soldiers are called the **infantry.** They use assault rifles and other light weapons (such as mines and machine guns) as well as heavy artillery of various types. Artillery is extremely destructive and not very discriminating: It usually causes the most damage and casualties in wars. *Armor* refers to tanks and armored vehicles. In open terrain, such as desert, mechanized ground forces typically combine armor, artillery, and infantry. In close terrain, such as jungles and cities, however, foot soldiers are more important. For this reason, the armies of industrialized states have a greater advantage over poor armies in open conventional warfare, such as in the Kuwaiti desert. In jungle, mountain, or urban warfare, however—as in Afghan mountains and Iraqi cities—such advantages are eroded, and a cheaper and more lightly armed force of motivated foot soldiers or guerrillas may ultimately prevail over an expensive conventional army.

infantry Foot soldiers who use assault rifles and other light weapons (mines, machine guns, etc.).

Public Opinion and International Relations
Military Spending in the United States

As shown in Table 6.1, the United States spends far more on its military than any other country. Indeed, the United States spends more than most of the rest of the world combined. During the early period of the Cold War, most Americans were quite supportive of high military spending: Competition with the Soviet Union in arms spending led to fast-growing budgets. During the Vietnam War, which became very unpopular in the United States, public support for large military budgets declined rapidly. For example, in Figure 6.2, note that the high point for Americans feeling that "too much" is spent on the military happened in the 1970s—the final years of the Vietnam War (which America withdrew from in 1973).

Yet, soon after the end of Vietnam, the proportion of Americans feeling the government spent "too little" on the military steadily grew. This fell again during the 1980s, as Americans began to feel there was "too much" spending—a sentiment that reached a peak as the Cold War came to an end.

It is also important to note that, other than during the Vietnam War and until very recently, the plurality of Americans has felt that military spending was "about right." Military budgets in the United States did vary markedly over this time period. After Vietnam, spending fell, but budgets increased significantly under President Ronald Reagan (1980–1988). After the end of the Cold War (1989), budgets began to fall again as the need to compete with the Soviet Union (now Russia) had ended.

Interestingly, after the 9/11 terrorist attacks on the United States, public opinion actually became divided. Until this point, the number of Americans feeling that "too little" or "too much" was spent moved in roughly equal and opposite directions. Yet, after 2001, the total percentage of Americans in those categories grew together, as the number feeling that defense spending was "about right" continued to fall. Again, this suggests a growing divide in the U.S. public: Now, growing percentages believe that military spending levels are not quite right, but those respondents are divided between thinking it is "too much" and "too little."

This suggests that, like many issues in the current American political system, strong public divisions (often referred to as polarization) have grown and could continue to increase.

Figure 6.2 Views of Military Spending in the United States

Source: Roper Center for Public Opinion Research, 2017.

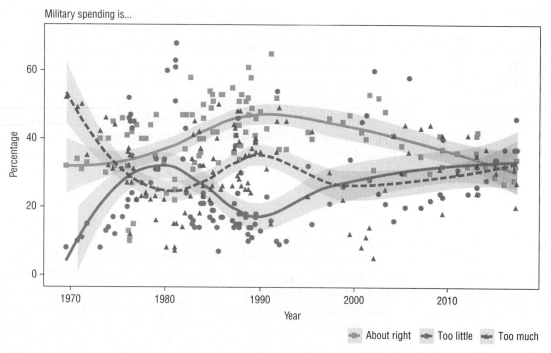

The superiority of conventional armed forces to irregular forces in open battle was graphically demonstrated in Somalia at the end of 2006. An Islamist militia had taken control of most of the country and the capital, leaving a transitional government near Ethiopia's border, backed by Ethiopia's large conventional military. The Islamists closed schools and sent teenagers with rifles in pickup trucks to attack the provisional government. They were no match for the Ethiopian army, which then ousted them from the whole country in two weeks. The Islamists, like most irregular forces, then had to fall back to guerrilla attacks rather than taking and holding territory. Here, in turn, the conventional Ethiopian military proved no match, and the Islamists gained ground steadily until the Ethiopian army gave up and left in January 2009. After its departure, Somali-Islamist groups captured most of the country's territory, overpowering Somali government forces and fighting peacekeepers from the African Union (AU). Somalia's government incorporated mod-

WINNING HEARTS AND MINDS Counterinsurgency warfare has become central to the missions of uniformed military forces worldwide. The U.S. military rewrote its counterinsurgency manual and changed its tactics in Iraq and Afghanistan to emphasize political and economic activities and positive relations with civilian populations. Here, in the capital of Somalia, human rights advisers instruct African Union peacekeeping soldiers on international law in hopes that their behavior will be consistent with international standards in civilian protection, 2014.

Michelle Shephard/Toronto Star/Getty Images

erate Islamist factions but continued to fight more radical Islamist groups. Forces from the AU were continuing to battle the Islamist forces into 2018, although talks were under way to coordinate an AU withdrawal during the year.

counterinsurgency An effort to combat guerrilla armies, often including programs to "win the hearts and minds" of rural populations so that they stop sheltering guerrillas.

Counterinsurgency has received growing attention in recent years because of Iraq and Afghanistan, but it is central to nearly all the wars currently in progress worldwide. Counterinsurgency warfare often includes programs to try to "win the hearts and minds" of populations so that they stop sheltering the guerrillas. In some ways, because counterinsurgency warfare is as much about political gains as military strategy, it is the most complex type of warfare. While battling armed factions of an insurgency, a government must essentially conduct a public relations campaign to persuade the population to abandon the movement while providing public services (such as education and welfare programs) to show a government's responsiveness to the population. A government must be strong militarily, but it cannot be too brutal in the application of force lest more of the population begin to support the guerrillas.

U.S. military forces conducted counterinsurgency campaigns in Iraq and Afghanistan for years. The campaigns included the use of lethal military force, payments to key tribal leaders to support American efforts, assisting the formation of local government, and training new police and military forces to combat the insurgency. These types of activities place tremendous stress on militaries, which are usually trained only to fight wars, not to undertake rebuilding distant governments.

Counterinsurgency campaigns are costly and labor-intensive. For example, the U.S. Army's counterinsurgency manual suggests deploying 20 troops for every 1,000 citizens to be protected from insurgents. Few states can afford such campaigns for long periods of time. Indeed, even including allied forces, the United States never reached such a ratio of troops-to-population in Iraq or Afghanistan. Such a ratio would require 600,000 troops for Afghanistan, compared with the 130,000 international troops actually deployed there at the peak in 2010 (down to 14,000 by 2018).

A common tool of guerrillas, insurgents, and the governments fighting them are **landmines**, which are simple, small, and cheap containers of explosives with a trigger activated by contact or sensor. These mines were a particular focus of public attention in the 1990s because in places such as Angola, Afghanistan, Cambodia, and Bosnia, they were used extensively by irregular military forces that never disarmed them. Long after such a war ends, landmines continue to maim and kill civilians who try to reestablish their lives in former war zones. Landmines have also become a lethal weapon for nonstate actors. It is estimated that more than 15 million landmines are still buried in the desert of Egypt's Sinai Peninsula. Recently, various terrorist groups have begun to dig them up to use them as explosives to attack their own targets. Globally, as many as 100 million landmines remain from wars; they kill or injure about 5,000 people a year (a third of whom are children). Although they are cheap to deploy, it costs about $1,000 per mine to find and disarm them.

Public opinion and nongovernmental organizations (NGOs) have pressured governments to restrict the use of landmines. More than 100 countries signed a treaty to ban landmines at a 1997 conference organized by Canada. Russia and Japan signed on shortly afterward, but not China or the United States (which said mines would be needed to slow any North Korean invasion of South Korea). By 2018, more than 50 million landmines had been destroyed under the treaty, with 87 countries eliminating their stockpiles. A new norm seems to be emerging, but its effect on actual military practice is not yet clear.

6.1.2 Naval Forces: Controlling the Seas

Navies are adapted primarily to control passage through the seas and to attack land near coastlines. Controlling the seas in wartime allows states to move their own goods and military forces by sea while preventing enemies from doing so. Navies can also blockade enemy ports, as, for example, Israel does to control sea access to Hamas-ruled Gaza.

In 2008–2012, navies of the Western powers responded to the rapid growth of piracy in three of the world's vital shipping lanes—off Somalia south of the Suez Canal; the Straits of Malacca in Indonesia connecting the Indian Ocean with East Asia; and, more recently, the waters off West Africa. The Somali pirates, taking advantage of near-anarchy in that country, established safe havens onshore and ventured out to capture dozens of ships, holding the vessels, cargoes, and crews for ransom. Shipping companies generally paid millions of dollars per ship rather than lose valuable goods and people. The pirates pushed the limits by capturing first a Ukrainian freighter loaded with tanks and weapons and then a huge Saudi oil tanker with $100 million of oil. Racing to ships in very small, fast boats, armed with automatic rifles and grenade launchers, they toss up grappling hooks, climb the sides, and subdue the crew, typically within about ten minutes.

The world's navies patrolled the area to deter piracy (see Figure 6.3). In 2008, the UN Security Council unanimously called for international cooperation in fighting the surge in hijackings. Many states responded, including the five permanent members of the Security Council. European Union (EU) attack helicopters raided an onshore pirate base in 2012. Many cargo ships began carrying armed guards. These efforts, among others, led to a sharp decline in Somali hijackings in 2012. A notorious pirate leader, "Big Mouth," who had once seized the Ukrainian ship full of tanks, announced his disarmament and retirement in 2013. Yet this substantial success near Somalia brought unintended consequences. By 2017, piracy was growing in West Africa and in East Asia as groups in those areas expanded their efforts as the world's navies had focused on Somalia. The sheer size of the oceans and the number of potential targets for pirates make piracy a difficult problem to solve.

Aircraft carriers—mobile platforms for attack aircraft—are instruments of **power projection** that can attack almost any state in the world. Merely sending an

---

landmines Concealed explosive devices, often left behind by irregular armies, that kill or maim civilians after wars end. Such mines number more than 100 million, primarily in Angola, Bosnia, Afghanistan, and Cambodia. A movement to ban landmines is under way; more than 100 states have agreed to do so.

power projection The ability to use military force in areas far from a country's region or sphere of influence.

Figure 6.3 Pirate Attacks Around the World, 2017

Source: Pirate Attacks Around the World, 2017, Based on ICC-CCS map, 2017. https://www.icc-ccs.org/index.php/piracy-reporting-centre/live-piracy-map/piracy-map-2017.

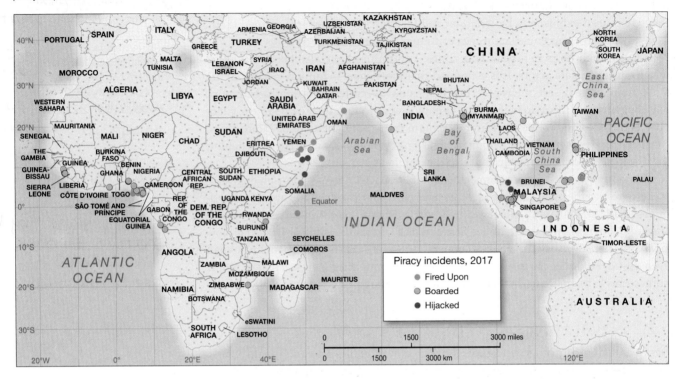

aircraft carrier sailing to the vicinity of an international conflict implies a threat to use force—a modern version of nineteenth-century "gunboat diplomacy." Aircraft carriers are extremely expensive and typically require 20 to 25 supporting ships for protection and supply. Few states can afford even one. The United States operates the largest number of carriers—10 of them, costing more than $5 billion each. In 2017, the U.S. Navy launched a newly designed carrier, costing $14 billion. China launched one renovated carrier in 2012, although only for training purposes. In 2017, it began initial operations of its first home-built carrier and announced the building of a second carrier. Eight other countries (France, India, Russia, Spain, Brazil, Italy, Thailand, and the United Kingdom) maintain smaller carriers that use helicopters or small airplanes.

Surface ships, which account for the majority of warships, rely increasingly on guided missiles and are in turn vulnerable to attack by missiles (fired from ships, planes, submarines, or land). Because the ranges of small missiles now reach from dozens to hundreds of miles, naval warfare emphasizes detection at great distances without being detected oneself—a cat-and-mouse game of radar surveillance and electronic countermeasures.

Marines (part of the navy in the United States, Britain, and Russia) move to battle in ships but fight on land—amphibious warfare. Marines are also useful for great power intervention in distant conflicts where they can insert themselves quickly and establish local control.

6.1.3 Air Forces: Controlling the Skies

Air forces serve several purposes—strategic bombing of land or sea targets; "close air support" (battlefield bombing); interception of other aircraft; reconnaissance; and airlift of supplies, weapons, and troops. Missiles—whether fired from air, land, or sea—are increasingly important. Air forces have developed various means to try to fool

[Handwritten notes in margin:]
- Military Logistics
1. US fully possesses these capabilities
2. Brit. & France are close second
3. US & Russia have mil. cap in space

6.1.4 Coordinating Forces: Logistics and Intelligence

All military operations rely heavily on logistical support such as food, fuel, and ordnance (weapons and ammunition). Military logistics is a huge operation, and in most armed forces the majority of soldiers are not combat troops. Global-reach capabilities combine long-distance logistical support with various power-projection forces. These capabilities allow a great power to project military power to distant corners of the world and to maintain a military presence in most of the world's regions simultaneously. Only the United States today fully possesses such a capability—with worldwide military alliances, air and naval bases, troops stationed overseas, and aircraft carriers plying the world's oceans (see Table 6.2). Britain and France are in a distant second place, able to mount occasional distant operations of modest size such as the Falklands War. Russia is preoccupied with internal conflicts and its near neighbors, and China's military forces are oriented toward regional conflicts and are not global in scope (although China is currently attempting to build a navy capable of better power projection).

Space forces are military forces designed to attack in or from outer space. Ballistic missiles, which travel through space briefly, are not generally included in this category. Only the United States and Russia have substantial military capabilities in space. China put an astronaut in orbit in 2003, successfully tested an antisatellite missile, launched a lunar orbiter in 2007, and plans to launch a lunar lander in 2018. Although its space capabilities (civilian and military) lag behind those of the United States, China is catching up quickly, routinely putting satellites in earth's orbit. The development of space weapons has been constrained by the technical challenges and expenses of space operations, and by norms against militarizing space.

The far more common uses of space by the military are for command and coordination purposes. Satellites are used extensively for military purposes, but these purposes thus far do not include attack. Satellites perform military surveillance and mapping, communications, weather assessment, and early warning of ballistic missile launches. Satellites also provide navigational information to military forces—army units, ships, planes, and even guided missiles in flight. Locations are calculated to within about 50 feet by small receivers, which pick up beacons transmitted from a network of 24 U.S. satellites known as a *Global Positioning System* (*GPS*). Handheld receivers are available commercially, so the military forces of other countries can free-ride on these satellite navigation beacons. Poorer states can buy satellite photos—including high-resolution pictures that Russia sells for hard currency. In fact, access to such information has diffused to the point that the terrorists who attacked Mumbai, India, in 2008 planned their attack using satellite images available through Google Earth and coordinated it in real time from Pakistan using satellite phones. In the 2006 war

Table 6.2 Location of U.S. Military Forces, 2017

Region	Personnel	Distribution of Forces Abroad
United States	1,120,000	—
Europe	60,000	31%
Japan/Pacific	74,000	38%
Russia/CIS	100	0%
Middle East	40,000	20%
Latin America	1,300	1%
Africa	4,100	2%
South Asia	13,000	7%
Total abroad	192,500	100%

Note: Totals do not include personnel afloat in the region.
Source: U.S. Department of Defense.

between Hezbollah and Israel in Lebanon, Hezbollah forces used GPS jammers to complicate Israeli air support and targeting operations. But generally, in outer space, great powers have advantages over smaller or poorer states.

Intelligence gathering also relies on various other means such as electronic monitoring of telephone lines and other communications, reports from embassies, and information in the open press. Some kinds of information are obtained by sending agents into foreign countries as spies. They use ingenuity (plus money and technology) to penetrate walls of secrecy that foreign governments have constructed around their plans and capabilities. For example, in 1999 a Russian spy taped conversations from a listening device planted in a high-level conference room at the U.S. State Department. The 2001 terrorist attacks showed a weakness in U.S. "human intelligence" capabilities, in that the United States had not penetrated a large terrorist network based in Afghanistan and operating globally. U.S. "signal intelligence" capabilities are more impressive. The largest U.S. military intelligence agency is the National Security Agency (NSA), whose mission is encoding U.S. communications and breaking the codes of foreign communications. The NSA intercepts truly massive amounts of information from sources such as undersea phone cables, then sifts through the information to find significant conversations. The NSA employs more mathematics Ph.D.s than anyone in the world, is the second largest electricity consumer in the state of Maryland, has a budget larger than that of the Central Intelligence Agency (CIA), and is believed to have the most powerful computer facility in the world. These operations, taken together, are very large and are growing in importance as the information revolution proceeds and as the war on terror makes their mission more central. The full extent of the NSA's operations were revealed in 2013 when a former NSA contractor leaked millions of documents revealing that the NSA had secretly gathered massive amounts of data on American citizens and foreign diplomats, including telephone and Internet records. The revelation of these programs led to outrage among U.S. allies and to calls for expanded oversight of spy agencies by the American public.

6.2 Evolving Technologies

Evaluate the importance of new technologies in transforming the nature of war.

Technological developments have changed the nature of military force in several ways. First, the resort to force in international conflicts now has more profound costs and consequences. Great powers in particular can no longer use force to settle disputes among themselves without risking massive destruction and economic ruin. Also, military engagements now occur across greater standoff distances between opposing forces. Missiles of all types are accelerating this trend. These technological advances undermine the territorial basis of war and the "hard shell" of the state itself.

In recent years, this trend has accelerated with the use of unmanned aerial vehicles (UAVs), or **drones**. Drones have been used for many years and in many wars, including the Vietnam War in the 1970s, the Iran-Iraq War, and the 1991 Gulf War. But after the 9/11 terrorist attacks, the United States began expanding its use of drones, especially those that could undertake direct strikes on targets. These included drones armed with missiles used in U.S. military efforts in Afghanistan, Pakistan, Yemen, and Libya.

In addition to America's hundreds of armed drones, other countries have been rapidly acquiring them. Over 30 countries, including China, Russia, India, Pakistan, Turkey, Italy, Germany, France, and Iran, have or are developing heavy and medium-weight attack drones. An Iranian-made drone was shot down over Israel in 2012. Britain and Israel have used drones for attacks for several years, and in just the past three

drones Another term for unmanned aerial vehicles; these small flying vehicles, which can be armed or unarmed, are increasingly used in combat and reconnaissance operations.

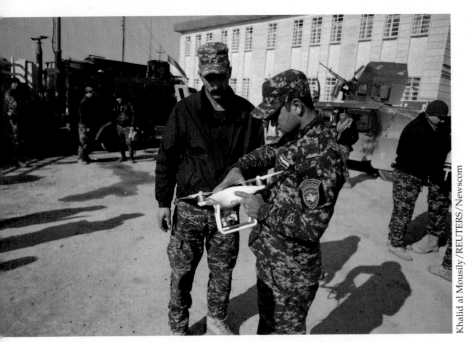

Khalid al Mousily/REUTERS/Newscom

EYES IN THE SKY Nearly every government now uses nonlethal drones as a military tool. The drones, similar in many ways to those available to consumers, allow for efficient gathering of intelligence, especially when it would be dangerous for military personnel to do so. Here, members of the Iraqi Special Forces deploy a drone in Mosul, a city recently taken from ISIS, 2017. The drone will allow the search of buildings for any remaining ISIS fighters.

years, Nigeria, Iraq, and Pakistan have also used armed drones to strike at militant groups. In some cases, countries have built their own armed drone programs, but certain countries, such as Nigeria, Iraq, and Pakistan, have purchased their armed drones from China. Israel and the United States have also sold armed drones to countries such as Germany and Italy.

Many countries also use nonlethal drones in the service of war fighting, usually for intelligence gathering. Nearly 80 countries have developed or purchased these nonlethal surveillance drones. They often use surveillance drones in support of military operations or to gather intelligence on militant groups operating within the state. Some experts note that dictators can use surveillance drones to gather intelligence about anti-regime activity. U.S. underwater sea drones for mine clearing, produced by Germany, were sent to the Persian Gulf in 2012 as tensions with Iran escalated.

Even businesses and private citizens use drones in ways that can affect international relations (IR)—in late 2014, a European soccer match between Serbia and Albania was interrupted by a drone carrying an Albanian nationalist flag flying near midfield. The incident led to diplomatic tension between the two countries.

The expanded use of military drones, especially attack drones, has created several controversies in recent years. First, there is concern that the technology will spread quickly, including to states or groups that could use drones to attack civilians. For example, China has been especially active in selling drones to countries to which the United States has refused to provide this technology. Unlike nuclear weapons (see Weapons of Mass Destruction), drone technology is fairly simple and within the grasp of most states, raising the possibility of proliferation.

Second, the use of armed drones to kill individuals is questioned under international law. The laws of war (see Chapter 7) require states to limit hostilities to those geographic areas where there are active conflicts. That is, when two countries are fighting each other, they are not supposed to get nearby countries involved in the fighting. This not only protects nearby civilians from war but also limits how widespread fighting can become. Yet, in the war against al Qaeda, the United States has used drones extensively outside Afghanistan, including in Pakistan and Yemen. Should the United States be required to declare war on Pakistan and Yemen to attack targets there?

On one hand, advocates of drone strikes say no—the United States is not at war with those countries, just some people who live there. Yet, critics of drone strikes point to several problems, including a lack of due process for the targets. For example, if a suspected terrorist were caught in the United States, the suspect would be tried in a court before being punished. If the same terrorist were in the area of conflict, he or she would be an acceptable target under the laws of war. But should the suspected terrorist be in a third country, that country's laws should apply. Yet drone strikes are routinely carried out without the consent of the third country. These challenging international law issues have not yet been resolved.

It is no surprise that the use of drones, especially in counterinsurgency and counterterrorism operations, has increased. The drones offer militaries, but especially political leaders, the chance to strike at an enemy from far away without risking the lives of their countries' own troops. Historically, an operation to capture a terrorist, or strike a stockpile of weapons, would require deploying ground troops who could be vulnerable in small operations. Even using aircraft to strike targets would risk having a pilot killed in an operation. Drones can accomplish many of the same tasks without risk of life to a country's own soldiers. Yet, many are concerned it makes these operations too easy to carry out. If operations entail low or no costs, states have an incentive to order them very frequently. Indeed, during 2008–2017, the United States reported over 400 drone strikes in Pakistan alone.

Electronic warfare (now broadened to *information warfare*) refers to the uses of the electromagnetic spectrum (radio waves, radar, infrared, etc.) in war and is critical to all technologically advanced military forces. Strategies for *cyberwar*—disrupting enemy computer networks to degrade command and control, or even hacking into bank accounts electronically—may figure prominently in future wars, although they have not yet. The United States decided against using cyberattacks to disable Libya's air defenses in 2011 out of fear of the precedent such an action could set. In the future, terrorist attacks could also target computer networks, including the Internet and critical infrastructure such as electricity grids.

electronic warfare Use of the electromagnetic spectrum (radio waves, radar, infrared, etc.) in war, such as employing electromagnetic signals for one's own benefit while denying their use to an enemy.

Policy Perspectives
President of the United States, Donald Trump

PROBLEM   *How do you balance the trade-offs in the use of force to combat nontraditional security threats?*

NASA Image Collection / Alamy Stock Photo

BACKGROUND   As a presidential candidate in 2016, you publicly suggested that the war in Afghanistan was a "total disaster" and pledged to end U.S. involvement in that war. By August 2017, however, you had announced that you planned to increase the number of American troops stationed in Afghanistan in the future.

Large parts of Afghanistan are still unstable after the 17-year-long war. International troops still routinely confront hostile forces or are attacked by them. The Taliban, and its allies in the Haqqani network, continue to attack local Afghan security forces as well. These attacks often result in significant military and civilian casualties.

DOMESTIC CONSIDERATIONS   Terrorism and the war in Afghanistan are still key issues in U.S. public opinion. The American public has grown quite weary of the war in Afghanistan, and after the death of Osama bin Laden, growing numbers question the continued military presence there. Public opinion polls showed support for your proposal to withdraw all combat troops from that conflict.

SCENARIO   Imagine that the war in Afghanistan suddenly escalates. The Taliban, with help from the Haqqani network and ISIS resources from Iraq and Syria, has escalated the war against the Afghan government and international forces in several key provinces. Attacks against American troops increase significantly, leading to significant U.S. casualties. The American public is upset: The growing number of troop deaths has received increased media attention and has become a major foreign policy issue. Your own advisers are also divided: Some suggest that a victory by pro-Taliban forces would be a threat to the United States, while others contend that the 12-year-long war permanently reduced the threat from the Taliban against the U.S. mainland.

CHOOSE YOUR POLICY   How do you respond to the possibility of civil war in Afghanistan? Do you send even more troops into the conflict? Doing so could stop the Taliban advances but would lead to further U.S. casualties. Do you leave Afghanistan to its fate, as you had initially promised? That would be popular at home, but it would risk the reemergence of anti-U.S. forces that America intervened to topple after the 9/11 attacks. How do you balance the competing domestic and international pressures in confronting nontraditional security threats?

Cyberattacks are an issue of growing importance in IR, with Chinese, Russian, and American hackers constantly probing each other's systems. In 2010, the U.S.-Israeli Stuxnet virus targeted Iran's nuclear centrifuges, and in 2012, the Flame virus was found on thousands of computers across the Middle East, mostly in Iran. It could grab screenshots and keystrokes, and remotely turn on computer microphones to help the creators (again, presumably Americans and Israelis) spy on operations in the Iranian nuclear program. A few months later, probably in response, a virus deleted files on the computers of a major Saudi oil company, replacing them with an image of a burning American flag.

Russia has been using cyberattacks in an attempt to expand its influence for many years. In 2008, Russian government hackers shut down nearly all Internet access to the country of Estonia after the removal there of a statue commemorating Russian war veterans. During Russia's military conflict with Georgia in 2008, cyberattacks increased against official Georgian Web sites. Several countries, including the United States, have accused Russia of meddling in their democratic elections. U.S. intelligence agencies have supported these accusations. Relatedly, Russian hackers have also been accused of programming automatic "bots" to spread fake news stories through social media to influence public opinion around the time of elections.

It is clear that cyberattacks, whether in the service of a direct military campaign, or as an attempt to influence electoral outcomes, are becoming an increasingly important tool of leverage in IR. Given that access to the Internet is easy and growing quickly (indeed nearly universal in some parts of the world—see Chapter 10), it is not surprising that both states and nonstate actors have adapted their strategies to use cyberspace as a place to influence international politics.

stealth technology The use of special radar-absorbent materials and unusual shapes in the design of aircraft, missiles, and ships to scatter enemy radar.

On the more traditional military side is **stealth technology**, which uses special radar-absorbent materials and unusual shapes in aircraft, missiles, and ships to scatter enemy radar. However, stealth is expensive (the B-2 stealth bomber costs about $2 billion per plane) and is prone to technical problems.

Military historians refer to a period of rapid change in the conduct of war as a "revolution in military affairs." These periods usually combine innovative applications of new technology with changes in military doctrine, organization, or operations. Such revolutions may arise from innovations in organization, as when revolutionary France first mobilized an entire nation into a war machine two centuries ago. Or they may arise from new military doctrine, as when Germany used the blitzkrieg to overwhelm Poland and France at the outset of World War II, or from technology alone, as with the invention of nuclear weapons. Many military analysts consider the present period, starting with the 1991 Gulf War, a revolution in military affairs, especially in U.S. forces. Management of information is central to this revolution. Two centuries ago, the German military strategist Carl von Clausewitz described as a "fog of war" the confusion and uncertainty that greatly reduce the effectiveness of armies in battle. Today's U.S. forces are attempting to pierce that fog for themselves while thickening it for their enemies. As the fog of war becomes transparent, U.S. forces can also disperse light forces widely rather than

KHALIL MAZRAAWI/AFP/Getty Images

SMALL IS BEAUTIFUL The information revolution is making smaller weapons and smaller dispersed units more potent. The "revolution in military affairs" is driving changes in military strategy worldwide, including the expanding use of unmanned drones. Here, Prince Faisal and the chairman of the chiefs of staff of the Jordanian military examine a micro drone, 2016.

massing concentrations of heavy units, as Clausewitz emphasized. The ability to conduct precision strikes and the increasing use of space in warfare are two other aspects of the present revolution.

The revolutionary potentials were first apparent in the lopsided 1991 victory over Iraq's large but not technologically advanced army, and the 1999 Kosovo campaign was notable in achieving its war aims without loss of a single U.S. life to hostile fire. But the 2001 Afghanistan campaign best exemplified the revolution. Small groups of lightly armed U.S. special forces, inserted across the country, used lasers to illuminate targets for smart bombs dropped by high-flying aircraft. The integration of these diverse forces using information-rich battle management systems resulted in a stunningly effective bombing campaign that destroyed the Taliban as an effective army and handed victory to the smaller anti-Taliban armies, all with just a handful of U.S. casualties. The 2003 invasion of Iraq seemed to continue this success, but then the postinvasion security situation in Iraq unraveled over several years despite the revolutionary technologies of U.S. forces.

Because of their more modest cost, drone technology and cyberwarfare are well within the reach of many states, not just great powers. A more unsettling thought is that the revolution in military affairs may work for nonstate actors, including terrorists, as well as for states. The September 2001 attackers used information technology, such as encrypted Internet communications, to coordinate forces while keeping U.S. authorities in the dark. They carried out precision strikes over long distances with very small, dispersed units. As a result, 19 attackers killed nearly 3,000 people, and an expenditure of under $1 million caused tens of *billions* of dollars in damage.

6.3 Terrorism

Assess potential advantages and disadvantages to two different approaches to counterterrorism.

The U.S. State Department listed 61 foreign terrorist organizations in 2018. Some are motivated by religion (for example, al Qaeda) but others by class ideology (for example, Shining Path in Peru) or by ethnic conflict and nationalism (for example, Basque Fatherland and Liberty). In Chapter 5, we discussed conflicts involving armed Islamist militias and terrorist networks. Here we will discuss terrorism itself as a tactic. Since September 2001, governments and ordinary people have paid much more attention to terrorism than ever before. But terrorism itself is not new.

Terrorism refers to political violence that targets civilians deliberately and indiscriminately. Beyond this basic definition, other criteria can be applied, but the definitions become politically motivated: One person's freedom fighter is another's terrorist. More than guerrilla warfare, terrorism is a shadowy world of faceless enemies and irregular tactics marked by extreme brutality.

Traditionally, the purpose of terrorism is to demoralize a civilian population in order to use its discontent as leverage on national governments or other parties to a conflict. Related to this is the aim of creating drama in order to gain media attention for a cause. When the Irish Republican Army (IRA) planted bombs in London in the 1960s and 1970s, it hoped to make life miserable enough for Londoners that they would insist their government settle the Northern Ireland issue. The bombing also sought to keep the issue of Northern Ireland in the news, in the hope that the British government would then be pressured to concede to terms more favorable to the IRA than would otherwise be the case. Terrorism is seldom mindless; rather, it is usually a calculated use of violence as leverage. However, the motives and the means of terrorism vary widely, having in common only that some actor is using violence to influence other actors.

The primary effect of terrorism is psychological. In part, the effectiveness of terrorism in capturing attention is due to the dramatic nature of the incidents, especially as shown on television news. Terrorism also gains attention because of the randomness of victims. Although only a few dozen people may be injured by a bomb left in a market, millions of people realize "It could have been me" because they, too, shop in markets. Attacks on airplanes augment this fear because many people already fear flying. Terrorism thus amplifies a small amount of power by its psychological effect on large populations; this is why it is usually a tool of the weak.

However, al Qaeda's attacks follow a somewhat different pattern, planned less to create fear than simply to kill as many Americans and their allies as possible—and ultimately to touch off apocalyptic violence that al Qaeda's followers believe will bring about God's intervention. Indeed, terrorist attacks in general have become more deadly over the past 50 years as terrorist tactics have increasingly employed more violent means to injure or kill civilians. The psychological effect is aimed at Muslim populations worldwide rather than at Americans.

In the shockingly destructive attacks on the World Trade Center, the Pentagon, and the flight that crashed in Somerset County, Pennsylvania, tangible damage was far greater than in previous terrorist attacks—reaching into thousands of lives and tens of billions of dollars. The psychological impact was even stronger than the physical damage—changing the U.S. political and cultural landscape instantly. And the same terrorist network was trying to obtain nuclear weapons (see Weapons of Mass Destruction) with which to kill not thousands, but hundreds of thousands of Americans.

The classic cases of terrorism—from the 1970s to the 2001 attacks—are those in which a *nonstate* actor uses attacks against *civilians* by secret *nonuniformed* forces, operating *across international borders*, as leverage against *state* actors. Radical political factions or separatist groups hijack or blow up airplanes or plant bombs in cafés, clubs, or other crowded places. For example, Chechen radicals seized a school in Beslan, a small city in the Caucasus region, in 2004. For three days, they held nearly 1,200 children, parents, and teachers without food or water. When Russian troops stormed the school, more than 300 people died, including 172 children.

Such tactics create spectacular incidents that draw attention to the terrorists' cause. For example, the bombing of the Boston Marathon in 2013 was an unsophisticated attack by two brothers, yet it preoccupied news media for weeks afterward. Often terrorism is used by radical factions of movements that have not been able to get attention or develop other effective means of leverage. It is often a tactic of desperation, and it almost always reflects weakness in the power position of the attacker. For instance, Palestinian radicals in 1972 had seen Arab states defeated by Israel in war and could not see a way to gain even a hearing for their cause. By capturing media attention worldwide with dramatic incidents of violence—even at the cost of rallying world public opinion against their cause—the radicals hoped to make Palestinian aspirations an issue that Western governments could not ignore when deciding on policies toward the Middle East.

Yet the persistence of terrorism is in some ways puzzling because the tactic has a mixed record of success. Suicide bombers were arguably effective at convincing the United States to leave Lebanon in 1983, but the Chechen terrorists' 2004 school attack marked their end as a serious force in Chechnya. The Palestinians did not win a state through terrorism. Videos of beheadings of hostages by ISIS fighters rallied global efforts to defeat that movement in Iraq and Syria. In addition, even large numbers of suicide bombers have yet to be effective in gaining a state for the Tamils in Sri Lanka or providing leverage for Hamas or Islamic jihad against Israel. Clearly, terrorist activities do not reliably achieve political ends.

Some research has attempted to analyze systematically when particular types of terrorism, such as suicide bombings, are effective at achieving the goals of terrorist

Figure 6.4 Location of Suicide Attacks, 1974–2016

Source: Data from Chicago Project on Security and Terrorism (CPOST). 2016. *Suicide Attack Database* (October 12, 2016 Release). [Data File. Retrieved from http://cpostdata.uchicago.edu/.]

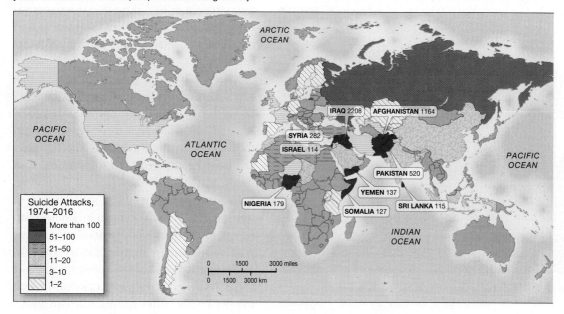

organizations. According to one study, suicide bombings are not an irrational use of violence by terrorist groups and follow strategic patterns (see Figure 6.4). In particular, they occur most frequently against democracies rather than autocracies, presumably because democracies are thought to be strongly influenced by public opinion. Still, this same study concludes that this terror tactic has not been particularly successful at achieving significant goals.

Terrorists are more willing than states are to violate the norms of the international system because, unlike states, they do not have a stake in that system. Conversely, when a political group gains some power or legitimacy, its use of terrorism usually diminishes. This was true of the Palestine Liberation Organization during the peace process in 1993–2000 as well as the IRA starting in 1995.

States themselves carry out acts designed to terrorize their own populations or those of other states, but scholars tend to avoid the label "terrorism" for such acts, preferring to call it repression or war. In fact, no violent act taken during a civil or international war—by or toward a warring party—can necessarily fit neatly into the category of terrorism. Of course, because war is hard to define, so is terrorism; warring parties often call each other terrorists. The narrowest definition of terrorism would exclude acts either by or against *uniformed military forces* rather than civilians. This definition would exclude the killing of 243 U.S. Marines by a car bomb in Lebanon in 1983 and the 2001 attack on the Pentagon because they were directed at military targets. It would also exclude the bombing of German cities in World War II, although the purpose was to terrorize civilians. But in today's world of undeclared war, guerrilla war, civil war, and ethnic violence, a large gray zone surrounds clear cases of terrorism.

State-sponsored terrorism refers to the use of terrorist groups by states—usually under control of the state's intelligence agency—to achieve political aims. In 1988, a bomb scattered pieces of Pan Am flight 103 over the Scottish countryside. Combing the fields for debris, investigators found fragments of a tape recorder that had contained a sophisticated plastic explosive bomb. The U.S. and British governments identified the Libyan intelligence agents responsible, and in 1992, backed by the UN Security Council, they demanded that Libya turn over the agents for trial. When Libya refused, the UN imposed sanctions, including a ban on international flights to or from Libya. In 1999, Libya turned over the suspects for trial—two received life in

state-sponsored terrorism The use of terrorist groups by states, usually under control of a state's intelligence agency, to achieve political aims.

Masatomo Kuriya/Getty Images

ASYMMETRIC CONFLICT Terrorist attacks often reflect the weakness of the perpetrators and their lack of access to other means of leverage. Terror can sometimes amplify a small group's power and affect outcomes. Al Qaeda's September 11, 2001, attacks, staged by a relatively small nonstate actor, ultimately led to the withdrawal of U.S. troops from Saudi Arabia, drew the United States into a counterinsurgency war in Iraq, and brought al Qaeda itself a surge of recruits for new attacks worldwide.

prison while a third was acquitted—and the UN suspended its sanctions. In 2003, Libya formally took responsibility for the bombing, struck a multibillion-dollar compensation deal with the victims' families, and regained a normal place in the international community.

As of 2018, the United States has accused four states of supporting international terrorism—Iran, Syria, Sudan, and North Korea. The first three have been on the list for more than a decade. The U.S. government has barred U.S. companies from doing business in those states. However, these kinds of unilateral U.S. sanctions are of limited effect. Syria can do business with Egypt, as can Iran with Russia. North Korea was removed from the list in 2008 in exchange for promises to halt its nuclear weapons program, but it was placed back on the list in 2017 after testing nuclear weapons. Cuba was removed from the list in 2015 after normalization of relations with the United States.

6.3.1 Counterterrorism

Just as the methods used by terrorists have become more diverse over the past decades, so have the policies implemented to prevent terrorist incidents. Debates over how best to prevent terrorist attacks are often heated because there are also debates about why individuals engage in terrorist attacks in the first place.

Policies to combat terrorism can be placed along a spectrum involving more or less force in confronting terrorism and terrorist organizations. On the nonviolent end of the spectrum are calls for economic development. Advocates of these programs point out that, in very poor states, people are especially vulnerable to recruitment by terrorist organizations. With no bright future ahead of them and little opportunities to better themselves, people will naturally lose hope, become angry, and undertake seemingly irrational acts because they feel they have nothing to lose. And although there is little direct evidence that factors like poverty correlate directly with terrorist activities, it is clear that very poor states with weak central governments have served as recruiting grounds for international terrorist organizations.

In the middle of the spectrum are policing activities, which involve efforts by domestic police, usually in cooperation with other countries' police forces, to apprehend or kill terrorists while breaking up terrorist organizations. In one famous example of effective counterterrorist policing, the government of Peru, using an elite investigative team of the national police force, arrested the leader of the Shining Path movement, which at one point controlled over 20,000 well-armed militia members and had assassinated several Peruvian political leaders. The police arrested the movement's leader after staking out a dance studio (which he lived above) and digging through trash from the studio to find clues. After his capture, the Shining Path movement largely collapsed.

At the other end of the counterterrorism spectrum is organized military conflict. States may undertake small- or large-scale conflicts to counter terrorist organizations. In 1998, the United States launched cruise missile strikes against a plant in Sudan believed to be producing chemical weapons for al Qaeda, but it turned out to be making infant formula. In addition, the U.S.-led war in Afghanistan was a response to the 9/11 attacks on the United States.

Of course, nearly every state that undertakes counterterrorism policies uses some combination of these methods. In the United States, for example, foreign aid is often justified in terms of assisting development and economic growth to decrease the possibility that the poor and uneducated can be drafted easily into terrorist organizations. The FBI and local law enforcement cooperate with many international partners to track and detain suspected terrorists, while U.S. soldiers assist other states with training and weapons in their fight against terrorists. Finally, the war in Afghanistan was a large war undertaken against the Taliban government that had protected al Qaeda.

6.4 Weapons of Mass Destruction

Contrast the effectiveness of the global regime to prevent the spread of nuclear weapons with that of the global regime to prevent the spread of chemical weapons.

Weapons of mass destruction (WMDs) comprise three general types: nuclear, chemical, and biological weapons. They are distinguished from conventional weapons by their enormous potential lethality, given their small size and modest costs, and by their relative lack of discrimination in whom they kill. When deployed on ballistic missiles, they can potentially be fired from the home territory of one state and wreak great destruction on the home territory of another state. Until now this has never happened. But the mere threat of such an action undermines the territorial integrity and security of states in the international system. Of central concern today are the potentials for proliferation—the possession of weapons of mass destruction by more and more states.

Weapons of mass destruction serve different purposes than conventional weapons. With a few exceptions, their purpose is to deter attack (especially by other weapons of mass destruction) by giving state leaders the means to inflict great pain against a would-be conqueror or destroyer. For middle powers, these weapons also provide destructive power more in line with that of the great powers, thus serving as symbolic equalizers. For terrorists, potentially, their purpose is to kill a great many people.

weapons of mass destruction (WMDs) Nuclear, chemical, and biological weapons, all distinguished from conventional weapons by their enormous potential lethality and their relative lack of discrimination in whom they kill.

- WMDs
  - nuclear
  - biological
  - chemical
- Reasons for WMD
  - deter attack
  - kill masses of people

6.4.1 Nuclear Weapons

Nuclear weapons are, in sheer power, the world's most destructive weapons. A single weapon the size of a refrigerator can destroy a city. Defending against nuclear weapons is extremely difficult at best. To understand the potentials for nuclear proliferation, one has to know something about how nuclear weapons work. There are two types. *Fission weapons* (atomic bombs or A-bombs) are simpler and less expensive than *fusion weapons* (also called thermonuclear bombs, hydrogen bombs, or H-bombs).

When a fission weapon explodes, one type of atom (element) is split, or *fissioned*, into new types with less total mass. The lost mass is transformed into energy according to Albert Einstein's famous formula, $E = mc^2$, which shows that a little bit of mass is equivalent to a great deal of energy. In fact, the fission bomb that destroyed Nagasaki, Japan, in 1945 converted to energy roughly the amount of mass in a single penny. Two elements can be split in this way, and each has been used to make fission weapons. These elements—known as **fissionable material**—are uranium-235 (or U-235) and plutonium. Fission weapons were invented 75 years ago by U.S. scientists in a secret World War II science program known as the *Manhattan Project*. In 1945, one uranium bomb and one plutonium bomb were used to destroy Hiroshima and Nagasaki, killing 100,000 civilians in each city and inducing Japan to surrender unconditionally. By today's standards, those bombs were crude, low-yield weapons. But they are the kind of weapon that might be built by a developing state or a nonstate actor.

- Types of nuclear weapons:
  1. Fission (a-bombs)
  2. Fusion (thermonuclear bombs, H-bombs)

fissionable material The elements uranium-235 and plutonium, whose atoms split apart and release energy via a chain reaction when an atomic bomb explodes.

Alejandro A. Alvarez/Rapport Press/Newscom

NUKE IN A BOX Nuclear weapons were invented during World War II and used on two Japanese cities in 1945. Tens of thousands have been built, and nine states now possess them. Obtaining fissionable materials is the main difficulty in making nuclear weapons. Terrorists' efforts to obtain them pose a grave threat. Here, in 1999, a U.S. congressman displays a mock-up of the Soviet-built nuclear "suitcase bomb" that, in the wrong hands, could kill hundreds of thousands of people.

- Countries w/ U-235
  - N. Korea
  - Iran
  - Iraq
  - Libya

- Iran Nuclear Deal
  - allowed Iran to enrich uranium under Inspection
  - US left in 2018

Fission weapons work by taking subcritical masses of the fissionable material—amounts not dense enough to start a chain reaction—and compressing them into a critical mass, which explodes as the splitting atoms release neutrons that split more atoms in a chain reaction. In the simplest design, one piece of uranium is propelled down a tube (by conventional explosives) into another piece of uranium. A more efficient but technically demanding design arranges high explosives precisely around a hollow sphere of plutonium to implode the sphere and create a critical mass.

Although these designs require sophisticated engineering, they are well within the capabilities of many states and some private groups. The obstacle is obtaining fissionable material. Only 10 to 100 pounds are required for each bomb, but even these small amounts are not easily obtained. U-235, which can be used in the simplest bomb designs, is especially difficult to obtain. Natural uranium (mined in various countries) has less than 1 percent U-235, mixed with nonfissionable uranium. Extracting the fissionable U-235, referred to as enriching the uranium up to weapons grade (or high grade), is slow, expensive, and technically complex—a major obstacle to proliferation. But North Korea, Iran, Iraq, and Libya all have built the infrastructure to do so in recent years. North Korea promised to end its uranium program and dismantle its nuclear complex (after testing a bomb in 2006 and 2009), but has since resumed its program, testing three nuclear bombs from 2016 to 2017. Iran defied several UN Security Council demands to stop enriching uranium, insisting on its sovereign right to enrich uranium for what it calls peaceful purposes. In 2015, Iran reached a deal with the five permanent members of the UN Security Council and Germany that allowed it to continue to process uranium to low levels of enrichment while allowing international inspections of nuclear sites. Skeptics of the agreement feared that Iran would not comply with the deal, while advocates argued that Iran's program would be slowed by many years. In 2018, the United States withdrew from the agreement, casting doubt on its future.

Plutonium is more easily produced from low-grade uranium in nuclear power reactors—although extracting the plutonium requires a separation plant. But a plutonium bomb is more difficult to build than a uranium one—another obstacle to proliferation. Plutonium is also used in commercial breeder reactors, which Japan and other countries have built recently—another source of fissionable material. (Thus, if it decided to do so in the future, which is unlikely, Japan could quickly build a formidable nuclear arsenal.) North Korea tested a plutonium bomb in 2006, achieving fission, although with a low yield.

Fusion weapons are extremely expensive and technically demanding; they are for only the richest, largest, most technologically capable states. Here two small atoms (variants of hydrogen) fuse together into a larger atom, releasing energy. This reaction occurs only at very high temperatures (the sun "burns" hydrogen through fusion). Weapons designers use fission weapons to create these high energies and trigger an explosive fusion reaction. The explosive power of most fission weapons is between 1 and 200 kilo-tons (each kiloton is the equivalent of 1,000 tons of conventional explosive). The power of fusion weapons can reach 20 megatons (a megaton is 1,000 kilotons). In the post–Cold War era, megaton weapons have become irrelevant because they are too powerful for any actor to use productively and too difficult for terrorists or small states to build.

The effects of nuclear weapons include not only the blast of the explosion but also heat and radiation. Heat can potentially create a self-sustaining firestorm in a city. Radiation creates radiation sickness, which at high doses kills people in a few days and at low doses creates long-term health problems, especially cancers. Radiation is most intense in the local vicinity of (and downwind from) a nuclear explosion, but some radiation is carried up into the atmosphere and falls in more distant locations as nuclear fallout. Nuclear weapons also create an electromagnetic pulse (EMP) that can disrupt and destroy electronic equipment.

6.4.2 Ballistic Missiles and Other Delivery Systems

Delivery systems for getting nuclear weapons to their targets—much more than the weapons themselves—are the basis of states' nuclear arsenals and strategies (discussed shortly). Inasmuch as nuclear warheads can be made quite small—weighing a few hundred pounds or even less—they are adaptable to a wide variety of delivery systems.

During the Cold War, nuclear delivery systems were divided into two categories. *Strategic* nuclear weapons could hit an enemy's homeland, usually at long range (for instance, Moscow from Nebraska). *Tactical* nuclear weapons were designed for battle-field use. In the Cold War years, both superpowers integrated tactical nuclear weapons into their conventional air, sea, and land forces using a variety of delivery systems—gravity bombs, artillery shells, short-range missiles, landmines, depth charges, and so forth. However, the tens of thousands of nuclear warheads integrated into superpower conventional forces posed dangers such as theft or accident. Their actual use would have entailed grave risks of escalation to strategic nuclear war, putting home cities at risk. Thus, both superpowers phased out tactical nuclear weapons almost entirely when the Cold War ended.

The main strategic delivery vehicles are **ballistic missiles**; unlike airplanes, they are extremely difficult to defend against. Ballistic missiles carry a warhead up along a trajectory and let it drop on the target. A trajectory typically rises out of the atmosphere—at least 50 miles high—before descending. In addition, some missiles fire from fixed sites (silos), whereas others are mobile, firing from railroads or large trailer trucks (making them hard to target). The longest-range missiles are **intercontinental ballistic missiles (ICBMs)**, with ranges of more than 5,000 miles. In 2017, North Korea successfully tested missiles 13 times, including a new ICBM that traveled 2,800 miles into space. While experts question the reliability of North Korea's ICBMs, including their accuracy and ability to carry large payloads, it is clear North Korea's missile program has advanced in the past decade.

Of special interest today are short-range ballistic missiles (SRBMs), with ranges of well under 1,000 miles. The modified Scud missiles fired by Iraq at Saudi Arabia and Israel during the Gulf War were (conventionally armed) SRBMs. In regional conflicts, the long range of more powerful missiles may not be necessary. The largest cities of Syria and Israel are only 133 miles from each other; the capital cities of Iraq and Iran are less than 500 miles apart, as are those of India and Pakistan. All of these states own ballistic missiles. Short-range and some medium-range ballistic missiles are cheap enough to be obtained and even home-produced by small middle-income states. Table 6.3 lists the capabilities of the 32 states with ballistic missiles.

Many short-range ballistic missiles, including those used by Iraq during the Gulf War, are highly inaccurate but still very difficult to defend against. With conventional warheads, they have more psychological than military utility (demoralizing an enemy

ballistic missiles The major strategic delivery vehicle for nuclear weapons; it carries a warhead along a trajectory (typically rising at least 50 miles high) and lets it drop on the target. See also *intercontinental ballistic missiles (ICBMs)*.

intercontinental ballistic missiles (ICBMs) The longest-range ballistic missiles, able to travel 5,000 miles. See also *ballistic missiles*.

Table 6.3 Ballistic Missile Capabilities, 2018

Country	Range (Miles)	Potential Targets
United States[a]	13,000	(World)
Russia[a]	13,000	(World)
China[a]	13,000	(World)
North Korea[a]	13,000	(World)
Britain[a]	4,600	(World; submarine-launched)
France[a]	3,700 [4,600]	(World; submarine-launched)
Iran[b,c]	900 [3,500]	Iraq, Kuwait, Afghanistan, Israel [Europe to Asia]
Israel[a,c]	900 [3,500]	Syria, Iraq, Saudi Arabia, Egypt [Iran]
India[a,c]	1,500 [2,500]	Pakistan, China, Afghanistan, Iran, Turkey
Pakistan[a]	800 [2,000]	India [Russia, Turkey, Israel]
Saudi Arabia	1,700	Iran, Iraq, Syria, Israel, Turkey, Yemen, Egypt, Libya, Sudan
Syria	300 [400]	Israel, Jordan, Iraq, Turkey
Egypt	400	Libya, Sudan, Israel
Yemen	300	Saudi Arabia
Libya	200	Egypt, Tunisia, Algeria
United Arab Emirates	200	Saudi Arabia, Iran
Afghanistan	200	Pakistan, Tajikistan, Uzbekistan
Kazakhstan	200	Uzbekistan, Tajikistan, Kyrgyzstan, Russia
Romania	200	Ukraine, Hungary
Turkmenistan	200	Iran, Afghanistan, Uzbekistan, Tajikistan
Armenia	200	Azerbaijan
Belarus	200	Russia, Ukraine, Poland
Ukraine	200	Russia, Belarus, Poland, Hungary, Romania
Georgia	200	Russia, Armenia, Turkey
South Korea	200	North Korea
Vietnam	200	China, Cambodia
Bahrain	200	Saudi Arabia, Qatar
Taiwan	200	China
Greece	100	Turkey
Turkey	100	Greece
Iraq	100	Iran, Syria, Saudi Arabia
Slovakia	80	Czech Rep., Hungary, Poland
Japan[c]	—	
Number of states with ballistic missiles: 32		

[a]States that have nuclear weapons.

[b]States believed to be trying to build nuclear weapons.

[c]States developing space-launch missiles adaptable as long-range ballistic missiles.

Notes: Bracketed range numbers indicate missiles under development. List of potential targets includes both hostile and friendly states, and is suggestive rather than comprehensive. Missile ranges increase with smaller payloads. 200-mile ranges (Scud-B) and 300-mile ranges (Scud Mod-C) are approximate for a three-quarter-ton payload. Saudi range is for a two-ton payload; South Korean range is for a half-ton payload.

Source: Based on Carnegie Endowment of International Peace.

population by attacking cities indiscriminately). With nuclear, chemical, or biological warheads, however, these missiles could be deadlier. The accuracy of delivery systems of all ranges improves as one moves to great powers, especially the United States. After traveling thousands of miles, the best U.S. missiles can land within 50 feet of a target half of the time. The trend in the U.S. nuclear arsenal has been toward less powerful warheads but more accurate missiles, for flexibility.

The **cruise missile** is a small winged missile that can navigate across thousands of miles of previously mapped terrain to reach a target, with the help of satellite guidance. Cruise missiles can be launched from ships, submarines, airplanes, or land. The United States used cruise missiles extensively against Iraq in 1993, Serbian forces in Bosnia in 1995, Serbia in 1999, and Iraq in 2003.

The spread of ballistic missiles has been difficult to control. Through the **Missile Technology Control Regime**, industrialized states try to limit the flow of missile-relevant technology to states in the global South, but they have had limited success. Short- and medium-range missiles (with ranges of up to about 2,000 miles) apparently are being developed by Iran, Israel, Saudi Arabia, Pakistan, India, North Korea, and possibly Argentina and Brazil. In 2009, Iran alarmed the West by testing a missile that could reach Egypt, Israel, and parts of Europe.

Small states or terrorists that may acquire nuclear weapons in the future could deliver them through innovative means. Because nuclear weapons are small, one could be smuggled into a target state by car, by speedboat, or in diplomatic pouches.

Since 2001, the United States has run a container security initiative aimed at preventing weapons of mass destruction from reaching U.S. shores in seaborne shipping containers. But doing so without impeding the prosperity-inducing flow of international trade is a daunting challenge—nearly 8 million shipping containers pass through U.S. ports every year. In 2006, the U.S. Congress scuttled a deal that would have let a company based in Dubai, an Arab country, control some operations at several U.S. ports (as other foreign companies already do).

6.4.3 Chemical and Biological Weapons

A *chemical weapon* releases chemicals that disable and kill people. The chemicals vary from lethal ones such as nerve gas to merely irritating ones such as tear gas. Different chemicals interfere with the nervous system, blood, breathing, or other body functions. Some can be absorbed through the skin; others must be inhaled. Some persist in the target area long after their use; others disperse quickly.

It is possible to defend against most chemical weapons by dressing troops in protective clothing and gas masks and following elaborate procedures to decontaminate equipment. But protective suits are hot, and antichemical measures reduce the efficiency of armies. In addition, civilians are much less likely to have protection against chemicals than are military forces. Chemical weapons are by nature indiscriminate about whom they kill. Several times, chemical weapons have been deliberately used against civilians (notably by the Iraqi government against Iraqi Kurds in the 1980s).

Use of chemical weapons in war has been rare. Mustard gas, which produces skin blisters and lung damage, was widely used in artillery shells in World War I. After the horrors of that war, the use of chemical weapons was banned in the 1925 Geneva Protocol, still in effect today. In World War II, both sides were armed with chemical weapons but neither used them, for fear of retaliation. Since then (with possibly a few unclear exceptions), only Iraq has violated the treaty—against Iran in the 1980s. Unfortunately, Iraq's actions not only breached a psychological barrier against using chemical weapons but also showed such

cruise missile A small winged missile that can navigate across thousands of miles of previously mapped terrain to reach a particular target; it can carry either a nuclear or a conventional warhead.

Missile Technology Control Regime A set of agreements through which industrialized states try to limit the flow of missile-relevant technology to third world states.

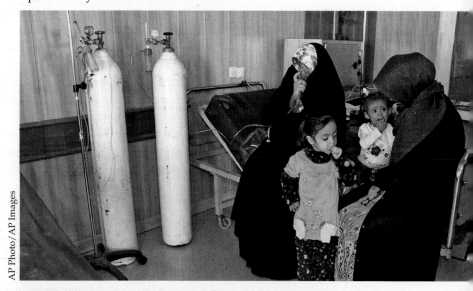
VULNERABLE Civilians are very vulnerable to weapons of mass destruction, especially chemical weapons. Here, victims exposed to a chemical attack by the Islamic State are treated at a hospital in northern Iraq, 2016.

AP Photo/AP Images

weapons to be cheap and effective against human waves of attackers without protective gear. This example stimulated dozens more poor states to begin acquiring chemical weapons. Chemical weapons are a cheap way for states to gain weapons of mass destruction. Chemical weapons can be produced using processes and facilities similar to those for pesticides, pharmaceuticals, and other civilian products, which makes it difficult to find chemical weapons facilities in suspect countries or to deny those states access to the needed chemicals and equipment.

The 1925 Geneva Protocol did not ban the production or possession of chemical weapons, only their use, and several dozen states built stockpiles of them. The United States and the Soviet Union maintained large arsenals of chemical weapons during the Cold War but have reduced them greatly in the past two decades. The 1992 **Chemical Weapons Convention** to ban the production and possession of chemical weapons has been signed by all the great powers and nearly all other states, with a few exceptions, including Egypt, Angola, and North Korea. The new treaty includes strict verification provisions and the threat of sanctions against violators, including nonparticipants in the treaty (an important extension). Several states (including India, China, South Korea, France, and Britain) admitted to having secret chemical weapons programs, which are now being dismantled under international oversight. Russia faced a long and costly task of destroying a 44,000-ton arsenal of chemical weapons built during the Cold War, yet in September 2017 announced that it had completed that task. The United States has until 2023 to complete the destruction of its stockpile. From 1997 to 2016, the treaty organization oversaw the elimination of more than half of the world's chemical weapons (nearly 70,000 metric tons).

In 2013, Syria admitted to possessing chemical weapons and agreed to the destruction of its weapons that were used against rebel groups in that country's civil war. Unfortunately, since 2013, there have been several suspected uses of chemical weapons in Syria and in neighboring Iraq. In 2016, the UN blamed the government of Syria for using chemical weapons in 2014 and 2015, and blamed the Islamic State for using mustard gas in 2015. Later, in 2018, the United States bombed Syrian targets in response to the use of chemical weapons by the Syrian government.

Biological weapons resemble chemical ones, but they use deadly microorganisms or biologically derived toxins. Some use viruses or bacteria that cause fatal diseases, such as smallpox, bubonic plague, and anthrax. Others cause nonfatal, but incapacitating, diseases or diseases that kill livestock. Theoretically, a single weapon could spark an epidemic in an entire population, but this would pose too great a danger, so less contagious microorganisms are preferred. Biological weapons have almost never been used in war (Japan tried some on a few Chinese villages in World War II). Their potential strikes many political leaders as a Pandora's box that could let loose uncontrollable forces if the box were opened.

For this reason, the development, production, and possession of biological weapons are banned under the 1972 **Biological Weapons Convention**, signed by more than 100 countries, including the great powers. The superpowers destroyed their stocks of biological weapons and had to restrict their biological weapons complexes to defensive research rather than the development of weapons. However, because the treaty makes no provision for inspection and because biological weapons programs are, like chemical ones, relatively easy to hide, several states remain under suspicion of having biological weapons. UN inspections of Iraq in the mid-1990s uncovered an active biological weapons program. Evidence surfaced after the collapse of the Soviet Union that a secret biological weapons program had been under way there as well. In 2001, the United States pulled out of talks to strengthen the 1972 treaty, declaring the proposed modifications unworkable.

Today the United States and perhaps a dozen other countries maintain biological weapons research (not banned by the treaty). Researchers try to ascertain the military implications of advances in biotechnology.

Chemical Weapons Convention (1992) An agreement that bans the production and possession of chemical weapons and includes strict verification provisions and the threat of sanctions against violators and nonparticipants in the treaty.

Biological Weapons Convention (1972) An agreement that prohibits the development, production, and possession of biological weapons but makes no provision for inspections.

6.4.4 Proliferation

Proliferation is the spread of weapons of mass destruction—nuclear weapons, ballistic missiles, and chemical or biological weapons—into the hands of more actors. The implications of proliferation for IR are difficult to predict but profound. Ballistic missiles with weapons of mass destruction remove the territorial protection offered by state borders and make each state vulnerable to others. Some realists, who believe in the rationality of state actions, are not so upset by this prospect, and some even welcome it. They reason that, in a world where the use of military force could lead to mutual annihilation, there would be fewer wars—just as during the arms race of the Cold War, the superpowers did not blow each other up. Other IR scholars who put less faith in the rationality of state leaders are much more alarmed by proliferation. They fear that, with more and more nuclear (or chemical/biological) actors, miscalculation or accident—or fanatical terrorism—could lead to the use of weapons of mass destruction on a scale unseen since 1945.

The leaders of the great powers tend to side with the second group. They have tried to restrict the most destructive weapons to the great powers. Proliferation erodes the great powers' advantage relative to middle powers. There is also a widespread fear that these weapons may fall into the hands of terrorists or other nonstate actors who would be immune to threats of retaliation (with no territory or cities to defend). Evidence captured during the 2001 war in Afghanistan showed that the al Qaeda organization was trying to obtain weapons of mass destruction and would have been willing to use them. Lax security at the vast, far-flung former Soviet nuclear complex increased fears that fissionable materials could reach terrorists.

Nuclear proliferation could occur simply by a state or nonstate actor's buying (or stealing) one or more nuclear weapons or the components to build one. The means to prevent this include covert intelligence, tight security measures, and safeguards to prevent a stolen weapon from being used. In 2007, two teams of armed assailants broke into the South African nuclear facility where atomic bombs had once been designed and produced. After reaching the control room and shooting one guard, they were repelled, leaving a mystery along with doubts about the security of such nuclear facilities. As broader political unrest occurs in other nuclear states, notably Pakistan, thoughts often turn toward the safety of nuclear weapons and materials.

A stronger form of nuclear proliferation is the development by states of nuclear complexes to produce their own nuclear weapons on an ongoing basis. Here, larger numbers of weapons are involved and strong potentials exist for arms races in regional conflicts and rivalries. The relevant regional conflicts are those between Israel and the Arab states, Iran and its Arab neighbors, India and Pakistan, the two Koreas, and possibly Taiwan and China. India and Pakistan each have dozens of nuclear weapons and the missiles to deliver them. North Korea tested weapons in 2006 and 2009. South Africa reported after the fact that it had built several nuclear weapons but then dismantled them in the 1980s before white minority rule ended.

In the 1990s, Pakistan's top nuclear scientist sold bomb kits with low-grade uranium, enrichment centrifuges, and bomb designs to Libya, North Korea, and Iran. Libya gave up its bomb-making program, North Korea negotiated but remained coy about its uranium program (while giving up its plutonium program), and Iran continues to enrich uranium. Israel has never officially admitted that it has nuclear weapons but is widely believed to have a hundred or more. Israel wants these capabilities to convince Arab leaders that military conquest of Israel is impossible. To prevent Iraq from developing nuclear weapons,

proliferation The spread of weapons of mass destruction (nuclear, chemical, or biological weapons) into the hands of more actors.

SOMETHING TO HIDE The most important hurdle in making nuclear weapons is access to fissionable materials (plutonium and uranium). Iran's enrichment of uranium could give that country nuclear bombs within the decade. Fueling Western suspicions, Iran has not been forthcoming with international inspectors. Iran bulldozed this large site and removed its topsoil in 2004 before letting inspectors in. Western states and the UN Security Council have applied sanctions against Iran, and a controversial nuclear deal was agreed to in 2015.

Israel carried out a bombing raid on the main facility of the Iraqi nuclear complex in 1981. In 2007, Israeli warplanes destroyed a site in Syria thought to be a nuclear reactor of North Korean design. Syria quickly cleared all traces of the building after the attack.

Non-Proliferation Treaty (NPT) (1968) A treaty that created a framework for controlling the spread of nuclear materials and expertise, including the International Atomic Energy Agency (IAEA), a UN agency based in Vienna that is charged with inspecting the nuclear power industry in NPT member states to prevent secret military diversions of nuclear materials.

The **Non-Proliferation Treaty (NPT)** of 1968 created a framework for controlling the spread of nuclear materials and expertise. The International Atomic Energy Agency (IAEA), a UN agency based in Austria, is charged with inspecting the nuclear power industry in member states to prevent secret military diversions of nuclear materials. However, a number of potential nuclear states (such as Israel) have not signed the NPT, and even states that have signed may sneak around its provisions by keeping some facilities secret (as Iraq and Iran did). Under the terms of the Gulf War cease-fire, Iraq's nuclear program was uncovered and dismantled by the IAEA. In 2006, a deal between the United States and India to share nuclear technology led many states to question the NPT because those benefits were supposedly reserved for only signatories. Nonetheless the deal received final U.S. and Indian approval in 2008.

North Korea withdrew from the IAEA in 1993 and then bargained with Western leaders to get economic assistance, including safer reactors, in exchange for freezing its nuclear program. North Korea's leader died months later, but the compromise held up. In 1999, North Korea allowed inspection of a disputed underground complex and agreed to suspend missile tests in exchange for aid and partial lifting of U.S. trade sanctions. Then in 2002, the United States confronted North Korea with evidence of a secret uranium enrichment program, which the North Koreans then admitted to having. North Korea then pulled out of the agreement and out of the IAEA; restarted its nuclear reactor; and apparently turned its existing plutonium into a half dozen bombs within months, one of which it tested in 2006. North Korea again agreed to give up its program in 2008, but after another nuclear test in 2009, it began processing nuclear material again. After increasing pressure from the international community in 2017, especially the United States, North Korea agreed to begin negotiations over its nuclear program in 2018.

At present, in addition to the "big five" Security Council members, nuclear states are Israel, India and Pakistan (with dozens of warheads each, and growing), and North Korea (with perhaps a half dozen, also growing).

Iran denies but appears to be working to develop nuclear weapons. Since 2003, Iran first agreed to suspend its uranium enrichment program and allow surprise IAEA inspections, then restarted enrichment, suspended it again, and restarted it again. In 2005, U.S.-backed efforts by Europe to reach a deal faltered. In 2006, the UN Security Council condemned Iran's actions and imposed mild sanctions. Iran insisted on its right to enrich uranium for what it called peaceful purposes. In 2008, Iran's behavior led to further UN Security Council sanctions, and in 2009, after a secret underground processing facility was discovered, Iran was engaged in talks over the program with Western powers. An interim deal was reached in late 2013 whereby Iran agreed to slow uranium processes in exchange for relief from sanctions. A final deal was reached in mid-2015 that allowed Iran to continue enrichment of uranium, but only to low levels that could not be used to make a weapon. Iran also agreed to allow increased inspections of its nuclear sites. In exchange, Western powers agreed to lift sanctions against Iran, although some of these sanctions will not be lifted until Iran dismantles certain parts of its nuclear program. That agreement was controversial in the United States and the Trump Administration withdrew from the agreement in 2018.

A number of middle powers and two great powers (Japan and Germany) have the potential to make nuclear weapons but have chosen not to do so. The reasons for deciding against "going nuclear" include norms against using nuclear weapons; fears of retaliation; and practical constraints, including cost. Brazil and Argentina seemed to be headed for a nuclear arms race in the 1980s but then called it off as civilians replaced military governments in both countries. In 2004, after years of resistance, Brazil gave IAEA inspectors access to a controversial uranium enrichment plant (not part of a nuclear weapons program, evidently).

6.4.5 Nuclear Strategy and Arms Control

The term *nuclear strategy* refers to decisions about how many nuclear weapons to deploy, what delivery systems to put them on, and what policies to adopt regarding the circumstances in which they would be used.

The reason for possessing nuclear weapons is almost always to deter another state from a nuclear or conventional attack by threatening ruinous retaliation. This should work if state leaders are rational actors wanting to avoid the huge costs of a nuclear attack. But it will work only if other states believe that a state's threat to use nuclear weapons is credible. The search for a credible deterrent by two or more hostile states tends to lead to an ever-growing arsenal of nuclear weapons. To follow this logic, start with Pakistan's deployment of its first nuclear missile aimed at India (the example also works with the countries reversed). Then India would not attack—that is, unless it could prevent Pakistan from using its missile. India could do this by building offensive forces capable of wiping out the Pakistani missile (probably using nuclear weapons, but that is not the key point here). Then the Pakistani missile, rather than deter India, would merely spur India to destroy the missile before any other attack. An attack intended to destroy—largely or entirely—a state's nuclear weapons before they can be used is called a *first strike*.

Pakistan could make its missile survivable (probably by making it mobile). It could also build more nuclear missiles so that even if some were destroyed in an Indian first strike, some would survive with which to retaliate. Weapons that can take a first strike and still strike back give a state *second-strike* capabilities. Possession of second-strike capabilities by both sides is called **mutually assured destruction (MAD)** because neither side can prevent the other from destroying it. The term implies that the strategy, though reflecting "rationality," is actually insane (mad) because deviations from rationality could destroy both sides.

If India could not assuredly *destroy* Pakistan's missile, it would undoubtedly deploy its own nuclear missile(s) to *deter* Pakistan from using its missile. India, too, could achieve a second-strike capability. Now the question of credibility becomes important. In theory, India could launch a nonnuclear attack on Pakistan, knowing that rational Pakistani leaders would rather lose such a war than use their nuclear weapons and bring on an Indian nuclear response. The nuclear missiles in effect cancel each other out.

Defense has played little role in nuclear strategy because no effective defense against missile attack has been devised. However, the United States is spending billions of dollars a year to try to develop defenses that could shoot down incoming ballistic missiles. The program is called the **Strategic Defense Initiative (SDI)**, Star Wars, or Ballistic Missile Defense (BMD). It originated in President Ronald Reagan's 1983 call for a comprehensive shield that would make nuclear missiles obsolete. However, the mission soon shifted to defending some U.S. missiles in a massive Soviet attack. After the Cold War, the mission shifted again, to protecting U.S. territory from a very limited missile attack (at most a few missiles), such as might occur in an unauthorized launch, an accident, or an attack by a small state. Japan is spending $1 billion a year to build a

mutually assured destruction (MAD) The possession of second-strike nuclear capabilities, which ensures that neither of two adversaries could prevent the other from destroying it in an all-out war. See also *deterrence*.

Strategic Defense Initiative (SDI) A U.S. effort, also known as Star Wars, to develop defenses that could shoot down incoming ballistic missiles, spurred by President Ronald Reagan in 1983. Critics call it an expensive failure that will likely be ineffective. See also *Anti-Ballistic Missile (ABM) Treaty*.

Ilia Yefimovich/Getty Images

DEFENSIVE MOVE The nuclear arms race between the superpowers during the Cold War led to strategies and arms control agreements that helped develop norms and expectations about nuclear weapons and missiles. India and Pakistan have followed a similar arms race, leading to mutual deterrence. Recently, defense against missiles has begun to enter the strategic calculus. Here, Israel's Iron Dome system shoots down short-range missiles from Gaza, 2014.

U.S.-designed missile defense system, which it tested successfully in late 2007. North Korea has more than 600 ballistic missiles capable of hitting Japan, however.

As of 2010, the United States is deploying a multilayer system with 24 ground-based interceptor missiles in Alaska and California (directed toward the North Korean threat), 21 ship-based interceptors, about 500 Patriot missiles for short-range ballistic missile threats, and a series of radar and control centers. It had begun testing an airplane-based laser system and had concluded agreements with Poland and the Czech Republic to build missile defenses in those countries before reversing these plans in favor of a sea-based system to guard against any Iranian threat, with a radar system based in Turkey. In 2012 and 2014, Israel used a new Iron Dome defense system to shoot down short-range missiles fired by Hamas in large numbers.

In addition to the technical challenges of stopping incoming ballistic missile warheads, such as distinguishing warheads from decoys, a true strategic defense would also have to stop cruise missiles (possibly launched from submarines), airplanes, and more innovative delivery systems. If a rogue state or terrorist group struck the United States with a nuclear weapon, it would probably not use an ICBM to do so.

During the Cold War, the superpowers' nuclear forces grew and technologies developed. Those evolving force structures were codified (more than constrained) by a series of arms control agreements. *Arms control* is an effort by two or more states to regulate by formal agreement their acquisition of weapons, using the reciprocity principle to solve the collective goods problem of expensive arms races that ultimately benefit neither side (see the Seeking the Collective Good box). Arms control is broader than just nuclear weapons—for instance, after World War I the great

Seeking the Collective Good
Arms Control
COLLECTIVE GOOD: Limiting Nuclear Arsenals

BACKGROUND After the creation of nuclear weapons in World War II, the two superpowers (the United States and the Soviet Union) built large arsenals of them during the decades of the Cold War. Eventually, each side had tens of thousands. These nuclear weapons posed a grave danger that miscalculation or accident could lead to truly catastrophic consequences. Limiting and controlling nuclear arms, to avoid this catastrophic outcome, is a collective good. Both sides benefited if nuclear war was avoided, regardless of which side gave up however many weapons in a negotiated agreement.

CHALLENGE Arms races represent the dark side of the reciprocity principle, a downward spiral of relations in which each reciprocates the other's hostile actions—in this case, deploying more nuclear weapons. Since the 1960s, the two sides have used negotiated agreements to try to control the arms race. For decades the effort merely channeled and illuminated the steady buildup of arms on both sides.

SOLUTION The same reciprocity that fueled the arms race also fueled its reversal after the Cold War ended. Each side has matched the other's reductions in weapons, governed by a series of formal, verifiable treaties. The arsenals have shrunk dramatically as a result.

The U.S. and Russian presidents sign thick arms control treaty, 2010.

In 2010, the U.S. and Russian presidents signed a new nuclear arms control treaty. Over seven years it has cut strategic nuclear warheads by almost one-third, from 2,200 to 1,550 for each side. Each side also agreed to extensive monitoring to ensure that the other side is living up to its bargain (despite rising tensions in 2018, both sides certified they had fulfilled the terms of the agreement). Using the reciprocity principle, the former superpowers have used step-by-step measures, each side matching the other, first to limit and then to reduce greatly their stockpiles of nuclear weapons.

powers negotiated limits on sizes of navies—but in the Cold War, nuclear weapons were the main focus of arms control. Arms control agreements typically require long, formal negotiations with many technical discussions, culminating in a treaty. Some arms control treaties are multilateral, but during the Cold War most were bilateral (U.S.-Soviet). Some stay in effect indefinitely; others have a limited term.

Several treaties in the 1970s locked in the superpowers' basic parity in nuclear capabilities under MAD. The 1972 **Anti-Ballistic Missile (ABM) Treaty** prevented either side from using a ballistic missile defense as a shield from which to launch a first strike. However, to allow full-scale testing of missile-defense technologies, the United States withdrew from the ABM Treaty with six months' notice (as provided in the treaty) in 2002. President Bush called the treaty a relic of the Cold War, but critics called U.S. missile defense a costly blunder

MPI / Getty Images

THE WAR IS OVER U.S. and Russian nuclear forces were greatly reduced in the 1990s. Here, U.S. B-52 bombers are being chopped up, under the eye of Russian satellites, to bring force levels down.

that could induce China to enlarge its minimal nuclear arsenal greatly (which, in turn, could accelerate India's nuclear weapons production and thus Pakistan's as well).

The Strategic Arms Limitation Treaties (SALT) in the 1970s put formal ceilings on the growth of both sides' strategic weapons. More recent arms control agreements regulated the substantial reduction of nuclear forces after the end of the Cold War. The U.S. arsenal peaked in the 1960s at more than 30,000 warheads; the Soviet arsenal peaked in the 1980s at more than 40,000. The 1991 Strategic Arms Reduction Treaty (START) limited warheads to 6,000 on each side. Meanwhile, the 2002 Strategic Offensive Reductions Treaty (SORT) called for further reductions to 2,200 each by 2012, but it relies on START mechanisms for verification. In March 2010, the sides signed a treaty (referred to as New START) that will lower the number of warheads to 1,550 and also creates additional verification mechanisms for both sides. The reciprocity principle that helped fuel the arms race also enables its step-by-step reversal.

China, France, and Britain each have several hundred weapons—France's and Britain's mostly on submarine-launched missiles and China's mostly on long-range bombers and intermediate-range missiles.

A **Comprehensive Test Ban Treaty (CTBT)** to halt all nuclear test explosions was signed in 1996 after decades of stalemate. It aims to impede the development of new types of nuclear weapons. However, the treaty does not take effect until signed and ratified by all 44 states believed capable of building at least a crude nuclear weapon. India did not sign the CTBT and defied it in 1998 with five nuclear tests. Pakistan followed suit with its own tests. The U.S. Senate voted in 1999 against ratifying the CTBT. Russia ratified it in 2000. Although no nuclear tests occurred worldwide in 1999–2005, North Korea's nuclear tests in 2006, 2009, 2013, 2016, and 2017 dealt more setbacks to the CTBT.

All the weapons of mass destruction are relatively difficult and expensive to build, yet they provide only specialized capabilities that are rarely if ever actually used. This is why most states that could technically acquire them have decided not to do so. Such cost-benefit thinking also applies more broadly to states' decisions about the acquisition of all kinds of military forces.

Anti-Ballistic Missile (ABM) Treaty (1972) A treaty that prohibited either the United States or the Soviet Union from using a ballistic missile defense as a shield, which would have undermined mutually assured destruction and the basis of deterrence. See also *mutually assured destruction (MAD)* and *Strategic Defense Initiative (SDI)*.

Comprehensive Test Ban Treaty (CTBT) (1996) A treaty that bans all nuclear weapons testing, thereby broadening the ban on atmospheric testing negotiated in 1963.

6.5 States and Militaries

Explain how tensions in civil-military relations can undermine military operations and even threaten political stability.

Given the range of military capabilities available to states (at various costs), how much and what types should state leaders choose to acquire? This question confronts all states, but they answer it in different ways.

6.5.1 Military Economics

Choices about military forces depend on the connection between a state's military spending and its economic health. People in the United States once believed that "war is good for the economy" because, seemingly, military spending had helped end the Great Depression in the late 1930s. If this were true, state leaders would not face difficult choices in setting military budgets. High military spending would give them both more military capabilities for use in international conflicts *and* more economic growth for domestic needs (buying popular and political support in various ways). Unfortunately for state leaders, allocating economic resources for military purposes deprives the rest of the economy and reduces its long-term growth.

Negative effects of war

Both the long- and short-term effects of military spending are magnified by actual warfare. War not only stimulates high military spending, but it also destroys capital (people, cities, farms, and factories in battle areas) and causes inflation (reducing the supply of various goods while increasing demand for them). Governments must pay for war goods by borrowing money (increasing government debt), by printing more currency (fueling inflation), or by raising taxes (reducing spending and investment). U.S. revolutionary Thomas Paine warned in 1787 that "war … has but one thing certain, and that is to increase taxes."[3]

Positive effects of war

Nonetheless, war and high military spending can have certain economic benefits. Short-term stimulation can result from a boost in military spending. Another potential benefit is the acquisition of territory (containing resources and capital). Serbian ultra-nationalists made fortunes off the plunder of Bosnians whom they "ethnically cleansed," and Congolese militia leaders enriched themselves with minerals exported during the civil war. Another potential economic benefit of war is to stir up a population's patriotism so that it will work harder for less pay. But overall, the economic costs of war usually far surpass any benefits.

States vary widely in military spending, from Costa Rica, with almost no military spending at all, to North Korea, which devotes 20 percent or more of gross domestic product (GDP) to military purposes. If military budgets are too low, states may be unprepared to meet a security threat; in the worst case, they may even be overrun and conquered militarily. But if leaders set military budgets too high, they will overburden and stifle the national economy.

World military spending is 2.2 percent of the total goods and services in the world economy—about $1.7 trillion every year, or roughly $1 million every 20 seconds. Most is spent by a few big states, about 40 percent by the United States alone. World military spending is a vast flow of money that could, if redirected to other purposes, change the world profoundly and improve major world problems. Of course, "the world" does not spend this money or choose how to direct it; states do.

In the global South, military spending varies greatly across countries, depending in part on the government in power (military or civilian). Spending also depends heavily on available hard currency, from exports of oil or other products, to pay for arms purchases.

Most arms sales worldwide go to the global South. In recent decades, about half of these arms imports have been in the Middle East, but lately India and China have taken

---

[3] Paine, Thomas. *The Writings of Thomas Paine.* Vol. 2. Knickerbocker, 1894.

a growing share. The great majority of international arms exports come from the United States, with Russia, France, and Britain also ranking. In the immediate post–Cold War era, global arms sales fell, but they have since climbed back to near–Cold War levels.

Activists have called attention to the sales of small arms, especially assault rifles, to unstable conflict zones where irregular armies commit brutalities. In 2001, 140 states agreed to a voluntary pact to curb small-arms sales to conflict zones. The United States, by far the largest exporter of small arms, blocked proposals to restrict sales of military weapons to rebel movements and to civilians. The Arms Trade Treaty passed the UN General Assembly in 2013 with only Iran, North Korea, and Syria voting no. The treaty entered into force in December 2014. While 94 countries have ratified the treaty, ratification by the U.S. Senate appears unlikely.

Beyond these considerations about the size of military forces, the configuration of a state's military forces also presents difficult choices. Different missions require different forces. During the Cold War, about half of all military spending in the U.S. budget—and of world military spending—was directed toward the East-West conflict in Europe. Now other missions such as intervention in regional conflicts and counterinsurgency are more important. And other new missions for military forces include humanitarian assistance, drug interdiction, and aid to other nations in building roads and schools.

6.5.2 Control of Military Forces

One cannot take for granted the ability of a state leader to make military forces take desired actions. At best, military forces are large and complex institutions operating in especially difficult conditions during wartime. At worst, military forces have a mind of their own. Sometimes, the state leader appears to exert only incomplete control over the military.

States control military forces through a **chain of command**, running from the highest authority through a hierarchy spreading out to the lowest-level soldiers. The highest authority, or commander in chief, is usually the top political leader. The importance of this military hierarchy is illustrated by a story from ancient China in which a king was thinking of hiring Sun Tzu as an adviser. As a test, the king asked Sun Tzu to turn the king's harem of 200 concubines into troops. Sun Tzu divided them into two units, commanded by the king's two favorites. He explained the signals to face forward, backward, right, and left. But when he gave the signals, the women just laughed. Sun Tzu then had the two "officers" executed on the spot and put the next most senior concubines in their places. When he gave the signals again, the women obeyed flawlessly. Sun Tzu declared that the troops are in good order and may be deployed as the king desires. Thus, military hierarchy and discipline make armed forces function as instruments of state power—at the price of brutality and loss of individual freedom.

In actual battle conditions, controlling armed forces is especially difficult because of complex operations, rapid change, and the fog of war created by the gap between battlefield activity and command-level information. Participants are pumped up with adrenaline,

chain of command A hierarchy of officials (often civilian as well as military) through which states control military forces.

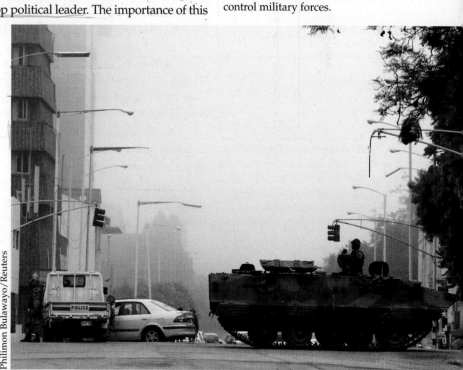

Philimon Bulawayo/Reuters

INTO THE STREETS Through a hierarchical chain of command, states control the actions of millions of individual soldiers, creating leverage in the hands of state leaders. But armed forces still sometimes defy civilian control. Here, a tank takes up position in a busy intersection in Harare, Zimbabwe, after the military there arrested the longtime ruler, forcing him from power, 2017.

deafened by noise, and confused by a mass of activity that—from the middle of it—may seem to make no sense. They are called on to perform actions that may run against basic instincts as well as moral norms—killing people and risking death. It is difficult to coordinate forces effectively in order to carry out overall plans of action. Military forces counteract these problems through military discipline. Insubordination, mutiny, and deserting are serious offenses punishable by prison or death. But discipline depends not only on punishment but also on patriotism and professionalism on the part of soldiers. Officers play to nationalist sentiments, reminding soldiers that they fight for their nation and family. Combat, logistics, communication, and command all depend on individual performance; motivation matters.

Military units also rely on soldiers' sense of group solidarity. Soldiers risk their lives because their "buddies" depend on them. Abstractions such as nationalism, patriotism, and religious fervor are important, but loyalty to the immediate group (along with a survival instinct) is a stronger motivator. Recent debates about participation of women in the U.S. armed forces revolve around whether their presence disrupts group solidarity. (Evidence suggests that it need not, and in 2011, the ban on U.S. gay soldiers was lifted for similar reasons.)

Finally, officers and political leaders need accurate intelligence to make good decisions. Of course, even the most advanced intelligence systems cannot stop human error. Friendly-fire incidents account for a substantial fraction of U.S. military fatalities. In late 2001, U.S. special forces were traveling with Hamid Karzai, believed at the time to be the only person who could lead a united, U.S.-allied Afghan government. As a U.S. soldier called in airstrikes on an enemy position, the battery in his GPS unit needed changing, and the unit's coordinates defaulted to its own position. A U.S. warplane dropped a bomb right on that target, killing three U.S. soldiers and five Afghan allies and nearly killing Karzai himself.

6.5.3 Civil-Military Relations

Beyond overcoming chaos and complexity, state leaders sometimes must confront challenges from within their own military ranks as well. Many states, especially democratic states, adhere to a principle of *civilian supremacy*. This is the idea that civilian leaders (who are either elected or appointed) are at the top of the chain of command. Civilians, not military officers, decide when and where the military fights. The officers, by contrast, are supposed to control how the military fights.

This division of labor between civilians and militaries inevitably leads to tensions. The interaction of civilian with military leaders—called **civil-military relations**—is an important factor in how states use force. Military leaders may undermine the authority of civilian leaders in carrying out foreign policies, or they may even threaten civilian supremacy if certain actions are taken in international conflicts. Military officers also want autonomy of decision once force is committed in order to avoid the problems created in the Vietnam War when President Johnson sat in the White House situation room daily picking targets for bombing raids. Worse yet, in the North Atlantic Treaty Organization's (NATO's) 1999 bombing of Serbia, politicians in multiple countries had to approve specific targets. In 2010, the commanding American general in Afghanistan lost his job after publicly questioning President Obama's Afghanistan policies.

Even outside the context of ongoing warfare, differences between civilian and military leaders can lead to tensions. In the United States, opinion surveys consistently show that military officers, on average, maintain different opinions than civilians on issues such as the use of force as a tool of leverage. Scholars have begun to study why this gap between civilians and the military has developed and its implications for American foreign policy.

Similar tensions exist in other democracies. In Turkey, tensions have grown between the Islamic government and its military. Historically, Turkey's military has intervened numerous times to take control from elected leaders when military officers felt the

civil-military relations The relations between a state's civilian leaders and the military leadership. In most countries, the military takes orders from civilian leaders. In extreme cases, poor civil-military relations can lead to military coups.

government was threatening the secular nature of Turkey. Recently, however, the civilian government has been aggressive in arresting officers who it believes were plotting a coup. These actions have led to a fragile situation in that country. In the 2011 Arab Spring, the Egyptian military refused to fire on protesters, whereas Syrian forces did use lethal fire.

If tensions become too sharp between civilian leaders and their military forces, a **coup d'état** (French for "blow against the state") can result. A coup is the seizure of political power by domestic military forces—a change of political power outside the state's constitutional order. The outcome of a coup attempt is hard to predict. If most or all of the military go along with the coup, civilian leaders are generally helpless to stop it. But if most of the military officers follow the existing chain of command, the coup is doomed. In the Philippines in the late 1980s, the top general, Fidel Ramos, remained loyal to the civilian president, Corazón Aquino, in seven coup attempts by subordinate officers. In each case, the bulk of the Philippine military forces stayed loyal to Ramos, and the coups failed.

International pressures, such as sanctions, may also convince military leaders to step down. In late 2009, military leaders took power in Honduras after deposing its president. The international community, including the Organization of American States (OAS), pressured Honduras after the 2009 coup. Elections were held in the fall of 2009, restoring a democratic government, but Hondurans remain divided over the legitimacy of the new government.

If a coup is successful, military forces themselves control the government. These **military governments** tend to be the most common in poor countries, where the military may be the only large modern institution in the country. Ironically, the disciplined central command of military forces, which makes them effective as tools of state influence, also lets the state lose control of them to military officers. Soldiers are trained to follow the orders of their commanding officers, not to think about politics.

Covert operations can also get out of the control of governments. Several thousand such operations were mounted during the Cold War, when the CIA and its Soviet counterpart, the KGB, waged an ongoing worldwide secret war. CIA covert operations in the 1950s overthrew unfriendly foreign governments—in Iran and Guatemala—by organizing coups against them. The CIA-organized Bay of Pigs invasion in Cuba, in 1961, was its first big failure, followed by other failed efforts against the Castro government (including eight assassination attempts). CIA covert activities were sharply scaled back after congressional hearings in the 1970s revealed scandals. After September 2001, the executive branch enjoyed greater authority in conducting covert operations with less congressional scrutiny.

Overall, states face complex choices regarding the configuration of their military forces in the post–Cold War era. Not only have the immediate contingencies and threats changed drastically but the nature of threats in the new era is unclear. Perhaps most important, world order itself is evolving even as military technologies do. The next chapter will discuss the evolving structures and norms governing international political relations and how they are changing the nature of world order.

coup d'état French for "blow against the state"; a term that refers to the seizure of political power by domestic military forces—that is, a change of political power outside the state's constitutional order.

military governments States in which military forces control the government; they are most common in third world countries, where the military may be the only large modern institution.

Chapter Review

Summary

- Military forces include a wide variety of capabilities suited to different purposes. Conventional warfare requires different kinds of forces than those needed to threaten the use of nuclear, chemical, or biological weapons.

- Control of territory is fundamental to state sovereignty and is accomplished primarily with ground forces.

- Air war, using precision-guided bombs against battlefield targets, proved extremely effective in the U.S.

campaigns in Iraq in 1991, Serbia in 1999, Afghanistan in 2001, and Iraq in 2003.

- Drones and electronic warfare are increasingly important tools of leverage for states and nonstate actors.

- Terrorism is effective if it damages morale in a population and gains media exposure for the cause.

- The September 2001 attacks differed from earlier terrorism both in their scale of destruction and in the long reach of the global al Qaeda terrorist network. The attacks forced dramatic changes in U.S. and worldwide security arrangements and sparked U.S. military intervention in Afghanistan to overthrow the Taliban regime and destroy the al Qaeda bases there.

- Weapons of mass destruction—nuclear, chemical, and biological—have rarely been used in war.

- The production of nuclear weapons is technically within the means of many states and some nonstate actors, but the necessary fissionable material (uranium-235 or plutonium) is very difficult to obtain.

- Most industrialized states, and many poor ones, have refrained voluntarily from acquiring nuclear weapons. These states include two great powers, Germany and Japan.

- More states are acquiring ballistic missiles capable of striking other states from hundreds of miles away (or farther, depending on the missile's range). But no state has ever attacked another with weapons of mass destruction mounted on ballistic missiles.

- Chemical weapons are cheaper to build than nuclear weapons, they have similar threat value, and their production is harder to detect. More middle powers have chemical weapons than nuclear ones. A new treaty bans the possession and use of chemical weapons.

- Several states conduct research into biological warfare, but by treaty the possession of such weapons is banned.

- Slowing the proliferation of ballistic missiles and weapons of mass destruction in the global South is a central concern of the great powers.

- The United States is testing systems to defend against ballistic missile attack, although none has yet proven feasible, and has withdrawn from the ABM Treaty with Russia to pursue this program.

- The United States and Russia have arsenals of thousands of nuclear weapons; China, Britain, and France have hundreds. Israel, India, and Pakistan each have scores. Weapons deployments are guided by nuclear strategy based on the concept of deterrence.

- Arms control agreements formally define the contours of an arms race or mutual disarmament process. Arms control helped build confidence between the superpowers during the Cold War.

- Political leaders face difficult choices in configuring military forces and paying for them. Military spending tends to stimulate economic growth in the short term but reduce growth over the long term.

- In the 1990s, military forces and expenditures of the great powers—especially Russia—were reduced and restructured.

- Except in times of civil war, state leaders—whether civilian or military—control military forces through a single hierarchical chain of command.

- Military forces can threaten the domestic power of state leaders, who are vulnerable to being overthrown by coups d'état.

Key Terms

infantry 174
counterinsurgency 176
landmines 177
power projection 177
drones 181
electronic warfare 183
stealth technology 184
state-sponsored terrorism 187
weapons of mass destruction
    (WMDs) 189
fissionable material 189
ballistic missiles 191

intercontinental ballistic missiles
    (ICBMs) 191
cruise missile 193
Missile Technology Control
    Regime 193
Chemical Weapons
    Convention 194
Biological Weapons
    Convention 194
proliferation 195
Non-Proliferation Treaty
    (NPT) 196

mutually assured destruction
    (MAD) 197
Strategic Defense Initiative
    (SDI) 197
Anti-Ballistic Missile
    (ABM) Treaty 199
Comprehensive Test Ban Treaty
    (CTBT) 199
chain of command 201
civil-military relations 202
coup d'état 203
military governments 203

Critical Thinking Questions

1. If you were the leader of, say, Vietnam, what size and kinds of military forces would you want your country to have? To meet what kinds of threats would you choose each type of capability?

2. Suppose that Iran turned out to have obtained three tactical nuclear warheads from the former Soviet arsenal and was keeping them in unknown locations. What, if anything, should the great powers do about this? What consequences might follow from their actions?

3. Imagine a world in which most of the states, rather than just a few, had nuclear weapons and long-range ballistic missiles. Would it be more peaceful or more war-prone? Why?

4. Most of the great powers are reconfiguring their military forces in the post–Cold War era. What kinds of capabilities do you think your own country needs in this period? Why?

5. World military spending is nearly $2 trillion every year. If you could redirect these funds, how would you use them? Would such uses be better or worse for the states involved? Do you think there is a realistic chance of redirecting military spending in the way you suggest?

Suggested Readings

Feaver, Peter D., and Christopher Gelpi. *Choosing Your Battles: American Civil-Military Relations and the Use of Force.* Princeton, 2005.

Gat, Azar. *The Causes of War and the Spread of Peace.* Oxford, 2017.

Hoffman, Bruce, and Fernando Reinares, eds. *The Evolution of the Global Terrorist Threat.* Columbia, 2016.

Hoffman, Peter J., and Thomas G. Weiss. *Sword and Salve: Confronting New Wars and Humanitarian Crises.* Rowman & Littlefield, 2006.

Narang, Vipin. *Nuclear Strategy in the Modern Era: Regional Powers and International Conflict.* Princeton, 2014.

Pape, Robert. *Dying to Win: The Strategic Logic of Suicide Terrorism.* Random House, 2005.

Let's Debate the Issue
Negotiations with North Korea: Progress Toward Disarmament or Fool's Errand?

Overview

For nearly two decades, North Korea has defied the international community and proceeded with its nuclear weapons program. Several times, North Korea has agreed to give up its nuclear program, only to renege on those promises. In 2006, North Korea tested a nuclear weapon. Although the test had only a small yield, North Korea clearly possesses the knowledge, resources, and ability to produce nuclear weapons.

In 2007, an agreement was reached in which North Korea promised to halt its nuclear program in exchange for international assistance, including fuel and food aid. It then destroyed part of its nuclear processing facilities but restarted its program when the United States delayed removing North Korea from its list of terror-supporting states. Once North Korea was removed from the list in the fall of 2008, it promised to allow nuclear inspectors to verify the stopping of its program. When the time came to formalize the agreement in writing, however, North Korea refused. By 2017, North Korea had fully resumed nuclear weapon and missile testing. In 2018, President Trump and North Korean leader Kim Jung Un to negotiate, but only a statement of principle was reached.

Based on this history of failed agreements and tense negotiations, some have suggested ending negotiations with North Korea over its nuclear program. Others point to the potential danger posed by a North Korean nuclear program and urge continuation of the talks. Should the United States continue the multilateral talks aimed at disarming North Korea?

ARGUMENT 1

The United States Should Continue to Pursue North Korean Talks

U.S. allies favor negotiations. Although they are concerned that North Korea not be rewarded for its bad behavior, South Korea and Japan both would like negotiations to continue. While these U.S. allies do not want to reach an agreement at any cost because any conflict with North Korea would be exceedingly costly to one or both of them, they would prefer a diplomatic solution to this problem.

A war over the North Korean program would be disastrous. North Korea's nuclear weapons, ironically, are not the biggest threat to its neighbor to the south. Rather, experts estimate that conventional artillery that is aimed at the South Korean capital, Seoul, could do significant damage in a short period of time.

Isolating North Korea could be the most dangerous policy of all. The most likely scenario for North Korean leadership to use their nuclear arsenal would be a time when they felt backed into a corner. Walking away from negotiations to leave them in isolation would accomplish exactly that goal. North Korea could lash out militarily at South Korea or Japan, two important U.S. allies.

ARGUMENT 2

The United States Should Give Up Its Quest for a North Korean Deal

North Korea has never kept its promises. After its rejection of the NPT in the 1990s, North Korea has not only refused to honor many of the commitments but also actively cheated on them to continue its nuclear weapons program. Even if an agreement were reached, there would be no guarantee that North Korea would not cheat.

The North Korean regime is untrustworthy. North Korean leaders do not care about the welfare of citizens and care even less about international reputation. While North Korea may rely on international aid to stay afloat, it could extract even more aid if it had a more successful nuclear program.

Only a collapse of the North Korean regime will bring true change. As long as the current regime is in power, nothing will change in North Korea. The faster international isolation undermines the regime, the better. Without fuel and food aid from the United States or nearby countries, the regime may collapse more quickly.

Questions

- Do you think North Korea is a trustworthy negotiating partner? How many chances should it be given to live up to its agreements? What realistic alternatives are there to negotiations?
- How much say should U.S. allies have in the negotiations? Does the proximity of South Korea and Japan to North Korea make their negotiating interests more important than those of the United States?
- What might be some of the potential problems if the United States took unilateral steps for the permanent disarmament of North Korea? Those unilateral steps could

include more sanctions; war; or, at the other extreme, massive flows of financial aid to pay North Korea for giving up its nuclear arsenal.

For Further Reading

Cha, Victor, and David Kang. *Nuclear North Korea: A Debate on Engagement Strategies.* Columbia, 2005.

O'Hanlon, Michael, and Mike Mochizuiki. *Crisis on the Korean Peninsula: How to Deal with a Nuclear North Korea.* McGraw-Hill, 2003.

Rozman, Gilbert. *Strategic Thinking About the Korean Nuclear Crisis: Four Parties Caught Between North Korea and the United States.* Palgrave Macmillan, 2007.

Wit, Joel S. *Going Critical: The First North Korean Nuclear Crisis.* Brookings, 2005.

Chapter 7

International Organizations, Law, and Human Rights

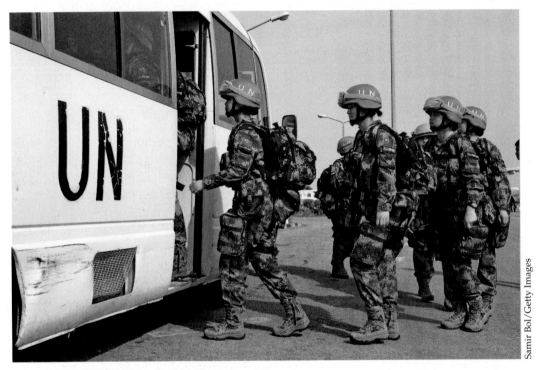

CHINESE PEACEKEEPERS ARRIVE IN SOUTH SUDAN, 2015.

Samir Bol/Getty Images

 Learning Objectives

7.1 Identify the differences between intergovernmental organizations (IGOs) and nongovernmental organizations (NGOs) in both form and function.

7.2 Describe the structure and rules of the UN Security Council, including identification of the five permanent members.

7.3 Evaluate the arguments over the effectiveness or ineffectiveness of international law in restraining state behavior.

7.4 Summarize the distinction between just wars and wars of aggression.

7.5 Contrast the effectiveness of international law, NGOs, and states in advancing the cause of human rights around the globe.

7.1 Roles of International Organizations

Identify the differences between intergovernmental organizations (IGOs) and nongovernmental organizations (NGOs) in both form and function.

Most international conflicts are not settled by military force. Despite the anarchic nature of the international system based on state sovereignty, the security dilemma does not usually lead to a breakdown in basic cooperation among states. States generally refrain from taking maximum short-term advantage of each other (such as by invading and conquering). Rather, states usually work *with* other states for mutual gain and take advantage of each other only in limited circumstances. Unfortunately, the day-to-day cooperative activities of international actors often are less newsworthy than their conflicts.

States work together by following rules they develop to govern their interactions. States usually *do* follow the rules. Over time, the rules become more firmly established and institutions grow up around them. States then develop the habit of working through those institutions and within the rules. They do so because of self-interest. Great gains can be realized by regulating international interactions through institutions and rules, thereby avoiding the costly outcomes associated with a breakdown of cooperation (see Chapter 3).

The rules that govern most interactions in international relations (IR) are rooted in norms. **International norms** are the expectations actors hold about normal international relations. The invasion of Kuwait by Iraq in 1990 not only was illegal but also was widely viewed as immoral—beyond the acceptable range of behavior of states. Political leaders in the United States and around the world drew on moral norms to generate support for a collective response to Iraq. Of course, many also viewed the U.S. invasion of Iraq in 2003 as both illegal and immoral, with numerous U.S. allies refusing to support the invasion because of this perceived violation of norms. Thus, morality is an element of power (see Elements of Power in Chapter 2) drawing on the core principle of identity (most state leaders want their publics and other leaders to see them as upholding high morals).

Some norms, such as sovereignty and respect for treaties, are widely held; they shape expectations about state behavior and set standards that make deviations stand out. Constructivist scholars in IR (see Chapter 3) emphasize the importance of these global norms and standards. The attempt to define international norms follows a centuries-long philosophical tradition. Philosophers such as Kant argued that it was natural for autonomous individuals (or states) to cooperate for mutual benefit because they could see that pursuing their narrow individual interests would end up hurting all. Thus, sovereign states could work together through structures and organizations (such as Kant's proposed world federation) that would respect each member's autonomy and not create a world government over them. In the nineteenth century, such ideas were embodied in practical organizations in which states participated to manage specific issues such as international postal service and control of traffic on European rivers.

Agreed norms of behavior, institutionalized through such organizations, become *habitual* over time and gain *legitimacy*. State leaders become used to behaving in a normal way and stop calculating whether violating norms would pay off for each possible action. For example, at the turn of the nineteenth century, U.S. war planners had active war plans for the possibility of a major naval conflict between the United States and Great Britain. Today, such plans seem ridiculous. Over time, states refrain from behavior not only for cost-benefit reasons (as emphasized by realists and liberals) but also for normative reasons having little to do with material calculations (as emphasized by constructivists). Legitimacy and habit explain why international norms can be effective even when they are not codified and enforced.

international norms The expectations held by participants about typical interactions among states.

NOT THE NORM International norms are evolving in such areas as humanitarian intervention, human rights, and the laws of war. These norms help define the roles of international organizations. One of their areas of concern is the use of child soldiers, like this Yemeni boy joining newly recruited Houthi fighters in 2017. The civil war in Yemen has created concerns about the violation of several international norms including the withholding of food as a weapon, the intentional targeting of hospitals, and the use of child soldiers.

The power of international norms and standards of morality, however, may vary when different states or world regions hold different expectations of what is normal. To the United States, it was a moral imperative to remove Saddam Hussein from power in 2003. But from the perspective of Arab populations, the U.S. invasion was an unjust violation of territorial sovereignty. In cases of diverging norms, morality can be a factor for misunderstanding and conflict rather than a force of stability. Realists point to examples such as these to suggest that international norms do not hold much sway on important matters of IR. Rather, realists point out, many of the accepted norms were shaped by the powerful states in the system (the dominance principle), and these same powerful states are often responsible for their interpretation. Yet constructivist scholars point out that even if international norms are violated, states (even the United States) go to tremendous lengths to justify behaviors that violate the norms. This suggests that strong norms do exist and are recognized by even the most powerful states.

Especially in times of change, when shared norms and habits may not suffice to solve international dilemmas and achieve mutual cooperation, institutions play a key role. They are concrete, tangible structures with specific functions and missions. These institutions have proliferated rapidly in recent decades and continue to play an increasingly important role in international affairs. **International organizations (IOs)** include *intergovernmental organizations (IGOs)*, such as the UN, and *nongovernmental organizations (NGOs)*, such as the International Committee of the Red Cross (ICRC).

international organizations (IOs) Intergovernmental organizations (IGOs) such as the UN and nongovernmental organizations (NGOs) such as the International Committee of the Red Cross (ICRC).

Liberals point out that, contrary to what realists or constructivists maintain, it is the codification of international norms in institutions that gives norms their power. As discussed in Chapter 3, these institutions create incentives to reciprocate behavior encouraged by a norm (the reciprocity principle) while also constraining the behavior of powerful states through rules that govern behavior. Liberals point to the large and growing number of international institutions as evidence of their power and importance.

The number of IOs has grown more than fivefold since 1945, to about 350 independent IGOs and tens of thousands of NGOs (depending somewhat on definitions). Figure 7.1 illustrates this growth. New NGOs are created around the world daily. This weaving together of people across national boundaries through specialized groups reflects interdependence (see Chapter 8).

Some IGOs are global in scope; others are regional or just bilateral (having only two states as members). Some are general in their purposes; others have specific functional purposes. Overall, the success of these IGOs has been mixed; the regional ones have had more success than the global ones, and those with specific functional or technical purposes have worked better than those with broad purposes (see Chapter 10). IGOs hold together because they promote the national interests (or enhance the leverage) of their member states—not because of vague ideals.

Among *regional* IGOs, the European Union (EU) encompasses some of the most important organizations (see Chapter 10), but it is not the only example. Other important regional IGOs are the Association of South East Asian Nations (ASEAN), the Southern Cone Common Market (MERCOSUR), and the African Union (AU). The

Figure 7.1 States and IGOs in the World, 1815–2015

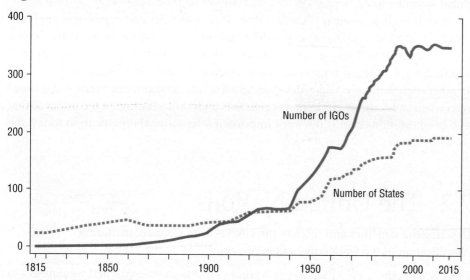

functional roles of IOs are important to their overall effect on international relations, but those roles are taken up in Chapter 10 on international integration. Here we will rely on the more general theoretical discussion of international institutions begun in Chapter 3.

Global IGOs (aside from the UN) usually have functional purposes involving coordinating actions of some set of states around the world. The IGO called Intelsat, for example, is a consortium of governments and private businesses that operates communications satellites. Members of the Organization of the Petroleum Exporting Countries (OPEC) are major oil producers who meet periodically in Vienna, Austria, to set production quotas for members in an effort to keep world oil prices high and stable. Note that, although the key members of IGOs are states, NGOs, businesses, or individuals can have important advisory and consulting roles in IGOs.

NGOs tend to be more specialized in function than IGOs. For instance, someone wanting to meet political scientists from other countries can join the International Political Science Association. Many NGOs have economic or business-related functions. The International Air Transport Association coordinates the work of airline companies. Other NGOs have global political purposes—for example, Amnesty International for human rights and Planned Parenthood for reproductive rights and family planning. Still others have cultural purposes—for example, the International Olympic Committee.

Religious groups are among the largest NGOs—their memberships often span many countries. Both in today's world and historically, sects of Christianity, Islam, Buddhism, Judaism, Hinduism, and other world religions have organized themselves across state borders, often in the face of hostility from one or more national governments. Missionaries have deliberately built and nurtured these transnational links. The Catholic Church historically held a special position in the European international system, especially before the seventeenth century.

Today, many NGOs desire access to IGOs to help shape rules and norms. NGOs with broad purposes and geographical scope often maintain observer status in the UN so that they can participate in UN meetings about issues of concern. For example, Greenpeace attends UN meetings about the global environment. Many NGOs covet a "seat at the table"—the right to attend IGO meetings, have their voices heard, and even vote. This is especially true when difficult problems are on the table. For example, meetings such as the annual conference of parties for the Intergovernmental Panel on Climate Change (IPCC) are attended by nearly all states, dozens of other IGOs, hundreds of NGOs, and thousands of citizens, all in an effort to shape solutions to global warming (see Chapter 11).

A web of international organizations of various sizes and types now connects people in all countries. The rapid growth of this network, and the increasingly intense communications and interactions that occur within it, indicates rising international interdependence. These organizations in turn provide the institutional mesh to hold together some kind of world order even when leaders and contexts come and go, and even when sudden changes in power relations undermine norms. At the center of that web of connections stands the most important international organization today, the United Nations.

7.2   The United Nations

Describe the structure and rules of the UN Security Council, including identification of the five permanent members.

The UN and other international organizations have both strengths and weaknesses in the anarchic international system. State sovereignty creates a real need for such organizations on a practical level because no central world government performs the function of coordinating the actions of states for mutual benefit. However, state sovereignty also severely limits the power of the UN and other IOs because governments reserve power for themselves and are stingy in delegating it to the UN or anyone else. The UN has had a mixed record due to these strengths and weaknesses—in some ways providing remarkable global-level management and in other ways appearing helpless against the sovereignty of even modest-sized states (not to mention great powers).

7.2.1 The UN System

The UN is a relatively new institution, over 70 years old. Even newer is the more prominent role that the UN has played in international security affairs since the end of the Cold War. Despite this more recent prominence, the main purposes of the UN are the same now as when it was founded after World War II.

PURPOSES OF THE UN   The UN is the closest thing to a world government that has ever existed, but it is not a world government. Its members are sovereign states that have not empowered the UN to enforce its will within states' territories except with the consent of those states' governments. Thus, although the UN strengthens world order, its design acknowledges the realities of international anarchy and the unwillingness of states to surrender their sovereignty. Within these limits, the basic purpose of the UN is to provide a global institutional structure through which states can sometimes settle conflicts with less reliance on the use of force.

The **UN Charter** is based on the principles that states are *equal* under international law; that states have full *sovereignty* over their own affairs; that states should have full *independence* and *territorial integrity*; and that states should carry out their international *obligations*, such as respecting diplomatic privileges, refraining from committing aggression, and observing the terms of treaties they sign. The UN Charter also lays out the structure of the UN and the methods by which it operates.

The UN does not exist because it has power to force its will on the world's states; rather, it exists because states have created it to serve their needs. A state's membership in the UN is essentially a form of indirect leverage. States gain leverage by using the UN to seek more beneficial outcomes in conflicts (especially on general multilateral issues for which a global forum brings all parties together). The cost of this leverage is modest: UN dues and the expenses of diplomatic representatives, in addition to the agreement to behave in accordance with the UN Charter (most of the time).

UN Charter The founding document of the United Nations; it is based on the principles that states are equal, have sovereignty over their own affairs, enjoy independence and territorial integrity, and must fulfill international obligations. The Charter also lays out the structure and methods of the UN.

States get several benefits from the UN. Foremost among these is the international stability (especially in security affairs) that the UN tries to safeguard; this allows states to realize gains from trade and other forms of exchange (see Chapter 8). The UN is a *symbol* of international order and even of global identity. It is also a *forum* where states promote their views and bring their disputes. And it is a *mechanism* for conflict resolution in international security affairs. The UN also promotes and coordinates development assistance (see Chapter 13) and other programs of economic and social development in the global South. These programs reflect the belief that economic and social problems—above all, poverty—are an important source of international conflict and war. Finally, the UN is a coordinating system for *information* and planning by hundreds of internal and external agencies and programs, and for the publication of international data.

Despite its heavy tasks, the UN is still a small and fragile institution. Compare, for instance, what states spend on two types of leverage for settling conflicts: military forces and the UN. Every year, the world spends almost $2 *trillion* on the military, and about $5 *billion* on the UN regular budget. The whole budget of UN operations, peacekeeping, programs, and agencies combined is less than 3 percent of world military spending. That proportion is even more extreme in the United States: more than 150 to 1. Each U.S. citizen pays (on average) about $2,000 a year for U.S. military spending but only about $15 a year for U.S. payments of UN dues, assessments, and voluntary contributions to UN programs and agencies combined.

Sometimes the UN succeeds and sometimes it fails. The UN deals with the issues that are perhaps the most difficult in the world. If groups of states could easily solve problems such as ethnic conflicts, human rights, refugees, and world hunger themselves, they most likely would have done so. Instead, states turn many of these difficult problems over to the UN and hope it can take care of them.

Karamallah Daher / Reuters

KEEPING AN EYE OUT The United Nations has very limited powers and resources, yet the world places some of the most important tasks on the UN, including peacekeeping between former belligerents. Here, UN peacekeepers from an observer force in Lebanon keep watch on the border with Israel, 2017.

STRUCTURE OF THE UN   The UN's structure, shown in Figure 7.2, centers on the **UN General Assembly**, where representatives of all states sit together in a huge room, listen to speeches, and pass resolutions. The General Assembly coordinates a variety of development programs and other autonomous agencies through the *Economic and Social Council (ECOSOC)*. Parallel to the General Assembly is the **UN Security Council**, in which five great powers and ten rotating member states make decisions about international peace and security. The Security Council dispatches peacekeeping forces to trouble spots. The administration of the UN takes place through the **UN Secretariat** (executive branch), led by the Secretary General of the UN. The *World Court* (International Court of Justice), discussed later in the chapter, is a judicial arm of the UN. (A *Trusteeship Council* oversaw the transition of a handful of former colonial territories to full independence, but with the last trust territory's independence in 1994, the Trusteeship Council suspended operations.)

National delegations to the UN, headed by ambassadors from each member state, work and meet together at UN headquarters in New York City. They have diplomatic status in the United States, which as host country also assumes certain other obligations to facilitate the UN's functioning. For example, the U.S. government has permitted people such as Fidel Castro—normally barred from entry to the United States—to visit New York long enough to address the UN.

UN General Assembly A body composed of representatives of all states that allocates UN funds, passes nonbinding resolutions, and coordinates third world development programs and various autonomous agencies through the Economic and Social Council (ECOSOC).

UN Security Council A body of five great powers (which can veto resolutions) and ten rotating member states that makes decisions about international peace and security, including the dispatch of UN peacekeeping forces.

UN Secretariat The UN's executive branch, led by the Secretary General.

Figure 7.2 The United Nations

Source: Based on United Nations.

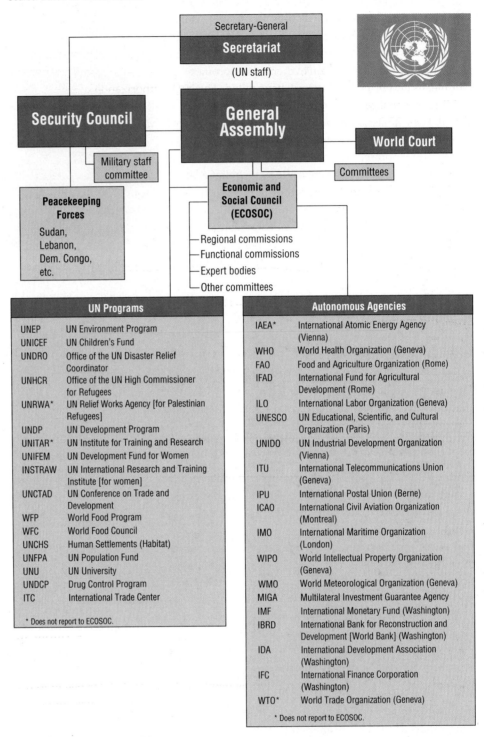

A major strength of the UN structure is the *universality of its membership*. The UN had 193 members in 2018. Almost every territory in the world is either a UN member or formally a province or colony of a UN member. (Taiwan is considered part of China; Switzerland, traditionally neutral, joined in 2003; and Palestine became a nonmember observer state in 2012.) Formal agreement on the UN Charter, even if sometimes breached, commits all states to a set of basic rules governing their relations. The old League of Nations, by contrast, was flawed by the absence of several important actors.

One way the UN induced all the great powers to join was to reassure them that their participation in the UN would not harm their national interests. Recognizing the role of power in world order, the UN Charter gave five great powers each a veto over the substantive decisions of the Security Council.

The UN Charter establishes a mechanism for *collective security*—the banding together of the world's states to stop an aggressor. Chapter 7 of the Charter explicitly authorizes the Security Council to use military force against aggression if the nonviolent means called for in Chapter 6 have failed. The 2011 authorization of a no-fly zone in Libya, for instance, was taken under Chapter 7. Because of the great power veto, however, the UN cannot effectively stop aggression by (or supported by) a great power. As often happens with the dominance principle, this structure creates resentments by smaller powers. In 2006, Iran's president asked the General Assembly, "If the governments of the United States or the United Kingdom commit atrocities or violate international law, which of the organizations in the United Nations can take them to account?"[1] (None of them, of course, is the answer.) Chapter 7 of the Charter was used only once during the Cold War—in the Korean War when the Soviet delegation unwisely boycotted the proceedings (and when China's seat was held by the nationalists on Taiwan).

HISTORY OF THE UN   The UN was founded in 1945 in San Francisco by 51 states. It was the successor to the League of Nations, which had failed to counter aggression effectively in the 1930s. Like the League, the UN was founded to increase international order and the rule of law to prevent another world war.

A certain tension has long existed between the UN and the United States as the world's most powerful state. (The United States had not joined the League of Nations, and it was partly to ensure U.S. interest that UN headquarters was placed in New York City.) The UN in some ways constrains the United States by creating the one coalition that can rival U.S. power—that of all the states. A certain isolationist streak in U.S. foreign policy runs counter to the UN concept. However, the UN *amplifies* U.S. power when the United States leads the global UN coalition. The United States is not rich or strong enough to keep order in the world by itself. And, as a great trading nation, the United States benefits from the stability and order that the UN helps create.

In the 1950s and 1960s, the UN's membership more than doubled as colonies in Asia and Africa won independence. This expansion changed the character of the General Assembly, in which each state has one vote regardless of size. The new members had different concerns from those of the Western industrialized countries and in many cases resented having been colonized by Westerners. Many states in the global South believed that the United States enjoyed too much power in the UN. They noticed that the UN is usually effective in international security affairs only when the United States leads the effort (which happens when U.S. interests are at stake).

The growth in membership thus affected voting patterns in the UN. During the UN's first two decades, the General Assembly had regularly sided with the United States, and the Soviet Union was the main power to use its veto in the Security Council to counterbalance that tendency. But as newly independent states began to predominate, the United States found itself in the minority on many issues, and by the 1970s and 1980s, it had become the main user of the veto.

Until 1971, China's seat on the Security Council (and in the General Assembly) was occupied by the nationalist government on the island of Taiwan, which had lost power in mainland China in 1949. The exclusion of communist China was an exception to the UN principle of universal membership and, in 1971, the Chinese seat was taken from the nationalists and given to the communist government. Today, the government of Taiwan—which functions autonomously in many international matters despite its formal status as a Chinese province—is not a member of the UN. But it is the only important such case.

---

[1] (2006, September 19). Transcript of Ahmadinejad's U.N. Speech. National Public Radio. Retrieved from https://www.npr.org/templates/story/story.php?storyId=6107339.

Throughout the Cold War, the UN had few successes in international security because the U.S.-Soviet conflict prevented consensus. The UN appeared somewhat irrelevant in a world order structured by two opposing alliance blocs. A few notable exceptions exist, such as defending South Korea during the Korean War and agreeing to station peacekeeping forces in the Middle East, but the UN did not play a central role in solving international conflicts. The General Assembly, with its predominantly third world membership, concentrated on the economic and social problems of poor countries, and these became the main work of the UN.

States in the global South also used the UN as a forum to criticize rich countries in general and the United States in particular. By the 1980s, the U.S. government showed its displeasure with this trend by withholding U.S. dues to the UN (eventually worth more than $1 billion), paying up only years later after UN reforms.

After the Cold War, the great powers could finally agree on measures regarding international security. In this context, the UN moved to center stage in international security affairs. The UN had several major successes in the late 1980s in ending violent regional conflicts (in Central America and the Iran-Iraq War) while introducing peace-keepers to monitor the cease-fires. In Namibia, a UN force oversaw independence from South Africa and the nation's first free elections. By the 1990s, the UN had emerged as the world's most important tool for settling international conflicts. Between 1987 and 1993, Security Council resolutions increased from 15 to 78; peace-keeping missions, from 5 to 17; peacekeepers, from 12,000 to 78,000; and countries sending troops, from 26 to 76.

The new missions ran into serious problems, however. Inadequate funding and management problems undermined peacekeeping efforts in Angola, Somalia, and Cambodia. In the former Yugoslavia in 1993–1995, the UN undertook a large peace-keeping mission before a cease-fire was in place. In response to these problems (and to the unpaid U.S. dues), the UN scaled back peacekeeping operations in 1995–1997 (from 78,000 to 19,000 troops) and carried out reductions and reforms in the UN Secretariat and UN programs.

For years, the United States failed to pay its bills, even though a new Secretary General shrank budgets and jobs as the United States had demanded. This U.S. free riding shows that support of intergovernmental organizations presents a difficult collective goods problem (see the Seeking the Collective Good box in Chapter 3). Finally, after criticism from allies, the United States agreed to pay up but under renegotiated terms for the future.

The 2003 Iraq War, however, triggered serious divisions among the great powers that sidelined the UN. After reaching consensus to insist on Iraqi disarmament and send back UN weapons inspectors, the Security Council split on whether to authorize force against Iraq—the United States and Britain in favor; France, Russia, and China against. UN Secretary General Kofi Annan later called the war "illegal." To aggravate U.S.-UN tensions further, documents recovered during the Iraq War showed that high-ranking UN, French, Chinese, and Russian officials (and American oil companies) illegally profited from the UN's $64 billion oil-for-food program for Iraq, which was supposed to ease the civilian suffering caused by economic sanctions in the 1990s. In 2005, an independent investigation found the program corrupt and heavily criticized the UN for mismanagement and poor oversight of the program.

Currently, the UN follows a principle of "three pillars"—security, economic development, and human rights—which are considered mutually necessary for any of them to succeed. At the end of 2006, the outgoing and incoming Secretaries General both referred to this principle. In a postwar conflict situation, in particular, each of the three reinforces the others.

The UN is in some ways just beginning to work as it was originally intended to, through a concert of great powers and universal recognition of the Charter. However, as states turned increasingly to the UN after the Cold War, its modest size and resources became seriously overburdened, leading to contraction of missions and funding. Today, the UN is more important than ever, yet it is still in danger of failing. In the coming few years, the UN must continue to grapple with the challenges of its evolving role given the limitations of its budget and the continuing strength of state sovereignty.

7.2.2 The Security Council

The Security Council is responsible for maintaining international peace and security and for restoring peace when it breaks down. Its decisions are *binding* on all UN member states. The Security Council has tremendous power to *define* the existence and nature of a security threat, to *structure* the response to such a threat, and to *enforce* its decisions through mandatory directives to UN members (such as to halt trade with an aggressor).

Since 1945, the Council has passed nearly 2,400 resolutions, with new ones added every week. These resolutions represent the great powers' blueprints for resolving the world's various security disputes, especially in regional conflicts. (Because of the veto system, the Council avoids conflicts among great powers themselves, such as on arms control.)

The five *permanent members* of the Council—the United States, Britain, France, Russia, and China—are the most important. What they can agree on, generally the world must go along with. Issues on which they disagree can quickly become contentious. In 2008, after the Security Council failed to decide whether the Serbian province of Kosovo should be independent, Kosovars unilaterally declared their independence from Serbia. Kosovo was quickly recognized by some Security Council members (the United States, France, and Britain) but not by others (China and Russia). Angry Serbians rejected Kosovo's declaration and blamed the Western powers for encouraging it. In 2010, the World Court held Kosovo's *declaration* to be legal, but its substantive status remains bitterly disputed. As of 2018, 108 UN members have recognized Kosovo's independence.

Security Council resolutions require nine votes from among the 15 members. But a no vote by any permanent member defeats the resolution—the *veto* power. Many resolutions have been vetoed by the permanent members, and many more have never been proposed because they would have faced certain veto. Since 1995, however, the use of the veto has dropped abruptly, to just 34 vetoes—18 by Russia, 14 by the United States, and 10 by China (multiple states can veto the same resolution).

In the past few years, Russia (and occasionally China) has used its veto power to shield the Syrian government from resolutions that, in Russia's opinion, would violate Syrian sovereignty in the context of its civil war. That war, which has killed thousands, displaced millions, and even included the use of chemical weapons, illustrates some of the limits of UN power when the permanent veto players (mostly Russia and the United States) are directly involved in a conflict. While the Security Council has been able to create some cease-fires to facilitate humanitarian aid, stronger resolutions (usually created by the United States) have been vetoed (usually by Russia).

The Security Council's ten *nonpermanent members* rotate onto the Council for two-year terms. Nonpermanent members are elected (five each year) by the General Assembly from a list prepared by informal regional caucuses. Usually there is a mix of regions and country sizes, though not by any strict formula. Often, countries lobby vigorously for a seat on the Council, producing books, advertisements, and memos to gain votes from other members of the regional caucuses. In 2006, Venezuela campaigned for the upcoming Latin American seat on the Council, seeking a platform to lead a growing, virulently anti-American coalition. Its president, in his speech to the General Assembly, called the U.S. president "the devil" and said the room still smelled of sulfur from his speech the previous day. Guatemala, with U.S. support, also

Table 7.1 Regional Representation on the UN Security Council

Region	Permanent Members[a]	Nonpermanent Members[b]			Possible Contenders for New Permanent Seats[c]
		2018	2017	2016	
North America	United States				
W. Europe	Britain France	Netherlands Poland Sweden	Italy Sweden	Spain	Germany
Japan/Pacific			Japan	New Zealand Japan	Japan
Russia/CIS	Russia	Kazakhstan	Kazakhstan Ukraine	Ukraine	
China	China				
Middle East		Kuwait	Egypt	Egypt	Egypt?
Latin America		Bolivia Peru	Bolivia Uruguay	Venezuela Uruguay	Brazil? Mexico?
South Asia				Malaysia	India? Indonesia?
Africa		Ethiopia Ivory Coast Equatorial Guinea	Ethiopia Senegal	Angola Senegal	Nigeria? South Africa?

[a]The five permanent members hold veto power.
[b]Nonpermanent members are elected for two-year terms by the General Assembly, based on nominations by regional caucuses.
[c]Possible new permanent seats might have fewer if any veto powers.

campaigned for the seat. In the General Assembly, neither country could achieve the required two-thirds majority for election to the Council. After voting 47 times, the Assembly finally gave the seat to Panama as a compromise. In 2008, Iran campaigned for a seat but gained only a handful of votes, while Turkey was voted onto the Council for the first time in more than 45 years.

In 2014, Saudi Arabia won a coveted Security Council seat but then refused to accept it. It became the first state to refuse a seat on the Council. This high-profile protest came after Saudi Arabia heavily criticized what it considered weak responses by the UN to the conflict in Syria and to negotiations with Iran over that country's nuclear program.

Table 7.1 shows the recent rotations of members onto the Security Council. The system of nomination by regional caucuses has worked to keep the regional balance on the Council fairly constant as individual states come and go. Major regional actors tend to rotate onto the Council more often than do less important states.

Members can *abstain* on resolutions, an option that some permanent members use to register misgivings about a resolution without vetoing. China regularly abstains when its own security is not directly affected, and the United States has abstained several times to register a middle position on resolutions critical of Israel.

The Security Council *meets irregularly* (in the New York City UN headquarters) upon request of a UN member—often a state with a grievance regarding another state's actions. When Kuwait was invaded, and when Bosnia was being overrun, the victims called on the Security Council—a kind of 911 phone number for the world (but one without a standing police force). Because international security continues to be troublesome in many regions and because these troubles often drag on for months or years, meetings of the Security Council are frequent.

The Security Council's power is limited in two major ways; both reflect the strength of state sovereignty in the international system. First, the Council's decisions depend entirely on the interests of its member states (see Figure 7.3). The ambassadors who represent those states cannot change a Security Council resolution without authorization from their governments. Second, although Security Council resolutions in

Figure 7.3 Divergent Interests on the UN Security Council

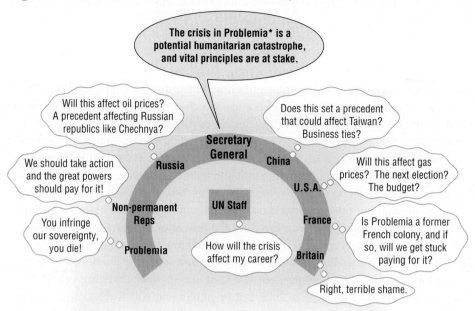

Problemia could be Kurdish Iraq in 1991 or Darfur, Sudan, in 2007.

theory bind all UN members, member states in practice often try to evade or soften their effect. For instance, trade sanctions are difficult to enforce. A Security Council resolution can be enforced in practice only if enough powerful states care about it.

Even when the Security Council cannot agree on means of enforcement, its resolutions shape the way disputes are seen and ultimately how they are resolved. Security Council Resolution 242 after the Arab-Israeli war of 1967 laid out the principles for a just peace in that conflict—primarily the right of all states in the region to live within secure and well-defined borders and the return by Israel of territories captured in the 1967 war. (The parties are still arguing about whether territories to be returned by Israel means "all" territories.) Reaffirmed in Resolution 338 after the 1973 war, these resolutions helped shape the 1978 Camp David agreement and later formed the basis for peace negotiations between Israel and its Arab neighbors that began in 1991. If a Palestinian-Israeli settlement is ever reached, it surely will follow the outlines of UN Resolutions 242 and 338.

PROPOSED CHANGES The structure of the Security Council is not without problems. Japan and Germany are great powers that contribute substantial UN dues (based on economic size) and make large contributions to UN programs and peacekeeping operations. Yet they have exactly the same formal representation in the UN as tiny states with less than one-hundredth of their populations: one vote in the General Assembly and the chance to rotate onto the Security Council (in practice they rotate onto the

Xinhua/Sipa USA/Newscom

COUNCIL OF UNEQUALS The UN Security Council can help advance peace and security when its permanent members (the P5) work in unison. When division exists, the Council cannot authorize military interventions, grant humanitarian assistance, or approve investigations during conflicts. Here, the Russian ambassador to the UN casts a no vote—a veto—against a resolution to investigate responsibility for chemical weapon attacks in Syria, defeating the resolution, 2017.

Council more often than the tiny states). As global trading powers, Japan and Germany have huge stakes in the ground rules for international security affairs and would like seats at the table.

But including Japan and Germany as permanent Security Council members would not be simple. If Germany were to join, three of the seven permanent members would be European, giving that region unfair weight. The three European seats could be combined into one (a rotating seat or one representing the European Union), but this would water down the power of Britain and France, which can veto any such change in the UN Charter. Japan's bid for a seat faces Chinese opposition. Also, if Japan or Germany got a seat, then what about India, with 20 percent of the world's population? And what about an Islamic country such as Indonesia? Finally, what about Latin America and Africa? Possible new permanent members could include Germany, Japan, India, Brazil, Egypt, and either Nigeria or South Africa. None of these plans has made much progress. Any overhaul of the Security Council would require a change in the UN Charter, and a change in membership would reduce the power of the current five permanent members, any of which could veto the change, making any change very difficult. In late 2004, an expert panel appointed by Annan recommended expanding the Security Council to 24 members under either of two formulas, neither changing veto powers. These proposals were debated in 2005, but no agreement was reached and the issue was put on hold. During the debate, 42 million people in China and 40 other countries signed a petition against Japan's getting a Security Council seat until it recognizes and sincerely apologizes for its war crimes in World War II.

7.2.3 Peacekeeping Forces

Peacekeeping forces are not mentioned in the UN Charter. Secretary General Dag Hammarskjöld in the 1960s joked that they were allowed under "Chapter Six and a Half"—somewhere between the nonviolent dispute resolution called for in Chapter 6 of the Charter and the authorization of force provided for in Chapter 7. The UN Charter requires member states to place military forces at the disposal of the UN, but such forces were envisioned as being used in response to aggression (under collective security). In practice, when the UN has authorized force to reverse aggression—as in the Gulf War in 1990—the forces involved have been *national* forces not under UN command. These forces, such as the Australian-led force in East Timor, display neither UN insignia nor flags.

The UN's *own* forces—borrowed from armies of member states but under the flag and command of the UN—have been *peacekeeping* forces to calm regional conflicts, playing a neutral role between warring forces. These forces won the Nobel Peace Prize in 1988 in recognition of their growing importance and success. As was learned in Bosnia, however, such neutral forces do not succeed well in a situation in which the Security Council has identified one side as the aggressor.

PEACEKEEPING MISSIONS   The Secretary General assembles a peacekeeping force for each mission, usually from a few states totally uninvolved in the conflict, and puts it under a single commander. The soldiers are commonly called *blue helmets*. Peacekeeping forces serve at the invitation of a host government and must leave if that government orders them out.

Authority for peacekeeping forces is granted by the Security Council, usually for a period of three to six months, which may be renewed—in some cases for decades. In one early case, the Suez crisis in 1956, the General Assembly authorized the forces under the "Uniting for Peace" resolution, which allowed the General Assembly to take up security matters when the Security Council was deadlocked. In the Congo in 1960, the Secretary General took the initiative. But today the Security Council firmly controls peacekeeping operations.

Funds must be voted on by the General Assembly, and lack of funds is today the single greatest constraint on the use of peacekeeping forces. Special assessments

Table 7.2 UN Peacekeeping Missions as of May 2018

Location	Region	Personnel	Annual Cost (million $)	Role	Since
Democratic Congo	Africa	20,600	$1,100	Enforce cease-fire; protect civilians	2010
Sudan/South Sudan	Africa	18,000	1,100	Support peace agreement	2011
Sudan/Darfur	Africa	16,000	500	Protect civilians	2007
Mali	Africa	15,000	1,050	Protect civilians for elections	2013
Central African Rep.	Africa	14,000	900	Protect civilians; demobilization	2014
Lebanon	Middle East	11,000	500	Monitor cease-fire on Israeli border	1978
Sudan/Abyei	Africa	4,800	300	Monitor disputed town on border	2011
Haiti	Latin America	4,000	100	Assist transitional govt.	2004
Liberia	Africa	1,600	100	Assist transitional govt.	2003
Cyprus	Middle East	1,100	60	Monitor Greek-Turkish cease-fire	1964
Syria (Golan Heights)	Middle East	1,000	60	Monitor Israel-Syria cease-fire	1974
Western Sahara	Africa	500	55	Organize referendum in territory	1991
Israel	Middle East	350	70	Observe Arab-Israeli truce	1948
Kosovo	Europe	350	40	Civil administration; relief	1999
India/Pakistan	South Asia	100	20	Observe India-Pakistan cease-fire	1949
Total		109,000	6,000		

Note: Size indicates total international personnel (mostly troops but some civilian administrators and police).
Source: Based on United Nations.

against member states pay for peacekeeping operations. With the expansion of peace-keeping since 1988, the expenses of these forces (over $6 billion in 2018) are several times larger than the regular UN budget.

RECENT MISSIONS As of 2018, the UN maintained about 109,000 international personnel (including troops, military observers, police, and administrators) in 15 peacekeeping or observing missions that spanned five world regions and used military personnel from 128 countries (see Table 7.2).

The two largest peacekeeping missions in 2018 were in the Democratic Congo and in the Darfur region of Sudan. In the Congo mission, over 20,000 peacekeepers monitored a cease-fire and protected civilians after a civil war. In 2012, these UN peacekeepers proved weak when a rebel movement in the unstable east of the country went on the attack, displacing civilians. A decade after the main war ended, such recurrent attacks proved vexing for UN forces. Additional troops were added in 2013–2014 to help confront local rebels.

In 2007, the Security Council approved a nearly 20,000-troop peacekeeping force for the Darfur region in Sudan, after several years of resistance from the Sudanese government. As of 2018, that force still maintains a strength of nearly 16,000 troops and police personnel. The UN troops joined an already deployed (but small) AU contingent. It took several more years for all of the authorized troops to arrive because of numerous objections from Sudan, and attacks on civilians continued despite their presence. In 2012, fighting between government and rebel forces drove 25,000 civilians out of one refugee camp. The Darfur mission is in addition to nearly 18,000 UN troops enforcing a cease-fire between Sudan and newly independent South Sudan, as well as an interim UN security force of nearly 5,000 troops, focused on the disputed town of Abyei on the border between Sudan and South Sudan.

The UN's other largest peacekeeping operations were in Mali (trying to maintain stability during a government transition), the Central African Republic (protecting civilians after the end of a civil war), and Lebanon (following the 2006 Israeli-Hezbollah war). The largest recent missions reflect the resurgence of UN peacekeeping after a shakeout in the mid-1990s.

In the 1990s, the UN had several spectacular failures in peacekeeping, in the former Yugoslavia, Rwanda, Angola, and Somalia. Less newsworthy were the successful missions in that period. In Cambodia, 15,000 peacekeepers worked with a large force of UN administrators who largely took over the Cambodian government after a long and devastating civil war. Despite many difficulties, the UN held elections in 1993 and helped stabilize Cambodian politics to some extent. The lessons learned in Cambodia helped the UN accomplish a similar mission in Mozambique. A peace agreement ended a long and devastating civil war there, setting up mechanisms for disarmament, the integration of military forces, and the holding of internationally supervised elections for a new government. Missions in El Salvador and Namibia were also early successes for post–Cold War UN peacekeeping. These experiences helped the UN respond more effectively after civil wars in Sierra Leone, Ivory Coast, and Liberia in 2002–2003. But problems with sex-related crimes in UN peacekeeping operations and the importance of women in postwar societies spurred the Security Council to pass Resolution 1325 in 2000 to focus attention on gender issues in UN peacekeeping and reconstruction (see Chapter 3).

As UN peacekeeping has become more intensive in recent years, new missions have expanded the range of what are now called broadly *peace operations*. These operations include not only traditional peacekeeping but also the use of force to protect civilians (as in Democratic Congo), the supervision of elections (as in Liberia), and even running the government while a society gets back on its feet (as in Cambodia, East Timor, and Kosovo). These expanded operations after conflicts are called **peacebuilding**. In an effort to provide longer-term support after wars, in 2005 the UN created a Peacebuilding Commission to coordinate reconstruction, institution building, and economic recovery efforts after peacekeeping missions end.

peacebuilding The use of military peacekeepers, civilian administrators, police trainers, and similar efforts to sustain peace agreements and build stable, democratic governments in societies recovering from civil wars. Since 2005, a UN Peacebuilding Commission has coordinated and supported these activities.

OBSERVING AND PEACEKEEPING Peacekeepers actually perform two different functions: observing and peacekeeping. *Observers* are unarmed military officers sent to a conflict area in small numbers simply to watch what happens and report back to the UN. With the UN watching, the parties to a conflict are often less likely to break a cease-fire. Observers can monitor various aspects of a country's situation—cease-fires, elections, respect for human rights, and other areas.

The function of *peacekeeping* is carried out by lightly armed soldiers (in armored vehicles with automatic rifles but without artillery, tanks, and other heavy weapons). Such forces play several roles. They can *interpose* themselves physically between warring parties to keep them apart (more accurately, to make them attack the UN forces in order to get to their enemy). UN peacekeepers often try to *negotiate* with military officers on both sides. This channel of communication can bring about tactical actions and understandings that support a cease-fire. But the UN forces in a war zone cannot easily get from one side's positions to those of the other to conduct negotiations.

Peacekeeping is much more difficult if one side sees the UN forces as being biased toward the other side. Israel feels this way about UN forces in southern Lebanon, for example. On occasion, Israeli forces have broken through UN lines to attack enemies, and they allegedly have targeted UN outposts on occasion. In Cambodia and the former Yugoslavia in the early 1990s, one party deliberately attacked UN forces many times, causing a number of deaths. In general, when cease-fires break down, UN troops get caught in the middle. More than 3,300 peacekeepers have been killed over the years.

Many countries contribute their national military forces to UN peacekeeping missions. In 2017, the five leading contributors (with troop and police numbers) were Ethiopia (8,400), Bangladesh (7,100), India (6,400), Rwanda (6,300), and Pakistan (6,300). Reasons for troop contributions to UN peacekeeping vary. Some states feel that, by contributing to a common good, they are advancing the interest of peace while simultaneously projecting the image of a strong military power. In this way, states may serve to increase their soft power. Alternatively, some states find contributing to these missions financially beneficial because peacekeeping forces are paid by UN contributions. In a few countries such as Nepal and Sierra Leone, sending military forces out of the country for peacekeeping is useful for domestic political stability after a civil war.

In some conflicts, peacekeepers organized outside the UN framework have been used instead of UN-commanded forces. Some 3,500 French peacekeepers—not under UN command—served in Ivory Coast alongside nearly 12,000 UN peacekeepers, between 2003 and 2017. When government airstrikes killed nine French soldiers in 2004, the French forces retaliated robustly, destroying the government's air force. In 2011, after the incumbent president lost an election but refused to leave, UN and French troops helped the winner dislodge him by force. After a series of more peaceful elections, UN representatives and the Security Council determined that the forces were no longer needed to guarantee stability, leading to a withdrawal of French and UN forces in 2017.

Peacekeepers from regional organizations have also been deployed to monitor and enforce cease-fire agreements and transitions after civil war. In 2012, the Economic Community of West African States (ECOWAS) sent out multinational military forces to Guinea-Bissau after a military coup there. After overseeing peaceful elections in 2014 and ensuring a peaceful transition, those forces began to withdraw in 2017.

Peacekeeping forces have generally been unable to make peace, only to keep it. To go into a shooting war and suppress hostilities requires military forces far beyond those of past UN peacekeeping missions. Thus, peacekeepers are usually not sent until a cease-fire has been arranged, has taken effect, and has held up for some time. Often, dozens of cease-fires are broken before one sticks. Wars may simmer along for years, taking a terrible toll, before the UN gets its chance to send peacekeepers.

To address this problem, the Secretary General in 1992 proposed the creation of UN *peacemaking* (or *peace enforcement*) units that would not only monitor a cease-fire but also enforce it if it broke down. The Secretary General called for member states to make available, on a rapid deployment basis, 1,000 soldiers each—specially trained volunteers—to create a standby UN army that could respond quickly to crises. Not only did the member states refuse the request for soldiers, they criticized the idea of peacemaking altogether. Since then, the UN has authorized member states to provide real military forces, not peacekeepers, when fighting may be required. In an exception that may or may not indicate a trend, the Security Council broadened the mandate of UN peacekeepers in Democratic Congo to let them protect civilians (which UN forces have been criticized for not doing). In 2005, Pakistani peacekeepers in that operation in the Democratic Congo killed 50 militia fighters after nine peacekeepers from Bangladesh were killed in an ambush. The Democratic Congo operation remains violent: As recently as 2017, 15 Tanzanian peacekeepers were killed in an attack by militants.

In the late 1990s, seven countries—Denmark, Norway, Sweden, Poland, the Netherlands, Austria, and Canada—formed a 4,000-troop UN Standby High Readiness Brigade. Headquartered in Denmark and available to deploy to conflict areas in two to four weeks rather than months, the brigade is controlled by the Security Council. It participated in the UN mission to Ethiopia-Eritrea in 2000–2001. In early 2005, the brigade deployed to Sudan to support a peace agreement between northern and southern regions after a long civil war.

Generally speaking, the permanent members of the Security Council have not contributed extensive numbers of peacekeeping troops, but rather have been asked to pay for the missions. A growing exception to this trend is China, which has placed over 2,500 troops under UN control in recent missions. China, unlike Britain and France, has no history of colonizing other territory, and unlike the United States and Russia, has not been considered a global superpower. These factors make China's involvement more acceptable to states asked to host peacekeeping troops. China is outspoken, however, in its demand that the peacekeeping forces respect state sovereignty. It labels its contributed military troops "comprehensive security forces" rather than military personnel.

7.2.4 The Secretariat

The Secretary General of the UN is the closest thing to a "president of the world" that exists. But the Secretary General represents member states—not the world's 7.6 billion people. Where the great powers do not have consensus, it is hard for the Secretary General to make anything happen.

The Secretary General is nominated by the Security Council—requiring the consent of all five permanent members—and must be approved by the General Assembly. The term of office is five years and may be renewed. Past Secretaries General have come from various regions of the world but never from a great power.

Secretary General Antonio Guterres began his term in 2017. Guterres, the former prime minister of Portugal, as well as the former UN High Commissioner for Refugees, will focus his first term on the many humanitarian crises stemming from international conflicts, especially the growing numbers of refugees around the globe. His predecessor, Ban Ki-moon, concentrated on UN reform, economic development, human rights, terrorism, proliferation, environmental problems, and HIV/AIDS. Former Secretary General Kofi Annan, who served from 1997 to 2006, helped reinvigorate the UN, winning the one-hundredth-anniversary Nobel Peace Prize for his efforts.

The Secretariat of the UN is its executive branch, headed by the Secretary General. It is a bureaucracy for administering UN policy and programs, just as the State Department is a bureaucracy for U.S. foreign policy. In security matters, the Secretary General personally works with the Security Council. The Secretariat is divided into functional areas, with undersecretaries general and assistant secretaries general.

The UN staff in these areas includes administrative personnel as well as technical experts and economic advisers working on various programs and projects. The staff numbers about 40,000 people, and the total number of employees in the UN system (including the World Bank and International Monetary Fund) is 75,000. UN-related agency offices are concentrated in Geneva, Switzerland. Geneva is a frequent site of international negotiations and is seen by some as more neutral than New York.

One purpose of the UN Secretariat is to develop an *international civil service* of diplomats and bureaucrats whose loyalties lie at the global level, not with their states of origin. The UN Charter sets the Secretary General and staff apart from the authority of national governments and calls on member states to respect the staff's "exclusively international character." The UN has been fairly successful in this regard; the Secretary General is most often seen as an independent diplomat thinking about the whole world's interests, not acting as a pawn of any state. But in the early 1990s, the UN bureaucracy came under increasing criticism for both inefficiency and corruption. These criticisms, coming especially from the United States, which saw itself as bearing an unfair share of the costs, led to a reform program. By the late 1990s, UN staff was reduced by one-quarter compared to a decade earlier, and budgets were scaled back year by year. By winter 2002, a strapped UN could not keep

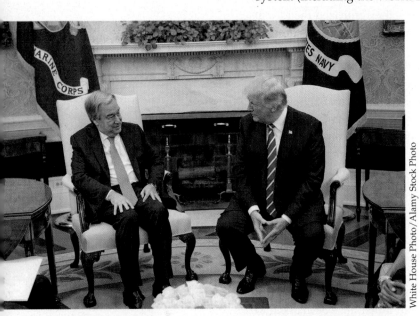

White House Photo/Alamy Stock Photo

CHIEF EXECUTIVES The UN Secretary General has a lofty mission but limited power and resources. Here, new UN Secretary General Antonio Guterres meets with President Donald Trump to discuss UN reform. The Secretary General must attempt to persuade member states, especially the great powers, to take action in a number of issue areas including development, human rights, and peace and security.

its New York City headquarters building heated. Since then, the situation has improved, but money remains extremely tight.

The Secretary General is more than a bureaucratic manager. He (it has not yet been a she) is a visible public figure whose personal attention to a regional conflict can move it toward resolution. The UN Charter allows the Secretary General to use the UN's good offices to serve as a neutral mediator in international conflicts—to bring hostile parties together in negotiations.

The Secretary General also works to bring together the great power consensus on which Security Council action depends. The Secretary General has the power under the UN Charter to bring to the Security Council any matter that might threaten international peace and security, and so to play a major role in setting the UN's agenda in international security affairs. Still, the Secretary General experiences tensions with the Security Council. When the Secretary General asks for authority for a peacekeeping mission for six months, the Security Council is likely to say three months. If the Secretary General asks for $10 million, he might get $5 million. Thus the Secretary General remains, like the entire UN system, constrained by state sovereignty.

7.2.5 The General Assembly

The General Assembly is made up of all 193 member states of the UN, each with one vote. It usually meets every year, from late September through January, in *plenary session*. State leaders or foreign ministers, including the U.S. president, generally come through one by one to address this assemblage. The General Assembly sessions, like most UN deliberations, are simultaneously translated into dozens of languages so that delegates from around the world can carry on a single conversation. This global town hall is a unique institution and provides a powerful medium for states to put forward their ideas and arguments. Presiding over it is a president elected by the Assembly—a post without much power.

The Assembly convenes for *special sessions* every few years on general topics such as economic cooperation. The UN special session on disarmament in June 1982 provided the occasion for one of the largest political rallies in U.S. history—a peace demonstration of a million people in New York. The Assembly has met in *emergency session* in the past to deal with an immediate threat to international peace and security, but this has happened only nine times and has now become uncommon.

The General Assembly has the power to accredit national delegations as members of the UN (through its Credentials Committee). For instance, in 1971, the delegation of the People's Republic of China was given China's seat in the UN (including on the Security Council) in place of the nationalists in Taiwan. For decades, neither North Korea nor South Korea became a member of the UN (because both claimed the whole

Chip East/Reuters

ASSEMBLY OF EQUALS The universal membership of the United Nations is one of its strengths. All member states have a voice and a vote in the General Assembly, where state leaders rotate through each autumn. Here, the president of Nauru, an island state of eight square miles and about 9,000 people, addresses the General Assembly, 2014.

of Korea), but they finally took seats as separate delegations in 1991. Some political entities that fall short of state status send *permanent observer missions* to the UN. These missions participate without a vote in the General Assembly. They include the Vatican (Holy See) and the Palestinian Authority.

The General Assembly's main power lies in its control of finances for UN programs and operations, including peacekeeping. It can also pass resolutions on various matters, but these are purely advisory and at times have served largely to vent frustrations of the majority of poor countries. The Assembly also elects members of certain UN agencies and programs. Finally, the Assembly coordinates UN programs and agencies through its own system of committees, commissions, councils, and so forth.

The Assembly coordinates UN programs and agencies through the Economic and Social Council (ECOSOC), which has 54 member states elected by the General Assembly for three-year terms. ECOSOC manages the overlapping work of a large number of programs and agencies. Its *regional commissions* look at how UN programs work together in a particular region; its *functional commissions* deal with global topics such as population growth, narcotics trafficking, human rights, and the status of women; and its *expert bodies* work on technical subjects that cut across various UN programs in areas such as crime prevention and public finances. Outside ECOSOC, the General Assembly operates many other *specialized committees*. Standing committees ease the work of the Assembly in issue areas such as decolonization, legal matters, and disarmament.

Many of the activities associated with the UN do not take place under tight control of either the General Assembly or the Security Council. They occur in functional agencies and programs that have various amounts of autonomy from UN control.

7.2.6 UN Programs

Through the Economic and Social Council, the General Assembly oversees more than a dozen major programs to advance economic development and social stability in poor states of the global South. Through its programs, the UN helps manage global North-South relations: It organizes a flow of resources and skills from the richer parts of the world to support development in the poorer parts.

The programs are funded partly by General Assembly allocations and partly by contributions that the programs raise directly from member states, businesses, or private charitable contributors. The degree of General Assembly funding, and of operational autonomy from the Assembly, varies from one program to another. Each UN program has a staff, a headquarters, and various operations in the field where it works with host governments in member states.

Several of these programs are of growing importance. The *UN Environment Program (UNEP)* became more prominent in the 1990s as the economic development of the global South and the growing economies of the industrialized world took a toll on the world environment (see Chapter 11). The UNEP grapples with global environmental strategies. It provides technical assistance to member states, monitors environmental conditions globally, develops standards, and recommends alternative energy sources.

UNICEF is the UN Children's Fund, which gives technical and financial assistance to poor countries for programs benefiting children. Unfortunately, the needs of children in many countries are still urgent, and UNICEF is kept busy. Financed by voluntary contributions, UNICEF has for decades organized U.S. children in an annual Halloween fund drive on behalf of their counterparts in poorer countries.

The *Office of the UN High Commissioner for Refugees (UNHCR)* is also busy. UNHCR coordinates efforts to protect, assist, and eventually repatriate the many refugees who flee across international borders each year to escape war and political violence. The longer-standing problem of Palestinian refugees is handled by a different program, the *UN Relief Works Agency (UNRWA)*.

The *UN Development Program (UNDP)*, funded by voluntary contributions, coordinates all UN efforts related to development in poor countries. With about 5,000 projects operating simultaneously around the world, UNDP is the world's largest international agency for technical development assistance. The UN also runs several development-related agencies for training and for promoting women's role in development.

Many poor countries depend on export revenues to finance economic development, making them vulnerable to fluctuations in commodity prices and other international trade problems. The **UN Conference on Trade and Development (UNCTAD)** negotiates international trade agreements to stabilize commodity prices and promote development. Because countries of the global South do not have much power in the international economy, however, UNCTAD has little leverage to promote their interests in trade. The World Trade Organization (WTO) has thus become the main organization dealing with trade issues (see Chapter 8).

> **UN Conference on Trade and Development (UNCTAD)** A structure established in 1964 to promote third world development through various trade proposals.

In 2006, the UN created a new Human Rights Council, replacing a Human Rights Commission notorious for including human rights abusers as member states. The new council has expanded powers and more selective membership (47 states). On more than one occasion, a state with a questionable human rights record (e.g., Sudan and Syria) has been left off the Human Rights Council ballot to prevent it from serving.

Other UN programs manage problems such as disaster relief, food aid, housing, and population issues. Throughout the poorer countries, the UN maintains an active presence in economic and social affairs.

7.2.7 Autonomous Agencies

In addition to its own programs, the UN General Assembly maintains formal ties with about 20 autonomous international agencies not under its control. Most are specialized technical organizations through which states pool their efforts to address problems such as health care and labor conditions.

> **World Health Organization (WHO)** An organization based in Geneva that provides technical assistance to improve health conditions in the third world and conducts major immunization campaigns.

The only such agency in international security affairs is the *International Atomic Energy Agency (IAEA)*, headquartered in Vienna, Austria. It was established under the UN but is formally autonomous. Although the IAEA has an economic role in helping develop civilian nuclear power plants, it mainly works to prevent nuclear proliferation (see Chapter 6). The IAEA was responsible for inspections in Iraq in 2002–2003, which found no evidence of a secret nuclear weapons program. It has been involved in monitoring Iran's nuclear program. The IAEA won the 2005 Nobel Peace Prize.

In the area of health care, the Geneva-based **World Health Organization (WHO)** provides technical assistance to improve conditions and conduct major immunization campaigns in poor countries. In the 1960s and 1970s, WHO led one of the great public health victories of all time—the worldwide eradication of smallpox. Today, WHO is a leading player in the worldwide effort to respond to global health epidemics and in the fight to control AIDS (see Chapter 11).

In agriculture, the *Food and Agriculture Organization (FAO)* is the lead agency. In labor standards, it is the *International Labor Organization (ILO)*. The *UN Industrial Development Organization (UNIDO)* promotes industrialization in the global South.

UNESCO—the *UN Educational, Scientific and Cultural Organization*—facilitates international communication and scientific collaboration. The United

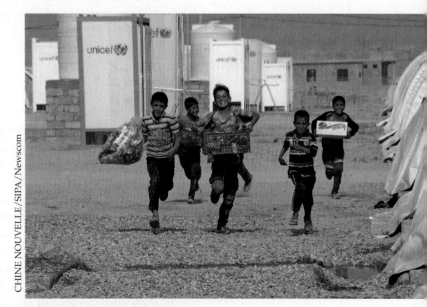

CHINE NOUVELLE/SIPA/Newscom

HELPING WHERE NEEDED An array of UN programs, operating under the General Assembly, aim to help countries in the global South to overcome social and economic problems. These programs play a crucial role in times of natural disasters and military conflicts. Here, UN relief supplies arrive in camps in Iraq during the conflict there against ISIS, 2016.

States has a contentious relationship with UNESCO. Twice the United States has withdrawn from the organization, citing bias in the organization's activities. The most recent withdrawal, in 2017, accused UNESCO of an anti-Israeli bias.

The longest-established IOs, with some of the most successful records, are specialized agencies dealing with technical aspects of international coordination such as aviation and postal exchange. For instance, the *International Telecommunications Union (ITU)* allocates radio frequencies. The *Universal Postal Union (UPU)* sets standards for international mail. The *International Civil Aviation Organization (ICAO)* sets binding standards for international air traffic. The *International Maritime Organization (IMO)* facilitates international cooperation on shipping at sea. The *World Intellectual Property Organization (WIPO)* seeks world compliance with copyrights and patents, and promotes development and technology transfer within a legal framework that protects such intellectual property (see Chapter 8). Finally, the *World Meteorological Organization (WMO)* oversees a world weather watch and promotes the exchange of weather information.

The major coordinating agencies of the world economy (discussed in Chapters 8, 9, and 13) are also UN-affiliated agencies, although they operate as essentially stand-alone IGOs. The World Bank and the International Monetary Fund (IMF) give loans, grants, and technical assistance for economic development (and the IMF manages international balance-of-payments accounting). The World Trade Organization (WTO) sets rules for international trade.

Overall, the density of connections across national borders, both in the UN system and through other IOs, is increasing year by year. In a less tangible way, people are also becoming connected across international borders through the meshing of ideas, including norms and rules. And gradually the rules are becoming international laws.

7.3 International Law

Evaluate the arguments over the effectiveness or ineffectiveness of international law in restraining state behavior.

International law, unlike national laws, derives not from actions of a legislative branch or other central authority but from tradition and agreements signed by states. It also differs in the difficulty of enforcement, which depends not on the power and authority of central government but on reciprocity, collective action, and international norms.

7.3.1 Sources of International Law

Laws within states come from central authorities—legislatures or dictators. Because states are sovereign and recognize no central authority, international law rests on a different basis. The declarations of the UN General Assembly are not laws and most do not bind the members. The Security Council can compel certain actions by states, but these are commands rather than laws: They are specific to a situation. No body of international law has been passed by a national legislative body. Four sources of international law are recognized: treaties, custom, general principles of law (such as equity), and legal scholarship (including past judicial decisions).

Treaties and other written conventions signed by states are the most important source. International treaties now fill more than a thousand thick volumes, with tens of thousands of individual agreements. A principle in international law states that treaties, once signed and ratified, must be observed (*pacta sunt servanda*). States violate the terms of treaties they have signed only if the matter is very important or if the penalties for such a violation seem very small. In the United States, treaties duly ratified by the Senate are considered the highest law of the land, equal with acts passed by Congress.

Treaties and other international obligations such as debts are binding on successor governments whether the new government takes power through an election, a coup, or a revolution. For example, after the revolutions in Eastern Europe around 1990, newly democratic governments were held responsible for debts incurred by their communist predecessors. Even when the Soviet Union broke up, Russia as the successor state had to guarantee that Soviet debts would be paid and Soviet treaties honored. Although revolution does not free a state from its obligations, some treaties have built-in escape clauses that let states legally withdraw from them, after giving due notice, without violating international law. For example, the United States in 2001 invoked the six-month opt-out provision of the Anti-Ballistic Missile (ABM) Treaty.

Because of the universal commitment by all states to respect certain basic principles of international law, the UN Charter is one of the world's most important treaties. Its implications are broad and far-reaching, in contrast to more specific treaties such as a fishery management agreement. However, the specialized agreements are usually easier to interpret and more enforceable than broad treaties such as the Charter. Another key treaty in international law is the 1949 Geneva Conventions (expanding an 1864 convention), which defines the laws of war regarding the protection of civilians and prisoners, among related issues.

Custom is the second major source of international law. If states behave toward each other in a certain way for long enough, their behavior may become generally accepted practice with the status of law. Western international law (though not Islamic law) tends to be *positivist* in this regard—it draws on actual customs, the practical realities of self-interest, and the need for consent rather than on an abstract concept of divine or natural law.

General principles of law also serve as a source of international law. Actions such as theft and assault recognized in most national legal systems as crimes tend to have the same meaning in an international context. Iraq's invasion of Kuwait was illegal under treaties signed by Iraq (including the UN Charter and that of the Arab League) and under the custom Iraq and Kuwait had established of living in peace as sovereign states. Beyond treaty or custom, the invasion violated international law because of the general principle that one state may not overrun its neighbor's territory and annex it by force. (Of course, a state may still think it can get away with such a violation of international law.)

The fourth source of international law, recognized by the World Court as subsidiary to the others, is *legal scholarship*—the written arguments of judges and lawyers around the world on the issues in question. Only the writings of the most highly qualified and respected legal figures can be taken into account, and then only to resolve points not resolved by the first three sources of international law.

Often international law lags behind changes in norms; law is quite tradition-bound. Certain activities such as espionage are technically illegal but are so widely condoned that they cannot be said to violate international norms. Other activities are still legal but have come to be frowned upon and seen as abnormal. For example, China's shooting of student demonstrators in 1989 violated international norms but not international law.

7.3.2 Enforcement of International Law

Although these sources of international law distinguish it from national law, an even greater difference exists as to the *enforcement* of the two types of law. International law is much more difficult to enforce. There is no world police force. Enforcement of international law depends on the power of states themselves, individually or collectively, to punish transgressors.

Enforcement of international law depends heavily on the reciprocity principle (see Chapter 1). States follow international law most of the time because they want other states to do so. The reason neither side in World War II used chemical weapons was not that anyone could *enforce* the treaty banning use of such weapons. It was that the other side would probably respond by using chemical weapons, too, and the subsequent costs would be high to both sides. International law recognizes in certain circumstances the legitimacy of *reprisals*: Actions that would have been illegal under international law may sometimes be legal if taken in response to the illegal actions of another state.

A state that breaks international law may face a collective response by a group of states, such as the imposition of *sanctions*—agreements among other states to stop trading with the violator or to stop some particular commodity trade (most often military goods) as punishment for its violation. Over time, a sanctioned state can become a pariah in the community of nations, cut off from normal relations with others. This is very costly in today's world, in which economic well-being everywhere depends on trade and economic exchange in world markets. Libya suffered for decades from its isolated status in the international community, and it decided in 2003 to make a clean break and regain normal status. Libya admitted responsibility for past terrorism; began to compensate victims; and agreed to disclose and dismantle its nuclear, chemical, and biological weapons programs.

Even the world's superpower constrains its behavior, at least some of the time, to adhere to international law. For example, in late 2002 a North Korean freighter was caught en route to Yemen with a hidden load of 15 Scud missiles. The United States, fighting the war on terrorism, had an evident national interest in preventing such proliferation and had the power to prevent it. But when U.S. government lawyers determined that the shipment did not violate international law, the United States backed off and let the delivery continue. Yet, in 2017, two North Korean ships were stopped that were carrying chemicals to Syria that could have been used to make chemical weapons. Because of a legal agreement concerning chemical weapons in Syria, those ships were not allowed to continue.

International law enforcement through reciprocity and collective response has one great weakness—it depends entirely on national power. Reciprocity works only if the aggrieved state has the power to inflict costs on the violator. Collective response works only if the collective cares enough about an issue to respond. Thus, it is relatively easy to cheat on small issues (or to get away with major violations if one has enough power).

If international law extends only as far as power reaches, what good is it? The answer lies in the uncertainties of power (see Chapter 2). Without common expectations regarding the rules of the game and adherence to those rules most of the time by most actors, power alone would create great instability in the anarchic international system. International law, even without perfect enforcement, creates expectations about what constitutes legal behavior by states. Because violations or divergences from those expectations stand out, it is easier to identify and punish states that deviate from accepted rules. When states agree to the rules by signing treaties (such as the UN Charter), violations become more visible and clearly illegitimate. In most cases, although power continues to reside in states, international law establishes workable rules for those states to follow. The resulting stability is so beneficial that usually the costs of breaking the rules outweigh the short-term benefits that could be gained from such violations.

World Court Also called the International Court of Justice (ICJ). The judicial arm of the UN; located in The Hague, it hears only cases between states.

International Court of Justice (ICJ) See *World Court*.

7.3.3 The World Court

As international law has developed, a general world legal framework in which states can pursue grievances against each other has begun to take shape. The rudiments of such a system now exist in the **World Court** (formally called the **International Court of Justice [ICJ]**), although its jurisdiction is limited and its caseload light. The World Court is a branch of the UN.

Only states, not individuals or businesses, can sue or be sued in the World Court. When a state has a grievance against another, it can take the case to the World Court for an impartial hearing. The Security Council or General Assembly may also request advisory Court opinions on matters of international law. For example, the 2010 Court ruling declaring Kosovo's declaration of independence legal was an advisory opinion requested by the General Assembly.

The World Court is a panel of 15 judges elected for nine-year terms (five judges every three years) by a majority of both the Security Council and General Assembly. The Court meets in The Hague, Netherlands. It is customary for permanent members of the Security Council to have one of their nationals as a judge at all times, although this is only custom and not a formal rule. Ad hoc judges may be added to the 15 if a party to a case does not already have one of its nationals as a judge.

ALL RISE The World Court hears international disputes but with little power to enforce judgments. Here, in 2004, the judges rule in favor of Mexico's complaint that the U.S. death penalty against Mexican citizens violated a 1963 treaty.

The great weakness of the World Court is that states have not agreed in a comprehensive way to subject themselves to its jurisdiction or obey its decisions. Almost all states have signed the treaty creating the Court, but only about a third have signed the *optional clause* in the treaty agreeing to give the Court jurisdiction in certain cases—and even many of those signatories have added their own stipulations reserving their rights and limiting the degree to which the Court can infringe on national sovereignty. Colombia withdrew from a treaty giving the Court jurisdiction in 2012 after the Court awarded disputed territorial waters to Nicaragua. Similarly, Iran refused to acknowledge the jurisdiction of the Court when sued by the United States in 1979 over its seizure of the U.S. embassy in Iran. In such a case, the Court may hear the case anyway and usually rules in favor of the participating side—but it has no means to enforce the ruling. Justice can also move slowly. In 2007, the Court issued a ruling against Bosnia's case accusing Serbia of genocide after 14 years of preliminary maneuvering.

In one of its most notable successes, the World Court in 1992 settled a complex border dispute between El Salvador and Honduras dating from 1861. In 2002, the World Court settled a long-standing and sometimes violent dispute over an oil-rich peninsula on the Cameroon-Nigeria border. It gave ownership to Cameroon, and Nigeria (which is more powerful) pulled troops out in 2006.

A main use of the World Court now is to arbitrate issues of secondary importance between countries with friendly relations overall. The United States has settled commercial disputes with Canada and with Italy through the Court. Because security interests are not at stake and because the overall friendly relations are more important than the particular issue, states have been willing to submit to the Court's jurisdiction. In 2004, the World Court ordered the United States to review death sentences of Mexican nationals to see whether their lack of access to Mexican officials had harmed their legal case. Under the 1963 Vienna Convention on Consular Relations, citizens arrested in a foreign country must be advised of their right to meet with their home country's representatives. The United States had often failed to do so despite demanding this right for Americans abroad. The World Court suggested that U.S. courts add relevant language to the Miranda warning for cases when police arrest foreign nationals. Figure 7.4 illustrates one of the Court's recent cases, a dispute between Argentina and Uruguay.

Figure 7.4 World Court Case of Argentina v. Uruguay

Source: Based on The International Court of Justice.

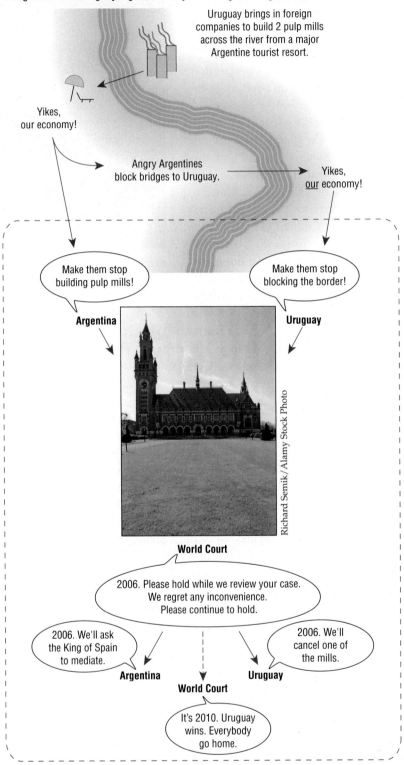

Because of the difficulty of winning enforceable agreements on major con-flicts through the World Court, states have used the Court infrequently over the years—a dozen or fewer cases per year (about 150 judgments and advisory opin-ions since 1947).

7.3.4 International Cases in National Courts

Most legal cases concerning international matters—whether brought by governments or by private individuals or companies—remain entirely within the legal systems of one or more states. National courts hear cases brought under national laws and can enforce judgments by collecting damages (in civil suits) or imposing punishments (in criminal ones).

A party with a dispute that crosses national boundaries gains several advantages by pursuing the matter through the national courts of one or more of the relevant states, rather than through international channels. First, judgments are enforceable. The party that wins a lawsuit in a national court can collect from the other party's assets within the state. Second, individuals and companies can pursue legal complaints through national courts (as can subnational governmental bodies), whereas in most areas of international law, states must themselves bring suits on behalf of their citizens. (In truth, even national governments pursue most of their legal actions against each other through national courts.)

Third, there is often a choice of more than one state within which a case could legally be heard; one can pick the legal system most favorable to one's case. Each state's court system must decide whether it has *jurisdiction* in a case (the right to hear it), and courts tend to extend their own authority with a broad interpretation. Traditionally, a national court may hear cases concerning any activity on its national territory, any actions of its own citizens anywhere in the world, and actions taken toward its citizens elsewhere in the world. Noncitizens can use the national courts to enforce damages against citizens because the national court has authority to impose fines and, if necessary, to seize bank accounts and property.

The United States is a favorite jurisdiction within which to bring cases for two reasons. First, U.S. juries have a reputation for awarding bigger settlements in lawsuits than juries elsewhere in the world (if only because the United States is a rich country). Second, because many people and governments do business in the United States, it is often possible to collect damages awarded by a U.S. court. For these reasons, U.S. courts in recent years have ruled on human rights cases brought by Chinese dissidents over the 1989 Tiananmen massacre, Cuban exiles against the Cuban government, and a Paraguayan doctor suing a Paraguayan police official for torturing the doctor's son. In 2003, U.S. courts ordered large payments by Iraq and Iran to U.S. victims of terrorism and torture. The Alien Tort Claims Act of 1789 gives federal courts jurisdiction over civil lawsuits against foreigners for "violation of the law of nations." Human rights activists have used the law against repressive governments in recent years, as when they sued U.S. oil companies ExxonMobil and Unocal for aiding abusive regimes in Indonesia and Burma, respectively. But in 2013, the U.S. Supreme Court sharply limited this extension of U.S. legal jurisdiction, throwing out a case against the Dutch company Shell for facilitating government atrocities in Nigeria.

Belgium's national courts are a favorite venue for international human rights cases because a 1993 law gives them jurisdiction over any violation of the Geneva Conventions. In 2001, four people accused of war crimes in Rwanda in 1994 were sent to prison by a Belgian jury. (Rwanda is a former Belgian colony, and ten Belgian soldiers had been killed in the genocide there.) In 2005, Belgium indicted a former leader of Chad accused of 40,000 political murders in Chad in the 1980s, and Senegal (where he lived) asked the AU to rule on whether it should extradite him. The AU encouraged Senegal to try him domestically instead.

There are important limits, however, to the use of national courts to resolve international disputes. Most important is that the authority of national courts stops at the state's borders, where sovereignty ends. A court in Zambia cannot compel a resident of Thailand to come and testify; it cannot authorize the seizure of a British bank account to pay damages; it cannot arrest a criminal suspect (Zambian or foreigner) except on Zambian soil. To take such actions beyond national borders, states must persuade other states to cooperate. In 2012, a U.S. hedge fund that had lost $370 million in Argentina's 2002 debt default convinced Ghana to seize a visiting Argentinean ship to pay the debt, but Ghana released the ship after a ruling by a UN maritime tribunal.

To bring a person outside a state's territory to trial, the state's government must ask a second government to arrest the person on the second state's territory and hand him or her over for trial. Called *extradition*, this is a matter of international law because it is a legal treaty arrangement between states. Hundreds of such treaties exist, many dating back hundreds of years. If no such treaty exists, the individual generally remains immune from a state's courts by staying off its territory. For example, Russia has declared that it will not extradite American hacker Edward Snowden, instead offering him political asylum in 2013.

Some U.S. allies do not usually extradite to the United States suspects who would face the death penalty. For example, in 2012 the European Court of Justice (see Chapter 10) allowed Great Britain to extradite a Muslim cleric suspected of terrorist activities to the United States after nearly ten years of legal hearings. The European Court had feared the suspect would receive ill treatment in the U.S. prison system and thus delayed his extradition for nearly a decade.

In one particularly high-profile debate about extradition, the former Chilean military dictator Augusto Pinochet was arrested in England in 1999 on a Spanish warrant, based on crimes committed against Spanish citizens in Chile during Pinochet's rule. His supporters claimed that he should have immunity for acts taken as head of state, but because he was not an accredited diplomat in England (where he had gone for medical treatment) and no longer head of state, the British courts held him on Spain's request to extradite him. However, the British government eventually let him return to Chile, citing his medical condition, and a Chilean court suspended his case on health grounds. He died in 2006 without standing trial.

Gray areas exist in the jurisdiction of national courts over foreigners. If a government can lure a suspect onto the high seas, it can nab the person without violating another country's territoriality. More troublesome are cases in which a government obtains a foreign citizen from a foreign country for trial without going through extradition procedures. In a famous case in the 1980s, a Mexican doctor was wanted by U.S. authorities for allegedly participating in the torture and murder of a U.S. drug agent in Mexico. The U.S. government paid a group of bounty hunters to kidnap the doctor in Mexico, carry him forcibly across the border, and deliver him to the custody of U.S. courts. The U.S. Supreme Court gave the U.S. courts jurisdiction in the case—showing the tendency to extend state sovereignty wherever possible—although international lawyers and Mexican officials objected strongly. The U.S. government had to reassure the Mexican government that it would not kidnap Mexican citizens for trial in the United States in the future. The doctor returned home after the case was thrown out for lack of evidence.

immigration law National law(s) that establish the conditions under which foreigners may travel and visit within a state's territory, work within the state, and sometimes become citizens of the state (naturalization).

The principle of territoriality also governs **immigration law**. When people cross a border into a new country, the decision about whether they can remain there, and under what conditions, is up to the new state. The state of origin cannot compel their return. National laws establish conditions for foreigners to travel and visit on a state's territory, to work there, and sometimes to become citizens (*naturalization*). Many other legal issues are raised by people traveling or living outside their own country—passports and visas, babies born in foreign countries, marriages to foreign nationals, bank accounts, businesses, taxes, and so forth. Practices vary from country to country, but the general principle is that national laws prevail on the territory of a state.

Despite the continued importance of national court systems in international legal affairs and the lack of enforcement powers of the World Court, it would be wrong to conclude that state sovereignty is supreme and international law impotent. Rather, a balance of sovereignty and law exists in international interactions.

7.4 Law and Sovereignty

Summarize the distinction between just wars and wars of aggression.

The remainder of this chapter discusses particular areas of international law, from the most firmly rooted and widely respected to newer and less-established areas. In each area, the influence of law and norms runs counter to the unimpeded exercise of state sovereignty. This struggle becomes more intense as one moves from long-standing traditions of diplomatic law to recent norms governing human rights.

7.4.1 Laws of Diplomacy

The bedrock of international law is respect for the rights of diplomats. The standards of behavior in this area are spelled out in detail, applied universally, and taken very seriously. The ability to conduct diplomacy is necessary for all other kinds of relations among states, except perhaps all-out war. Since the rise of the international system five centuries ago, it has been considered unjustifiable to harm an emissary sent from another state as a means of influencing the other state. Such a norm has not always existed; it is natural in some ways to kill the messenger who brings an unpleasant message, or to use another state's official as a hostage or bargaining chip. But today, this kind of behavior is universally condemned, though it still happens from time to time.

The status of embassies and of an ambassador as an official state representative is explicitly defined in the process of **diplomatic recognition**. Diplomats are *accredited* to each other's governments (they present "credentials"), and thereafter the individuals so defined enjoy certain rights and protections as foreign diplomats in the host country. Diplomats have the right to occupy an *embassy* in a host country, within which the host country's laws may not be enforced without the consent of the embassy's country. For this reason, embassies occasionally shelter dissidents who take refuge there from their own governments.

diplomatic recognition The process by which the status of embassies and that of an ambassador as an official state representative are explicitly defined.

A flagrant violation of the sanctity of embassies occurred in Iran after Islamic revolutionaries took power in 1979. Iranian students seized and occupied the U.S. embassy compound, holding the U.S. diplomats hostage for more than a year. The Iranian government did not directly commit this act but did condone it and did refuse to force the students out of the embassy. (Host countries are expected, if necessary, to use force against their own citizens to protect a foreign embassy.)

Diplomats enjoy **diplomatic immunity** even when they leave the embassy grounds. The right to travel varies from one country to another; diplomats may be restricted to one city or free to roam about the countryside. Alone among all foreign nationals, diplomats are beyond enforcement of the host country's national courts. If they commit crimes, from jaywalking to murder, they may be shielded from arrest. All the host country can do is take away a diplomat's accreditation and expel the person from the host country. However, strong countries sometimes pressure weaker ones to lift immunity so that a diplomat may face trial for a crime. This happened twice in 1997, for example, when the United States and France were allowed to prosecute diplomats from Georgia and Zaire, respectively, for reckless driving that killed children.

diplomatic immunity A privilege under which diplomats' activities fall outside the jurisdiction of the host country's national courts.

U.S. commitments as host country to the UN include extending diplomatic immunity to the diplomats accredited to the UN. Given this immunity, delegates simply tear up thousands of parking tickets each year, for example. It is estimated that the city of New York is owed $16 million in unpaid tickets. The parking ticket matter has become a sensitive political issue, as the State Department now reserves the right to revoke driver's licenses, license plates, and even reduce foreign aid based on outstanding parking tickets. In London three cars driven by Sudanese diplomats received over 800 tickets tallying over $100,000 in fines.

OUT OF REACH International law prohibits attacks on diplomats and embassies. This fundamental principle, like others in international law, is ultimately enforced through reciprocity. When the founder of WikiLeaks took refuge in the Ecuadorian embassy in London to avoid extradition to Sweden, the British government considered coming in and taking him, but thought better of it. Here, in the spring of 2017, he delivers a speech from the embassy balcony announcing he will continue to live in the embassy, where he has resided since 2012.

Because of diplomatic immunity, espionage activities are commonly conducted through the diplomatic corps, out of an embassy. Spies are often posted to low-level positions in embassies, such as cultural attaché, press liaison, or military attaché. If the host country catches them spying, it cannot prosecute them, so it merely expels them. Diplomatic norms (though not law) call for politeness when expelling spies; the standard reason given is "for activities not consistent with his or her diplomatic status." If a spy operates under cover of being a businessperson or tourist, then no immunity applies; the person can be arrested and prosecuted under the host country's laws. Such was the case in 2010, when the U.S. government arrested ten Russian spies who were leading lives as ordinary citizens in America. Before the prosecution of the accused spies could proceed in New York courts, however, the United States and Russia agreed to an exchange of accused spies.

A *diplomatic pouch* is a package sent between an embassy and its home country. As the name implies, it started out historically as a small and occasional shipment, but today a large and steady volume of such shipments travel all over the world. Diplomatic pouches, too, enjoy the status of home country territoriality: They cannot be opened, searched, or confiscated by a host country. Although we do not know how much mischief goes on in diplomatic pouches (because they are secret), it is safe to assume that illicit goods such as guns and drugs regularly find their way across borders in diplomatic pouches.

To *break diplomatic relations* means to withdraw one's diplomats from a state and expel that state's diplomats from one's own state. This tactic is used to show displeasure with another government; it is a refusal to do business as usual. When a revolutionary government comes into power, some countries may withdraw recognition. And when small states recognize Taiwan diplomatically, China withdraws recognition of them.

When two countries lack diplomatic relations, they often do business through a third country willing to represent a country's interests formally through its own embassy. This is called an *interests section* in the third country's embassy. Thus, the practical needs of diplomacy can overcome a formal lack of relations between states. For instance, during their long period of mutual nonrecognition, U.S. interests were represented by the Swiss embassy in Cuba, and Cuban interests were represented by the Swiss embassy in the United States. In practice, these interest sections were located in the former U.S. and Cuban embassies and staffed with U.S. and Cuban diplomats.

Diplomatic relationships can also become entangled in sanctions. In 2016, as a part of sanctions against Russia for meddling in the U.S. presidential election of that year, the United States closed two diplomatic compounds in Maryland and New York. Russia responded to this action (and other sanction-related actions) by expelling 755 U.S. diplomats in 2017.

States register lower levels of displeasure by *recalling their ambassadors* home for some period of time; diplomatic norms call for a trip home "for consultations" even when everyone knows the purpose is to signal annoyance. Milder still is the expression of displeasure by a *formal complaint*. Usually the complaining government does so in its own capital city, to the other's ambassador.

The law of diplomacy is repeatedly violated in one context—terrorism (see Chapter 6). Because states care so much about the sanctity of diplomats, the diplomats make a tempting target for terrorists, and because terrorist groups do not enjoy the benefits of diplomatic law (as states do), they are willing to break diplomatic norms and laws. An attack on diplomats or embassies is an attack on the territory of the state itself—yet can be carried out far from the state's home territory. Many diplomats have been killed in recent decades. In 1998, al Qaeda terrorists bombed the U.S. embassies in Kenya and Tanzania, killing more than 200 people. In late 2004, terrorists stormed a U.S. consulate in Saudi Arabia, killing several guards, and in 2012, terrorists burned the U.S. consulate in Benghazi, Libya, killing the ambassador.

7.4.2 Just-War Doctrine

After the law of diplomacy, international law regarding war is one of the most developed areas of international law. Laws concerning war are divided into two areas— laws *of* war (when war is permissible) and laws *in* war (how wars are fought).

To begin with the laws of war, international law distinguishes **just wars** (which are legal) from wars of aggression (which are illegal). (We discuss laws in war later in the context of human rights.) This area of law grows out of centuries-old religious writings about just wars (which once could be enforced by threats to excommunicate individuals from the church). Today, the UN Charter, which outlaws aggression, defines the legality of war. Above and beyond its legal standing, just-war doctrine has become a strong international norm, not one that all states follow but an important part of the modern intellectual tradition governing matters of war and peace that evolved in Europe.

just wars A category in international law and political theory that defines when wars can be justly started (*jus ad bellum*) and how they can be justly fought (*jus in bello*). See also *war crimes*.

The idea of aggression, around which the doctrine of just war evolved, is based on a violation of the sovereignty and territorial integrity of states. *Aggression* refers to a state's use of force, or an imminent threat to do so, against another state's territory or sovereignty—unless the use of force is in response to aggression. Tanks swarming across the border constitute aggression, but so do tanks massing at the border if their state has threatened to invade its neighbor. The lines are somewhat fuzzy. But for a threat to constitute aggression (and justify the use of force in response), it must be a clear threat of using force, not just a hostile policy or general rivalry.

States have the right to respond to aggression in the only manner thought to be reliable—military force. Just-war doctrine is thus not based on nonviolence. Responses can include both *repelling* the attack itself and *punishing* the aggressor. Responses can be made by the victim of aggression or by other states not directly affected—as a way of maintaining the norm of nonaggression in the international system. The collective actions of UN members against Iraq after its invasion of Kuwait are a classic case of such a response.

Response to aggression is the only allowable use of military force according to just-war doctrine. The just-war approach thus explicitly rules out war as an instrument to change another state's government or policies, or in ethnic and religious conflicts. In fact, the UN Charter makes no provision for "war" but rather for "international police actions" against aggressors. The analogy is with law and order in a national society, enforced by police when necessary. Because only aggression justifies military force, if all states obeyed the law against aggression, there would be no international war.

For a war to be *morally* just, it must be more than a response to aggression; it must be waged for the *purpose* of responding to aggression. The *intent* must be just. A state may not take advantage of another's aggression to wage a war that is essentially aggressive. Although the U.S.-led war effort to oust Iraq from Kuwait in 1991 was certainly a response to aggression, critics found the justness of the war to be compromised by the U.S. interest in obtaining cheap oil from the Middle East—not an allowable reason for waging war.

Just-war doctrine has been undermined, even more seriously than have laws of war crimes, by the changing nature of warfare. In civil wars and low-intensity conflicts, the belligerents range from poorly organized militias to national armies, and the battleground is often a patchwork of enclaves and positions with no clear front lines (much less borders). It is thus harder to identify an aggressor in such situations and harder to balance the relative merits of peace and justice.

7.5 Human Rights

Contrast the effectiveness of international law, NGOs, and states in advancing the cause of human rights around the globe.

human rights The rights of all people to be free from abuses such as torture or imprisonment for their political beliefs (political and civil rights) and to enjoy certain minimum economic and social protections (economic and social rights).

One of the newest areas of international law concerns **human rights**—the rights of human beings against certain abuses of their *own* governments.

7.5.1 Individual Rights Versus Sovereignty

The very idea of human rights flies in the face of the sovereignty and territorial integrity of states. Sovereignty gives states the right to do as they please in their own territory: Nobody can tell them how to treat their own citizens.

Thus, a consensus on what are the most important human rights is difficult to reach. One approach to human rights argues that rights are *universal*. No matter where a person resides; no matter his or her ethnic nationality; and no matter his or her local religious, ethnic, or clan traditions, that person has certain rights that must be respected. The other approach to human rights is often labeled *relativism*. According to this idea, local traditions and histories should be given due respect, even if this means limiting rights that others outside that local context find important. Efforts to promote human rights are routinely criticized by governments with poor human rights records by Western standards (including China and Russia) as "interference in our internal affairs." This charge puts human rights law on shaky ground and reflects a more relativist stance.

The concept of human rights arises from at least three sources. The first is religion. Nearly every major world religion has at its foundation the idea that humans were created in an image of a higher power and that therefore all humans are to be afforded the dignity and respect that are due that higher power. Nowhere is this idea more clearly spelled out than in the American Declaration of Independence, written by Thomas Jefferson, that all people are "endowed by their Creator with certain unalienable rights."[3]

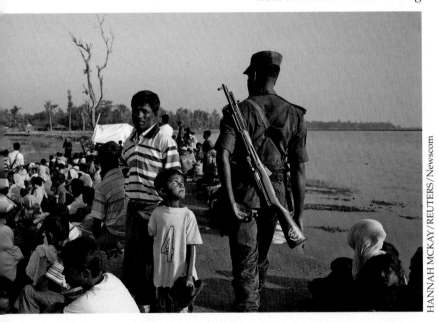

CLASHING NORMS International norms concerning human rights conflict with state sovereignty, causing friction in relationships such as that of Burma (Myanmar) with the international community. In 2017, Burma began violently forcing hundreds of thousands of members of an ethnic minority into neighboring Bangladesh. And while Bangladesh honored the norm of accepting those fleeing persecution, it also requested assistance in dealing with the over 300,000 refugees. Here, from an overfilled refugee camp, a Bangladeshi troop watches refugees fleeing from Burma.

HANNAH MCKAY/REUTERS/Newscom

Second, political and legal philosophy for centuries has discussed the idea of natural law and natural rights. From Aristotle to John Locke, to Immanuel Kant, to Jean-Jacques Rousseau, political philosophers have developed the idea that a natural law exists that grants all humans the right to life, liberty, property, and happiness.

---

[3]U.S. National Archives and Records Administration. [https://www.archives.gov/founding-docs/declaration-transcript].

Finally, political revolutions in the eighteenth century, such as the American and French Revolutions, translated the theory of natural law and natural rights into practice. In the United States, the Declaration of Independence, and in France, the Declaration of the Rights of Man and of the Citizen, engendered laws that solidified the idea that humans have certain rights that no state or other individuals can take away.

Of course, criticisms of these ideas of human rights exist, on both a theoretical and a practical level. Theoretically, relativists point out that much of the origin and development of human rights ideas (at least two of the three sources discussed) are Western in origin. Non-Western societies have different philosophical traditions and may choose to emphasize group or family rights, for example, over individual ones. At a practical level, many (especially non-Western) critics are quick to point out that even after the eighteenth-century revolutions in Europe and America, rights were still not universal. Women, children, and usually nonwhites were not assumed to enjoy the same rights as landholding white males, making the very idea of universal rights misleading.

Partially because of this controversy, no globally agreed-upon definitions of the essential human rights exist. Rights are often divided into two broad types: civil-political and economic-social. Civil-political rights are sometimes referred to as negative rights and include what are considered traditional Western rights such as free speech, freedom of religion, equal protection under the law, and freedom from arbitrary imprisonment. It is generally thought that these rights are best guaranteed by limiting the power of governments over their people. Economic-social rights are referred to as positive rights and include rights to good living conditions, food, health care, social security, and education. It is often held that these rights are best promoted by the expansion of governments to provide minimal standards to their people.

No state has a perfect record on any type of human rights, and states differ as to which areas they respect or violate. When the United States criticizes China for prohibiting free speech, limiting access to certain Internet sites, using prison labor, and torturing political dissidents (civil-political rights), China notes that the United States has 40 million poor people, the highest ratio of prison inmates in the world, and a history of racism and violence (economic-social rights). During the Cold War, the United States and its allies consistently criticized the Soviet Union and China for violations of civil-political rights yet refused to endorse treaties championing economic-social rights. Likewise, communist states encouraged the development of the latter rights while ignoring calls for the former. Overall, despite the poor record of the world's states on some points, progress has been made on others. For example, slavery—once considered normal worldwide—has mostly been abandoned in the past 150 years.

Historically, a significant global shift in human rights occurred at the end of World War II. Horrified by Nazi Germany's attempt to exterminate the Jewish population and by Japanese abuses of Chinese citizens, many scholars and practitioners began to suggest that there were limits to state sovereignty. States could not claim to be sovereign and above interference if they attempted to massacre their own people. In the aftermath of World War II and the creation of the United Nations, some of the most significant international attempts to codify and enforce human rights began. In the next section, we will examine some of these agreements and institutions.

7.5.2 Human Rights Institutions

In 1948, the UN General Assembly adopted what is considered the core international document concerning human rights: the **Universal Declaration of Human Rights (UDHR)**. The UDHR does not have the force of international law, but it sets forth (hoped-for) international norms regarding behavior by governments toward their own citizens and foreigners alike. The declaration roots itself in the principle that violations of human rights upset international order (causing outrage, sparking rebellion, etc.) and in the fact that the UN Charter commits states to respect fundamental

Universal Declaration of Human Rights (UDHR) (1948) The core UN document on human rights; although it lacks the force of international law, it sets forth international norms regarding behavior by governments toward their own citizens and foreigners alike.

Table 7.3 Ratification Status of Nine Core UN Human Rights Treaties, 2018

Treaty	Date in Force	Number of Parties	Key Nonmembers
International Convention on the Elimination of All Forms of Racial Discrimination (CERD)	January 4, 1969	178	Burma, Malaysia, North Korea
International Covenant on Economic, Social and Cultural Rights (CESCR)	January 3, 1976	165	Botswana, Saudi Arabia, U.S.
International Covenant on Civil and Political Rights (CCPR)	March 23, 1976	169	Burma, China, Saudi Arabia
Convention on the Elimination of All Forms of Discrimination Against Women (CEDAW)	September 3, 1981	189	Iran, Somalia, Sudan, U.S.
Convention Against Torture (CAT)	June 26, 1987	162	Angola, Burma, India, Iran, Sudan
Convention on the Rights of the Child (CRC)	September 2, 1990	196	U.S.
International Convention on the Protection of the Rights of All Migrant Workers and Members of Their Families (CMW)	July 1, 2003	51	France, Great Britain, China, Russia, U.S.
Convention on the Rights of Persons with Disabilities (CRPD)	May 3, 2008	175	Chad, Libya, U.S.
International Convention for the Protection of All Persons from Enforced Disappearance (CPED)	December 23, 2010	57	Australia, China, Russia, U.S.

Source: United Nations.

freedoms. The declaration proclaims that "all human beings are born free and equal"[4] without regard to race, sex, language, religion, political affiliation, or the status of the territory in which they were born. It goes on to promote norms in a wide variety of areas, including banning torture, guaranteeing religious and political freedom, and ensuring the right of economic well-being.

Since the adoption of the UDHR, the UN has opened nine treaties for state signature to further define protections of human rights (see Table 7.3). Unlike the UDHR, these treaties are legally binding contracts signed by states. Of course, international law is only as good as the enforcement mechanisms behind it. Yet these nine treaties are important in outlining the basic protections for individuals expected by the international community.

Two key treaties are the *International Covenant on Civil and Political Rights* (CCPR) and the *International Covenant on Economic, Social and Cultural Rights* (CESCR). These two treaties, both of which entered into force in 1976, codify the promises of the UDHR while dividing the list of rights in the UDHR into civil-political and economic-social rights, respectively. These two covenants, along with the UDHR, are often referred to as the International Bill of Human Rights.

The remaining treaties each deal with a particular group that the international community considers vulnerable. The International Convention on the Elimination of All Forms of Racial Discrimination (CERD), enacted in 1969, bans discrimination against individuals based on race, ethnicity, religion, or national origin. The CERD does not include language concerning gender discrimination. The Convention on the Elimination of All Forms of Discrimination Against Women (CEDAW), however, fills this void by banning discrimination against women. CEDAW entered into force in 1981.

The Convention Against Torture (CAT), instituted in 1987, bans dehumanizing, degrading, and inhumane treatment of individuals even in times of war. The Convention on the Rights of the Child (CRC), enacted in 1990, promotes children's health, education, and physical well-being (every country in the world except the United States has approved the CRC). The International Convention on the Protection of the Rights of All Migrant Workers and Members of Their Families (CMW) entered into force in 2003. The CMW attempts to protect the political, labor, and social rights of the nearly 100 million migrant workers around the globe.

The Convention on the Rights of Persons with Disabilities (CRPD), which entered into force in 2008, promotes dignity, equality of legal protection, and reasonable

---

[4]Universal Declaration of Human Rights (UDHR), Paris, France. (December 10, 1948). [http://www.un.org/en/universal-declaration-human-rights/].

accommodation for disabled persons in all signatory states. The most recent core human rights treaty is the International Convention for the Protection of All Persons from Enforced Disappearance (CPED), which became active in 2010. This treaty protects individuals from forced disappearance, which is defined, in part, as a "deprivation of liberty" followed by a concealment of that deprivation.

Equally important as these UN treaties themselves are the *optional protocols* that are attached to several of the treaties. These protocols can be thought of as addendums to the treaties because they contain additional protections not included in the original documents. In general, far fewer states sign these optional protocols because the protections contained in them were too controversial for the original documents. In addition, some of the optional protocols contain stronger enforcement mechanisms, such as giving individuals in signatory states the right to go to the UN monitoring bodies without the approval of their governments. States that are not party to the original treaty may sign them, as is the case with the United States, which has not signed the CRC but has signed its two optional protocols.

Besides the UN-related human rights treaties, several regional IOs have promoted the protection of human rights. Nowhere is this more true than in Europe, where the European Union, the Council of Europe, and the European Court of Human Rights all work to ensure that all states in the region respect human rights (see Chapter 10). In Latin America, the *Inter-American Court of Human Rights* has had some success in promoting human rights, yet it has also been limited by state refusal to abide by its decisions. Finally, the AU helps support the African Commission on Human and Peoples' Rights, but the commission has been hampered by its lack of monetary and political support from African states.

In the past two decades, developed states have begun to use other international organizations to pressure developing states to improve human rights conditions. Free trade agreements (see Chapter 8) frequently contain provisions that condition trade benefits on the respect for human rights, especially workers' rights. Because these treaties provide policies beneficial to the developing states, they create a ready mechanism to punish countries that abuse their citizens. Others argue, however, that limiting economic benefits to countries harms their economic development, which is likely only to make the human rights situation worse.

Today, NGOs play a key role in efforts to win basic political rights in authoritarian countries—including a halt to the torture, execution, and imprisonment of those expressing political or religious beliefs. The leading organization pressing this struggle is **Amnesty International**, an NGO that operates globally to monitor and try to rectify glaring abuses of human rights. Amnesty International has a reputation for impartiality and has criticized abuses in many countries, including the United States. Other groups, such as Human Rights Watch, work in a similar way but often with a more regional or national focus. NGOs often provide information and advocacy for UN and other regional organizations. They essentially serve as a bridge between the global or regional organizations and efforts to promote human rights "on the ground."

Amnesty International An influential nongovernmental organization (NGO) that operates globally to monitor and try to rectify glaring abuses of political (not economic or social) human rights.

Enforcing norms of human rights is difficult because it involves interfering in a state's internal affairs. Cutting off trade or contact with a government that violates human rights tends to hurt the citizens whose rights are being violated by further isolating them. Yet such measures keep those suffering from human rights abuses in the global spotlight, drawing more attention to their plight.

The most effective method yet discovered is a combination of *publicity* and *pressure*. Publicity entails digging up information about human rights abuses, as Amnesty International does. Through a process some scholars have dubbed "naming and shaming," supporters of human rights hope that publicity will embarrass the regime and change its behavior. The publicity also serves to alert those traveling to or doing business with offending regimes to the conditions in those countries. Human rights activists hope this negative attention will convince individuals to stop their interactions with the state in question, putting further economic pressure on it.

The pressure of other governments, as well as private individuals and businesses, consists of threats to punish the offender in some way through nonviolent means. But because most governments seek to maintain normal relations with each other most of the time, this kind of intrusive punishment by one government of another's human rights violations is rare—and not reliably successful.

Also rare are humanitarian interventions using military force to overcome armed resistance by local authorities or warlords and bring help to civilian victims of wars and disasters. However, international norms have increasingly shifted against sovereignty and toward protecting endangered civilians. A major summit of world leaders in 2005 enshrined the concept of the **responsibility to protect (R2P)**, which holds that governments worldwide must act to save civilians from genocide or crimes against humanity perpetrated or allowed by their own governments. Three important humanitarian interventions in the 1990s were in Kurdish areas of Iraq, in Somalia, and in Kosovo (Serbia). The UN-authorized NATO campaign in Libya in 2011 followed from the R2P concept. Yet the people of Syria did not get protection in 2011–2018 as tens of thousands were killed by their government, and starting in 2014 also by Islamic State rebels (see the Public Opinion and International Relations box).

The U.S. State Department has actively pursued human rights since the late 1970s. An annual U.S. government report assesses human rights in states around the world. In states where abuses are severe or becoming worse, U.S. foreign aid has been withheld. (But in other cases, CIA funding has supported the abusers.) In response to these reports, China produces its own human rights report on the state of U.S. human rights, releasing it on the same day as the U.S. State Department report.

responsibility to protect (R2P) Principle adopted by world leaders in 2005 holding governments responsible for protecting civilians from genocide and crimes against humanity perpetrated within a sovereign state.

7.5.3 War Crimes and the ICC

Large-scale abuses of human rights often occur during war. Serious violations of this kind are considered **war crimes**. In wartime, international law is especially difficult to enforce, but extensive norms of legal conduct in war as well as international treaties are widely followed. After a war, losers can be punished for violations of the laws of war, as Germans were in the Nuremberg trials after World War II. Because the Nazi murders of civilians did not violate German law, the Nuremberg Tribunal treated them as a new category, **crimes against humanity**, conceived as inhumane acts and persecutions against civilians on a vast scale in the pursuit of unjust ends (see the Seeking the Collective Good box).

In the 1990s, for the first time since World War II, the UN Security Council authorized an international war crimes tribunal, directed against war crimes in the former Yugoslavia. Similar tribunals were later established for genocide in Rwanda and Sierra Leone. The tribunal on the former Yugoslavia, headquartered in The Hague, Netherlands, issued indictments against the top Bosnian Serb leaders and other Serbian and Croatian officers, and in 1999 against Serbian strongman Slobodan Milosevic for his expulsion of Albanians from Kosovo. The tribunal was hampered by lack of funding and by its lack of power to arrest suspects who enjoyed the sanctity of Serbia and Croatia. After Milosevic lost power in Serbia, the new Serbian government turned him over to the tribunal in 2001, and he died in custody in 2006. By 2011, no Bosnia war criminals remained at large, and at the end of 2012, the Rwanda tribunal also completed all of its 71 cases. One of the final prosecutions in Bosnia ended in 2017 with a guilty verdict against a former

war crimes Violations of the law governing the conduct of warfare, such as mistreatment of prisoners of war or the unnecessary targeting of civilians. See also *just wars*.

crimes against humanity A category of legal offenses created at the Nuremberg trials after World War II to encompass genocide and other acts committed by the political and military leaders of the Third Reich (Nazi Germany). See also *dehumanization* and *genocide*.

Public Opinion and International Relations
U.S. Public Opinion and Human Rights

The subject of human rights is often on the mind of the American public. Figure 7.5 shows two clear trends in public opinion data from the United States over the last 15-plus years. First, only a small percentage of the public believes that human rights should not be a priority in American foreign policy. This number looks to hover around 10 percent for most of the last two decades. Second, the percentage of the public who believe human rights should be a "top priority" has been growing steadily for the past decade. This could be in response to the deadly war in Syria over that time or the massive flow of refugees created by the conflict there and in Libya.

American opinion on international human rights, however, is not a story of unconditional support. Public opinion in the United States becomes quite mixed when actual policies to promote human rights (or to end large-scale violations of human rights) are discussed. The clearest evidence of this can be found in opinions regarding humanitarian interventions—the use of the U.S. military to stop conflicts that are leading to mass human rights violations. When asked about specific interventions to stop these conflicts, opinions of the American public vary widely. Figure 7.6 shows the results of four different polls concerning four different conflicts where significant human rights violations were present. In these polls, there is less evidence of any clear trend. When polls ask about "genocide," support for intervention seems to rise, but in general, support for military intervention into ethnic conflicts is not high.

What do we conclude about American public opinion on human rights? Americans are traditionally skeptical about intervening in other country's ethnic conflicts—a tradition that perhaps

Figure 7.6 United States Public Opinion Toward International Interventions

NOTE: Figures may not add to 100% because of rounding.
Source: Pew Research Center March 10–13, 2011.

Few Say U.S. Has Responsibility to Act in Libya

Does the U.S. have a responsiblity to do something about …	Yes %	No %	DK %
Fighting in Libya (3/2011)	27	63	10 = 100
Ethnic genocide in Darfur (12/2006)	51	36	13 = 100
Ethnic fighting in Kosovo (3/1999)	47	46	7 = 100
Fighting between Serbs and Bosnians (6/1995)	30	64	6 = 100

grows from the American experience in Vietnam and, more recently, Afghanistan and Iraq. Yet, it is in these very conflicts where widespread violations of human rights occur: war crimes, crimes against humanity, and genocide. Thus, it is difficult to build political support for acting in the actual cases that threaten human rights the most.

Short of intervention in conflicts, Americans are generally more willing for the government to use sanctions or to cut economic or military aid to states that abuse human rights. In that way, the U.S. public is willing to pay the costs of defending human rights around the world. It would be fair to say that Americans are supportive of foreign policies to promote human rights—but only to a point, and that point is overt military intervention.

Figure 7.5 Human Rights as a United States Foreign Policy Priority

Source: Roper Center for Public Opinion.

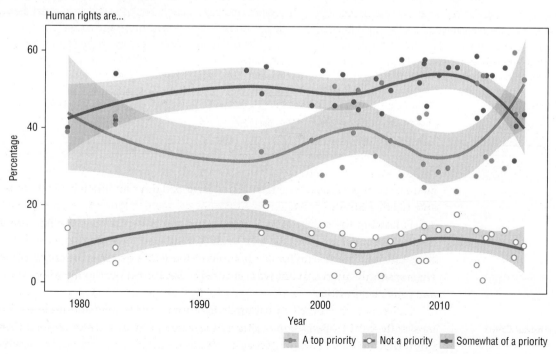

Human rights are...

A top priority   Not a priority   Somewhat of a priority

Seeking the Collective Good
Responsibility to Protect
COLLECTIVE GOOD: Stopping Atrocities Against Civilians

BACKGROUND: The international system based on sovereignty has historically treated serious human rights abuses as domestic problems of no concern to outside countries. Over the years, however, a norm has developed that treats the most serious atrocities as matters of concern for all of humanity. For instance, after the horrors of the Nazi Holocaust during World War II, the world's countries signed the Convention on the Prevention and Punishment of the Crime of Genocide (Genocide Convention) in 1948. Signatories (currently 146 states) pledge to "prevent and punish" genocide in both war and peacetime. Many scholars of international law interpret this as a commitment by states to intervene in recognized cases of genocide to stop the killing.

The concept that the international community must stop abuses by governments against their own people has gained momentum over the years since then, with various treaties and practices moving in this direction. The International Criminal Court (ICC) and several international war crimes tribunals have tried individuals accused of war crimes, crimes against humanity, and genocide. In 2005, human rights advocates proposed the overarching concept of responsibility to protect (R2P). The international community should try prevention and diplomacy first, but ultimately must use military intervention as a last resort if necessary to stop mass atrocities.

Everyone agrees that the world would be better off without atrocities, which degrade humanity and undermine norms of peaceful politics. These ideals, however, are a collective good, enjoyed by all countries regardless of which ones put money and lives on the line.

CHALLENGE: Mass atrocities continue to occur despite the Genocide Convention, the human rights treaties, the tribunals, and the R2P concept. In 1994, in Rwanda, ultranationalists seized power and slaughtered more than half a million ethnic minority members and political opponents. In 2004, Sudan used an armed militia to murder and displace large numbers of inhabitants of the Darfur region, where rebels opposed the government. In these and other cases, no states intervened effectively

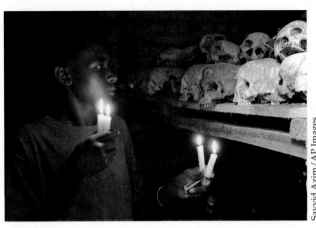

Rwandan survivor visits memorial on tenth anniversary of the 1994 genocide.

to stop the atrocities. But in 2011, outsiders did halt an imminent slaughter by Libya's dictator.

SOLUTION: Human rights organizations rely on the identity principle to try to spur action by the international community. They publicize crises and goad the governments of democracies to act in the name of humanity. In the case of Darfur, a well-funded campaign with plenty of popular support called for strong action to stop the Sudanese government. These appeals have brought meager results, however, because Western governments do not want to spend blood and treasure to intervene in messy foreign conflicts. The reciprocity principle has also come up short: The ICC, which the world's countries are supposed to mutually support, has been unable to arrest the president of Sudan after indicting him for war crimes.

The dominance principle, then, governs the response to atrocities. When great powers see action as in their national interest, they act. Otherwise, they do not. Until the world's strong military powers decide to act against mass atrocities, the provision of the collective good embodied by R2P will continue to fall short.

Bosnian Serb general whose trial lasted over 500 days and included 500 witnesses and 10,000 exhibits.

Following the civil war in Sierra Leone, the government there has run a war crimes tribunal jointly with the UN. In 2003, it indicted the sitting state leader in next-door Liberia, Charles Taylor, for his role in the war's extreme brutality. He fled to Nigeria shortly afterward but was captured there, turned over to the tribunal in 2006, and convicted in 2012.

Following up on the UN tribunals for former Yugoslavia and Rwanda, in 1998 most of the world's states signed a treaty to create a permanent **International Criminal Court (ICC)**. It hears cases of genocide, war crimes, and crimes against humanity from anywhere in the world. The ICC opened for business in 2003 in The Hague, with

International Criminal Court (ICC) A permanent tribunal for war crimes and crimes against humanity.

18 judges sworn in from around the world (but not the United States). In 2008, the ICC began its first trial, of a militia leader from Democratic Congo accused of drafting children under age 15 and killing civilians. He was convicted in 2012.

What makes the ICC different (and controversial) is the idea of *universal jurisdiction*—that the ICC has the ability to prosecute individuals of any state. This distinguishes the ICC from the World Court, before which only states are complainants and defendants. Under the ICC, individuals can be prosecuted for their roles in violations of human rights. Three mechanisms can trigger an ICC trial. First, a state can turn over an individual for trial if the state agrees to do so. Second, against the wishes of a state, a special prosecutor at the ICC can begin a trial if the crimes occurred in the territory of a signatory to the ICC. Third, the UN Security Council can begin proceedings even against individuals from nonsignatory states. It is hoped that the ICC, in addition to prosecuting individual cases of war crimes, will serve to deter potential violators of these norms because of the threat of prosecution.

Adam Jones

REMAINS OF WAR CRIMES War crimes include unnecessary targeting of civilians and mistreatment of prisoners of war (POWs). The most notorious war crime in Europe since World War II was the massacre of more than 7,000 men and boys by Serbian forces who overran the UN "safe area" of Srebrenica, Bosnia, in 1995. Here, a mass grave there is excavated in 2007.

The United States has refused to ratify the ICC agreement and shows little interest in doing so (President George W. Bush removed the U.S. signature from the treaty). In addition, the United States has pressured many ICC member states to sign immunity agreements (known as Bilateral Immunity Agreements [BIAs]) to protect American soldiers serving in those countries from prosecution. In 2005, after several ICC members refused to sign a BIA, Congress voted to cut foreign aid to those states. U.S. leaders are concerned that American soldiers, serving in peacekeeping missions or with NATO allies, will fall under the jurisdiction of the ICC rather than under the American military's own justice system. Indeed, in 2017, the lead ICC prosecutor suggested that American troops may have committed war crimes in Afghanistan—likely eliminating any possibility that the United States would join the court in the near future.

War crimes in Darfur, Sudan—which a UN commission found grave but short of "genocide"—have also been referred to the ICC after the United States dropped its objections in 2005 (when exemptions for U.S. soldiers serving in peacekeeping operations were restored). The Darfur case is a difficult challenge for the ICC. In 2009, the ICC indicted the sitting Sudanese president, Omar al-Bashir, on charges of war crimes and crimes against humanity, and issued a warrant for his arrest. The indictment angered the Sudanese government, which then expelled humanitarian organizations from Darfur. In 2010, al-Bashir left Sudan for the first time, but his destination country of Chad refused to arrest him, citing bias in the ICC. The ICC faces a difficult balance in holding officials in Sudan accountable yet being sensitive to efforts to end the violence in Darfur.

This difficulty has grown in recent years as more African nations have accused the ICC of bias against African leaders. In 2015, South Africa refused to arrest al-Bashir when he attended a summit of African leaders in that country. The ICC subsequently criticized South Africa for failing to uphold international law, which led South Africa to announce its withdrawal from the ICC, along with fellow African states Burundi and Gambia (later, South Africa and Gambia would reverse their decisions to leave). Many African leaders are quick to point out that nearly all of the ICC activity has occurred on their continent. They contend that non-African states should also be investigated. (In a sign of solidarity, Russia removed its signature from the ICC treaty in 2016.)

The most important principle in the laws of war is the effort to limit warfare to the combatants and to protect civilians. It is illegal to target civilians in a war. It is not illegal, however, to target military forces knowing civilians will be killed. Even then, the amount of force used must be *proportional* to the military gain, and only the *necessary* amount of force can be used.

In 2017, the government of Burma responded to an attack on a security outpost by a Muslim minority group, called Rohingya, by targeting hundreds of predominantly Rohingya villages. Thousands of homes were burned and reports of mass killings emerged in the ensuing weeks. At the same time, thousands of Rohingya fled Burma into neighboring Bangladesh. NGOs estimated nearly 600,000 Rohingya migrated as a result of the violence, perpetrated by the army, which rules Burma. Many countries, including the United States, labeled Burma's behavior "ethnic cleansing." These countries argued that because Burma's army response was non-proportional and exceeded necessary amounts of force, it constituted war crimes.

To help separate combatants from civilians, soldiers must wear uniforms and insignia, such as a shoulder patch with a national flag. This provision is frequently violated in guerrilla warfare, making that form of warfare particularly brutal and destructive of civilian life. If one cannot tell the difference between a bystander and a combatant, one is likely to kill both when in doubt. By contrast, in a large-scale conventional war, it is much easier to distinguish civilians from soldiers, although the effort is never completely successful. When U.S. special forces in Afghanistan made friends with local fighters by operating out of uniform and with bushy beards, humanitarian-aid agencies complained and the Pentagon ordered the soldiers back into uniform. In the Iraq War, insurgents have repeatedly targeted civilians and attacked in civilian clothes, from hospitals and schools, and after feigning surrender—all against the laws of war.

In recent years, the unprecedented rise in the use of private military forces in wars, especially in Iraq, has challenged the laws of war. Because these private forces are not members of a country's military, the international laws of war do not necessarily apply to them (only states, not corporations, sign the Geneva Conventions). In Iraq, the U.S. government had granted a waiver to these companies to ensure that they could not be prosecuted for violations of international law, only local law. But because there was no formal Iraqi government, no one could enforce violations of domestic law committed by these companies. Several high-profile incidents (including abuses at the Abu Ghraib prison and several shootings of civilians) led Congress, the UN, and Iraq to hold private forces accountable.

prisoners of war (POWs) Soldiers who have surrendered and who thereby receive special status under the laws of war.

Soldiers have the right under the laws of war to surrender, which is to abandon their status as combatants and become **prisoners of war (POWs)**. They give up their weapons and their right to fight, and earn instead the right (like civilians) not to be targeted. POWs may not be killed, mistreated, or forced to disclose information beyond their name, rank, and serial number. The law of POWs is enforced through practical reciprocity. Once, late in World War II, German forces executed 80 POWs from the French partisan forces (whom Germany did not recognize as legitimate belligerents). The partisans responded by executing 80 German POWs.

International Committee of the Red Cross (ICRC) A nongovernmental organization (NGO) that provides practical support, such as medical care, food, and letters from home, to civilians caught in wars and to prisoners of war (POWs). Exchanges of POWs are usually negotiated through the ICRC.

The laws of war reserve a special role for the **International Committee of the Red Cross (ICRC)**. The ICRC provides practical support—such as medical care, food, and letters from home—to civilians caught in wars and to POWs. Exchanges of POWs are usually negotiated through the ICRC. Armed forces must respect the neutrality of the Red Cross, and usually do so (again, guerrilla war is problematic). In the current war on terrorism, the United States does not consider the "enemy combatants" it detains to be POWs but has granted the ICRC access to most (though not all) of them. More controversial is the U.S. policy called extraordinary rendition, which lets terrorist suspects captured overseas be transferred to other countries, including some that use torture, for questioning.

The laws of warfare impose moral responsibility on individuals, as well as on states, in wartime. The Nuremberg Tribunal established that participants can be held accountable for war crimes they commit. German officers defended their actions as "just following orders," but this reasoning was rejected; the officers were punished, and some executed, for their war crimes.

Not all Nuremberg defendants were found guilty, however. For example, laws of war limit the use of force against civilians to what is necessary and proportional to military objectives. In World War II, the German army besieged the Russian city of Leningrad (St. Petersburg) for two years, and civilians in the city were starving. Sieges of this kind are permitted under international law if an army cannot easily capture a city.

CHANGING CONTEXT   The changing nature of war has undermined the laws of warfare. Conventional wars by defined armed forces on defined battlegrounds are giving way to irregular and asymmetrical wars fought by guerrillas and death squads in cities or jungles. The lines between civilians and soldiers blur in these situations, and war crimes become more commonplace. In the Vietnam War, one of the largest problems faced by the United States was an enemy that seemed to be everywhere and nowhere. This led frustrated U.S. forces to attack civilian villages seen as supporting the guerrillas. In one infamous case, a U.S. officer was court-martialed for ordering his soldiers to massacre hundreds of unarmed civilians in the village of My Lai in 1968 (he was convicted but given a light sentence). In today's irregular warfare, frequently inflamed by ethnic and religious conflicts, the laws of war are increasingly difficult to uphold.

Another factor undermining laws of war is that states rarely issue a *declaration of war* setting out whom they are warring against and the cause of their action. Ironically, such declarations are historically the exception, not the rule. This trend continues today because declarations of war bring little benefit to the state declaring war and incur obligations under international law. In many cases, such as revolutionary and counterrevolutionary civil wars, a declaration would not even be appropriate because wars are declared only against states, not internal groups. In undeclared wars, the distinctions between participants and nonparticipants are undermined (along with the protection of the latter). The Bush administration called the 2001 terrorist attacks acts of war, and the response a war on terror, but Congress did not formally declare war (just as it had not during the Korean and Vietnam Wars).

7.5.4 The Evolution of World Order

The most powerful states, especially hegemons, have great influence on the rules and values that have become embedded over time in a body of international law. For example, the principle of free passage on the open seas is now formally established in international law. But at one time warships from one state did not hesitate to seize the ships of other states and make off with their cargoes. This practice was profitable to the state that pulled off such raids, but its own ships could be raided, of course, in return. Such behavior made long-distance trade itself more dangerous, less predictable, and less profitable. The trading states could benefit more by getting rid of the practice. So, over time, a norm developed around the concept of freedom of navigation on the high seas. It became one of the first areas of international law developed by the Dutch legal scholar Hugo Grotius in the mid-1600s—a time when the Dutch dominated world trade and could benefit most from free navigation.

Thus, Dutch power provided the backbone for the international legal concept of freedom of the seas. Later, when Britain was dominant, it enforced the principle of free seas through the cannons of its warships. As the world's main trading state, Britain benefited from a worldwide norm of free shipping and trade. And with the world's most powerful navy, it was in a position to define and enforce the rules for the world's oceans.

Likewise, twentieth-century world order depended heavily on the power of the United States (and, for a few decades, on the division of power between the United States and the Soviet Union). The United States at times came close to adopting the

Policy Perspectives
International Criminal Court Chief Prosecutor, Fatou Bensouda

PROBLEM *How do you balance respect for international legal principles and national interests?*

ISAAC KASAMANI/AFP/Getty Images

BACKGROUND Prior to the 2001 invasion of Afghanistan, especially after the Soviet Union's 1979 invasion, conflict was the rule rather the exception in Afghanistan. Since the U.S.-led war in 2001 to overthrow the Taliban, an uneasy peace has held. That peace is occasionally broken by a re-formed Taliban or other anti-Western groups, such as the Haqqani network, opposed to the government supported by the United States.

You are the chief prosecutor for the International Criminal Court (ICC). In 2003, Afghanistan became a member of the ICC. In 2016, you opened a preliminary fact-finding investigation to examine the possibility of war crimes by Taliban forces during and after the 2001 invasion. In the fall of 2017, you asked for authorization for a full investigation of the possibility of war crimes committed by Taliban and Haqqani network forces. Moreover, you also asked for permission to investigate the possibility that Afghan government and Western military forces (including U.S. troops) committed torture during the conflict.

DOMESTIC CONSIDERATIONS Violence and conflict are still common in Afghanistan. A slow-moving peace process appears to be close to ending violence between the government and Islamist rebels such as the Taliban. This peace has been elusive, and at various points in the negotiations, both the government and its opponents have walked away from the talks. Many diplomats believe that the key to establishing stability in Afghanistan will be to have a comprehensive peace agreement signed between the warring parties.

SCENARIO Imagine that the U.S. government and the Afghan government request that you halt the war crimes investigation in Afghanistan. Afghanistan's government threatens to walk away from the talks if any members of its military are prosecuted. Diplomats argue the investigations could scare rebel groups away from peace talks. The United States demands that you end the investigation or it could be forced to withdraw all American troops from Afghanistan. Human rights groups, on the other hand, point out that the Afghan people do not trust the Afghan government or Islamist rebel groups, in part because of the atrocities that each have committed. They argue that without the pursuit of justice for victims of war crimes, the public will never support the government or the peace process.

CHOOSE YOUR POLICY Do you suspend the ICC's efforts to prosecute the various actors in the Afghanistan conflict for war crimes? How do you balance the demands of the Afghan government, the rebel groups, and the United States? How do you balance your desire to bring justice to the victims of the conflict in Afghanistan with the reality of the peace process, which hangs in the balance? Can justice be delayed to save lives in the short term? If justice is delayed, will it ever be achieved?

explicit role of "world police force." But in truth the world is too large for any single state—even a hegemon—to police effectively. Rather, the world's states usually go along with the rules established by the most powerful state without constant policing. Meanwhile, they try to influence the rules by working through international institutions (to which the hegemon cedes some of its power). In this way, although states do not yield their sovereignty, they vest some power and authority in international institutions and laws and generally work within that framework.

Three factors combined to shake up international norms in the post–Cold War era—the end of the Cold War, the shifts in economic position of various regions and states, and the effects of technological change in creating a smaller world. Domestic and local politics now play out on a global stage. These new norms still remain unsettled. New expectations are emerging in areas such as human rights, UN peacekeeping, humanitarian interventions, Russia's and China's roles as great powers, and the U.S. role as a superpower. However, core norms and stable institutions shape international political economy—the subject of the remaining chapters of this book—with more stability than in international security. We return to the pinnacle of international organization, the EU, in Chapter 10. But first, we review key world economic arrangements.

Careers in International Relations: International Law

Summary

Jobs in international law can pay well and offer opportunities to work on a wide variety of international issues, but such jobs require extra schooling that can be expensive.

BENEFITS AND COSTS Many jobs exist in the field of international law. As in the practice of law in the domestic context, lawyers may specialize in any of the various areas of international law that exist. Indeed, many traditional areas of legal study and practice—such as contract law, tax law, and regulation law—have international specializations. Thus, a wide variety of potential areas of legal practice exist, ranging from the laws of war, to human rights law, to international business and contract law.

Indeed, many lawyers cite the wide variety of issues in international law as a benefit to such employment—each case brings new challenges, sometimes pushing the practitioner into different areas of study. An international lawyer could be negotiating contracts between businesses in a number of countries one day, then advising a client about environmental regulations in yet another country the next. In addition, most (but not all) jobs in international law pay relatively well.

While there are many jobs in international law, like in domestic law, the jobs dealing with high-profile positions are rare and hard to get. That is, you are more likely to end up helping firms in different countries solve contract disputes than to be helping two countries solve a border dispute or to be helping an individual solve a human rights problem.

International law jobs almost always require graduation from law school. Admission to law school is growing more difficult. Today, law schools admit nearly 18,000 fewer applicants than they did in 2010. In addition, law school is expensive and financial assistance is relatively rare: Because many who finish law school find high-paying jobs, it is assumed these lawyers will be able to pay back their loans with little difficulty. In 2017, the average cost of the tuition at the top ten law schools in the United States was over $60,000 per year (not including books or living expenses).

SKILLS TO HONE Law school admissions criteria are similar irrespective of what type of law you intend to practice. Strong writing and analytical skills are important. Law schools expect students to be able to read complex cases, spot critical issues in them, and write succinctly about what the law says about those issues.

Tony Tallec/Alamy Stock Photo

Oral presentation skills are also important to many aspects of law. Whether it is arguing in front of a court or communicating clearly with a client, strong communication skills are critical. Relatedly, as with any international-oriented job, foreign language skills are helpful, especially if your work in law would require you to familiarize yourself with the law of other countries.

Finally, while political science is traditionally a "feeder" major into law school, students hoping to attend law school should take courses in a number of different fields. Being a political science major is not a disadvantage, but law school admissions committees often value a candidate's broad range of experiences and knowledge, not just a knowledge of government and politics.

Resources

Rist, D. Wes. *ASIL Careers in International Law: A Guide to Career Paths in International Law.* American Society for International Law, 2013.

Swartz, Salli A. *Careers in International Law.* 4th ed. American Bar Association, 2013.

https://www.asil.org

https://www.americanbar.org/groups/international_law.html

Chapter Review

Summary

- International anarchy is balanced by world order—rules and institutions through which states cooperate for mutual benefit.

- States follow the rules—both moral norms and formal international laws—much more often than not. These rules operate through institutions (IOs), with the UN at the center of the institutional network.

- The UN embodies a tension between state sovereignty and supranational authority. In part because of its deference to state sovereignty, the UN has attracted nearly universal membership of the world's states, including all the great powers.

- The UN particularly defers to the sovereignty of great powers, five of whom as permanent Security Council members can each block any security-related resolution binding on UN member states. The five permanent members of the Security Council are the United States, France, Great Britain, China, and Russia.

- Each of the 193 UN member states has one vote in the General Assembly, which serves mainly as a world forum and an umbrella organization for social and economic development efforts.

- The UN is administered by international civil servants in the Secretariat, headed by the Secretary General.

- The regular UN budget plus all peacekeeping missions together amount to less than 3 percent of what the world spends on military forces.

- UN peacekeeping forces are deployed in regional conflicts in five world regions. Their main role is to monitor compliance with agreements such as cease-fires, disarmament plans, and fair election rules. They were scaled back dramatically in 1995–1997, then have grown rapidly since 1998.

- UN peacekeepers operate under the UN flag and command. Sometimes national troops operate under their own flag and command to carry out UN resolutions.

- IOs include UN programs (mostly on economic and social issues), autonomous UN agencies, and organizations with no formal tie to the UN. This institutional network helps strengthen and stabilize the rules of IR.

- International law, the formal body of rules for state relations, derives from treaties (most important), custom, general principles, and legal scholarship—not from legislation passed by any government.

- International law is difficult to enforce and is enforced in practice by national power, international coalitions, and the practice of reciprocity.

- The World Court hears grievances of one state against another but cannot infringe on state sovereignty in most cases. It is an increasingly useful avenue for arbitrating relatively minor conflicts.

- A permanent International Criminal Court (ICC) began operations in 2003. Taking over from two UN tribunals, it hears cases of genocide, war crimes, and crimes against humanity.

- In international law, diplomats have long had special status. Embassies are considered the territory of their home country.

- Laws of war are also long-standing and well established. They distinguish combatants from civilians, giving each certain rights and responsibilities. Guerrilla wars and ethnic conflicts have blurred these distinctions.

- International norms concerning human rights are becoming stronger and more widely accepted. However, human rights law is problematic because it entails interference by one state in another's internal affairs.

Key Terms

Critical Thinking Questions

1. Suppose you were asked to recommend changes in the structure of the UN Security Council (especially in permanent membership and the veto). What changes would you recommend, if any? Based on what logic?

2. The former UN Secretary General Boutros Boutros-Ghali proposed (without success) the creation of a standby army of peacemaking forces loaned by member states. This would reduce state sovereignty a bit and increase supranational authority. Discuss this plan's merits and drawbacks.

3. Collective security against aggression depends on states' willingness to bear the costs of fighting wars to repel and punish aggressors. Sometimes great powers have been willing to bear such costs; at other times they have not. What considerations do you think should guide such decisions? Give examples of situations (actual or potential) that would and would not merit the intervention of great powers to reverse aggression.

4. Given the difficulty of enforcing international law, how might the role of the World Court be strengthened in the future? What obstacles might such plans encounter? How would these obstacles change the Court's role if they were effective?

5. Although international norms concerning human rights are becoming stronger, China and many other states continue to consider human rights an internal affair over which the state has sovereignty within its territory. Do you think human rights issues are a legitimate subject for one state to raise with another? If so, how do you reconcile the tensions between state autonomy and universal rights? What practical steps could be taken to get sovereign states to acknowledge universal human rights?

Suggested Readings

Autessere, Severine. *Peaceland: Conflict Resolution and the Everyday Politics of International Intervention.* Cambridge, 2014.

Barnett, Michael N., and Martha Finnemore. *Rules for the World: International Organizations and Global Politics.* Cornell, 2004.

Evans, Gareth. *The Responsibility to Protect: Ending Mass Atrocity Crimes Once and for All.* Brookings, 2008.

Fortna, Virginia Page. *Does Peacekeeping Work? Shaping Belligerents' Choices After Civil War.* Princeton, 2008.

Goodheart, Michael. *Human Rights: Politics and Practice.* 3rd ed. Oxford, 2016.

Keck, Margaret, and Kathryn Sikkink. *Activists Beyond Borders: Advocacy Networks in International Politics.* Cornell, 1998.

Risse, Thomas, Stephen C. Ropp, and Kathryn Sikkink, eds. *The Persistent Power of Human Rights: From Commitment to Compliance.* Cambridge, 2013.

Straus, Scott. *Making and Unmaking Nations: War, Leadership, and Genocide in Modern Africa.* Cornell, 2015.

Walzer, Michael. *Arguing About War.* Yale, 2004.

Weiss, Thomas G. *What's Wrong with the United Nations and How to Fix It.* 3rd ed. Polity, 2016.

Let's Debate the Issue
Human Rights: A Hollow Promise to the World?

Overview

Since the adoption of the UN Universal Declaration of Human Rights over 70 years ago, states have been committed to advancing human rights. Nine different UN treaties, signed by the majority of the world's states, guarantee the protection and advancement of human rights in several areas, including the rights of women, the rights of children, the rights of migrant workers, and protection from torture. Numerous other regional treaties and protocols promote economic well-being, protect due process rights, and endorse self-determination.

State leaders consistently tout the importance of human rights in promoting fairness, justice, and equality. This is true of both democratic and nondemocratic states. In rhetoric, the importance of promoting and protecting human rights does seem universal.

Yet violations of all these treaties still occur and indeed, at times, seem commonplace. Violations range from small (lack of equal protection for minorities in some states, the allowing of torture of a few individuals) to large (genocide in Darfur). No matter the scale of the violations, all show a brazen disregard for the importance of human rights. This leads many to ask, Is the promise of global human rights one that states will ever attempt to fulfill? Can individuals count on state governments to promote and protect human rights?

ARGUMENT 1

States Make Few Efforts to Promote and Protect Human Rights

Most UN treaties concerning human rights are not enforced. The core UN human rights treaties have little, if any, enforcement attached to them. In fact, some of the worst violators of human rights are often the first to sign these documents because they know there will be no enforcement of the rules. The treaties are only pieces of paper.

Political goals will always subvert the promotion of human rights. When push comes to shove, states will ignore human rights abuses to achieve other political goals. Whether it is the United States ignoring political repression in China, China ignoring genocide in Sudan, or South Africa ignoring a crackdown in Zimbabwe, states of all types will turn a blind eye to human rights abuses if doing so serves their purposes.

Human rights standards are applied unevenly. When attention is paid to human rights violations, it is done so unevenly. More often than not, violations are brought to light only against states that are considered enemies or politically unimportant. Meanwhile, similar violations are ignored in allied or politically powerful states.

ARGUMENT 2

States Do Help to Promote Human Rights

Emerging norms of democracy are promoting human rights. The growing number of democratic countries around the globe is serving to increase respect for human rights. Democracies are more likely to protect and promote human rights. Many Western countries have expanded their support for young democracies, which will help human rights worldwide.

NGOs continue to work with states to promote human rights. NGOs such as Amnesty International and Human Rights Watch continue to provide information to states and their citizens concerning human rights abuses. While states do not act on all of these instances, they do respond to some of these grassroots efforts to improve global respect for human rights. NGOs are thus important agents for states wanting to advance the cause of human rights.

States promote human rights through other institutions. Many states are beginning to condition foreign aid and free trade policies on human rights behavior. The European Union requires all signatories to trade agreements to abide by certain human rights standards, while the United States requires all free trade partners to acknowledge workers' and children's rights. These requirements, embedded in economically important treaties, are more likely to be enforced.

Questions

- Do states, especially Western states, effectively advance human rights? Do you think there has been more or less enforcement of human rights standards in the past decade? Are there important cases of states supporting human rights? Or of states ignoring violations of them?

- How can human rights standards be promoted more effectively? Is it more effective to use sticks (threats of punishment) or carrots (promises of rewards for better behavior) to improve respect for human rights?

- Is promoting human rights standards forcing a particular set of morals and norms on non-Western states? Is there such a thing as universal human rights?

For Further Reading

Donnelly, Jack, and Daniel Whelan. *International Human Rights.* 5th ed. Westview, 2017.

Hafner-Burton, Emilie. *Making Human Rights a Reality.* Princeton, 2013.

Mahoney, Jack. *The Challenge of Human Rights: Origin, Development and Significance.* Wiley-Blackwell, 2006.

Simmons, Beth. *Mobilizing for Human Rights: International Law in Domestic Politics.* Cambridge, 2009.

Chapter 8
International Trade

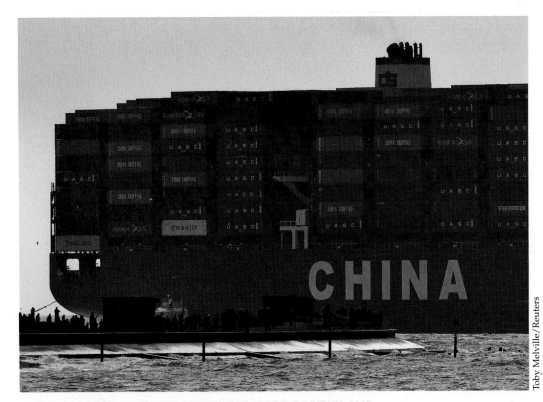

Toby Melville/Reuters

WORLD'S LARGEST CONTAINER SHIP DOCKS IN GREAT BRITAIN, 2015.

 Learning Objectives

8.1 Describe three policies that interfere with the free trade of goods and services in international markets.

8.2 Identify at least one factor behind the current impasse in World Trade Organization (WTO) negotiations.

8.3 Describe at least two ways in which countries or individual citizens are resisting global trade.

8.1 Theories of Trade

Describe three policies that interfere with the free trade of goods and services in international markets.

International trade amounts to one-sixth of the total economic activity in the world. Nearly $21 trillion of goods and services cross international borders each year. This is a very large amount, many times larger than the world's military spending, for example. The great volume of international trade reflects the fact that trade is profitable.

The role of trade in the economy varies somewhat from one nation to another, but overall it is at least as important in the global South as in the industrialized North. The global South accounts for a relatively small part of all trade in the world economy, but this is because its economic activity itself is only about 40 percent of the world total (see Chapter 1).

Trade is not only an economic issue but also a highly political one. It crosses state-defined borders, is regulated by states that are pressured by interest groups, and occurs within trade regimes maintained by and negotiated among states.

Scholars of *international political economy* (*IPE*) thus study the politics of international economic activities. The most frequently studied of these activities are trade, monetary relations, and multinational corporations (see this chapter and Chapter 9). In addition, two topics of special interest in recent years are the economic integration of Europe and other regions (Chapter 10) and the international politics of the global environment (Chapter 11). Most scholars of IPE focus on the industrialized regions of the world, where most of the world's economic activity occurs. However, the global South has received growing attention as globalization integrates parts of the South into the world economy more intensely (Chapters 12 and 13). Although these issues overlap (to varying degrees) with international security matters, they all deal primarily with political bargaining over economic issues and thus fit within IPE broadly defined.

The core principles laid out in Chapter 1 and the concepts of power and bargaining developed initially in Chapter 2 apply to IPE. States are the most important actors in IPE, but they are not as important as in international security. Actors in IPE, as in security affairs, tend to act in their own interests. As Brazil's foreign minister explained in 2001, his country shared with the United States the same guiding principle in negotiating a hemisphere-wide free trade area (FTA): "What's in it for us?"

8.1.1 Liberalism and Mercantilism

Two major approaches within IPE differ on their views of trade. One approach, called **mercantilism**, generally shares with realism the belief that each state must protect its own interests at the expense of others—not relying on international organizations to create a framework for mutual gains. Mercantilists therefore emphasize relative power (as do realists): What matters is not so much a state's absolute amount of well-being as its position relative to rival states.

In addition, mercantilism (like realism) holds that the importance of economic transactions lies in their implications for the military. States worry about relative wealth and trade because these can be translated directly into military power. Thus, although military power is generally not useful in economic negotiations, mercantilists believe that the outcome of economic negotiations matters for military power.

Economic liberalism, an alternative approach, generally shares with liberal internationalism a belief in the possibility of cooperation to realize common gains (see Chapter 3). It holds that, by building international organizations, institutions, and norms, states can mutually benefit from economic exchanges. It matters little to liberals whether one state gains more or less than another—just whether the state's wealth is increasing in *absolute* terms.

mercantilism An economic theory and a political ideology opposed to free trade; it shares with realism the belief that each state must protect its own interests without seeking mutual gains through international organizations. See also *economic liberalism*.

economic liberalism In the context of international political economy (IPE), an approach that generally shares the assumption of anarchy (the lack of a world government) but does not see this condition as precluding extensive cooperation to realize common gains from economic exchanges. It emphasizes absolute over relative gains and, in practice, a commitment to free trade, free capital flows, and an "open" world economy. See also *mercantilism* and *neoliberal*.

Liberalism and mercantilism are *theories* of economics and also *ideologies* that shape state policies. Liberalism is the dominant approach in Western economics, though more so in *microeconomics* (the study of firms and households) than in *macroeconomics* (the study of national economies). Marxism is often treated as a third theoretical/ideological approach to IPE, along with mercantilism and liberalism (see Chapter 3). Marxist approaches are attuned to economic exploitation as a force that shapes political relations. We will explore Marxist theories in depth in Chapter 12; they find their greatest explanatory power in North-South relations.

Most international economic exchanges (as well as security relationships) contain some element of mutual interests—joint gains that can be realized through cooperation—and some element of conflicting interests. Game theorists call this a "mixed interest" game. For example, in the game of Chicken (see Chapter 2), the two drivers share an interest in avoiding a head-on collision, yet their interests diverge in that one can be a hero only if the other is a chicken. In international trade, even when two states both benefit from a trade (a shared interest), one or the other will benefit more (a conflicting interest).

Liberalism emphasizes the shared interests in economic exchanges, whereas mercantilism emphasizes the conflicting interests. For liberals, the most important goal of economic policy is to create a maximum of total wealth by achieving optimal *efficiency* (maximizing output, minimizing waste). For mercantilists, the most important goal is to create the most favorable possible *distribution* of wealth (see Figure 8.1).

Liberal economists believe in markets. The terms of an exchange are defined by the price at which goods are traded. Often the *bargaining space*—the difference between the lowest price a seller would accept and the highest price a buyer would pay—is quite large. For example, Saudi Arabia would be willing to sell a barrel of oil (if it had no better option) for as little as, say, $10 a barrel, and industrialized countries are willing to pay more than $100 a barrel for the oil. (In practice, oil prices have fluctuated in this broad range in recent decades.) How are prices determined within this range? That is, how do the participants decide on the distribution of benefits from the exchange?

When there are multiple buyers and sellers of a good (or equivalent goods that can be substituted for it), prices are determined by market competition. In practice, free markets are supposed to (and sometimes do) produce stable patterns of buying and selling at a fairly uniform price. At this *market price*, sellers know that an effort to

---

Figure 8.1 Joint and Individual Benefits

Any deal struck, such as at point A, yields certain benefits to each actor (dotted lines). Joint benefits are maximized at the Pareto-optimal frontier, but the distribution of those benefits, as between points B and C (both of which are better than A for both actors), is a matter for bargaining. Liberalism is more concerned with joint benefits, mercantilism more with the relative distribution.

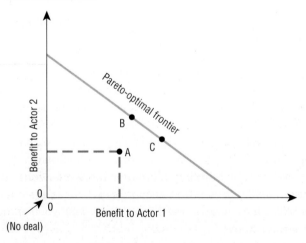

raise the price would drive the buyer to seek another seller, and buyers know that an effort to lower the price would drive the seller to seek another buyer. Thus, in liberal economics, *bilateral* relations between states are less important than they are in security affairs. The existence of world markets reduces the leverage that one state can exert over another in economic affairs (because the second state can simply find other partners). For example, U.S. sanctions on Iran, a major oil exporter, invited Indian companies to fill the void in recent years. In IPE, then, power is more diffuse and involves more actors at once than in international security.

Buyers vary in the value they place on an item (such as a barrel of oil); if the price rises, fewer people are willing to buy it, and if the price drops, more people are willing to buy it. This is called the *demand curve* for the item. Sellers also vary in the value they place on the item. If the price rises, more sellers are willing to supply the item to buyers; if the price drops, fewer sellers are willing to supply the item. This is called the *supply curve*. In a free market, the price at which the supply and demand curves cross is the *equilibrium price*. At this price, sellers are willing to supply the same number of units that buyers are willing to purchase. (In practice, prices reflect *expectations* about supply and demand in the near future.)

The supply and demand system does not always produce stability, however. Such a failure can be seen with oil, arguably the most important commodity in the world economy and the most traded one by value. The price of a barrel of oil has fluctuated radically over recent years. Each time world economic growth accelerates, demand for oil rises and so does its price. But each time oil prices spike up, Western economies go into recession because high prices for this key commodity undermine the whole economy. These recessions in turn reduce demand, and oil prices drop. The amount of economic activity may vary by only 5 or 10 percent, but the price of oil doubles or triples, then drops in half. The two most recent cases of this cycle have occurred in the past decade. Starting in 2007, spectacular, unprecedented (and unsustainable) increases in oil prices left oil at $140 a barrel, up from around $70 a barrel. This rise was driven by new demand in fast-growing Asian economies, among other factors. The world economy then entered a spectacular, unprecedented recession, and oil prices dropped in just a few months back to $40 a barrel.

Then, between 2008 and 2011, oil prices spiked again, nearing $120 a barrel, only to plummet again to around $30 a barrel by the beginning of 2016. (In early 2018, the price of a barrel of oil hovered around $60.) This kind of instability in the price of a key commodity is terrible for the world economy, and creates a big incentive for governments to take political actions rather than rely entirely on market forces.

Liberalism sees individual households and firms as the key actors in the economy and views government's most useful role as one of noninterference in economics, except to regulate markets in order to help them function efficiently (and to create infrastructure such as roads, which also help the economy function efficiently). Politics, in this view, should serve the interests of economic efficiency. With the hand of government removed from markets, the "invisible hand" of supply and demand can work out the most efficient patterns of production, exchange, and consumption (through the mechanism of prices). Because of the benefits of **free trade** among countries, liberals disdain realists' obsession with international borders because borders constrain the

Justin Chin/Getty Images

POWER AND PLENTY Mercantilists emphasize that trade should serve political ends, including expanding a state's military power. China has used its trade surplus to increase its defense spending and modernize its military. Here, China's new aircraft carrier sails into Hong Kong while a large container ship sets out to sea, adding to China's trade surplus.

free trade The flow of goods and services across national boundaries unimpeded by tariffs or other restrictions; in principle (if not always in practice), free trade was a key aspect of Britain's policy after 1846 and of U.S. policy after 1945.

maximum efficiency of exchange. Trade-based wealth depends on international political cooperation, and violence usually does not work well in pursuing such wealth. Thus, liberals argue that interdependence inherently promotes peace, an idea introduced earlier (see Chapter 3). (Then again, some observers saw similar trends in international interdependence just before World War I, but war occurred anyway.)

For mercantilists, by contrast, economics should serve politics: The creation of wealth underlies state power. Because power is relative, trade is desirable only when the distribution of benefits favors one's own state over rivals. The terms of exchange shape the relative rates at which states accumulate power and thus shape the way power distributions in the international system change over time.

Mercantilism achieved prominence several hundred years ago, and Britain used trade to rise in relative power in the international system around the eighteenth century. At that time mercantilism meant specifically the creation of a trade surplus in order to stockpile money in the form of precious metal (gold and silver), which could then be used to buy military capabilities (mercenary armies and weapons) in time of war.

Mercantilism declined in the nineteenth century as Britain decided it had more to gain from free trade than from protectionism. It returned as a major approach in the period between World War I and World War II, when liberal global trading relations broke down.

Mercantilists' preferred means of making trade serve a state's political interests—even at the cost of some lost wealth that free markets might have created—is to create a favorable balance of trade. The **balance of trade** is the value of a state's imports relative to its exports. A state that exports more than it imports has a *positive balance of trade* (*trade surplus*). China has run a large trade surplus for years, over $440 billion in 2017. It gets more money for the many goods it exports than it pays for raw materials and other imported goods (see Figure 8.2). A state that imports more than it exports has a *negative balance of trade* (*trade deficit*). A trade deficit is different from a budget deficit in government spending (see Chapter 9). Since the late 1990s, the U.S. trade deficit has grown steadily to hundreds of billions of dollars per year, exceeding $560 billion in 2017, with about a quarter accounted for by China and another quarter by oil imports.

States must ultimately reconcile the balance of trade. It is tracked financially through the system of national accounts (see Chapter 9). In the short term, a state can trade for a

balance of trade The value of a state's exports relative to its imports.

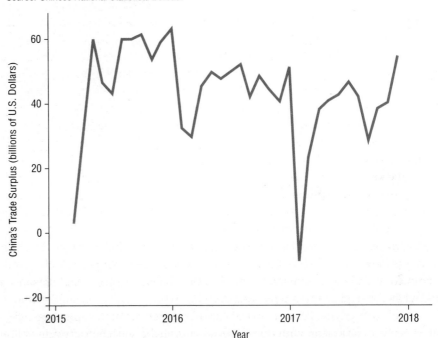

Figure 8.2 China's Growing Trade Surplus

Source: Chinese National Statistical Bureau.

few years at a deficit and then a few years at a surplus. The imbalances are carried on the national accounts as a kind of loan. But a trade deficit that persists for years becomes a problem. In recent years, to balance its trade deficit, the United States has "exported" currency (dollars) to China, Japan, Europe, and other countries, which use the dollars to buy items such as shares of U.S. companies, U.S. Treasury bills, or U.S. real estate. Economists worry that if foreigners lose their taste for investments in the United States, the U.S. economy could suffer.

This is one reason why mercantilists favor national economic policies to create a trade surplus. Then, rather than being unable to find the money it might need to cope with a crisis or fight a war, the state sits on a pile of money representing potential power. Historically, mercantilism literally meant stockpiling gold (gained from running a trade surplus) as a fungible form of power (see Figure 8.3). Such a strategy is attuned to realism's emphasis on relative power and is an example of the dominance principle. For one state to have a trade surplus, another must have a deficit.

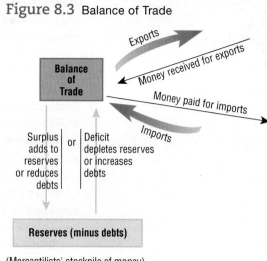

Figure 8.3 Balance of Trade

(Mercantilists' stockpile of money)

8.1.2 Comparative Advantage

The overall success of liberal economics is due to the substantial gains that can be realized through trade. These gains result from the **comparative advantage** that different states enjoy in producing different goods (a concept pioneered by economists Adam Smith and David Ricardo more than 200 years ago). States differ in their abilities to produce certain goods because of differences in natural resources, labor force characteristics, technology, and other such factors. To maximize the overall creation of wealth, each state should specialize in producing the goods for which it has a comparative advantage and then trade for goods that another state produces best. Of course, the costs of transportation and of processing the information in the trade (called *transaction costs*) must be included in the costs of producing an item. But increasingly, as globalization proceeds, both of these are low relative to the differences in the cost of producing items in different locations.

> **comparative advantage** The principle that says states should specialize in trading goods that they produce with the greatest relative efficiency and at the lowest relative cost (relative, that is, to other goods produced by the same state).

Two commodities of great importance in the world are oil and cars. It is much cheaper to produce oil (or another energy source) in Saudi Arabia than in Japan, and much cheaper to produce cars in Japan than in Saudi Arabia. Japan needs oil to run its industry (including its car industry), and Saudi Arabia needs cars to travel its vast territory (including reaching its remote oil wells). Even with shipping and transaction costs, shipping Japanese cars to Saudi Arabia and Saudi oil to Japan saves a huge amount of money, compared to the costs if each tried to be self-sufficient.

A state need not have an absolute advantage (that is, be the most efficient producer in the world) in producing one kind of good in order to make specialization pay. It need only specialize in producing goods that are relatively lower in cost than other goods. Imagine that Japan discovered a way to produce synthetic oil using the same mix of labor and capital that it now uses to produce cars, and that this synthetic oil could be produced a bit more cheaply than what it costs Saudi Arabia to produce oil, but that Japan could still produce cars *much* more cheaply than Saudi Arabia. It might seem intuitive that Japan should produce synthetic oil rather than pay extra for Saudi oil. But this is wrong. From a strictly economic point of view, Japan should keep producing cars (where it has a huge comparative advantage) and not divert capital and labor to make synthetic oil (where it has only a slight advantage). The extra profits Japan would make from exporting more cars would more than compensate for the slightly higher price it would pay to import oil.

Thus, international trade generally expands the Pareto-optimal frontier (see Figure 8.1) by increasing the overall efficiency of production. Free trade allocates global resources to states that have the greatest comparative advantage in producing each kind of commodity. As a result, prices are both lower overall and more consistent worldwide. Increasingly, production is oriented to the world market.

The economic benefits of trade, however, come with some political drawbacks. First, long-term benefits may incur short-term costs. When a state begins to import goods that it had been producing domestically, its economy may be disrupted; workers may need to retrain and find new jobs, and capital may not be easy to convert to new uses. Thus, state leaders may feel political pressure to become involved in economic policy (see Resistance to Trade). Also, the benefits and costs of trade tend to be unevenly distributed *within* a state. Some industries or communities may benefit at the expense of others. For example, if a U.S. manufacturing company moves its factory to Mexico to take advantage of cheaper labor there and exports its goods back to the United States, the workers at the old U.S. factory lose their jobs, but U.S. consumers enjoy cheaper goods. The costs of such a move fall heavily on a few workers, but the benefits are spread thinly across many consumers.

By the same logic, protectionist measures benefit a few people greatly, and cost many people a bit. By one estimate, a 20 percent steel tariff enacted by the George W. Bush administration in 2002–2003 cost consumers $7 billion and saved 7,300 U.S. jobs—a pricey $326,000 per job. Yet those 7,300 workers (and their unions and companies) benefit greatly, whereas the roughly $20 cost per U.S. citizen goes unnoticed. Similarly, the Trump administration's 30 percent tariff on solar panels in 2018, while meant to save manufacturing jobs, was predicted to lead to an overall loss of jobs. The rising cost of solar panels created by the tariff could lead to lower sales, resulting in job losses in the solar panel installation industry. This kind of unequal distribution of costs and benefits often creates political problems for free trade even when the *overall* economic benefits outweigh the costs. Worker or industry interest groups will form against the concentrated costs (losing jobs) far more often than consumer groups will form against the diffuse losses.

8.1.3 Political Interference in Markets

A free and efficient market requires many buyers and sellers with fairly complete information about the market. Also, the willingness of participants to deal with each other should not be distorted by personal (or political) preferences but should be governed only by price and quality considerations. Deviations from these conditions, called *market imperfections*, reduce efficiency. Most political intrusions into economic transactions are market imperfections.

International trade occurs more often at world market prices than does *domestic* economic exchange. No world government owns industries, provides subsidies, or regulates prices. Nonetheless, world markets are often affected by politics. When states are the principal actors in international economic affairs, the number of participants is often small. When there is just one supplier of an item—a *monopoly*—the supplier can set the price quite high. For example, the South African company De Beers produces over one-third of the world supply and controls two-thirds of the world market for uncut diamonds. An *oligopoly* is a monopoly shared by just a few large sellers—often allowing for tacit or explicit coordination to force the price of a product up. For example, members of the Organization of the Petroleum Exporting Countries (OPEC) agree to limit oil production to keep prices up. To the extent that companies band together along national lines, monopolies and oligopolies are more likely.

Another common market imperfection in international trade is *corruption*; individuals may receive payoffs to trade at nonmarket prices. The government or company involved may lose some of the benefits being distributed, but the individual government official or company negotiator gets increased benefits (see Chapter 13).

Politics provides a *legal framework* for markets—ensuring that participants keep their commitments, contracts are binding, buyers pay for goods they purchase, counterfeit money is not used, and so forth. In the international economy, lacking a central government authority, rules are less easily enforced. As in security affairs, such rules can be codified in international treaties, but enforcement depends on practical reciprocity (see Chapter 3).

Taxation is another political influence on markets. Taxes are used both to generate revenue for the government and to regulate economic activity by incentives. For instance, a government may keep taxes low on foreign companies in hopes of attracting them to locate and invest in the country. Taxes applied to international trade itself, called *tariffs*, are a frequent source of international conflict (see Protectionism).

SANCTIONS Political interference in free markets is most explicit when governments apply *sanctions* against economic interactions of certain kinds or between certain actors. Political power then prohibits an economic exchange that would otherwise have been mutually beneficial. In 2018, the United States had trade restrictions on 16 states in response to those states' political actions, such as human rights violations.

Enforcing sanctions is always a difficult task because participants have a financial incentive to break the sanctions through black markets or other means. Without broad, multilateral support for international sanctions, they generally fail. For instance, in 2012, India—Iran's top oil customer—sent a trade delegation to Iran to take advantage of openings created by Western sanctions. The difficulty of applying sanctions reflects a more general point made earlier—that power in IPE is more diffused among states than it is in security affairs. Refusing to participate in mutually profitable economic trade often harms oneself more than the target of one's actions, unless nearly all other states follow suit (note that sanctions enforcement is a form of the collective goods problem). In the case of Iran, it took quite a few years to get European and other major powers on board with the United States (notwithstanding India's reticence) to apply sanctions that hurt Iran's economy. One concern regarding the 2015 nuclear deal between Western powers and Iran (which removed sanctions in exchange for limits on Iran's nuclear program) was that, if Iran cheated, the sanctions would be nearly impossible to impose again on Iran because of the difficulty of international cooperation.

AUTARKY One obvious way to avoid becoming dependent on other states, especially for a weak state whose trading partners would tend to be more powerful, is to avoid trading and instead to try to produce everything that state needs by itself. Such a strategy is called *self-reliance* or **autarky**. But it has proven ineffective. A self-reliant state pays a very high cost to produce goods for which it does not have a comparative advantage. As other states cooperate among themselves to maximize their joint creation of wealth, the relative power of the autarkic state in the international system tends to fall.

States that have relied on a policy of autarky have indeed lagged behind others. A classic case in recent decades was the small state of Albania in southeast Europe. A communist state that split from both the Soviet Union and China, Albania for decades did not participate in world markets but relied on a centrally planned economy designed for self-sufficiency. Few foreigners could visit, little trade took place, and Albania pursued autarky to prevent outsiders from gaining power over it. When this

Fernando Llano/AP Images

SANCTIONS BITE Economic sanctions, such as the current international restrictions on trade and business with Iran, are among the most obvious ways that politics interferes in markets. Sanctions are hard to enforce, especially when not all countries participate, because doing business is profitable. The heavy sanctions imposed on Venezuela by the United States and the European Union have contributed to an economic crisis. In order to deal with this crisis, Venezuela printed all new currency in 2017. Here, individuals trade in their old currency, in hopes that the new money will hold its value.

autarky A policy of self-reliance, avoiding or minimizing trade and trying to produce everything one needs (or the most vital things) by oneself.

curtain of isolation finally fell in 1991, Albania was as poor as it had been decades earlier and had missed out on the prosperity that came to the rest of Europe.

China's experience also illustrates the problems with autarky. China's economic isolation in the 1950s and 1960s, resulting from an economic embargo imposed by the United States and its allies, deepened during its Cultural Revolution in the late 1960s when it broke ties with the Soviet Union as well. In that period, China rejected all things foreign. When China opened up to the world economy in the 1980s, the pattern reversed. The rapid expansion of trade, along with some market-oriented reforms in its domestic economy, resulted in rapid economic growth. By contrast, North Korea maintained a policy of self-reliance and isolation even after the Cold War, and experienced mass starvation in the 1990s.

8.1.4 Protectionism

protectionism The protection of domestic industries against international competition, by trade tariffs and other means.

Although few states pursue strategies of autarky, many states try to manipulate international trade to strengthen one or more domestic industries and shelter them from world markets. Such policies are broadly known as **protectionism**—protection of domestic industries from international competition. Although this term encompasses a variety of trade policies arising from various motivations, all are contrary to liberalism because they seek to distort free markets to gain an advantage for the state (or for substate actors within it), generally by discouraging imports of competing goods or services.

A state's *motivation* to protect domestic industry can arise from several sources. Often governments simply cater to the political demands of important domestic industries and interests, regardless of the overall national interest. An industry may lobby or give campaign contributions in order to win special tax breaks, subsidies, or restrictions on competing imports (see Industries and Interest Groups later in this chapter).

States often attempt to protect an *infant industry* as it starts up in the state for the first time, until it can compete on world markets. For instance, when South Korea first developed an automobile industry, it was not yet competitive with imports, so the government gave consumers incentives to buy Korean cars. Eventually the industry developed and could compete with foreign producers and even export cars profitably. In a number of poor states, the *textile* trade has been a favored infant industry (adding value without heavy capital requirements) that governments have protected. Protection of infant industry is considered a relatively legitimate reason for (temporary) protectionism.

Another motivation for protection is to give a domestic industry breathing room when market conditions shift or new competitors arrive on the scene. Sometimes domestic industry requires time to adapt and can emerge a few years later in a healthy condition. When gas prices jumped in the 1970s, U.S. auto producers were slow to shift to smaller cars, and smaller Japanese cars gained a great advantage in the U.S. market. The U.S. government used a variety of measures, including import quotas and loan guarantees, to help the U.S. industry through this transition. (Yet when gas prices jumped again in early 2008, U.S. auto producers again were unprepared and needed government help to stay afloat during the 2008–2009 recession.)

Jorge Silva/Reuters

JUST A TRUCK FULL OF SUGAR Protectionism uses various means to keep foreign imports from competing with domestic products. Agricultural producers in the global South complain that subsidies and other protectionist measures in Europe and the United States prevent poor farmers in developing countries from exporting to world markets. Here, sugar cane awaits processing in Thailand, where low prices for sugar have hurt farmers badly, 2016.

Government also protects industries considered vital to national security. In the 1980s, U.S. officials sought to protect the U.S. electronics and computer industries against being driven out of business by Japanese competitors because those industries were considered crucial to military production. The government sponsored a consortium of U.S. computer chip companies to promote the U.S. capability to produce chips cheaply (ordinarily the government would discourage such a consortium as an antitrust violation). Autarky may not pay in most economic activities, but for military goods, states will sacrifice some economic efficiency for the sake of self-sufficiency to reduce vulnerability in the event of war.

Finally, protection may be motivated by a defensive effort to ward off predatory practices by foreign companies or states. *Predatory* generally refers to efforts to capture unfairly a large share of world markets, or even to create a near-monopoly, so that eventually the predator can raise prices without fearing competition. Most often these efforts entail **dumping** products in foreign markets at prices below the minimum level necessary to make a profit. Within a domestic economy, the government can use antitrust laws to break up an impending monopoly, but because no such mechanism exists in international relations (IR), governments try to restrict imports in such situations to protect their states' industries. Such restrictions are recognized as legitimate, although great disagreements exist about whether a given price level is predatory or merely competitive. These conflicts generally are now resolved through the World Trade Organization (WTO) (see Trade Regimes).

dumping The sale of products in foreign markets at prices below the minimum level necessary to make a profit (or below cost).

Dumping complaints are usually lodged by particular industries that feel they have been harmed by foreign competitors. They must first convince their own government that they have been unfairly targeted. Then, after their government places tariffs on imports of the good, the foreign government may file a complaint with the WTO. In 2007, the WTO ruled against the United States in a complaint brought by Japanese manufacturers who claimed they had been unfairly accused of dumping industrial goods on the American market. Ironically, rather than denying that Japan had dumped goods on the American market, the WTO criticized how the United States had computed the tariff on Japanese goods, ruling that it was set too high to create a level playing field. The United States was then forced to review how it proceeds with dumping complaints because of the WTO ruling.

Just as there are several motivations for protectionism, so too governments use several tools to implement this policy. The simplest is a **tariff** or *duty*—a tax imposed on certain types of imported goods (usually as a percentage of their value) as they enter the country. Tariffs not only restrict imports but also can be an important source of state revenues. If a state is to engage in protectionism, international norms favor tariffs as the preferred method of protection because they are straightforward and not hidden. Most states maintain a long and complex schedule of tariffs based on thousands of categories and subcategories of goods that are organized by industry.

tariff A duty or tax levied on certain types of imports (usually as a percentage of their value) as they enter a country.

Other means to discourage imports are **nontariff barriers** to trade. Imports can be limited by a *quota*. Quotas are ceilings on how many goods of a certain kind can be imported; they are imposed to restrict the growth of such imports. The extreme version is a flat prohibition against importing a certain type of good (or goods from a certain country). The U.S. government used quotas to restrict the number of Japanese-made cars that could enter the United States in the 1980s, when the U.S. automobile industry was losing ground rapidly to Japanese imports. Most of those quotas were *voluntary* in that Japan and the United States negotiated a level that both could live with.

nontariff barriers Forms of restricting imports other than tariffs, such as quotas (ceilings on how many goods of a certain kind can be imported).

The two nontariff barriers that are the most fought about in the WTO are subsidies and regulation. *Subsidies* are payments by a government to a domestic industry that allow it to lower its prices without losing money. Such subsidies are extensive in, but not limited to, state-owned industries. Subsidies to an industry struggling to get established or facing strong foreign competition include *tax breaks, loans* (or guaranteed private loans) on favorable terms, and high *guaranteed prices* paid by governments.

Subsidies to farmers have been the major sticking point between rich and poor countries in the Doha Round trade talks. In 2010, the United States and Brazil settled a WTO case over American subsidies to cotton growers. Prior to the settlement, Brazil was set to begin imposing nearly $830 million in sanctions against the United States.

Subsidies are also a frequent source of U.S.-European conflict, often involving EU policies regarding the Common Agricultural Policy (see Chapter 10). Subsidies outside the agricultural sector can also be sensitive politically. A European aerospace company that receives EU subsidies now actively bids on American defense department projects. American manufacturers complain that the subsidies given to the EU-based company make it difficult for them to compete because the subsidies allow the European company to place a lower bid. Thus, subsidies have moved from an issue in trade policy to the security area as well.

Imports can also be limited by *restrictions* and *regulations* that make it hard to distribute and market a product even when it can be imported. In marketing U.S. products in Japan, U.S. manufacturers complain of complex bureaucratic regulations and a tight system of corporate alliances funneling the supply of parts from Japanese suppliers to Japanese manufacturers. Environmental and labor regulations can function as nontariff barriers as well. This has caused great controversy in the WTO, such as when Europe banned genetically modified crops that happened to come mostly from the United States. Finally, when a state nationalizes an entire industry, such as oil production or banking, foreign competition is shut out.

Sometimes a country's culture, rather than state action, discourages imports. Citizens may (with or without government encouragement) follow a philosophy of *economic nationalism*—use of economics to influence international power and relative standing in the international system (a form of mercantilism). For example, U.S. citizens sometimes ignore the advice of liberal economists to buy the best products at the best price and instead "buy American" even if it means paying more for an equivalent product. Although such a bias reduces the overall efficiency of world production, it does benefit U.S. workers.

Protectionism has both positive and negative effects on an economy, most often helping producers but hurting consumers. For instance, although U.S. automobile manufacturers were aided somewhat by the restrictions imposed on Japanese imports in the 1980s, U.S. automobile consumers paid more for cars as a result (several hundred dollars more per car by some estimates). Another problem with protectionism is that domestic industry may use protection to avoid needed improvements and may therefore remain inefficient and uncompetitive—especially if protection continues over many years.

Still, temporary protectionism can have a stabilizing effect under certain conditions. When U.S. motorcycle manufacturer Harley-Davidson lost half its U.S. market share in just four years, the U.S. government imposed tariffs on imported Japanese motorcycles. The tariffs started at 45 percent in 1983, were to decline each year for five years, and then be eliminated. With the clock running, Harley scrambled to improve efficiency and raise quality. As a result, Harley regained its market share, and the tariffs were lifted a year early. In the late 1980s, a reinvigorated Harley expanded its market share and began exporting to Japan. Protectionism worked in this case because it was short term and straightforward.

8.2 Trade Regimes

Identify at least one factor behind the current impasse in World Trade Organization (WTO) negotiations.

As technology links the world across space, a global integration process based on free trade is shaping the international economic agenda. The World Trade Organization plays the central role in this process.

8.2.1 The World Trade Organization

The **World Trade Organization (WTO)** is a global, multilateral intergovernmental organization (IGO) that promotes, monitors, and adjudicates international trade. Together with the regional and bilateral arrangements described shortly, the WTO shapes the overall expectations and practices of states regarding international trade. The WTO is the successor organization to the **General Agreement on Tariffs and Trade (GATT)**, which was created in 1947 to facilitate freer trade on a multilateral basis. The GATT was more of a negotiating framework than an administrative institution. It did not actually regulate trade. Before the GATT, proposals for a stronger institutional agency had been rejected because of U.S. fears that overregulation would stifle free trade. The GATT had little institutional infrastructure until the mid-1990s, with just a small secretariat headquartered in Geneva, Switzerland (where the WTO remains). In addition to its main role as a negotiating forum, the GATT helped arbitrate trade disputes, clarifying the rules and helping states observe them.

In 1995, the GATT became the WTO, which incorporated the GATT agreements on manufactured goods and extended the agenda to include trade in services and intellectual property. The WTO has some powers of enforcement and an international bureaucracy (more than 600 people) that monitors trade policies and practices in each member state and adjudicates disputes among members. The WTO wields some power over states, but as with most international institutions, this power is limited. An ongoing public backlash against free trade (see Resistance to Trade) reflects uneasiness about the potential power of a foreign and secretive organization to force changes in democratically enacted national laws. But the WTO is the central international institution governing trade and therefore one that almost all countries want to participate in and develop.

Over time, the membership of the WTO has grown. By 2018, 164 countries—including all of the world's major trading states—had joined the WTO. Russia's membership bid succeeded in 2011 after 17 years, when neighboring Georgia agreed not to block it (a consensus of all members is needed). Politically unstable Afghanistan joined in 2016. More than 20 states are seeking admission, the most important of which are Iran and Iraq. After more than a decade of negotiations, China joined in 2001. The United States and other countries usually demand, as a condition of membership, liberalization of the trading practices of would-be members. These new practices have affected China's economic and political development (see Chapter 9).

The WTO framework rests on the principle of reciprocity—matching states' lowering of trade barriers to one another. It also uses the concept of nondiscrimination, embodied in the **most-favored nation (MFN)** concept, which says that trade restrictions imposed by a WTO member on its most-favored trading partner must be applied equally to all WTO members. If Australia applies a 20 percent tariff on auto parts imported from France, it must not apply a 40 percent tariff on auto parts imported from the United States. Thus, the WTO does not get rid of barriers to trade altogether but equalizes them in a global framework to create a level playing field for all member states. States are not prevented from protecting their own industries but cannot play favorites among their trading partners. States may also extend MFN status to others that are not WTO members, as the United States did with China before it joined the WTO.

An exception to the MFN system is the **Generalized System of Preferences (GSP)**, dating from the 1970s, by which rich states give trade concessions to poor ones to help their economic development. Preferences amount to a promise by rich states to allow imports from poor ones under lower tariffs than those imposed under MFN.

The WTO continues the GATT's role as a negotiating forum for multilateral trade agreements that lower trade barriers on a fair and reciprocal basis. These detailed and complex agreements specify commitments to lower certain trade barriers by certain amounts on fixed schedules. Almost every commitment entails domestic political

World Trade Organization (WTO) An organization begun in 1995 that replaced the GATT and expanded its traditional focus on manufactured goods. The WTO created monitoring and enforcement mechanisms. See also *General Agreement on Tariffs and Trade (GATT)* and *Uruguay Round*.

General Agreement on Tariffs and Trade (GATT) A world organization established in 1947 to work for freer trade on a multilateral basis; the GATT was more of a negotiating framework than an administrative institution. It became the World Trade Organization (WTO) in 1995.

Members
- total: 164
- Russia (2017)
- Afghanistan (2016)
- China (2001)

most-favored nation (MFN) A principle by which one state, by granting another state MFN status, promises to give it the same treatment given to the first state's most-favored trading partner. See also *Generalized System of Preferences (GSP)*.

Generalized System of Preferences (GSP) A mechanism by which some industrialized states began, in the 1970s, to give tariff concessions to third world states on certain imports; an exception to the most-favored nation (MFN) principle. See also *most-favored nation (MFN)*.

costs because domestic industries lose protection against foreign competition. Even when other states agree to make similar commitments in other areas, lowering trade barriers is often hard for national governments.

As a result, negotiations on these multilateral agreements are long and difficult, typically stretching on for years in a *round of negotiations*. Among the five rounds of GATT negotiations from 1947 to 1995, the Kennedy Round in the 1960s—so called because it started during the Kennedy administration—paid special attention to the growing role of European integration, which the United States found somewhat threatening. The Tokyo Round (begun in Tokyo) in the 1970s had to adjust rules to new conditions of world interdependence when, for instance, OPEC raised oil prices and Japan began to dominate the automobile export business.

Uruguay Round A series of negotiations under the General Agreement on Tariffs and Trade (GATT) that began in Uruguay in 1986 and concluded in 1994 with agreement to create the World Trade Organization. The Uruguay Round followed earlier GATT negotiations such as the Kennedy Round and the Tokyo Round. See also *World Trade Organization (WTO)*.

The **Uruguay Round** started in 1986 (in Uruguay). Although the rough outlines of a new GATT agreement emerged after a few years, closure eluded five successive Group of Seven (G7) summit meetings in 1990–1994. As the round dragged on year after year, participants said the GATT should be renamed the "General Agreement to Talk and Talk." A successful conclusion to the round would add more than $100 billion to the world economy annually. But that money was a collective good, to be enjoyed both by states that made concessions in the final negotiations and by states that did not. Agreement was finally reached in late 1994. The United States had pressured Europe to reduce agricultural subsidies and states in the global South to protect intellectual property rights. In the end, the United States got some, but not all, of what it wanted. For example, France held out adamantly and won the right to protect its film industry against U.S. films.

From 1947 onward, the GATT encouraged states to use import tariffs rather than nontariff barriers to protect industries and to lower those tariffs over time. The GATT concentrated on manufactured goods and succeeded in substantially reducing the average tariffs, from 40 percent of the goods' value decades ago to 3 percent by 2002 (under the Uruguay Round agreement). Tariff rates in the global South are much higher, around 15 percent (reflecting the greater protection that industry there apparently needs).

Doha Round A series of negotiations under the World Trade Organization that began in Doha, Qatar, in 2001. It followed the Uruguay Round and has focused on agricultural subsidies, intellectual property, and other issues. See also *Uruguay Round.*

Agricultural trade is politically more sensitive than trade in manufactured goods and came into play only in the Uruguay Round. Trade in services, such as banking and insurance, is another current major focus of the WTO. Such trade neared 25 percent of the total value of world trade in 2017.

The problems in expanding into these and other sensitive areas became obvious at a 1999 Seattle WTO conference, where trade ministers had hoped to launch a new, post–Uruguay Round of trade negotiations. Representatives of poor countries argued that they needed trade to raise incomes and could not meet the standards of industrialized countries (which, after all, had allowed low wages, harsh working conditions, and environmental destruction when *they* began industrializing). Environmental and labor activists, joined by window-smashing anarchists, staged street protests that delayed the conference opening by a day. The meeting ended in failure.

In 2001, after the failure in Seattle, trade ministers meeting in Doha, Qatar, agreed to launch a new round of trade negotiations, the **Doha Round**. The issues under negotiation included agriculture, services, industrial products, intellectual property,

Paul Yeung/Reuters

MAKING MAGIC Rounds of trade negotiations, such as the current Doha Round begun in 2001, last for years as members negotiate complex deals that must be approved by consensus of all 164 member states. A conference of trade ministers in December 2005 tried to regain momentum for the stalled Doha Round, with mixed success. Here, then–WTO head Pascal Lamy opens the conference with the tool he hopes will bring success—a magic wand. The talks remained stalled in 2018.

WTO rules (including how to handle antidumping cases), dispute settlement, and some trade and environmental questions. At the 2003 meeting in Cancun, Mexico, states from the global South walked out after the industrialized countries would not agree to lift their agricultural subsidies, which were shutting out poor countries' agricultural exports. At the 2005 Hong Kong meeting, wealthy states agreed to end the export subsidies, but tough negotiations continued over tariffs on manufactured goods, protection of intellectual property, and opening financial sectors. The main obstacle remains the resistance of the industrialized West to cut agricultural subsidies as demanded by countries in the global South (see the Seeking the Collective Good box).

In explaining the difficulty in wrapping up a major trade agreement such as the Doha Round, game theorists might look to the game of Chicken (see Chapter 2) as an explanatory model. In most trade disputes, each state would rather get to a deal, even on terms that somewhat favor the other state if need be. But each would like, if possible, to get a deal on its own terms. Similarly, in a game of Chicken, each player wants to avoid a head-on collision, and being a hero or a chicken is a secondary consideration. In trade negotiations, both states hold out for their own terms (not swerving) for as long as possible, then come to agreement only when faced with an imminent collision—the expiration of a deadline beyond which there will be no deal at all. In the game of Chicken, there is no incentive to give ground before the last minute.

The Doha Round of WTO negotiations stretched from 2001 to 2015 without conclusion. In 2007, participants tried to use a key deadline—expiration of the fast-track authorization by the U.S. Congress, after which U.S. approvals of a new WTO agreement

Seeking the Collective Good
Free Trade

COLLECTIVE GOOD: A Doha Round WTO Agreement

BACKGROUND: Over the decades, the world has substantially lowered trade barriers and enjoyed rising prosperity as a result of trade. Negotiating through the World Trade Organization (WTO), countries have concluded successive rounds of trade agreements, in which each state reciprocates the concessions of other states. These negotiations require every single member—almost all the world's major trading powers—to agree before any can enjoy the benefits of an agreement.

A new WTO agreement is a collective good because all the member states profit from relaxing trade restrictions, regardless of which of them made the concessions needed to reach a deal. For example, in the previous Uruguay Round, the entire deal was held up while France and the United States fought about French restrictions on U.S. films. Whether France or the United States hung tough to win on this issue, both would benefit overall from the deal. But if both hung tough, the entire deal would break down and the collective good would not be provided. (In the end, France was able to free-ride, and the trade deal went forward.)

CHALLENGE: The Doha Round had been stalled for years and was eventually suspended. Countries want the overall freer trade that an agreement would bring—worth many billions of dollars to the world—but are fighting about agricultural subsidies and other issues. Until the participants find agreement on these pesky remaining issues, nobody can enjoy the economic boost that a new WTO agreement will bring.

Here, WTO trade ministers meet in Argentina, 2017.

SOLUTION: Only reciprocity can solve this dilemma. No feel-good shared identity can compete with the dollars in the pockets of participating states and their constituents (industries, citizens, etc.). And the entire structure of world trade relies on the formal equality of all participants, so dominance does not play a major role. Certainly, military force cannot resolve trade disputes as it might have done centuries ago.

Consistent with reciprocity solutions generally, trade agreements have great complexity and fine-level detail, and require considerable effort to monitor compliance. When a new global trade agreement finally emerges, it will result from breaking the disagreements into many tiny pieces and finding reciprocal compromises—everyone giving some ground—on each one.

would become difficult—to inspire a final agreement. After that deadline passed, other deadlines came and went as well. As each such deadline passed, it became harder to believe that the next deadline was real, that the head-on collision loomed if states did not "swerve" in time. The Chicken game may help us understand such dynamics. One drawback of the model, however, is that it does not predict the outcomes, because the game is inherently unstable. What it does predict is that an agreement, if reached, will arrive suddenly, ahead of a credible deadline, and that a disastrous failure will come as an unpleasant surprise to participants ("Why didn't he swerve?").

Smaller agreements within the WTO negotiations kept some hope alive that the Doha Round would end with a new global trade agreement. A deal between the United States and India in 2014 concerning agricultural subsidies for the stockpiling of food brought renewed hopes of a breakthrough, but those hopes came to an end in 2015, when the WTO officially suspended the Doha Round. The WTO continues to hold annual ministerial meetings, but there is little hope for a multilateral trade agreement given the deep differences that remain between member states. At the 2017 ministerial meeting, many states declared it was time to work in smaller "like-minded" groups in order to make progress on resolving some issues. How those smaller agreements, if they are made, would turn into a larger, global trade deal remains an open question.

In general, states continue to participate in the WTO because the benefits, in terms of global wealth creation, outweigh the costs, in terms of harm to domestic industries and painful adjustments in national economies. States try to change the rules in their favor during negotiations, and between rounds they may evade the rules in minor ways. But the overall benefits are too great to jeopardize by nonparticipation or frequent trade wars.

8.2.2 Bilateral and Regional Agreements

Although the WTO provides an overall framework for multilateral trade in a worldwide market, most international trade also takes place under more specific international political agreements—bilateral trade agreements and regional free-trade areas.

BILATERAL AGREEMENTS Bilateral agreements covering trade are reciprocal arrangements to lower barriers to trade between two states. Usually they are very specific. For instance, one country may reduce its prohibition on imports of product X (which the second country exports at competitive prices) while the second country lowers its tariff on product Y (which the first country exports). A sweeping agreement, such as that between Canada and India in 2007, generally contains mind-numbing levels of detail concerning specific industries and products. As with most agreements based on the reciprocity principle, trade treaties involve great complexity and constant monitoring. U.S. free-trade deals with South Korea, Panama, and Colombia took effect in 2011.

Part of the idea behind the GATT/WTO was to strip away the maze of bilateral agreements on trade and simplify the system of tariffs and preferences. This effort has only partially succeeded, however, because bilateral trade agreements continue to play an important role. They have the advantages of reducing the collective goods problem inherent in multilateral negotiations and facilitating reciprocity as a means to achieve cooperation. When WTO negotiations bog down, bilateral agreements can keep trade momentum going. Because most states do most of their trading with a few partners, a few bilateral agreements can go a long way in structuring a state's trade relations. The number of bilateral agreements has grown substantially in the past decade, and their numbers far overwhelm all other types of agreements combined.

FREE TRADE AREAS Regional free-trade areas also matter in the structure of world trade. In such areas, groups of neighboring states agree to remove most or all trade barriers within their area. Beyond free trade areas, states may reduce trade barriers *and* adopt a common tariff toward states that are not members of the agreement. This is known as a *customs union*. If members of a customs union decide to coordinate other policies such as monetary exchange, the customs union becomes a *common market*. The creation of a regional trade agreement (of any type) allows a group of states to cooperate in increasing their wealth without waiting for the rest of the world.

The most important free trade area is in Europe; it is connected with the European Union but has a somewhat larger membership. Because Europe contains a number of small industrialized states living close together, the creation of a single integrated market allows these states to gain the economic advantages that come inherently to a large state such as the United States. The European free-trade experiment has been a great success overall, contributing to Europe's accumulation of wealth since World War II (see Chapter 10).

The United States, Canada, and Mexico signed the **North American Free Trade Agreement (NAFTA)** in 1994, following a U.S.-Canadian free-trade agreement in 1988. In NAFTA's first decade, U.S. imports from both Mexico and Canada more than doubled, then fell back somewhat (after 1999). Canada and Mexico were the largest and third-largest U.S. trading partners, respectively (Japan was second). Initially, Mexico's currency dropped drastically relative to the dollar in 1994–1995. U.S. opponents of NAFTA, including various U.S. labor unions, criticized the low wages and poor labor laws in Mexico, which they feared would drag down U.S. labor standards. Environmentalists similarly criticized Mexico's lax environmental laws (relative to those of the United States) and saw NAFTA as giving U.S. corporations license to pollute by moving south of the border. But over more than 25 years, neither the great benefits predicted by NAFTA supporters nor the disasters predicted by its opponents have materialized (see the Public Opinion and International Relations box).

Politicians in North and South America have long spoken of creating a single free trade area in the Western Hemisphere, from Alaska to Argentina—the *Free Trade Area of the Americas (FTAA)*. To empower him to do so, President Clinton asked Congress in 1997 to reinstate fast-track legislation. But Democrats in Congress defeated the measure, demanding that free trade agreements include requirements for labor and environmental standards for other countries—points on which they found NAFTA's record wanting. President Bush had more success winning fast-track authority from Congress, and FTAA negotiations began in 2003 with a target date of 2005. But by then several factors had created pressures against the FTAA. The 2001 recession and post–September 11 security measures reduced trade; China provided U.S. companies with a better source of cheap labor; and left-leaning governments, wary of liberal economic advice, came to power in most of the Latin American countries. Those countries cared most about tariff-free trade, while the U.S. position emphasized a range of other issues such as services, intellectual property, and financial openness. Currently, the FTAA talks remain in hibernation. Meanwhile, the United States reached free trade agreements with several Latin American countries.

In 2007, the ten Association of South East Asian Nations (ASEAN) countries met with China, Japan, India, Australia, and New Zealand to begin negotiating an East Asian free-trade area. The group, unlike some other Asia-Pacific IGOs, does not include the United States, but it does include half the world's population and some of its most dynamic economies. The negotiations between ASEAN states and China were successful, and in 2010, a free trade area went into effect among these countries. The ASEAN-China FTA is the world's third-largest free trade area, after the EU and NAFTA.

In the wake of the failed FTAA talks, however, the United States has entered negotiations to explore the formation of what are being called mega-FTAs. EU and U.S. officials were negotiating the Transatlantic Trade and Investment Partnership (*T-TIP*), which would provide lower tariffs and lower barriers to investment between the United States and the European Union. In addition, the United States had negotiated

North American Free Trade Agreement (NAFTA) A free trade zone encompassing the United States, Canada, and Mexico since 1994.

Public Opinion and International Relations
NAFTA

On January 1, 1994, the North American Free Trade Agreement (NAFTA) came into force. The primary goal of the agreement was to eliminate trade and investment barriers between Canada, Mexico, and the United States. The agreement replaced a free trade agreement between the United States and Canada, which had gone into effect in 1988.

NAFTA was controversial from the start. In the United States, environmental groups, labor groups, and some industries vehemently opposed the agreement. Opponents of the agreement argued it would lead to large job losses in the United States as well as human rights and environmental problems given the lack of labor and environmental standards in Mexico. Yet, it also received significant support from many business groups who argued the agreement would bring lower prices to Americans, better economic growth, and, in the long run, more jobs to the United States. The U.S. House and Senate approved the agreement by comfortable margins after President Clinton negotiated two additional NAFTA protocols: one on labor rights, the other on environmental standards.

The controversy over NAFTA receded in the 1990s as the U.S. economy grew and thrived. But during the mid-2000s, the critics of NAFTA began to raise their voices again—less about labor violations or environmental problems and more about job losses, especially in the industrial sector in the United States. By the time the 2016 presidential campaign began, two candidates from the major parties, Republican Donald Trump and Democrat Bernie Sanders, both argued that NAFTA was a bad deal for the United States and had been a mistake.

How has the American public felt about NAFTA over this time period? As Figure 8.4 shows, there has been a lot of change in opinion about the agreement. Interestingly, in the immediate aftermath of entering NAFTA, despite its controversial nature, many Americans had no strong opinion about the agreement. (Note in the early polls, when adding the two responses, the sum falls far short of 100 percent of respondents.) Since 2005, however, opinion has been quite mixed: Those feeling NAFTA was good for the United States were the largest group in 2005 and then again after 2016.

Around the time of the 2016 U.S. presidential election, there is a marked shift in opinion, with NAFTA becoming more popular. This move, ironically, is against President Trump's position that NAFTA is bad for the United States. One possible explanation for this change in public mood is that President Trump's attacks on the agreement have forced its supporters to become more vocal about the benefits of the agreement.

The controversy over NAFTA in the United States is far from settled. Despite President Trump's promises to end NAFTA if it cannot be renegotiated, large numbers of business and industry groups have opposed this position. Negotiations to change NAFTA continue into 2018, but this would change only some portions of the agreement, leaving most of it untouched.

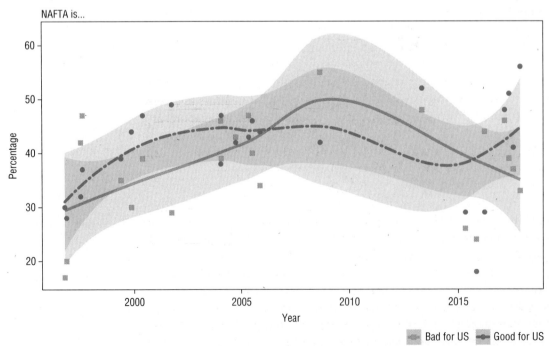

Figure 8.4 United States Public Opinion Toward NAFTA

Source: Roper Center for Public Opinion.

Policy Perspectives
President of Mexico, Andrés Manuel López Obrador

PROBLEM *How do you balance the demands of a key trading partner with domestic economic needs?*

BACKGROUND Imagine that you are the president of Mexico. Over the past 20 years, your country's economic situation has improved dramatically. Your economy is now the fifteenth largest in the world (eleventh if adjusted for purchasing power parity). Economic growth has been strong, growing at 3 percent in recent years. Your country's exports have increased and your oil reserves provide an important source of cash for your economy.

- The United States, Canada, China, Japan, and Germany are your key export partners. Yet, the United States accounts for 80 percent of your exports and nearly 50 percent of your imports. China and Germany are also important export and import partners, but both pale in comparison to the United States.

Since the election of Donald Trump as president, formal relations with the United States have been tense. President Trump campaigned on a platform of renegotiating NAFTA at Mexico's expense. He called for building a wall between the United States and Mexico to stop illegal immigration and pledged to make Mexico pay for its construction. He has referred to Mexican people in degrading terms. In late 2018, your predecessor reached an agreement to revise NAFTA, creating a new agreement with the United States and Canada.

DOMESTIC CONSIDERATIONS NAFTA was popular among the public in your country. Yet, President Trump is very unpopular in Mexico - the Mexican public is angry and feels disrespected. The new trade agreement should continue to benefit Mexico as NAFTA did. Any move to cancel or greatly alter the new agreement would be a threat to your economy.

SCENARIO Now imagine that important trading partners (China, Brazil, and Germany) approach you to negotiate bilateral trade agreements with them. Under the provisions of the new trade agreement, you will not be able to export those goods into the United States, but you could find ways to add enough value to some of those products to label them "Made in Mexico" and send them to the United States.

But by accepting any of these offers, you will likely anger the United States. And while President Trump is unpopular in your country, trade with the United States is crucial to your economic success. If the United States attempted to shut down that trade, it would be disastrous for your economy. Yet, any U.S. threat to do so is not entirely credible—the United States depends on your market to export many of its agricultural goods, so a trade war would harm both sides (although it would damage Mexico more).

CHOOSE YOUR POLICY Do you accept the offers from your other trading partners? Do you attempt to find alternative markets to the United States to hedge your bets, knowing you can never completely replace these markets? How do you balance the demands of competing (and important) trade partners while trying to achieve the best outcome for your public?

---

the Trans-Pacific Partnership (TPP), which would bring together economies as diverse as those in Japan, Chile, New Zealand, Vietnam, Canada, Malaysia, Singapore, and others. TPP negotiations concluded in 2015, but before Congress could approve the pact, President Trump removed the United States from the TPP agreement and announced the United States would not take part in T-TIP. The prospective TPP member states, led by Japan, went ahead with the agreement without the United States. And when the Trump administration in early 2018 suggested reopening T-TIP negotiations, the EU (led by France) responded by that it would not negotiate trade deals with states that had not signed the Paris Agreement on climate change (which President Trump had withdrawn from; see Chapter 11).

During the Cold War, the Soviet Union and its satellites maintained their own trading bloc. After the Soviet Union collapsed, the members scrambled to join the world economy. The Commonwealth of Independent States (CIS), formed by 12 former Soviet republics, remains economically integrated (although Georgia quit after its 2008 war with Russia). It was previously a free trade zone by virtue of being part of a single state with integrated transportation, communication, and other infrastructure links.

Latin America has followed a winding path toward free trade. The Southern Cone Common Market (MERCOSUR) began in the early 1990s with Brazil, Argentina, Uruguay, and Paraguay, which opposed letting Venezuela in. After Paraguay's president was hastily impeached in 2012, Brazil engineered Paraguay's suspension from MERCOSUR for ten months, during which Venezuela was admitted. Chile, Bolivia, Colombia, Ecuador, and Peru have joined as associate members. MERCOSUR members trade more with the United States than they do with each other, but they played a leading role in blocking a proposed free trade area of North and South America. In 2002, the countries agreed to allow their 250 million citizens free movement and residency across countries. A Caribbean common market (CARICOM) was created in 1973, but the area is neither large enough nor rich enough to make regional free trade a very important accelerator of economic growth. In 1969, Colombia, Ecuador, Peru, and Bolivia created a group now known as the Andean Community of Nations, which has had modest successes and counts the MERCOSUR members as associate members. Finally, in 2008, a single continent-wide Union of South American Nations (UNASUR) began taking shape, to merge MERCOSUR and the Andean Community of Nations in an effort to follow the example of the European Union. UNASUR came into being in 2010 with its ratification by Uruguay.

If regional free-trade areas such as now exist in Europe and in North America gain strength and new ones arise, it may weaken the WTO. The more that states meet the political requirements of economic growth through bilateral and regional agreements, the less they may depend on the worldwide agreements developed through the WTO. Furthermore, the overlap of WTO rules and regional agreements can create confusion. For example, in 2006, a WTO panel upheld U.S. duties on Canadian softwood lumber, while a NAFTA panel overturned the duties and ordered refunds to Canada. (On appeal, the WTO reversed its ruling, and the two countries promptly signed a new agreement, with the United States refunding more than $4 billion.) Ultimately, regional agreements might divide the world into three competing trading blocs, each internally integrated but not very open to the other two blocs. Regional free-trade areas in Europe and the Americas, and perhaps in Asia in the future, raise the possibility of trading zones practicing liberalism inwardly and mercantilism outwardly.

8.2.3 Cartels

cartel An association of producers or consumers (or both) of a certain product, formed for the purpose of manipulating its price on the world market.

A **cartel** is an association of producers or consumers, or both, of a certain product—formed to manipulate its price on the world market. It is an unusual but interesting form of trade regime. Most often producers, and not consumers, form cartels because there are usually fewer producers than consumers, and it seems possible for them to coordinate to keep prices high. Cartels can use a variety of means to affect prices; the most effective is to coordinate limits on production by each member and thus lower the supply of, relative to the demand for, the good.

Organization of the Petroleum Exporting Countries (OPEC) The most prominent cartel in the international economy; its members control about half the world's total oil exports, enough to affect the world price of oil significantly.

The most prominent cartel in the international economy is the **Organization of the Petroleum Exporting Countries (OPEC)**. Its member states together control hundreds of billions of dollars in oil exports annually—about 43 percent of the world total and enough to affect the price significantly. (A cartel need not hold a monopoly on production of a good to affect its price.) At OPEC's peak of strength in the 1970s, the proportion was even higher. OPEC maintains a headquarters in Vienna, Austria, and holds negotiations several times a year to set quotas for each country's production of oil in order to keep world oil prices in a target range. Saudi Arabia is by far the largest oil exporter (although the United States is the largest oil producer) and therefore occupies a unique position in the world economy (see Table 8.1).

OPEC illustrates the potential that a cartel creates for collective goods problems. Individual members of OPEC can cheat by exceeding their production quotas while still enjoying the collective good of high oil prices. The collective good breaks down

Table 8.1 OPEC Members and Oil Production, 2018

Member State	Millions of Barrels/Day
Saudi Arabia	10.0
Iran	3.8
Venezuela	1.8
Iraq	4.4
Kuwait	2.7
United Arab Emirates	2.9
Nigeria	1.7
Angola	1.6
Libya	1.0
Algeria	1.0
Qatar	0.6
Ecuador	0.5
Total OPEC	32.0
Percent of World	43%

Note: Major oil exporters not in OPEC include Russia, Kazakhstan, Mexico, China, Britain, and Norway. Gabon left OPEC in 1995.

Source: Data adapted from OPEC Monthly Oil Market Report.

when too many members exceed their quotas, as has happened repeatedly to OPEC. Then world oil prices drop. Iraq's accusations that fellow OPEC member Kuwait was exceeding production quotas and driving oil prices down was one factor in Iraq's invasion of Kuwait in 1990.

OPEC may work as well as it does only because one member, Saudi Arabia, has enough oil unilaterally to manipulate supply enough to drive prices up or down—a form of hegemonic stability (see Chapter 2) within the cartel. Saudi Arabia can take up the slack from some cheating in OPEC (cutting back its own production) and keep prices up. Or if too many OPEC members are cheating on their quotas, it can punish them by flooding the market with oil and driving prices down until the other OPEC members collectively come to their senses.

Consumers usually do not form cartels. In response to OPEC, however, the major oil-importing states formed their own organization, the *International Energy Agency (IEA)*, which partly functions as a cartel. The IEA coordinates the energy policies of major industrialized states—such as the maintenance of oil stockpiles in case of a shortage on world markets—in order to keep world oil prices low and stable. The largest importers of oil are the members of the G7 (large industrialized states). Considering the importance of oil to the world economy and the existence of both producer and consumer cartels, the price of oil has been surprisingly unstable. This shows the limits of cartels in affecting prices.

For a few commodities that are subject to large price fluctuations on world markets—detrimental to both producers and consumers—joint producer-consumer cartels have been formed. To keep prices stable, producing and consuming states use the cartel to coordinate the overall supply and demand globally. Such cartels exist for coffee, several minerals, and some other products. Nongovernmental organizations (NGOs) introduced fair trade coffee, and later chocolate and other products, guaranteeing farmers a price above their production costs through the price booms and busts. More than a million farmers in 70 countries benefit from these arrangements.

In general, the idea of cartels runs counter to liberal economics because cartels deliberately distort free markets. Cartels usually are not as powerful as market forces in determining overall world price levels: Too many producers and suppliers exist— and too many substitute goods can replace ones that become too expensive—for a cartel to corner the market.

Sipa via AP Images

MAKING HAY Agriculture is at the top of the agenda of international trade negotiations, as developing countries push richer ones to end farm subsidies. Here, French farmers protest negotiations between MERCOSUR and the EU by blocking roads with tractors and spraying hay at government buildings in western France, 2018.

industrial policy The strategies by which a government works actively with industries to promote their growth and tailor trade policy to their needs.

8.2.4 Industries and Interest Groups

Industries and other domestic political actors often seek to influence a state's foreign economic policies (see Interest Groups in Chapter 4). These pressures do not always favor protectionism. Industries that are advanced and competitive in world markets try to influence their governments to adopt free trade policies. This strategy promotes a global free-trade system in which such industries can prosper. By contrast, industries that lag behind their global competitors tend to seek protection.

Means to influence foreign economic policy include lobbying, forming interest groups, paying bribes, and even encouraging coups. Actors include industry-sponsored groups, companies, labor unions, and individuals. Within an industry, such efforts usually work in a common direction because, despite competition among companies and between management and labor, all share common interests regarding the trade policies. However, a different industry may be pushing in a different direction. For instance, some U.S. industries supported NAFTA; others opposed it.

In many countries, government not only responds to industry influence but also works actively with industries to promote their growth and tailor trade policy to their needs. Such **industrial policy** is especially common in states where one or two industries are crucial to the entire economy (and, of course, where states own industries directly).

Interest groups not organized along industry lines also have particular interests in state trade policies. U.S. environmentalists, for example, do not want U.S. companies to use NAFTA to avoid pollution controls by relocating to Mexico (where environmental laws are less strict). U.S. labor unions do not want companies to use NAFTA to avoid paying high wages. However, Mexican American citizens' groups in the United States tend to support NAFTA because it strengthens ties to relatives in Mexico.

Several industries are particularly important in trade negotiations currently. Atop the list is the agricultural sector. Traditionally, agriculture has been protected because self-sufficiency in food reduces national vulnerability (especially in time of war). Although such security concerns have now faded somewhat, farmers are well-organized and powerful domestic political actors in Europe, the United States, Japan, and other countries. For instance, Japanese farmers argue that Japan's rice-centered culture demands self-sufficiency in rice production. In the Doha Round of WTO negotiations, agricultural subsidies were a key sticking point. The talks collapsed in 2003 in Cancun, Mexico, over the subsidies, but they were revived the next year by U.S. promises to cut farm subsidies 20 percent. At the 2005 Hong Kong talks, wealthy countries agreed to end all farm export subsidies by 2013—a goal that was not reached.

A second important focus in recent years has been the textile and garment sector. As of 2005, textile quotas worldwide were dropped as part of previously negotiated WTO deals. At the same time, China began dominating world clothing exports, with whole cities specializing in one type of garment produced for mass export to giant retailers. With vast pools of cheap and disciplined labor, China threatened to drive U.S. textile and clothing producers out of business and give stiff new competition to exporters such as Pakistan and Bangladesh, where textiles make up 70 percent of exports. Later in 2005, the European Union and the United States each reached bilateral agreements with China to reimpose textile quotas for a few years. Now, countries such as Vietnam have begun to take textile business away from China by providing even lower production costs.

Intellectual property rights are a third contentious area of trade negotiations. Intellectual property rights are the rights of creators of books, films, computer software, and similar products to receive royalties when their products are sold. The United States has a major conflict with some states over piracy of computer software, music, films, and other creative works—products in which the United States has a strong comparative advantage globally. It is technically easy and cheap to copy such works and sell them in violation of copyright, patent, or trademark laws. Because U.S. laws cannot be enforced in foreign countries, the U.S. government wants foreign governments to prevent and punish such violations. Countries that reportedly pirate large amounts of computer software and music and entertainment products include China, Taiwan, India, Thailand, and Brazil.

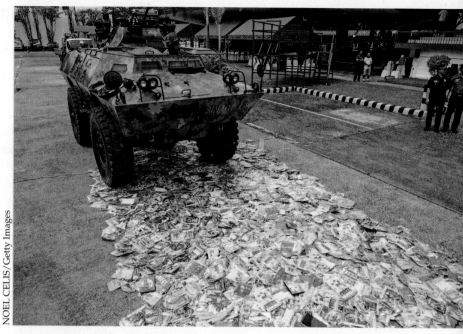

HEAP OF TROUBLE Intellectual property rights have been an important focus of recent trade negotiations. In many countries, pirated copies of videos, music, and software sell cheaply on the street with no royalty payments. Here, an armored personnel carrier in the Philippines drives over illegal DVDs in that government's efforts against piracy, 2016.

NOEL CELIS/Getty Images

Of course, stopping individual piracy activity is difficult, even if such activity is widespread. For example, a 2017 survey found that 16 percent of consumers in Indonesia and Egypt admitted to having pirated entertainment content more than once a week. In a 33-country survey (including the United States) in 2017, 57 percent of respondents admitted to having pirated at least one piece of software for their computer. Infringement of intellectual property rights is widespread in many third world countries, on products such as DVDs and prescription drugs.

In response, the international community has developed an IGO with 186 UN member states, the World Intellectual Property Organization (WIPO), which tries to regularize patent and copyright law across borders. Most states have signed an important 1994 patent treaty and a 1996 copyright treaty. The WTO oversees the world's most important multilateral agreement on intellectual property, called Trade-Related aspects of Intellectual Property Rights (TRIPS). Most industrialized countries prefer to use TRIPS rules because these rules are stronger than WIPO safeguards and can be relaxed only if all WTO members agree. WIPO rules require only a majority vote to change.

The 2001 WTO meeting at Doha led to a declaration that states could exempt certain drugs from TRIPS rules to deal with serious domestic health crises, such as an HIV/AIDS epidemic. (The U.S. government supported this move after it had threatened to take over production of a powerful antibiotic drug, Cipro, during the post-9/11 anthrax scare.) Although procedures were established for these exceptions, only a few developing countries have used them. For several years, these disputes slowed the effective distribution of medicines to millions of Africans with AIDS, though progress picked up after 2004.

Companies trying to protect intellectual property in an international context cannot rely on the same enforcement of rules as in domestic contexts. Instead, they need to bring their own state's government to bear, as well as use their own resources. Because of state sovereignty in legal matters, private international economic conflicts easily become government-to-government issues.

A fourth key trade issue is the openness of countries to trade in the **service sector** of the economy. This sector includes many services, especially those concerning

intellectual property rights
The legal protection of the original works of inventors, authors, creators, and performers under patent, copyright, and trademark law. Such rights became a contentious area of trade negotiations in the 1990s.

service sector The part of an economy that concerns services (as opposed to the production of tangible goods); the key focus in international trade negotiations is on banking, insurance, and related financial services.

information, but the key focus in international trade negotiations is on banking, insurance, and related financial services. U.S. companies, and some in Asia, enjoy a comparative advantage in these areas because of their information-processing technologies and experience in financial management. In general, as telecommunications becomes cheaper and more pervasive, services offered by companies in one country can be used efficiently by consumers in other countries. U.S. consumers phoning customer service at U.S. companies and connecting to India or another English-speaking developing country engage in a long-distance trade in services.

Another especially important industry in international trade is the arms trade, which operates largely outside the framework of normal commercial transactions because of its national security implications. Governments in industrialized countries want to protect their domestic arms industries rather than rely on imports to meet their weapons needs. And those domestic arms industries become stronger and more economically viable by exporting their products (as well as supplying their own governments). Governments usually participate actively in the military-industrial sector of the economy, even in countries such as the United States that lack industrial policy in other economic sectors. For example, fighter jets are a product in which the United States enjoys a global comparative advantage. In the 1990s, the U.S. arms industry, like the tobacco industry, looked overseas for new customers to offset declining demand at home. The Middle East has been the leading arms-importing region of the global South, with India and China increasing recently.

A different problem is presented by the "industry" of illicit trade, or *smuggling*. No matter what restrictions governments put on trading certain goods, someone is usually willing to risk punishment to make a profit in such trade. Illegal goods, and legal goods imported illegally, often are sold in black markets—unofficial, sometimes secret markets. This deprives governments of significant revenue. Black markets also exist for foreign currency exchange (see Chapter 9).

The extent of illicit trade varies from one country and industry to another, depending on profitability and enforcement. Drugs and weapons are most profitable, and worldwide illegal trade networks exist for both. International black markets for weapons trade, beyond government controls, are notorious. A state with enough money can buy—although at premium prices—most kinds of weapons.

8.2.5 Enforcement of Trade Rules

As with international law generally, economic agreements among states depend strongly on the reciprocity principle for enforcement (see Chapter 7). If one state protects its industries, or puts tariffs on the goods of other states, or violates the copyright on works produced in other countries, the main resort that other states have is to apply similar measures against the offending state. The use of reciprocity to enforce equal terms of exchange is especially important in international trade, in which states often negotiate complex agreements—commodity by commodity, industry by industry—based on reciprocity. Trade disputes and retaliatory measures are common. States keep close track of the exact terms of trade. Large bureaucracies monitor international economic transactions (prices relative to world market levels, tariffs, etc.) and develop detailed policies to reciprocate any other state's deviations from cooperation.

Enforcement of equal terms of trade is complicated by differing interpretations of what is "fair." States generally decide which practices of other states they consider unfair (often prodded by affected domestic industries) and then take (or threaten) retaliatory actions to punish those practices. A U.S. law, the Super 301 provision, mandates retaliation against states that restrict access of U.S. goods to their markets. If the other state does not agree that its practices are unfair, however, the retaliatory actions may themselves seem unfair and call for retaliation. One disadvantage of reciprocity is that it can lead to a downward spiral of noncooperation, popularly called a trade war (the economic equivalent of an arms race; see Chapter 2). To prevent this, states often negotiate agreements regarding what practices they consider unfair. In some cases, third-party arbitration can also be used to resolve trade disputes. Currently, the World Trade Organization hears complaints and sets levels of acceptable retaliation. Some regional trade agreements also establish mechanisms to hear and resolve complaints.

Retaliation for unfair trade practices usually tries to match the violation in type and extent. Under WTO rules, a state may impose retaliatory tariffs equivalent to the losses caused by another state's unfair trade practices (as determined by WTO hearings). But the retaliatory measures do not necessarily need to stay in the same sector. For instance, in 2013, Antigua and Barbuda received permission to punish the United States for blocking its online gambling sites, costing the tiny Caribbean country $21 million a year. (Because various forms of gambling are widely available domestically, the U.S. government failed to show why its citizens should be protected from "imported" gambling online.) The WTO said Antigua and Barbuda could steal $21 million annually in U.S. intellectual property by, for example, putting movies and TV shows online without paying for U.S. copyrights.

In cases of dumping, retaliation aims to offset the advantage enjoyed from goods imported at prices below the world market. Retaliatory tariffs raise the price back to market levels. In 2001, the weakened U.S. steel industry pleaded for U.S. government protection from cheap foreign steel, under an antidumping rationale. Before such tariffs are imposed, a U.S. government agency, the International Trade Commission (ITC), decides whether the low-priced imports have actually hurt the U.S. industry. The ITC ruled that U.S. steelmakers had indeed been hurt, and the U.S. government imposed 30 percent tariffs in 2002. But the WTO ruled against the United States in 2003 and gave other countries the right to impose $2 billion in retaliatory tariffs. As Europeans drew up their list of tariffs, targeting maximum damage to swing electoral states in 2004, President Bush backed down and abolished the steel tariffs (declaring them successful and no longer needed). By making the cost of tariffs higher than the benefits, the WTO effectively changed U.S. policy—an indication of the WTO's growing power. This example also shows how closely international trade connects with domestic politics.

Trade cooperation is easier to achieve under hegemony (see Hegemony in Chapter 2). The efficient operation of markets depends on a stable political framework such as hegemony can provide. Political power can protect economic exchange from the distorting influences of violent leverage, of unfair or fraudulent trade practices, and of uncertainties in international currency rates. A hegemon can provide a world currency in which value can be universally calculated. It can punish the use of violence and can enforce norms of fair trade. Because its economy is so large and dominating, the hegemon can threaten to break off trade ties even without resorting to military force. For example, to be denied access to U.S. markets today would seriously hurt export industries in many states. U.S. hegemony thus helped create the major norms and institutions of international trade in the post–1945 era. Now that U.S. hegemony seems to be giving way to a more multipolar world—especially in economic affairs among the great powers—institutions are even more important for the success of the world trading system.

States have found it worthwhile to expand trade steadily, using a variety of regimes and institutions to do so—the WTO, free trade areas, bilateral agreements, and cartels. Overall, despite some loss of state sovereignty as a result of growing interdependence, these efforts have benefited participating states. Stable political rules governing trade allow states to realize the great economic gains that can result from international exchange.

8.3 Economic Globalization

Describe at least two ways in which countries or individual citizens are resisting global trade.

We introduced the process of *globalization* in Chapter 1 in general terms, and will now consider some specifically economic aspects of globalization. The expansion of trade is a central aspect of globalization in the international political economy, but it is hardly the only one. Globalization is transforming not only trade but also money, business, integration, communication, environmental management, and the economic development of poor countries—the subjects of the remaining chapters of this book. Today's accelerating pace of economic activity grows out of a long history of world economic expansion, which serves as the foundation for globalization.

8.3.1 The Evolving World Economy

In 1750, Britain, the world's most advanced economy, had a gross domestic product (GDP) of about $1,200 per capita (in today's dollars). That is less than the present level of most of the global South. Today, however, Britain produces more than ten times that much per person (and with a much larger population than in 1750). This accomplishment is due to **industrialization**—the use of energy to drive machinery and the accumulation of such machinery along with the products created by it. The Industrial Revolution started in Britain in the eighteenth century, underpinned Britain's emerging leadership role in the world economy, and spread to the other advanced economies (see Figure 8.5).

industrialization The use of fossil-fuel energy to drive machinery and the accumulation of such machinery along with the products created by it.

By around 1850, the wooden sailing ships of earlier centuries had given way to larger and faster coal-powered iron steamships. Coal-fueled steam engines also drove factories producing textiles and other commodities. The great age of railroad building was taking off. These developments not only increased the volume of world production and trade but also tied distant locations more closely together economically. The day trip across France by railroad contrasted with the same route a hundred years earlier, which took three weeks to complete. In this period of mechanization, however, factory conditions were extremely harsh, especially for women and children operating machines.

Britain dominated world trade in this period. Because Britain's economy was the most technologically advanced in the world, its products were competitive world-wide. Thus, British policy favored free trade. In addition to its central role in world trade, Britain served as the financial capital of the world, managing an increasingly complex world market in goods and services in the nineteenth century. The British currency, pounds sterling (silver), became the world standard. International monetary relations were still based on the value of precious metals, as they had been in the sixteenth century when Spain bought its armies with Mexican silver and gold.

By the outset of the twentieth century, however, the world's largest and most advanced economy was no longer Britain but the United States. The industrialization of the U.S. economy was fueled by territorial expansion throughout the nineteenth century, adding vast natural resources. The U.S. economy attracted huge pools of immigrant labor from Europe as well. The United States led the world in converting from coal to oil and from horse-drawn transportation to motor vehicles. New technical innovations, from electricity to airplanes, also helped push the U.S. economy into a dominant world position.

In the 1930s, the U.S. and world economies suffered a severe setback in the Great Depression. The protectionist Smoot-Hawley Tariff Act adopted by the United States in 1930, which imposed tariffs on imports, contributed to the severity of the depression by provoking retaliation and reducing world trade. Adopting the principles of *Keynesian economics*, the U.S. government used deficit spending to stimulate the economy, paying itself back from new wealth generated by economic recovery. The government's role in the economy intensified during World War II.

Following World War II, the capitalist world economy was restructured under U.S. leadership. Today's international economic institutions, such as the World Bank and the International Monetary Fund (IMF), date from this period. The United States provided massive assistance to resuscitate the Western European economies (through the Marshall Plan) as well as Japan's economy. World trade greatly expanded, and the world market became woven together more closely through air transportation and telecommunications. Electronics emerged as a new leading sector, and technological progress accelerated throughout the twentieth century.

Figure 8.5 The World Economy, 1750–2000

Sources: Based on North, Douglass C., and Robert Paul Thomas. *The Rise of the Western World: A New Economic History*. Cambridge, 1973. Hobsbawm, E. J. *Industry and Empire: From 1750 to the Present Day*. Penguin-Pelican, 1969. Tracy, James D., ed. *The Political Economy of Merchant Empires: State Power and World Trade, 1350–1750*. Cambridge, 1991.

	1750	1800	1850	1900	1950	2000
Production		industrialization		assembly line; WWI; world depression; Soviet industrialization	WWII; postwar prosperity; Cold War arms race; Japanese & German growth	globalization; Soviet collapse
Energy		coal		oil	nuclear power	nat. gas
Leading Sectors		steam engine; cotton gin	iron & steam; textiles	steel; electricity; motor vehicles	plastics; electronics; computers	biotech
Transportation		(wooden sailing ships)	iron steamships; railroads; Suez Canal	Trans-Siberian Railroad; Panama Canal; airplanes; automobiles	jets; freeways	high-speed rail
Trade		British dominance	(free trade)	protectionism	U.S. dominance; GATT; European integration	WTO; NAFTA
Money			pound sterling (British) as world currency	post-WWI inflation; Keynes; Bretton Woods; IMF	Marshall Plan; IMF; U.S. dollar as world currency; U.S. drops gold standard	debt crises; Russia joins IMF
Communication			telegraph	telephone invented; transoceanic cables; radio	communication satellites; information revolution	Internet; fax, modem, cellular, etc.

centrally planned economy
An economy in which political authorities set prices and decide on quotas for production and consumption of each commodity according to a long-term plan.

Standing apart from this world capitalist economy, the economies of the Soviet Union and Eastern Europe followed communist principles of central planning and state ownership. In a **centrally planned economy** (or *command economy*), political authorities set prices and decide on quotas for production and consumption of each commodity according to a long-term plan, and international trade occurs at government-controlled prices. The proponents of central planning claimed that it would make economies both more rational and more just. By controlling the economy, governments could guarantee the basic needs of citizens and could mobilize the state fully for war if necessary. Proponents of central planning also hoped that governments' long-term view of resources and needs would smooth out the "boom and bust" fluctuations of capitalist economies (known as business cycles).

The Soviet economy had some notable successes in rapidly industrializing the country in the 1930s, surviving the German assault in the 1940s, and developing world-class aerospace and military production capability in the 1950s and 1960s. The Soviet Union launched the world's first satellite (*Sputnik*) in 1957, and in the early 1960s, its leaders boasted that communist economies would outperform capitalist ones within decades. Instead, the Soviet bloc economies stagnated under the weight of bureaucracy, ideological rigidity, environmental destruction, corruption, and high military spending. Centrally planned economies proved hopelessly inefficient.

transitional economies Countries in Russia and Eastern Europe that are trying to convert from communism to capitalism, with various degrees of success.

Now the former Soviet republics and Eastern Europe are **transitional economies**, changing over to a market-based economy connected to the world capitalist economy. This transition has proved difficult. In the first half of the 1990s, the total GDP of the region *shrank* by about 35 percent—a depression worse than the Great Depression that the United States had experienced in the early 1930s. Living standards dropped dramatically. In Boris Yeltsin's administration (1991–1999), Russia's economy remained dysfunctional because of depression, corruption, tax delinquency, and the vast differences between the old communist and new capitalist models. President Vladimir Putin (2000–2008 and 2012–present) brought new energy to economic reform, and high prices for crude oil, a major Russian export, buoyed its economy in the new century; but Putin's centralization of political power could choke off capitalist growth.

China, whose government continues to follow a Marxist *political* line (central control by the Communist Party), has shifted substantially toward a market *economy*. (The state still controls major industries.) This transition has dramatically increased China's economic growth since the 1980s. Growth reached a sustained annual rate of about 10 percent throughout the 1990s and is nearly as fast in recent years (see The Chinese Experience in Chapter 13).

Today, the world's economic activity follows the principles of free markets more than central planning but often falls somewhere between the extremes. Many governments control domestic prices on some goods (for instance, subsidizing certain goods to win political support). Many states *own* (all or part of) industries thought to be vital for the national economy—**state-owned industries** such as oil production companies or national airlines. And the government sector of the economy (military spending, road building, Social Security, and so on) makes up a substantial fraction of the industrialized countries' economies. Because they contain both some government control and some private ownership, the economies of the industrialized West are often called **mixed economies**.

state-owned industries Industries such as oil-production companies and airlines that are owned wholly or partly by the state because they are thought to be vital to the national economy.

mixed economies Economies such as those in the industrialized West that contain both some government control and some private ownership.

Today there is a single integrated world economy that almost no country can resist joining. At the same time, the imperfections and problems of that world economy are evident in periodic crises and recessions and in the sharpening of disparities between the richest and poorest world regions. At no time have these imperfections been more glaring than during the 2008–2009 global financial crisis and ensuing world recession. Starting with the subprime mortgage collapse in the United States, economic troubles quickly spread to Europe as major banks and investment companies lost hundreds of billions of dollars. These losses led to a global slowdown in consumer spending and production that caused large job losses in countries like the United

States, China, and India. The subsequent fall in consumer demand for goods led to declines in global trade of 9 percent—the largest decline since World War II.

8.3.2 Resistance to Trade

The globalization of the world economy has fueled a countercurrent of growing nationalism in several world regions where people believe their identities and communities are threatened by the penetration of foreign influences. In addition, the material dislocations caused by globalization directly affect the self-interests of certain segments of countries' populations.

Workers in industrialized countries in industries that face increasing competition from low-wage countries in the global South—such as steel, automobiles, electronics, and clothing—are among the most adversely affected by free trade. Inevitably, the competition from low-wage countries holds down wages in those industries in the industrialized countries. It also creates pressures to relax standards of labor regulation, such as those protecting worker safety, and it can lead to job losses if manufacturers close down plants in high-wage countries and move operations to the global South. Not surprisingly, labor unions have been among the strongest political opponents of unfettered trade expansion. (Although the United States stands at the center of these debates, other industrialized countries face similar issues.)

Human rights NGOs have joined labor unions in pushing for trade agreements to include requirements for low-wage countries to improve working conditions such as minimum wages, child labor, and worker safety. The United States bans imports of goods (mostly rugs) made by South Asia's 17 million indentured (slave) child laborers. Companies stung by criticism of conditions in their Asian factories have adopted voluntary measures to end the worst abuses, as Apple Computer did in 2012 after its Chinese supplier Foxconn faced worker protests and media attention over working conditions. More than 200 million children under age 14 work in the global South, more than half in hazardous labor, according to the International Labor Organization. In Ivory Coast, the world's largest exporter of cocoa (for chocolate consumed in the global North), tens of thousands of children work for low wages, or even as slaves, on cocoa plantations.

In April 2013, a factory collapse in Bangladesh killed over 1,100 workers and injured over 2,000 and brought new attention to worker safety issues. The garment factory collapse, the worst industrial accident in the history of Bangladesh, led to efforts by NGOs to increase labor standards by demanding that retailers commit to new safety standards for workers. By 2015, two different agreements had emerged: one signed by mostly European retailers and another signed mostly by American retailers. Labor groups have criticized the American agreement as lacking strong legal penalties for violating the agreement.

Environmental groups have also actively opposed the unrestricted expansion of trade, which they see as undermining environmental laws in industrialized countries and promoting environmentally harmful practices worldwide (see Chapter 11). For example, U.S. regulations require commercial shrimp boats to use devices that prevent endangered species of sea turtles from drowning in shrimp nets. Indonesia, Malaysia, Thailand, and Pakistan, whose shrimp exports to the United States were blocked because they do

Ahmed Salahuddin/AP Images

COSTLY LABOR Labor, environmental, and human rights organizations have all criticized unrestricted free trade. They argue that free trade agreements encourage multinational corporations (MNCs) to produce goods under unfair and unhealthy conditions, including the use of child labor. Here, a woman grieves over a missing family member at the site of the eight-story garment factory that collapsed in Bangladesh in 2013. The collapse killed more than 1,100 workers.

[Handwritten annotation in right margin:] Countries w/ child labor - Ivory Coast (cocoa) - China (foxconn)

not require the use of such devices, filed a complaint with the WTO, arguing that the U.S. regulation unfairly discriminated against them. In 1998, the United States lost the WTO ruling and appeal. Sea turtles became a symbol of environmentalist opposition to the WTO. (In 2001, the WTO ruled the U.S. law acceptable after changes had made application of the law more even-handed.) In 1996, Brazil and Venezuela took the United States to the WTO and forced a change in U.S. environmental rules regarding imported gasoline, claiming that regulations under the Clean Air Act were functioning as nontariff barriers.

In general, unrestricted trade tends to force countries to equalize their regulations in a variety of areas not limited to labor and environmental rules. For example, the WTO ruled in 1997 that Europeans' fears about the use of growth hormones in beef were not scientifically warranted, and therefore EU regulations could not be used to exclude U.S. beef containing hormones. When the European Union persisted, the United States was allowed to retaliate by imposing high tariffs on a list of EU exports such as French cheeses. Similarly, in 2006, the WTO ruled that European restrictions on imports of genetically modified food from the United States violated trade rules.

These examples illustrate the variety of sources of backlash against free trade agreements. Labor, environmental, and consumer groups all portray the WTO as a secretive bureaucracy outside democratic control that serves the interests of big corporations at the expense of ordinary people in both the global North and the global South. More fundamentally, these critics distrust the corporate-driven globalization, of which the WTO is just one aspect. Recent U.S. surveys show a drop in the belief that trade is good for the economy. According to a late 2017 survey, 72 percent believe trade is "an opportunity" for the United States, while 23 percent say it is "a threat"—up several percentage points from just a few years earlier. Globally, public opinion supports trade: A 2014 poll in 44 countries found that, on average, 81 percent of respondents saw international trade as a good thing, despite concerns about negative cultural and environmental effects. Support was especially high in export-dependent economies—above 90 percent in Vietnam, Israel, South Korea, and Germany, for example.

The benefits of free trade, as noted earlier, are much more diffuse than the costs. U.S. consumers enjoy lower prices on goods imported from low-wage countries. The consumers may therefore spend more money on other products and services, eventually employing more U.S. workers. Cheap imports also help keep inflation low, which benefits citizens. This is small comfort, however, if you are the one who just lost your job.

Of course, international trade requires money to facilitate exchange. In the era of globalization, a significant amount of international trade is conducted through multinational corporations. The next chapter takes up these two issues in the context of the global economy.

Chapter Review

Summary

- Liberal economics emphasizes international cooperation—especially through worldwide free trade—to increase the total creation of wealth (regardless of its distribution among states).

- Mercantilism emphasizes the use of economic policy to increase state power relative to that of other states. It mirrors realism in many ways. Mercantilists favor trade policies that produce a trade surplus for their own state. Such a positive trade balance generates money that can be used to enhance state power.

- Trade creates wealth by allowing states to specialize in producing goods and services for which they have a comparative advantage (and importing other needed goods).

- The distribution of benefits from an exchange is determined by the price of the goods exchanged. With many buyers and sellers, prices are generally determined by market equilibrium (supply and demand).

- Politics interferes in international markets in many ways, including the use of economic sanctions as political leverage on a target state. However, sanctions are difficult to enforce unless all major economic actors agree to abide by them.

- States that have reduced their dependence on others by pursuing self-sufficient autarky have failed to generate new wealth to increase their well-being. Self-reliance, like central planning, has been largely discredited as a viable economic strategy.

- Through protectionist policies, many states try to protect certain domestic industries from international competition. Such policies tend to slow down the global creation of wealth but do help the particular industry in question. Protectionism can be pursued through various means, including import tariffs (the favored method), quotas, subsidies, and other nontariff barriers.

- The volume of world trade is very large—about one-sixth of global economic activity—and is concentrated heavily in the states of the industrialized West (Western Europe, North America, and Japan) and China.

- Over time, the rules embodied in trade regimes (and other issue areas in IR) become the basis for permanent institutions whose administrative functions provide yet further stability and efficiency in global trade.

- The World Trade Organization (WTO), formerly the GATT, is the most important multilateral global trade agreement. The GATT was institutionalized in 1995 with the creation of the WTO, which expanded the focus on manufactured goods to consider agriculture and services. Intellectual property is another recent focus.

- In successive rounds of GATT negotiations over 50 years, states have lowered overall tariff rates (especially on manufactured goods). The Uruguay Round of the GATT, completed in 1994, added hundreds of billions of dollars to the global creation of wealth. The Doha Round began in 2001 and was suspended in 2015. Meanwhile textile tariffs were dropped worldwide in January 2005.

- Although the WTO provides a global framework, states continue to operate under thousands of bilateral trade agreements specifying the rules for trade in specific products between specific countries.

- Regional free-trade areas (with few if any tariffs or nontariff barriers) have been created in Europe, North America, and several other regions. NAFTA includes Canada, Mexico, and the United States.

- International cartels are occasionally used by leading producers (sometimes in conjunction with leading consumers) to control and stabilize prices for a commodity on world markets. The most visible example in recent decades has been the oil producers' cartel, OPEC, whose members control more than half the world's exports of a vital commodity, oil.

- Industries often lobby their own governments for protection. Governments in many states develop industrial policies to guide their efforts to strengthen domestic industries in the context of global markets.

- Certain economic sectors—especially agriculture, intellectual property, services, and military goods—tend to deviate more than others from market principles. Political conflicts among states concerning trade in these sectors are frequent.

- Because there is no world government to enforce rules of trade, such enforcement depends on reciprocity and state power. In particular, states reciprocate each other's cooperation in opening markets (or punish each other's refusal to let in foreign products). Although it leads to trade wars on occasion, reciprocity has achieved substantial cooperation in trade.

- The world economy has generated wealth at an accelerating pace in the past two centuries and is increasingly integrated on a global scale, although with huge inequalities.

- Communist states during the Cold War operated centrally planned economies in which national governments set prices and allocated resources. Almost all these states are now in transition toward market-based economies, which generate wealth more efficiently.

- Free trade agreements have led to a backlash from politically active interest groups adversely affected by globalization; these groups include labor unions, environmental and human rights NGOs, and certain consumers.

Key Terms

mercantilism 255
economic liberalism 255
free trade 257
balance of trade 258

comparative advantage 259
autarky 261
protectionism 262
dumping 263

tariff 263
nontariff barriers 263
World Trade Organization
(WTO) 265

Critical Thinking Questions

1. Suppose your state had a chance to reach a major trade agreement by making substantial concessions. The agreement would produce $5 billion in new wealth for your state, as well as $10 billion for each of the other states involved (which are political allies but economic rivals). What advice would a mercantilist give your state's leader about making such a deal? What arguments would support the advice? How would liberal advice and arguments differ?

2. China has made a successful transition to market economics and is growing rapidly. It is the world's second-largest economy. Do you think this is a good thing or a bad thing for your state? Does your reasoning reflect mercantilist or liberal assumptions?

3. Given the theory of hegemonic stability (see Chapter 2), what effects might a resurgence of U.S. power in the post–Cold War era have on the world trading system? How might those effects show up in concrete ways?

4. Before you read this chapter, to what extent did you prefer to buy products made in your own country? Has reading this chapter changed your views on that subject? How?

5. Imagine a Free Trade Area of the Americas that would join Canada and the United States with Latin American countries, where wages are lower and technology is less developed. Which U.S. industries do you think would gain from such a trade area? Specifically, do you think labor-intensive industries or high-technology industries would be winners? Why?

Suggested Readings

Bernstein, William J. *A Splendid Exchange: How Trade Shaped the World.* Grove, 2009.

Blackwill, Robert D., and Jennifer M. Harris. *War by Other Means: Geoeconomics and Statecraft.* Belknap, 2017.

Hufbauer, Gary Clyde, Jeffrey Schott, Kimberly Ann Elliot, and Barbara Oegg. *Economic Sanctions Reconsidered.* Peterson Institute, 2008.

Irwin, Douglas. *Against the Tide: An Intellectual History of Free Trade.* Princeton, 1996.

North, Douglass C., and Robert Paul Thomas. *The Rise of the Western World: A New Economic History.* Cambridge, 1973.

Rivoli, Pietra. *The Travels of a T-Shirt in the Global Economy: An Economist Examines the Markets, Power, and Politics of World Trade.* Wiley, 2014.

Let's Debate the Issue

Are Free Trade Agreements Good for the Global Economy?

Overview

In the past twenty-five years, the number of bilateral and multilateral free-trade agreements (FTAs) has skyrocketed. Today, nearly every country is a party to at least one FTA. Many countries are party to multiple FTAs, and nearly all FTAs cover states that are members of the WTO.

There are several reasons offered for the recent explosion of these arrangements. Some attribute the popularity of the neoliberal economic model and its emphasis on free trade as a source of motivation for these agreements. Others point to the suspension of the Doha Round of the WTO negotiations. If the WTO ceases to expand in scope, groups of states will do so on their own by signing an FTA. Finally, some point to business pressure to join these arrangements because, under an FTA, a multinational corporation (MNC) with factories in multiple states can ship goods between those factories tariff-free.

Despite the prevalence of these agreements, they are controversial. As discussed in this chapter, free trade brings diffuse benefits but concentrated costs, but there are always opponents to these agreements within member states. Economists are also divided on whether FTAs are beneficial because states may be less likely to cooperate to achieve global free trade (the best outcome for economists) if they are happy with free trade among their key trading partners. Yet others contend they are acceptable stepping-stones to a world of global free trade. Are FTAs good for the global economy, or do they bring more difficulties domestically and internationally?

ARGUMENT 1

FTAs Are Beneficial to the Global Economy

FTAs usually increase trade. Several studies in economics have shown that free trade areas do increase the amount of trade between countries. This trade can be beneficial to consumers and producers, and helps increase economic growth. Given the slow rate of progress at the WTO talks, other solutions are needed to increase trade.

Free trade lowers costs for consumers. Once tariffs are removed from goods, these goods may be sold at a cheaper price. Consumers benefit from these cheaper prices. In extreme cases, FTAs can lower tariffs that effectively exclude goods from entering a market, giving consumers more choice in the products they buy.

FTAs increase foreign investment. Because FTAs eliminate or lower trade barriers, they encourage companies located in states outside the FTAs to locate new factories within the FTAs in order to take advantage of lower tariffs. Some research has shown that FTAs lure increased foreign investment to member states—an important way to increase economic growth, especially in poor countries.

ARGUMENT 2

FTAs Are Harmful to the Global Economy

FTAs hinder the advancement of global free trade. Most economists agree that the ideal situation in the global economy is the complete elimination of trade barriers through a large agreement like the WTO. Once states have secured their best trading partners in an FTA, they have no incentive to advance the WTO process.

FTAs are exclusionary and discriminatory. By definition, FTAs provide lower tariffs for only a small number of states. They do not address tariffs levied against nonmembers, and states may have incentives to increase tariffs against nonmembers to encourage trade within the FTA and discourage imports from outside it.

FTAs threaten jobs and general economic well-being. Because FTAs make it easier for goods to cross borders, companies can locate in other member states where labor costs or environmental standards are lower and thus cut their production costs. This means fewer jobs in some member states and can lead to further degradation of the natural environment.

Questions

- Do you feel that FTAs are helpful or harmful to the global economy? Would the global economy be better off with no FTAs, leaving only the WTO to liberalize trade?

- As the global economy has emerged from the recession of 2008–2009, will we see a move back to free trade? How much of the current opinion toward the effects of free trade has been influenced by the global economic recession?

- Suppose WTO negotiations continue to be deadlocked, with no hope in sight for a more extensive global trade agreement. Does this change your opinion of whether more FTAs should be concluded? Or are the domestic implications (price changes versus job losses) more important in your thinking?

For Further Reading

Chang, Ha-Joon. *Bad Samaritans: The Myth of Free Trade and the Secret History of Capitalism.* Bloomsbury, 2007.

Irwin, Douglas. *Free Trade Under Fire.* 4th ed. Princeton, 2015.

Rodrik, Dani. *Straight Talk on Trade: Ideas for a Sane World Economy.* Princeton, 2017.

Stiglitz, Joseph, and Andrew Charlton. *Fair Trade for All: How Trade Can Promote Development.* Oxford, 2006.

Chapter 9
Global Finance and Business

WORLD STOCK MARKET INDICATOR, TOKYO, 2018.

⌄ Learning Objectives

9.1 Describe the effects of the 2008–2009 global financial crisis.

9.2 Summarize the three types of exchange rate systems adopted by states.

9.3 Compare and contrast the financial positions of the United States and Russia in regard to the potential for future economic growth.

9.4 Identify two risks to firms that engage in foreign direct investment and two risks to countries that host foreign direct investment.

9.1 Globalization and Finance

Describe the effects of the 2008–2009 global financial crisis.

Globalization has led to momentous changes in many areas of international relations (IR). So far, we have discussed how globalization has influenced global security and international trade relations. Yet globalization has had its most profound influence in the way states, businesses, and individuals deal with financial markets.

Today, global financial markets are as integrated as they have ever been. Investors in one country buy and sell assets or exchange currency with a few taps on a phone. Banks' investment portfolios often contain millions of dollars in assets (real estate, land, stocks) located in other countries. About $3 trillion a day is exchanged on currency markets because investors need various currencies to do business in other countries and also to bet on the rise and fall of currencies, which we will discuss momentarily.

This financial integration has tremendous advantages. It offers investors and businesses access to overseas markets to spur economic growth. It allows for the possibility of better returns on investment for individuals investing for college tuition or retirement. But financial integration also carries risks. An economic crisis in one state can quickly spread to another, then another. The spread of economic difficulties can quickly lead to a global economic crisis affecting small and large economies alike.

Such was the case in 2008. As an economic downturn began in the United States, many Americans who had taken out loans on their homes found themselves unable to pay back these loans. At the same time, the value of their homes began to fall, so that even if banks were to reclaim them, the banks could not recover the money they had loaned. Moreover, these loans had been resold by the banks to other businesses as investments, often in other countries. Several large U.S. banks then announced that they were on the verge of failing because they had too much money tied up in these bad home loans. This was a problem not only for the banks and the individuals who could not pay for their homes but also for those businesses who had purchased these loans as investments.

Given the global integration of financial markets, this housing crisis led quickly to a global banking crisis. Several British banks then announced they were near bankruptcy. The U.S. government responded with a rescue package of $800 billion to help shore up failing banks. Britain also created a rescue package of nearly $450 billion. The entire banking sector of Iceland was taken over by the government, and Iceland, a prosperous country, needed a loan from the International Monetary Fund (IMF) to rescue the government from bankruptcy.

Global stock markets tumbled dramatically as a result of this financial crisis, by a third, a half, and even two-thirds in the case of China. Unemployment increased worldwide. What began as trouble in the U.S. housing market ended as a global financial meltdown.

The world economy recovered in the years after 2008 but soon faced the ripple effects of a debt crisis in Europe. The financial problems there, which began in Greece and spread to Spain, Portugal, and even Italy, threatened the European Union (EU) as a whole while holding back growth in the United States (see Chapter 10). The spread of these financial problems dramatically illustrates the financial interdependence of today's world. While most experts agree that the global economy has recovered from the financial crisis, the Greek debt crisis continues to plague Europe.

This chapter will investigate two central pillars of our global financial markets: the politics of the world monetary system and the role of private companies as non-state actors in the world economy.

9.2 The Currency System

Summarize the three types of exchange rate systems adopted by states.

Nearly every state prints its own money. The ability to print one's own currency is one of the hallmarks of state sovereignty. Yet in a globalized system of trade and finance, businesses and individuals often need other states' currencies to do business.

9.2.1 About Money

Because of the nature of state sovereignty, the international economy is based on national currencies, not a world currency. One of the main powers of a national government is to create its own currency as the sole legal currency in the territory it controls. The national currencies are of no inherent value in another country, but they can be exchanged one for another.

Traditionally, for centuries, the European state system used *precious metals* as a global currency, valued in all countries. *Gold* was most important, and *silver* was second. These metals had inherent value because they looked pretty and were easily molded into jewelry or similar objects. They were relatively rare, and the mining of new gold and silver was relatively slow. These metals lasted a long time, and they were difficult to dilute or counterfeit.

Over time, gold and silver became valuable *because* they were a world currency—because other people around the world trusted that the metals could be exchanged for future goods—and this overshadowed any inherent functional value of gold or silver. States held bars of gold and silver as a kind of bank account denominated in an international currency. These piles of gold (literal and figurative) were the object of mercantilist trade policies in past centuries (see Chapters 2 and 8). Gold has long been a key power resource with which states could buy armies or other means of leverage.

In recent years the world has not used such a **gold standard** but has developed an international monetary system divorced from any tangible medium such as precious metals. Even today, some private investors buy stocks of gold or silver at times of political instability as a haven that would reliably have future value. But gold and silver have now become basically like other commodities, with unpredictable fluctuations in price. The change in the world economy away from bars of gold to purely abstract money makes international economics more efficient; the only drawback is that, without tangible backing in gold, currencies may seem less worthy of people's confidence.

gold standard A system in international monetary relations, prominent for a century before the 1970s, in which the value of national currencies was pegged to the value of gold or other precious metals.

exchange rate The rate at which one state's currency can be exchanged for the currency of another state. Since 1973, the international monetary system has depended mainly on floating rather than fixed exchange rates. See also *convertible currency; fixed exchange rates;* and *managed float.*

WHAT'S IT WORTH TO YOU? Money has value only because people trust its worth. Inflation erodes a currency's value if governments print too much money or if political instability erodes public confidence. Constant minor adjustments set currencies' values; this Ukrainian exchange in 2015 reacts to increased violence in the eastern portion of that country, further eroding the value of its currency.

9.2.2 International Currency Exchange

Today, national currencies are valued against each other, not against gold or silver. Each state's currency can be exchanged for a different state's currency according to an **exchange rate**—defining, for instance, how many Canadian dollars are equivalent to one U.S. dollar. These exchange rates affect almost every international economic transaction—trade, investment, tourism, and so forth.

Most exchange rates are expressed in terms of the world's most important currencies—the U.S. dollar, the Japanese yen, and the EU's euro. Thus, the rate for exchanging Danish kroner for Brazilian reals depends on the value of each relative to these world currencies. Exchange rates that most affect the world economy are those *within* the largest economies—U.S. dollars, euros, yen, British pounds, and Canadian dollars.

The relative values of currencies at a given point in time are arbitrary; only the *changes* in values over time are meaningful. For instance, the euro happens to be fairly close to the U.S. dollar in value, whereas the Japanese yen is denominated in units closer to the U.S. penny. In itself this disparity says nothing about the desirability of these currencies or the financial positions of their states. However, when the value of the euro rises (or falls) *relative* to the dollar, because euros are considered more (or less) valuable than before, the euro is said to be strong (or weak). A strong currency makes imports more affordable, while a weak currency makes exports more competitive. For example, when the U.S. dollar's value fell in 2001–2006, the exports of 200 large U.S. companies with substantial foreign sales rose from 32 to 44 percent of their total sales.

Some states do not have **convertible currencies**. The holder of such money has no guarantee of being able to trade it for another currency. Such is the case in states cut off from the world capitalist economy, such as the former Soviet Union. In practice, even nonconvertible currency can often be sold, in black markets or by dealing directly with the government issuing the currency, but the price may be extremely low. Some currencies are practically nonconvertible because they are inflating so rapidly that holding them for even a short period means losing money. Inflation reduces a currency's value relative to more stable (more slowly inflating) currencies.

convertible currency The guarantee that the holder of a particular currency can exchange it for another currency. Some states' currencies are nonconvertible. See also *hard currency*.

The industrialized West has kept inflation relatively low—mostly below 5 percent annually—since 1980. (The 1970s saw inflation of more than 10 percent per year in many industrialized economies, including the United States.) Inflation in most of the global South is lower than it was 25 years ago (see Table 9.1). Latin America brought inflation from 750 percent to around 5 percent, while China and the Middle East got inflation rates below 5 percent. Most dramatically, in Russia and other former Soviet republics, inflation rates of more than 1,000 percent came down to 5 percent.

Extremely high, uncontrolled inflation—more than 50 percent per month, or 13,000 percent per year—is called **hyperinflation**. The $100 trillion notes introduced by Zimbabwe in 2009 quickly lost most of their initial value (about $30 U.S.) under hyperinflation exceeding 200 million percent per year. More recently, Venezuela's inflation rate rose to 4,000 percent in the fall of 2017, leading the government to print new money, including issuing an online currency backed by the country's oil reserves.

hyperinflation An extremely rapid, uncontrolled rise in prices, such as occurred in Germany in the 1920s and in some third world countries more recently.

Table 9.1 Inflation Rates by Region, 1993–2018

Region	Inflation Rate (percent per year)		
	1993	2009	2018[a]
Industrialized West	3	0.1	2
Russia/CIS	1,400	11	5
China	15	−0.5	3
Middle East	27	4	4
Latin America	750	6	5
South Asia	6	7	9
Africa	112	11	6

[a]Data are estimates based on partial data for 2017.

Note: Regions are not identical to those used elsewhere in this book.

Source: World Economic Situation and Prospects 2018. United Nations, 2017.

Even just moderately high inflation causes money to lose value weekly, making it hard to conduct business.

hard currency Money that can be readily converted to leading world currencies. See also *convertible currency.*

In contrast with nonconvertible currency, **hard currency** is money that can be readily converted to leading world currencies (which now have relatively low inflation). For example, a Chinese computer producer can export its products and receive payment in dollars, euros, or another hard currency, which it can use to pay for components that it needs to import from abroad. But a Chinese farmer paid in Chinese currency for rice could not simply use that currency to buy imported goods. Rather, the exchange for foreign currency would be controlled by the Chinese government at rates the government set. In a few countries, such as Cuba, two versions of currency circulate, one convertible to foreign hard currency and one for internal use only. Cubans complain that needed goods are available only at stores taking the hard version (such as stores selling to tourists), whereas their salaries are paid in the soft version. Generally, as economies develop and join the global marketplace, their currencies also develop, from the shaky versions based on beer cans or prone to hyperinflation to the much more stable versions such as China's today and eventually to the fully convertible model.

reserves Hard-currency stockpiles kept by states.

States maintain **reserves** of hard currency. These reserves are the equivalent of the stockpiles of gold in centuries past. National currencies are now backed by hard-currency reserves, not gold. Some states continue to maintain gold reserves as well. In 2010, Saudi Arabia disclosed that it maintained over 300 tons of gold in reserve, worth more than $10 billion. By 2018, both China and Russia had amassed nearly 2,000 tons of gold in reserve. The industrialized countries have financial reserves roughly in proportion to the size of their economies.

fixed exchange rates The official rates of exchange for currencies set by governments; not a dominant mechanism in the international monetary system since 1973. See also *floating exchange rates.*

One form of currency exchange uses **fixed exchange rates**. Here, governments decide, individually or jointly, to establish official rates of exchange for their currencies. For example, the Canadian and U.S. dollars were equal in value for many years; a fixed rate of one to one was maintained (this is no longer true). States have various means for trying to maintain, or modify, such fixed rates in the face of changing economic conditions (see Why Currencies Rise or Fall later in this chapter).

floating exchange rates The rates determined by global currency markets in which private investors and governments alike buy and sell currencies. See also *fixed exchange rates.*

Floating exchange rates are now more commonly used for the world's major currencies. Rates are determined by global currency markets in which private investors and governments alike buy and sell currencies. There is a supply and demand for each state's currency, with prices constantly adjusting in response to market conditions. Just as investors might buy shares of Apple or Walmart stock if they expected its value to rise, so they would buy a pile of Japanese yen if they expected that currency's value to rise in the future. Through short-term speculative trading in international currencies, exchange rates adjust to changes in the longer-term supply and demand for currencies.

Major international currency markets operate in a handful of cities—the most important being New York, London, Zurich (Switzerland), Tokyo, and Hong Kong—linked together by instantaneous computerized communications. These markets are driven in the short term by one question: What will a state's currency be worth in the future relative to what it is worth today? These international currency markets involve huge amounts of money—$3 trillion every day—moving around the world (of course, only the computerized information actually moves). They are private markets and are not as strongly regulated by governments as are stock markets.

managed float A system of occasional multinational government interventions in currency markets to manage otherwise free-floating currency rates.

National governments periodically *intervene* in financial markets, buying and selling currencies in order to manipulate their value. (These interventions may also involve changing interest rates paid by the government; see "discount rate" in the Central Banks section later in this chapter.) Such government intervention to manage the otherwise free-floating currency rates is called a **managed float** system. The leading industrialized states often, but not always, work together in such interventions. If the price of the U.S. dollar, for instance, goes down too much relative to other important currencies (a political judgment), governments step into the currency markets, side by side with private investors, and buy dollars. With this higher demand for dollars, the price may then stabilize and perhaps rise again. (If the price gets too high, governments step in to sell dollars, increasing supply and driving the price down.) Such interventions usually happen quickly, in one day, but may be repeated several times within a few weeks in order to have the desired effect. Note that monetary intervention requires costly multilateral cooperation among states. Liberals point to such cooperation as evidence that states recognize their long-term interest in a mutually beneficial international economy (see the Seeking the Collective Good box).

In their interventions in international currency markets, governments are at a disadvantage because, even when acting together, they control only a small fraction of the money moving on such markets; most of it is privately owned. However, governments have one advantage: They can work together to have enough impact on the market to make at least modest changes in price. Governments can also operate in secret, keeping private investors in the dark regarding how much currency governments may eventually buy or sell, and at what price. Only *after* a coordinated multinational intervention into markets does the public find out about it. (If speculators knew in advance, they could make money at the government's expense.) Note that this is an area where states have a common interest (making sure a large economy does not collapse) aligned against transnational actors (investors who are trying to make money at the expense of states).

Seeking the Collective Good
Currency Stability

COLLECTIVE GOOD: Stable Currency Exchange Rates for World Business

BACKGROUND: Globalization has brought great wealth to the world as business increasingly operates internationally. The ability to do business internationally depends on the stability of currency exchange rates in different countries. Whatever the exchange rate, businesspeople can plan on investments, imports, or purchases based on knowing what these items will cost if paid for in a foreign currency. This stability is a collective good for the world. If the world's major countries maintain stability by coordinating their financial policies, all enjoy the benefit. That stability can be achieved even if some states free-ride by manipulating their own currency exchange rates to their own advantage. If too many countries do so, the collective good is not achieved, as shown in the competitive devaluations of major currencies in the 1930s, which worsened the Great Depression.

Dollars and euros anchor the currency system, 2010.

CHALLENGE: China has kept its currency pegged to the U.S. dollar for years, even as economic conditions in the two countries have diverged and a huge trade imbalance developed. Most economists expect that, if allowed to float freely like the world's other major currencies, the Chinese currency would rise substantially. This would help American exports and harm Chinese exports, reducing the trade imbalance somewhat. Recently, China has begun to allow its currency to move more substantially, but many experts believe this movement is still controlled by the Chinese government.

SOLUTION: Unlike the trade system based on equality and reciprocity, the international financial system more closely resembles a dominance hierarchy. The IMF uses a weighted voting system that gives power to the largest economies. Until recently, major world currency decisions were made by the Group of Seven (G7) countries. This was expanded to the larger and more inclusive G20—a flattening of the dominance hierarchy in response to the world economic crisis—but still leaves the top countries calling the shots. World currency markets are dominated by the U.S. dollar, the euro, and the Japanese yen.

By keeping its currency artificially low, China is free riding on the world currency system by boosting its own exports. However, China is not a large enough piece of the world economy as a whole to bring down the currency system by its nonparticipation.

A successful intervention can make money for governments at the expense of private speculators. If, for example, the Group of Twenty (G20) governments step in to raise the price of U.S. dollars by buying them around the world (selling other hard currencies), and if they succeed, the governments can then sell again and pocket a profit. However, if the intervention fails and the price of dollars keeps falling, the governments *lose* money and may have to keep buying and buying in order to stop the slide. In fact, if investors become aware of such moves, they may interpret this action as a signal that the currency being bought is weak, which could depress the price even further. In extreme cases, the governments may run out of their stockpiles of hard currencies before then and have to absorb a huge loss. Thus governments must be realistic about the limited effects they can have on currency prices.

These limits were well illustrated in the 2001 Argentine financial collapse. Argentina in the 1990s had pegged the value of its currency at a fixed rate to the U.S. dollar—a wonderfully effective way to stop the runaway inflation that had recently wreaked devastation on Argentina's economy. Tying the peso to the dollar, however, represented a loss of sovereignty over monetary policy, one of the key levers to control an economy. Argentina and the United States in the late 1990s had different needs. As a historic U.S. expansion brought unprecedented prosperity (allowing interest rates to be kept relatively high), Argentina suffered four years of recession but could not lower interest rates to stimulate growth. Argentina accumulated more than $100 billion in foreign loans and could not service its debts. Assistance from the IMF in restructuring debt was contingent on a tight financial policy of tax increases and spending cuts—a mistake during a major multiyear recession, according to critics. In 2001, as the United States and the IMF stood by, Argentina's economy collapsed; two presidents resigned in short order; and a populist took power, defaulted on foreign debts, and devalued the peso to create jobs—an embarrassing chapter for the IMF and a painful one for Argentina. In 2003, Argentina defaulted on a $3 billion payment to the IMF, the largest default in IMF history. Its economy turned around and it paid the IMF in 2006, though negotiations with foreign government creditors continued.

Another Latin American case, Venezuela, demonstrates the harmful effects of poor currency policy choices. Beginning in 2003, Venezuela imposed a differentiated exchange rate—the official exchange rate varied depending on what was being bought and sold. Because some imported goods were bought at a more favorable exchange rate, certain "expensive" goods became very cheap (luxury cars and liquor), while staple goods (milk) became expensive. By 2018, the Venezuelan economy was experiencing hyperinflation and hard currency was very difficult to find in the country.

More recently, pressures built up in a vastly more important case—China's currency. As in Argentina in 2001, the current policy of pegging China's currency to the dollar did not adjust to different economic conditions in China and the United States. China runs a big trade surplus (see Chapter 8) while the United States runs a big trade deficit—over $375 billion with China alone in 2017 and over $550 billion in total. Critics charge that the dollar–yuan ratio is held artificially high, making China's exports to the United States cheaper and contributing to the trade imbalance and the loss of U.S. manufacturing jobs—an issue in U.S. domestic politics. These dynamics were one reason for the United States to raise its tariffs on several goods from China in 2017–2018, including solar panels, washing machines, and steel. Pressure on China to reform its currency has grown. Yet China is concerned about domestic stability—for employment to stay high, China must export goods. China's undervalued currency keeps exports cheap and workers employed. China has only slowly allowed its currency to appreciate in value. A study by the U.S. Federal Reserve Board in 2017 argued that China's currency was moving as if it were a floating currency, but also suggested that the Chinese government's policy allowing this float could change quickly.

In 2006, China, Japan, and South Korea announced plans to work toward coordinating their currency policies. In 2017, South Korea extended a currency exchange agreement, worth over $50 billion, with China, even though the two countries were in the midst of a diplomatic dispute over South Korea placing an American missile defense system on its territory. Along with the Association of South East Asian Nations (ASEAN) countries, China, Japan, and South Korea are also studying the creation of an Asian currency unit that would track the aggregate value of the region's currencies. Both measures are possible early steps toward the eventual creation of an Asian currency like the euro. But such a major move is in the early stages at best.

9.2.3 Why Currencies Rise or Fall

In the short term, exchange rates depend on speculation about the future value of currencies. But over the long term, the value of a state's currency tends to rise or fall relative to others because of changes in the long-term supply and demand for the currency. *Supply* is determined by the amount of money a government prints. Printing money is a quick way to generate revenue for the government, but the more money that is printed, the lower its price. Domestically, printing too much money creates inflation because the amount of goods in the economy is unchanged, but more money is circulating to buy the goods with. *Demand* for a currency depends on the state's economic health and political stability. People do not want to own the currency of an unstable country because political instability leads to the breakdown of economic efficiency and of trust in the currency. Conversely, political stability boosts a currency's value. For instance, in 2001, when a new Indonesian president took office after a period of political and economic turmoil, the Indonesian currency jumped 13 percent in two days because of expectations of greater stability.

Currency stability is hard to achieve. In the last few years, the U.S. dollar dropped from over 90 Japanese yen to under 80, then rose to 120, only to settle back at around 105. This kind of instability in exchange rates disrupts business in trade-oriented sectors because companies face sudden and unpredictable changes in their plans for income and expenses (for example, changes in the cost of computer chips from Japan needed to manufacture U.S. computers, or U.S. software needed in Japan). States also have a shared interest in currency stability because instability tends to be profitable for speculators at the expense of central banks. States also share an interest in the integrity of their currencies against counterfeiting, but so-called rogue states may feel otherwise. In 2006, the United States accused North Korea of passing off tens of millions of dollars in extremely realistic counterfeit $100 bills—a direct gain for the North Korean regime at the expense of the U.S. Treasury.

Despite these shared interests in currency stability, states also experience *conflicts* over currency exchange. States often prefer a *low* value for their own currency relative to others because a low value promotes exports and helps turn trade deficits into surpluses—as mercantilists especially favor (see Chapter 8). For instance, as Canada's dollar rose 25 percent in 2009–2012 relative to the U.S. dollar, American automakers shifted production, and thousands of jobs, out of Canada and into the United States.

Justin Sullivan/Getty Images

PRICES SUBJECT TO CHANGE Changes in the value of the dollar—reflecting underlying trends in U.S. and foreign economies as well as governments' monetary policies—directly affect the prices of imported goods such as gasoline, here rising in California in 2015.

Exchange rates and trade surpluses or deficits tend to adjust automatically toward equilibrium (the preferred outcome for liberals). An *overvalued* currency, whose exchange rate is too high, creates a chronic trade deficit. The deficit can be covered by printing more money, which waters down the currency's value and brings down the exchange rate (assuming it is allowed to float freely). Because liberals see such adjustments as harmless, they view these changes as positive mechanisms for the world economy to work out inefficiencies and maximize overall growth.

A unilateral move to reduce the value of one's own currency by changing a fixed or official exchange rate is called a **devaluation**. Generally, devaluation is a quick fix for financial problems in the short term, but it can create new problems. It causes losses to foreigners who hold one's currency (which suddenly loses value). Such losses reduce the trust people place in the currency. As a result, demand for the currency drops, even at the new lower rate. Investors become wary of future devaluations, and indeed such devaluations often follow one after another in unstable economies. In the first three weeks of 2009, Russia devalued its ruble six times after the price of its main export, oil, plummeted. A currency may be devalued by being allowed to float freely after a period of fixed exchange rates, often bringing a single sharp drop in values. In general, any sharp or artificial change in exchange rates tends to disrupt smooth international trade and interfere with the creation of wealth.

Relatively stable exchange rates for international currency can be seen as a collective good because all members of the international economy benefit from a stable framework for making investments and sales, yet an individual country can benefit from devaluing its own currency. (Whether such benefits are actually economic, or merely political benefits tied to perceptions of national interest, does not matter here, as long as state leaders perceive that defection from existing exchange rates can benefit their countries.) According to the theory of collective goods, international exchange rate stability should be achieved more readily in two circumstances—under hegemony (the dominance principle) and under an arrangement among a small group of key states (where the reciprocity principle operates effectively). Hegemonic stability, in this theory, includes providing backing for world currency stability, using the hegemon's own economic clout and its influence over other great powers. Lacking a hegemon, collective goods are thought to be easiest to ensure if controlled by a small group. In the small-group setting, defectors stand out and mutual cooperation is enforced more readily.

In recent years, a new phenomenon known as electronic currencies has gained attention around the world. None of these currencies exist in physical form. The most widely used of these currencies, bitcoin, is now accepted by many businesses around the world. These currencies may be traded for traditional currencies on a number of Web-based trading firms. Bitcoin, worth as little as $0.05 at its creation, traded for nearly $1,000 in the summer of 2014, settled back to around $300 by 2015, only to skyrocket in value to over $11,000 in 2018. What makes electronic currencies unique is that they are not issued by states, yet individuals use them to buy and sell goods (initially, mostly illegal goods on international markets). Whether these new currencies will play a bigger role in everyday global commerce remains to be seen (see Chapter 10).

devaluation A unilateral move to reduce the value of a currency by changing a fixed or official exchange rate. See also *exchange rate*.

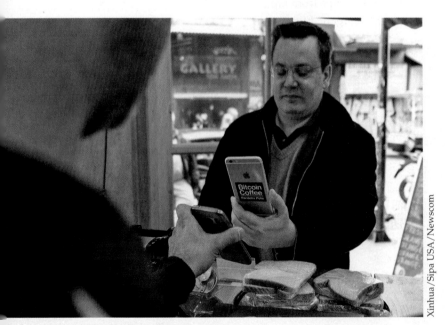

Xinhua/Sipa USA/Newscom

TAP HERE TO PAY Virtual currencies, such as bitcoin, are gaining in popularity although they account for only a small fraction of economic transactions. Virtual currencies are used increasingly in countries with currency issues. Here, a customer pays with bitcoin in an Athens coffee shop, 2018. Bitcoin is growing in popularity in Greece because while the government has placed controls on the circulation of euros, it has not regulated the circulation of virtual currencies.

Policy Perspectives
President of Taiwan, Tsai Ing-wen

PROBLEM   *How do you balance international political pressures with domestic economic concerns?*

Fabian Hamacher/Reuters

BACKGROUND   Imagine that you are the president of Taiwan. Your economy has experienced strong economic growth in the past decade, thanks to an advanced industry that produces manufactured and high-technology goods. Although most states of the world do not formally recognize your country diplomatically, they still engage in extensive amounts of trade with your country. Even though you are a small island country, you rank fifteenth globally in total exports. You have an excellent balance of trade and extensive currency reserves—by one estimate, only five countries have more currency reserves than Taiwan.

Because exports are such an important part of your economy, the level of the exchange rate is very important to the country's overall economic health. A cheap New Taiwan Dollar (NTD) makes your goods cheaper, helping your exports. Your currency has maintained stability against other important currencies like China's Remnimbi and the U.S. dollar, but in 2016, the U.S. government accused your government of intervening too much in currency markets to hold down the value of the NTD. The United States placed Taiwan on a "watch list" and threatened Taiwan with cuts in foreign aid if it manipulated its currency too much.

DOMESTIC CONSIDERATIONS   Economic growth, driven by exports, is important for your country. You were elected to the presidency on a promise of continuing economic growth and lowering political corruption in Taiwan. Youth unemployment is higher than normal in Taiwan. Wages have remained stagnant in the country, leading to complaints about your government's ability to manage the economy.

Taiwan is a relatively wealthy country on a per capita basis (around $50,000 per year). Most citizens are very engaged politically and are quick to hold leaders accountable for the state of the economy. Keeping exports high to promote economic growth is an important promise you made to voters as a presidential candidate.

SCENARIO   Now imagine that, because of slower global economic growth, your exports to China and the United States begin to decline dramatically. This only adds to the stagnation in wages and increases unemployment as there are fewer jobs in the manufacturing sector. One policy that could help reignite your export levels would be to spend some of your reserves in an attempt to lower the value of your currency, making your goods more attractive.

Of course, this policy has some risks. First, there is a chance it would not work. It can be difficult for states to manipulate the value of their currencies. Second, if the United States finds out that you are trying to lower the value of your currency, it could attempt to punish you by cutting aid or asking the IMF to investigate your economic policy.

CHOOSE YOUR POLICY   Do you intervene in international currency markets to depress the value of the NTD? If you do, how can you deal with the threat of punishment from the United States if it notices your policies? If you do not, how do you deal with the growing economic troubles of your country and the threat to your exports? How do you balance the needs of your country against the pressures of other states and the international economy?

9.2.4 Central Banks

Governments control the printing of money. In some states, the politicians or generals who control the government directly control the amounts of money printed. It is not surprising that inflation tends to be high in those states because political problems can often be solved by printing more money. But in most industrialized countries, politicians know they cannot trust themselves with day-to-day decisions about printing money. To enforce self-discipline and enhance public trust in the value of money, these decisions are turned over to a **central bank**.

central bank An institution common in industrialized countries whose major tasks are to maintain the value of the state's currency and to control inflation.

The economists and technical experts who run the central bank seek to maintain the value of the state's currency by limiting the amount of money printed and not allowing high inflation. Politicians appoint the people who run the bank, but generally for long terms that do not coincide with those of the politicians. Thus, central bank managers try to run the bank in the national interest, a step removed from partisan politics. If a state leader orders a military intervention, the generals obey, but if the leader orders an intervention in currency markets, the central bank does not have to comply. In practice, the autonomy of central banks varies. For instance, the prime minister of Thailand fired the head of the country's central bank in a dispute over interest rates in 2001.

In the United States, the central bank is the *Federal Reserve*, or the Fed. The "reserve" is the government's stockpile of hard currency. The Fed can affect the economy by releasing or hoarding its money. Internationally, it does this by intervening in currency markets (as described earlier). Multilateral interventions are usually coordinated by the heads of central banks and treasury (finance) ministries in the leading countries. The long-term, relatively nonpartisan perspective of central bankers makes it easier for states to achieve the collective good of a stable world monetary system.

discount rate The interest rate charged by governments when they lend money to private banks. The discount rate is set by countries' central banks.

Domestically, the Fed exercises its power mainly by setting the **discount rate**—the interest rate the government charges when it loans money to private banks. (Central banks have only private banks, not individuals and corporations, as their customers.) In effect, this rate controls how fast money is injected into the economy. If the Fed sets too low a discount rate, too much money will enter into circulation and inflation will result. If it sets the rate too high, too little money will circulate and consumers and businesses will find it hard to borrow as much or as cheaply from private banks; economic growth will be depressed.

Central bank decisions about the discount rate have important international consequences. If interest rates are higher in one state than in another, foreign capital tends to be attracted to the state with the higher rate. And if economic growth is high in a foreign country, more goods can be exported to it. So states care about other states' monetary policies. The resulting international conflicts can be resolved only politically (such as at G20 meetings), not technically, because each central bank, although removed from domestic politics, still looks out for its own state's interests.

Although central banks control sizable reserves of currency, they are constrained by the limited share of world money they own. Private banks and corporations control most wealth. As economic actors, states do not drive the direction of the world economy; in many ways, they follow it, at least over the long run. As we have seen in the recent global economic crises, however, states still play a key role in the global economy. In the short run, states can adopt massive financial stimulus packages, can rescue private banks and corporations that teeter on bankruptcy, and can prosecute individuals who act illegally to cause economic hardship.

9.2.5 The World Bank and the IMF

Because of the importance of international cooperation for a stable world monetary system and because of the need to overcome collective goods problems, international regimes and institutions have developed around norms of behavior in monetary relations. Just as the UN institutionally supports regimes based on norms of behavior in international security affairs, the same is true in the world monetary regime.

Bretton Woods system A post–World War II arrangement for managing the world economy, established at a meeting in Bretton Woods, New Hampshire, in 1944. Its main institutional components are the World Bank and the International Monetary Fund (IMF).

World Bank Formally the International Bank for Reconstruction and Development (IBRD), an organization that was established in 1944 as a source of loans to help reconstruct the European economies. Later, the main borrowers were third world countries and, in the 1990s, Eastern European ones.

As in security affairs, the main international economic institutions were created near the end of World War II. The **Bretton Woods system** was adopted at a conference of the winning states in 1944 (at Bretton Woods, New Hampshire). It established the *International Bank for Reconstruction and Development (IBRD)*, more commonly called the **World Bank**, as a source of loans to reconstruct the Western European economies after the war and to help states through future financial difficulties. (Later, the main borrowers were developing countries and, in the 1990s, Eastern European ones.) Closely linked with the World Bank is the **International Monetary Fund (IMF)**. The IMF coordinates international currency exchange, the balance of international payments, and national accounts (discussed shortly). The World Bank and the IMF continue to be the pillars of the international financial system. (The roles of the World Bank and the IMF in international development are taken up in Chapter 13.)

Bretton Woods set a regime of stable monetary exchange, based on the U.S. dollar and backed by gold, that lasted from 1944 to 1971. During this period, the dollar had a fixed value equal to $\frac{1}{35}$ of an ounce of gold, and the U.S. government guaranteed to buy dollars for gold at this rate (from a stockpile in Fort Knox, Kentucky). Other states' currencies were exchanged at fixed rates relative to the dollar. The IMF set these fixed exchange rates based on the long-term equilibrium level that could be sustained for each currency (rather than short-term political considerations). The international currency markets operated within a narrow range around the fixed rate. If a country's currency fell more than 1 percent from the fixed rate, the country had to use its hard-currency reserves to buy its own currency back and thus shore up the price. If the price rose more than 1 percent, it had to sell its currency to drive the price down.

The gold standard was abandoned in 1971—an event sometimes called the "collapse of Bretton Woods." The term is not quite appropriate: The institutions survived, and even the monetary regime underwent more of an adjustment than a collapse. The U.S. economy no longer held the overwhelming dominance it had in 1944—mostly because of European and Japanese recovery from World War II, but also because of U.S. overspending on the Vietnam War and the outflow of U.S. dollars to buy oil. As a result, the dollar became seriously overvalued. By 1971, the dollar was no longer worth $\frac{1}{35}$ of an ounce of gold, and the United States had to abandon its fixed exchange rate. President Nixon unilaterally dumped the dollar–gold system and allowed the dollar to float freely. Soon it had fallen to a fraction of its former value relative to gold.

The abandonment of the gold standard was good for the United States and bad for Japan and Europe, where leaders expressed shock at the unilateral U.S. actions. The interdependence of the world capitalist economy, which had produced record economic growth for all the Western countries after World War II, had also created the conditions for new international conflicts.

To replace gold as a world standard, the IMF created a new world currency, the **Special Drawing Right (SDR)**. The SDR has been called "paper gold" because it is created in limited amounts by the IMF, is held as a hard-currency reserve by states' central banks, and can be exchanged for various international currencies. The SDR is today the closest thing to a world currency that exists, but it cannot buy goods—only currencies. And it is owned only by states (central banks), not by individuals or companies. SDRs are linked in value to a basket of several key international currencies (but one that the IMF periodically adjusts to reflect the dollar's strength or weakness). When one currency rises a bit and another falls, the SDR does not change value much; but if all currencies rise (worldwide inflation), the SDR rises with them.

Since the early 1970s, the managed float system has governed the major national currencies. Transition from the dollar–gold regime to the managed float regime was difficult. States had to bargain politically over the targets for currency exchange rates in the meetings known as the Group of Six (G6) summits. The G6 was later expanded to the G8 with the addition of Canada (in 1976) and Russia (in 1997) (Russia's membership was suspended in 2014, after its annexation of Crimea). In 2009, it was announced that the G20, including far more developed and developing countries, would begin to replace the G8 in undertaking major financial deliberations.

The technical mechanisms of the IMF are based on each member state's depositing financial reserves with the IMF. Upon joining the IMF, a state is assigned a *quota* for such deposits, partly of hard currency and partly of the state's own currency (this quota is not related to the concept of trade quotas, which are import restrictions). The quota is based

International Monetary Fund (IMF) An intergovernmental organization (IGO) that coordinates international currency exchange, the balance of international payments, and national accounts. Along with the World Bank, it is a pillar of the international financial system. See also *IMF conditionality*.

Special Drawing Right (SDR) A world currency created by the International Monetary Fund (IMF) to replace gold as a world standard. Valued by a "basket" of national currencies, the SDR has been called "paper gold."

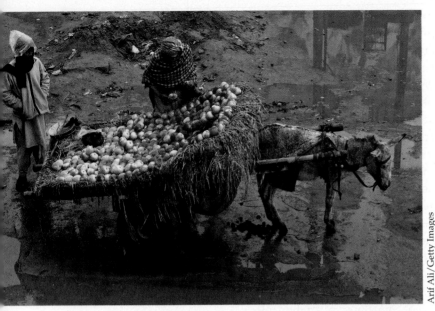

Arif Ali/Getty Images

SEEDS OF DEVELOPMENT The World Bank works to stabilize and develop economies in poor and middle-income countries. In Pakistan, the Bank runs programs to increase agricultural productivity and improve nutrition. This vendor in Lahore sells apples from his donkey cart, 2012.

on the size and strength of a state's economy. A state can then borrow against its quota (even exceeding it somewhat) to stabilize its economy in difficult times and repay the IMF in subsequent years. In 2009, world leaders pledged to pay an additional $1 trillion to the IMF so it could help developing countries cope with the global financial crisis.

Unlike the WTO or UN General Assembly, the IMF and the World Bank use a *weighted voting* system—each state has a vote equal to its quota. Thus the advanced economies control the IMF, although nearly all the world's states are members. The United States has the single largest vote (17 percent), and Washington, DC, is headquarters for both the IMF and the World Bank. In 2008, the IMF adjusted the voting formula, increasing modestly the quota and voting power of China (from about 3 to 3.7 percent of the total) and other developing countries.

Since 1944, the IMF and the World Bank have tried to accomplish three major missions. First they sought to provide stability and access to capital for states ravaged by World War II, especially Japan and the states of Western Europe. This mission was a great success, leading to growth and prosperity in those states. Second, especially in the 1970s and 1980s but still continuing today, the World Bank and the IMF have tried to promote economic development. That mission has been far less successful—as seen in the lingering poverty in much of the global South (see Chapter 12). The third mission, in the 1990s, was the integration of Eastern Europe and Russia into the world capitalist economy. This effort posted a mixed record but has had general success.

9.3 State Financial Positions

Compare and contrast the financial positions of the United States and Russia in regard to the potential for future economic growth.

As currency rates change and state economies grow, the overall positions of states relative to each other shift.

9.3.1 National Accounts

balance of payments A summary of all the flows of money into and out of a country. It includes three types of international transactions: the current account (including the merchandise trade balance), flows of capital, and changes in reserves.

The IMF maintains a system of *national accounts* statistics to keep track of the overall monetary position of each state. A state's **balance of payments** is like the financial statement of a company: It summarizes all the flows of money into and out of the country. The system itself is technical and not political in nature. Essentially, three types of international transactions go into the balance of payments: the current account, flows of capital, and changes in reserves.

The *current account* is basically the balance of trade discussed in Chapter 8. Money flows out of a state to pay for imports and flows into the state to pay for exports. The goods imported or exported include both merchandise and services. For instance, money spent by a British tourist in Florida is equivalent to money spent by a British consumer buying Florida oranges in a London market; in both cases money flows into the U.S. current account. The current account includes two other items. *Government transactions* are military and foreign aid grants, as well as salaries and pensions paid to government employees abroad. *Remittances* are funds sent home by companies or individuals outside a country (see Chapter 12). For example, a Honda subsidiary in America may send profits back to Honda in Japan. Or a British citizen working in New York may send money to her parents in London.

The second category in the accounts, *capital flows*, is composed of foreign investments in, and by, a country. Capital flows are measured in *net* terms—the total investments and loans foreigners make *in* a country minus the investments and loans that country's companies, citizens, and government invest in *other* countries. Most of such investment is private, although some is by (or in) government agencies and state-owned industries. Capital flows are divided into *foreign direct investment* (or *direct foreign investment*)—such as owning a factory, company, or real estate in a foreign country—and indirect *portfolio investment*, such as buying stocks and bonds or making loans to a foreign company. These various kinds of capital flows have somewhat different political consequences (see the International Debt and Foreign Direct Investment sections later in this chapter), but they are basically equivalent in the overall national accounts picture.

The third category, *changes in foreign exchange reserves*, makes the national accounts balance. Any difference between the inflows and outflows of money (in the current account and capital flows combined) is made up by an equal but opposite change in reserves. These changes in reserves consist of the state's purchases and sales of SDRs, gold, and hard currencies other than its own, and changes in its deposits with the IMF. If a state has more money flowing out than in, it gets that money from its reserves. If it has more money flowing in than out, it puts that money in its reserves. Thus, national accounts always balance in the end. At least, they almost balance; there is a residual category—errors and omissions—because even the most efficient and honest government (many governments are neither) cannot keep track of every bit of money crossing its borders.

9.3.2 International Debt

In one sense, an economy is constantly in motion as money moves through the processes of production, trade, and consumption. But economies also contain *standing wealth*. The hard-currency reserves owned by governments are one form of standing wealth, but not the most important. Most standing wealth is in the form of homes and cars, farms and factories, ports and railroads. In particular, *capital* goods (such as factories) are products that can be used as inputs for further production. Nothing lasts forever, but standing wealth lasts for enough years to be treated differently from goods that are quickly consumed. The main difference is that capital can be used to create more wealth: Factories produce goods, railroads support commerce, and so forth. Standing wealth creates new wealth, so the economy tends to grow over time. As it grows, more standing wealth is created. In a capitalist economy, money makes more money.

Interest rates reflect this inherent growth dynamic. *Real interest rates* are the rates for borrowing money above and beyond the rate of inflation (for instance, if money is loaned at an annual interest rate of 8 percent but inflation is 3 percent, the real interest rate is 5 percent). Businesses and households borrow money because they think they can use it to create new wealth faster than the rate of interest on the loan.

If a state's economy is healthy, it can borrow money from foreign governments, banks, or companies and create enough new wealth to repay the debts a few years later. But states, like businesses, sometimes operate at a loss; then their debts mount up. In a vicious circle, more and more of the income they generate goes to pay interest, and more money must be borrowed to keep the state in operation. If its fortunes reverse, a state or business can create wealth again and over time pay back the principal on its debts to climb out of the hole. If not, it will have to begin selling off part of its standing wealth (buildings, airplanes, factories, and the like). The *net worth* of the state or business (all its assets minus all its liabilities) will decrease.

austerity measures Government policies that severely cut government spending or raise taxes (or both). The policies are adopted to reduce government budget deficits, usually to pay off debt.

Keynesian economics The principles articulated by British economist John Maynard Keynes, used successfully in the Great Depression of the 1930s, including the view that governments should sometimes use deficit spending to stimulate economic growth.

fiscal policy A government's decisions about spending and taxation, and one of the two major tools of macroeconomic policy making (the other being monetary policy).

monetary policy A government's decisions about printing and circulating money, and one of the two major tools of macroeconomic policy making (the other being fiscal policy).

Failure to repay debts makes it hard to borrow in the future, a huge impediment to economic growth. When debts become unpayable, the lenders (banks and governments) have to write them off the books or settle them at a fraction of their official value. In 2001, when Argentina collapsed under more than $100 billion of debt accumulated over the prior decade, creditors had to accept less than one-third of their money in a 2005 restructuring deal. In 2010–2012, financial markets repeatedly slumped in reaction to fears of a Greek default on large debts, and possible contagion to larger economies—Spain, Portugal, Ireland, and perhaps Italy. In 2012, several bailouts stabilized the crisis but not until **austerity measures**, government policies that cut government spending or raise taxes to pay debts, had driven the entire eurozone into a recession.

In 2015, fed up with tough austerity measures, Greeks elected a new government that promised to renegotiate Greek debt and lift austerity measures. The new Greek government had difficulty convincing its creditors that it would not default if these tough reforms were brought to an end. By mid-2015, the new Greek government accepted more loans to avoid default and accepted tough austerity measures, and the government called for new elections. Although the government did win reelection, budget cuts in Greece remained unpopular. By early 2018, Greece had experienced four straight quarters of economic growth, but unemployment remained very high (over 20 percent).

Why do states go into debt? One major reason is a trade deficit. In the balance of payments, a trade deficit must somehow be made up. It is common to borrow money to pay for a trade deficit. A second reason is the income and consumption pattern among households and businesses. If people and firms spend more than they take in, they must borrow to pay their bills. The credit card they use may be from a local bank, but that bank may be getting the money it lends to them from foreign lenders.

A third reason for national debt is government spending relative to taxation. Under the principles of **Keynesian economics** (named for late economist John Maynard Keynes), governments sometimes spend more on programs than they take in from tax revenue—*deficit spending*—to stimulate economic growth. Many G8 countries, especially the United States, adopted this strategy during the last financial crisis. If this strategy works, increased economic growth eventually generates higher tax revenues to make up the deficit. If it does not, a state finds itself with a poor economy in even deeper debt.

Government decisions about spending and taxation are called **fiscal policy**; decisions about printing and circulating money are called **monetary policy**. These are the two main tools available for governments to manage an economy. There is no free lunch: High taxation chokes off economic growth, printing excess money causes inflation, and borrowing to cover a deficit places a mortgage on the state's standing wealth. Thus, for all the complexities of governmental economic policies and international economic transactions, a state's wealth and power ultimately depend more than anything on the underlying health of its economy—the education and training of its labor force, the amount and modernity of its capital goods, the morale of its population, and the skill of its managers. In the long run, international debt reflects these underlying realities.

DEBT HURTS Failure to make payments on international debt, called a default, is a very serious action because it can cut off a country's access to future investment and loans. Nonetheless, several states have defaulted on debts rather than inflict painful budget cuts that would hurt the population. In 2011–2012, Greece narrowly averted defaulting on its huge debts, accepting EU bailouts. Today, Greece still struggles with debt and has cut many social programs to save money in order to repay that debt. Here, Greek protesters face off with police over new austerity measures passed by the Greek government, 2018.

Kostas Pikoulas/CrowdSpark/Newscom

Shifts in financial fortune among the great powers often accompany changing power relations. Consider how the past two decades have changed the financial positions of the United States, of Russia and Eastern Europe, and of Asia. (The position of Europe, including the new European currency, is discussed in Chapter 10.)

9.3.3 The Position of the United States

The United States is an extraordinarily wealthy and powerful state. Its most *unique* strengths may be in the area of international security—as the world's only super-power—but its economic strengths are also striking. It is not only the world's largest economy but also the most technologically advanced one in growth sectors such as computers, telecommunications, aviation and aerospace, and biotechnology. The U.S. position in scientific research and higher education is unparalleled in the world.

The U.S. position in the international economy, however, has shifted over the decades. U.S. hegemony peaked after World War II, then it gradually eroded as competitors gained relative ground (especially in Western Europe and Asia). In the early 1950s, the U.S. economy (gross domestic product [GDP]) was about twice the size of the next six advanced industrial states *combined*. By the 1980s, its relative share of world GDP had dropped almost by half. In 1950, the United States held 50 percent of the world's financial reserves; by 1980, it held less than 10 percent. This long-term decline after the extraordinary post–1945 U.S. hegemony was a natural and probably unavoidable one. The shifting U.S. financial position since the 1980s is illustrated in Figure 9.1. In the early 1980s, the trade deficit (exports minus imports) grew from near zero to $200 billion in just a few years. The trade deficit shrank back, but then grew to more than $700 billion a year by 2007. After shrinking again during the 2008–2009 recession, the trade deficit began to grow again in 2010 and ran above $500 billion in 2017. The budget deficit meanwhile jumped to $300 billion per year in the early 1980s, then closed in the 1990s and briefly became a large surplus, only to exceed $1 trillion a year in 2008–2012 as a result of war spending, tax cuts, and a Keynesian effort to

Figure 9.1 U.S. Financial Position, 1960–2017

For decades the United States has imported more than it has exported (the current account balance or trade deficit), and its government has spent more than its income (the budget deficit). The budget deficit results in a large national debt.

Source: Congressional Budget Office.

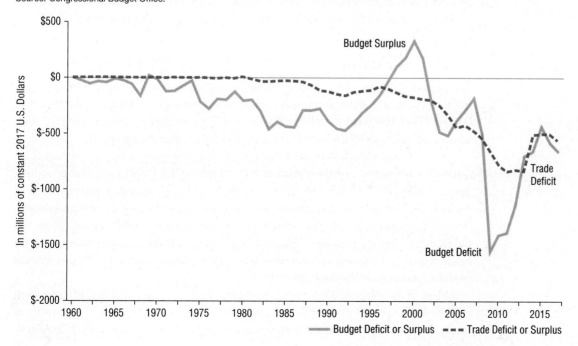

stimulate economic growth during the economic recession. These trends have caused alarm regarding U.S. international economic leadership.

The U.S. economy began the twenty-first century hitting a number of rough patches, after a decade of relative prosperity in the 1990s. The bursting of an Internet investment bubble was followed by a worldwide recession in 2001 and then the economic disruptions that followed the September 2001 terrorist attacks. Tax cuts and war spending primed growth in 2002–2006, but at the cost of rising debt. In 2008, another recession arrived, the so-called Great Recession, the worst downturn since the Great Depression of the 1930s (although not nearly that bad). Growth resumed in 2009 but remained sluggish, with persistently high unemployment, ever-rising debt, and contentious government decision making. By 2013, stock markets had fully recovered from the 2008 crash, yet unemployment remained persistent and did not return to pre-recession levels until 2017.

The combination of many of these economic factors—stubborn unemployment rates, high trade deficits, and rising national debt—led to a resurgence of frustration with many aspects of U.S. foreign policy in 2016, no doubt contributing to the election of Donald Trump as president. A vocal critic of trade agreements, Trump openly blamed unemployment and the trade deficit on free trade agreements signed by previous American presidents. Once elected, President Trump's actions continued this theme: withdrawing the United States from a major Asian trade agreement, placing tariffs on goods such as aluminum and steel, and demanding that other states renegotiate existing trade agreements. These actions were met with significant controversy, even from those within Trump's own party who feared tariffs would lead to worse unemployment and economic stagnation.

national debt The amount a government owes in debt as a result of deficit spending.

In addition, the accumulated debt from decades of deficit spending remains. The U.S. government's **national debt** grew from about $1 trillion in 1980 to $3 trillion in 1990, $5 trillion in 2000, and $20 trillion in 2018. The interest payments are equivalent to what would otherwise be a healthy rate of economic growth. The United States was once the world's leading lender state; now it is the world's leading debtor state.

These U.S. financial trends have profound implications for the entire world political economy. They first undermined (in the 1980s), then reconstructed (in the 1990s), and then undermined again (since 2000) the leading U.S. role in stabilizing international trade and monetary relations, in ensuring the provision of collective goods, and in providing capital for the economic development of other world regions. In a more decentralized, more privatized world economy with an uncertain U.S. role, collective goods problems would be harder to solve and free trade harder to achieve.

9.3.4 The Position of Russia and Eastern Europe

The United States provided limited capital (investments, loans, and grants) to help get the Russian and Eastern European region on its feet again after the Cold War. The United States has not repeated in Russia and Eastern Europe the aid program that stimulated new growth in Western Europe and Japan after World War II.

Instead, states in this region faced daunting challenges as they converted from centrally planned to capitalist economies and joined the world capitalist economy. These challenges included integrating into the world trading system (membership in the WTO, bilateral trade agreements, and so forth) and attracting foreign investment. Among the most difficult tasks were the attempts of states in this region to join the international monetary system. Effectively dealing with these issues matters greatly because having a stable and convertible currency is a key element in attracting foreign business and expanding international trade.

Most of the states of the former Soviet bloc became members of the IMF and were assigned quotas. But the IMF and the World Bank would not make loans available freely to these states until their governments took strong action to curb inflation,

Table 9.2 Economic Collapse in Russia and Eastern Europe

Country	Cumulative (10-Year) Change in GDP, 1990–1999
Russia/CIS	–50%
Former Yugoslavia	–35%
Estonia, Latvia, and Lithuania	–29%
Bulgaria	–29%
Romania	–28%
Albania	–12%
Czech Republic	–11%
Slovakia	–1%
Hungary	–1%
Poland	+21%

Source: Based upon United Nations, *World Economic and Social Survey 1999.* United Nations, 1999, p. 263.

balance government budgets, and ensure economic stability. Such stability would have been easier to achieve with the foreign loans, however, creating a chicken-and-egg problem.

All the economies of the region experienced a deep depression (shrinking GDP) in the years following the end of the Cold War. The economies of the former Soviet Union shrank by half over seven years before climbing again (see Table 9.2). In general, the Eastern European countries have turned around their economies more effectively than have the former Soviet republics. Among the latter, Russia was better off than some others; it had inherited much of the Soviet Union's economic infrastructure and natural resources, especially oil, and was large enough to gain the attention of the West. But internal power struggles created political instability in Russia, discouraging foreign investment. Inflation reached 1,500 percent in 1992.

Organized crime emerged as a major problem in the 1990s. So-called plutocrats seized formerly state-owned companies and drained their wealth into private bank accounts. The chaos of transition also provided fertile ground for corruption among government officials. In 2004, President Vladimir Putin shut down Russia's largest oil company (Yukos) because of nonpayment of a $10 billion tax bill, only to have its assets purchased by a state-owned business. (Yukos's owner was an opponent of Putin.) The state has consolidated its control of major companies and the media again, using its powers to either put the plutocrats under its control or push them aside.

After a financial crisis in 1998, Russia registered strong economic growth for a decade and reduced runaway inflation to less than 10 percent a year. The 2008–2009 global recession hit the economy quite hard as the price of oil plummeted. While Russians were hopeful that the return of Vladimir Putin to the presidency in 2012 would provide greater economic stability, the continuing decline of oil prices and slowing investment kept growth rates modest. Russia's conflict with Ukraine in 2014 brought more economic instability, and Russia's growth slowed to around 1 percent. Perceptions of increasing political repression in Russia further harmed investment. Russia's economic future will likely be dictated by the price of oil and how investors perceive Russia's political stability.

9.3.5 The Position of Asia

Following decades of robust growth since the devastation of World War II, Japan by the 1980s seemed to be emerging as a possible rival to the United States as the world's leading industrial power. Japanese auto manufacturers gained ground on U.S. rivals when smaller cars became popular after the oil-price shocks of the 1970s. In electronics and other fields, Japanese products began to dominate world markets, and Japanese

Eugene Hoshiko/Associated Press

BODY CHECK East Asia's economies have grown robustly in the decade since the 1997 financial crisis, but many of the causes of instability remain. Poor quality control in China's fast-growing export sector has sent tainted foods, drugs, and toys to Western markets. Chinese authorities opened this toy-testing lab in response, 2007.

capital became a major economic force in nearby developing economies (such as China and Thailand) and even in the United States, where Japanese creditors financed much of the growing U.S. national debt.

These successes, however, masked serious problems. The economic growth of the 1980s drove prices of stocks and real estate to unrealistic levels based on speculation rather than inherent value. When these collapsed at the end of the 1980s, many banks were left with bad loans backed by deflated stocks and real estate. These losses were covered up, and the underlying problems—lax banking regulation, political cronyism, and outright corruption—persisted through the 1990s.

Despite the example of Japan's financial system, these mistakes were repeated almost exactly in the 1990s by other countries of East and Southeast Asia. Real estate and stocks became overvalued as rapid economic growth led to speculation and ever-rising expectations. Banks made massive bad loans based on the overvalued assets and got away with it because of political corruption and cronyism. In 1997, these economies suffered a serious financial crisis, which jumped across international borders and sent shock waves around the globe that reverberated for two years. The *1997 Asian financial crisis* began when currency speculators began selling off the currencies of Southeast Asian countries. Thailand, the Philippines, Malaysia, and Indonesia were forced to let their currencies be devalued. The currency problems of Asian countries led to stock market crashes in several of them. Other so-called *emerging markets* around the world—notably Brazil—suffered as investors feared the problems in Asia were present in other regions as well.

The Philippines addressed the problem in the manner that international agencies and foreign investors preferred. After losing $1 billion by unsuccessfully defending its currency's value, the Philippines let its currency float and then asked the IMF for a $1 billion stabilization loan, which the IMF approved in a week. In return for the IMF loan, the Filipino government agreed to keep interest rates high and budget deficits low (to reduce inflation), to pass a tax reform law, and to tighten control of banks that had made bad real estate loans. These kinds of tough measures create political problems, especially when banks are politically connected or when governments are corrupt. The Philippines, by addressing such problems, won international approval.

Other Asian countries did not act decisively and suffered greater economic setbacks. The currency speculators attacked Indonesia, which had to let its currency fall, raise interest rates, and let its stock market drop. Within months, Indonesia too sought tens of billions of dollars in IMF loans, with the usual conditions attached. But Indonesia resisted implementing the promised reforms, and its economy continued to slide (as did its political stability) in 1998. Riots and student protests eventually forced President Suharto to resign after 30 years of dictatorship in Indonesia. Overall, in Thailand, Malaysia, and Indonesia, stock markets lost about half their value and currencies about a quarter of their value.

When South Korea caught this "Asian flu" in 1997, its stock markets collapsed and its banks were saddled with $50 billion in bad loans based on cronyism. The IMF stepped in with a $60 billion international bailout—the largest ever—and Koreans elected a new reformist president. Thus, in South Korea, as in Thailand and Indonesia, the financial crisis brought about reform as well as pain.

China escaped harm from the 1997 crisis for several reasons: Its economic growth had been less speculative (although rapid), its currency was not freely convertible, it held massive reserves of hard currency, and its government had shown the discipline necessary to bring inflation under control. The government reduced inflation from 20 percent to less than 4 percent in 1995–1997, and the engineer of this tight-money policy, Zhu Rongji, became the Chinese prime minister in 1998. (Successful inflation fighters also became presidents of Brazil and Argentina in the 1990s.)

In theory, the instant free flow of capital around the world—a result of global communications technologies—should stabilize economies. Investors can shift money quickly, and thus incrementally, as conditions indicate the shifting strengths and weaknesses of different currencies and economies. Instead of waiting for governments to devalue or revalue currencies when problems are far along, markets can gradually adjust values day by day. In practice, however, the global liquidity of capital has also shown a destabilizing tendency, as small events can be amplified and reverberate in distant locations. Thus, the problems of Thailand became an Asian crisis, and then an emerging-markets crisis, as liquid capital fled for cover at the speed of light. These events foreshadowed the financial crisis in 2008 when events in one country and sector again quickly spread worldwide.

Governments face a dilemma because politically desirable policies—from stimulating growth and keeping taxes low to supporting banks and businesses owned by friends and relatives—tend to undermine currency stability. If allowed to continue, such policies may lead to an economic collapse and the loss of foreign investment, but tough policies to maintain currency stability may cause a government to lose power.

In all the regions just discussed—the United States, Russia and Eastern Europe, and Asia—the role of private businesses is expanding relative to that of the state. Throughout the remainder of the world, private business plays a role in the economy that exceeds that of the state. The remainder of this chapter considers the international political issues related to the operation of private businesses across state borders.

9.4 Multinational Business

Identify two risks to firms that engage in foreign direct investment and two risks to countries that host foreign direct investment.

Although states are the main rule makers for currency exchange and other international economic transactions, those transactions are carried out mainly by private firms and individuals, not governments. Most important among these private actors are multinational corporations.

9.4.1 Multinational Corporations

Multinational corporations (MNCs) are companies based in one state with affiliated branches or subsidiaries operating in other states. There is no exact definition, but the clearest case of an MNC is a large corporation that operates on a worldwide basis in many countries simultaneously, with fixed facilities and employees in each. There is also no exact count of the total number of MNCs, but most estimates are in the tens of thousands worldwide.

Most important are *industrial corporations*, which make goods in factories in various countries and sell them to businesses and consumers in various countries. The automobile, oil, and electronics industries have the largest MNCs. Almost all of the largest MNCs are based in G8 states.

multinational corporation (MNC) A company based in one state with affiliated branches or subsidiaries operating in other states. See also *home country* and *host country*.

Wong Maye-E / AP Images

DOING BUSINESS WORLDWIDE Multinational corporations (MNCs) play important roles in international relations and are powerful actors with considerable resources in negotiating with governments. Here, Airbus, a division of a European MNC, shows off its new super-jumbo jet at the Singapore Airshow, 2008.

Financial corporations (the most important being banks) also operate multinationally—although often with more restrictions than industrial MNCs. Among the largest commercial banks worldwide, the United States does not hold a leading position—reflecting the traditional U.S. antitrust policy that limits banks' geographic expansion. The growing international integration of financial markets was spectacularly illustrated in 1995, when a single 28-year-old trader in Singapore lost $1 billion speculating on Japanese stock and bond markets and bankrupted his employer, a 200-year-old British investment bank.

Some MNCs sell *services*. The McDonald's fast-food chain and American Telephone and Telegraph (AT&T) are good examples. So are the international airlines, which sell tickets in dozens of states (and currencies) for travel all over the world. More down-to-earth service businesses such as retail grocery stores can also become MNCs. The United States predominates in service MNCs as it does in industrial ones.

The role of MNCs in international political relations is complex and in some dispute. Some scholars see MNCs as nearly being agents of their home national governments. This view resonates with mercantilism, in which economic activity ultimately serves political authorities; thus MNCs have clear national identities and act as members of their national society under state authority. A variant of this theme (from a more revolutionary worldview) considers national governments as being agents of their MNCs; state interventions (economic and military) serve private, monied interests.

Others see MNCs as citizens of the world beholden to no government. The head of Dow Chemical once said that he dreamed of buying an island beyond any state's territory and putting Dow's world headquarters there. In such a view, MNCs act globally in the interests of their (international) stockholders and owe loyalty to no state. In any case, MNCs are motivated by the need to maximize profits. Only in the case of state-owned MNCs—an important exception but a small minority of the total companies worldwide—do MNC actions reflect state interests. Even then, managers of state-owned MNCs have won greater autonomy to pursue profit in recent years (as part of the economic reforms instituted in many countries), and in many cases state-owned enterprises are being sold off (privatized).

As independent actors in the international arena, MNCs are increasingly powerful. Dozens of industrial MNCs have annual sales of tens of billions of dollars each (hundreds of billions of dollars for the top corporations). Only 25 states had more economic activity per year (GDP) in 2017 than did the largest MNC, Walmart, at nearly $500 billion. However, the largest state (the United States) has government revenues above $3 *trillion*—six times that of Walmart. Thus, the power of MNCs does not rival that of the largest states but exceeds that of many poorer states; this affects MNC operations in the global South.

Giant MNCs contribute to global interdependence. They are so deeply entwined in so many states that they have a profound interest in the stable operation of the international system—in security affairs as well as in trade and monetary relations. MNCs prosper in a stable international atmosphere that permits freedom of trade, of movement, and of capital flows (investments)—all governed by market forces with minimal government interference. Thus MNCs are, overall, a strong force for liberalism in the world economy, despite the fact that particular MNCs in particular industries push for certain mercantilist policies to protect their own interests.

Most MNCs have a world management system based on *subsidiaries* in each state in which they operate. The operations within a given state are subject to the legal authority of that state's government. But the parent MNC in the home country owns the foreign subsidiaries (in whole or in substantial part). Thus, the parent MNC hires and fires the top managers of its foreign subsidiaries. The business infrastructure is a key aspect of *transnational relations*—linkages among people and groups across national borders.

In addition to the direct connections among members of a single MNC, the operations of MNCs support a global business infrastructure connecting a transnational community of businesspeople. A U.S. manager arriving in Seoul, South Korea, for instance, does not find a bewildering scene of unfamiliar languages, locations, and customs. Rather, he or she moves through a familiar sequence of airport lounges, telephone calls and faxes, international hotels, business conference rooms, and CNN broadcasts—most likely hearing English spoken in all.

9.4.2 Foreign Direct Investment

MNCs do not just operate in foreign countries, they also own capital there—buildings, factories, cars, and so forth. For instance, U.S. and German MNCs own some of the capital located in Japan, and Japanese MNCs own capital located in the United States and Germany. *Investment* means exchanging money for ownership of capital (for the purpose of producing a stream of income that will, over time, more than compensate for the money invested). Investments in foreign countries are among the most important, and politically sensitive, activities of MNCs. Figure 9.2 illustrates the growth of foreign direct investment. Although there is a strong trend toward more foreign direct investment, these flows rise and fall with the global economy.

Unlike portfolio investment (on paper), **foreign direct investment** (FDI) involves tangible goods such as factories and office buildings (including ownership of a sizable fraction of a company's total stock, as opposed to a portfolio with little bits of many companies). Paper can be traded on a global market relatively freely, but direct investments cannot be freely moved from one state to another when conditions change.

foreign direct investment The acquisition by residents of one country of control over a new or existing business in another country. Also called *direct foreign investment*.

Figure 9.2 Foreign Direct Investment, World Totals, 1990–2016

Source: UNCTAD data.

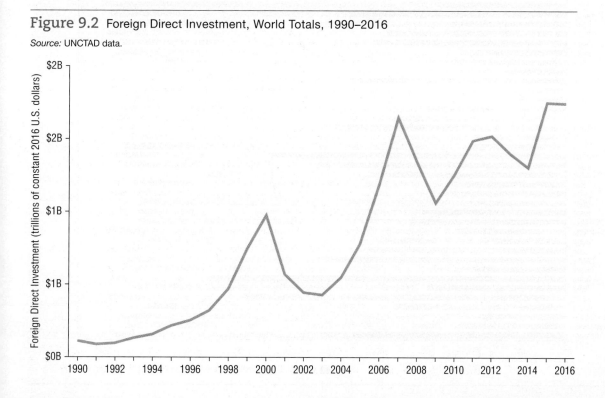

Direct investment is long term, and it is more visible than portfolio investment. Investments in the manufacturing sector usually entail the greatest investment in fixed facilities and in training workers and managers. Investments in the service sector tend to be less expensive and easier to walk away from if conditions change.

Public Opinion and International Relations
Foreign Investment

Foreign direct investment (FDI) can be controversial in host states where large MNCs place their investments. Depending on how a particular company interacts with local conditions and residents, such investments can turn out to be popular or unpopular, as we have discussed in this section. In 2014, a survey of residents of 43 countries asked about their feelings toward foreign businesses and whether ties with those businesses were helpful.

The results of the poll are presented in Figure 9.3. The vast majority of respondents in each country describe their impressions of foreign business ties as somewhat or very good. In fact, combining these two responses shows a clear majority in every country surveyed feels foreign business ties are helpful to their country in some way. In certain countries, larger segments of respondents are skeptical of foreign business ties, rating them as very or somewhat bad. Interestingly, these countries are quite varied—ranging from Italy to Egypt to Turkey to Thailand.

What might explain this high level of support across countries for foreign businesses? One possibility is that individuals around the world have come to internalize globalization: All countries depend somewhat on goods and services from other countries. Many have come to view the presence of those foreign companies as a net positive for local hosts, especially when the business ties in question could be selling popular brands like Apple or Samsung or Gap. A related possibility is that respondents know that these investments often produce jobs or economic growth.

Given how controversial FDI is considered, should we have reason to doubt these positive numbers? Without more data, it is difficult to know what "foreign business ties" mean to a typical respondent. It could mean jobs and growth. It could mean cultural imperialism. It could simply mean the ability to buy a foreign-made product locally. What we can say from these data is that populations of many countries in the world do not view foreign economic ties in an inherently skeptical manner.

Figure 9.3 Public Opinion About Foreign Businesses in 43 Countries

Source: Pew Research Center.

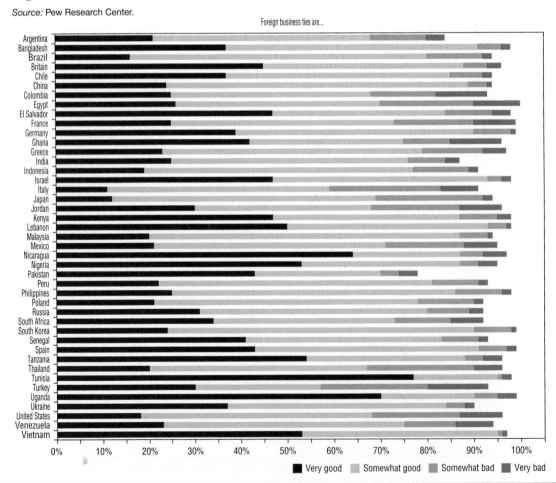

Mercantilists tend to view foreign investments in their own country suspiciously. In developing countries, foreign direct investment (FDI) often evokes concerns about a loss of sovereignty because governments may be less powerful (and possibly less wealthy) than the MNCs that invest in their country. These fears also reflect the historical fact that most foreign investment in the global South once came from colonizers. Furthermore, although such investments create jobs, they also bring dislocations of traditional ways of life and cultures (see the Public Opinion and International Relations box).

But because many poor and transitional states also desperately need capital from any source to stimulate economic growth, they welcome and encourage FDI despite the fears of economic nationalists (North-South investment is discussed further in the next section). Most foreign direct investment (like most portfolio investment) is not in the global South, however, but in industrialized countries.

Economic nationalists in industrialized countries also worry about losing power and sovereignty from foreign investment. In Canada, for instance, mercantilists are alarmed that U.S. firms own more than half of Canada's manufacturing industry and more than two-thirds of Canada's oil and gas industry. Canada is much smaller than the United States, yet it depends heavily on U.S. trade. In this asymmetrical situation, some Canadians worry that they are being turned into an annex of the United States— economically, culturally, and ultimately politically—losing their own national culture and control of their economy.

Meanwhile, U.S. economic nationalists have similar concerns over FDI in the United States. Partly this reflects alarm over the accumulation of U.S. debts. Mercantilists see a loss of power when foreign investors buy up companies and real estate in a debtor country. Such concerns seem stronger when a foreign MNC buys an existing company or building than when it builds a new factory or other facility. For example, in 2005, an outcry in the United States forced a Chinese oil company to withdraw its bid to buy the U.S. company Unocal, which ended up selling itself for a lower price to a U.S. company. (Chinese business and government leaders resented what they saw as a U.S. double standard.) But when Honda builds a new car factory in Ohio, adding jobs and facilities to the U.S. economy, Americans perceive no such loss.

Liberalism does not condone such arguments. Liberal economists emphasize that global efficiency and the increased generation of wealth result from the ability of MNCs to invest freely across international borders. Investment decisions should be made solely on economic grounds, not nationalistic ones. In the view of liberal economists, foreign investments in the United States help, rather than hurt, the U.S. economy. Many of the benefits of a profitable Japanese factory in the United States accrue to U.S. workers at the plant and U.S. consumers of its products, even if some profits go back to Japan (and even those profits may be reinvested in the United States). Because U.S. MNCs have more than $6 trillion of FDI outside the United States, the picture is by no means one-sided.

9.4.3 Host and Home Government Relations

A state in which a foreign MNC operates is called the **host country**; the state in which the MNC has its headquarters is called its **home country**. MNC operations create a variety of problems and opportunities for both the host and home countries' governments. Conflicts between the host government and the MNC may spill over to become an interstate conflict between the host government and home government. For example, if a host government takes an MNC's property without compensation or arrests its executives, the home government may step in to help the MNC.

Because host governments can regulate activities on their own territories, an MNC cannot operate in a state against the wishes of its government. Conversely, because MNCs have many states to choose from, a host government cannot generally force an MNC to do business in the country against the MNC's wishes. At least in

host country A state in which a foreign multinational corporation (MNC) operates. See also *home country*.

home country The state in which a multinational corporation (MNC) has its headquarters. See also *host country*.

theory, MNCs operate in host countries only when it is in the interests of both the MNC and the host government. Common interests result from the creation of wealth in the host country by the MNC. Both the MNC and the host government benefit—the MNC from profits, the government directly by taxation and indirectly through economic growth (generating future taxes and political support).

However, conflicts also arise in the relationship. One obvious conflict concerns the distribution of new wealth between the MNC and the host government. This distribution depends on the rate at which MNC activities or profits are taxed, as well as on the ground rules for MNC operations. Before an MNC invests or opens a subsidiary in a host country, it sits down with the government to negotiate these issues. Threats of violent leverage are largely irrelevant. Rather, the government's main leverage is to promise a favorable climate for doing business and making money; the MNC's main leverage is to threaten to take its capital elsewhere.

Governments can offer a variety of incentives to MNCs to invest. Special terms of taxation and of regulation are common. In cases of resource extraction, negotiations may revolve around the rates the government will charge to lease land and mineral rights to the MNC. National and local governments may offer to provide business infrastructure—such as roads, airports, or phone lines—at the government's expense. (An MNC could also offer to build such infrastructure if allowed to operate on favorable terms in the country.) Over time, certain locations may develop a strong business infrastructure and gain a comparative advantage in luring MNCs to locate there.

In addition to these relatively straightforward questions of distribution, MNC relations with host governments contain several other sources of possible conflict. One is the potential for governments to break their agreements with MNCs and change the terms of taxes, regulations, or other conditions. The extreme case is nationalization, in which a host government takes ownership of MNC facilities and assets in the host country (with or without compensation). In recent years, Russia, Venezuela, Bolivia, and Ecuador have all taken significant state ownership in what had been foreign assets in those countries' oil and gas sectors. Once an MNC has invested in fixed facilities, it loses much of its leverage over the government because it cannot move to another country without incurring huge expenses. However, governments hesitate to break their word with MNCs because then other MNCs may not invest there in the future. In fact, for this reason, FDI in Bolivia dropped by 90 percent from 1999 to 2005. Nationalization of foreign assets is rare now.

Another source of conflict is the trade policies of the host government. Government restrictions on trade seldom help foreign MNCs; more often they help the host country's own industries—which frequently compete directly with foreign MNCs. Ironically, although they favor global free trade, MNCs may funnel direct investment to states that restrict imports because MNCs can avoid the import restrictions by producing goods in the host country (rather than exporting from the home country). Trade restrictions are thus another form of leverage that states have in luring foreign direct investment.

Trade regulations often seek to create as many jobs and as much taxable income as possible within the host country. If Toyota assembles cars at a factory in the United States (perhaps to

IT'S A JOB Foreign direct investment is often sought by host governments because it stimulates employment and economic growth, though at wages that home countries would not tolerate. Here, women assemble Santa Claus in eastern China. Note that along with investment, a host country imports certain cultural trappings of the MNC's activity—such as the importance of Santa Claus to a Christian holiday in a predominantly non-Christian country.

STR/AFP/Getty Images

avoid U.S. import restrictions), the U.S. government tends to pressure Toyota to use more U.S. parts in building the cars (such "domestic content" rules were part of NAFTA). MNCs generally want the freedom to assemble goods anywhere from parts made anywhere; governments, by contrast, want to maximize the amount of wealth created within their own territories. With parts and supplies now routinely converging from many countries to go into a product completed in one country, it is very difficult to say exactly where the product was made. The question is a complex one that entails long negotiations between MNCs and host governments.

Monetary policy also leads to conflicts between MNCs and host governments. When a state's currency is devalued, imports suddenly become more expensive. A foreign MNC selling an imported product (or a product assembled from imported parts) in the host country can be devastated by such a change. For example, if the dollar falls relative to the yen, Toyota USA may have to charge more U.S. dollars for its cars in order to pay for the parts it brings in from Japan. Therefore, an MNC making a long-term investment in a host country wants that country's currency to be reasonably stable.

Finally, MNCs may conflict with host governments on issues of international security as well as domestic political stability. When an MNC invests in a country, it assumes that its facilities there will operate profitably over a number of years. If a war or revolution takes away the MNC's facility, the company loses not only income but also capital—the standing wealth embodied in that facility. In 2001, ExxonMobil suspended operations at gas fields in Aceh province of Indonesia for three months until the Indonesian government—which earns $1 billion a year from the operation—brought in military forces to suppress armed separatists who had been attacking ExxonMobil. In 2003, Chevron Texaco, Shell, and Total had to shut down oil production in Nigeria for weeks because of ethnic violence.

In negotiating over these different sources of conflict, MNCs use a variety of means to influence host governments. These generally follow the same patterns as those used by domestic corporations. MNCs hire lobbyists, use advertisements to influence public opinion, and offer incentives to host-country politicians (such as locating facilities in their districts). Such activities are politically sensitive because host-country citizens and politicians may resent foreigners' trying to influence them.

Corruption is another means of influence over host governments that cannot be overlooked. Nobody knows the full extent to which MNCs use payoffs, kickbacks, gifts, and similar methods to win the approval of individual government officials for policies favorable to the MNCs. Certainly this occurs frequently with host governments in the global South (where government officials may be more desperate for income), but corruption also occurs regularly in rich industrialized countries.

MNCs have a range of conflicts with their home governments (where their headquarters are located), just as they do with their host states. Some MNC conflicts with home governments resemble the conflicts with host governments. Taxation is an important one. Trade policies are another. A recurrent complaint of MNCs against home governments is that policies adopted to punish political adversaries—economic sanctions and less extreme restrictions—end up harming the home-country MNCs more than the intended target. Usually, a competing MNC from another country is able to step into the gap when a government restricts its own MNCs. Unless they are prohibited from doing so, MNCs tend to go on doing business wherever it is profitable, with little regard for the political preferences of their governments.

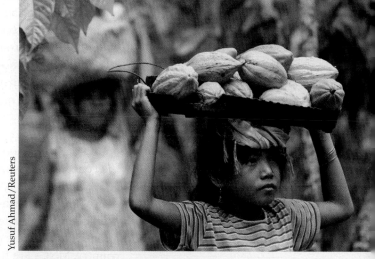

Yusuf Ahmad / Reuters

THE CHILDREN BEHIND THE CHOCOLATE International business prospers in stable political environments in host countries, but the relationship of a host country with an investing multinational corporation (MNC) can be complex. Foreign investors are wary of putting money into business environments marked by inflation, crime, corruption, and especially armed violence that could hit their facilities and employees. Host countries and nongovernmental organizations (NGOs) are concerned that MNCs will commit labor abuses. The global cocoa industry is one that depends, in many countries, on child labor. Here, young girls carry cocoa pods in Indonesia, 2010.

Sometimes governments do prevail because MNCs often need the support of their home governments. In the 1990s, the U.S.-based Conoco oil company agreed to a billion-dollar oil development project in Iran, just when the U.S. government was trying to isolate Iran as a rogue state. Under pressure from the U.S. government, Conoco quickly decided to back out of the deal. This move saved Conoco a fight with its home government, but it cost Conoco a lucrative contract that went instead to a European company.

The location of an MNC's headquarters determines its home nationality. The shareholders and top executives of an MNC are mostly from its home country. But as the world economy becomes more integrated, this is becoming less true. Just as MNCs are increasingly doing business all over the world and assembling products from parts made in many countries, so are shareholders and managers becoming more international in composition.

All business activity takes place in an environment shaped by politics. The international business environment most conducive to the creation of wealth by MNCs is one of stable international security. It is difficult and risky to make money in a situation of international conflict, especially one that threatens to degenerate into violence and war. War destroys wealth, reduces the supply of labor, and distorts markets in many ways. Certainly some businesses profit from international instability and the threat of war—such as arms merchants and smugglers—but these are the exceptions.

Beyond these international security concerns, MNCs favor political stability in the broader rules of the game governing international business. In monetary policy, international business benefits from the stability of rates that the managed float system tries to achieve. In trade policy, business benefits from the stability of tariff levels in the slowly shifting WTO framework. According to norms of international law, business benefits from the traditions holding governments responsible for their predecessors' debts and requiring compensation for nationalized foreign assets.

Occasionally, MNCs can get their home governments to provide security when host governments fail to do so. IR scholars continue to study the relationships between the international economic activities of MNCs and the international security activities of their home governments.

Corporate alliances involving MNCs often have international implications. When business alliances in an industry that has international markets occur within a single state, the alliances may in effect promote economic nationalism. Increasingly, however, corporate alliances are forming across national borders. Such alliances tend to promote liberalism rather than economic nationalism.

These international business alliances undermine both economic nationalism and the concept of a world splitting into rival trading blocs based in Europe, North America, and East Asia. In fact, international business alliances create interdependence among their home states. National interests become more intertwined and conflicts between states tend to be reduced. By operating in multiple countries at once, all MNCs have these effects to some degree. But because they are based in one home country, MNCs are foreigners in other countries. International alliances of MNCs, however, are at home in several countries at once.

We do not yet live in a world without national borders—not by a long shot—but the international activities of MNCs are moving us in that direction. Chapter 10 explores some of the ways in which people, companies, and ideas are becoming globally integrated across states.

Careers in International Business

Summary

Jobs in international business offer high pay, interesting work, and demanding hours for those with language and cultural skills.

BENEFITS AND COSTS As the pace and scope of globalization have accelerated, opportunities to work in international business have blossomed. For many large companies, the domestic/global distinction has ceased to exist. This new context provides opportunities and challenges for potential employees.

Careers in international business offer many advantages. Business jobs can pay substantially more than those in governments or NGOs and can open opportunities to travel extensively and network globally. Foreign-based jobs mean relocation to another country to work and immerse oneself in another culture.

Such a career choice also has potential costs, however. Many jobs require extensive hours, grueling travel, and frequent relocation. As with any job, promotion and advancement may fall victim to external circumstances such as global business cycles. And these jobs can be especially hard on families.

International opportunities arise in many business sectors. Banking, marketing (public relations), sales, and computing/telecommunications have seen tremendous growth in recent years. These jobs fall into three broad categories: (1) those located domestically, yet involving significant interactions with firms abroad; (2) domestic jobs working for foreign-based companies; and (3) those based abroad, for foreign or domestic firms.

SKILLS TO HONE One key to landing a job in the international business world is to develop two families of skills: those related to international relations and those related to business operations. Traditional masters in business administration (MBAs) and business school programs will be helpful for all three categories of jobs. Yet for jobs based abroad, employers often also look for a broader set of skills taught in economics, political science, and communications. Thus, not only traditional business skills but also language and cultural skills are essential. Employers look for those who have knowledge of a country's human and economic geography as well as culture. Experience with study abroad, especially including working abroad, can help show an ability to adapt and function well in other cultures. Strong analytical and especially writing abilities also matter greatly to employers.

Andersen Ross/Getty Images

Research also helps in landing a job. Employers often look for knowledge of a particular industry or company in order to make best use of an employee's language and cultural skills. Of course, while experience in noninternational business never hurts, be mindful that the practices, customs, and models of business in one country may not apply well abroad. Cross-cultural skills combined with substantive business knowledge in order to translate the operational needs of companies from the business world to the global realm are highly valued.

Resources

Mueller, Sherry Lee, and Mark Overmann. *Working World: Careers in International Education, Exchange, and Development*. 2nd ed. Georgetown, 2014.

Penrith, Deborah, ed. *The Directory of Jobs and Careers Abroad*. 13th ed. Vacation, 2007.

https://www.myperfectresume.com/how-to/career-resources/internat/

https://jobs.goabroad.com

http://www.transitionsabroad.com/listings/work/careers/index.shtml

Chapter Review

Summary

- Each state uses its own currency (except the 19 states that share the euro). These currencies have no inherent value but depend on the belief that they can be traded for future goods and services.

- Gold and silver were once used as world currencies that had value in different countries. Today's system is more abstract: National currencies are valued against each other through exchange rates.

- The most important currencies—against which most other states' currencies are compared—are the U.S. dollar, the euro, and the Japanese yen.

- Inflation, most often resulting from the printing of currency faster than the creation of new goods and services, causes the value of a currency to fall relative to other currencies. Inflation rates vary widely but are generally much higher in the global South and former Soviet bloc than in the industrialized West.

- States maintain reserves of hard currency and gold. These reserves back a national currency and cover short-term imbalances in international financial flows.

- Fixed exchange rates can be used to set the relative value of currencies, but more often states use floating exchange rates driven by supply and demand on world currency markets.

- Governments cooperate to manage the fluctuations of (floating) exchange rates but are limited in this effort by the fact that most money traded on world markets is privately owned.

- Over the long term, the relative values of national currencies are determined by the underlying health of the national economies and by the monetary policies of governments (how much money they print).

- Governments often prefer a low (weak) value for their own currency because this promotes exports, discourages imports, and hence improves the state's balance of trade. However, a sudden unilateral devaluation of the currency is a risky strategy because it undermines confidence in the currency.

- To ensure discipline in printing money—and to avoid inflation—industrialized states turn monetary policy over to semiautonomous central banks, such as the U.S. Federal Reserve. By adjusting interest rates on government money loaned to private banks, a central bank can control the supply of money in the national economy.

- The World Bank and the International Monetary Fund (IMF) work with states' central banks to maintain stable international monetary relations. From 1945 to 1971, this was done by pegging state currencies to the U.S. dollar and the dollar in turn to gold. Since 1971, the system has used Special Drawing Rights (SDRs)—a kind of world currency controlled by the IMF—in place of gold.

- The IMF operates a system of national accounts to keep track of the flow of money into and out of states. The balance of trade (exports minus imports) must be balanced by capital flows (investments and loans) and changes in reserves.

- International debt results from a protracted imbalance in capital flows—a state borrowing more than it lends—to cover a chronic trade deficit or government budget deficit.

- The U.S. financial position declined naturally from its extraordinary predominance immediately after World War II. The fall of the dollar–gold standard in 1971 reflects this decline.

- The positions of Russia and the other states of the former Soviet bloc declined drastically as they made the difficult transition from communism to capitalism. Though the uncontrolled inflation of the early 1990s has subsided, the economies of the former Soviet republics are still not fully integrated into the world economy.

- Multinational corporations (MNCs) do business in more than one state simultaneously. The largest are based in the leading industrialized states, and most are privately owned. MNCs are increasingly powerful in international economic affairs.

- MNCs contribute to international interdependence in various ways. States depend on MNCs to create new wealth, and MNCs depend on states to maintain international stability conducive to doing business globally.

- MNCs try to negotiate favorable terms and look for states with stable currencies and political environments in which to make direct investments. Governments seek such foreign investments on their territories to benefit from the future stream of income.

- MNCs try to influence the international political policies of both their home (headquarters) state and the other states in which they operate. Generally, MNCs promote policies favorable to business—low taxes, light regulation, stable currencies, and free trade. They also support stable international security relations because war generally disrupts business.

- Increasingly, MNCs headquartered in different states are forming international alliances with each other.

These inter-MNC alliances, even more than other MNC operations across national borders, are creating international interdependence and promoting liberal international cooperation.

Key Terms

gold standard 288
exchange rate 288
convertible currency 289
hyperinflation 289
hard currency 290
reserves 290
fixed exchange rates 290
floating exchange rates 290
managed float 290

devaluation 294
central bank 295
discount rate 296
Bretton Woods system 296
World Bank 296
International Monetary
    Fund (IMF) 297
Special Drawing Right (SDR) 297
balance of payments 298

austerity measures 300
Keynesian economics 300
fiscal policy 300
monetary policy 300
national debt 302
multinational corporation (MNC) 305
foreign direct investment 307
host country 309
home country 309

Critical Thinking Questions

1. Find a recent news article about a change in currency exchange rates (usually located in the business section of the newspaper or Web site). Analyze the various influences that may have been at work in the change of currency values—monetary policies, the underlying state of national economies, the actions of central banks (separately or in coordination), and factors such as political uncertainty that affect investors' confidence in a currency.

2. The IMF's Special Drawing Rights (SDRs) are a world currency used only by governments for international currency management and national accounts. Do you think SDRs could become a currency used by businesses and individuals, and how could this happen (or why couldn't it)? What would be the effects on world business and on the ability of sovereign states to manage their own economies?

3. Many scholars and politicians alike think private international investment is the best hope for the economies of Russia and Eastern Europe. Given the current economic and political disarray in that region,

what kinds of investors from the industrialized West might be willing to invest there? What actions could the governments of Western states take to encourage such investment? What pitfalls would the governments and investors have to watch out for?

4. If you were representing an MNC such as Toyota in negotiations over building an automobile factory in a foreign country, what kinds of concessions would you ask the host government for? What would you offer as incentives? In your report to Toyota's top management regarding the deal, what points would you emphasize as most important? If instead you were representing the host state in the negotiations and reporting to top state leaders, what would be your negotiating goals and the focus of your report?

5. Suppose that the head of Dow Chemical had his way and established Dow's world headquarters on an island outside all state territories. How do you think such a location would change Dow's strategies or business operations? What problems might it create for Dow?

Suggested Readings

Aliber, Robert Z. *The New International Money Game.* 7th ed. Palgrave, 2011.

Baker, Andrew. *Governing Financial Globalization: International Political Economy and Multi-Level Governance.* Routledge, 2008.

Cohen, Benjamin J. *Currency Power: Understanding Monetary Rivalry.* Princeton, 2015.

Eichengreen, Barry, Arnaud Mehl, and Livia Chitu. *How Global Currencies Work: Past, Present, and Future.* Princeton, 2017.

Stiglitz, Joseph. *Globalization and Its Discontents Revisited: Anti-Globalization in the Era of Trump.* W. W. Norton, 2017.

Let's Debate the Issue

Foreign Direct Investment: Engine of Growth or Tool of Exploitation?

Overview

Foreign direct investment (FDI) is a central part of the international economy. Over $2.5 trillion a year flows across borders as investments. Today, most of this amount flows to developing countries (especially China). Over $600 billion flows from developed countries in the global North to developing countries in the global South. In 2017, five of the top ten investment recipients were developing economies.

Historically, most FDI flowed between countries in the global North. In fact, until the 1960s, the United States accounted for a large majority of FDI. Yet with the growth of the global economy and the rise of globalization, FDI has become a global phenomenon. Throughout the 1970s and 1980s, FDI in developing countries remained low, averaging less than $20 billion as the 1990s approached. By the end of the 1990s, however, over $200 billion in investments entered developing economies from abroad. That number continued to expand to its current level of over $600 billion.

These flows to the global South are not without controversy. While some find these FDI flows necessary to spur economic growth, others argue that the money is not worth the political and social costs. Some states have attempted to lure FDI, especially from large Western MNCs, by undertaking domestic economic reforms. Other states do little to encourage FDI, fearful of potential negative environmental, social, and political impacts. Is FDI a positive resource for the developing world?

ARGUMENT 1

FDI Brings Positive Benefits to Developing Countries

FDI brings capital investment that is key to economic growth. What developing countries need more than anything to spur growth is capital. It is difficult for developing economies to generate this capital from within, so foreign investment is an excellent source of it to increase the potential for economic growth.

FDI brings more employment to developing economies. FDI often comes in the form of factories that bring increased employment for developing countries. While some argue that these jobs do not pay well, by local standards they often pay better than jobs generated locally.

FDI contributes to global interdependence. As firms and MNCs spread their manufacturing around the globe,

they increase economic interdependence between states and thus foster better relationships. As investors put more money into other states' economies, they may care more about those states' policies in other areas such as human rights or the environment. This could lead to pressure on FDI recipients to improve standards in areas such as labor practices or pollution.

ARGUMENT 2

FDI Brings Problems to Developing Countries

FDI's impact on developing economies is limited. Often, a very small number of individuals benefit from FDI, leaving the rest of the population unaffected by this external investment. Thus, even when FDI does add to economic growth, this growth is distributed very unevenly, leading to a large rich–poor gap in recipient states.

Policies to lure FDI hurt recipient states. To lure large amounts of foreign investment, states will often adopt policies to please investors such as large MNCs. These policies can include tax breaks (thus removing a source of state income), lax environmental standards (leading to problems such as pollution), or weak labor standards (leading to abusive labor practices such as child labor).

Jobs created by FDI are of poor quality. Regardless of their pay, jobs created by FDI are of poor quality. Almost all lack any significant benefits, and unionization is nearly always prohibited. The jobs can be very temporary as well—if a lower-cost labor supply is found, MNCs will pick up and move to other locations at a moment's notice. These are not the types of jobs that bring long-term stability to developing economies.

Questions

- On balance, do you believe that FDI is good or bad for developing countries? Given the expansion of MNCs and investment in this time of globalization, can a developing country forgo FDI if it hopes to achieve economic growth?

- Assuming that some harm comes to recipients of FDI, how can the harm be mitigated? Would it be easier to change the policies of the states that accept FDI or the behavior of the investors and businesses that invest in developing states?

- What leverage do leaders in developing countries have against MNCs that want to invest in their states? What are the dangers in making demands about the nature of FDI that enters the state?

For Further Reading

Jensen, Nathan. *Nation-States and the Multinational Corporation: A Political Economy of Foreign Direct Investment.* Princeton, 2008.

Moran, Theodore. *Foreign Direct Investment and Development: Launching a Second Generation of Policy Research.* Peterson Institute, 2011.

Pinto, Pablo. *Partisan Investment in the Global Economy: Why the Left Loves Foreign Direct Investment and Why FDI Loves the Left.* Cambridge, 2013.

Razin, Assaf, and Efraim Sadka. *Foreign Direct Investment: Analysis of Aggregate Flows.* Princeton, 2016.

Chapter 10
International Integration

Frank Augstein/AP Images

BREXIT PROTEST, 2018.

∨ Learning Objectives

10.1 Identify the contradictory forces faced by all international organizations.

10.2 Use functionalist theory to explain the founding and the growth of the European Union (EU).

10.3 Describe the growth of the EU in terms of the number of members and identify two challenges arising from the increase in membership.

10.4 Explain two ways in which information can be a tool for governments and two ways in which information can be a tool used against governments.

10.1 Globalization and Integration

Identify the contradictory forces faced by all international organizations.

Common to most discussions of globalization is a sense that there are forces in the world bringing us all closer together. Some of these forces are the result of state decisions—as we discussed in Chapter 8, states have attempted to integrate their economies through free trade agreements. Still other forces are, for example, technological changes that influence how states, nonstate actors, and even individual citizens function on a day-to-day basis.

This chapter discusses the sources of this "coming together." First, we will discuss state decisions to cooperate in order to create international organizations that are **supranational**—they subsume a number of states and their functions within a larger whole. The United Nations (UN), as we have seen, has some supranational aspects, though they are limited by the UN Charter, which is based on state sovereignty. On a regional level, the European Union (EU) is a somewhat more supranational entity than the UN; other regional organizations have tried to follow Europe's path as well, but with only limited success.

supranational Larger institutions and groupings such as the European Union to which state authority or national identity is subordinated.

Challenges realism

These intergovernmental organizations (IGOs) all contain a struggle between the contradictory forces of *nationalism* and *supranationalism*—between state sovereignty and the higher authority of supranational structures. The growing backlash against globalization is relevant to the topic of integration as well. No instance drives home the competing forces of nationalism and supranationalism more than Great Britain's decision in 2016 to leave the EU. A majority of British citizens voted to prioritize nationalism over the European integration project, triggering a lengthy negotiation between the British government and the EU on how to unwind decades of cooperation. Great Britain is scheduled to leave the EU in March 2019.

The other source of "coming together" we examine is technological change, specifically the revolution in information technologies such as the Internet. These technologies may be even more far-reaching because they operate globally and regionally across state boundaries without formal political structures. Nearly all of us have been affected by information technology that has brought us closer together within a state, across a region, or around the world.

Whether the sources of integration are from states or nonstate actors, the process of integration always involves transnational actors or issues. *Transnational actors* (for example, multinational corporations [MNCs] and nongovernmental organizations [NGOs]) bridge national borders, creating new avenues of interdependence among states. *Transnational issues* (for example, global warming or the spread of information technology) are processes that force states to work together because they cannot solve or manage these issues alone. This chapter explores how transnational actors and issues can lead to integration either through the actions of states or through technological change.

10.2 Integration Theory

Use functionalist theory to explain the founding and the growth of the European Union (EU).

The theory of international integration attempts to explain why states choose supranationalism, which challenges once again the foundations of realism (state sovereignty and territorial integrity). **International integration** refers to the process by which supranational institutions replace national ones—the gradual shifting upward of some sovereignty from state to regional or global structures. The ultimate expression of integration would be the merger of several (or many) states into a single state—or ultimately into a single world government. Such a shift in sovereignty to the supranational level would

international integration The process by which supranational institutions come to replace national ones; the gradual shifting upward of some sovereignty from the state to regional or global structures.

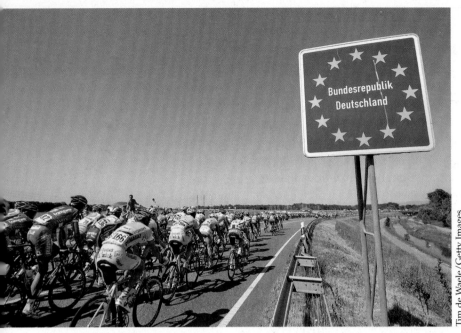

CROSSING THE BORDER Integration processes in Europe and elsewhere are making state borders more permeable to people, goods, and ideas—increasing interdependence. The European Union is deepening economic integration while expanding eastward. Here, in 2006, the Tour de France crosses into Germany, passing only a road sign where in centuries past, great armies faced off across massive fortifications.

probably entail some version of federalism, in which states or other political units recognize the sovereignty of a central government while retaining certain powers for themselves. This is the form of government adopted (after some debate) in the U.S. Constitution.

In practice, the process of integration has never gone beyond a partial and uneasy sharing of power between state and supranational levels. States have been unwilling to give up their exclusive claim to sovereignty and have limited the power and authority of supranational institutions. The UN certainly falls far short of a federal model (see Chapter 7). It represents only a step in the direction of international integration. Other modest examples of the integration process have been encountered in previous chapters—for example, the North American Free Trade Agreement (NAFTA) and the World Trade Organization (WTO). But these arrangements hardly challenge states' territorial integrity and usually challenge political sovereignty on only a handful of issues (such as trade).

The most successful example of the process of integration by far—though even that success is only partial—is the European Union. The regional coordination now occurring in Western Europe is a new historical phenomenon achieved only since World War II.

Until 70 years ago, the European continent was the embodiment of national sovereignty, state rivalry, and war. For 500 years, until 1945, the states of Europe were locked in chronic intermittent warfare; in the twentieth century alone, two world wars left the continent in ruins. The European states have historical and present-day religious, ethnic, and cultural differences. At the beginning of 2018, the 28 members of the EU spoke 24 different official languages. If ever there were a candidate for the failure of integration, Europe would appear to be it. Even more surprising, European integration began with the cooperation of Europe's two bitterest enemies over the previous 100 years, enemies in three major wars since 1870—France and Germany (references to "Germany" refer to West Germany from 1944 to 1990, and unified Germany since).

That Western European states began forming supranational institutions and creating an economic community to promote free trade and coordinate economic policies caught the attention of international relations (IR) scholars, who used the term *integration* to describe what they observed. Seemingly, integration challenged the realist assumption that states were strictly autonomous and would never yield power or sovereignty.

These scholars proposed that European moves toward integration could be explained by *functionalism*—growth of specialized technical organizations that cross national borders. According to functionalists, technological and economic development lead to more and more supranational structures as states seek practical means to fulfill necessary *functions* such as delivering mail from one country to another or coordinating the use of rivers that cross borders. As these connections became denser and the flows faster, functionalism predicted that states would be drawn together into stronger international economic structures.

The European experience, however, went beyond the creation of specialized agencies to include the development of more general, more political supranational bodies, such as the European Parliament. **Neofunctionalism** is a modification of

neofunctionalism A theory that holds that economic integration (functionalism) generates a "spillover" effect, resulting in increased political integration.

Tim de Waele/Getty Images

functional theory by IR scholars to explain these developments. Neofunctionalists argue that economic integration (functionalism) generates a *political* dynamic that drives integration further. Closer economic ties require more political coordination in order to operate effectively and eventually lead to political integration as well—a process called *spillover*.

Some scholars focused on the less tangible *sense of community* ("we" feeling) that began to develop among Europeans, running contrary to nationalist feelings that still existed as well. The low expectation of violence among the states of Western Europe created a **security community** in which such feelings could grow. This is a prime example of the identity principle discussed in Chapter 1.

> **security community** A situation in which low expectations of interstate violence permit a high degree of political cooperation—as, for example, among NATO members.

Elsewhere in the world, economies were becoming more interdependent at both the regional and global levels. In Asia, the Association of South East Asian Nations (ASEAN), founded in 1967, chalked up some successes in promoting regional economic coordination over several decades. The Andean Common Market, begun in 1969, promoted a limited degree of regional integration in the member states of Venezuela, Colombia, Ecuador, Peru, and Bolivia. Other South American countries (Argentina, Brazil, Paraguay, and Uruguay) founded MERCOSUR in 1991 to increase economic trade and integration. More recently, in 2002 the countries of Africa formed the African Union (AU), an ambitious plan to coordinate economic and foreign policies, elect an African parliament, and create a stronger infrastructure than the predecessor, Organisation of African Unity (OAU). Of course, none of these organizations have experienced the success of the EU, but their aims are often similar.

The new wave of integration in Europe and elsewhere has encountered limits and setbacks. Integration reduces states' ability to shield themselves and their citizens from the world's many problems and conflicts. For example, in the early 1990s, Venezuela found that its open border with Colombia brought in large transshipments of cocaine bound for the United States. Moreover, as states increasingly fear transnational terrorism, the prospects of open borders can give state leaders pause. As tens of thousands of refugees fleeing the Syrian civil war began pouring into Europe in 2015, European states started to place restrictions on border crossings that had previously been open to any to cross, even without a passport.

Integration can mean greater centralization at a time when individuals, local groups, and national populations demand more say over their own affairs. The centralization of political authority, information, and culture as a result of integration can threaten both individual and group freedom. Ethnic groups want to safeguard their own cultures, languages, and institutions against the bland homogeneity that a global or regional melting pot would create. As a result, a growing number of states and their citizens, in Europe and elsewhere, have responded to the new wave of integration with resurgent nationalism.

Indeed, these forces have set in motion a wave of *disintegration* of states running counter to (though simultaneous with) the integrating tendencies in today's world. The wave of disintegration in some ways began with the decolonization of former European empires in Africa, Asia, and the Middle East after World War II. After the Cold War, disintegration centered on Russia and Eastern Europe—especially in the former Soviet Union and former Yugoslavia. States in other regions—Somalia, Democratic Congo, Syria, and Iraq—appear in danger of breaking into pieces, in practice if not formally. A current challenge to integration theorists is to account for these new trends running counter to integration.

The forces of disintegration or separation are not limited to the developing world. The rise of economic nationalism was clear in Great Britain in its vote in 2016 to leave the EU. In the United States, President Donald Trump campaigned on a platform of "America first"—a message of national pride and antiglobalization. In other European countries, the past five years have marked the rise of nationalistic parties resisting EU integration efforts.

Throughout the successful and unsuccessful efforts at integration runs a common thread—the tension between nationalism and supranational loyalties (regionalism or globalism). In the less successful integration attempts, nationalism stands nearly unchallenged, and even in the most successful cases, nationalism remains a potent force locked in continual struggle with supranationalism. This struggle is a central theme even in the most successful case of integration—the European Union.

10.3 The European Union

Describe the growth of the EU in terms of the number of members and identify two challenges arising from the increase in membership.

European Union (EU) The official term for the European Community (formerly the European Economic Community) and associated treaty organizations. At the beginning of 2018, the EU has 28 member states, although Great Britain voted in 2016 to exit the EU. See also *Maastricht Treaty.*

Like the UN, the **European Union (EU)** was created after World War II and has developed since. But whereas the UN structure has changed little since its Charter was adopted, the EU has gone through several waves of expansion in its scope, membership, and mission over the past 60 years. The EU today has nearly 500 million citizens and surpasses the U.S. economy in gross domestic product (GDP).

10.3.1 The Vision of a United Europe

Europe in 1945 was decimated by war. Most of the next decade was spent recovering with help from the United States through the Marshall Plan. But already, two French leaders, Jean Monnet and Robert Schuman, were developing a plan to implement the idea of functionalism in Europe—that future wars could be prevented by creating economic linkages that would eventually bind states together politically.

In 1950, Schuman as French foreign minister proposed a first modest step—the merger of the French and German steel (iron) and coal industries into a single framework that could use the two states' coal resources and steel mills most efficiently. Coal and steel were key to European recovery and growth. The Schuman plan gave birth in 1952 to the *European Coal and Steel Community (ECSC)*, in which France and Germany were joined by Italy (the third largest industrial country of continental Europe) and by three smaller countries—Belgium, the Netherlands, and Luxembourg (together called the *Benelux countries*). These six states (Britain did not join) worked through the ECSC to reduce trade barriers in coal and steel and to coordinate their coal and steel policies. The ECSC also established a high authority that to some extent could bypass governments and deal directly with companies, labor unions, and individuals.

If coal and steel sound like fairly boring topics, that was exactly the idea of functionalists. The issues involved were matters for engineers and technical experts, and did not threaten politicians. Since 1952, technical experts have served as the leaders of the integration process in other aspects of European life and outside Europe. (Of course, coal and steel were not chosen by accident: Both were essential to make war.) As mentioned in Chapter 7, technical IOs such as the Universal Postal Union came before political ones such as the UN.

International scientific communities deserve special mention in this regard. If German and French steel experts had more in common than German and French politicians, this is even truer of scientists. Today the European scientific community is one of the most internationally integrated areas of society. For example, the EU operates the European Space Agency and the European Molecular Biology Laboratory.

Although technical cooperation succeeded in 1952, political and military cooperation proved much more difficult. In line with the vision of a united Europe, the six ECSC states signed a second treaty in 1952 to create a European Defense Community to work toward integrating Europe's military forces under one budget and command. But the French parliament failed to ratify the treaty, and Britain refused to join such a force. The ECSC states also discussed formation of a European Political Community in 1953 but could not agree on its terms. Thus, in economic cooperation the supranational institutions succeeded, but in political and military affairs, state sovereignty prevailed.

10.3.2 The Treaty of Rome

In the **Treaty of Rome**, in 1957, the same six states (France, Germany, Italy, Belgium, the Netherlands, Luxembourg) created two new organizations. One extended the coal-and-steel idea into a new realm, atomic energy. **Euratom**, the European Atomic Energy Community, was formed to coordinate nuclear power development by pooling research, investment, and management. It continues to operate today with an expanded membership. The second organization was the *European Economic Community* (*EEC*), later renamed the *European Community* (*EC*).

As discussed briefly in Chapter 8, there are important differences between *free trade areas*, *customs unions*, and *common markets*. Creating a **free trade area** meant lifting tariffs and restrictions on the movement of goods across (EEC) borders, as was done shortly after 1957. Today the *European Free Trade Association* (*EFTA*) is an extended free trade area associated with the European Union; its members are Norway, Iceland, Liechtenstein, and Switzerland.

In a **customs union**, participating states adopt a unified set of tariffs with regard to goods coming in from outside the free trade area. Without unified tariffs, each type of good could be imported into the state with the lowest tariff and then reexported (tariff-free) to the other states in the free trade area; this would be inefficient. The Treaty of Rome committed the six states to creating a customs union by 1969. A customs union creates free and open trade within its member states, bringing great economic benefits. Thus, the customs union remains the heart of the EU and the one aspect widely copied elsewhere in the world.

A **common market** means that, in addition to the customs union, member states allow labor and capital (as well as goods) to flow freely across borders. For instance, a Belgian financier can invest in Germany on the same terms as a German investor. Although the Treaty of Rome adopted the goal of a common market, even today it has been only partially accomplished.

One key aspect of a common market was achieved, at least in theory, in the 1960s when the EU (then the EC) adopted a **Common Agricultural Policy (CAP)**. In practice, the CAP has led to recurrent conflicts among member states and tensions between nationalism and regionalism. Recall that agriculture has been one of the most difficult sectors of the world economy in which to achieve free trade (see Chapter 8). To promote national self-sufficiency in food, many governments give subsidies to farmers. The CAP was based on the principle that a subsidy extended to farmers in any member state should be extended to farmers in all EU countries. That way, no member government would be forced to alienate politically powerful farmers by removing subsidies, yet the overall policy would be equalized throughout the community in line with the common market principle. As a result, subsidies to farmers today absorb about 40 percent of the total EU budget, with France as the main beneficiary, and are the single greatest source of trade friction between Europe and the United States.

The next step in the plan for European integration, after a free trade area, customs union, and common market, was an *economic and monetary union* (*EMU*), which would coordinate the overall economic policies of the member states for greatest efficiency and stability. In this step, a single currency would replace the separate national currencies now in use (see Monetary Union later in this chapter). A possible future step could be the supranational coordination of economic policies such as budgets and taxes.

Treaty of Rome (1957) The founding document of the European Economic Community (EEC), or Common Market, now subsumed by the European Union.

Euratom An organization created by the 1957 Treaty of Rome to coordinate nuclear power development by pooling research, investment, and management.

free trade area A zone in which there are no tariffs or other restrictions on the movement of goods and services across borders. See also *customs union*.

customs union A common external tariff adopted by members of a free trade area; that is, participating states adopt a unified set of tariffs with regard to goods coming in from outside. See also *free trade area*.

common market A zone in which labor and capital (as well as goods) flow freely across borders.

Common Agricultural Policy (CAP) A European Union policy based on the principle that a subsidy extended to farmers in any member country should be extended to farmers in all member countries.

dpa picture alliance / Alamy Stock Photo

PLANTING POLITICAL SEEDS Under the free trade area first created by the 1957 Treaty of Rome, goods can move freely across European borders to reach consumers in any member country. In agriculture, creating an integrated free market in Europe has not been easy; the EC adopted a Common Agricultural Policy in the 1960s to address the problem. Here, Belgian farmers block the European Commission headquarters in Brussels, Belgium, in 2018 to protest proposed agricultural policy changes.

To reduce state leaders' fears of losing sovereignty, the Treaty of Rome provides that changes in its provisions must be approved by all member states. For example, France vetoed Britain's application for membership in the EEC in 1963 and 1967. However, in 1973, Britain did finally join, along with Ireland and Denmark. This action expanded the organization's membership to nine, including the largest and richest countries in the region.

In 1981, Greece was admitted, and in 1986, Portugal and Spain joined. Inclusion of these poorer countries with less industry and lower standards of living created difficulties in effectively integrating Europe's economies (difficulties that persist today). Richer European states give substantial aid to the poorer ones in hopes of strengthening the weak links. Yet, by 2015, the debt problems of these poorer countries had led to wealthier member states spending billions in bailout funds, while continuing economic turmoil threatened the stability of the wider European economy.

10.3.3 Structure of the European Union

The structure of the EU reflects its roots in technical and economic cooperation. The coal and steel experts have been joined by experts on trade, agriculture, and finance at the heart of the community. The EU headquarters and staff have the reputation of being colorless bureaucrats—sometimes called *Eurocrats*—who care more about technical problem solving than about politics. These supranational bureaucrats are balanced in the EU structure by provisions that uphold the power of states and state leaders.

Although the rule of Eurocrats follows the functionalist plan, it has created problems as the EU has progressed. Politicians in member states have qualms about losing power to the Eurocrats. Citizens in those states have become more uncomfortable in recent years with the growing power of faceless Eurocrats over their lives. Citizens can throw their own political leaders out of office in national elections, but the Eurocrats seem less accountable.

The EU's structure is illustrated in Figure 10.1. The Eurocrats consist of a staff of 34,000, organized under the **European Commission** at EU headquarters in Brussels, Belgium. The Commission has 28 individual members—one from each member state—who are chosen for four-year renewable terms. Their role is to identify problems and propose solutions to the Council of the European Union. They select one of their members as the Commission president. These individuals are supposed to represent the interests of Europe as a whole (supranational interests), not of their own states, but this goal has been met only imperfectly.

The European Commission lacks formal autonomous power except for day-to-day EU operations. Formally, the Commission reports to, and implements policies of, the **Council of the European Union** (formerly named the Council of Ministers). The Council is a meeting of the relevant ministers (foreign, economic, agriculture, finance, etc.) of each member state—politicians who control the bureaucrats (or who try to).

European Commission A European Union body whose members, while appointed by states, are supposed to represent EU interests. Supported by a multinational civil service in Brussels, the Commission's role is to identify problems and propose solutions to the Council of the European Union. See also *Council of the European Union*.

Council of the European Union A European Union institution in which the relevant ministers (foreign, economic, agriculture, finance, etc.) of each member state meet to enact legislation and reconcile national interests. Formerly known as the Council of Ministers. When the meeting takes place among the state leaders, it is called the "European Council." See also *European Commission*.

Figure 10.1 Structure of the European Union (EU)

Source: European Commission in the European Union.

For instance, in 2015, the 28 foreign ministers met to discuss improving counterterrorism efforts and political relations with Russia. This formal structure reflects states' resistance to yielding sovereignty. It also means that the individuals making up the Council of the European Union vary from one meeting to the next, and that technical issues receive priority over political ones. The arrangement thus gives some advantage back to the Commission staff. Recall the similar tension between politicians and career bureaucrats in national foreign policy making (see Bureaucracies in Chapter 4).

The Council of the European Union in theory has functioned using weighted voting based on each state's population, but in practice it has operated by consensus on major policy issues (all members must agree). After adoption of the Lisbon Treaty (see later in the chapter), nearly all issues are now decided by qualified majority voting. The Treaty's definition of a qualified majority is that at least 55 percent of EU members, representing 65 percent of EU citizens, must vote in favor to secure passage. The Council has a rotating presidency (with limited power). The Council of the European Union must approve the policies of the European Commission and give it general directions.

In the 1970s, state leaders (prime ministers or presidents) created a special place for themselves in the EC, to oversee the direction of the community; this structure again shows state leaders' resistance to being governed by any supranational body. This *European Council* of the 28 state leaders meets with the European Commission president twice a year. They are the ones with the power to get things done in their respective national governments (which still control most of the money and power in Europe).

There is a **European Parliament**, which falls somewhat short of a true legislature passing laws for all of Europe. At present, it operates partly as a watchdog over the Commission, but with some power to legislate. It must approve the Commission's budget but cannot control it item by item. The parliament shares power with the Council under a "co-decision procedure" in areas such as migration, employment, health, and consumer protection. The 2009 Lisbon Treaty significantly expanded the areas in which the co-decision procedure applies. It also serves as a debating forum and a symbol of European unity. In 1999, an independent commission created by the parliament found waste and fraud in the European Commission, leading all 20 commissioners to resign. Since 1979, voters throughout Europe have directly elected their representatives according to population—750 members representing over 500 million citizens. Each member state has at least 6 and no more than 96 members. Political parties are organized across national lines.

European Parliament A quasi-legislative body of the European Union that operates as a watchdog over the European Commission and has limited legislative power.

The *Economic and Social Committee* discusses continent-wide issues that affect particular industries or constituencies. This committee is purely advisory; it lobbies the European Commission on matters it deems important. It is designed as a forum in which companies, labor unions, and interest groups can bargain transnationally.

The **European Court of Justice** in Luxembourg adjudicates disputes on matters covered by the Treaty of Rome—which covers many issues. Unlike the World Court (see Chapter 7), the European Court has actively established its jurisdiction and does not serve merely as a mechanism of international mediation. The European Court can overrule national laws that conflict with EU law—giving it unique powers among international courts. In addition, it hears cases brought by individuals, not just governments. In hundreds of cases, the Court has ruled on matters ranging from discrimination in the workplace to the pensions of Commission staff members.

European Court of Justice
A judicial arm of the European Union, based in Luxembourg. The court has actively established its jurisdiction and its right to overrule national law when it conflicts with EU law.

10.3.4 The Single European Act

European integration has proceeded in a step-by-step process that produces tangible successes, reduces politicians' fears of losing sovereignty, and creates pressures to continue the process. Often major steps forward are followed by periods of stagnation or even reversals in integration. The first major revision of the Treaty of Rome—the 1985 **Single European Act**—began a new phase of accelerated integration. The EU set a target date of the end of 1992 for the creation of a true common market in Europe. This comprehensive set of changes was nicknamed *Europe 1992* and centered on about 300 directives from the European Commission, aimed at eliminating nontariff barriers to free trade in goods, services, labor, and capital within the EC. The issues tended to be complex and technical. For instance, professionals licensed in one state should be free to practice in another, but Spain's licensing requirements for, say, physical therapists may have differed from those of Britain. The Commission bureaucrats worked to smooth out such inconsistencies and create a uniform set of standards. Each national government had to pass laws to implement these measures.

Single European Act (1985) An act that set a target date of the end of 1992 for the creation of a true common market (free cross-border movement of goods, capital, people, and services) in the European Community (EC).

For example, a dispute raged for decades over the definition of chocolate. Belgium—famous for its chocolates—requires the exclusive use of cocoa butter for a product to be called chocolate; Britain and other countries use a cheaper process that partially substitutes other vegetable oils. With deepening integration and seamless trade, Belgium worried that it would lose its competitive advantage in the $30 billion worldwide chocolate market (half of which came from Europe). Britain and six other EU countries that joined the EU since 1973 won an exemption from the all–cocoa butter rule that applies to the other eight EU members. Under the pressure of integration, however, the EU is moving to unify standards such as food regulations. The chocolate wars illustrate that the seemingly simple concept of economic integration sets in motion forces of change that reach into every corner of society and affect the daily lives of millions of people.

The Single European Act also gave a new push to the creation of a European Central Bank (in Frankfurt, Germany), and a single currency and monetary system—long-standing goals that have since been accomplished. As long as the economies of the EU members were tied to separate states (with separate central banks), efforts to maintain fixed exchange rates were difficult. For example, British politicians in 1992 were reluctant to deepen a recession by keeping interest rates high just to save German politicians from inflation that might result from lowering rates.

The 1992 process moved economic integration into more political and controversial areas, eroding sovereignty more visibly than before. It also deepened a trend toward the EU's dealing directly with provinces rather than the states they belong to—thus beginning to "hollow out" the state from below (stronger provincial governments) as well as from above (stronger Europe-wide government). However, Europe 1992 continued to put aside for the future the difficult problems of political and military integration.

10.3.5 The Maastricht Treaty

The **Maastricht Treaty**, signed in the Dutch city of Maastricht in 1992, renamed the EC as the EU and committed it to further progress in three main areas. The first was monetary union (discussed shortly), in which the existing national currencies were abolished and replaced by a single European currency. A second set of changes, regarding justice and home affairs, created a European police agency and responded to the new reality that borders were opening to immigrants, criminals, sex traffickers, and contraband. It also expanded the idea of citizenship so that, for example, a French citizen living in Germany can vote in local elections there. A third goal of Maastricht—political and military integration—was even more controversial. The Treaty commits European states to work toward a common foreign policy with a goal of eventually establishing a joint military force.

Some citizens of Europe began to react strongly against the loss of national identity and sovereignty implicit in the Maastricht Treaty. As an amendment to the Treaty of Rome, Maastricht had to be ratified by all (then 12) members. The ratification process stirred up strong public feelings against closer European union in several countries. Suddenly, citizens and leaders in several countries seemed to realize that the faceless Eurocrats in Brussels were stripping away their national sovereignty! In the end, the EU implemented the Maastricht Treaty, although more slowly and with fewer participating countries than had been originally hoped. Economic and technical integration, including the new monetary union among 12 members, maintained momentum.

Europe's economic integration has begun to reshape political economy at a global level. The EU now sets the rules for access to one of the world's largest markets, for a vast production and technology network, and for the world's strongest currency. Europe's new power is illustrated in its environmental initiatives. The U.S. chemical industry operated under U.S. regulations that exempt 80 percent of chemicals. But the EU adopted stricter chemical regulations, requiring tests of health effects of all chemicals used in products and mandating efforts to substitute for toxic chemicals in everyday products. As a result, several major U.S. cosmetics companies reformulated their products to comply with the new EU cosmetics regulations calling for removal of unhealthy substances. And Japanese car manufacturers adapted production processes to meet the EU's requirement that new cars consist of 95 percent recyclable components as of 2015.

Political and military integration have been much more problematic. The struggle between nationalism and supranationalism seems precariously balanced between the two; the transition to supranationalism has not yet been accomplished in the realms of sovereignty and foreign and military policy. Even after 60 years of preparation, spillover from economic integration into political issues is elusive.

10.3.6 Monetary Union

A European currency, the **euro**, has replaced national currencies in 19 EU member states, as mandated in the Maastricht Treaty. After several years as an abstract unit like the International Monetary Fund's (IMF) SDR (see Chapter 9), used by national governments and for international exchange, the euro came into full circulation in 2002 and the national currencies ceased to exist. The European Central Bank took over the functions of states' central banks.

Monetary union is difficult for both economic and political reasons. In participating states, fundamental economic and financial conditions must be equalized. One state cannot stimulate its economy with low interest rates (for example, because of a recession) while another cools inflation with high interest rates (because of high economic growth). For example, in January 2018, the unemployment rate was over 17 percent in Spain but only 3 percent in Germany. In an integrated economy that is

Maastricht Treaty A treaty signed in the Dutch city of Maastricht and ratified in 1992; it commits the European Union to monetary union (a single currency and European Central Bank) and to a common foreign policy. See also *European Union (EU)*.

euro Also called the ECU (European currency unit); a single European currency used by 19 members of the European Union (EU).

Nicolas Liponne/NurPhoto/Sipa/AP Images

FIGHTING FOR A JOB The Maastricht Treaty called for a monetary union with a common currency. In 2002, the euro currency came into effect smoothly in 12 (now 19) countries and emerged as a world currency that rivals the U.S. dollar. But the Great Recession of 2008 exposed underlying problems that triggered a eurozone debt crisis and a second recession in 2012. Unemployment remains a problem in many EU member states after these crises. Here, workers in France protest a proposed labor law intended to ease unemployment, 2018.

also politically centralized, the central government can reallocate resources, as the United States might do if Texas were booming and Massachusetts were in recession. But the EU does not have centralized powers of taxation or control of national budgets. This split of fiscal and monetary policy is unusual.

One solution is to work toward equalizing Europe's economies. For example, to reduce the disparity between rich and poor EU states, the Maastricht Treaty increased the EU budget by $25 billion annually to provide economic assistance to the poorer members. But the richer EU members pay the cost for this aid—in effect carrying the poor countries as free riders on the collective good of EU integration. Partly for this reason, $25 billion annually was far too small to truly equalize the rich and poor countries.

The main solution adopted at Maastricht was to restrict membership in the monetary union, at least in the first round, to only those countries with enough financial stability not to jeopardize the union. To join the unified currency, a state had to achieve a budget deficit of less than 3 percent of GDP, a national debt of less than 60 percent of GDP, an inflation rate no more than 1.5 percentage points above the average of the three lowest-inflation EU members, and stable interest rates and national currency values.

This meant hard choices by governments in France, Spain, Italy, and other countries to cut budgets and benefits and to take other politically unpopular moves. French workers responded with massive strikes on several occasions. Governments fell to opposition parties in several countries, but the new leaders generally kept to the same course. As a result of their newfound fiscal discipline, all 12 EU members that wanted to participate in the euro qualified. Slovenia joined in 2007; Cyprus and Malta, in 2008; Slovakia, in 2009; Estonia, in 2011; Latvia, in 2014; and Lithuania, in 2015. Britain, Denmark, and Sweden opted to retain their national currencies.

Money is more political than steel tariffs or chocolate ingredients. A monetary union infringes on a core prerogative of states—the right to print currency. Because citizens use money every day, a European currency along these lines could deepen citizens' sense of identification with Europe—a victory for supranationalism over nationalism. When the euro went into circulation in 2002, people for the first time could "put Europe in their pocket." Precisely for this reason, however, some state leaders and citizens resisted the idea of giving up the symbolic value of their national currencies. These problems were reflected in the task of designing euro banknotes and coins. How could any country's leaders or monuments become Europe-wide symbols? The solution was to put generic architectural elements (not identifiable by country) on the front of the banknotes and a map of Europe on the back. Coins come in various member-state designs (all valid throughout the eurozone).

Conflicts have arisen within the eurozone. In 2004, the European Commission challenged the EU member states for voting to let France and Germany break the euro rules by running high budget deficits. And Latvia's government lost power within six months of the country's joining the EU, under pressure of unpopular budget cuts needed to meet the euro rules within four years.

In 2010, new challenges to the euro arose. Greece, which had previously admitted to falsifying economic data in order to be admitted to the eurozone, had for years borrowed more than it could repay and needed a European bailout to survive the global financial crisis. Because Greece used the euro, its troubles affected global investors' impressions of all euro states.

Worse, the debt problems soon spread beyond Greece. In fact, in 2010, only two states in the EU (Finland and Luxembourg) actually met the EU targets for debt levels. Greece, Spain, Portugal, Ireland, and Italy all undertook large-scale economic reforms, and governments lost power in Greece, Italy, and other EU states. Germany and France fought over who would help bail out the euro states in trouble. After Germany's economic minister stated that Germany "would not offer Greece a cent," cooler heads prevailed and the EU countries banded together to support one another's economies.

By 2012, the EU had patched together a bailout system, backed by more than $1 trillion, capable of propping up its members' economies when needed (see the Seeking the Collective Good box). But the EU's decision process remained cumbersome, and citizens took to the streets frequently in countries such as Greece and Spain that had to implement harsh austerity budgets in exchange for bailouts. The austerity measures not only drove up unemployment, around 25 percent in the case of Spain in 2015 (50 percent unemployment for those under age 25), but also slowed economic activity in the whole eurozone. In 2014, fed up with austerity measures,

Seeking the Collective Good
Bailing Out Greece

COLLECTIVE GOOD: European Financial Health

BACKGROUND: The 19 states that make up the eurozone have given up their national currencies in favor of a common one. As a result, each is affected by the financial policies of the others. For instance, deficit spending on politically popular programs normally affects just that country's currency, but if the country is in the eurozone, then that effect is spread across all the other euro countries. To avoid the temptation to free-ride, the European Union set up rules for fiscal responsibility (including low deficits) before a country could adopt the euro. As later became clear, several countries, including Greece, fudged those requirements when they first joined the eurozone.

The health of the euro currency is thus a collective good depending on the fiscal discipline of its members. Free riding threatens all eurozone members because an economic crisis in one country can easily spread to others through the common currency.

CHALLENGE: In 2010, Greek fiscal policies combined with the aftermath of the global recession to put Greece into a debt crisis, nearing bankruptcy. This instability threatened to spread to the other high-deficit euro members (Spain, Portugal, and Ireland). The value of the euro began to drop and world financial markets fell as anxiety increased.

SOLUTION: In response, the European Union and IMF put together a $141 billion rescue package for Greece. To take effect, the package needed approval from all 16 (at that time) eurozone members. In Germany, where fiscal discipline is a tradition, angry voters did not want to bail out the irresponsible Greeks, and

President of the European Central Bank speaks with Greece's finance minister, 2018.

the governing party's slim majority in parliament was threatened. The German government thus faced both domestic costs and a direct price tag of $28 billion for Germany's share of the bailout.

Identity played a role in the German government's decision to approve the deal. The European Union's identity as a continent in common meant that Germany saw the collective good of euro stability as its own good. However, reciprocity also played a role because the German government supported the bailout only after the problem threatened to spread and destabilize the euro, directly harming Germany if it did not approve the deal. Just the thought of fellow Europeans in need did not alone make Germany want to help.

Greece elected a new leftist government on the promise of negotiating less harsh conditions from the EU. The new Greek government failed to do so, and in 2015, Greece accepted new emergency loans from the EU, which included demands for difficult cuts in the budget. Since 2015, Greece has continued to struggle with high unemployment. In 2017, however, Greece finally achieved economic growth for the first time since the Great Recession, and unemployment began to fall. Although the road to recovery is still long for Greece, 2018 brought some optimism that it was on its way down that long road.

Despite these recent problems in the eurozone, the creation of a European currency is arguably the largest financial overhaul ever attempted in history, and in its first 16 years, it has been mostly successful.

10.3.7 Expanding the European Union

The EU's success has attracted neighboring states that want to join. The EU has expanded from 15 members to 28 since 2004, with potentially far-reaching changes in how the EU operates.

Spain and Portugal, admitted in 1986 as the eleventh and twelfth members, filled out the western side of Europe. In 1995, Austria, Sweden, and Finland joined the EU. They are located on the immediate fringe of the present EU area, and as relatively rich countries, they did not disrupt the EU economy. Norway applied to join and was accepted, but its citizens voted down the idea in a referendum in 1994, leaving the EU with 15 members after 1995—all but two of the main states of Western Europe. (Switzerland's plans to join were, like Norway's, halted by a popular referendum in the early 1990s.)

The EU's current expansion is guided by the 2000 Treaty of Nice, which came into effect in 2003 after Irish voters reversed an earlier vote and approved it (the last country to ratify it). Ten new members joined in 2004: Poland, the Czech Republic, Slovakia, Hungary, Slovenia, Estonia, Latvia, Lithuania, Malta, and Cyprus. The European Commission expanded to 25 members, without the five largest having two seats, and with new voting rules that moved away from a requirement for consensus. In 2007, Romania and Bulgaria brought the EU's membership to 27. Croatia joined in 2013 as the twenty-eighth member, showing that despite its financial problems the EU continues to expand, albeit slowly.

Turkey continues to seek membership, although Turkey's president said in 2018 it would not "beg" for membership. Although it rebuffed Turkey in 2002, the EU later agreed to begin formal entry negotiations with Turkey in 2005—the start of a years-long process. The EU has not reached a consensus on admitting Turkey as a full member. Proponents note that Turkey has made major economic and political changes, including abolishing the death penalty and improving human rights, to try to win EU membership. Granting full membership would reward these changes, keeping an implicit promise to reciprocate Turkey's actions. Turkey's GDP, growing rapidly in recent years, would add about 5 percent to the EU's economy. And Turkish workers could help alleviate a labor shortage in Western Europe. Supporters also argue that Turkey as an EU member would serve as a bridge between Europe and the important but unstable Middle East region and as an example of secular democracy to other Middle Eastern countries. Turkey has helped Europe by accepting many Syrian refugees, for which the EU has paid Turkey nearly $6 billion under an agreement reached in 2015.

Opponents note that Turkey would be the only Muslim country in the EU yet would become the second most populous EU member after Germany. With 2 million Turks already living in Germany, opponents argue that EU membership would open the floodgates for immigration from a large, poor country, overwhelming the smaller and richer EU members. In economic terms, Turkey would be the poorest member

Figure 10.2 Income Levels of Old and New EU Members, 2017

Source: World Bank Data

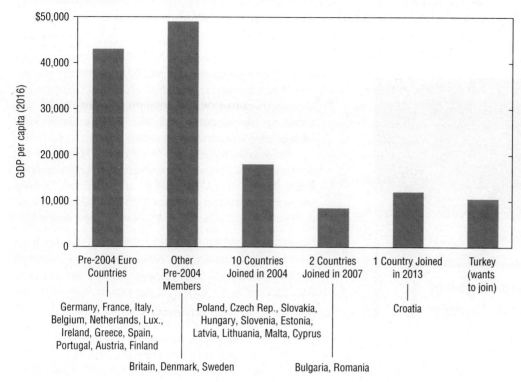

(see Figure 10.2). Costs to subsidize Turkish farmers and expand social programs could reach tens of billions of euros. Finally, opponents want Turkey to remove its military forces from EU member Cyprus, where a Greek-Turkish partition has endured for decades. Since 2010, the financial crisis in the eurozone has pushed aside the question of admitting Turkey or other new members.

As the new members joined the EU since 2004, the ability of the EU to reach decisions by consensus became more complicated, a point underscored by Slovakia's single-handed veto of a massive euro bailout in 2011 (Slovakia eventually changed its vote). The working time required to make decisions in the Council of the European Union expanded, with potential conflicts and alliances on a particular issue among 28 rather than 15 members. Recall that collective goods are generally harder to provide in larger groups, where free riding is less obvious, than in smaller ones.

Furthermore, by Western European standards, the new members are relatively poor. Existing EU members were wary of being dragged down by these economies, most of which are still embroiled in the painful transition from socialism to capitalism and sometimes lack stable currencies. In fact, however, the recent debt crisis and recession centered on the older members such as Greece, Spain, and Portugal, not the new members.

Perhaps as a result of these pressures, the EU in the last decade has shown signs of dividing into "inner" and "outer" layers—with states such as France and Germany joining a currency union and deepening their integration, and those such as Britain and perhaps the new members operating at the edges of the EU with more autonomy. Still, in some areas, there have been strides toward integration. Since 1995, the EU has established and expanded the *Schengen Area*, a zone in which border controls have been abolished. Goods and people move freely within the zone without stopping at borders. The Schengen countries include the major EU states (except Britain, by its choice). Norway, Iceland, and Switzerland also belong, although they are not EU members.

[handwritten margin note:]

Schengen States:
- Norway
- Iceland
- Switzerland
- NOT BRITAIN

Policy Perspectives
Chancellor of Germany, Angela Merkel

PROBLEM *How do you balance competing forces in the EU while satisfying domestic public opinion?*

Martin Meissner/Associated Press

BACKGROUND For decades, Turkey has desired full membership in the European Union. For many reasons, Turkey's application has been stalled. It would be the poorest member of the EU, it would be the only non-Christian EU member, it has not settled past conflicts with current members Cyprus and Greece, and it has never admitted its role in the genocide of Armenians during World War I.

Yet many observers argue that Turkey is too important to leave out of the EU: It serves as a vital link between Europe and the Middle East; it is a NATO member; and it has undertaken many of the reforms asked of it by EU states, in human rights, minority rights, and democracy. It has also agreed to host over a million Syrian refugees so they do not seek asylum in central and Western Europe. Your own country maintains extensive economic ties with Turkey as well—Germany is Turkey's top source of imports and biggest market for exports. An economically healthy Turkey in the EU would be good for German businesses.

Past German leaders have differed on their views on Turkey's application, ranging from outright opposition to strong support. You have attempted to provide a compromise solution: the idea of a "privileged partnership," which would provide some economic benefits to Turkey, but not full membership. Turkish leaders oppose this option, and other European leaders have not supported your compromise to date.

While Turkey's application to the EU has supporters and detractors across Europe, no country opposes Turkish membership more than France. The current French president, Emmanuel Macron, announced in January 2018 that the EU should end the "hypocrisy" of pretending that Turkey will ever enter the EU.

DOMESTIC CONSIDERATIONS Turkish membership in the EU is not popular domestically. Native Germans are concerned that immigrants could freely come to Germany and take jobs. They also fear that a wave of cheap exports from Turkey will undermine German workers. Already, more than 2.1 million Turks live in Germany, making them the largest ethnic minority in your country. There have been ethnic tensions between the Turkish immigrants and native Germans, leading for calls for tight restrictions on Turkish immigration. Yet many of the Turks in Germany are voting and taxpaying citizens who have urged you to support Turkey's membership.

SCENARIO Imagine that France proposes to kill permanently Turkey's membership application to the EU. France asks for your support in ensuring that Turkey will never become a member of the EU. Upon hearing of France's proposal, ethnic Turks begin large protests in several cities in Germany to urge your support of Turkey's application.

CHOOSE YOUR POLICY Do you support France's attempt to keep Turkey out of the EU? Do you continue to push for your idea of a "privileged partnership" even though the idea has received little support at home or abroad? How do you balance demands from important EU partners with your own policy preferences and a difficult domestic situation?

10.3.8 The Lisbon Treaty

To grapple with the implications of an expanding EU, the 25 leaders signed an EU constitution in late 2004, and the European Parliament gave it a strong vote of support in 2005. To take effect, it had to be ratified by all 25 states, including several requiring referenda. The constitution would establish a stronger president of the EU, as well as a foreign minister, and would replace the requirement for consensus in EU decision making with majority voting in more cases. It also guaranteed fundamental rights to all EU citizens. But voters in France and the Netherlands rejected the constitution and the process halted.

At the end of 2007, the EU moved forward with another new proposed constitution, the **Lisbon Treaty**. The Treaty was similar to the previous constitution but faced a popular referendum only in Ireland. (The Lisbon Treaty did not require

Lisbon Treaty A European Union agreement that replaces a failed attempt at an EU constitution with a similar set of reforms strengthening central EU authority and modifying voting procedures among the EU's expanded membership.

more state-level votes because it only amended previous EU treaties rather than replacing them as the constitution proposed to do.) The Treaty came into force in 2009.

The Treaty created numerous changes in both the structure and the day-to-day operations of the EU. Some of those changes promote more supranational decision making. For example, a charter of human rights was made legally binding on all member states. A new position called the High Representative for Foreign Affairs and Security Policy was created to better coordinate foreign policy among member states. (This position immediately became controversial when a relatively unknown British lord was chosen to fill the position.)

On the other hand, some changes allow state members and individual citizens to place more checks on EU power. Now, national parliaments can have more say in who is admitted to the EU (likely bad news for Turkey). National parliaments will now also receive draft legislation to evaluate and respond to before it is enacted in Brussels. The Treaty also attempts to increase transparency by requiring European Council meetings to be held in public. And in an attempt to engage EU citizens directly, the Commission must now take up any proposal or petition that receives 1 million signatures.

10.3.9 Immigration, Brexit, and the Future of the Europe

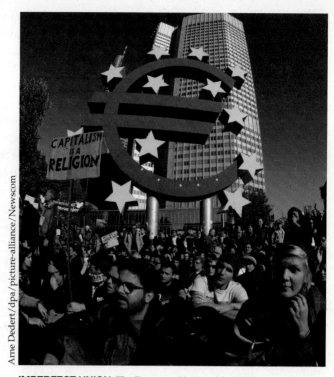

IMPERFECT UNION The European Union added 12 members, mostly from Eastern Europe, in 2004 and 2007. Efforts to update European governance with the new Lisbon Treaty finally succeeded in 2009. But much complexity remains to be worked out, as shown in the muddled response to the Greek financial crisis in 2011. Here, protesters demonstrate at the European Central Bank in Frankfurt, Germany, 2011.

Arne Dedert/dpa/picture-alliance/Newscom

European political crises began to take their toll on support for the EU over the past decade. After the 2008–2009 Great Recession and the fallout from the Greek debt crisis, Europe was hit with a migration crisis in 2015. Between January 2015 and March 2016, a million refugees entered the EU through Greece, most of them arriving by boat from Turkey. These migrants were fleeing conflicts in Syria, Libya, and Iraq.

The EU responded by approving a plan to resettle many of the refugees, despite objections from the Czech Republic, Slovakia, Hungary, and Romania. This plan strained relations between Germany and newer Eastern European members. The EU agreed to pay Turkey to take back refugees who had arrived in Greece after March 2016. For each refugee that Turkey took back from Greece, the EU would resettle a refugee living in Turkey (Turkey hosts over 1 million refugees from the Syrian civil war). The EU also agreed to pay Turkey 3 billion euros to help pay for the cost of the refugee crisis as well as to allow Turkish citizens to travel between several European states without obtaining travel visas.

Many EU members and human rights organizations criticized the deal. Largely due to economic and political concerns, EU members did not wish to resettle Syrian refugees in their own countries. Several member states were still struggling with unemployment after the Great Recession and the Greek debt crisis. Member states also raised concerns about terrorists from ISIS, which controlled parts of Syria, entering through the asylum program. These concerns, among others, led to an increase in support for anti-EU parties in several countries, including France, Hungary, Finland, and Denmark.

These same anti-EU sentiments in Great Britain reached a fevered pitch in June 2015, with the British prime minister scheduling a vote on the future of British membership in the EU in one year. The election about British exit ("Brexit") from the EU was expected to be close, but most observers predicted the forces of supranationalism would prevail. After all, despite membership in the EU, Great Britain had maintained autonomy in important areas such as finance (the British did not use the euro) and foreign policy.

Yet, in June 2016, British citizens voted by a slim margin (51.9 percent in favor) for leaving the EU. On March 29, 2017, Great Britain triggered the exit clause in the Lisbon Treaty, setting off a two-year period of negotiations. Under EU rules, Great Britain must leave the EU by March 29, 2019.

Negotiations over Brexit will need to cover many issues. Britain must pay a fee to leave the EU—an amount that must be negotiated between Britain and the remaining EU members. The status of EU citizens in Britain and British citizens living in Europe needs to be clarified. Crossing the border between Ireland and Great Britain will need new rules since Ireland plans to remain in the EU. What will be the status of trade tariffs between the EU and Great Britain? In short, the disintegration process is complicated and highly political. While many in the EU would love to punish the British for leaving—charging a large leaving fee, raising tariffs, and the like—Great Britain remains a major trading partner of many EU states and is a member of NATO. As institutionalist theorists would emphasize, the shadow of the future is still present between the parties, influencing cooperation today. As of 2018, many details remain to be negotiated for Brexit to take place in the spring of 2019.

Beyond the EU itself, Europe is a patchwork of overlapping structures with varying memberships (see Figure 10.3). Despite the Single European Act, there are still many Europes. Within the EU are the "inner six" and the new arrivals, each with its own concerns. Around the edges are the EFTA states participating in the European Economic Area. NATO membership overlaps partly with the EU. Russia and even the United States are European actors in some respects but not others. One truly universal IGO exists in Europe—the *Organization for Security and Cooperation in Europe* (*OSCE*). Operating by consensus, with a large and universal membership of 56 states, the OSCE has little power except to act as a forum for discussions of security issues.

Thus, international integration is not a matter of a single group or organization but more a mosaic of structures tying states together. These various structures of the European political system, centered on the EU, are IGOs composed of states as members. But a less-tangible aspect of integration is the sense of identity that develops over time as economic (and other functional) ties bring people closer together across borders. Supranational identity, culture, and communication are also aspects of international integration. The remainder of this chapter considers how information technologies are bypassing states and bringing about this kind of integration globally.

10.4 The Power of Information

Explain two ways in which information can be a tool for governments and two ways in which information can be a tool used against governments.

Global telecommunications are profoundly changing how information and culture function in IR. These technological advances, at the center of globalization, are bringing the identity principle to the fore as communities interact across distances and borders. Newly empowered individuals and groups are creating new transnational networks worldwide, bypassing states.

10.4.1 Connecting the World

New international political possibilities arise from technological developments. The media over which information travels—telephones, television, films, magazines, and so forth—shape the way ideas take form and spread from one place to another. The media with the strongest political impact are television, radio, phones, and the Internet.

Figure 10.3 Overlapping Memberships of European States

TV AND RADIO   There are 1.4 billion households around the world with a TV set while an estimated 5 billion people around the world listen to radio. Radio and increasingly TV reach the poorest rural areas of the global South. Ordinary over-the-air TV and radio signals are radio waves of specific frequencies, which are a limited resource in high demand, regulated by governments. Because radio waves do not respect national borders, the allocation of frequencies is a subject of interstate bargaining. International regimes have grown up around the regulation of communications technologies, centered on the International Telecommunication Union (ITU).

Satellite TV bypasses states' control and fortifies transnational or supranational identity politics by allowing, for example, all Arabs in the world to see Arab satellite TV coverage of the Palestinian issue. The Qatar-based al Jazeera, begun in 1996, is a force in Middle Eastern politics and reaches an influential audience worldwide. Polls in Arab countries consistently list al Jazeera as the main source of international news by a large margin over any other satellite TV network. Several Arab governments, including Egypt, Saudi Arabia, and Jordan, have heavily criticized the network because of their diplomatic tensions with Qatar.

TELEPHONE AND INTERNET   Even more empowering of ordinary citizens are telephones and the Internet. Both provide ways for users to interact among themselves without a centralized information source. In 2017, the world had over 7.5 billion cell phone subscriptions, almost as many as people and far outnumbering the nearly 1 billion landlines. More than 4 billion people had mobile broadband Internet capability, including 100 percent of the population in South Korea and Singapore. India has nearly increased the number of cell phone subscribers since 2007 by five times, while China had nearly 1.4 billion cell phone subscribers as of 2017. The explosion of international phone traffic worldwide and of home and mobile access to the Internet is a clear indicator of globalization (see Figure 10.4).

Figure 10.4 World Phone and Internet Use, 2005–2017

Source: International Telecommunication Union (ITU) data

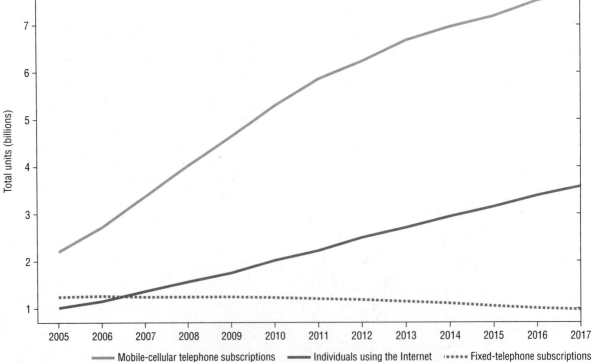

Mobile-cellular telephone subscriptions   Individuals using the Internet   Fixed-telephone subscriptions

One of the most politically important features of these technologies is the cell phone camera. It has empowered ordinary citizens to create visual records, such as videos of political demonstrations in one country that end up on TV in another country. In the 2011–2012 Arab Spring revolutions, especially in Syria, cell phone videos played a critical role in winning support by showing governments brutally murdering citizens. A related technological development of paramount political importance is the growth of social media such as Facebook and Twitter, which build communities and allow sharing of ideas (including those cell phone videos) outside government control and across international borders.

In Africa, cheap cell phones with cheap prepaid calling cards have let millions of relatively poor individuals communicate. In about a decade, sub-Saharan Africa saw subscribers increase to over 750 million by 2017. These phones empower individuals, for example, by letting farmers check market prices before deciding when to harvest crops. In one notable African success, Kenya has become the world's leader in using cell phones for banking. The country has 10 million banking transactions daily (averaging $20), but half the population lacks a bank account, so entrepreneurs developed the M-Pesa mobile payment system. City dwellers can transfer money to their home villages by phone instead of taking a wad of cash for a long bus ride. By 2017, these mobile fund transfers by over 20 million users (about two-thirds of the population) made up one-fourth of Kenya's GDP.

Deep political divisions over the Internet came into focus in December 2012, at a conference of the ITU in Dubai to develop a new treaty on the Internet and global telecommunications. Russia, China, and others saw the Internet as a system of government-controlled networks, while the United States and others, including Google and various NGOs, saw it as a more amorphous entity to facilitate the free flow of information. The U.S. House of Representatives, in a rare moment of bipartisanship, unanimously opposed the new treaty. In the end, 89 countries supported it, but 55 others would not sign.

THE DIGITAL DIVIDE   Taken on its own, the addition of phone and Internet capability in poor countries is impressive. But in comparison with rich regions, the gap persists (see Figure 10.5). A person living in the global North is far more likely than a person in the global South to have a landline, cell phone, and Internet access. This gap, along with the gap in access to information technologies *within* countries, is known as the **digital divide**.

digital divide The gap in access to information technologies between rich and poor people, and between the global North and the global South.

Figure 10.5 The North-South Digital Divide, 1994–2017

Source: International Telecommunication Union (ITU) data

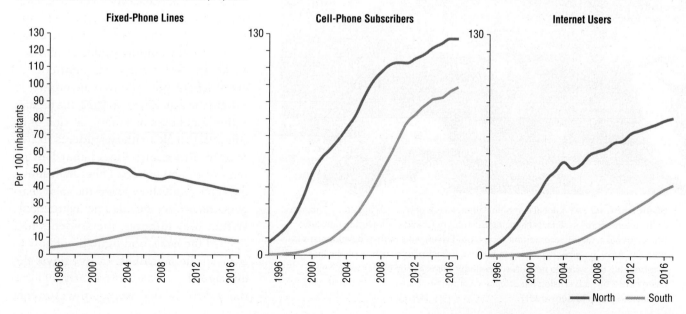

■— North   ■— South

As the Internet connects parts of the world into a tight network centered on the United States, Europe, and East Asia—where most Web users or netizens live—other regions are well behind in Internet access, especially via high-speed connections. In 2015, the Internet bandwidth per user was 25 times higher in Europe than in Africa. Less than 2 percent of individuals in the developing world have high-speed, broadband connections, compared to 25 percent in the developed world. The Internet reaches 85 percent of households in the global North but only 40 percent in the global South. The numbers for mobile phone Internet are 97 percent in the North and less than 50 percent in the South. Despite the growth of Internet use in the global South, a deep digital divide remains, favoring the wealthier North.

Some activists hope that the Internet can transform poor villages in the global South, partly by letting them produce traditional goods locally and market them globally. In one successful experiment in India in recent years, a businessman placed computer screens with pointing and clicking devices and high-speed Internet access in walls and kiosks in very poor slums. In each location, neighborhood kids quickly gathered, taught themselves to browse the Internet, and even invented their own terminology to describe the unfamiliar cursor and icons on the screen. This small-scale "hole-in-the-wall experiment" shows that simple methods can go far to break down the digital divide between the world's rich and poor.

A model project in Cambodia in 2001 helped revive a village silk-weaving industry by marketing locally made scarves on a village Web site. However, critics noted that the project was feasible only because a satellite company owned by the Thai prime minister donated $18,000 per year of link time. A U.S. aid organization provided the computers, training, Web site design, and credit card processing required to sell scarves from the village. The reality is that most poor villages cannot afford the Internet, cannot read the language of most Web sites, and cannot maintain computers and Web sites without extensive training.

Since 2007, the One Laptop per Child project has been mass-producing an inexpensive Web-capable wireless personal computer, priced at $200. The computers, designed by an MIT professor, can communicate with Internet access points, such as at school, and network with each other to extend Internet access along a chain, say, from school to students' homes. The laptops can be hand-powered, with one minute of exertion charging the battery for ten minutes of use. Several countries have ordered millions for their children, and about 3 million have shipped to 40 countries, notwithstanding problems and setbacks. In 2009, Uruguay bought one for every school-age child in that country. In a dramatic experiment in 2012, the organization sent boxes of a tablet version of its computer to elementary students in two remote Ethiopian villages that had no schools and no literacy. Other than showing some adults how to use the solar chargers, the project included no instructions. Within four minutes, the students had opened the boxes and figured out how to turn on the machines. In five days, the average child was using nearly 50 apps daily. Within two weeks, the students

SCAN HERE TO PAY Global communication, a very new capability on the timeline of the international system, is changing the rules of IR and empowering nonstate transnational actors. Telecommunications could change the path of development in poor countries, possibly bypassing traditional infrastructure such as phone lines and leapfrogging to a wireless networked economy. Here, a shop owner waits for customers while advertising the acceptance of the M-Pesa system—a mobile payments system in Kenya, 2017.

Noor Khamis/REUTERS

were singing ABC songs and teaching themselves to read. And in five months, they had hacked into the Android operating system to enable a camera and customize the desktop.

10.4.2 Information as a Tool of Governments

With more information traveling around the world than ever before, information has become an important instrument of governments' power (domestic and interstate). After the Soviet Union collapsed, leaders of the newly independent republics asked the U.S. secretary of state, "How do I get CNN?"[1] They wanted information. Today, governments can gather, organize, and store huge amounts of information. In this respect, the information revolution empowers governments more than ever. In the past, a wanted criminal, drug lord, or terrorist could slip over the border and take refuge in a foreign country. The terrorists who attacked the United States in 2001 demonstrated how easy this was. Today, however, it is more likely that a routine traffic ticket in the foreign country could trigger an instant directive to arrest the person. On the other hand, information technologies give repressive governments more power to keep tabs on citizens, spy on dissidents, and manipulate public opinion. Those technologies are now being mobilized in force to strengthen counterterrorism.

Just as citizens and terrorists find it harder to hide from governments, so are state governments finding it harder to hide information from each other. The military importance of satellite reconnaissance has been mentioned (see Chapter 6). A powerful state such as the United States can increase its power through information technologies. It can and does monitor phone calls, faxes, data transmissions, and radio conversations in foreign countries. The revelation in 2013 that the National Security Agency (NSA) and other American agencies had mass surveillance programs showed that even democratically accountable governments can use technology to monitor their own citizens.

In the Arab Spring movements in 2011, protesters were not the only ones to deploy Internet capabilities; governments did as well. Egypt successfully blocked a choke point and cut off international Web access. And Syria's government used its own hackers to track down the identities of protesters anonymously posting antigovernment videos and messages on the Web. The U.S. government in response trained democracy activists in technologies of the Internet and social media and created shadow Internet and cell phone networks inside foreign countries whose governments were trying to shut down communications.

As the cost of information technology decreases, it comes into reach of more states. Now small states can gain some of the same capabilities electronically. Even sophisticated information is more available and cheaper—high-resolution satellite photos are now available commercially and are cheap or free. These images can be used for both military purposes and natural resource management—for example, knowing which states (including one's own) have resources such as oil, minerals, forests, and farmland, and the rate at which they are being used.

Most governments create explicit channels of information dissemination to influence domestic and international audiences. Stations such as Radio Moscow broadcast radio programs in dozens of languages aimed at all the world's regions. The United States operates the Voice of America (VOA) shortwave radio network, which is picked up in many remote regions.

Governments spread false as well as true information as a means of international influence. This is called *disinformation*. In the 1930s, the Nazis discovered that the "big lie," if repeated enough times, would be accepted as truth by most people. It is harder to fool international audiences these days, but domestic ones can still respond to propagandistic misinformation.

---

[1] Peter Arnett. (1992). *Exporting the First Amendment to the World.* Published by University of Arizona.

Indeed, the 2016 U.S. presidential election was the target of Russia hackers, including a Russian organization known as the Internet Research Agency. Dozens of Russians posted on Facebook and Twitter to disparage some presidential candidates (Hillary Clinton and Ted Cruz) and support others (Donald Trump and Bernie Sanders). These "trolls," to use the slang for frequent Internet posters who attempt to sow discord on the Internet, posted thousands of times on Facebook and Twitter in attempts to influence voters and even created fake political events to encourage partisan fights. Whether these attempts had any influence on the outcome of the election or not, it is clear that Russia (among other states) has decided to use cyberattacks as a tool of leverage to influence other states (see the Public Opinion and International Relations box).

Public Opinion and International Relations
The Danger of Cyberattacks

The 2016 presidential election in the United States drew attention to the growing use of cyberattacks and espionage to disrupt day-to-day activities of governments and individuals. Yet, the actions of Russia during the U.S. elections were not aimed at disrupting daily life, as with its past attacks against other countries. Nor is Russia alone in its efforts to use the Internet as a tool of leverage: China, the United States, and many other countries have used the Internet as a military or diplomatic tool to influence world politics.

Because of the growing usage of the Internet as a foreign policy tool, global citizens have become more aware that the Internet can be used against them and their country. A 2016 survey asked citizens of 13 countries whether they felt cyberattacks were a major threat, a minor threat, or not a threat to their country (see Figure 10.6). The perceived level of threat from cyberattacks varied, although majorities in nine of the 13 countries felt potential attacks were a major threat.

Interestingly, the country with the least fear of cyberattacks is China—a country with extensive experience in conducting

such attacks. Just over 20 percent of Chinese citizens consider cyberattacks a major threat, while approximately 25 percent see no threat at all. China's neighbor, Japan, has the highest level of concern about cyberattacks, above 80 percent.

Two other countries show somewhat less concern about cyberattacks than do other states: Greece and India. For Greece, other issues may loom as more threatening to its public as that country continues to struggle in the aftermath of its debt crisis. India, like China, is home to a large number of sophisticated programmers, which could account for that country's lower level of concern. It is also possible that because the Internet is still less widespread in China and India's poorer regions, few respondents in those areas would find cyberattacks to be of any concern.

Despite these three cases of lower concern, most citizens of these states are concerned about cyberattacks. As stories of cyberattacks, espionage, and other uses of the Internet to serve state power become more common, these numbers will no doubt remain high.

Figure 10.6 Public Opinion Concerning Cyberattacks in 13 Countries

Source: Pew Research Center.

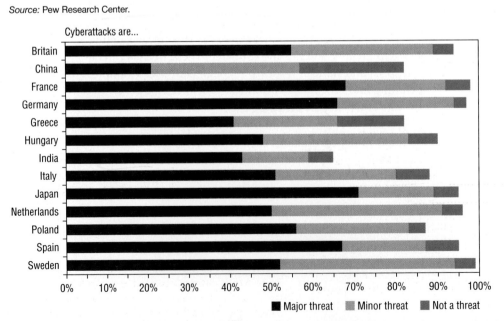

Most governments (but not the U.S. government) own and operate at least one main TV station, and many hold a monopoly on TV stations. Thus, TV signals often rank with military equipment and currency as capabilities so important to a government that it must control them itself. Indeed, in a military coup d'état, usually one of the first and most important targets seized is the television broadcasting facility.

10.4.3 Information as a Tool Used Against Governments

Information can be used against governments as well, by foreign governments, NGOs, or domestic political opponents. Governments, especially repressive ones, fear the free flow of information, for good reason. New information technologies have become powerful tools of domestic opposition movements and their allies in foreign governments. Television coverage has fed popular discontent regarding the current U.S. war in Iraq, as it did for the Vietnam War and the Russian war in Chechnya.

More than 700 million Chinese use the Internet, though that use is not uncensored. It is estimated that the Chinese government censors over 6 million Web sites. In Iran, where millions of people have used the Internet to discuss taboo topics such as sex, fashion, and politics, the government was widely criticized for cracking down on protesters after a disputed election in 2009. That crackdown was broadcast on Internet sites such as Twitter and Facebook as opposition members posted videos and pictures of beatings and even the shooting death of a female protester. The Arab Spring protesters later adopted these methods.

In the Philippines in 2001, huge protests that swept a president from office were organized through text messages on cell phones. In Ghana, very popular talk shows on private FM radio programs—allowed after 1995—gave voice to ordinary people who then threw out the ruling party in 2000. Antigovernment protesters used common Twitter hashtags to coordinate protests against Ukraine's president in the spring of 2014.

To counteract such uses of information, governments throughout the world try to limit the flow of unfavorable information—especially information from foreign sources. These efforts can include censorship of individual sites or services or can extend to a complete shutdown of the Internet. China, for example, channels all access to the Internet through a few state-controlled service providers, and it filters the hundreds of billions of text messages exchanged annually among over 1 billion Chinese cell phone subscribers. China has famously banned Facebook and Twitter, yet Chinese alternatives to these social media sites, such as WeChat and Weibo, have many millions of users (WeChat has nearly 1 billion users, and Weibo surpassed Twitter in 2017 with over 350 million users).

Internet companies based in the United States have differed in their response to Chinese censorship, known in the West as "the Great Firewall." In 2010, Google announced that it would no longer comply with Chinese law that censors Internet searches by blocking politically sensitive words from its Chinese search engine. Later, Google compromised with the Chinese

Majdi Fathi/Newscom

HOT OFF THE PRESS Information, which easily crosses state borders, is a major factor in both international and domestic politics. Governments have many ways to try to control information. Here, Palestinian journalists protest in solidarity with al Jazeera after reports that the Israeli government was considering shutting down the station's offices in Jerusalem, 2017.

[handwritten notes in margin:]
States w/ Internet Censor.
- China
- Iran
- Turkey
- North Korea
- Vietnam
- Saudi Arabia
- Democratic Congo

government, angering some U.S. critics. In 2017, Apple agreed that all data posted in its cloud servers would be moved to servers physically located in China. Thus, while U.S. companies may object to Chinese government censorship, it is hard to resist hundreds of millions of Chinese Internet users as a customer base.

Other countries maintain extensive restrictions on the Internet as well. Iran bans Twitter, Turkey banned access to Wikipedia in 2017, only 4 percent of North Koreans can use the Internet, Saudi Arabia blocks over 400,000 sites, and Vietnam forces all Internet providers to turn over information on all bloggers. Countries can also choose to shut down the entire Internet at times. For example, in response to protests against its president in 2015, the Democratic Congo imposed an Internet blackout to stop protests from growing.

Information technologies have security implications. Capabilities such as fiber-optic cables or satellite communications serve governments in conducting their foreign and military policies (see Evolving Technologies in Chapter 6). Nonstate actors such as terrorist organizations have also harnessed the power of cell phones and the Internet to recruit operatives, raise money, and coordinate attacks—even to detonate improvised explosive devices remotely with a cell phone's ring triggering the bomb when called. Recall that new "smart weapons" technologies empower foot soldiers relative to large weapons systems. New communications technologies may be doing the same for ordinary citizens relative to governments and political parties.

The Internet in many ways empowers small fringe groups relative to states and leaves states vulnerable in new ways. Hackers have taken over control of U.S. government computers and have unleashed costly viruses against businesses and people worldwide. These cyberattacks by small-scale actors may target foreign countries, including their governments, businesses, and universities. In 2015, Penn State University was forced to disconnect computers in its engineering school after it was discovered that Chinese hackers had stolen sensitive research information.

Another challenge to governments is the growing popularity of cryptocurrencies, or **virtual currencies**. Users create these currencies as a way to facilitate the exchange of goods and services beyond the control of governments. Neither governments nor banks control virtual currencies (at the moment). The advantage of virtual currencies is that their value is global: No single country sets the market value of such currencies, and they can be used anywhere that will accept them as a form of payment. One risk is that, without government backing, there is little to stabilize the value of the currencies and they are thus subject to wide swings in value. There is also a risk that governments could try to make transactions using virtual currencies illegal (China banned some virtual currency activities in 2017).

Bitcoin is the most popular virtual currency, but many others exist. The creation and usage of virtual currencies illustrate the idea, promoted by constructivist theories (see Chapter 3), that money is a social construct. All currencies, whether virtual or government backed, have value because of a shared understanding among individuals. Virtual currencies show that one does not even need a piece of paper as a symbol for

virtual currencies Currencies created by users as a way to facilitate the exchange of goods and services beyond the control of governments.

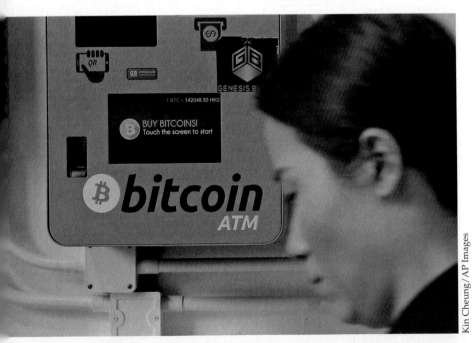

Kin Cheung/ AP Images

VIRTUAL MONEY States do not control the global flow of information, which has become a potent force in world politics, challenging state power. This challenge has even spread to the world of money, which is traditionally printed and controlled by states. Virtual currencies, like bitcoin, are not controlled by governments or banks and can be spent anonymously. Here, a woman in Hong Kong walks by a bitcoin ATM, 2017.

that value to exist. These new currencies remain controversial among some financial experts who fear they are simply a trendy investment, while others argue they have the potential to transform global finance.

A growing number of governments worry that terrorists could use the Internet to cause massive disruptions in daily life. In 2017, an ISIS-affiliated hacker group took over several British national health care Web sites to display gruesome pictures of Syrian war victims. American military officials have stressed the dangers of cyberattacks on defense systems as well. As discussed in Chapter 6, in the world of military conflicts, cyberspace is now a field of battle similar to air, land, and sea.

All in all, the tide of technology seems to be running against governments. Information gets through, and no political power seems capable of holding it back for long. As more and more communication channels carry more information to more places, governments become just another player in a crowded field.

10.4.4 Telecommunications and Global Culture

As the information revolution continues to unfold, it will further increase international interdependence, making actions in one state reverberate in other states more strongly than in the past. Information is thus slowly undermining realists' assumptions of state sovereignty and territorial integrity. At the same time, by empowering substate and transnational actors, information technology is undermining the centrality of states themselves in world affairs.

The information revolution greatly increases *transparency* in IR. As a result, states do not need to arm against unknown potential threats because they see the real threats. Similarly, the ability to monitor performance of agreements makes collective goods problems easier to resolve because cheaters and free riders can be identified. Moreover, the availability of instant communications channels enhances the ability of governments to bargain effectively with each other and to reach mutually beneficial outcomes. In these ways, the increased transparency allowed by new technologies strengthens the reciprocity principle as a solution to IR conflicts. The complex monitoring and accounting required in international agreements based on reciprocity—from trade deals to arms control—becomes much easier in a transparent world.

Telecommunications, with its ability to connect communities beyond geographic space, is also strengthening the identity principle in IR because people's identities have new sources and new avenues of expression that often transcend national borders. In the past, nationalism has tapped into the psychological dynamics of group identity in a powerful way that has legitimized the state as the ultimate embodiment of its people's aspirations and identity. Now the information revolution may aid the development of transnational or supranational identities. Journalists, scientists, and church members, among others, work in communities spanning national borders. So do members of transnational movements, such as those linking women from various countries, or

Kyodo/AP Images

SPORTS AS DIPLOMACY The power of information can create and strengthen global communities that cross or even transcend national borders. The Olympics are watched on TV and the Internet around the world, as athletes compete in a spirit of friendly global competition. The 2018 Winter Olympics, hosted by South Korea, occurred during a time of significant military tensions on the Korean peninsula. Nonetheless, the North and South Korean Olympic teams decided to enter as a unified team during the opening ceremonies.

environmentalists, or human rights activists. The links forged in such transnational communities may create a new functionalism that could encourage international integration on a global scale.

Sports also create transnational communities. Citizens of different states share their admiration of sports stars, who become international celebrities. The Olympics (run by the International Olympic Committee, an NGO) is a global event with a worldwide audience. The U.S.-Chinese rapprochement of 1971 was so delicate that political cooperation was impossible until sports had first paved the way—the U.S. table tennis team that made the first official U.S. visit to China.

Finally, tourism also builds transnational communities. International tourists cross borders over 600 million times a year. Tourism ranks among the top export industries worldwide. People who travel to other countries often develop both a deeper understanding and a deeper appreciation for those countries. Added to these contacts are exchange students and those who attend college in a foreign country.

Like international integration and globalization generally, global culture has its downside. The emerging global culture is primarily the culture of white Europeans and their descendants in rich areas of the world (mixed slightly with cultural elements of Japan and local elites in the global South). This cultural dominance has been referred to as **cultural imperialism**. For many people, especially in the global South, the information revolution carrying global culture into their midst is, despite its empowering potential, an invasive force in practice. Because cultures are being subsumed, half of the world's nearly 7,000 languages risk extinction this century, according to UNESCO.

Above all, the emerging global culture is dominated by the world's superpower, the United States; U.S. cultural influence is at least as strong as U.S. military influence. Culture may be just another economic product, to be produced in the place of greatest comparative advantage, but culture is also central to national identity and politics. The prospect of cultural imperialism thus opens another front in the conflict of liberalism and mercantilism. Even the architecture of cyberspace assumes the United States as the default in domain names such as .gov (U.S. government) and .mil (U.S. military). At the UN-sponsored World Summit on the Information Society in 2005, Europe and developing countries tried unsuccessfully to break the monopoly held by a U.S. consortium over registering domain names, including country-code domains such as ".uk" (Britain) and ".cn" (China) that states want to control as a matter of national sovereignty. By 2009, however, the Internet's governing body, the Internet Corporation for Assigned Names and Numbers (ICANN), announced that Internet addresses can now contain non-Latin characters. This will allow addresses to contain Chinese, Cyrillic, Japanese, Arabic, or any number of non-Latin-based characters to form a Web address.

Recent trends seem to be moving toward a more multilateral world culture. For example, South Korea's Ministry of Culture has supported the mass production of a new, fast growing, billion-dollar export product, Korean pop music (K-pop). Boy and girl bands are systematically recruited and developed, then marketed globally via social media. Another highly successful cultural export product can be found in Brazilian soap operas.

These supranational cultural influences are still in their infancy. Over the coming years and decades, their shape will become clearer, and scholars will be able to determine more accurately how they influence world politics and state sovereignty. We need not wait as long to see the effects of a different kind of supranational influence, however. Environmental problems, which rarely recognize national borders, have forced states into ever-closer cooperation as political leaders find that the only effective responses are at a supranational level. These issues will be discussed in Chapter 11.

cultural imperialism A term critical of U.S. dominance of the emerging global culture.

Chapter Review

Summary

- Supranational processes bring states together in larger structures and identities. These processes generally lead to an ongoing struggle between nationalism and supranationalism.

- International integration—the partial shifting of sovereignty from the state toward supranational institutions—is considered an outgrowth of international cooperation in functional (technical and economic) issue areas.

- Integration theorists thought that functional cooperation would spill over into political integration in foreign policy and military issue areas. Instead, forces of disintegration tore apart previously existing states such as the Soviet Union.

- The European Union (EU) is the most advanced case of integration. Its 28 member states have given considerable power to the EU in economic decision making. However, national power still outweighs supranational power even in the EU.

- Since the founding of the European Coal and Steel Community (ECSC) in 1952, the mission and membership of what is now the EU have expanded continually.

- The most important and most successful element in the EU is its customs union (and the associated free trade area). Goods can cross borders of member states freely, and the members can adopt unified tariffs with regard to goods entering from outside the EU.

- Under the EU's Common Agricultural Policy (CAP), subsidies to farmers are made uniform within the community. Carrying out the CAP consumes 40 percent of the EU's budget. EU agricultural subsidies are a major source of trade conflict with the United States.

- The EU has a monetary union with a single European currency (the euro) in 19 of the 28 EU states. It is the biggest experiment with money in history and had great success in its first years, but it hit a crisis in 2010–2015 over members' debts. A monetary union requires roughly comparable inflation rates and financial stability in participating states.

- In structure, the EU revolves around the permanent staff of Eurocrats under the European Commission. The Commission's president, individual members, and staff all serve Europe as a whole—a supranational role. However, the Council of the European Union representing member states (in national roles) has power over the Commission.

- The European Parliament has members directly elected by citizens in EU states, but it has few powers and cannot legislate the rules for the Community. The European Court of Justice also has limited powers, but it has extended its jurisdiction more successfully than any other international court and can overrule national laws.

- The 1991 Maastricht Treaty on closer European integration (monetary union and political-military coordination) provoked a public backlash in several countries against the power of EU bureaucrats.

- Twelve new members, mostly Eastern European, joined the EU in 2004 and 2007. The EU's structures and procedures were adapted as it moved from 15 to 28 members. The EU faces challenges in deciding how far to expand its membership, particularly regarding Turkey.

- The nationalist backlash to globalization has generated significant debates about the EU, including the British decision in 2016 to leave the EU. Nationalist, anti-EU political parties have gained support in several central European EU members.

- A different type of international integration can be seen in the growing role of communication and information operating across national borders. New information technologies—especially mass media such as TV, radio, and the Internet—are fostering supranational relationships and identities, although the process is still in an early stage.

- Internet governance is under negotiation at UN meetings, notably one in 2012, where 89 countries supported a new treaty giving governments more power, but 55 others would not sign.

- Governments use the dissemination of information across borders as a means of influencing other states. Government access to information can also increase the stability of international relationships because the security dilemma and other collective goods problems become less difficult in a transparent world.

- The greater and freer flow of information around the world can undermine the authority and power of governments as well. Virtual currencies are a way for individuals and groups to engage in transactions without the oversight of governments. In addition, authoritarian governments find it hard to limit the flow of information into and out of their states, despite extensive efforts to do so.

• Telecommunications are contributing to the development of global cultural integration. This process may hold the potential for the development of a single world culture. However, some politicians and citizens worry about cultural imperialism—that such a culture would be too strongly dominated by the United States.

Key Terms

supranational 319
international integration 319
neofunctionalism 320
security community 321
European Union (EU) 322
Treaty of Rome 323
Euratom 323
free trade area 323

customs union 323
common market 323
Common Agricultural Policy
    (CAP) 323
European Commission 324
Council of the European Union 324
European Parliament 325
European Court of Justice 326

Single European Act 326
Maastricht Treaty 327
euro 327
Lisbon Treaty 332
digital divide 337
virtual currencies 342
cultural imperialism 344

Critical Thinking Questions

1. Functional economic ties among European states have contributed to the emergence of a supranational political structure, the EU, which has considerable though not unlimited power. Do you think the same thing could happen in North America? Could the United States, Canada, and Mexico form a future North American Union like the EU? What problems would it be likely to face, given the experience of the EU?

2. Suppose you happened to be chatting with the president of the European Commission, who is complaining about the public reaction in European states against the growing power of the Commission's Eurocrats. What advice would you give? What steps could the Commission take to calm such fears without reversing the process of integration? How would your suggestions address the resentments that many European citizens or governments feel against the European Commission?

3. What are the implications of Great Britain voting to leave the European Union? Is this the first sign that nationalist sentiment will unravel the EU or will the forces of supranationalism emerge stronger?

4. Information technologies are strengthening transnational and supranational communications and identity. However, they are also providing states with new instruments of power and control. Which aspect do you find predominant now? Are these new capabilities helpful or harmful to state governments? Why? Do you expect your answer to change in the future as technology continues to develop?

5. What are the good and bad effects, in your opinion, of the emergence of global communications and culture? Should we be cheering or lamenting the possibility of one world culture? Does the answer depend on where one lives in the world? Give concrete examples of the effects you discuss.

Suggested Readings

Dinan, Desmond, Neill Nugent, and William E. Paterson. *The European Union in Crisis.* Palgrave, 2017.

Hanson, Elizabeth C. *The Information Revolution in World Politics.* Rowman & Littlefield, 2008.

Moravcsik, Andrew. *The Choice for Europe: Social Purpose and State Power from Messina to Maastricht.* Cornell, 1998.

Pollack, Mark A. *The Engines of Integration: Delegation, Agency, and Agenda Setting in the European Union.* Oxford, 2003.

Ragnedda, Massimo, and Glenn W. Muschert, eds. *The Digital Divide: The Internet and Social Inequality in International Perspective.* Routledge, 2015.

Let's Debate the Issue
Has European Integration Gone as Far as Possible?

Overview

Since the creation of the European Coal and Steel Community, there appears to be a forward-moving process of integration in Europe. The European Union is now the major political force in Europe. It is economically large, with an aggregate GDP greater than that of the United States. It is a powerful force diplomatically, mediating international disputes and conflicts, even those involving other great powers. It possesses significant influence inside and outside Europe.

Yet the EU has lately had difficulty furthering the integration process. After the adoption of the euro, the EU changed its focus from deepening integration (taking over more policy areas from member states) to broadening membership by admitting former Eastern European states to membership. This expansion has extended the economic and political power of the EU, but it has also resulted in challenges. The global economic recession also put strains on the EU, with the Hungarian prime minister warning in 2009 of a "new iron curtain" between rich (Western European) and poor (Eastern European) states. The refugee crisis of 2015 and the subsequent decision of the British to leave the EU are significant events that threaten EU integration efforts.

Some now wonder whether European integration has run its course. Have the last steps toward deepening integration already taken place? Are there more issues on which states will surrender their sovereignty in favor of supranationalism, or is the EU left only to add more members?

ARGUMENT 1

The Progress of the EU Integration Process Is Finished

Troubles with the proposed Constitution and new Lisbon Treaty prove there are difficulties. The rejection of the proposed European Constitution in 2007 and the initial rejection of the Lisbon Treaty in 2008 show that considerable challenges lie ahead when it comes to implementing major EU policy changes. Even the attempt to guarantee individual rights in Europe created controversy.

The number of members makes it nearly impossible to accomplish major change. Many of the major EU changes, including the Single European Act and the Maastricht Treaty, began when the EU had 12 or 15 members. Now, with 28 members, finding agreement among all the states will be extremely difficult, especially on issues that require unanimous consent.

Public opinion is skeptical of further integration. "Euroskeptics," as they are labeled, are increasingly common in Europe and now powerful in several member state parliaments. While public support may not directly influence EU policy, the public may begin to vote for leaders and political parties that will put a halt to EU integration (and possibly expansion as well), as the British did in 2016.

ARGUMENT 2

The EU Integration Process Will Continue to Advance

Obstacles have been overcome in the past. Few observers gave the EU much of a chance to get the euro off the ground, yet it has succeeded in doing so. Soon after the defeat of the Lisbon Treaty in Ireland, a new agreement was reached to allow a second vote. EU ministers have been persistent and creative in their attempts to deepen the integration process. The same will likely be true of Brexit negotiations.

External factors will drive deepening integration. With the failure of the Doha Round of WTO negotiations and tensions with the United States over when and where NATO forces should be used, the EU has strong incentives to deepen cooperation among its members. It now knows it cannot rely only on the WTO to further trade liberalization or on the United States for military leadership.

The EU is flexible enough to deal with large numbers of members. Many cooks in the kitchen does not necessarily mean bad broth. The EU has been and remains flexible about how member states respond to the deepening of cooperation. The euro is a perfect example—not all members use the euro, some from economic necessity but some by choice (for example, Britain). Thus, further integration does not require unanimous adoption of all policies.

Questions

- Will the EU branch out into new issue areas or focus only on expanding to new members for the foreseeable future? Is there a natural geographic limit to the boundaries of the EU? How will the potential exit of Great Britain influence the future?

- Could the EU separate into two tiers: the wealthier Western European states and the poorer Eastern

European states? Would the EU be as important politically and economically if only certain states cooperated on some issues? Could a euro-like solution work in other policy areas?

• What other functions could the EU attempt to perform? What would the prospects for success be in deepening military cooperation or budgetary coordination? How would increasing military cooperation fit with many EU states' existing commitment to NATO?

For Further Reading

Kahanec, Martin, and Klaus F. Zimmermann, eds. *Labor Migration, EU Enlargement, and the Great Recession.* Springer, 2016.

Schimmelfennig, Frank. *The Politics of European Union Enlargement: Theoretical Approaches.* Routledge, 2005.

Sjursen, Helene. *Questioning EU Enlargement.* Routledge, 2006.

Szcerbiak, Aleks, and Paul Taggart, eds. *EU Enlargement and Referendums.* Routledge, 2013.

Chapter 11
Environment and Population

WINDMILL AND NUCLEAR POWER PLANT, BRITAIN, MID-1980S.

 Learning Objectives

11.1 Illustrate the collective action problem facing the international community by focusing on one global environmental issue.

11.2 Evaluate the roadblocks to achieving a successful international agreement to address the problem of global warming.

11.3 Describe three ways in which the need for natural resources can create international conflict.

11.4 Explain the demographic transition and why some states are vulnerable to rapid population growth.

11.1 Interdependence and the Environment

Illustrate the collective action problem facing the international community by focusing on one global environmental issue.

Global threats to the natural environment are a growing source of interdependence. States' actions regarding pollution, conservation, and natural resources routinely affect other states. Because environmental effects tend to be diffuse and long term and because such effects easily spread from one location to another, international environmental politics creates difficult collective goods problems (see Chapter 1). A sustainable natural environment is a collective good, and states bargain over how to distribute the costs of providing that good. The technical, scientific, and ethical aspects of managing the environment are complex, but the basic nature of states' interests is not. The collective goods problem arises in each issue area concerning the environment, resources, and population.

For example, the world's major fisheries in international waters are not owned by any state; they are a collective good. The various fishing states must cooperate (partly by regulating nonstate actors such as multinational corporations [MNCs]) to avoid depleting the stocks of fish. If too many states fail to cooperate, the fish populations decline and everyone's catch drops. And indeed, in 1997–2007, catches worldwide declined significantly. It is estimated that 90 percent of large fish stocks have disappeared. Fishers have moved on to new species of seafood after depleting earlier ones, but they have already depleted a third of the species, with the rest projected to go by midcentury. Because the world's states did not solve the collective goods problem of world fisheries, they are paying $20 billion a year in subsidies to bankrupt fishing industries in their respective countries. An effort to end these subsidies failed at the 2017 WTO meetings, prompting the European Union's (EU) trade commissioner to lament: "we cannot even agree to stop subsidizing illegal fishing!"

This depletion occurred because each additional fishing boat—and the MNC that owns it as well as its state of origin—gains by catching an additional fish. The benefits of that fish go entirely to the one catching it, whereas the eventual costs of depleted stocks will be shared by all who fish there. But what is a state's fair quota of fish? No world government exists to decide such a question, so states must enter into multilateral negotiations, agreements, and regimes. Such efforts create not only new avenues for functionalism and international integration, but also new potentials for conflict and instances of the Prisoner's Dilemma.

In 1999, a UN-sponsored agreement among all the world's major fishing states set goals to reduce fleet overcapacity. (Four million fishing boats operate worldwide, of which 40,000 are ships larger than 100 tons.) Participating nations are capping the size of fishing fleets and then scaling them back gradually, while reducing subsidies. The pain of unemployment and economic adjustment should thus be shared. However, the agreement is voluntary; its implementation delayed; and its effect on collapsing fisheries probably too little, too late.

This type of collective goods dilemma has been called the **tragedy of the commons**. Centuries ago, the commons were shared grazing land in Britain. As with fisheries, if too many people kept too many sheep, the commons would be overgrazed. Yet adding one more sheep was profitable to that sheep's owner. Britain solved the problem by **enclosure** of the commons—splitting it into privately owned pieces on each of which a single owner would have an incentive to manage resources responsibly. The world's states have taken a similar approach to coastal fisheries by extending territorial waters to put more fish under the control of single states (see Chapter 5). The *global commons* refers to the shared parts of the earth, such as the oceans and outer space.

tragedy of the commons
A collective goods dilemma that is created when common environmental assets (such as the world's fisheries) are depleted or degraded through the failure of states to cooperate effectively. One solution is to "enclose" the commons (split them into individually owned pieces); international regimes can also be a (partial) solution.

enclosure The splitting of a common area or good into privately owned pieces, giving individual owners an incentive to manage resources responsibly.

As in other areas of international political economy (IPE), the solution of environmental collective goods problems is based on achieving shared benefits that depend on overcoming conflicting interests. *Regimes* are an important part of the solution (see Chapter 3), providing rules based on the reciprocity principle to govern bargaining over who gets the benefits and bears the costs of environmental protection. Functional international organizations (IOs) specialize in technical and management aspects of the environment.

Increasingly, these IOs overlap with broader communities of experts from various states that structure the way states manage environmental issues; these have been called *epistemic communities* (knowledge-based communities). For example, the transnational community of experts and policy makers concerned with pollution in the Mediterranean is an epistemic community.

In global environmental politics, it is hard to manage collective goods problems because of the large number of actors. Collective goods are easier to provide in small groups, in which individual actions have more impact on the total picture and cheating is more noticeable. The opposite is true with the environment. The actions of nearly 200 states (albeit some more than others) aggregate to cause indirect but serious consequences throughout the world.

Dake Kang/AP Images

SOMETHING FISHY The depletion of global fish stocks is an example of the tragedy of the commons, where public goods (here, fish) are overused, depriving everyone. Agreements can be made to allocate public goods to different countries, but those agreements must be enforced or the tragedy of the commons will reemerge. Here, members of Thailand's navy check a boat for illegal fishing, 2016.

Interest in the environment has grown steadily since the first Earth Day organized by environmental activists in 1970. The first UN conference on the international environment took place in Stockholm, Sweden, in 1972. It adopted general principles—that one state's actions should not cause environmental damage to another, for instance—and raised awareness about international aspects of environmental damage. A second conference was held, with less publicity, in 1982 in Nairobi, Kenya (headquarters of the UN Environment Program). The larger and more ambitious 1992 Earth Summit in Rio de Janeiro, Brazil, brought together more than 100 state leaders.

11.1.1 Sustainable Development

A major theme of these conferences is *sustainable* development. This refers to economic growth that does not deplete resources and destroy ecosystems so quickly that the basis of that economic growth is itself undermined. The concept applies to both the industrialized regions and the global South.

The 1992 Earth Summit established the *Commission on Sustainable Development*, which monitors states' compliance with the promises they made at the Earth Summit and hears evidence from environmental nongovernmental organizations (NGOs) such as Greenpeace. In 2013 the High-Level Political Forum on Sustainable Development replaced the Commission. But this new forum, like its predecessor, lacks powers of enforcement over national governments—again reflecting the preeminence of state sovereignty over supranational authority. All UN members can participate in the forum. The forum's ability to monitor and publicize state actions is supposed to discourage states from cheating (a version of "naming and shaming" discussed by constructivist scholars). But progress has been slow.

China and other developing countries in Asia stand at the center of the debate over sustainable development. In the drive for rapid economic growth, these countries have created serious pollution and other environmental problems. In early 2013, Beijing's smog far exceeded dangerous levels, and residents who ventured outside suffered burning lungs and stinging eyes. Because of China's size, any success in developing its economy along Western industrialized lines (for example, with mass ownership of automobiles) could create shocks to the global environment. In recent years, while China has been scouring the planet for raw materials, it has also become a leader in the development of green technology. For example, China now dominates the production of solar panels. And after the 2013 air pollution crisis, the Chinese government implemented tight restrictions on pollution. But much of China's growth has been powered by polluting, coal-burning power plants.

11.2 Managing the Environment

Evaluate the roadblocks to achieving a successful international agreement to address the problem of global warming.

Most global environmental problems are those that involve collective goods for all states and people in the world.

11.2.1 The Atmosphere

global warming A slow, long-term rise in the average world temperature caused by the emission of greenhouse gases produced by burning fossil fuels—oil, coal, and natural gas. See also *greenhouse gases*.

Preserving the health of the earth's atmosphere is a benefit that affects people throughout the world without regard for their own state's contribution to the problem or its solution. Two problems of the atmosphere have become major international issues—global warming and depletion of the ozone layer.

NOT SUSTAINABLE Developing countries such as China rely heavily on coal and other dirty technologies for the energy and raw materials they need. As it grows rapidly, China is literally choking on its own pollution. In 2013, the Beijing air quality far exceeded the most dangerous end of the pollution scale, leading the Chinese government to greatly restrict the burning of fossil fuels. While air pollution has improved under these new policies, significant pollution remains. Here, a family takes a photo with smog-covered Shanghai in the background, 2018.

Zhong Yang / AP Images

GLOBAL WARMING Global climate change, or **global warming**, is a long-term rise in the average world temperature. Growing and compelling evidence shows that global warming is a real problem, that it is caused by the emission of carbon dioxide and other gases, and that it will get much worse in the future. The issue of global warming has risen high on the political agenda in the past decade because of massive melt-offs of Arctic ice; freakish weather; and devastating storms, including three major hurricanes in 2017 that caused over $250 billion in damage. Unfortunately, the international community has had little success solving the problem.

Over the coming decades, according to most estimates, global temperatures may rise by between 3 and 10 degrees Fahrenheit if nothing is done. Possibly within a few decades, the polar ice caps will begin to melt and cause the sea level to rise by as much as a few feet. Studies in 2012 confirmed that the warming trend is accelerating, faster than what had been seen as worst-case scenarios. The ten warmest years on record have happened since 1998, with the five warmest recorded since 2010. Global warming could flood many coastal cities and devastate low-lying areas such as the heavily populated coastal areas of Bangladesh and China. Urgent calls for action to avert global warming come from island states in the Pacific that will likely disappear this century. Indeed, reflecting an all-too-realistic lack of faith in international action, the low-lying state of the Maldives created a fund to buy land in another country to move its 300,000 residents as its territory disappears.

Global climate change has begun to alter weather patterns in many regions, causing droughts, floods, freezes, and widespread disruption of natural ecosystems. It is also possible that climate changes could *benefit* some regions and make agriculture more productive. Melting of polar ice is opening new shipping routes north of Canada and Russia that could potentially cut weeks off the transit time from northern Europe or America to Asia (see Figure 11.1), a huge savings for global business. Furthermore, the Arctic seas hold large deposits of oil and gas, which will become commercially accessible as the ice melts (and, ironically, contribute to even more global warming).

The **UN Environment Program (UNEP)**, whose main function is to monitor environmental conditions, works with the World Meteorological Organization to measure changes in global climate from year to year. Since 1989, the UN-sponsored *Intergovernmental Panel on Climate Change (IPCC)* has served as a negotiating forum for this issue. In 2013, the IPCC issued a report from scientists around the world concluding that global warming is "unequivocally" caused by human behavior.

It is costly to reduce the emissions of gases—mainly carbon dioxide—that cause global warming. These gases result from the broad spectrum of activities that drive an industrial economy. They are a by-product of burning *fossil fuels*—oil, coal, and natural gas—to run cars, tractors, furnaces, factories, and so forth. These activities create **greenhouse gases**—so named because, when concentrated in the atmosphere, these gases act like the glass in a greenhouse: They let energy in as short-wavelength solar radiation but reflect it back when it tries to exit again as longer-wavelength heat waves. The greenhouse gases are *carbon dioxide* (responsible for two-thirds of the effect), *methane gas*, *chlorofluorocarbons* (CFCs), and *nitrous oxide*. Particulate matter from diesel engines (in the global North) and dirty cookstoves (in the South) are also major contributors. Ironically, data stored in "the cloud," seemingly free from earthly concerns, actually live in data centers that use vast amounts of electricity and run large diesel generators that contribute to global warming.

UN Environment Program (UNEP) A program that monitors environmental conditions and, among other activities, works with the World Meteorological Organization to measure changes in global climate.

greenhouse gases Carbon dioxide and other gases that, when concentrated in the atmosphere, act like the glass in a greenhouse, holding energy in and leading to global warming.

Figure 11.1 Potential Arctic Shipping Routes

Source: Based on United Nations Environment Program.

Northwest Passage
8,500 miles

Northern Sea Route
8,000 miles

Panama Canal Route
15,000 miles

Suez Canal Route
13,000 miles

Thus, reducing the greenhouse effect means curbing economic growth or shifting it onto entirely new technological paths, both of which are extremely expensive. The political costs of such actions—which would likely increase unemployment, reduce corporate profits, and lower personal incomes—could be severe. If Arctic sea ice melts, polar bears may go extinct, but they do not have a seat at the table in international climate negotiations. Neither do today's children, who cannot vote but will live with the long-term consequences of their elders' actions.

For individual states, the costs of reducing greenhouse emissions are almost unrelated to the benefits of a solution. If one state reduces its industrial production or makes expensive investments in new technologies, this will have little effect on the long-term outcome unless other states do likewise. And if most states took such steps, a free rider that did not go along would save money and still benefit from the solution.

Global warming thus presents states with a triple dilemma. First, there is the dilemma of short-term (and predictable) costs to gain long-term (and less predictable) benefits. Second, specific constituencies such as oil companies and industrial workers pay the costs, whereas the benefits are distributed more generally across domestic societies and international states. Third, there is the collective goods dilemma among states: Benefits are shared globally, but costs must be extracted from each state individually (see the Public Opinion and International Relations box).

This third dilemma is complicated by the North-South divide. How can the industrialization of today's poor countries (China and India in particular) take place without pushing greenhouse emissions to unacceptable levels? Greenhouse gases are produced by each state roughly in proportion to its industrial activity. Seventy percent of greenhouse gases now come from China, the United States, EU states, Japan, Russia, and India. Forty-five percent of all greenhouse emissions come from the United States and China. U.S. carbon dioxide emissions amount to over 15 tons per person annually, about twice the European and Chinese rate (although China's aggregate emissions exceed those of the United States and Canada combined). Yet the most severe impacts of global warming are likely to be felt in the global South. In densely populated countries such as Bangladesh, hundreds of millions of people stand to lose their homes and farmland under a rising sea. Offsetting these North-South divisions, however, is the emerging realization that global climate change could cause environmental catastrophes across both North and South.

Kyoto Protocol (1997) A major international treaty on global warming, which entered into effect in 2005 and mandated cuts in carbon emissions. Almost all the world's major countries, except the United States, were participants.

All these elements make for a difficult multilateral bargaining situation, one not yet resolved. The *Framework Convention on Climate Change* adopted at the 1992 Earth Summit set a nonbinding goal to limit greenhouse emissions to 1990 levels by the year 2000. That goal was not met. The treaty did not commit the signatory states to meet target levels of greenhouse emissions by a particular date because of U.S. objections to such a commitment. Western Europe and Japan have been more willing to regulate greenhouse emissions than has the United States (which burns more fossil fuel per person).

The 1997 **Kyoto Protocol** adopted a complex formula for reducing greenhouse emissions to 1990 levels in the global North over about a decade. Countries in the global South received preferential treatment because their levels (per capita) were much lower. Yet China's fast-growing, coal-burning economy is a

David J. Phillip / AP Images

GLIMPSE OF THE FUTURE International treaties have been much more successful at addressing ozone depletion than global warming, mostly because of costs. While international agreements like the 1997 Kyoto Protocol or the 2016 Paris Agreement on climate set modest goals for industrialized countries to reduce their output of carbon dioxide and related gases, progress has fallen short. Extreme weather in recent years has offered an early warning sign. Here flooding hits Houston, Texas, after Hurricane Harvey, 2017.

Public Opinion and International Relations
Climate Change

The issue of climate change and its threat to our natural environment has become a key political issue in many countries around the world. Policies to address the threat of global warming are discussed, debated, and enacted at the international, national, regional, and local levels. These policies, moreover, can be quite controversial.

As discussed in this chapter, much of the controversy over policies to mitigate global warming involves their expense and who pays for them. Furthermore, there are differences among individuals within countries as to the severity of the threat. Some individuals see the threat of climate change as severe and thus argue for immediate changes in policy to mitigate the threat. Others see climate change as less of a threat.

In 2017 a Pew Global Attitudes survey asked individuals in 38 countries about their perceptions of the threat of global warming. Figure 11.2 shows the results of this survey. In a majority of states, over half of the population sees climate change as a major threat (the median across all countries was 61 percent). Moving to examine the views of those in individual countries yields interesting patterns, although each pattern has exceptions. For example, larger percentages of residents of countries with extensive coastlines, which could suffer the most from the consequences of global warming, are concerned about climate change. Over 75 percent of residents of Chile, Greece, Peru, South Korea, and Spain believe climate change is a major threat. Yet, exceptions to this pattern exist: Low numbers of Israelis and Indians, who live in two states that could suffer tremendous damage from rising sea levels, feel global warming is a threat.

Those in Middle Eastern states, in general, seem less concerned about global warming. Israel, Jordan, Tunisia, and Turkey all rank in the bottom half of numbers concerned about climate change. Yet concern in Lebanon (a coastal state) nears 60 percent of the population. Wealth seems to correlate with concern about climate change. States with lower levels of per capita GDP seem to have lower percentages of residents concerned: Ghana, India,

Jordan, Nigeria, and Tunisia all rank toward the bottom half of the list. Yet, Kenyans and Tanzanians rank as some of the most concerned.

Of course, even if large numbers of the population agree that climate change is a threat, there is no guarantee that a country will take action. This could be because the government is nondemocratic and thus not responsive to public opinion. Or interest groups that push policy one way or another may influence the government's policies. For example, the survey found that while 56 percent of Americans see climate change as a major threat, in the same year the Trump administration withdrew the United States from the Paris Agreement.

These multifaceted patterns illustrate the complexity of the climate change issue and why international agreements have proved difficult to forge. Coalitions of states are more difficult to form regarding this issue. This state of affairs, combined with the cost of combating greenhouse gases, has led to slow progress at the international level.

Figure 11.2 Climate Change Is a Major Threat
Source: Pew Research Center.

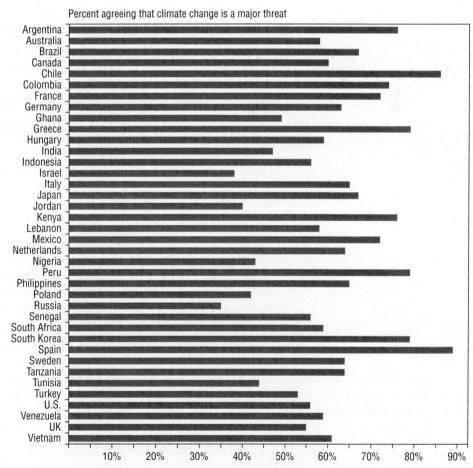

Figure 11.3 Projected U.S. and Chinese Carbon Dioxide Emissions, 1990–2030

Source: International Energy Agency.

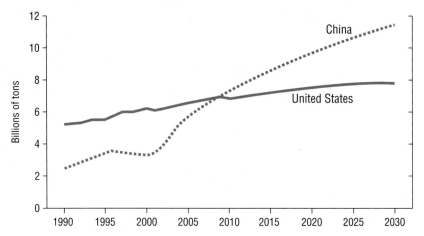

major factor in global warming (see Figure 11.3). India is another large source of carbon dioxide. The United States signed the treaty, but Congress would not ratify it.

Moving forward without U.S. support, 160 countries in 2001 agreed to implement Kyoto. The agreement called for 40 industrialized countries to reduce emissions to 5 percent below 1990 levels, by 2012, with binding penalties for failure. The EU pledged $400 million per year to help the global South reduce its emissions. After enough states ratified it, the treaty came into effect in 2005, and mandatory carbon cuts began in 2008, but they generally fell short of targets.

The European Union established markets to trade carbon emission credits among 11,000 industrial facilities across Europe. However, the economic slowdown in Europe led to a drastic price drop for carbon credits in 2011. Those prices stayed very low through 2014, leading some to question the future of the European emissions trading market. At the same time, however, other countries created similar emissions trading schemes, including South Korea, China, and Japan. All these carbon markets use free market principles to make reduction in carbon emissions more efficient. For example, a venture in Brazil earned carbon credits by burning methane gas from a garbage dump (to generate electricity) instead of venting it as a strong greenhouse gas. European investors bought the credits and could then sell them to, say, a polluting factory in Eastern Europe where reducing carbon might be especially expensive.

With the Kyoto Protocol set to expire after 2012, 180 states negotiated for years about what to do next. The United States rejoined these talks. In late 2011, states at a meeting in Durban, South Africa, agreed to extend the Kyoto framework to 2013–2017. At a meeting late in 2014 in Peru, participants agreed on the principle that all states— rich and poor—should commit to limit greenhouse emissions.

Meanwhile, the United States and China agreed in late 2014 that both countries would accelerate their efforts to reduce emissions. The United States agreed to reduce its emissions by over 25 percent (below 2005 levels) by 2025, while China agreed to continue its shift away from coal plants toward alternative energy sources. Even before this agreement, both countries have shown movement toward these goals. By 2013, the United States was 10 percent below 2005 emission levels and, that same year, China's use of coal declined for the first time in a century. In 2015, global emissions declined for the first time since the Great Recession of 2008–2009 (emissions usually fall during economic crises since many factories shut down). The 2015 decline was due to lower emissions in the United States, the EU, and China.

Paris Climate Agreement The main international agreement on global warming signed in 2015. Calls for keeping a global temperature rise this century well below 2 degrees Celsius above preindustrial levels. Nearly all countries of the world are participants.

The **Paris Climate Agreement** of 2015 was an important agreement concerning global climate politics. The agreement began as nearly universal—195 parties signed the agreement (some UN observers were allowed to sign). The agreement calls on states to limit the global rise in temperatures to above 2 degrees Celsius below preindustrial temperatures. It does so by calling on states to set their own emissions targets and self-reporting their compliance with those targets. The agreement contains no enforcement mechanism that would punish states for not meeting their goals.

In the summer of 2017, the Trump administration announced it would no longer remain a member of the Paris Agreement. The withdrawal will not take effect until 2020 because of the provisions of the agreement. The withdrawal led to global condemnation of the U.S. position. European Union states, in particular, responded by making future treaty partnerships (e.g., trade agreements) conditional on partner states signing the Paris Agreement.

The medium- and long-term implications of the U.S. withdrawal from the Paris Agreement are unclear. On one hand, the United States helped design the Paris Agreement and attempted to bring other states on board. As a major source of emissions, U.S. policy is important to efforts to reduce global warming. Lack of U.S. leadership on climate change could be a danger to global efforts to combat warming. Yet, other states are important too: China, India, and EU countries. Those states remain committed to the Paris Agreement. Many global MNCs, even those in the energy sector, also remain committed to moving away from fossil fuels, as do many U.S. states and cities.

To date, states have begun to implement their Paris Agreement targets through a host of measures. France has pledged to stop burning coal to produce electricity by 2022. China has doubled its expected use of solar energy by 2020 and created new coal consumption restrictions. India has greatly increased its projected use of renewable energy to lessen growing air pollution problems.

In addition, about half the states of the United States (notably California), and a number of cities, began taking steps to limit greenhouse emissions. Yet none of these moves are broad enough, or soon enough, to reverse the direction of climate change decisively. The dilemma of global warming remains fundamentally unsolved, and although experts hope that the Paris Agreement will lead to declines in emissions and a stabilization of temperatures, its lack of strong enforcement measures means that it is up to states to self-monitor their compliance with their targets (see the Seeking the Collective Good box).

OZONE DEPLETION   A second major atmospheric problem negotiated by the world's governments is the depletion of the world's **ozone layer**. Ozone high in the atmosphere screens out harmful ultraviolet rays from the sun. Certain chemicals expelled by industrial economies float to the top of the atmosphere and interact with ozone in a way that breaks it down. The chief culprits are CFCs, until recently widely used in refrigeration and in aerosol sprays. (Unfortunately, ozone produced by burning fossil fuels does not replace the high-level ozone but only pollutes the lower atmosphere.) As the ozone layer thins, more ultraviolet radiation reaches the earth's surface. Over Antarctica, a seasonal hole in the ozone grew larger year by year. If ozone levels were to keep lowering, the increased radiation could eventually kill off vegetation, reduce agricultural yields, and disrupt ecosystems.

ozone layer The part of the atmosphere that screens out harmful ultraviolet rays from the sun. Certain chemicals used in industrial economies break down the ozone layer.

Clearly, this was another collective goods problem in that one state could benefit by allowing the use of CFCs in its economy, provided that most other states prohibited their use. But the costs of replacing CFCs were much lower than the costs of addressing global warming: CFCs could be replaced with other chemicals at relatively modest costs. Furthermore, the consequences of ozone depletion were both better understood and more immediate than those of global warming.

Perhaps because of these cost issues, states had much more success in negotiating agreements and developing regimes to manage ozone depletion than global warming. In the 1987 **Montreal Protocol**, 22 states agreed to reduce CFCs by 50 percent by 1998. In 1990, the timetable was accelerated and the signatories expanded: Eighty-one states agreed to eliminate all CFCs by 2000. In 1992, as evidence of ozone depletion mounted, the schedule was again accelerated, with major industrial states phasing out CFCs by 1995. The signatories agreed

Montreal Protocol (1987) An agreement on protection of the ozone layer in which states pledged to reduce and then eliminate use of chlorofluorocarbons (CFCs). It is the most successful environmental treaty to date.

Seeking the Collective Good
Global Warming

COLLECTIVE GOOD: Enforcing a Climate Agreement

BACKGROUND: The prevention of global warming is a collective good that affects the entire world but results from the actions of the world's states individually. Those affected most actually will be those least responsible for causing it. Weather disasters such as the 2017 catastrophic hurricanes in Puerto Rico and the southern United States will become more common if the world does not address the problem effectively.

The costs of required actions are high, however, and states have been hesitant to pay them. Governments tend to focus on short-term outcomes. Thus, the international community has had tremendous difficulty addressing the very serious problem of global warming. Major players such as the United States did not ratify the Kyoto Protocol, and although it helped design the Paris Agreement, it announced its withdrawal from it in 2017.

CHALLENGE: In late 2015, the world's states gathered in Paris to negotiate a new treaty on global warming to follow Kyoto. The resulting document is considered a landmark agreement that attempts to address climate change by allowing states to set their own individual goals and adopt their own methods for ameliorating rising carbon dioxide emissions. The agreement includes provisions for wealthy states to assist poorer states to achieve their emission reduction goals. Yet, the arrangement does not contain a strong enforcement provision—states are left to self-monitor their progress and do not face punishment from other states if they fail to meet their goals.

SOLUTION: For many years, the focus of the world was on how to get an agreement on climate. Now attention turns to enforcement. The Paris Agreement is not legally binding—countries

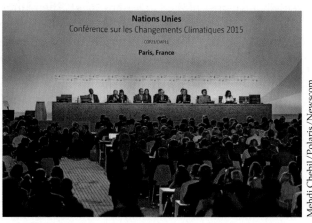

Announcing the Paris Agreement on climate, 2015.

Mehdi Chebil/Polaris/Newscom

must monitor their own (and others') compliance with the agreement. Two principles will be key. First, reciprocity will be important: One state's decrease in fossil fuel usage could spur others to comply. In this way, states can be reassured others are bearing the cost of lowering emissions. Second, identity will matter. Given the lack of a binding legal treaty, those states that do not comply with their commitment cannot be punished, except by naming and shaming. If enough countries do comply, gaining an identity of a free rider could be a badge of shame for polluters.

The new climate treaty still faces significant collective action problems. Whether future agreements will result from more reciprocity, dominance solutions, or identity principles is unknown. But given the magnitude of the stakes, it is likely all three will be relevant in finding solutions.

in principle to establish a fund to help developing countries pay for alternative refrigeration technologies not based on CFCs. Without such an effort, the states of the global South would be tempted to free-ride and could ultimately undermine the effort. These countries were also given until 2010 to phase out production. The Montreal Protocol was revised and strengthened again in 1997 and 1999. Rich countries stopped making CFCs in 1996 and have contributed about $3 billion to the fund. This money, supporting thousands of projects in more than a hundred countries, has helped the global South reduce emissions over the past two decades. The ozone hole is projected to shrink back slowly over the coming 40–50 years if current arrangements continue. In fact, calculations in 2018 showed that between 2005 and 2016, ozone depletion declined by 20 percent.

The Montreal Protocol on CFCs is the most important success yet achieved in international negotiations to preserve the global environment. Indeed, UN Secretary General Kofi Annan called it "perhaps the single most successful international agreement to date." It showed that states can agree to take action on urgent environmental threats, agree on targets and measures to counter such threats, and allocate the costs of such measures in a mutually acceptable way and actually pay up when the bill comes. But the international cooperation on the ozone problem has not been widely repeated on other environmental issues.

Environmental negotiations resemble trade talks in that they rely on the reciprocity principle as the prime mover of agreement. If each country contributes, and all the others contribute, a goal such as restoring the ozone layer can be accomplished. As with trade, the agreements and regimes are complicated and require monitoring of compliance to prevent free riding. The biggest difference from trade talks is that when trade talks succeed in solving a collective goods problem, the participants get a short-term, tangible benefit of billions of dollars added to the world economy. When environmental collective goods problems are solved, the participants get a short-term, tangible bill to pay, and then long-term benefits. The size of that bill seems to be the major difference between very difficult, expensive global warming solutions and reasonably affordable ozone solutions. Reciprocity, evidently, solves collective goods problems better with low costs or tangible benefits (ozone; trade) than with high costs and distant benefits (climate change).

11.2.2 Biodiversity

Biodiversity refers to the tremendous diversity of plant and animal species making up the earth's (global, regional, and local) ecosystems. Because of humans' destruction of ecosystems, large numbers of species are already *extinct*. Extinction results from overhunting, overfishing, and introducing non-native species that crowd out previous inhabitants. But the most important cause is *loss of habitat*—the destruction of rain forests, pollution of lakes and streams, and loss of agricultural lands to urban sprawl. Because ecosystems are based on complex interrelationships among species, the extinction of a few species can cause deeper changes in the environment. For example, the loss of native microorganisms can lead to chronic pollution of rivers or to transformation of arable land into deserts.

Because ecosystems are so complex, it is usually impossible to predict the consequences of a species' extinction or of the loss of a habitat or ecosystem. Generally, the activities that lead to habitat loss are economically profitable, so real costs are associated with limiting such activities. Species preservation is thus a collective good resembling global warming; the costs are immediate and substantial but the benefits are long term and ill defined.

It has been difficult to reach international agreement on sharing the costs of preserving biodiversity. A UN convention on trade in endangered species has reduced but not eliminated such trade. At the 1992 Earth Summit, a treaty on biodiversity committed signatories to preserving habitats and got rich states to pay poor ones for the rights to use commercially profitable biological products extracted from rare species in protected habitats (such as medicines from rain forest trees). However, because of fears that the treaty could limit U.S. patent rights in biotechnology, the United States never ratified it—and is the only UN member not to do so. As of 2018, the treaty had 196 member states. The United States does, however, participate in other biological treaties, such as a 1971 wetlands convention and the 1973 Convention on International Trade in Endangered Species (CITES).

International regimes to protect whales and dolphins have had limited success. The **International Whaling Commission** (an intergovernmental organization [IGO]) sets quotas for hunting certain whale species, but participation is voluntary and governments are not bound by decisions they object to.

biodiversity The tremendous diversity of plant and animal species making up the earth's (global, regional, and local) ecosystems.

International Whaling Commission An intergovernmental organization (IGO) that sets quotas for hunting certain whale species; states' participation is voluntary.

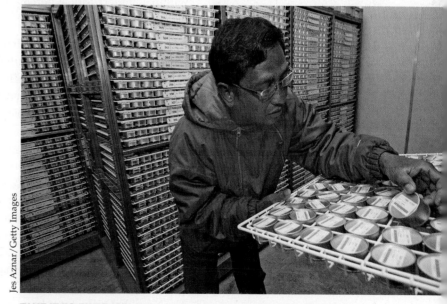

Jes Aznar/Getty Images

TAKE IT TO THE BANK Some environmentalists criticize the World Bank and other international institutions promoting economic development in poor countries for interfering destructively in local ecosystems such as rain forests. The green revolution increased yields but shifted patterns of agriculture in complex ways, such as by increasing pesticide and fertilizer runoff. Now genetically engineered crops promise further increases in agricultural productivity—more food on the table—but with environmental consequences that are not fully understood. This gene bank in the Philippines stores rice varieties from around the world.

The *Inter-American Tropical Tuna Commission* (another IGO) regulates methods used to fish for tuna and aims to minimize dolphin losses. The United States, which consumes half the world's tuna catch, has gone further and unilaterally requires—in the Marine Mammal Protection Act—that dolphin-safe methods be used for tuna sold in U.S. territory. Other countries have challenged the act through international trade organizations as an unfair restriction on tuna exports to the United States. Such conflicts portend future battles between environmentalists and free trade advocates. Free traders argue that states must not use domestic legislation to seek global environmental goals. Environmentalists do not want to give up national laws that they worked for decades to enact, over the opposition of industrial corporations.

For example, the U.S. Clean Air Act successfully reduced air pollution in U.S. cities, but the regulations had to be revised in 1997, on order of the World Trade Organization (WTO), to allow gasoline refined in Venezuela and Brazil to compete in U.S. markets. Environmentalists adopted the sea turtle as a symbol of their opposition to the WTO after the WTO overturned U.S. regulations that required shrimp to be caught in nets from which sea turtles (an endangered species) can escape. Recent conflicts have arisen over U.S. laws restricting imports of foods with pesticide residues, and over European laws on imports of genetically engineered agricultural and pharmaceutical products, which the United States wants to export worldwide.

Thus, unilateral approaches to biodiversity issues are problematic because they disrupt free trade; multilateral approaches are problematic because of the collective goods problem. It is not surprising that the international response has been fairly ineffective to date.

11.2.3 Forests and Oceans

Two types of habitat—tropical rain forests and oceans—are especially important to biodiversity *and* the atmosphere. Both are also reservoirs of commercially profitable resources such as wood and fish. They differ in that forests are located almost entirely within state territory, whereas oceans are largely beyond any state territory, in the global commons.

RAIN FORESTS   As many as half of all the world's species live in *rain forests*, which replenish oxygen and reduce carbon dioxide in the atmosphere—slowing down global warming. Rain forests thus benefit all the world's states; they are collective goods.

International bargaining on the preservation of rain forests has made considerable progress, probably because most rain forests belong to a few states. These few states have the power to speed up or slow down the destruction of forests—and international bargaining amounts to agreements to shift costs from those few states onto the broader group of states benefiting from the rain forests.

Although some rich states (including the United States) have large forests, most of the largest rain forests are in poor states such as Brazil, Indonesia, Malaysia, and Madagascar. Such states can benefit economically from exploiting the forests—freely cutting lumber, clearing land for agriculture, and mining. Until recently (and still to an extent), leaders of rich states have been most interested in encouraging maximum economic growth in poor states so that foreign debts could be paid—with little regard for environmental damage.

Now that rich states have an interest in protecting rain forests, they are using development assistance as leverage to induce poorer states to protect their forests rather than exploit them. Under international agreements reached in the early 1990s, rich countries contribute hundreds of millions of dollars in foreign aid for this purpose. In some poor countries burdened by large foreign debts, environmentalists and bankers from rich countries have worked out so-called debt-for-nature swaps in which a debt is canceled in exchange for the state's agreement to preserve forests. In 2006, for example, the U.S. government and NGOs helped Guatemala cancel more

Policy Perspectives
Prime Minister of Ireland, Leo Varadkar

PROBLEM   *How do you balance environmental and economic concerns?*

PACIFIC PRESS / Alamy Stock Photo

BACKGROUND   Imagine that you are the president of Ireland. Genetically modified organisms (GMOs) are highly controversial in Europe, and this certainly includes your country. In 1997, for example, Ireland reluctantly approved a permit for the global MNC Monsanto to grow sugar beets near Dublin. After several legal attempts to halt the planting of the crop failed, activists destroyed the crop in the ground before it could be harvested.

Your country has quietly supported several Irish biotechnology firms in the past with joint ventures in research. These have produced a variety of advances that give Ireland a significant advantage in this field over other European states. Several MNCs stand to benefit from this research, providing you with investment and tax income.

DOMESTIC CONSIDERATIONS   Unfortunately, this "positive but precautionary" approach is unpopular with the public. Some worry that Ireland's reputation as "the Green Island" will suffer, possibly posing a threat to tourism—a major source of income for your country. Others join the chorus of European opposition to GMOs based on concerns over the possible environmental effects of these products.

In the spring of 2004, the European Union (EU) approved an end to the moratorium on GMO product sales (with your country voting in the majority), partially under a threat from the United States to enforce a WTO ruling that found the GMO ban illegal. The United States is your largest single trade partner, but other EU states, when taken together, form your most significant export market. In 2015, the European Parliament rejected a law that would have allowed member states to ban GMOs. And while there was public support for that law in Ireland, some major organizations such as the Irish Farmers' Association, opposed the ban.

SCENARIO   Imagine that, in light of the recent EU legislation, interest groups pressure your party to ban GMOs in Ireland. These groups threaten to support opposition parties in the next election should you refuse.

GMO crops could provide economic benefits to your country. Given your comparative technological advantage in this area, your economy stands to profit from expanding GMO use through increased agricultural output and increased business activity from MNCs. The United States has no regulations concerning the importation of GMO products and would be open to exports of these crops.

GMOs carry possible dangers as well. Some environmentalists warn that GMOs could have negative effects on ecology, wildlife, and human health. Many of your EU partners will shun your GMO products, robbing you of a large export market for these goods. Domestically, expanding the production of GMOs will be controversial.

CHOOSE YOUR POLICY   Do you continue to work quietly, encouraging the advance of GMO crops? Do you move for a unilateral ban on the production of GMOs because of interest-group pressure to respect the long-term environmental concerns raised by these products? Do you work with MNCs to use your comparative advantage for economic gain? How do you balance economic prosperity with a concern for the environment?

than $20 million in debts in exchange for expanded conservation programs. In 2014, Liberia and Peru agreed to end deforestation in exchange for a significant foreign aid pledge from Norway. In 2008, Brazil announced that it planned to end deforestation within a decade. Environmentalists thought the plan was overly optimistic and Brazil now says it hopes to slow deforestation by 2020.

OCEANS   The *oceans*, covering 70 percent of the earth's surface, are (like the rain forest) a key to regulating climate and preserving biodiversity. Oceans, like forests, are attractive targets for short-term economic uses that cause long-term environmental damage. Such uses include overfishing, dumping toxic and nuclear waste (and other garbage), and long-distance oil shipments with their recurrent spills. Unlike rain forests, oceans belong to no state but are a global commons. This makes the collective goods problem more difficult because no authority exists to enforce regulations. Preserving the oceans depends on the cooperation of more than 100 states and thousands of nonstate actors. Free riders have great opportunities to profit. For example, *drift nets* are huge fishing nets, miles long, that scoop up everything in their path. They are very profitable but destructive of a sustainable ocean environment. Most states have now banned their use (under pressure from the environmental movement). However, no state has the authority to go onto the **high seas** (nonterritorial waters) and stop illegal use of these nets.

high seas The portion of the oceans considered common territory, not under any kind of exclusive state jurisdiction. See also *territorial waters*.

One solution that states have pursued involves "enclosing" more of the ocean. Territorial waters have expanded to hundreds of miles off the coast (and around islands), so that state sovereignty encloses substantial resources such as fisheries and offshore oil and mineral deposits. This solution has been pursued in the context of larger multilateral negotiations on ocean management.

UN Convention on the Law of the Sea (UNCLOS) A world treaty (1982) governing use of the oceans. The UNCLOS treaty established rules on territorial waters and a 200-mile exclusive economic zone (EEZ). See also *territorial waters*.

The **UN Convention on the Law of the Sea (UNCLOS)**, negotiated from 1973 to 1982, governs the uses of the oceans. After more than a decade's delay and renegotiation of some of the deep-sea mining aspects, the United States signed UNCLOS in 1994 but has yet to ratify the treaty. The UNCLOS treaty established rules on territorial waters—12 miles for shipping and a 200-mile exclusive economic zone (EEZ) for economic activities, such as fishing and mining. The 200-mile limit placed a substantial share of the economically profitable ocean resources in the control of about a dozen states (see Figure 11.4).

Varying interpretations leave economic rights in dispute in a number of locations. In the South China Sea, China, the Philippines, Malaysia, Taiwan, Brunei, and Vietnam all claim small islands and reefs. The islands and reefs are near oil reserves that would be extremely valuable to the state granted the claim. In the past five years, China has used dozens of large sand dredgers to add land to reefs. China has claimed these new human-made islands and has used them as military bases for naval and air capabilities.

UNCLOS also developed the general principle that the oceans are a common heritage of humankind. A mechanism was created, through the International Seabed Authority, for sharing some of the wealth that rich states might gain from extracting minerals on the ocean floor (beyond 200 miles).

ANTARCTICA Like the oceans, *Antarctica* belongs to no state. The continent's strategic and commercial value is limited, however, and not many states care about it. Thus, states have been successful in reaching agreements on Antarctica because the costs were low and the players few. The *Antarctic Treaty of 1959*—one of the first multilateral treaties concerning the environment—forbids military activity as well as the presence of nuclear weapons or the dumping of nuclear waste. It sets aside territorial claims on the continent for future resolution and establishes a regime under which various states conduct scientific research in Antarctica. All states with interests in the area, including both superpowers, signed the treaty. By 1991, Greenpeace had persuaded the treaty signatories to turn the continent into a "world park." Antarctica is largely a success story in international environmental politics.

11.2.4 Pollution

Pollution generally creates a collective goods problem, but one that is not usually global in scale. Pollution is more often a regional or bilateral issue. With some exceptions—such as dumping at sea—the effects of pollution are limited to the state where it occurs and its close neighbors; U.S. industrial smokestack emissions cause acid rain in Canada but do not directly affect distant states. China's terrible air pollution kills nearly half a million Chinese a year, but few foreigners. Even when pollution crosses state borders, it often has its strongest effects closest to the source. This localized effect makes for a somewhat less intractable collective goods problem because a state that pollutes can seldom free-ride, and few actors are involved.

Figure 11.4 State-Controlled Waters

Overfishing and similar problems of managing the "commons" of world oceans have been addressed by enclosing the most important ocean areas under the exclusive control of states. Shaded areas are within the 200-mile exclusive economic zones controlled by states under terms of the UNCLOS treaty.

Source: Based on Andrew Boyd, *An Atlas of World Affairs*, 9th ed. New York: Routledge, 1992.

200 mile offshore economic zone

363

Wissam Nassar/dpa/picture-alliance/Newscom

DIRTY WATERS Water pollution is both an international and a national threat to health and safety. For example, due to fuel shortages, Gaza has been unable to keep its main sewage treatment plant operating. Excess sewage is often released from holding pools into the ocean. Here, a Palestinian child plays near a raw sewage pool, 2018.

acid rain Rain caused by air pollution that damages trees and often crosses borders. Limiting acid rain (via limiting nitrogen oxide emissions) has been the subject of several regional agreements.

In several regions—notably Western and Eastern Europe and the Middle East—states are closely packed in the same air, river, or sea basins. In such situations, pollution controls must often be negotiated multilaterally. In Europe during the Cold War, the international pollution problem was exacerbated by the inability of Western European states to impose any limits on Eastern European ones, whose pollution was notorious.

Several regional agreements seek to limit **acid rain**, caused by air pollution. European states—whose forests have been heavily damaged—have agreed to limit air pollution and acid rain for their mutual benefit. In 1988, 24 European states signed a treaty to limit nitrogen oxide emissions to 1988 levels by 1995. After long negotiations, the United States and Canada signed bilateral agreements to limit such pollution as well. These regional agreements have worked fairly well.

Water pollution often crosses borders as well, especially because industrial pollution, human sewage, and agricultural fertilizers and pesticides all tend to run into rivers and seas. For instance, in 2005, a huge chemical spill in northeast China polluted a river that flows into Russia. Long-standing regional agencies that regulate shipping on heavily used European rivers now also deal with pollution. The Mediterranean basin is severely polluted and difficult to manage because so many states border it. In 2010, the largest accidental oil spill in history occurred in the Gulf of Mexico. The spill resulted from an explosion on an oil platform. The leakage took months to contain and highlighted the dangers associated with deep-water oil drilling. British Petroleum, the company that operated the well, agreed to set aside billions of dollars to pay damages to residents of several southern U.S. states affected by the spill.

Toxic and *nuclear wastes* are a special problem because of their long-term dangers. States occasionally try to ship such wastes out of the country. However, international agreements now ban the dumping of toxic and nuclear wastes at sea (an obvious collective goods problem). But such wastes have been sent to developing countries for disposal, for a fee. For instance, toxic ash from Pennsylvania became material for bricks in Guinea, and Italian nuclear waste was shipped to Nigeria.

Norms have developed in recent years against exporting toxic wastes—a practice seen as exploitive of the receiving country. In 1989, 100 states signed a treaty under UN auspices to regulate shipments of toxic and nuclear wastes and prevent their secret movements under corrupt deals. Forty more countries, in Africa, did not sign the treaty but called for a complete halt to toxic waste shipments to Africa. Nonetheless, in 2006, a multinational company based in Singapore tried to dispose of toxic waste from a tanker ship in the Netherlands. When it discovered the Netherlands has raised its fees to dispose of the waste, it sailed back to look for another location to dump the waste. Six weeks later, the ship unloaded the toxic sludge in Abidjan, Ivory Coast, where a local company dumped it at locations around the city. Thousands of residents got sick and eight people died. In 2007, the company agreed to pay $200 million to settle claims.

Chernobyl A city in Ukraine that was the site of a 1986 meltdown at a Soviet nuclear power plant.

In 1986, a meltdown at the Soviet nuclear power plant at **Chernobyl**, in Ukraine, created airborne radioactivity that spread over much of Europe, from Italy to Sweden. The accident exemplified the new reality—that economic and technical decisions made in one state can have grave environmental consequences for other countries. Soviet leaders made matters worse by failing to notify neighbors promptly of the accident.

On the various issues of water and air pollution, both unilateral state actions and international agreements have often been feasible and effective. In recent decades, river water quality has improved in most industrialized regions. Market economies have begun to deal with pollution as just another cost of production that should be charged to the polluter instead of to society at large. Some governments have begun to allocate "pollution rights" that companies can buy and sell on a free market.

In the former Soviet bloc, decades of centrally planned industrialization created more severe environmental problems. With staggering environmental damage and human health effects, the economically strapped former Soviet republics had to bargain over limiting pollution and repairing the damage. For example, the severely polluted Aral Sea, formerly contained within one state, the Soviet Union, is now shared by two, Kazakhstan and Uzbekistan. Once the world's fourth-largest inland sea, it shrank in half, its huge fisheries destroyed, after a Soviet-era mega-irrigation project to grow cotton in the desert diverted the Aral Sea's inlet rivers and polluted them with pesticides. Former fishing towns found themselves many miles from the shoreline. After local and international political leaders failed to implement plans to address the problem, local populations suffered from widespread health effects of the disaster.

11.3 Natural Resources

Describe three ways in which the need for natural resources can create international conflict.

The natural environment is not only a delicate ecosystem requiring protection but also a repository of natural resources. Because the extraction of resources brings states wealth, these resources regularly fuel international conflicts. Because they are mostly located within individual states, however, they do not present a collective goods problem. Rather, states bargain over these vital resources.

Three aspects of natural resources shape their role in international conflict. First, they are required for the operation of an industrial economy (sometimes even an agrarian one). Second, their sources—mineral deposits, rivers, and so forth—are associated with particular territories over which states may fight for control. Third, natural resources tend to be unevenly distributed, with plentiful supplies in some states and an absence in others. These aspects mean that trade in natural resources is extremely profitable; much additional wealth is created by such trade. They also mean that trade in resources is fairly politicized—creating market imperfections such as monopoly, oligopoly, and price manipulation, sometimes by cartels (see Chapter 8).

11.3.1 World Energy

Of the various natural resources required by states, energy resources (fuels) are central. The commercial fuels that power the world's industrial economies are oil (about 40 percent of world energy consumption), coal (30 percent), natural gas (25 percent), and hydroelectric and nuclear power (5 percent). The fossil fuels (coal, oil, gas) thus account for 95 percent of world energy consumption. Some energy consumed as electricity comes from hydroelectric dams or nuclear power plants, but most of it comes from burning fossil fuels in electric-generating plants.

Imagine a pile of coal weighing 65 pounds. The energy released by burning that much coal is equivalent to the amount of energy North Americans use per person every day. Wealthier people, of course, consume more energy per person than do poorer people, but 65 pounds is the average. The North American's pile of coal would be four times larger than that of a person in China, 20 times that of an African.

366 Chapter 11 Environment and Population

Table 11.1 Per Capita Energy Consumption and Net Energy Trade, 2015

	Per Capita Consumption (million BTU)	Total Net Energy Exports[a] (quadrillion BTU)
North America	285	−3
Europe	135	−37
Japan/Pacific	180	−40
Russia/CIS	155	+31
China	80	−12
Middle East	140	+47
Latin America	60	+3
South Asia	18	−6
Africa	16	+13
World as a whole	75	

[a]Net exports refers to production minus consumption. Net exports worldwide do not equal net imports for technical reasons.

Source: Calculated from U.S. Department of Energy. Energy Information Adminstration. See http://www.ela.doe.gov/iea

Table 11.1 shows energy consumption per person in the nine world regions. The four industrialized regions of the North use much more energy per person than those of the South. Because South Asia and Africa have little industry, North America uses 15 times as much per person as those two regions. Among industrialized countries there are differences in the *efficiency* of energy use—gross domestic product (GDP) produced per unit of energy consumed. The least efficient are the former Soviet Republics; North America is also rather inefficient; Europe and Japan are the most energy efficient.

International trade in energy thus plays a vital role in the world economy. As Table 11.1 shows, the regions of the industrialized West are all large net importers of energy. The Middle East, Africa, and Russia are exporters of energy. Although all forms of energy are traded internationally, the most important by far is oil, the cheapest to transport over long distances. Russia receives vital hard-currency earnings from exporting oil. Venezuela and Mexico (in Latin America) and Nigeria and Angola (in Africa) are also major oil exporters. But by far the largest source of oil exports is the Middle East—especially the countries around the Persian Gulf (Saudi Arabia; Kuwait; Iraq; Iran; and the small sheikdoms of United Arab Emirates, Qatar, Bahrain, and Oman). Saudi Arabia is the largest oil exporter and holds the largest oil reserves (see Table 8.1). The politics of world energy revolve around Middle Eastern oil shipped to Western Europe, China, Japan, and North America.

The importance of oil in the industrialized economies helps explain the political importance of the Middle East in world politics. Not only is energy a crucial economic sector (on which all industrial activity depends), but it is also one of the most politically sensitive because of the dependence of the West on energy imported from the Middle East and the rest of the global South.

To secure a supply of oil coming from the Middle East, Britain and other European countries colonized the area early in the twentieth century, carving up territory into protectorates in which European power kept local monarchs on their thrones. The United States did not claim colonies or protectorates, but U.S. MNCs were heavily involved in the development of oil resources in the area from the 1920s through the 1960s—often wielding vast power. These U.S. and European oil companies kept the price paid to local states low and their own profits high, yet local rulers depended on the expertise and capital investment of these companies.

After World War II, the British gave up colonial claims in the Middle East, but the Western oil companies kept producing cheap oil there for Western consumption. Then in 1973, during an Arab-Israeli war, the oil-producing Arab states of the region decided to punish the United States for supporting Israel. They cut off their oil exports to the United States and curtailed their overall exports. This supply disruption sent world oil prices skyrocketing. The Organization of the Petroleum Exporting Countries (OPEC) realized its potential power and the high price the world was willing to pay for oil. This 1973 *oil shock* had a profound effect on the world economy and on world politics. Huge amounts of hard currency accumulated in the treasuries of the Middle East oil-exporting countries, which in turn invested them around the world (these were called *petrodollars*). High inflation plagued the United States and Europe for years afterward. The economic instability and sense of U.S. helplessness—coming on top of the Vietnam War—seemed to mark a decline in American power and perhaps the rise of the global South.

In 1979, the revolution in Iran led to a second oil shock. But higher oil prices led to the expansion of oil production in new locations outside OPEC—in the North Sea (Britain and Norway), Alaska, Angola, Russia, and elsewhere. By the mid-1980s, the Middle East was rapidly losing its market share of world trade in oil. At the same time, industrialized economies learned to be more *energy efficient*. With supply up and demand down, oil prices dropped in the late 1980s to historic lows of less than $20 a barrel.

In the late 1990s, the Caspian Sea region beckoned as a new and largely untapped oil source (see Figure 11.5). However, the oil must travel overland by pipeline to reach world markets (the Caspian is an inland sea). But the main pipeline from oil-producing Azerbaijan to the Black Sea (where tanker ships could load) traveled through war-torn Chechnya in southern Russia. Russia then built a bypass route around Chechnya that carries a large and growing amount of Caspian oil for export through the Black Sea. Western powers sought other pipeline routes that did not cross Russia, while Turkey

Figure 11.5 Dividing the Caspian Sea

The Caspian Sea is the world's largest inland body of water. It could be defined under international law as either a lake or a sea.[a] A *lake* has a joint area in the middle (in green on the left panel) that can be exploited only if the countries agree on terms. There are also coastal zones under each country's sole control. In a *sea* less than 400 miles across, the bordering countries' 200-mile exclusive economic zones (EEZs) split up the whole sea (right panel). If the whole area is split as in the map on the right, the sectors can be defined by median lines (dashed line) or by a division into five sectors of equal area (dotted line), giving Iran a larger sector. In 2010, with major oil development underway in all five countries' coastal areas, a summit meeting agreed to give each a 25-mile zone. In 2012, Russia held joint military exercises with Kazakhstan to practice defense of oil facilities from an Iranian attack. This conflict was largely resolved, however, not through dominance, but through reciprocity. In 2018, the five countries bordering finally reached a solution, signing a treaty to treat the water as both a sea and a lake. The agreement treats the surface of the water as an international zone and the sea bed as territorial zones.

[a]Sciolino, Elaine. "It's a Sea! It's a Lake! No. It's a Pool of Oil!" *The New York Times*, June 21, 1998. Kucera, Joshua. "The Great Caspian Arms Race." *Foreign Policy*, June 22, 2012.

sought to control a larger market share and reduce environmental damage to the Bosporus waterway (through which Russian tankers must travel). After long negotiations, in 2002–2004, states and oil companies built a large-capacity pipeline, costing billions of dollars, through Azerbaijan and Georgia to Turkey's Mediterranean coast.

Violent conflicts make pipeline routes particularly complex. All three countries on the new pipeline route were at war in the past 20 years. A dozen other existing and proposed oil pipelines for Caspian Sea oil are no easier. Across the Caspian Sea, Turkmenistan wants to export natural gas to Pakistan, and from there to Asia, but a pipeline would have to cross war-torn Afghanistan. Meanwhile in 2003, a new $4 billion pipeline began carrying oil from Chad through Cameroon for export, promising to help both countries alleviate poverty, but as rebels based in Sudan attacked in Chad, oil money was diverted to military purposes. Although borders and geopolitics may be less and less important in communications and business, they still matter greatly in international economic transactions such as oil pipelines.

Oil prices stayed relatively high after 2000, ultimately shooting up to $140 a barrel in 2008 and pushing U.S. gas prices to more than $4 a gallon. These high oil prices had two major benefits. First, burning oil contributes to global warming, and high prices made it profitable to burn less oil and be more energy efficient. Second, high oil prices increase the export earnings of oil-producing countries. Countries such as Venezuela and Mexico count on oil revenues in their economic development plans and to repay foreign debts. These countries eased their debt problems as a result of higher prices, which also played a crucial part in Russia's economic recovery. Oil exporters can have too much of a good thing, however. The easy money concentrated in a few hands allowed dictators to rule and extremism to flourish in states such as Iran, Saudi Arabia, and Venezuela.

The global recession of 2008–2009 eventually pushed oil prices lower. Between 2015 and 2018, oil prices were relatively low. Lower prices have been a result of high productivity among OPEC countries (especially Saudi Arabia) and growing oil production in the United States, which was the world's largest oil producer in 2017. The exporting countries and their recently rich governments suddenly found themselves cash poor—contributing to economic instability in Russia and Iran.

11.3.2 Minerals

To build the infrastructure and other manufactured goods that create wealth in a national economy, states need other raw materials in addition to energy. These include metals, other minerals, and related materials extracted through mining. The political economy of minerals—iron, copper, platinum, and so forth—differs from that of world energy. The value of international trade in oil is many times that of any mineral. Moreover, mineral supply is not so concentrated in one region of the world. Industrialized countries have also reduced their vulnerability by stockpiling strategic minerals.

Most important to industrialized economies are the minerals that go into making industrial equipment. Iron is traditionally the most important; it is used to make steel. The leading producers of steel are the former Soviet Union, Japan, the United States, China, and Germany, followed by Brazil, Italy, South Korea, France, and Britain. Thus, major industrialized countries produce their own steel (Germany and Japan are the leading exporters worldwide). To preserve self-sufficiency in steel production, the United States and others have used trade policies to protect domestic steel industries (such as the 2018 U.S. steel tariffs). Some industrialized countries, notably Japan, depend heavily on importing iron ore for their steel industry. Iron ore is not concentrated in one location but is exported from developing and industrialized countries around the world.

For other important industrial minerals such as copper, nickel, and zinc, the pattern of supply and trade is much more diffuse than for oil, and the industrialized countries are largely self-sufficient. Even when poor states are the main suppliers, as with tin and bauxite, they have not gained the power of OPEC. There is a producer cartel in some cases (copper), a producer-consumer cartel in some (tin), and separate producer and consumer cartels in others (bauxite). China currently holds a near-monopoly on the world's supply of rare earth minerals vital (in small amounts) to the production of electronics. China has cut exports at times to boost these minerals' prices. In the last eight years, however, countries such as Vietnam have begun to produce some of these elements to challenge China's grip on the market.

Certain agricultural products have spawned producer cartels such as the Union of Banana Exporting Countries (UBEC) and the African Groundnut Council. Like minerals, some export crops come mainly from just a few countries. These include sugar (Cuba), cocoa (Ivory Coast, Ghana, Nigeria), tea (India, Sri Lanka, China), and coffee (Brazil, Colombia). Despite the concentrations, producer cartels have not been very successful in boosting prices of these products, which are less essential than energy.

11.3.3 Water

In addition to energy and minerals, states need water. This need increases as a society industrializes, as it intensifies agriculture, and as its population grows. World water use is 35 times that of just a few centuries ago, and grew twice as fast as population in the twentieth century. Yet water supplies are relatively unchanging and are becoming depleted in many places. One-fifth of the world's population lacks safe drinking water, and 80 countries suffer water shortages. Water supplies—rivers and water tables—often cross international boundaries; thus, access to water is increasingly a source of international conflict. Sometimes—as when several states share access to a single water table—these conflicts are collective goods problems.

Water problems are especially important in the Middle East. For instance, the Euphrates River runs from Turkey through Syria to Iraq before reaching the Persian Gulf. Iraq objects to Syrian diversion of water from the river, and both Iraq and Syria object to Turkey's diversion.

The Jordan River originates in Syria and Lebanon and runs through Israel to Jordan. In the 1950s, Israel began building a canal to take water from the Jordan River to "make the desert bloom." Jordan and its Arab neighbors complained to the UN Security Council, but it failed in efforts to mediate the dispute, and each state went ahead with its own water plans (Israel and Jordan agreeing, however, to stay within UN-proposed allocations). In 1964, Syria and Lebanon tried to build dams and divert water before it reached Israel, rendering Israel's new water system worthless. Israeli air and artillery attacks on the construction site forced Syria to abandon its diversion project, and Israel's 1967 capture of the Golan Heights precluded Syria from renewing such efforts. Thus, the dominance principle comes into play in resolving conflicts over natural resources.

A common theme runs through the conflicts over fuels, minerals, agricultural products, and territorial waters. They are produced in fixed locations but traded to distant places. Control of these locations gives a state both greater self-sufficiency (valued by mercantilists) and market commodities generating wealth (valued by liberals).

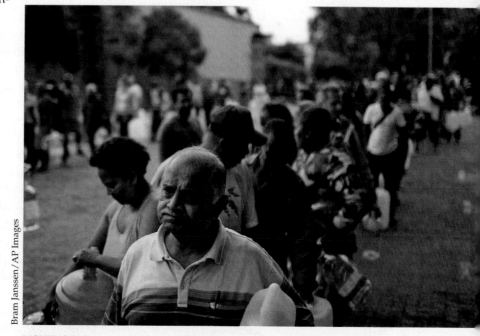

Bram Janssen/AP Images

LIQUID GOLD As population growth and economic development increase the demand for water, and as climate change induces changes in precipitation patterns, water has become an even more valuable resource. There is now concern that some high-population areas could suffer water shortages, leading to humanitarian and political crises. Here, South Africans near Cape Town line up for water, 2018.

Of course, these resources can also be directly related to international security. International relations (IR) scholars have expanded their studies of environmental politics to study systematically the relationship of military and security affairs to the environment. One side of this relationship is the role of the environment as a source of international conflict. We have seen how environmental degradation can lead to collective goods problems among large numbers of states and how competition for territory and resources can create conflicts among smaller groups of states.

As climate change induces shifts in weather and precipitation patterns, some areas have found they have far too much water, while others are experiencing new shortages in the form of droughts. In 2017, the city of Cape Town in South Africa announced it would run out of water in the spring of 2018. In response, the government placed strict limits on water usage, cutting daily usage in half. This pushed "zero day"—the day when water would run out—back several months. But unless new sources of water are found or rainfall increases, Cape Town will face an uncertain future with less water.

11.4 Population

Explain the demographic transition and why some states are vulnerable to rapid population growth.

Global population reached a record high today, as it does every day. World population, 7.6 billion in 2018, is growing by 80 million each year. Forecasting future population is easy in some respects. Barring a nuclear war or an environmental catastrophe, today's children will grow up and have children of their own. For the coming 20 to 30 years, world population growth will be driven, rather mechanistically, by the large number of children in today's populations in the global South. The projected world population in 2030 will be 8 to 9 billion people, and there is little anyone can do to change that projection.

Of the increase in population in that period, 96 percent will be in the global South. Currently, half the world's population growth occurs in just six countries: India, China, Pakistan, Nigeria, Bangladesh, and Indonesia. Among the world's poorest countries, population is expected to triple in the next 50 years, whereas many rich countries will see population shrink in that period.

Forecasting beyond 25 years is difficult. When today's children grow up, the number of children they bear will be affected by their incomes (because of the demographic transition, discussed shortly). To the extent that developing countries accumulate wealth—a subject taken up in Chapter 13—their populations will grow more slowly. A second factor affecting the rate of population growth will be government policies regarding women's rights and birth control.

Because of these two uncertainties, projections beyond a few decades have a range of uncertainty (see Figure 11.6). By 2050, world population could be 9 billion, with a final leveling out around 10 billion in the next 100 years. New data in 2002 showed that higher women's status and literacy are reducing population growth more than expected in large, poor countries. The actions of states and IOs *now* will determine the earth's population in 200 years.

Over two hundred years ago, the British writer Thomas Malthus warned that population tends to increase faster than food supply and predicted that population growth would limit itself through famine and disease. Today, experts and officials who warn against world overpopulation are sometimes called *Malthusian*. Critics of this view point out that

Figure 11.6 World Population Trends and Projections

Source: UN Population Office.

technology has kept pace with population in the past, allowing more food and other resources to be extracted from the environment even as population keeps growing.

11.4.1 The Demographic Transition

Population growth results from the difference between rates of birth (per 1,000 people) and rates of death. In agrarian (preindustrial) societies, both birthrates and death rates are high. Population growth is thus slow—even negative at times when death rates exceed birthrates (during a famine or plague, for instance).

The process of economic development—of industrialization and the accumulation of wealth on a per capita basis—brings about a change in birthrates and death rates that follows a fairly universal pattern called the **demographic transition** (see Figure 11.7). First, death rates fall as food supplies increase and access to health care expands. Later, birthrates fall as people become educated, more secure, and more urbanized, and as the status of women in society rises. At the end of the transition, as at the beginning, birthrates and death rates are fairly close to each other, and population growth is limited. But during the transition, when death rates have fallen more than birthrates, population grows rapidly.

One reason poor people tend to have many children is that under harsh poverty, a child's survival is not assured. Disease, malnutrition, or violence may claim the lives of many children, leaving parents with no one to look after them in their old age. Having many children helps ensure that some survive.

As a state makes the demographic transition, the structure of its population changes dramatically. At the beginning and middle of the process, most of the population is young. Families have many children, and adults do not have a long life expectancy. Because children are not very productive economically, the large number of children in poor countries tends to slow down the accumulation of wealth. But by the end of the demographic transition, because adults live longer and families have fewer children, the average age of the population is much older. Eventually a substantial section of the population is elderly—a different nonproductive population that the economy must support.

The industrialized countries have completed the demographic transition and now have slow population growth. Russia, Europe, and Japan have shrinking populations. Most developing countries are in the middle of the transition and have rapid population growth.

demographic transition The pattern of falling death rates, followed by falling birthrates, that generally accompanies industrialization and economic development.

Figure 11.7 The Demographic Transition

As income rises, first death rates and then birthrates fall. The gap between the two is the population growth rate. Early in the transition, the population contains a large proportion of children; later it contains a large proportion of elderly people.

Source: United Nations.

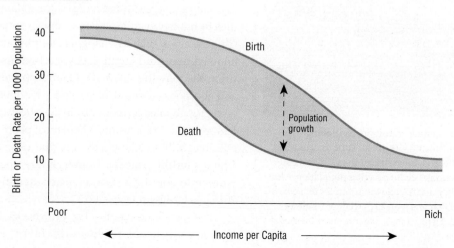

The dilemma of the demographic transition is this: Rapid population growth and a child-heavy population are powerful forces lowering per capita income. Yet the best way to slow population growth is to raise per capita income. Population growth thus contributes to a vicious cycle in many poor states. Where population rises at the same rate as overall wealth, the average person is no better off over time. Even when the economy grows faster than the population, so that the *average* income rises, the total *number* of poor people may increase.

The demographic transition tends to widen international disparities of wealth. States that manage to raise incomes a bit enter an upward spiral—as population growth slows, income levels per capita rise more, which further slows population growth, and so forth. Meanwhile, states that do not raise incomes have unabated population growth; per capita incomes stay low, which fuels more population growth—a downward spiral.

Globally, this disparity contributes to the gap in wealth between the North and South (see Chapter 12). Within the South, disparities are also sharpened as a few countries manage to slow population growth and raise incomes while others fail to do so. Even within a single country, the demographic transition sharpens disparities. Cities, richer classes, richer ethnic groups, and richer provinces tend to have low birthrates compared to the countryside and the poorer classes, poorer ethnic groups, and poorer provinces. In countries such as France, Israel, and the United States, wealthier ethnic groups have much slower population growth than poorer ethnic groups.

In recent decades, the global South seems to be splitting into two groups of states. The first group, including China and India, entered the phase of the demographic transition marked by falling birthrates in the 1970s. But in nearly 70 other poor states, death rates kept falling faster than birthrates, leading to accelerating population growth. These population trends contributed to disparities within the global South that emerged in the 1990s, notably between Africa and Asia.

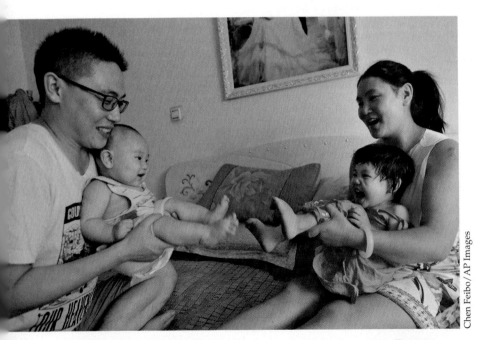

Chen Feibo / AP Images

TWO'S NOT A CROWD Because of the demographic transition, controlling population growth helps economic development and vice versa. Various countries use a wide range of population policies to this end, none stricter than China's one-child policy for urban couples. Yet, due to concerns about its aging population, China began to show flexibility in its one-child policy in 2013, allowing couples to have two children. Despite this change, it is estimated that less than 20 percent of Chinese families have applied to have a second child. Here, Chinese parents enjoy their two-child household, 2016.

11.4.2 Population Policies

The policies that governments adopt—not just economic and demographic conditions—influence the birthrate. Among the most important policies are those regarding birth control (contraception). State policies vary widely.

At one extreme, China uses its strong government control to try to enforce a limit of one child per couple. Penalties for having a second child include being charged for services that were free for the first child. China has started to encourage wealthy and more educated families to have two children, and now, in some Chinese cities such as Shanghai, couples are allowed two-child families. Beyond two children, the penalties escalate. Contraceptives and abortions are free. China's policy has lowered growth rates considerably in the cities but less so in the countryside, where most people still live. Still, in a single decade (the 1970s), China's fertility rate fell from 6 children per woman to about 2.5, a dramatic change. By 2015, the fertility rate was 1.6.

But the Chinese policy has drawbacks. It limits individual freedom in favor of government control. Forced or coerced abortions have been reported. In traditional Chinese society (as in some other countries), sons are valued more than daughters. Couples who have a daughter may keep trying until they have a son. In some cases, Chinese peasants have reportedly killed newborn daughters so that they could try for a son. Simply bribing officials or paying fines became more common routes around the one-child policy in the 1990s. Most often, parents in China (and some places in India) are using information technology—ultrasound scans—to determine their baby's gender and abort it if it is a female. China's 2000 census showed the percentage of female births at 0.85 per boy, rather than the normal 0.95, a difference that amounts to a million "missing" girls per year. In the countryside, the sex differential is twice as high as in the cities, reaching 140 men per 100 women in some areas where the one-child policy is strictly enforced. In recent years, young women living in neighboring states, such as Vietnam, have been kidnapped, taken to China, and sold as brides.

In response to this gender imbalance and to concerns of the aging working population, the Chinese government in 2013 began to relax its one-child policy. Urban residents with enough resources could apply to have a second child. Some couples immediately took advantage of the policy, having a second child. Yet, several studies have estimated that only 12 to 18 percent of eligible families have applied to have second children. In some cases, families blame the high cost of living in large Chinese cities, while others say they are deferring to the wishes of older children who wish to remain only children. The Chinese government has expressed disappointment that more couples have not taken advantage of this new opportunity.

India's policies are less extreme but have been slower to have an effect. The birthrate fell from nearly 6 per woman to about 4.7 in the 1970s and 2.4 in 2018. India's government, strongly committed to birth control, has tried to make information and means widely available, but as a democracy it does not have China's extreme government control over society. Countries whose citizens have somewhat higher incomes than in India or China can succeed in promoting lower birthrates more easily. For example, Mexico's strong but noncoercive family-planning program, adopted in 1974, cut birthrates in half over 15 years, to 2.7 per woman (and to just under 2.2 as of 2018).

At the other extreme from China are governments that encourage or force childbearing and outlaw or limit access to contraception. Such a policy is called **pronatalist** (pro-birth). Traditionally, many governments have adopted such policies because population was seen as an element of national power. More babies today meant more soldiers later.

Today, only a few governments have strongly pronatalist policies, but many do not make birth control or sex education available to poor women. In some such states, population is not considered a problem (and may even be seen as an asset); in other states, the government simply cannot afford effective measures to lower birthrates. According to the United Nations Population Fund (UNFPA), 200 million women do not have access to effective contraception.

Birthrates are heavily influenced by the status of women in society. In cultures that traditionally see women as valuable only in producing babies, great sanctions exist against women who stop doing so. Many women do not use birth control because their husbands will not allow them to. These husbands may think that having many children is proof of their manliness. However, as women's status improves and they can work in various occupations, own property, and vote, women gain the power as well as the education and money necessary to limit the size of their families. According to the UNFPA, improving the status of women is one of the most important means of controlling world population growth. Government policies about women's status vary from one state to another. International programs and agencies, such as the UN Commission on the Status of Women, are working to address this issue on a global scale.

pronatalist Describing government policy that encourages or forces childbearing, and outlaws or limits access to contraception.

11.4.3 Disease

Population growth is determined by the death rate as well as the birthrate. People die from many different causes at different ages. In poor countries, people tend to die younger, often from infectious diseases; in richer countries, people live longer and die more often from cancer and heart disease. The proportion of babies who die within their first year is the **infant mortality rate**. This rate is an excellent indicator of overall health because it reflects a population's access to nutrition, water, shelter, and health care. Infant mortality is 4 percent worldwide: 1 percent or less in rich countries but more than 10 percent in the poorest countries and even higher in local pockets of extreme poverty (especially in Africa and in recent war zones).

infant mortality rate The proportion of babies who die within their first year of life.

Although death rates vary greatly from one state or region to another, the overall trends are stable from decade to decade. Wars, droughts, epidemics, and disasters have an effect locally but hardly matter globally. In the poorest countries, which are working through the demographic transition, the death rate declined from nearly 30 deaths per thousand people in 1950 to fewer than 8 per thousand since 2014. In the industrialized countries, the death rate bottomed out around 10 per thousand by 1960, and now stands around 7 in the West. These stable trends in mortality mean that the death rate is not a means by which governments or international agencies can affect population growth—worsening poverty may cause famine and a rising death rate, but this is not a realistic way to control population growth. It would mean moving backward through the demographic transition, which would wreck any chance of lowering birthrates. Nor do wars kill enough people to reduce population growth. In short, most of the world is already at or near the end of the transition in *death* rates; the key question is how long birthrates take to complete the transition.

Three mortality factors, however—HIV/AIDS, other infectious diseases, and smoking—deserve special attention because they exact very high costs even if they do not much affect global population trends. In these cases, actions taken in the short term have long-term and often international consequences, and once again there are short-term costs and long-term benefits.

HIV/AIDS   In the worldwide AIDS epidemic, one state's success or failure in limiting the spread of HIV (human immunodeficiency virus) affects infections in other states as well. There is a delay of five to ten years after infection by the virus before symptoms appear, and during this period an infected individual can infect others (through sex or blood transfer). AIDS spreads internationally—through business, tourism, migration, and military operations—reflecting the interdependence of states.

By 2017, the HIV/AIDS epidemic had already killed about 35 million people, and an estimated 36–37 million more were infected—though most of them did not know it. Two-thirds of them live in Africa and half of the rest in South Asia (see Table 11.2). The epidemic has also left 16 million orphans worldwide (over 75 percent in Africa). Each year, about 1.8 million people are newly infected with HIV, and 1 million die from AIDS, including over 100,000 children.

In Africa, already the world's poorest region, AIDS has emerged as one of several powerful forces driving the region backward into deeper poverty. About 5 percent of adults are infected with HIV, more than half of them women. In the most affected African countries in southern Africa, one in six adults has HIV (one in four for Botswana, the worst case). Infection is also rampant in African armies, with direct implications for international security. In Angola, it was the *end* of a long civil war that opened borders and increased traffic with neighboring states that had high HIV infection rates. As Angola's infection rate began to climb, military officers took the initiative to set up education programs and comprehensive HIV testing within the army. In contrast to other African states with high military infection rates, Angola's aggressive program kept the rate as low as in the general population, below 10 percent.

Table 11.2 Population and AIDS by World Region, 2016

Region[a]	Population (millions)	Population Growth Rate 1992–2016	HIV Infections (millions)
World	7,600	1.3%	37
Global North	1,450	0.8	4
Global South	6,150	2.7	33
of which:			
China	1,450	0.8	1
Middle East	500	1.8	0.2
Latin America	660	1.4	2
South Asia	2,500	1.8	4
Africa (sub-Saharan)	1,050	2.7	25

[a]Regions do not exactly match those used elsewhere in this book.

Source: Calculated from World Development Indicators. World Bank, 2017. UNAIDS Data 2017. UNAIDS.

In North America and other industrialized regions, new drug therapies (which keep the virus in check for years) dramatically lowered the death rate from AIDS starting in the late 1990s. But these treatments were too expensive to help much in Africa and other poor regions. India and Brazil began to export cheap generic versions of these drugs, violating patent rights of Western drug companies. The U.S. government threatened to punish South Africa and other countries if they allowed import of these drugs without compensating U.S. corporations holding patents. It filed a complaint against Brazil with the WTO. In response, AIDS activists demonstrated loudly and mobilized public opinion to get the policies changed.

The United States withdrew its complaint against Brazil in 2001. Meanwhile, drug companies began offering lower prices to poor countries, but delivery of the drugs to millions of poor people remained painfully slow. In 2004, the international community finally initiated the large-scale delivery of antiviral drugs to AIDS patients in poor countries. Now, tremendous progress has been made in delivering these drugs. In the past ten years, the number of people receiving treatment has increased dramatically, with UNAIDS now estimating that nearly 20 million people have access to these drugs.

This increased access to drugs and other care was facilitated by a marked increase in funds made available to treat the disease. In 2001, during a special UN session on AIDS, then–UN Secretary General Kofi Annan proposed a $7 billion to $10 billion per year global budget to combat AIDS (a fivefold increase in funding). The G8 states responded with pledges of a bit more than $1 billion—"laudable" but "not enough," in Annan's view. In 2003, President Bush pledged $15 billion over five years to help slow AIDS in Africa. That program has since been expanded dramatically. Since 2003,

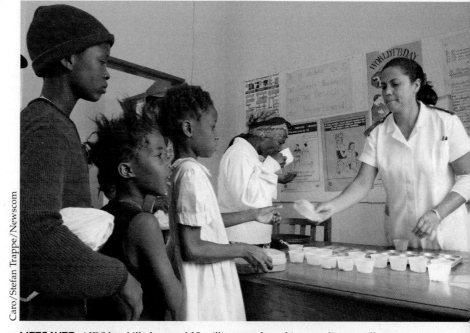

Caro/Stefan Trappe/Newscom

LIFESAVER AIDS has killed around 35 million people and is spreading rapidly in South Asia and China. The worldwide effort to slow AIDS, coordinated by the World Health Organization (WHO), illustrates how global-level problems such as AIDS are making IOs such as WHO more important. Currently, international efforts focus on trying to get antiviral medicines to more of the world's 36 million infected people. Tens of thousands of people who cannot afford the drugs and do not have access to a free program are dying of AIDS. Here, children receive medication to treat AIDS and TB in Namibia, 2016.

the United States has provided nearly $20 billion to combat AIDS. Between 2009 and 2014, the U.S. government pledged $48 billion to combat AIDS, tuberculosis (TB), and malaria. In 2006, five countries—France, Britain, Norway, Brazil, and Chile—agreed to raise $300 million a year to buy medications for children with AIDS, TB, and malaria. Most of it will come from taxing airline tickets (typically $5 coach and $50 first class). While observers have applauded these increased efforts, much more work remains, including care for the estimated 12 million children orphaned by AIDS in sub-Saharan Africa.

In some ways, AIDS has deepened the global North-South division. The 2001 UN session also revealed sharp differences between Western, secular states and a number of Islamic states that objected to any reference to gay people. This point was underscored when the then-president of Iran, in a 2007 speech at Columbia University, claimed there were no gay people in Iran. Catholic authorities worldwide have objected to programs that encourage condom use. As these examples show, some of the most effective prevention measures (public education, outreach to at-risk groups, condom distribution, free needles to drug users) are culturally and politically sensitive issues.

States must cooperate with each other if they are to bring the epidemic under control. These international efforts are coordinated primarily by the World Health Organization (WHO) and funded mainly by the industrialized countries. But the entire WHO budget is equivalent to that of a midsize hospital in the global North. WHO depends on national governments to provide information and carry out policies, and governments have been slow to respond. Some governments falsify statistics to underreport the number of cases (lest tourists be driven away), and many governments are reluctant to condone or sponsor sex education and distribution of condoms because of religious or cultural taboos.

In recent years, HIV has spread rapidly in South Asia, China, and Russia/Eastern Europe, where prostitution and drug use are growing. Thailand was especially vulnerable because of its huge prostitution industry, acceptance of male promiscuity, and large tourism industry. It was one of the first developing countries to develop an effective anti-AIDS program, which focuses on public education, and it dramatically lowered the infection rate in the 1990s.

In China, the government has been slow to act, and a stigma still prevents effective identification or treatment of the rapidly growing HIV-positive population. Unscrupulous cash-for-blood businesses, especially in one rural region, caused massive HIV infection. In rural China, medical practice relies heavily on shots—often with poorly sterilized needles—when other forms of treatment would be as effective. As a result, 60 percent of China's population has had hepatitis B, compared with 1 percent in the United States and Japan—a danger sign for the future growth of HIV in China. China had an estimated 1 million infected people in 2018, although these numbers are hard to confirm.

AIDS illustrates the transnational linkages that make international borders less meaningful than in the past. Effective international cooperation could save millions of lives and significantly enhance the prospects for economic development in the poorest countries in the coming decades. But once again, a

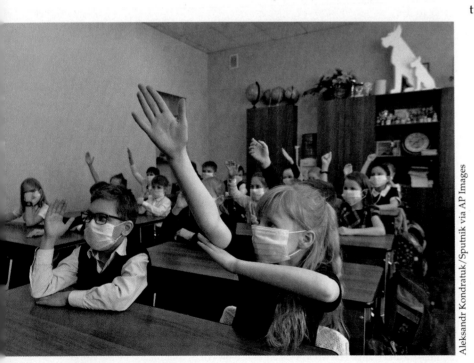

Aleksandr Kondratuk/Sputnik via AP Images

PANDEMIC PREVENTION With millions of people crossing borders around the world each year, there is always a concern that an isolated outbreak of an infectious disease could spread quickly. In 2017, the United States suffered one of the worst flu seasons in recent history with an estimated 4,000 deaths per week. Other countries, such as Canada, Russia, and China, also experienced worse than normal flu seasons. Here, schoolchildren in Russia wear masks to prevent catching the flu, 2018.

collective goods problem exists regarding the allocation of costs and benefits. A dollar spent by WHO has the same effect regardless of which country contributed it.

OTHER INFECTIOUS DISEASES   AIDS is not the only concern. TB, malaria, hepatitis, dengue fever, and cholera have all reemerged or spread in recent decades, often mutating into drug-resistant forms. TB now kills 1.7 million people per year (in addition to AIDS patients who also contract TB). Malaria sickens hundreds of millions of people and kills more than a million per year, nearly all in Africa. New campaigns have distributed millions of mosquito nets in Africa to reduce malaria—a proven, cost-effective measure. A malaria vaccine approved for usage in 2015 could cut malaria cases in half. Programs to evaluate the widespread use of the vaccine began in 2018. Vaccination programs have reduced the incidence of both polio and measles in recent years. A measles vaccination campaign now reaches 85 percent of infants worldwide, reducing deaths by 80 percent since 2000. Sadly, a polio vaccination drive in Pakistan was cut short in 2012 after Taliban militants killed health workers, claiming the vaccine was a Western plot to sterilize Muslim children.

In 2014, the world dealt with a significant disease crisis in West Africa. The Ebola virus became widespread in Guinea, Liberia, and Sierra Leone. It is estimated that nearly 10,000 people died as a result of the disease. Concern spread throughout the world as cases began appearing outside Africa, including the United States and Spain. Countries adopted travel restrictions and quarantine policies for those suspected of having the virus. Billions of dollars of aid was provided to these West African states to stop the virus and improve health care for its victims. It was yet another example of how, in the interconnected and globalized world, diseases may spread quickly over wide areas, even across oceans.

Iodine deficiency has historically received little attention, although it affects as many as 2 billion people worldwide. Even moderate deficiencies in unborn babies can lower intelligence by 10 to 15 IQ points, and serious deficiencies can stunt growth and cause mental retardation and goiter (enlarged thyroid gland). For about 5 cents per person yearly, adding iodine to salt can completely prevent the deficiency, but many countries in the global South and former Soviet bloc still do not do so. An international campaign did increase the use of iodized salt from 25 percent of households worldwide in 1990 to 66 percent in 2006.

Epidemics among animals have major effects as well. Currently, scientists fear that bird flu could mutate and spread person to person, sparking a global pandemic that could potentially kill millions. In 2009–2010, swine flu spread quickly around the globe, leading various countries to restrict travel to Mexico (where the flu originated). This strain of swine flu (H1N1) was found in numerous countries, many of which adopted quarantine policies for patients.

SMOKING   Worldwide, more than 1 billion people smoke, five-sixths of them in developing countries, and 5 million people a year die from tobacco-related disease. States that fail to curb the spread of nicotine addiction face high future costs in health care—costs that are just beginning to come due in many poor countries. The costs are largely limited to the state itself; its own citizens and economy pay the price. Nonetheless, the tobacco trade makes smoking an international issue. Tobacco companies' marketing campaigns targeting women in the global South could produce a huge increase in smokers in that group, according to WHO. The gender differences in smoking in developing countries are striking: Around 4 percent of women smoke in most developing countries, whereas the corresponding number for males runs as high as 60 percent (in China). By contrast, in the United States, about 20 percent of men smoke compared to 15 percent of women.

In 2001, tobacco companies with some U.S. support sought to weaken a new proposed treaty, the Framework Convention on Tobacco Control, but in 2003, the United States dropped its objections and WHO member states adopted the treaty, which entered into force in 2005. Member states pledge to ban tobacco advertising and are encouraged to raise taxes on tobacco 5 percent a year above the inflation rate. The United States, alone among the world's major powers, still had not ratified the treaty by 2018.

Population issues are sometimes portrayed as simply too many people using up too little food and natural resources. However, the idea that overpopulation is the cause of hunger in today's world is not really accurate. Poverty and politics—more than population—are the causes of malnutrition and hunger today (see World Hunger in Chapter 12). There is enough food, water, petroleum, land, and so forth—but these resources are unequally distributed.

This unequal distribution is directly related to the gap between the global North and the global South. Strains on the environment and on natural resources are global in scope, yet in the North they arise from industrialization (growing GDP per capita), whereas in the South they are more affected by growing populations. These differences in environmental impacts are by no means the only such North-South difference. The next two chapters turn to that global North-South divide.

Chapter Review

Summary

- Environmental problems are an example of international interdependence and often create collective goods problems for the states involved. The large numbers of actors involved in global environmental problems make them more difficult to solve.

- To resolve such collective goods problems, states have used international regimes and IOs and have, in some cases, extended state sovereignty (notably over territorial waters) to make management a national rather than an international matter.

- International efforts to solve environmental problems aim to bring about sustainable economic development.

- Global warming results from burning fossil fuels—the basis of industrial economies today. The industrialized states are much more responsible for the problem than are developing countries, but countries such as China and India also contribute to the problem. Solutions are difficult to reach because costs are substantial and dangers are somewhat distant and uncertain.

- Damage to the earth's ozone layer results from the use of specific chemicals, which are now being phased out under international agreements. Unlike global warming, the costs of solutions are much lower and the problem is better understood.

- Many species are threatened with extinction due to loss of habitats such as rain forests. An international treaty on biodiversity and an agreement on forests aim to reduce the destruction of local ecosystems, with costs spread among states.

- The UN Convention on the Law of the Sea (UNCLOS) establishes an ocean regime that puts most commercial fisheries and offshore oil under control of states as territorial waters.

- Pollution—including acid rain, water and air pollution, and toxic and nuclear waste—tends to be more localized than global and has been addressed mainly through unilateral, bilateral, and regional measures rather than global ones.

- Most Western states import energy resources, mostly oil, whereas the other world regions export them. Oil prices rose dramatically in the 1970s but declined in the 1980s as the world economy adjusted by increasing supply and reducing demand. Prices spiked again around 1991 and 2007–2008 before collapsing in 2008. Such fluctuations undermine world economic stability.

- The most important source of oil traded worldwide is the Persian Gulf area of the Middle East. Consequently, this area has long been a focal point of international political conflict.

- World population—now at 7.6 billion—may eventually level out around 10 billion. Almost all of the increase will come in the global South.

- Future world population growth will be largely driven by the demographic transition. Death rates have fallen throughout the world, but birthrates will fall proportionally only as per capita incomes go up. The faster the economies of poor states develop, the sooner their populations will level out.

- Government policies can reduce birthrates somewhat at a given level of per capita income. Effective policies are those that improve access to birth control and raise the status of women in society. Actual policies vary, from China's very strict rules on childbearing to pronatalist governments that encourage maximum birthrates and outlaw birth control.

- The global HIV/AIDS epidemic creates huge costs for many poor states. Currently over 35 million people are infected with HIV, and around 37 million more have died. Most are in Africa, but new infections are growing rapidly in Asia and Russia.

Key Terms

tragedy of the commons   350
enclosure   350
global warming   352
UN Environment Program
   (UNEP)   353
greenhouse gases   353
Kyoto Protocol   354

Paris Climate Agreement   356
ozone layer   357
Montreal Protocol   357
biodiversity   359
International Whaling
   Commission   359
high seas   362

UN Convention on the
   Law of the Sea (UNCLOS)   362
acid rain   364
Chernobyl   364
demographic transition   371
pronatalist   373
infant mortality rate   374

Critical Thinking Questions

1. Given the collective goods problem in managing environmental issues—heightened by the participation of large numbers of actors—what new international organizations or agreements could be created in the coming years to help solve this problem? Are there ways to reduce the number of actors participating in the management of global problems such as global warming? What problems might your proposals run into?

2. Few effective international agreements have been reached to solve the problem of global warming. Given the several difficulties associated with managing this problem, what creative international solutions can you think of? What would be the strengths and weaknesses of your solutions in both the short and the long term?

3. Does the record of the international community on environmental management reflect the views of mercantilists, liberals, or both? In what ways?

4. Some politicians call for the Western industrialized countries, including the United States, to be more self-sufficient in energy resources in order to reduce dependence on oil imports. In light of the overall world energy picture and the economics of international trade, what are the pros and cons of such a proposal?

5. Dozens of poor states appear to be stuck midway through the demographic transition: Death rates have fallen, birthrates remain high, and per capita incomes are not increasing. How do you think these states, with or without foreign assistance, can best get unstuck and complete the demographic transition?

Suggested Readings

Barkin, J. Samuel, and Elizabeth R. DeSombre. *Saving Global Fisheries: Reducing Fishing Capacity to Promote Sustainability*. MIT, 2013.

Blewit, John. *Understanding Sustainable Development*. 3rd ed. Routledge, 2018.

DeSombre, Elizabeth R. *The Global Environment and World Politics: International Relations for the 21st Century*. 2nd ed. Continuum, 2007.

Hudson, Valerie M., and Andrea M. Den Boer. *Bare Branches: The Security Implications of Asia's Surplus Male Population*. MIT, 2004.

Kahl, Colin H. *States, Scarcity, and Civil Strife in the Developing World*. Princeton, 2006.

Sachs, Jeffrey. *The Age of Sustainable Development*. Columbia, 2015.

Young, Oran R. *On Environmental Governance: Sustainability, Efficiency, and Equity*. Paradigm, 2013.

Let's Debate the Issue
Stopping Global Warming: Who Should Pay?

Overview

The Paris Agreement on climate is the latest attempt to control the pollutants that lead to global warming. Its predecessor, the Kyoto Protocol, used a market mechanism to allocate caps on the amount of emissions that can come from various countries. Yet only developed countries were required to meet the targets under Kyoto. Developing countries did not have binding caps on their emissions.

To move forward at the Paris negotiations, states agreed to drop binding restrictions for all countries. This allows countries flexibility in how they set targets to reduce emissions as well as flexibility in how those targets are met. Politically, the flexibility was necessary to get states to sign the Paris Climate Agreement. Developed states continued to demand that developing states (especially China and India) play an active role in preventing global warming, while developing states continued to demand resources (money and technology) to offset the costs of doing so.

The Paris Agreement includes provisions to provide up to $100 billion per year to developing countries to adapt economically and to mitigate global warming. Those pledges must be achieved by 2020 and run until 2025. Should developing countries, such as China, be asked to contribute to stopping global warming? Who should be required to contribute to the provision of this public good?

ARGUMENT 1

Developing Countries Should Pay Their Share to Stop Global Warming

Developing countries contribute to global warming, so they should pay. Developing countries contribute large amounts of carbon dioxide to the global atmosphere. They should not be allowed to free-ride on the efforts of the wealthy states who want to slow down global warming.

Technologies will keep costs low in the long run. While the cost to slow down global warming will be high initially, over time, technology will help states keep costs low while lessening emissions. Thus, one should not be overly concerned that the costs of policy change in developing states will be overwhelming.

Developing countries could benefit economically from climate agreements. Like the Kyoto Protocol, the Paris Agreement contains similar market-based mechanisms, which could benefit developing countries economically. If these countries can bring emissions down below their targets, they can sell their "unused" pollution allowance to recoup some of the costs of implementing the agreement.

ARGUMENT 2

Only Developed Countries Should Pay to Stop Global Warming

The costs to developing countries will undermine development. The costs of slowing global warming will be large. Placing even some of these costs on developing countries will lead to economic hardship, which will further undermine development, which in turn could increase emissions because these states would have no money to invest in better technologies or to develop cleaner industries.

Developed countries were allowed to pollute to develop. For many years, developed countries paid little attention to the environment as they built industries, achieved economic growth, and became successful. Now, with India and China threatening to become economically successful, Western states want to place limitations on how other states can develop and how they can treat the environment. Non-Western states should be allowed the same development path as Western states.

It is really the developed countries' pollution. Although developing countries do their fair share of polluting, many of these emissions come from industries that have been shipped from developed states. Western states did not want these polluting industries in their backyards, so they sent them abroad, and now demand that the host countries pay the bill for the cleanup.

Questions

- Should developed countries be bound by the Paris Agreement and pay the cost of reducing emissions in developing countries? Does this requirement make the success of the Paris Agreement (i.e., lowering temperatures) more or less likely?

- Do you believe that environmental issues like global warming will be more or less difficult to solve during this period of rising antiglobalization movements? Why or why not?

- Do you think that technological solutions will be developed to help solve the problem of global warming? Or will fundamental changes in how individuals consume energy be a better path to reduce the problem of global warming?

For Further Reading

Klein, Daniel, Maria Pia Carazo, Meinhard Doelle, Jane
Bulmer, and Andrew Higham, eds. *The Paris Agreement on
Climate Change: Analysis and Commentary.* Oxford, 2017.

Nordhaus, William D. *The Climate Casino: Risk, Uncertainty,
and Economics for a Warming World.* Yale, 2015.

Vogler, John. *Climate Change in World Politics.* Palgrave,
2016.

Zedillo, Ernesto. *Global Warming: Looking Beyond Kyoto.*
Brookings, 2008.

Chapter 12
The North-South Gap

AFRICAN MIGRANTS BOARDING SHIP, ITALY, 2015.

∨ Learning Objectives

12.1 Identify at least four basic human needs and describe how at least one region in the global South is meeting those needs.

12.2 Give examples of states that world-system theory would identify as members of the core, semiperiphery, and periphery.

12.3 Compare three different effects of colonialism and explain how these effects have led to problems with economic development in the global South.

12.1 The State of the South

Identify at least four basic human needs and describe how at least one region in the global South is meeting those needs.

This and the following chapter concern the world's poor regions—the global South—where most people live. States in these regions are called by various names, used interchangeably: third world countries, **less-developed countries (LDCs)**, *underdeveloped countries* (UDCs), or **developing countries**. This chapter discusses the gap in wealth between the industrialized regions (the North) and the rest of the world (the South). It develops the theories of imperialism introduced in Chapter 3 that try to explain this gap in terms of historical colonization of the South by the North. Chapter 13 discusses international aspects of economic development in the South.

International relations (IR) scholars do not agree on the causes or implications of poverty in the global South, nor do they agree on solutions (if any) to the problem. Thus, they also disagree about the nature of relations between rich and poor states (North-South relations). Everyone agrees, however, that much of the global South is poor, and some of it extremely poor.

In all, about 1 billion people live in abject poverty, without access to basic nutrition or health care. They are concentrated in Africa, where income levels have lagged for decades. Two decades ago, the concentration was as strong in South Asia, but economic growth there has greatly reduced the numbers living in extreme poverty. Still, the average income per person in South Asia—home to 2 billion people—is only $6,000 per year, and in Africa it is only $3,700 (these numbers adjust for the lower costs of living in these regions compared to richer ones). Billions of people are rising out of poverty, but because of population growth, the number of very poor people does not decline very quickly.

The bottom line is that every ten seconds, somewhere in the world, a child dies as a result of malnutrition—by not eating enough food or not eating the right food to resist diseases. That is over 3 million children every year. The world produces enough food to nourish these children and enough income to afford to nourish them, but their own families or states do not have enough income. They die, ultimately, from poverty. Meanwhile, in that same ten seconds, the world spends over $500,000 on military forces, one-thousandth of which could save the child's life and more. Likewise, people lack water, shelter, health care, and other necessities because they cannot afford them. The widespread, grinding poverty of people who cannot afford necessities is less visible than the dramatic examples of starvation triggered by war or drought, but it affects many more people.

In 2000, the UN adopted the *Millennium Development Goals* (MDG), which set targets for basic needs measures to be achieved by 2015. The first of the eight goals was to cut in half the proportion of the world's population living in "extreme poverty," defined as income of less than $1.25 per day. This goal was met ahead of schedule in 2010, although Africa lagged far behind Asia in cutting poverty. Since 1990, 2 billion people have gained access to improved drinking water, but over 800 million remain hungry around the world.

Based on the experience with the MDGs, the UN announced new goals in 2015, called the **Sustainable Development Goals (SDGs)**, which set targets for 17 basic needs measures to be achieved by 2030. The goals cover a wide range of subjects including poverty, hunger, education, affordable energy, reduced inequality, climate change, and economic growth. Within each of the 17 goals, the SDGs outline targets, including measurable indicators that will allow for an assessment of whether the goals have been achieved, in whole or in part.

The five regions of the global South differ not only on poverty reduction but also on income level and growth. As Figure 12.1 shows, the regions experiencing the

less-developed countries (LDCs) The world's poorest regions—the global South—where most people live. Also called *underdeveloped countries* or *developing countries*.

developing countries States in the global South, the poorest regions of the world—also called *third world countries*, *less-developed countries*, or *underdeveloped countries*.

Sustainable Development Goals (SDGs) UN targets for basic needs measures such as reducing poverty and hunger, adopted in 2015.

Figure 12.1 Income Level and Growth Rate by World Region

Source: Based on World Bank data.

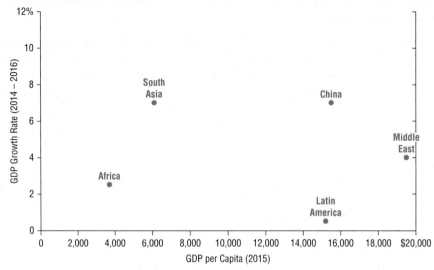

Note: For the global North overall, GDP per capita is $40,000.

fastest growth—China and South Asia—are neither the highest- nor the lowest-income regions. The Middle East is about as developed as China in terms of gross domestic product (GDP) per capita, but it is growing at only half the rate. Chapter 13 will explore the reasons for these differences in economic growth, but here we note simply that the world's regions vary on both income and growth, with no correlation between the two dimensions.

Experts disagree about how much poverty and inequality have decreased. Some argue that poverty has been halved through rapid economic growth and that the global distribution of income is shifting from having rich and poor extremes to having a bell curve distribution, with a large population at middle incomes—an emerging global middle class. The World Bank describes progress as slower. Between 1990 and 2015, incomes per person (adjusted for inflation and differential costs of living) in the global South as a whole rose from about $3,000 to about $8,900. In the global North, they rose from about $20,000 to about $40,000 per person. Does this indicate a slow closing of the gap because the ratio fell from about 6.7 to 5.0 as the result of a higher rate of growth in the South? Or does it indicate a widening of the gap between a person in the North and one in the South because, in absolute terms, incomes increased from $17,000 to under $32,000? Each has some truth.

12.1.1 Basic Human Needs

Some countries in the global South have made rapid progress in raising incomes, but others are caught in a cycle of poverty. Until incomes rise, the population will not move through the demographic transition (see Chapter 11); population growth will remain high and incomes low.

To put economic growth on a firm foundation, societies must meet the **basic human needs** of most of the population. People need food, shelter, and other necessities of daily life in order to feel secure. As long as people in the global South blame imperialism for a lack of basic needs, extreme poverty will fuel revolution, terrorism, and anti-Western sentiments.

Children are central to meeting a population's basic needs. In particular, education allows a new generation to meet other basic needs and move through the demographic transition. Literacy—which UNESCO defines as the ability to read and write a simple sentence—is the key component of education. A person who can read and

basic human needs The fundamental needs of people for adequate food, shelter, health care, sanitation, and education. Meeting such needs may be thought of as both a moral imperative and a form of investment in "human capital" essential for economic growth.

write can obtain a wealth of information about farming, health care, birth control, and so forth. Some poor countries have raised literacy rates substantially; others lag behind.

Great variation also exists in schooling. Primary-school enrollment in 2016 was more than 90 percent in most world regions, though only 70 percent for Africa. Secondary education—middle and high school—is another matter. In the North, about 90 percent of secondary-school-age children are enrolled, but in most of the global South, those numbers are significantly smaller. College is available to only a small fraction of the population.

According to UNICEF, in the global South, in 2017, one in four children suffered from malnutrition, one in seven lacked access to health care, and one in seven had no safe drinking water. The AIDS epidemic is undoing progress made over decades in reducing child mortality and increasing education.

Figure 12.2 shows the variation across regions in two key indicators of children's well-being at different stages—immunizations and secondary-school enrollments for males only (including females would lower these numbers). In both cases, achievement of these basic needs for children roughly correlates with the regions' respective income levels.

Effective health care in poor countries is not expensive—less than $5 per person per year for primary care. For instance, UNICEF has promoted four inexpensive methods that together are credited with saving the lives of millions of children each year. One method is growth monitoring. Experts estimate that regular weighing and advice can prevent half of all cases of malnutrition. A second method is oral rehydration therapy (ORT), which stops diarrhea in children before they die from dehydration. A facility that produced 300 packets per day of the simple sugar-salt remedy, at a cost of 1.5 cents each, was built in Guatemala for just $550. Child deaths from

Narinder Nanu/Getty Images

BABY BOOST Nearly a billion people in the global South—most of them in Africa and South Asia—live in abject poverty, lacking safe water, housing, food, and the ability to read. Natural disasters, droughts, and wars can displace subsistence farmers from their land and make matters worse. But sustained advances in health care, such as the prenatal checkup given these women in India in 2013, are bringing dramatic improvements.

Figure 12.2 Basic Needs Indicators by Region, 2016

Source: Based on World Bank data.

■ Measles immunization rate   ■ Secondary-school enrollments, male

Careers in International Relations: Nongovernmental Organizations (NGOs)

Summary

Jobs in NGOs provide personally rewarding experiences for those willing to work hard for a cause, but they pay poorly and are hard to obtain.

BENEFITS AND COSTS Nearly 40,000 NGOs exist, and that number grows daily. Thousands of individuals are interested in working in these organizations. Although all NGOs are different, many perform multiple functions: working in developing countries regarding a variety of issues, public outreach at home and abroad, lobbying governments to change their policies, designing projects to solve problems and attempting to find funding for their implementation.

Working for an NGO has many benefits. Workers often find themselves surrounded by others concerned about the same issues: improving the environment, protecting human rights, advancing economic development, or promoting better health care. The spirit of camaraderie can be exhilarating and rewarding.

While working for an NGO can be extremely rewarding personally, it is rarely rewarding financially. Most NGOs are nonprofit operations that pay workers meagerly for long hours. Moreover, many smaller NGOs engage in a constant fight for funding from governments, think tanks, private foundations, or individuals. The process of fundraising can be quite time consuming.

Despite the large number of NGOs, relatively low pay, and long hours, finding a job with an NGO can be difficult. One key is to be specific. Try to narrow your interests in terms of substantive areas (e.g., human rights, environment) and/or geographic region. Also think about whether you want to work in your own country or abroad. Positions abroad may be more rewarding but are in lower supply and higher demand.

SKILLS TO HONE NGOs are looking for self-starters. Most have little time and few resources for training. Basic office skills (for example, computer expertise) are essential, but employees also need to cover a range of duties every day. Anything and everything is in your job description. Writing and communication skills are key, especially when fundraising is part of the job. Foreign language skills also matter because many NGOs maintain or work with field offices abroad.

Often, NGOs ask potential employees to volunteer for a period while they train, before being hired. Increasingly, some companies place workers in an NGO or volunteer opportunity for a price. By

VLADIMIR VALISHVILI/AFP/Getty Images

paying to work, you can gain a probationary period to develop your skills and familiarize yourself with the operation and become efficient before going on the payroll.

Finally, in cities where NGOs cluster (for example, Washington, DC), personal networks play an important role in finding good opportunities. Workers often move from one organization to another. For this reason, many volunteer or accept jobs with NGOs not in their immediate area of interest to gain experience and contacts, which can help future career advancement.

Resources

King, Richard M. *From Making a Profit to Making a Difference: How to Launch Your New Career in Nonprofits*. Planning/Communications, 2000.

Weiss, David. Careers in International Development and Humanitarian Assistance NGOs. In *Careers in International Affairs*. 9th ed. Georgetown School of Foreign Service, 2014.

http://www.ngo.org/links/index.htm

http://www.idealist.org

http://www.wango.org/resources.aspx?section=ngodir

diarrhea were cut in half in one year. The third method is immunization against six common deadly diseases: measles, polio, tuberculosis (TB), tetanus, whooping cough, and diphtheria. In recent decades, the number of children immunized in poor countries has risen from 5 percent to more than 50 percent. By 2015, the number of children immunized at least once against measles had risen to 85 percent. The fourth method is the promotion of breast-feeding rather than infant formula (sometimes marketed unethically as more modern).

Since 1990, despite the daunting problems of war and the HIV/AIDS epidemic, public health in the global South has registered some important gains. Infant tetanus deaths were halved, and access to safe water was extended to a billion more people. Polio was nearly eliminated, but resistance to vaccination in parts of Nigeria let the disease begin to spread again, with three countries having indigenous virus populations as of 2016 (Pakistan, Afghanistan, and Nigeria—and the virus traveled from Pakistan to Egyptian sewage in 2013). In eight African countries in 2006, following successful trials in several other countries, authorities combined the distribution of insecticide-treated mosquito nets for malaria with measles and polio vaccines, deworming pills, vitamin A supplements, and educational materials—a combined approach proven to work. In 2016, deaths of children under five worldwide hit a record low, well below 6 million, having declined by half since 1990. Measles deaths dropped by three-quarters in just ten years, 2000–2010, an enormous success.

Still, the disparities in access to health care around the world are striking. Seventy-five percent of the world's people living in the global South have about 30 percent of the world's doctors and nurses. In medical research, less than 5 percent of world expenditures are directed at problems in developing countries, according to the World Health Organization (WHO). The biggest killers are AIDS, acute respiratory infections, diarrhea, TB, malaria, and hepatitis. More than 400 million people are infected with tropical diseases—200 million to 300 million with malaria alone. But because the people with such diseases are poor, there is often not a large enough market for drug companies (which are multinational corporations [MNCs]) in the industrialized world to invest in medicines for them. And when poor countries need medicines developed for rich markets, the drugs may be prohibitively expensive—as with the AIDS drugs (see Chapter 11). Despite this, efforts undertaken by the WHO as well as NGOs have reduced the mortality rate from malaria by 29 percent since 2010.

Safe water is another essential element of meeting basic human needs. In many rural locations, people must walk miles every day to fetch water. Note that access to water does not mean running water in every house but a clean well or faucet for a village. In 1990–2010, the number without access fell by half, meeting the MDG target early, but three in ten people worldwide still lack safe drinking water. Twice as many lack sanitation facilities (such as sewers and sanitary latrines). Some 4.5 billion people do not have access to sanitation. The result is recurrent epidemics and widespread diarrhea, which kill millions of children each year. Rural areas are worse than cities. Poor sanitation in Haiti allowed a cholera epidemic (ironically introduced by visiting Nepalese peacekeepers, sent to help Haiti) to kill thousands in 2010–2013.

Shelter is another key basic need. Of the world's 7.6 billion people, about one in six lives in substandard housing or is homeless altogether. For indicator after indicator, we find about a billion people left behind with nothing. The different indicators do not overlap perfectly, but basically the bottom billion of humanity, most living in rural areas, are in desperate poverty. The most important factors keeping these people in extreme poverty appear to be civil war, corruption, the "resource curse" (see Chapter 13), and landlocked locations without ready access to trade.

In theory, providing for basic needs should give poor people hope of progress and should ensure political stability. However, that is not always the result. In Sri Lanka, a progressive-minded government implemented one of the world's most successful basic needs strategies, addressing nutrition, health care, and literacy. The policy showed that even a very poor country could meet basic needs at low levels of per capita income. Then an ethnic civil war broke out. The war became more and more brutal—with death squads and indiscriminate reprisals on civilians—until it consumed the progress Sri Lanka had made.

War in the global South—both international and civil war—is a leading obstacle to the provision of basic needs. War causes much greater damage to society than merely the direct deaths and injuries it inflicts. In war zones, economic infrastructure

John Moore/AP Images

DO THE MATH Children are a main focus of efforts to provide basic human needs in the global South. Education is critical to both economic development and the demographic transition. Girls worldwide receive less education than boys, and in Afghanistan under the Taliban, they were banned from schools altogether. This math class in Kandahar, Afghanistan, in 2002 followed the Taliban's fall.

such as transportation is disrupted, as are government services such as health care and education. Wars drastically reduce the confidence in economic and political stability on which investment and trade depend.

Figure 12.3 maps the rates of access to safe water and food. The worldwide pattern somewhat resembles the map of wars in progress (see Chapter 5). If indeed there is a relationship between recent or present warfare and a lack of basic needs (in turn correlated with income level), what really causes what? Does being at war keep a society poor and prevent it from meeting its population's basic needs? Or does being poor, with unmet basic needs, make a society more war-prone? Probably both are true. War is often part of a vicious cycle for states unable to rise out of poverty.

The fragility of life in poor countries was demonstrated all too starkly in 2010 when a major earthquake devastated Haiti, already the poorest country in the Western hemisphere, with annual GDP of $1,300 per person. Because of poor construction, many buildings collapsed, and because of poor health and sanitation facilities, survivors faced desperate conditions. More than 100,000 people died and millions were left homeless. Haitians could only hope that international aid would help them rebuild from scratch.

12.1.2 World Hunger

malnutrition A lack of needed foods including protein and vitamins; about 3 million children die each year from malnutrition-related causes.

Of all the basic needs of people in the global South, the most central is *food*. **Malnutrition** (or malnourishment) refers to the lack of needed foods including protein and vitamins. The term *hunger* refers broadly to malnutrition or outright *undernourishment*—a lack of calories. Hunger does not usually kill people through outright starvation, but it weakens them and leaves them susceptible to infectious diseases that would not ordinarily be fatal.

About 800 million people—the vast majority in the Global South—are chronically undernourished (see Table 12.1). Their potential contribution to economic

Table 12.1 Global Undernourishment

Chronically Undernourished People by Region, c. 2016

Region	Number (millions)	Percentage of Population	15 Years Earlier
South Asia	270	15%	19%
Southeast Asia	65	10%	22%
China	135	10%	16%
Africa	205	21%	25%
Latin America	40	6%	11%
Middle East	40	9%	9%
Developing World	755	13%	18%

Sources: Based on Food and Agriculture Organization of the United Nations, *the State of food Inequality in the World*, 2017.

Figure 12.3 Rates of Access to Water and Food, 2015

Source: Based on World Health Organization.

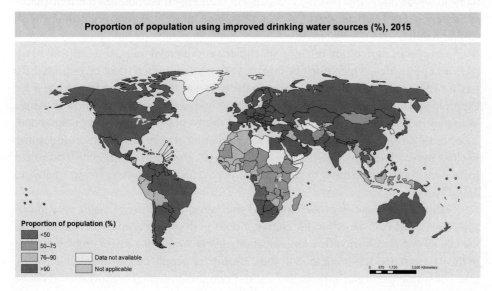

Proportion of population using improved drinking water sources (%), 2015

Proportion of population (%)

- <50
- 50–75
- 76–90
- >90
- Data not available
- Not applicable

PREVALENCE OF UNDERNOURISHMENT IN THE POPULATION
(PERCENT) IN 2014-16

LEGEND

- <5% Very low
- 5% —▷14.9% - Moderately low
- 15% —▷24.9% - Moderately high
- 25% —▷34.9% - High
- 35% and over - Very high
- Missing or insufficient data

accumulation is wasted because they cannot do even light work. And they are a potential source of political instability—including international instability—as long as they stay hungry. Record food prices in 2011 made the problem worse. At the World Food Summit in 1996, world leaders adopted a goal to cut hunger in half by 2015. The world came close to achieving this goal but did not quite make it. As a proportion of a growing population, the rate of hunger dropped from 19 to 11 percent from 1991 to 2014. In 2015, world leaders pledged to set development goals of ending hunger and extreme poverty by 2030.

China has made great progress in reducing child malnutrition, cutting these numbers in half since 1990. But progress in South Asia had been very slow and Africa was not moving forward. About one of every six of the world's children under age 5—and nearly half those in India—were underweight. By 2014, malnutrition among Indian children was declining, but not for the poorest 20 percent.

Traditionally, rural communities have grown their own food—**subsistence farming**. Colonialism disrupted this pattern, and the disruption has continued in postcolonial times. States in the global South shifted from subsistence to commercial

subsistence farming Rural communities growing food mainly for their own consumption rather than for sale in local or world markets.

agriculture. Small plots were merged into big plantations, often under the control of wealthy landlords. By concentrating capital and orienting the economy toward a niche in world trade, this process is consistent with liberal economics. But it displaces subsistence farmers from the land. Wars displace farmers even more quickly, with similar results.

cash crops Agricultural goods produced as commodities for export to world markets.

Commercial agriculture relies on machinery, commercial fuels, and artificial fertilizers and pesticides, which must be bought with cash and often must be imported. To pay for these supplies, big farms grow **cash crops**—agricultural goods produced for export to world markets. Such crops typically provide little nutrition to local peasants; examples include coffee, tea, and sugar cane. When a plantation is built or expanded, subsistence farmers end up working on the plantation at very low wages or migrating to cities in search of jobs. Often they end up hungry. Ironically, the higher food prices increase income for farmers in rural areas, yet at the cost of many being unable to afford food.

Natural disasters can exacerbate food shortages. The threat of major food shortages threatened Pakistan after devastating floods in the summer of 2010. According to the UN's Food and Agriculture Organization, nearly 2 million acres of crops were lost in the Pakistan flood, leaving food in short supply for people and farm animals. States, intergovernmental organizations (IGOs), and nongovernmental organization (NGOs) rushed food to Pakistan after the floods, hoping to avert a major humanitarian catastrophe.

International food aid itself can sometimes contribute to these problems. Agricultural assistance may favor mechanized commercial agriculture. And if an international agency floods an area with food, prices on local markets drop, which may force even more local farmers out of business and increase dependence on handouts from the government or international community. Also, people in a drought or famine often have to travel to feeding centers to receive the food, halting their work on their own land.

12.1.3 Rural and Urban Populations

The displacement of peasants from subsistence farming contributes to a massive population shift that typically accompanies the demographic transition. More and more people move to the cities from the countryside—**urbanization**. This is hard to measure exactly; there is no standard definition of when a town is considered a city. But industrialized states report that about 70 to 90 percent of their populations live in cities. By contrast, China was 55 percent urbanized in 2017 (the government target is 60 percent by 2020), while most states in Asia and Africa were between 30 and 40 percent. Most Middle Eastern states are more than 50 percent urbanized, and South American ones are 70 to 85 percent urban.

urbanization A shift of population from the countryside to the cities that typically accompanies economic development and is augmented by displacement of peasants from subsistence farming.

Urbanization is not caused by higher population growth in cities than in the countryside. In fact, the opposite is true. In cities, the people are generally better educated, with higher incomes. They are further along in the demographic transition and have lower birthrates than people in the countryside. Rather, the growth of urban population is caused by people moving to the cities from the countryside. They do so because of the higher income levels in the cities—economic opportunity—and the hope of more chances for an exciting life. They also move because population growth in the countryside stretches available food, water, arable land, and other resources.

land reform Policies that aim to break up large landholdings and redistribute land to poor peasants for use in subsistence farming.

In many cities, the influx of people cannot be accommodated with jobs, housing, and services. In slums, basic human needs often go unmet. Many states have considered policies to break up large landholdings and redistribute land to poor peasants for use in subsistence farming—**land reform**. The main opponents of land reform are large landowners, who often wield great political power because of their wealth and international connections to markets, MNCs, and other sources of hard currency.

12.1.4 Women in Development

Economic development in poor countries is closely tied to the status of women in those societies. This is a relatively recent revelation; most attention for decades had focused on men as supposedly the main generators of capital. Governments and international reports concentrated on work performed by male wage earners. Women's work, by contrast, often is not paid for in money and does not show up in financial statistics. But women in much of the world work harder than men and contribute more to the economic well-being of their families and communities. Women are key to efforts to improve the lot of children and reduce birthrates (see the Public Opinion and International Relations box). In nutrition, education, health care, and shelter, women are central to providing the basic needs of people in poor countries.

Yet women hold inferior social status to men in the countries of the South (even more so than in the North). For instance, when food is in short supply, men and boys often eat first, with women and girls getting what is left.

Discrimination against girls is widespread in education and literacy. Worldwide, two-thirds of the 775 million adults who cannot read or write are women. Across the global South, only in Latin America do women's literacy rates approach those of men. In Pakistan, three-quarters of boys but little more than half the girls receive primary education. Throughout Asia, Africa, and the Middle East (but not in Latin America), more boys receive education, especially at the secondary level, though the gap has closed considerably in recent years. At the university level, only 30 percent of students in the Middle East are women, a bit more than 20 percent in South Asia and Africa (but 45 percent in China and Latin America). The Taliban regime in Afghanistan (1996–2001) took extreme measures against women's education, banning all girls from school and all women from paid work.

States and international agencies have begun to pay attention to ending discrimination in schooling, ensuring women's access to health care and birth control, educating mothers about prenatal and child health, and generally raising women's status in society (allowing them a greater voice in decisions). For example, international agencies help women organize small businesses, farms, and other income-producing activities. UNICEF has helped women get bank loans on favorable terms to start small businesses in Egypt and Pakistan as well as cooperative farms in Indonesia. Women have organized cooperatives throughout the global South, often in rural areas, to produce income through weaving and other textile and clothing production, retail stores, agriculture, and so forth. In the slums of Addis Ababa, Ethiopia, women heads of household with no land for subsistence farming had been forced into begging and prostitution. Women taking part in the Integrated Holistic Approach Urban Development Project organized income-producing

BOUREIMA HAMA/AFP/Getty Images

WOMEN'S POWER The status of women in countries of the global South affects their prospects for economic development. Women are central to rural economies, to population strategies, and to the provision of basic human needs, including education. Here, women in Niger provide a guided tour of their urban garden entrepreneurship project, 2018.

businesses in areas such as food processing, cloth weaving, and garment production. These profitable businesses earned income for the women and helped subsidize health and sanitation services in the slums.

12.1.5 Migration and Refugees

The processes just outlined—basic needs deprivation, displacement from land, and urbanization—culminate in one of the biggest political issues affecting North-South relations: **migration** from poorer to richer states. Millions of people from the global South have crossed international borders, often illegally, to reach the North.

migration Movement between states, usually *emigration* from the old state and *immigration* to the new state.

Public Opinion and International Relations
Morality and Health

Access to some form of birth control is often identified as a key factor supporting women's health. Studies consistently report that access to birth control is vital to the health of women and children. Contraceptive use is found to prevent hundreds of thousands of maternal deaths in the developing world. Allowing more time between children could decrease under-5 child mortality by 25 percent.

Yet, religious beliefs, cultural norms, and family dynamics profoundly affect attitudes toward birth control. As such, individuals may hold very different views as to the morality of birth control. This can be true even within families: In one famous study, birth control was offered to some women in front of their husbands, while to others it was offered in private. Months later, those who were offered it in private were over 50 percent less likely to have an unwanted pregnancy.

Understandably, then, when asked whether the use of birth control as family planning is moral, variation of opinion exists across countries. A poll in 2013 conducted in 39 countries asked whether contraceptive use was morally acceptable, morally unacceptable, situationally moral, or not a moral issue at all. The results are presented in Figure 12.4.

For respondents in most countries, the most common response is that contraceptive use is morally acceptable. Indeed, for most countries of North America and Europe, the vast majority of the population responded that contraception is either morally acceptable or not a moral issue at all. In the developing world, however, there is more variation. In two countries, most respondents find contraception morally unacceptable: Pakistan and Nigeria. In other developing states, disapproval of contraceptive use is fairly high: Examples include Ghana, Tunisia, and Uganda. In Lebanon, relatively fewer people find contraception morally acceptable, yet few people find it morally unacceptable. Many people's responses in that country fall into the other two categories of situationally moral or not a moral issue.

If family planning is important to women and children's health, both of which are critical for economic development, informing and educating the public about this topic will need to be sensitive to different religious and cultural norms. A family-planning approach in Lebanon must be different from one in Pakistan. The implications of opinion on this topic are thus very important from a public policy standpoint.

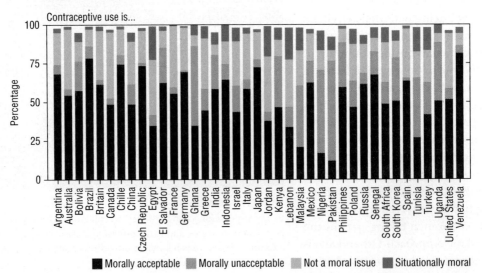

Figure 12.4 Global Views of Contraception Use

Source: Pew Research Center.

Someone who moves to a new country in search of better economic opportunities; a better professional environment; or better access to his or her family, culture, or religion is engaging in migration (emigration from the old state and immigration to the new state). Such migration is considered voluntary. The home state is not under any obligation to let such people leave, and, more important, no state is obligated to receive migrants. As with any trade issue, migration creates complex patterns of winners and losers. Immigrants often provide cheap labor, benefiting the host economy overall, but they also compete for jobs with (poor) citizens of the host country.

Most industrialized states try to limit immigration from the global South. Despite border guards and fences, many people migrate anyway, illegally. In the United States, such immigrants come from all over the world, but mostly from nearby Mexico, Central America, and the Caribbean. In Western Europe, they come largely from North Africa, Turkey, and Syria. Some Western European leaders worry that the loosening of border controls under the process of integration (see Chapter 10) will make it harder to keep out illegal immigrants. Indeed, fear of immigration is one reason why Swiss voters rejected membership in the EU. In 2004–2006, tens of thousands of migrants and refugees from sub-Saharan Africa came to Morocco and climbed over razor-wire fences to enter two tiny Spanish enclaves there. Once on Spanish soil, they could not be sent home if they kept authorities from determining their nationality. The increase in migrants trying to reach the enclaves in Morocco followed Spanish efforts to stem the flow of migrants crossing in boats from North Africa to Spain itself near the Gibraltar straits. In turn, when Spain cracked down on the crossings at the Moroccan enclaves, Africans set out in boats and rafts to reach the Spanish-owned Canary Islands in the Atlantic off Morocco (see the Seeking the Collective Good box).

International law and custom distinguish migrants from **refugees**, people fleeing to find refuge from war, natural disaster, or political persecution. (Fleeing from chronic discrimination may or may not be grounds for refugee status.) International norms obligate countries to accept refugees who arrive at their borders. Refugees from wars or natural disasters are generally housed in refugee camps temporarily until they can return home (though their stay can drag on for years). Refugees from political persecution may be granted asylum to stay in the new state. Acceptance of refugees—and the question of which states must bear the costs—is a collective goods problem.

refugees People fleeing their countries to find refuge from war, natural disaster, or political persecution. International law distinguishes them from migrants.

This problem came into sharp focus in 2015 when tens of thousands of refugees from Tunisia and Libya poured into Italy, from which they could pass freely into other nearby European countries. Thousands of migrants died in boats fleeing across the Mediterranean, while many hundreds of refugees suffered at the hands of smugglers, who would often leave them abandoned (or worse) as illegal immigrants. Central European states such as Hungary also faced waves of refugees fleeing conflicts in the Middle East, while EU leaders frantically debated how to handle the influx of migrants into Europe.

The number of international refugees in the world was over 25 million in 2017. About 40 million more people were displaced within their own countries. Three-fourths of these internally displaced persons (IDPs) resided in Colombia, Congo, Somalia, Sudan, Iraq, Afghanistan, and Syria. An additional 5 million Palestinian refugees fall under the responsibility of the

Radek Procyk / Alamy Stock Photo

ON THE MOVE Refugees are both a result of international conflict and a source of conflict. In addition to those fleeing war and repression and those seeking economic opportunity, hundreds of thousands of people each year cross borders as sex and labor slaves. These refugees are leaving Hungary, likely bound for Germany or Austria, 2015. Hungary became a major transit country for those fleeing Syria.

Seeking the Collective Good

The Refugee Regime

COLLECTIVE GOOD: The Well-Being of Refugees

BACKGROUND: Wars and disasters regularly displace millions of people from their homes, as they seek safety and survival by fleeing. Not infrequently, they show up at an international border seeking to cross and find refuge on the other side. A state that lets them in incurs costs in doing so. The world as a whole is served by helping refugees, because doing so heads off political and economic instability (as well as public health risks) that a desperate population out of control could pose. The care of refugees is thus a collective good for the world's states.

CHALLENGE: In 2017, the world had about 18 million refugees (and another 40 million displaced but still living within their countries). Eighty percent were in the global South. With most wars happening in poor regions of the world, the neighboring countries that are expected to absorb refugee populations often lack the resources to provide for them. Thus, there is a temptation to free-ride and turn refugees away at the border.

SOLUTION: The identity principle can play a role, as when refugees are a persecuted minority who cross the border into a country where their ethnic group is a majority. The host country then identifies with them and is more willing to provide for them. The main approach, however, is reciprocity—not expecting countries to take in refugees just from the goodness of their hearts but also not threatening them or forcing them to do so.

Rohingya refugees from Burma, fleeing ethnic cleansing, cross a river to enter Bangladesh, 2017.

The world's refugee regime is a reciprocity-based set of rules that the world's states have agreed to. All states are supposed to follow the same rules, which require them to take in war refugees. To assist the host countries, the international community has an international organization, the UN High Commissioner for Refugees (UNHCR), to help take care of refugee populations. UNHCR funding is itself a collective goods problem, and the agency often runs short of desperately needed supplies when the goods are not provided.

UN Relief and Works Agency (UNRWA). The majority of refugees and IDPs have been displaced by wars (see Table 12.2), most recently by the civil war in Syria, which by 2015 had generated 3 million refugees in Turkey, Lebanon, Iraq, and Jordan, and 6.5 million internally displaced persons, all fleeing violence in general and sexual violence in particular.

The political impact of refugees has been demonstrated repeatedly. The most politicized refugee problem for decades has been that of Palestinians displaced in the 1948 and 1967 Arab-Israeli wars (and their children and grandchildren). They live in

Table 12.2 Refugee Populations, 2017

Region	Millions	Main Concentrations
Middle East	22	Iraq, Syria, Iran, Turkey
Asia	8	Afghanistan, Pakistan, Thailand, Myanmar (Burma)
Palestinians under UNRWA	5	Palestine, Jordan, Lebanon
Africa	21	Nigeria, Somalia, Uganda, Sudan, D.R. Congo
Latin America	9	Colombia, United States
Europe	7	Germany, Ukraine
World Total	72	

Source: UN High Commissioner for Refugees (UNHCR). Includes refugees, asylum seekers, returned refugees, and internally displaced people.

Policy Perspectives
President of Botswana, Mokgweetski Masisi

PROBLEM *How do you confront a regional humanitarian crisis without sacrificing the well-being of your own population?*

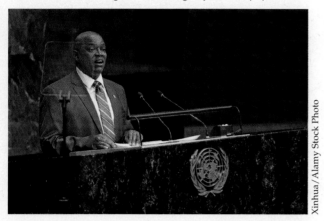

Xinhua / Alamy Stock Photo

BACKGROUND Imagine that you are the president of Botswana. Your neighbor to the east, Zimbabwe, has undergone years of political, economic, and social turmoil. Recently, however, a military coup unseated the long-time dictator of Zimbabwe, Robert Mugabe. This has brought hope that Zimbabwe will become more politically stable. Yet, the new government of Zimbabwe is struggling. There is a potential food shortage crisis due to drought conditions in parts of the country. Economically, Zimbabwe is in trouble as well, with an inflation rate above 200 million percent. Efforts by the new government to lure money back to the country have met with very limited success. Finally, Zimbabwe has experienced several outbreaks of cholera, which have killed thousands. To make matters worse, doctors in Zimbabwe have been on strike, taking a fragile health care system to the breaking point.

DOMESTIC CONSIDERATIONS Your own political and economic situation, however, is quite different. Over the past decade, your country has gone from being one of the poorest in Africa to one with a GDP of $16,000 per person. The economic situation of your country is solid and the political situation is relatively stable. This new wealth has let you put in place a comprehensive program to address the very high rate of HIV/AIDS infection (one in three adults) in your country and to begin reducing the high unemployment rate (40 percent by some estimates).

SCENARIO Now imagine that the new military regime in Zimbabwe begins to suffer from instability. Unable to turn around the economy, opponents begin to protest against the military government. The military responds with brutal repression, which escalates into a violent civil conflict between the military and opposition parties. The opposition parties flee to your country to take refuge, creating a migration crisis.

While your political and economic situation is certainly better than Zimbabwe's, it is not clear that you would be able to provide assistance or refuge for the tens of thousands of Zimbabweans fleeing to your country. In particular, your health care system, already strained by the AIDS epidemic, would be quickly overtaxed by refugees streaming in from Zimbabwe. And while your own public has some tolerance for a limited number of refugees, they would oppose accommodating all Zimbabweans who want assistance. Finally, there is also the chance that if you are seen protecting opponents of the Zimbabwean military, you could be drawn into a conflict with your neighbor.

CHOOSE YOUR POLICY What do you do with the refugees? Do you force them to return to Zimbabwe? This is against international refugee law and could add to the instability of Zimbabwe. Do you allow the refugees to stay in Botswana? This could lead to resentment on the part of your own population if the refugees take jobs, drain food supplies, or burden your health care system. It also risks open conflict with your neighbor. How do you balance humanitarian needs with a concern for your own people's physical and economic well-being?

"camps" that have become long-term neighborhoods, mainly in Jordan, Lebanon, and the Palestinian territories of Gaza and the West Bank. The poverty of the refugees in turn fuels radical political movements among the inhabitants. The question of Palestinian refugees' right to return to what is now Israel has challenged every attempt at a comprehensive peace settlement for years.

It is not always easy to distinguish a refugee fleeing war or political persecution from a migrant seeking economic opportunity. Illegal immigrants may claim to be refugees in order to be allowed to stay, when really they are seeking better economic opportunities. In recent decades this issue has become a major one throughout the North. In Germany, France, Austria, and elsewhere, resentment of foreign immigrants has fueled upsurges of right-wing nationalism in domestic politics.

REMITTANCES A crucial aspect of migration and immigration is **remittances**—money sent home by migrants to relatives in their country of origin. They are an important source of income for many poor countries. Remittances are important

remittances Money sent home by migrant workers to individuals (usually relatives) in their country of origin.

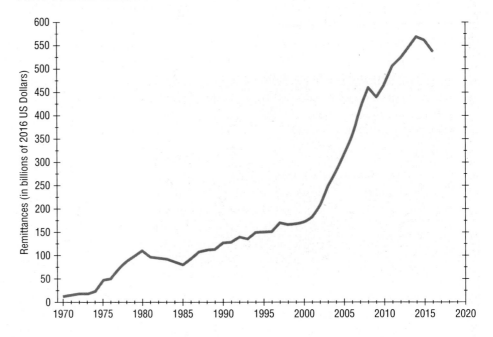

Figure 12.5 Global Flows of Remittances, 1970–2016

Source: World Bank calculations.

for states in many regions of the world. In 2016, worldwide remittances exceeded $500 billion, after tripling in a decade, and were three times as large as global foreign aid, according to the World Bank (which notes the true figure may be even higher).

Remittances are becoming an increasingly important part of the global economy (see Figure 12.5). Unlike foreign direct investment (FDI), remittances are not transferred between companies or wealthy individuals, but usually between families. Thus, remittances cannot be withdrawn from a recipient economy. They also are not handed out by governments and thus are not subject to corruption or governmental waste. Also, unlike foreign aid, remittances are not subject to conditions from donors. They are given freely from family to family. These characteristics of remittances (as well as their growing size) make them important yet also difficult to study.

Remittances help states in the global South. They give poorer households more disposable income. They have helped some poorer states, such as the Philippines and Bangladesh, improve their investment ratings and sell bonds, luring more foreign direct investment. However, remittance levels are very vulnerable to economic downturns in wealthy countries. Remittances also continue the cycle of dependency of poor states on wealthy ones. Should wealthy states close their borders or expel migrant populations, this would create hardships for individual families as well as for the economies of developing countries.

TRAFFICKING In addition to migration and refugees, a growing number of people—estimated at about 700,000 annually—are trafficked across international borders against their will. They include both sex slaves and labor slaves, with each category including females and males, adults and children. Perhaps 20,000 of these people are trafficked to the United States annually. In 2017, the U.S. State Department listed 23 countries making insufficient efforts to stop human trafficking, including Russia, Venezuela, China, and Belarus.

In general, South-North migration of all types creates problems for the industrialized states that, it seems, can be solved only by addressing the problems of the South itself.

12.2 Theories of Accumulation

Give examples of states that world-system theory would identify as members of the core, semiperiphery, and periphery.

How do we explain the enormous gap between income levels in the world's industrialized regions and those in the global South? What are the implications of that gap for international politics? There are several very different approaches to these questions; we will concentrate on two contrasting theories of wealth accumulation, based on more liberal and more revolutionary perspectives.

12.2.1 Economic Accumulation

A view of the problem from the perspective of capitalism is based on liberal economics—stressing overall efficiency in maximizing *economic growth*. This view sees the global South as merely lagging behind the industrialized North. More wealth creation in the North is a good thing, as is wealth creation in the South—the two are not in conflict.

A different view of things, from the perspective of socialism, is concerned with the distribution of wealth as much as the absolute creation of wealth. It sees the North-South divide as more of a zero-sum game in which the creation of wealth in the North most often comes at the expense of the South. It also gives politics (the state) more of a role in redistributing wealth and managing the economy than does capitalism. Socialism thus parallels mercantilism in some ways. But socialists see economic classes rather than states as the main actors in the political bargaining over the distribution of the world's wealth. And mercantilism promotes the idea of concentrating wealth (as a power element), whereas socialism promotes the broader distribution of wealth.

For socialists, international exchange is shaped by capitalists' exploitation of cheap labor and cheap resources—using states to help create the political conditions for this exploitation. (Some socialists focus on workers in poor countries, some on workers in richer industrialized countries, and some on both.) Thus, whereas mercantilists see political interests (of the state) as driving economic policies, socialists see economic interests (of capitalists and of workers) as driving political policies. In Latin America in recent years, several states have elected leftist presidents committed to changing course away from free market capitalism and toward a socialist philosophy with more state-owned industries. These countries are Venezuela, Bolivia, Ecuador, and Nicaragua.

Capitalist and socialist approaches are rather incompatible in their language and assumptions about the problem of poverty and its international implications. This chapter somewhat favors socialist approaches, focusing on the past history of imperialism as a central cause of the North-South divide, and on revolutionary strategies and massive redistribution of wealth as solutions to it. Chapter 13, in turn, leans toward capitalist approaches.

In reality, no state is purely capitalist. Almost all states have some form of mixed economy that includes both private and state ownership. In most capitalist countries, the government balances the inhuman side of capitalism by redistributing some wealth downward. A welfare state provides education, certain health benefits, welfare for the poor, and so forth. In the 2008–2009 financial crisis, some of the largest capitalist economies, including the United States and Great Britain, found themselves spending money to buy portions of private companies, such as insurance companies, automakers, and banks, to keep these businesses from going into bankruptcy.

Economic development is based on *capital accumulation*—the creation of standing wealth (capital) such as buildings, roads, and factories. For human populations and their capital to grow, they must produce an **economic surplus** by using capital to produce more capital. This is done by investing money in productive capital rather than

economic surplus A surplus created by investing money in productive capital rather than using it for consumption.

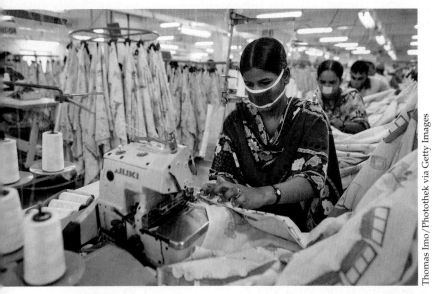

Thomas Imo/Photothek via Getty Images

LOW-TECH Production in the global South uses relatively little capital and much labor (at low wages), reflecting an early stage of industrialization. To develop economically, poor countries must generate self-sustaining capital accumulation. Agriculture, energy, and textiles are classic export products from the global South: They are relatively low-capital and labor-intensive. In Bangladesh, textiles such as these prepared for export in 2014 are a major source of export revenue.

using it for consumption. The more surplus an economy produces, the more resources are available for investment above the minimum level of consumption needed to sustain human life.

The Industrial Revolution of several centuries ago greatly accelerated the process of world accumulation, drawing on large amounts of energy from fossil fuels. But industrialization has occurred very unevenly from one world region to the next. The North has accumulated vast capital. Though the South produces spurts of wealth and has pockets of accumulation, in most areas it remains a preindustrial economy—the reason why the North consumes nearly ten times as much commercial energy per person as the South does (see Table 11.1).

Information technology now is making a fuel-burning infrastructure relatively less important in the advanced economies. The countries of the global South may need to pass through a phase of heavy industrialization, as countries in the North did, or perhaps they can develop economically along different paths, using new technology from the start. The problem is that, just as industrial infrastructure is located mostly in the North, so is the world's information infrastructure (see Chapter 10). While a generation of students in industrialized countries go online, poorer countries still struggle to extend literacy to rural populations.

12.2.2 The World-System

world-system A view of the world in terms of regional class divisions, with industrialized countries as the core, poorest countries as the periphery, and other areas (for example, some of the newly industrializing countries) as the semiperiphery.

Some IR scholars see the global system of regional class divisions as a **world-system** or a *capitalist world economy*. This view is Marxist in orientation (focusing on economic classes; see Chapter 3) and relies on a global level of analysis. In the world-system, class divisions are regionalized. Regions in the global South mostly extract raw materials (including agriculture)—work that uses much labor and little capital, and pays low wages. Industrialized regions mostly manufacture goods—work that uses more capital, requires more skilled labor, and pays workers higher wages. The manufacturing regions are called the *core* (or *center*) of the world-system; the extraction regions are called the *periphery*.

The most important class struggle today, in this view, is that between the core and the periphery of the world-system. The core uses its power (derived from its wealth) to concentrate surplus from the periphery, as it has done for about 500 years. Conflicts among great powers, including the two world wars and the Cold War, basically result from competition among core states over the right to exploit the periphery.

The core and the periphery are not sharply delineated. Within the periphery, there are also centers and peripheries (for instance, the city of Rio de Janeiro compared to the Amazon rain forest) as there are within the core (such as New York City compared to the Mississippi Delta). The whole global structure is one of overlapping hierarchies. The concentration of capital and the scale of wages each form a continuum rather than a sharp division into two categories.

In world-system theory, the *semiperiphery* is an area in which some manufacturing occurs and some capital concentrates, but not to the extent of the most advanced areas in the core. Eastern Europe and Russia are commonly considered semiperipheral, as are some of the newly industrializing countries such as Taiwan and Singapore. The semiperiphery acts as a kind of political buffer between the core and the periphery because poor states can aspire to join the semiperiphery instead of aspiring to rebel against domination by the core.

Over time, membership in the core, the semiperiphery, and the periphery changes somewhat, but the overall global system of class relations remains. Areas that once were beyond the reach of Europeans, such as the interior of Latin America, become incorporated as periphery. Areas of the periphery can become semiperiphery and even join the core, as North America did. And core states can slip into the semiperiphery if they fall behind in accumulation, as Spain did in the late sixteenth to early seventeenth century. Because world-system theory provides only general concepts but not firm definitions of what constitutes the core, semiperiphery, and periphery, it is hard to say exactly which states belong to each category.

The actual patterns of world trade support world-system theory to some extent. The industrialized West fits the profile of the core, exporting more than it imports in machinery, chemicals, and similar heavy manufactured goods. In the 1990s, all the other regions imported more than they exported in such goods. But in the 2000s, China (and other Asian countries) also became a net exporter of heavy manufactured goods. Asia also still has a niche in exporting light manufacturing including textile production. Such a pattern fits the semiperiphery category. The industrialized West imports these light manufactures. The shift of export-oriented manufacturing from the industrialized countries to Asia reflects globalization.

The net imports of energy by the industrialized West are an enormously important type of trade and another indication of globalization. Asia now also imports energy. The Middle East specializes in exporting oil; and Russia, Latin America, and Africa all export energy on balance as well. This is an extraction role typical of the periphery. Latin America has net exports in food, agricultural products, and minerals—also typical of the periphery. These regions' patterns of specialization must be kept in perspective, however. All regions both import and export all these types of goods.

Semiperiphery regions, which export manufactured products, are just those—China and South Asia—that have been growing very rapidly in recent years (see Figure 12.1). The three regions that engage with the globalizing world economy primarily as raw-material exporters (Africa, the Middle East, and Latin America) are growing more slowly.

Having exportable natural resources would seem a big plus for an economy, but in fact the problems of basing economic growth on resource exports have been called the **resource curse**. Even in a middle-income country, Chile, the quadrupling of the price of its main export commodity, copper, in 2003–2006 was a mixed blessing. Protesters demanded that the billions of dollars be spent on social services for the poor, but the president (although a socialist) warned against spending what could be a temporary windfall. Meanwhile the high export earnings strengthened Chile's currency, making it harder for other industries to export their products. Then in late 2008, the global recession caused a crash in copper prices, drastically cutting Chile's income.

resource curse The difficulties faced by resource-rich developing countries, including dependence on exporting one or a few commodities whose prices fluctuate, as well as potentials for corruption and inequality.

12.3 Imperialism

Compare three different effects of colonialism and explain how these effects have led to problems with economic development in the global South.

Both the disparities in wealth between the global North and global South and the regions' export specializations have long histories. In Chapter 3 we discussed Marxist theories of imperialism, which give a particular kind of explanation for

imperialism The acquisition of colonies by conquest or otherwise. Lenin's theory of imperialism argued that European capitalists were investing in colonies where they could earn big profits and then using part of those profits to buy off portions of the working class at home.

how the North-South gap evolved. Here we review how **imperialism** affected the South over the centuries and how its aftereffects are still felt around the world. Imperialism, especially in the sixteenth to mid-twentieth centuries, structured world order starkly around the dominance principle, with masters and slaves, conquerors and conquered peoples with their land, labor, and treasures. At the same time, imperialism depends on the identity principle to unite the global North around a common racial identity that defines nonwhite people as an out-group. (Although identity issues today are more complex, racism still affects North-South relations.)

12.3.1 World Civilizations

The present-day international system is the product of a particular civilization—Western civilization, centered in Europe. The international system as we know it developed among the European states of 300 to 500 years ago, was exported to the rest of the world, and has in the last century subsumed nearly all of the world's territory into sovereign states. Other civilizations existed in other world regions for centuries before Europeans ever arrived. These cultural traditions continue to exert an influence on IR, especially when the styles and expectations of these cultures come into play in international interactions (see Figure 12.6).

North America's indigenous cultures were largely exterminated or pushed aside by European settlers. Today's North American population is overwhelmingly descended from immigrants. In most of the world (especially in Africa and Asia), however, European empires incorporated rather than pushed aside indigenous populations. Today's populations are descended primarily from indigenous inhabitants, not immigrants. These populations are therefore more strongly rooted in their own cultural traditions and history than are most Americans.

European civilization evolved from roots in the Eastern Mediterranean—Egypt, Mesopotamia (Iraq), and especially Greece. Of special importance for IR is the classical period of Greek city-states around 400 B.C., which exemplified some of the fundamental principles of power politics (reflected in Thucydides's classic account of the Peloponnesian War between Athens and Sparta). By that time, states were carrying out sophisticated trade relations and warfare with each other in a broad swath of the world, from the Mediterranean through India to East Asia. Much of this area came under Greek influence with the conquests of Alexander the Great (around 300 B.C.), then under the Roman Empire (around A.D. 1), and then under the Arab caliphate (around A.D. 600).

China remained an independent civilization during all this time. In the "warring states" period, at about the same time as the Greek city-states, sophisticated states (organized as territorial political units) first used warfare as an instrument of power politics. This is described in the classic work *The Art of War*, by Sun Tzu. By about A.D. 800, when Europe was in its "dark age" and Arab civilization in its "golden age," China under the T'ang dynasty was a highly advanced civilization quite independent of Western influence. Japan, strongly influenced by Chinese civilization, flowered on its own in the centuries leading up to the shoguns (around A.D. 1200). Japan isolated itself from Western influence under the Tokugawa shogunate for several centuries, ending after 1850 when the Meiji restoration began Japanese industrialization and international trade. Latin America also had flourishing civilizations—the Mayans around A.D. 100 to 900 and the Aztecs and Incas around 1200—independent of Western influence until they were conquered by Spain around 1500. In Africa, the great kingdoms flowered after about A.D. 1000 (as early as A.D. 600 in Ghana) and were highly developed when the European slave traders arrived on the scene around 1500.

Figure 12.6 World Civilizations

Sources: Barraclough, Geoffrey, ed. *The Times Atlas of World History.* Hammond, 1978. Mozaffari, Mehdi, ed. *Globalization and Civilizations.* Routledge, 2002. Abu-Lughod, Janet. *Before European Hegemony: The World System, A.D. 1250–1350.* Oxford, 1989. Hodgson, Marshall G. S. *The Venture of Islam: Conscience and History in a World Civilization.* Chicago, 1974. Bozeman, Adda. *Politics and Culture in International History.* Princeton, 1960.

	Before A.D. 1000	A.D. 1000	1250	1500	1750	2000
Japan	Korean and Chinese influences	samurai	shoguns	Tokugawa isolation	Meiji restoration	WWII / prosperity
China	Dynasties; Great Wall begun; Taoism; Buddhism; paper, gunpowder	Sung dynasty	Mongol dynasty	Ming dynasty	Manchu dynasty	European dominance / People's Republic
S. Asia	Emergence of Hinduism, Buddhism; Ancient India; Arab conquest	Turkish period		Taj Mahal built	European colonialism →	independence
Africa	Kingdom of Ghana	Yoruba, Mali, Benin (kingdoms)	Congo	Zimbabwe / Buganda / slave trade	Ashanti / European colonialism	independence
Middle East	Mesopotamia, Egypt, Persia; Jews, Christians; Greeks/Romans; Islam	Crusades — Arab empire		Ottoman Empire	European colonialism	Arab nationalism / Islamic rev.
W. Europe	Ancient Greece; Roman Empire; Vikings; Feudalism	"Dark Ages"	Venice	Renaissance / Protestantism / Empires	French Revolution / German/Italian unifications	WWI/II / loss of empires
Russia & E. Europe	Khazars		Genghis Khan	Ivan the Terrible / czars	Lenin / USSR	WWII / CIS
N. America	(Preagricultural)			European colonization	American Revolution / westward expansion / U.S. Civil War	WWII / Cold War
Latin America	Mayans		Aztec & Inca Empires	Portuguese & Spanish conquest	colonialism / European & U.S. interventions / independence	wars, debts, dictators, revolutions

The Arab caliphate of about A.D. 600 to 1200 played a special role in the international relations of the Middle East. Almost the whole of the region was once united in this empire, which arose and spread with the religion of Islam. European invasions—the Crusades—were driven out. In the sixteenth to nineteenth centuries, the Eastern Mediterranean came under the Turkish-based Ottoman Empire, which gave relative autonomy to local cultures if they paid tribute. This history of empires continued to influence the region in the twentieth century. For example, *Pan-Arabism* (or Arab nationalism), especially strong in the 1950s and 1960s, saw the region as potentially one nation again, with a single religion, language, and identity. Iraq's Saddam Hussein during the Gulf War likened himself to the ruler who had driven away the Crusaders a thousand years before. The strength of Islamic fundamentalism throughout the region today, as well as the emotions attached to the Arab-Israeli conflict, reflect the continuing importance of the Arab caliphate.

Europe itself began its rise to world dominance around 1500, after the Renaissance (when the Greek and Roman classics were rediscovered). The Italian city-states of the period also rediscovered the rules of interstate power politics, as described by an adviser to Renaissance princes named Niccolò Machiavelli. Feudal units began to merge into large territorial nation-states under single authoritarian rulers (monarchs). The military revolution of the period created the first modern armies. European monarchs put cannons on sailing ships and began to "discover" the world. The Industrial Revolution greatly accelerated the development of the international system, of imperialism, and of trade and war after about 1750. Ultimately the European conquest of the world brought about a single world civilization, albeit with regional variants and subcultures.

12.3.2 History of Imperialism, 1500–2000

European imperialism got its start in the fifteenth century with the development of oceangoing sailing ships in which a small crew could transport a sizable cargo over a long distance. Portugal pioneered the first voyages of exploration beyond Europe. Spain, France, and Britain soon followed. With superior military technology, Europeans gained control of coastal cities and of resupply outposts along major trade routes. Gradually this control extended farther inland, first in Latin America, then in North America, and later throughout Asia and Africa (see Figure 12.7).

In the sixteenth century, Spain and Portugal had extensive empires in Central America and Brazil, respectively. Britain and France had colonies in North America and the Caribbean. The imperialists bought slaves in Africa and shipped them to Mexico and Brazil, where they worked in tropical agriculture and in mining silver and gold. The wealth produced was exported to Europe, where monarchs used it to buy armies and build states.

These empires decimated indigenous populations and cultures, causing immense suffering. Over time, the economies of colonies developed with the creation of basic transportation and communication infrastructure, factories, and so forth. But these economies were often molded to the needs of the colonizers, not the local populations.

Decolonization began with the British colonists in the United States, who declared independence in 1776. Most of Latin America gained independence a few decades later. The new states in North America and Latin America were, of course, still run by the descendants of Europeans, to the disadvantage of Native Americans and African slaves.

Europe was still acquiring new colonies through the end of the nineteenth century, culminating in a scramble for colonies in Africa in the 1890s (which resulted in arbitrary territorial divisions as competing European armies rushed inland from all sides). India became Britain's largest and most important colony in the nineteenth century. Latecomers such as Germany and Italy were frustrated to find few attractive

Figure 12.7 History of Imperialism, 1500–2000

North America
- Columbus
- British & French colonization
- U.S. independence
- War of 1812
- Canada →

Latin America
- Brazil (Portuguese)
- Central & S. America (Spanish)
- Independence
- European & U.S. interventions →
- Mexican Revolution

East Asia
- Russian conquest of Siberia
- (China)
- Opium Wars
- T'ai P'ing Rebellion
- Boxer Rebellion
- Taiwan & Korea (Japanese)
- Japanese empire
- Communist China
- Korea split
- Taiwan autonomous
- Hong Kong to China

South Asia
- Dutch East Indies Company
- Indonesia (Dutch) →
- India (British)
- Philippines (U.S.)
- Indian independence
- Vietnam War

Africa
- European explorers
- Slave trade
- Angola, Mozambique (Portuguese)
- Scramble for colonies (Brit., Fr., Ger.)
- Independence

Middle East
- Ottoman Empire
- British & French mandates
- (Palestine)
- Algerian independence

Time axis: 1500 — 1600 — 1700 — 1800 — 1900 — 2000

403

territories remaining in the world when they tried to build overseas empires in the late nineteenth century. Ultimately, only a few non-European areas of the world retained their independence: Japan, most of China, Iran, Turkey, and a few other areas. Japan began building its own empire, as did the United States, at the end of the nineteenth century. China became weaker, and its coastal regions fell under the domination, if not the formal control, of European powers. Europe colonized most of the world's territory at one time or another (see Figure 12.8).

In the twentieth century, the world regions formerly dominated by Europe gained independence, with their own sovereign states participating in the international system. Independence came earlier in the Americas (around 1800). In Latin America, most of the nineteenth century was absorbed with wars, border changes, the rise and fall of dictatorships and republics, a chronic foreign debt problem, revolutions, and recurrent military incursions by European powers and the United States to recover debts.

In the wave of decolonization after World War II, it was not local colonists (as in the Americas) but indigenous populations in Asia and Africa who won independence. Decolonization continued through the mid-1970s until almost no European colonies remained. Most of the newly independent states have faced tremendous challenges and difficulties in the postcolonial era because of their colonial histories.

12.3.3 Effects of Colonialism

For most states in the global South, the history of having been colonized by Europeans is central to their national identity, foreign policy, and place in the world. For these states—and especially for those within them who favor socialist perspectives—international relations revolves around their asymmetrical power relationships with industrialized states. (Capitalist perspectives tend to pay less attention to history and to focus on present-day problems in the South such as unbalanced economies, unskilled workforces, and corrupt governments.)

Being colonized has a devastating effect on a people and culture. Foreigners overrun a territory with force and take it over. They install their own government, staffed by their own nationals. The inhabitants are forced to speak the language of the colonizers, to adopt their cultural practices, and to be educated at schools run under their guidance. The inhabitants are told that they are racially inferior to the foreigners.

White Europeans in third world colonies in Africa and Asia were greatly outnumbered by native inhabitants but maintained power by a combination of force and (more important) psychological conditioning. After generations under colonialism, most native inhabitants either saw white domination as normal or believed that nothing could be done about it. The whites often lived in a bubble world separated from the lives of the local inhabitants.

Colonialism also had negative *economic* implications. The most easily accessible minerals were dug up and shipped away. The best farmland was planted in export crops rather than subsistence crops, and was sometimes overworked and eroded. The infrastructure that was built served the purposes of imperialism rather than the local population—for instance, railroads going straight from mining areas to ports. The education and skills needed to run the economy were largely limited to whites.

The economic effects were not all negative, however. Colonialism often fostered local economic accumulation (although controlled by whites). Cities grew. Mines were dug and farms established. It was in the colonial administration's interest to foster local cycles of capital accumulation. Much of the infrastructure that exists today in many third world countries was created by colonizers. In some cases (though not all), colonization combined disparate communities into a cohesive political unit with a common religion, language, and culture, thus creating more opportunities for economic accumulation. In some cases, the local political cultures replaced by colonialism were themselves oppressive to the majority of the people.

Figure 12.8 Conquest of the World

Former colonial territories of European states.

Source: Adapted from Andrew Boyd, An Atlas of World Affairs. 9th ed. NY: Routledge, 1992, p. 91.

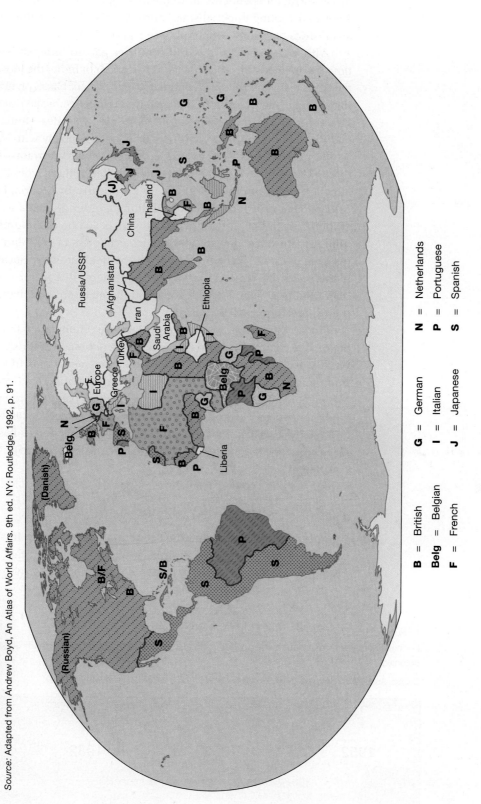

B = British	**G** = German	**N** = Netherlands	
Belg = Belgian	**I** = Italian	**P** = Portuguese	
F = French	**J** = Japanese	**S** = Spanish	

Wherever there were colonizers, there were anticolonial movements. Independence movements throughout Africa and Asia gained momentum during and after World War II, when the European powers were weakened. Through the 1960s, a wave of successful independence movements swept from one country to the next as people stopped accepting imperialism as normal or inevitable. Within a few decades, nearly all of Africa overthrew white rule (see Figure 12.9).

Although many third world countries gained independence around the same time, the methods by which they did so varied. In India, the most important colony of the largest empire (Britain), Gandhi led a movement based on nonviolent resistance to British rule (see Chapter 3). However, nonviolence broke down in the subsequent Hindu-Muslim civil war, which split India into two states—India mostly with Hindus, and Pakistan (including what is now Bangladesh) mostly with Muslims.

Some colonies—for example, Algeria and Vietnam—won independence through warfare to oust their European masters; others won it peacefully by negotiating a transfer of power with weary Europeans. In Algeria, France abandoned its colonial claims in 1962 only after fighting a bitter guerrilla war. Some colonial liberation movements fought guerrilla wars based on communist ideology. The Viet Minh, for instance, defeated the French occupiers in 1954 and established communist rule in all of Vietnam by 1975. The Soviet Union supported many such movements, and the United States opposed them. But in most cases the appeal of liberation movements was the general theme of anticolonialism rather than communist ideology.

Across the various methods and ideologies of liberation movements in the global South, one common feature was reliance on nationalism for strong popular support. Nationalism was only one idea that these movements took from Europe and used to undermine European control; others included democracy, freedom, progress, and Marxism. Leaders of liberation movements often had gone to European universities. Under European control, many states also developed infrastructures, educational and religious institutions, health care, and military forces based on the European model. Europe's conquest of the global South thus contributed tools to undo its conquest.

12.3.4 Postcolonial Dependency

If imperialism concentrated the accumulation of wealth in the core and drained economic surplus from the periphery, one might expect that accumulation in the global South would take off once colonialism was overthrown. Generally,

Figure 12.9 Areas of White Minority Rule in Africa, 1952–1994

Formal colonialism was swept away over 40 years. However, postcolonial dependency lingers on in many former colonies.

Source: Adapted from Andrew Boyd, *An Atlas of World Affairs.* 9th ed. Routledge, 1992, p. 91.

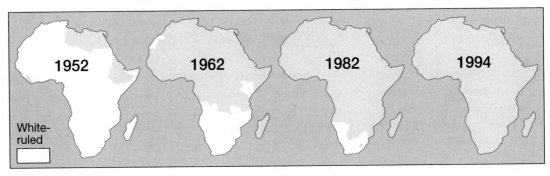

however, this was not the case. A few states, such as Singapore, have accumulated capital successfully since becoming independent. But others, including many African states, seem to be going backward, with little new capital accumulating to replace the old colonial infrastructure. Most former colonies are making only slow progress in accumulation. Political independence has not been a cure-all for poor countries.

One reason for these problems is that, under colonialism, the training and experience needed to manage the economy were often limited to white Europeans, leaving a huge gap in technical and administrative skills after independence.

Another problem faced by newly independent states was that, as colonies, their economies had been narrowly developed to serve the needs of the European home country. Many of these economies rested on the export of one or two products. For Zambia, it was copper ore; for El Salvador, coffee; for Botswana, diamonds. Such a narrow export economy would seem well suited to use the state's comparative advantage to specialize in one niche of the world economy. But it leaves the state vulnerable to price fluctuations on world markets (see the resource curse in Chapter 13). The liberal free trade regime based around the World Trade Organization (WTO) corrected only partially for the North's superior bargaining position in North-South trade. And the WTO has allowed agriculture (exported by the periphery) to remain protected in core states while promoting liberalization of trade in manufactured goods exported by the core (see Chapter 8).

It is not easy to restructure an economy away from the export of a few commodities. Nor do state leaders generally want to do so because the leaders benefit from the imports that can be bought with hard currency (including weapons). In any case, coffee plantations and copper mines take time and capital to create, and they represent capital accumulation—they cannot just be abandoned. In addition, local inhabitants' skills and training are likely to be concentrated in the existing industries. Infrastructure, such as railroads, most likely was set up to serve the export economy. For instance, in Angola and Namibia, the major railroads, built in colonial times, lead from mining or plantation districts to ports (see Figure 12.10).

The newly independent states inherited borders that were drawn in European capitals by foreign officers looking at maps. As a result, especially in Africa, the internal rivalries of ethnic groups and regions made it very difficult for the new states to implement coherent economic plans. In a number of cases, ethnic conflicts within former colonies led to civil wars, which halted or reversed capital accumulation.

Finally, the governments of many postcolonial states did not function very effectively, creating another obstacle to accumulation. In some cases, corruption became much worse after independence (see Corruption in Chapter 13). In other cases, governments tried to impose central control and planning on their national economy, based on nationalism, mercantilism, or socialism.

In sum, liberation from colonial control did not change underlying economic realities. The main trading partners of newly independent countries were usually their former colonial masters. The main products were usually those developed under colonialism. The administrative units and territorial borders were those created by Europeans. The state continued to occupy the same peripheral position in the world-system after independence as it had before. And in some cases, it continued to rely on its former colonizer for security.

For these reasons, the period after independence is sometimes called **neocolonialism**—the continuation of colonial exploitation without formal political control. This concept also covers the relationship of the global South with the United States, which (with a few exceptions) was not a formal colonizer. And it covers the North-South international relations of Latin American states, independent for almost two centuries.

neocolonialism The continuation, in a former colony, of colonial exploitation without formal political control.

Figure 12.10 Borders, Railroads, and Resources in Angola and Namibia

Despite the independence of Angola and Namibia, colonial times shaped the borders and infrastructure in the region.

dependency theory A Marxist-oriented theory that explains the lack of capital accumulation in the third world as a result of the interplay between domestic class relations and the forces of foreign capital. See also *enclave economy*.

enclave economy A historically important form of dependency in which foreign capital is invested in a third world country to extract a particular raw material in a particular place—usually a mine, oil well, or plantation. See also *dependency theory*.

DEPENDENCY Marxist IR scholars have developed **dependency theory** to explain the lack of capital accumulation in the third world. These scholars define dependency as a situation in which accumulation of capital cannot sustain itself internally. A dependent country must borrow capital to produce goods; its debt payments then reduce the accumulation of surplus. (Dependency is a form of international interdependence—rich regions need to loan out their money just as poor ones need to borrow it—but it is an interdependence with an extreme power imbalance.)

Dependency theorists focus not on the overall structure of the world-system (center and periphery) but on how a peripheral state's own internal class relationships play out. The development (or lack of development) of a third world state depends on its local conditions and history, though it is affected by the same global conditions as other countries located in the periphery.

One historically important configuration of dependency is the **enclave economy**, in which foreign capital is invested in a third world country to extract a particular raw material in a particular place—usually a mine, oil well, or plantation. Here, the cycle of capital accumulation is primed by foreign capital, is fueled by local resources (often people for their labor), and completes itself with the sale of products on foreign markets. Such an arrangement leaves the country's economy largely untouched except to give employment to a few local workers in the enclave and to provide taxes to the state (or line the pockets of some state officials). Over time, it leaves the state's natural resources depleted. Developing states often encourage these practices by creating *free trade zones*, which allow for products to move in and out of these enclaves tariff free.

Angola's Cabinda province, located up the coast from the rest of Angola, is a classic example of an enclave economy. Chevron pumps oil from a large field of offshore wells, with the money going to Angolan government officials, who spend some on weapons and pocket large sums in flagrant acts of corruption. The people of Cabinda, aside from a tiny number who work for Chevron, live in poverty with crumbling infrastructure, few government services, few jobs, and recurrent banditry by unpaid soldiers. Inside the Chevron compound, however, U.S. workers drive on paved roads, eat American food, and enjoy an 18-hole golf course. They spend 28 days there, working 12-hour days, then fly back to the United States for 28 days of rest. Traveling the 12 miles to the airport by helicopter, the Americans rarely leave the fenced compound, which Chevron reportedly surrounded with landmines.

A different historical pattern is that of nationally controlled production, in which a local capitalist class controls a cycle of accumulation based on producing export products. The cycle still depends on foreign markets, but the profits accrue to the local capitalists, building up a powerful class of rich owners within the country. This class—the local bourgeoisie—tends to behave in a manner consistent with the interests of rich industrialized countries (on whose markets the class depends). They are not unpatriotic, but their interests tend to converge with those of foreign capitalists. For instance, they want to keep local wages as low as possible and thus produce cheap goods for consumers in the rich countries. The local capitalists, in alliance with political authorities, enforce a system of domination that ultimately serves the foreign capitalists. This is another form of dependency.

MIGUEL ALVAREZ/AFP/Getty Images

WORKING IN THE ENCLAVE Multinational corporations (MNCs) will build factories abroad to produce goods with cheap inputs (materials or labor), then send the finished products to larger markets to be sold—the modern variant of an enclave economy. Here, a woman works sewing jeans in a free trade zone in Nicaragua, 2001. The factory is owned by a Taiwanese company and the jeans are bound for sale in the United States.

After World War II, a third form of dependency became more common—penetration of national economies by MNCs. Here the capital is provided externally (as with enclaves), but production is for local markets. For instance, a General Motors (GM) factory in Brazil produces cars mostly for sale within Brazil. To create local markets for such manufactured goods, income must be concentrated enough to create a middle class that can afford such goods. This sharpens disparities of income within the country (most people remain poor). The cycle of accumulation depends on local labor and local markets, but because MNCs provide the foreign capital, they take out much of the surplus as profit.

According to dependency theory, the particular constellation of forces within a country determines which coalitions form among the state, the military, big landowners, local capitalists, foreign capitalists (MNCs), foreign governments, and middle classes such as professionals and skilled industrial workers. On the other side, peasants, workers, and sometimes students and the church form alliances to work for more equal distribution of income, human and political rights, and local control of the economy. These class alliances and the resulting social relationships are not determined by any general rule but by concrete conditions and historical developments in each country. Like other Marxist theories, dependency theory pays special attention to class struggle as a source of social change.

Some people think that under conditions of dependency, economic development is almost impossible. Others think that development is possible under dependency, despite certain difficulties. We will return to these possibilities in Chapter 13.

12.3.5 Revolutionary Movements

Poverty and lack of access to basic human needs are prime causes of revolutions, especially when poor people see others living much better. Most revolutionary movements espouse egalitarian ideals—a more equal distribution of wealth and power.

During the Cold War years, the classic revolutionary movement was a communist insurgency based in the countryside. Usually "U.S. imperialism" or another such foreign presence was viewed as a friend of the state and an enemy of the revolution. Sometimes the U.S. government gave direct military aid to governments facing such revolutionary movements. In a number of countries, U.S. military advisers and even combat troops were sent to help put down the revolutions and keep communists from taking power. For its part, the Soviet Union often armed and helped train the revolutionaries. Thus, the domestic politics of poor countries became intertwined with great power politics in the context of the North-South gap. In reality, many of these governments and revolutions had little to do with global communism, capitalism, or imperialism. They were local power struggles—sometimes between the haves and the have-nots, sometimes between rival ethnic groups—into which great powers were drawn.

By the early 1990s, these communist revolutions seemed to have played themselves out—winning in some places, losing in others, and coming to a stalemate in a few countries. The end of the Cold War removed superpower support from both sides, and the collapse of the Soviet Union and the adoption of capitalist-oriented economic reforms in China undercut the ideological appeal of communist revolutions. Several Marxist revolutionary movements linger, however, including those in Colombia, Peru, and India. In Nepal, Maoist rebels fought for a decade until a 2006 peace agreement, then won elections and became the country's governing party.

In foreign policy, revolutionary governments often start out planning radically different relationships with neighbors and great powers. The pattern of international alliances often shifts after revolutions, as when a Cold War client of one superpower shifted to the other after a change of government. But the new government usually discovers that, once it holds power, it has the same interest as other states in promoting national sovereignty and territorial integrity. The rules of the international system now work for the revolutionaries instead of against them, once they control a state. Their state also has the same geographical location as before, the same historical conflicts with its

RARE SUCCESS South Africa's former president, Nelson Mandela (here shown at a march of the African National Congress in Boipatong, 1992), had unusual success in making the difficult transition from revolutionary to state leader, and then leaving office peacefully. He had the advantage of coming to power nonviolently (relatively speaking), enjoying tremendous world respect, and leading a country that is relatively prosperous (though with huge inequalities) in a very poor continent.

Uhan Kuus/Sipa Press

neighbors, and the same ethnic ties. So it is not unusual over time to find similar foreign policies emanating from a revolutionary government as from its predecessor. Although revolutions create short-term shifts in foreign policy, over the longer term the rules of international relations have tended to triumph over revolutionary challenges.

Overall, North-South relations show how difficult it has become to separate political economy from international security. The original political relations contained in European imperialism led to economic conditions in the South—such as high population growth, urbanization, and concentrations of wealth—that in turn led to political movements for independence, and later to revolutions. The various aspects of the North-South gap considered in this chapter—including hunger, refugees, and the structure of commodity exports—all contain both economic and political-military aspects.

Marxists emphasize that the economic realities of accumulation, or the lack of accumulation, lie beneath all the political struggles related to global North-South relations. But Marxists' strategies—from armed revolutions to self-reliance, to state ownership—have not been successful at changing those realities. Chapter 13 therefore examines in depth the question of how economies in the South can develop the accumulation process and what role the North can play in that process.

Chapter Review

Summary

- Most of the world's people live in poverty in the global South. About 1 billion live in extreme poverty, without access to adequate food, water, and other necessities.

- Wealth accumulation (including the demographic transition discussed in Chapter 11) depends on the meeting of basic human needs such as access to food, water, education, shelter, and health care. Third world states have had mixed success in meeting their populations' basic needs.

- Hunger and malnutrition are rampant in the global South. The most important cause is the displacement of subsistence farmers from their land because of war, population pressures, and the conversion of agricultural land into plantations growing export crops to earn hard currency.

- Urbanization is increasing throughout the global South as more people move from the countryside to cities. Huge slums have grown in the cities as poor people arrive and cannot find jobs.

- Women's central role in the process of accumulation has begun to be recognized. International agencies based in the North have started taking women's con-

tributions into account in analyzing economic development in the South.

- Poverty in the South has led huge numbers of migrants to seek a better life in the North; this has created international political frictions. War and repression in the South have generated millions of refugees seeking safe haven. Under international law and norms, states are generally supposed to accept refugees but do not have to accept migrants.

- War has been a major impediment to meeting basic needs, and to wealth accumulation generally, in poor countries. Almost all the wars of the past 50 years have been fought in the global South.

- Moving from poverty to well-being requires the accumulation of capital. Capitalism and socialism take different views on this process. Capitalism emphasizes overall growth with considerable concentration of wealth, whereas socialism emphasizes a fair distribution of wealth.

- Most states have a mixed economy with some degree of private ownership of capital and some degree of state ownership. However, state ownership has not been very successful in accumulating wealth. Consequently, many states have been selling off state-owned enterprises (privatization), especially in Russia and Eastern Europe.

- Since Lenin's time, many Marxists have attributed poverty in the South to the concentration of wealth in the North. In this theory, capitalists in the North exploit the South economically and use the wealth thus generated to buy off workers in the North. Revolutions thus occur in the South and are ultimately directed against the North.

- IR scholars in the world-system school argue that the North is a core region specializing in producing manufactured goods and the South is a periphery specializing in extracting raw materials through agriculture and mining. Between these are semiperiphery states with light manufacturing.

- Europeans conquered various world civilizations over several centuries and forcefully absorbed them into a single global international system initially centered in Europe. Today's North-South gap traces its roots to the past colonization of the southern world

regions by Europe. This colonization occurred at different times in different parts of the world, as did decolonization.

- Because of the negative impact of colonialism on local populations, anticolonial movements arose throughout the global South at various times and using various methods. These culminated in a wave of successful independence movements after World War II in Asia and Africa. (Latin American states gained independence much earlier.)

- Following independence, third world states were left with legacies of colonialism, including their basic economic infrastructures, that made wealth accumulation difficult in certain ways. These problems still remain in many countries.

- When revolutionaries succeed in taking power, they usually change their state's foreign policy. Over time, however, old national interests and strategies tend to reappear. After several decades in power, revolutionaries usually become conservative and in particular come to support the norms and rules of the international system (which are favorable to them as state leaders).

Key Terms

less-developed countries (LDCs)   383
developing countries   383
Sustainable Development Goals (SDGs)   383
basic human needs   385
malnutrition   388

subsistence farming   390
cash crops   390
urbanization   390
land reform   391
migration   393
refugees   394
remittances   396

economic surplus   398
world-system   398
resource curse   400
imperialism   400
neocolonialism   408
dependency theory   408
enclave economy   409

Critical Thinking Questions

1. In what ways does the North American Free Trade Agreement (NAFTA), discussed in Chapter 8, reflect the overall state of North-South relations as described in this chapter? How would capitalism and socialism as general approaches to the theory of wealth accumulation differ in their views of the agreement?

2. The zones of the world economy as described by world-system theorists treat the North as a core and the South as largely a periphery. Can you think of exceptions to this formula? How seriously do such exceptions challenge the overall concept as applied to

North-South relations generally? Be specific about why the exceptions do not fit the theory.

3. In North and South America, independence from colonialism was won by descendants of the colonists themselves. In Asia and Africa, it was won mainly by local populations with a long history of their own. How do you think this aspect has affected the postcolonial history of one or more specific countries from each group?

4. Suppose you lived in an extremely poor slum in the global South and had no money or job—but retained

all the knowledge you now have. What strategies would you adopt for your own survival and well-being? What strategies would you reject as infeasible? Would you adopt or reject the idea of revolution? Why?

5. Currently incomes in the global North are five times as high, per person, as in the global South. If you could magically redistribute the world's income so that everyone had equal income ($10,000 per person per year), would you? What effects would such a change make in the North and South?

Suggested Readings

Collier, Paul. *The Bottom Billion: Why the Poorest Countries Are Failing and What Can Be Done About It.* Oxford, 2007.

Food and Agriculture Organization. *The State of Food Security and Nutrition in the World: 2017.* FAO, 2018. http://www.fao.org/state-of-food-security-nutrition/en/.

Hulme, David. *Global Poverty: How Global Governance Is Failing the Poor.* Routledge, 2010.

Kevane, Michael. *Women and Development in Africa: How Gender Works.* 2nd ed. Lynne Rienner Publishers, 2014.

Martin, Susan F. *International Migration: Evolving Trends from the Early Twentieth Century to the Present.* Cambridge, 2014.

UN Development Program. *Human Development Report 2016.* UNDP, 2016. http://hdr.undp.org/en/2016-report.

UNCHR. *The Global Report: 2016.* UNHCR, 2017. http://www.unhcr.org/en-us/the-global-report.html.

U.S. Department of State. *Trafficking in Persons Report 2017.* U.S. Department of State, 2017.

Wallerstein, Immanuel. *World Systems Analysis: An Introduction.* Duke, 2004.

World Health Organization. *Health 2015: From MDGs to SDGs.* WHO, 2016.

legacies of Colonianism

Let's Debate the Issue

Immigration Reform: Should Illegal Immigrants in the United States Have a Path to Citizenship? Yes!

Overview

The movement of people across borders is one of the important issues that blends domestic politics and international relations. Although much of the debate is couched in terms of immigrants' (and migrants') impact on the economy of the host state, a variety of international factors shape the incentives of individuals to migrate, including global economic conditions, political conditions in neighboring states, and the status of military conflicts within and between states.

Nearly every country in the world engages in debates over immigration. In part, these issues are nettlesome because they combine important elements of economics (will immigrants drive down wages or take jobs?) with elements of national identity (who are we as a country and who will we be in the future?). Immigration policy must balance empathy for those abroad with a responsibility for those already here. Whether the debate is over war refugees in Africa, economic immigrants in Europe, or victims of natural disasters in Latin America, immigration policy is always a matter of intense debate.

The debate over immigration in the United States is no exception. The question of immigration policy has become one of extremely divided opinions in the United States—opinions that cross traditional ideological and political party lines. Particularly controversial is the idea of granting a way for immigrants currently in the United States illegally to earn a way to become citizens, giving them rights to vote, to education, and to social programs. Should the U.S. government provide a way for these illegal immigrants to become American citizens?

ARGUMENT 1

The U.S. Government Should Provide a Path to Citizenship for Illegal Immigrants

Legalizing illegal immigrants will lead to increases in tax revenue for governments. Because illegal immigrants often do not pay income taxes, they are a large untapped source of tax revenue. Many of these immigrants use social services, such as education, so allowing them to earn citizenship will allow them to "pay" for these services through taxes.

Remittances will help development in the immigrants' home countries. Workers who earn money inside the United States often send significant portions back to their home countries. This money helps to stabilize home countries economically, providing opportunities for family members and improving their quality of life.

Illegal immigrants are essential to the U.S. workforce. Absent immigration, the population of the United States is declining. Without the presence of these working immigrants (legal and illegal), some industries (agriculture and construction in particular) would experience labor shortages, which in turn would drive up prices for all Americans.

ARGUMENT 2

The U.S. Government Should Not Provide a Path to Citizenship for Illegal Immigrants

Granting citizenship rewards illegal behavior. There is already a legal path to citizenship that has been taken by millions of Americans. It would be unfair to reward with citizenship those who illegally entered the country after so many Americans had to undergo a long, arduous process to earn their rights.

Illegal immigrants compete for jobs in difficult economic times. During economic downturns, layoffs increase and jobs are harder to come by. Illegal immigrants compete for these scarce jobs. This competition is especially damaging to Americans of lower socioeconomic status, who are already threatened in other ways by economic downturns.

Increases in immigration resulting from the policy would create security risks. If a path to citizenship encourages surges in future immigration, it will be difficult to keep U.S. borders secure, leading to security risks. In this age of global terrorism, any factor increasing the large numbers of individuals passing across state borders can threaten a state's security.

Questions

- Do you think the U.S. government should provide a way for illegal immigrants to earn their citizenship? Are there other arguments you find convincing in this debate?

- Think about the NAFTA and EU member states. Why do you think the EU has been more willing to open borders to one another? Do you believe the EU will move to close borders in the future? Will NAFTA become more open in the future?

- How much do you feel that the arguments in this debate are influenced by international factors such as the state of the world economy? Do these factors affect similar debates concerning the rights of immigrants in other countries?

For Further Reading

Givens, Terri E., Gary P. Freeman, and David L. Leal, eds. *Immigration Policy and Security: U.S., European, and Commonwealth Perspectives.* Routledge, 2008.

Guskin, Jane, and David L. Wilson. *The Politics of Immigration: Questions and Answers.* 2nd ed. Monthly Review, 2017.

Hollifield, James F., Philip L. Martin, and Pia Orrenius, eds. *Controlling Immigration: A Global Perspective.* 3rd ed. Stanford, 2014.

Vecchio, Francesco. *Asylum Seeking and the Global City.* Routledge, 2016.

It is not illegal behavior, it is desperation, fear, and lack of security. No one wakes up and thinks: "I will leave my country to try a new life somewhere else." It is not like that; i

Chapter 13
International Development

CHINESE HOUSE WHOSE OWNERS WOULD NOT SELL, SHANGHAI, 2017.

 ## Learning Objectives

13.1 Compare and contrast the experiences of China and India in achieving economic development.

13.2 Identify and evaluate two different strategies that developing states have used in attempting to achieve economic growth.

13.3 Outline the ways in which large amounts of debt can hinder the process of economic development for countries of the global South.

13.4 Describe three reasons why countries might provide foreign aid to countries of the global South.

13.1 Experiences

Compare and contrast the experiences of China and India in achieving economic development.

Chapter 12 discussed the situation in the global South and how it came to be; this chapter takes up the question of what to do about it. **Economic development** refers to the combined processes of capital accumulation, rising per capita incomes (with consequent falling birthrates), increasing of skills in the population, adoption of new technological styles, and other related social and economic changes. The most central aspect is the accumulation of capital (with its ongoing wealth-generating potential). The concept of development has a subjective side that cannot be measured statistically—the judgment of whether a certain pattern of wealth creation and distribution is good for a state and its people. But one simple measure of economic development is the per capita gross domestic product (GDP)—the amount of economic activity per person. This measure was on the horizontal axis in Figure 12.1, and change in this measure was on the vertical axis.

By this measure, we can trace the successes and failures of the South as a whole and, more important, those of its regions and countries. The latter is more important because it contains the seeds of possible lessons and strategies that could build on the South's successes in the future. Most of the global South made progress on economic development in the 1970s, but per capita GDP *decreased* in the 1980s in Latin America, Africa, and the Middle East, with only China growing robustly. In the 1990s, real economic growth returned across much of the South—about 5–6 percent annual growth for the South as a whole, and even higher for China, compared to 2–3 percent in the global North. China stood out among the regions of the South as making rapid progress toward economic development.

In the twenty-first century, growth has accelerated in the South and now outpaces that in the North (see Figure 13.1). This growth has been uneven, however. South Asia (6–7 percent a year) has joined China (8–9 percent per year) in achieving rapid growth.

economic development The combined processes of capital accumulation, rising per capita incomes (with consequent falling birthrates), increasing of skills in the population, adoption of new technological styles, and other related social and economic changes.

Figure 13.1 Real GDP Growth of Selected Countries, 2016

Source: World Bank data.

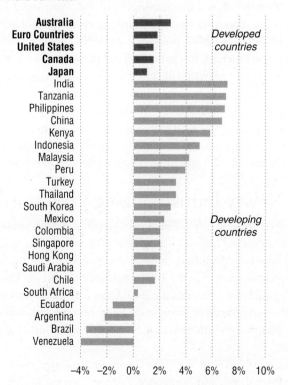

Figure 13.2 Per Capita GDP of South Korea, China, India, and Ghana, 1950–2016

Source: Based on World Bank data.

Because China and South Asia together contain the majority of the population in the global South, this development is very important.

This new growth shows that it is possible to rise out of poverty to relative prosperity. South Korea did so, followed by China, and India appears to be starting on the same curve (see Figure 13.2). In Africa, economies grew by 4 percent annually from 2011 to 2013 (led by, but not limited to, oil- and mineral-exporting nations). While the 2008–2009 global economic crisis threatened the developing world, most states in the global South emerged more quickly than their wealthy counterparts in the global North, a noteworthy trend. Between 2015 and 2017, economic growth slowed but remained strong in China, South Asia, and much of Africa. Latin America suffered a recession in 2015–2016, but economists predict that growth will slowly return in the coming years.

Today, much attention is given to a group of countries known as the BRICS (Brazil, Russia, India, China, and South Africa). While there are important economic differences between these states, they each have large economies and populations. They are considered an important group of countries that provides a strong voice to developing states, often in negotiation with wealthier North American and European states.

13.1.1 The Newly Industrializing Countries

newly industrializing countries (NICs) Third world states that have achieved self-sustaining capital accumulation, with impressive economic growth. The most successful are the "four tigers" or "four dragons" of East Asia: South Korea, Taiwan, Hong Kong, and Singapore.

"four tigers"/"four dragons" The most successful newly industrialized areas of East Asia: South Korea, Taiwan, Hong Kong, and Singapore.

Before China's growth took off, a handful of poor states—called the **newly industrializing countries (NICs)**—achieved self-sustaining capital accumulation, with impressive economic growth. These semiperiphery states, which export light manufactured goods, posted strong economic growth in the 1980s and early 1990s (see The World-System in Chapter 12). They suffered a setback in the 1997 Asian financial crisis because growth had been too fast, with overly idealistic loans, speculative investments, and corrupt deals. But the NICs quickly resumed growth and have developed much further and faster than most of the global South.

The most successful NICs are the **"four tigers"** or **"four dragons"** of East Asia: South Korea, Taiwan, Hong Kong, and Singapore. Each succeeded in developing particular sectors and industries that were competitive on world markets. These sectors and industries can create enough capital accumulation within each country to raise income levels not only among the small elite but also across the population more broadly. Scholars do not know whether the NICs are just the lucky few that have moved from the periphery to the semiperiphery of the world-system (see Chapter 12) or whether other countries throughout the global South can eventually replicate their success.

South Korea, with iron and coal resources, developed competitive steel and automobile industries that export globally, creating a trade surplus (see Chapter 8). Taiwan also used a strong state industrial policy, specializing in the electronics and computer industries and in other light manufacturing. Hong Kong—controlled by China since 1997—also has world-competitive electronics and other light industries, but its greatest strengths are in banking and trade. Singapore is a trading city located at the tip of the Malaysian peninsula—convenient to the South China Sea, the Indian Ocean, and Australia.

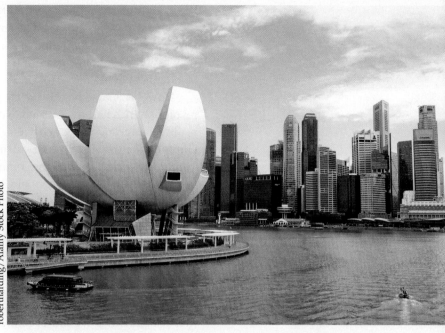

robertharding/ Alamy Stock Photo

A TIGER Singapore is one of the "four tigers" (with Hong Kong, Taiwan, and South Korea). Even after the setback of a 1997 financial crisis, their growth has made them prosperous by the standards of the global South. Other countries are trying to emulate the success of these NICs. But no single, simple lesson applicable to other states emerges from the NICs.

For different reasons, each of these states holds a somewhat unusual political status in the international system. South Korea and Taiwan were hot spots of international conflict that came under the U.S. security umbrella during the Cold War. Both were militarized, authoritarian states intolerant of dissent that later became democratic. U.S. spending in East Asia during the Cold War benefited South Korea and Taiwan. In these cases, military conflict did not impede development.

Hong Kong and Singapore have a different political profile. They are both former British colonies. They are more city-states than nation-states, and their cities are trading ports and financial centers. Although not as repressive or as militarized as South Korea and Taiwan during the Cold War era, Hong Kong and Singapore were not democracies either. Hong Kong was ruled by a British governor (and since 1997 by the government in Beijing), and Singapore by a dominant individual.

13.1.2 The Chinese Experience

If there was ever doubt that the successes of the NICs could be replicated elsewhere and on a larger scale, China ended those doubts. China has nearly 1.4 billion people, and this size alone makes China's efforts to generate self-sustaining accumulation worthy of study. But China has also had the world's fastest-growing economy since the early 1990s.

Between the communist victory of 1949 and the Cultural Revolution of the late 1960s, in the era of Chairman Mao Zedong, Chinese economic policy emphasized national self-sufficiency and communist ideology. The state controlled all economic activity through central planning and state ownership. An "iron rice bowl" policy guaranteed basic food needs to all Chinese citizens (at least in theory).

After Mao died in 1976, China under Deng Xiaoping instituted economic reforms and transformed its southern coastal provinces into *free economic zones* open to foreign investment and run on capitalist principles. Peasants worked their own fields, instead of collective farms, and got rich (by Chinese standards) if they did well. Entrepreneurs started companies, hired workers, and generated profits. Foreign investment flooded into southern China, taking advantage of its location, cheap labor, and relative political stability. Other areas of China gradually opened up to capitalist principles as well. The state required more industries to turn a profit and gave managers greater initiative to run their own companies and spend the profits as they saw fit. Economic growth has been rapid since these policies were instituted. Standards of living have risen substantially.

However, China has also re-created some of the features of capitalism that Mao's revolutionaries had overturned. New class disparities emerged, with rich entrepreneurs driving fancy imported cars while poor workers found themselves unemployed. Unprofitable state-owned industries laid off 10 million workers in the 1990s, with more coming each year. In the countryside, areas bypassed by development still contain 200 million desperately poor Chinese peasants. Social problems such as prostitution returned, as did economic problems such as inflation (since largely tamed). Most frustrating for ordinary Chinese is the widespread official corruption accompanying the get-rich atmosphere.

Popular resentment over problems such as inflation and corruption led industrial workers and even government officials to join students in antigovernment protests at Beijing's Tiananmen Square in 1989. Authorities used the military to suppress the protests violently, killing hundreds of people and signaling the government's determination to maintain tight political control while economic reform proceeded. Party leaders have repeatedly reaffirmed this policy of combining economic reform with political orthodoxy, and felt vindicated by subsequent economic performance. China then weathered the 1997 Asian financial crisis despite its widespread problems with bad bank loans, money-losing state industries, and corruption.

Foreign investments by multinational corporations (MNCs) primed rapid growth in Chinese exports—to $250 billion in 2000 and over $2.1 trillion in 2017. China became the world's largest exporter in 2010. In the coming years, it is poised to join the United States, Japan, and Germany as a major automobile exporter. China's World Trade Organization (WTO) membership since 2001 is accelerating these trends.

In 2012, a new generation of Chinese leaders took charge, led by President Xi Jinping. China had sustained its rapid economic growth (generally 10 percent annually) year after year, even after the 2008 global economic downturn hurt Chinese exports, with the help of large government infrastructure expenditures. But growing inequality and widespread corruption threatened the legitimacy of the Communist Party. An exposé by the *New York Times* in 2012 showed that family members of China's outgoing prime minister had amassed $3 billion of private wealth while he held power. In response, China blocked the *New York Times* Web site within the country. Despite efforts to clamp down on political expression, many Chinese citizens expressed their views not only in strikes and demonstrations but also on wildly popular microblogging sites, China's version of Twitter. In rural villages, peasants openly protested land seizures, taxes, pollution, and corruption by local officials. President Xi declared the battle against corruption a top priority, while continuing to discourage protests and writings that target party officials engaging in corrupt practices.

CAR CULTURE China's rapid economic growth has raised incomes dramatically, especially for a growing middle class. These successes followed China's opening to the world economy and adoption of market-oriented reforms. China is also attempting to develop its domestic market and grow consumer spending rather than relying so heavily on exports to fuel growth. Here, Chinese consumers do their part as they mob the Beijing auto show in 2017, hoping to get in on China's growing infatuation with that ultimate big-ticket consumer item, the automobile.

Imagine China/Newscom

With China now wired to the Internet, the economy gains great advantages, but citizens can also bypass government-controlled information. Some observers expect economic integration in an information era to open up China's political system inexorably and lead to democratization, whereas others think that as long as Chinese leaders deliver economic growth, the population will have little appetite for political change. Indeed, in 2018, the Chinese Communist Party removed term limits for the office of president—meaning that Xi Jinping could remain president for many years. This could allow him to consolidate power and further limit any political liberalization in the future.

China's economic success has given it both more prestige in the international system and a more global perspective on international relations (IR) far from China's borders. In 2013, China announced the formation of the *Asian Infrastructure Investment Bank (AIIB)*, its version of the Asian Development Bank and the World Bank. Many see this move as a way for China to create a new "World Bank" where it maintains control. So far, 61 countries have joined the AIIB. The United States has not done so and has criticized allies that have joined the bank (such as Great Britain). The AIIB has begun to make loans to develop infrastructure in Asia and its capital is at $100 billion—about half that of the World Bank.

China is also a key member of the Group of Twenty (G20) organization. In 2009, the large Western economies announced that the G20 would replace the G8 as the key international body to deal with questions of economic coordination, opening up a potentially new avenue of influence for China. China also has close economic ties with other Asian countries (see Figure 13.3). China's rising international standing was bolstered by its hosting of the 2008 Olympics, which were enormously successful.

China's economic miracle did hit a bump in the 2008–2009 economic crisis. China's investments in the United States, made with the trade surpluses China had accumulated over the years, lost a substantial fraction of their value in the financial meltdown. Chinese leaders announced a major stimulus package aimed at spurring domestic consumption in China, but this faced problems in the short term, including the cultural problem of getting people with a history of poverty to spend instead of save, and the economic problem of reorienting an export-driven economy to produce for domestic markets. Yet despite these dangers and risks, China's economy has forged ahead out of the economic crisis. For example, Chinese exports quickly returned to pre-recession levels after a drop in 2009 and have kept growing.

China's economy appears to have hit a second bump in the new millennium. Throughout 2015, China's stock markets dropped very significantly, leading many to question China's economic stability. China also undertook two surprise currency devaluations, lowered official interest rates, and increased public spending to stave off an economic downturn. These moves appear to have been successful—although China's growth rate has fallen in the past decade, it is still high compared to that of other developing countries at well above 6 percent.

One sign of potential trouble on the horizon for China could be the rise of nationalist and antiglobalization sentiment throughout the world. Just as many often blame the United States for spreading its culture through globalization, many around the world, especially in Western countries, blame China for their economic woes. Because of China's large balance of trade surplus, it is an easy target for those upset with trade under globalization. In 2017–2018, U.S. president Donald Trump began to place tariffs on imports from China, sparking a potential trade war. A global backlash against Chinese trade could put the Chinese economic model at risk, although it would also hurt consumers in countries that buy Chinese goods.

For years it appeared that China's huge population would supply limitless cheap labor to foreign investors making goods in China. In recent years, however, China's growth has begun to squeeze the available labor force and push wages up. Labor unrest has become more common throughout China as workers demand higher wages and better working conditions. MNCs have begun to move some light manufacturing to other Asian countries with even cheaper labor, such as Vietnam.

Figure 13.3 China's View of Its Neighborhood

China's continuing growth is the leading example of success of economic development in the global South. China's future path will affect all of Asia.

It is unclear what lessons China's economic success over the past decade holds for the rest of the global South. The shift away from central planning and toward private ownership was clearly a key factor in its success, yet the state continued to play a central role in overseeing the economy (even more than in the NICs). These topics are being debated vigorously as China navigates its new era of rising prosperity and rising expectations, finds its way in the newly turbulent world economy, and as other poor states look to China's experience for lessons.

13.1.3 India Takes Off

India, like China, deserves special attention because of its size and recent robust growth. From 1996 to 2016, India's average annual growth rate exceeded 6 percent. India's decade of success still does not compare to China's nearly three decades, and India's GDP per person is still not much more than half of China's. But India's success has started it toward what could be, in the coming years, a repetition of China's rise out of poverty.

India's economy was for decades based loosely on socialism and state control of large industries but on private capitalism in agriculture and consumer goods. The state subsidizes basic goods and gives special treatment to farmers. Unlike China, India has a democratic government, but a fractious one, with various autonomy movements and ethnic conflicts. India's government has suffered from corruption, although this has improved in recent years.

Indian state-owned industries, like those elsewhere, were largely unprofitable. To take an extreme example, 12 years after a fertilizer plant was built, it employed 3,000 workers but had not produced any fertilizer. India's socialist philosophy and widespread poverty also limited the growth of a middle class to support capital accumulation and state revenue: Less than 1 percent of the population paid any income tax. Furthermore, bureaucracy in India discouraged foreign investment. In the 1990s, China received many times the foreign investment that India did. The 1991 collapse of the Soviet Union—

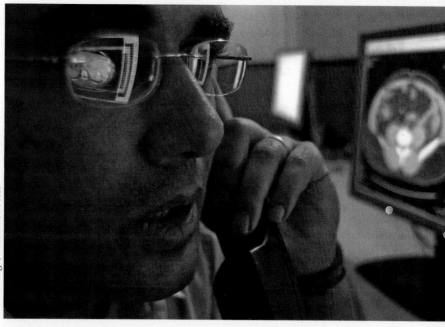

Gautam Singh/Associated Press

AT YOUR SERVICE India has grown rapidly in recent years, using its large, well-educated, English-speaking population to generate export revenues in the service sector—software companies, call centers serving American customers, and professional services in such areas as accounting, architecture, engineering, and medicine. This radiologist in Bangalore, India's technology capital, reads body scans from a U.S. hospital sent via the Internet and discusses the results by phone with the patient's doctor in Connecticut, 2004.

India's major trading partner—threw India into a severe economic crisis that nearly caused it to default on its international debts. India sought help from the International Monetary Fund (IMF) and the World Bank and committed itself to far-reaching economic reforms such as reducing bureaucracy and selling money-losing state-owned industries (see IMF Conditionality). Although reforms were imperfectly carried out, India saw robust economic growth return in the late 1990s. Recent economic growth comes despite continuing corruption and bureaucracy in India's government; Indians joke that the economy grows at night while the government is asleep.

In the era of globalization, India's niche in the globalized world economy is in the service and information sectors. Although the service sector accounts for less than 30 percent of India's labor force (most of which is still in agriculture), it contributes nearly 60 percent of GDP. Whereas South Korea specialized in exporting heavy manufactured goods and China in light manufactured goods, India specializes in exporting information products such as software and telephone call center services. Each country uses its labor force to add value to products that are exported worldwide, especially to the large American market. In India's case, the labor force is well educated and speaks English. India also uses its location to advantage by working during the nighttime hours in North America. Software companies can hand off projects daily for the India shift to work on overnight, and American hospitals can send medical notes for overnight transcription. MNCs widely use India's labor force to answer phone calls from around the world, such as technical support calls for a company's products.

India's future success or failure will bear strongly on several competing theories about economic development. In particular, China has had success under a harsh, centralized political system, whereas India has a freewheeling democracy. If India cannot sustain growth, then maybe authoritarian government helps development, and democracy should wait until a later stage. If India continues to succeed, however, then clearly authoritarian government is not a precondition.

Figure 13.4 compares China's and India's progress on two key indicators—infant mortality (a good overall measure of public health) and the fertility rate. In both cases,

Figure 13.4 Comparing Chinese and Indian Development

Source: Based on World Bank data.

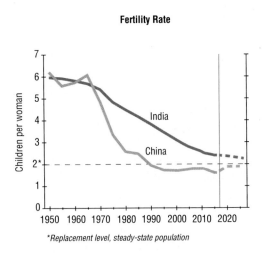

China was able to make dramatic improvements very quickly because of its authoritarian government, whose control (in theory) extended to every village and every bedroom. In the 1950s, China ordered mass campaigns in which citizens exterminated pests and set up sanitation facilities. As a result, in the 1960s, China's rates of epidemic diseases such as cholera and plague dropped, and so did the infant mortality rate. In the 1970s, with its heavy-handed one-child policy, China forced down the fertility rate. Women who objected could be forcibly sterilized. Thus, China relied on the dominance principle to force individuals to take actions that were in society's interest. Its successes in improving public health and lowering fertility provided a foundation for China's subsequent economic success, although obviously at a cost to individual freedom.

India, by contrast, has relied more on the identity principle, getting people to change their preferences and *want* to have fewer children and help improve public health. Without a dictatorship to force compliance, India's progress has been slower. Over time, however, India is moving toward the same results as China, albeit decades later, and doing so without giving up its own national identity as a democracy.

13.1.4 Other Experiments

Other sizable developing countries have pursued various development strategies, with mixed successes and failures. The best results have come from Asia. Figure 13.5 shows the income levels and growth rates of the 16 largest countries by population in the global South. The graph parallels that for world regions in Figure 12.1. Clearly the large countries of the South vary widely in income level. The five highest-income countries (Turkey, Iran, Thailand, Mexico, and China) come from three of the four regions and vary widely in their growth rates. Three of the fastest-growing countries (Bangladesh, India, and Ethiopia) at 7–8 percent are at the lower end of the income scale. Over the past 25 years, China has developed faster than the other 15 large countries of the global South, and with these growth rates, China has joined the ranks of the five highest-income countries in this group. Clearly, too, regional location makes a difference. The fact that the five regions of the global South can be mapped onto single contiguous zones in this figure shows that whole regions are moving together in distinct patterns.

In Asia, three of the first to try to follow the NICs were Indonesia, Malaysia, and Thailand. Indonesia set a goal in 1969 to become an NIC by 1994. It fell short of that goal, but made some progress in attracting foreign investment. With 250 million people and a GDP per capita near India's, Indonesia's major assets are cheap labor (a minimum wage of less than 50 cents per hour) and exportable natural resources, including oil. But Indonesia has had to import oil since 2004 because of decreasing production. The

Figure 13.5 Largest Countries' Income Levels and Growth Rates, 2016

Source: Based on World Bank data.

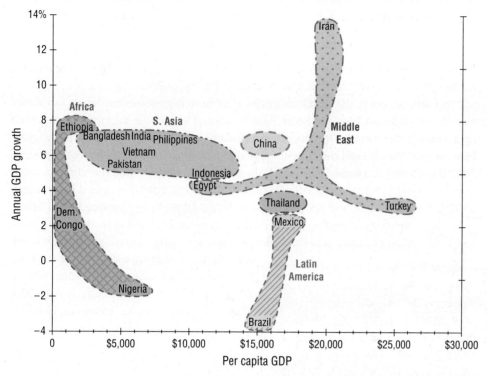

Note: Figure shows the 16 most populous developing countries.

position of the Philippines resembles that of Indonesia. After navigating the 1997 crisis smoothly, the Philippines got onto a growth curve, currently exceeding 5 percent a year, that is positive but not fast enough to address the widespread poverty in the country.

Malaysia also set out to follow closely in the footsteps of the tigers. Although it exports oil and gas, Malaysia focused its export industry heavily on electronics. It was hit hard by the information-sector dot-com crash of 2001–2002 but came back to grow at 5–7 percent per year in 2004–2008. Malaysia also recovered quickly from the 2008–2009 global recession. With income per person over $25,000, Malaysia has successfully risen to a middle-income level.

Thailand was often suggested as a potential "fifth tiger." It received enormous foreign investment in the 1980s (mostly from Japan) and created a sizable middle class. But its growth masked serious problems that were revealed in the 1997 financial crisis. Thailand recovered and posted strong growth, despite continuing problems with bad loans. But a coup in 2006 and political instability have made Thailand somewhat less attractive for foreign investment.

Since 2001, several Southeast Asian countries have also had to address problems of terrorism within their borders, and Indonesia faced simmering ethnic unrest in several islands (although the active secessionist war in Aceh province has ended). These factors held back the economic development of the would-be NICs of Southeast Asia.

Vietnam has found success similar to India's. Vietnam is a communist state following a reform model based on China's. Like China, Vietnam has few worries about terrorism and was largely unaffected by the 2008 economic crisis. Vietnam's growth since 1997 has averaged about 7 percent per year. This period of fast growth follows liberalization of the economy, which had been held back by decades of devastating war and centralized communist rule. Vietnam, which particularly exports textiles, joined the WTO in 2007. As with China, Vietnam did a good job of meeting basic human needs at very low average income levels and has reduced extreme poverty despite remaining a poor country.

The large Asian states of Bangladesh and Pakistan are more deeply mired in poverty and have dimmer prospects for capital accumulation in the coming years. They face problems with state bureaucracies, corruption, and political instability. Nonetheless, at the end of 2008, Bangladesh successfully ended emergency rule with fair elections that saw a huge turnout and brought new hopes for development and the curtailing of corruption. Pakistan, by contrast, continued to struggle with instability in areas bordering Afghanistan. With continued political infighting among its government, judiciary, and military, Pakistan's economic prospects hinge on finding political stability.

In Latin America, the major countries start from higher income levels but lower growth rates than in China and South Asia. Brazil and Mexico are the largest. Brazil built up a sizable internal market by concentrating income in a growing middle and upper class. However, its cities are still ringed with huge slums filled with desperately poor people. In 2003, the election of a leftist president, Lula da Silva, raised fears that spending on social programs would undermine Brazil's financial position, but instead he reined in spending, brought down inflation, and stabilized Brazil's financial position—proving that in Brazil, as in China, socialists can make good capitalists. Between 2012 and 2016, Brazil enjoyed a rare combination of steady growth, democracy, and shrinking inequality (although levels are still high), offering a development model for others to emulate. Brazil successfully hosted the 2014 soccer World Cup and the 2016 Summer Olympic Games, increasing its political prestige. Yet, in 2016, its president was impeached in a corruption scandal that deeply divided the country. Brazil's economy suffered as well, as it experienced negative economic growth for the first time since 1992.

Like Brazil, Mexico has pockets of deep poverty and a sizable foreign debt but, unlike Brazil, has oil to export. Mexico has also enjoyed relative political stability, though corruption is a problem. A reformist president was elected in 2000, though the long-standing ruling party regained power in 2012. In the two and a half decades since the North American Free Trade Agreement (NAFTA), despite periodic political and economic upheavals, Mexico has seen neither a breakthrough nor a disaster. However, drug-related violence threatens to undermine progress. In 2017 alone, nearly 30,000 murders occurred, many blamed on drug-related violence.

In Africa, Nigeria is the largest country and, with oil to export, should be one of the less impoverished. But at an income level of nearly $6,000 per person, its income is quite low, and corruption takes a steady toll on the economy. Nigeria seems to suffer from the "resource curse." Oil provides 95 percent of export earnings and provides revenue for two-thirds of the government's budget. After years of military dictatorship, elections were held in 1999, and Nigeria enjoyed more political stability in the twenty-first century, but a cease-fire with armed rebels in the oil-rich south was

Sameer Sehgal / Getty Images

GLOBALIZE THIS Globalization is creating winners and losers, leading to demands to place limits on markets. Debt, currency crises, IMF conditionality, foreign direct investment (FDI), and the privatization of state-owned enterprises are among the sources of upheaval and poverty in many poor countries. Here, traders in India protest against FDI and online retailers who they say are causing local businesses to shut down, 2014.

followed by an upsurge of Islamist terrorist bombings in the north. Since 2009, the main Islamist group, known as Boko Haram, has killed thousands of civilians, thus contributing to political instability. Nigeria's political and economic conditions remain fragile.

Elsewhere in Africa, Ethiopia and Democratic Congo are growing fast but starting from great poverty. Democratic Congo was poised to recover from decades of war, but persistent violence threatens progress. South Africa has a relatively high income ($13,000 per person) but tremendous inequality, high rates of HIV/AIDS, and high levels of corruption. A few African countries, however, such as Kenya and Mauritius, are emerging as model information-sector economies with bright prospects.

In the Middle East, Israel has developed economically in an unusual manner. It received sustained infusions of outside capital from several sources—German reparations, U.S. foreign aid, and contributions from Zionists in foreign countries. This outside assistance was particular to the history of German genocide against Jews during World War II and the efforts of Jews worldwide to help build a Jewish state afterward. Few if any developing countries could hope to receive such outside assistance (relative to Israel's small size). In common with other NICs, however, Israel had a strong state involvement in key industries and carved out a few niches for itself in world markets (notably in cut diamonds, computer software, and military technology).

The small countries with large oil exports—such as Saudi Arabia, Kuwait, Bahrain, and the United Arab Emirates—have done well economically. But they are in a special class; their experience is not one that others without oil can follow. Iran began to grow robustly and to attract foreign investment after the Iran-Iraq War ended in 1988. Most of the economy is state-controlled, however. In addition, Islamic radicalism creates frictions with Western powers and makes investors wary. Conflict over Iran's nuclear program led to a harsh sanctions regime that significantly undermined Iran's economic growth in 2012 and 2013. The nuclear deal reached in 2015 brought many eager Western firms to invest in Iran's economy, which includes 80 million consumers and up to $35 trillion in oil reserves. The Trump administration's abandonment of the nuclear deal in 2018 threatened not only access to Iran's market but also Iran's economy, leaving future opportunities uncertain.

Turkey was somewhat successful in developing its economy without oil revenues. Like South Korea and Taiwan, Turkey was an authoritarian state for many years but has allowed political liberalization since the 1990s. It has developed under a security umbrella (NATO) and has received considerable U.S. foreign aid. Like Mexico, Turkey is trying to join its richer neighbors—the European Union (EU) (see Chapter 10). Turkey's economy suffered during the 2008–2009 financial crisis but returned to stronger growth by 2010. Since 2011, conflict in Syria, Turkey's neighbor to the south, has put significant pressures on its economy.

Egypt is mired in poverty despite substantial U.S. aid since the late 1970s. The state owns much of the industry, operates the economy centrally, imposes high import tariffs, and provides patronage jobs and subsidized prices. Reforms in the 1990s brought economic growth, but remaining problems include high unemployment, a trade deficit, and widespread corruption. After the overthrow of its authoritarian ruler in 2011, Egypt looked forward to restarting its economy, which was seriously disrupted by the instability of the Arab Spring. Yet since 2011, Egypt has been unable to establish a pattern of strong economic growth.

13.2 Lessons

Identify and evaluate two different strategies that developing states have used in attempting to achieve economic growth.

The largest developing countries are following somewhat different strategies with somewhat different results. But several common themes recur. These themes concern trade, the concentration of capital, and corruption.

13.2.1 Import Substitution and Export-Led Growth

Throughout the global South, states are trying to use international trade as the basis of accumulation. For the reasons discussed in Chapter 8, a policy of self-reliance or autarky is at best an extremely slow way to build up wealth. But through the creation of a trade surplus, a state can accumulate hard currency and build industry and infrastructure.

One way to try to create a trade surplus, used frequently a few decades ago, is through **import substitution**—the development of local industries to produce items that a country had been importing. These industries may receive state subsidies or tariff protection. This might seem to be a good policy for reducing dependency—especially on the former colonial master—while shrinking a trade deficit or building a trade surplus. But it is against the principle of comparative advantage and has not proven effective in most cases. Some scholars think that import substitution is a useful policy only at a very early phase of economic development, after which it becomes counterproductive. Others think that it is never useful.

More and more states have shifted to a strategy of **export-led growth**, a strategy used by the NICs. This approach seeks to develop industries that can compete in specific niches in the world economy. These industries may receive special treatment such as subsidies and protected access to local markets. Exports from these industries generate hard currency and create a favorable trade balance. The state can then spend part of its money on imports of commodities produced more cheaply elsewhere. Such a strategy has risks, especially when a state specializes in the export of a few raw materials (see Postcolonial Dependency in Chapter 12). It leaves poor countries vulnerable to sudden price fluctuations for their exports.

Thus, states have looked to exporting manufactured goods, rather than raw materials, as the key to export-led growth. In seeking a niche for manufactured goods, however, a developing country must compete against industrialized countries with better technology, more educated workforces, and much more capital. It is not enough to subsidize and protect an industry until it grows in size; someday it has to be able to stand its own ground in a competitive world or it will not bring in a trade surplus.

import substitution A strategy of developing local industries, often conducted behind protectionist barriers, to produce items that a country had been importing.

export-led growth An economic development strategy that seeks to develop industries capable of competing in specific niches in the world economy.

13.2.2 Concentrating Capital for Manufacturing

Manufacturing emerges as a key factor in both export-led growth and self-sustaining industrialization (home production for home markets). To invest in manufacturing, these countries must *concentrate* what surplus their economies produce. Money spent building factories cannot be spent subsidizing food prices or building better schools. Thus, the concentration of capital for manufacturing can sharpen disparities in income. And because manufacturing industries in poor countries are not immediately competitive on world markets, one common strategy is first to build up the industry with sales to the home market (protected by tariffs and subsidies). But home markets for manufactured goods do not come from poor peasants in the countryside or the unemployed youth in city slums. Rather, wealth must be concentrated in a *middle class* that has the income to buy manufactured goods. These disparities may result in crowds rioting in the streets or guerrillas taking over the countryside.

Capital for manufacturing can come instead from foreign investment or foreign loans, but this reduces the amount of surplus available to the state in the long term. Another way to minimize capital needs is to start out in low-capital industries. These industries can begin generating capital, which can then be used to move into somewhat more technologically demanding and capital-intensive kinds of manufacturing. A favorite starter industry is *textiles*. The industry is fairly labor-intensive, giving an advantage to countries with cheap labor, and does not require huge investments of capital to get started. In 2005, textile tariffs were removed worldwide, so textile exporters in developing countries gained access to Western markets but faced intensified competition from China.

A related approach to capitalization in very poor countries, growing in popularity in recent years, is **microcredit** (or *microlending*). Based on a successful model in Bangladesh (the Grameen Bank, which won the 2006 Nobel Peace Prize and now operates more than 2,400 branch offices), microcredit uses small loans to poor people, especially women, to support economic self-sufficiency. The borrowers are organized into small groups and take responsibility for each other's success, including repaying the loans. Repayment rates have been high, and the idea has spread rapidly in several regions. In one popular application, village women used small loans to start businesses renting cell phone time. Rural farmers used the phone time to find out market conditions before making a long trek to sell their products. Thus, bringing the information revolution to isolated villages raised incomes for the farmers and the women alike, and the bank got its loans repaid. Micro-

Godong/Alamy Stock Photo

CAPITAL INVESTMENT Foreign investment, international debt, and domestic inequality all can help concentrate the necessary capital for manufacturing. In recent years, microcredit—very small loans made directly to very poor people—provides a way to use capital more diffusely. Here, women in Burkina Faso learn about microcredit in a seminar led by an NGO, 2017.

credit is now being applied on a macro scale. Tens of millions of families have received loans from thousands of institutions worldwide. Microcredit is the opposite of a trickle-down approach—it injects capital at the bottom of the economic hierarchy. A loan to buy a goat or cell phone may do more good, dollar for dollar, than a loan to build a dam.

microcredit The use of very small loans to small groups of individuals, often women, to stimulate economic development.

Capitalists tend to favor the concentration of capital as a way to spur investment rather than consumption (and to realize economies of scale and specialization). In line with liberalism, capitalists favor development paths that tie developing countries closely to the world economy and international trade. They argue that, although such development strategies defer equity, they maximize efficiency. Once a state has a self-sustaining cycle of accumulation under way, it can better redress poverty in the broad population. To do so too early would choke off economic growth, in this view. The same concept applies broadly to the world's development as a whole. From a capitalist perspective, capital accumulation is concentrated in the North. This unequal concentration creates faster economic growth, which ultimately will bring more wealth to the South as well. There is no practical way, in this view, to shift wealth from the North to the South without undermining the free market economics responsible for global economic growth.

Socialists, by contrast, argue that meaningful economic development should improve the position of the whole population and of the poor—sooner rather than later. Thus, socialists tend to advocate a more equitable distribution of wealth; they dispute the idea that greater equity will impede efficiency or slow down economic growth. Rather, by raising incomes among the poorer people, a strategy based on equity will speed up the demographic transition and lead more quickly to sustained accumulation. On a global level, socialists do not see the North-South disparities as justified by global growth benefits. They favor political actions to shift income from North to South in order to foster economic growth in the South. Such redistribution, in this view, would create faster, not slower, global economic growth—as well as more balanced and stable growth.

The capitalist theory that unequal income distributions are related to higher economic growth is only weakly supported by empirical evidence. Many states with fairly equitable income distributions have high growth rates (including South Korea, Taiwan, Singapore, and Hong Kong); many with unequal distributions have grown slowly if at all

(Mexico, Argentina, and Ghana). But there are also cases of relatively equitable countries that grow slowly and inequitable ones that grow rapidly. The World Bank reviewed evidence on the effect of income inequality on economic growth and concluded that inequality holds back growth by wasting human potential. The Bank recommends extending access to health care, education, and jobs—as well as to political power—to the poorest people in societies of the global South in order to spur faster economic growth.

13.2.3 Corruption

Corruption is an important negative factor in economic development in many states. Corruption centers on the government as the central actor in economic development, especially in its international aspects. Through foreign policy, the government mediates the national economy's relationship to the world economy. It regulates the conditions under which MNCs operate in the country. It enforces worker discipline—calling out the army if necessary to break strikes or suppress revolutions. It sets tax rates and wields other macroeconomic levers of control over the economy. And in most developing countries, it owns a sizable stake in major industries—a monopoly in some cases.

State officials decide whether to let an MNC into the country, which MNC to give drilling rights to, and what terms (leasing fees, percentages of sales, etc.) to insist on. These are complex deals struck after long negotiations. Corruption adds another player, the corrupt official, to share the benefits. For instance, a foreign oil company can pay off an official to award a favorable contract, and both can profit. In 2003, U.S. prosecutors indicted a ExxonMobil Oil executive for paying $78 million to two senior officials in Kazakhstan—with a kickback of $2 million for the ExxonMobil executive—to secure ExxonMobil's billion-dollar stake in a huge oil field there. He pleaded guilty to tax evasion, received a prison sentence, and had to pay taxes on the $2 million.

Corruption is by no means limited to the global South. But for several reasons, corruption has a deeper effect in poor countries. First, because there is simply less surplus to keep economic growth going, accumulation is fragile. Another difference is that, in developing countries that depend on exporting a few products, the revenue arrives in a very concentrated form—large payments in hard currency—presenting a greater opportunity for corruption than in a more diversified economy. This is a major element in the "resource curse" (see Chapter 12). Furthermore, in developing countries, incomes are often so low that corrupt officials are more tempted to accept payments.

Corruption in the global South presents a collective goods problem for states and MNCs in the global North: Individually, MNCs and their home states can profit by clinching a deal with a private payoff, but collectively, the MNCs and states of the North lose money by having to make these payoffs. Therefore, there is an incentive to clamp down on corruption only if other industrialized states do likewise. The United States in recent decades has barred U.S. companies from making corrupt deals abroad, but other countries of the North had not done so until recently. Germany and Canada even allowed their companies to deduct foreign bribes on their taxes.

Transparency helps solve collective goods problems. A Berlin-based NGO called Transparency International pushed successfully for action to stem corruption in international business deals. The group publishes annual surveys showing the countries that business executives consider most corrupt. The top five on the list in 2014 were Somalia, North Korea, Afghanistan, Sudan, and South Sudan. In

Qamar Sibtain/Getty Images

CLEAN IT UP! Corruption is a major impediment to economic development in both rich and poor countries but is more devastating to economies in the global South and to transitional former communist economies. In India, widespread corruption has held back economic development and equality for years. This Delhi supporter of hunger-striking anticorruption activist Anna Hazare holds a "key" to corrupt officials' Swiss bank locker, 2012.

1997, the world's 29 leading industrialized states agreed to forbid their companies from bribing foreign officials. And the Extractive Industries Transparency Initiative—a coalition of states, NGOs, and MNCs launched by Britain in 2002—fights corruption in the especially vulnerable oil, gas, and mineral sectors worldwide by getting companies to release information on payments they make to developing countries.

In Chad, in 1999, a consortium led by ExxonMobil and backed by World Bank loans struck a deal to build a $4 billion oil pipeline, with oil revenues going through a Citibank account in London to avoid corruption. Chad promised to use 72 percent of the money to reduce poverty. But in 2005, as the oil money flowed in, Chad's government—under attack by rebels based in Sudan—pulled out of the deal to use the money for its military, and the World Bank suspended its loans.

Careers in International Relations: Education and Research

Summary

Jobs in teaching and research offer freedom to pursue ideas and work with colleagues, but they require years of schooling.

BENEFITS AND COSTS People follow various paths to an interest in teaching and researching in the field of IR. Your own professor or instructor is likely to have a unique story about how he or she became interested in international affairs.

One advantage of an academic and research career, whether at a teaching-oriented institution or a large research university, is intellectual freedom. One can spend a career approaching a variety of topics that are interesting and constantly evolving, may involve travel abroad for fieldwork, and may let you network with hundreds of colleagues interested in similar topics.

Most research positions (for example, in think tanks) are different in two respects. First, these jobs often give more direction to an individual in terms of the research to be performed. Second, there is little or no teaching involved. Still, for those interested in IR research, such jobs can result in a wider dissemination of one's work to a broader audience that often includes policy makers.

To teach IR at an advanced level or to perform research for think tanks and government agencies usually requires an advanced degree—nearly always a masters degree, often a doctorate (Ph.D.). Masters degree programs often take between one and two years, while a Ph.D. in international relations usually requires a minimum of five years. Often, students take time off between their undergraduate and graduate educations to travel internationally or get work experience to hone their interests. Of course, many students never return to extend their education if they find a job that allows them to achieve their personal and career goals.

Finally, in completing most advanced degrees, a large amount of self-direction is necessary. Coursework is only one part of masters or Ph.D. programs: A thesis is also required. Writing a thesis entails working on your own time schedule, thereby balancing other duties (such as work as a teaching or research assistant) that can easily crowd out your own work. Many who complete the coursework for an advanced degree do not finish their thesis or take many years to do so.

SKILLS TO HONE Whether one wants to pursue an advanced degree for the purpose of teaching in an academic setting or engaging in applied research, there are important skill sets to develop.

First and foremost is critical thinking. Scholars and researchers must consider many alternatives as answers to questions, while being able to evaluate the validity or importance of those alternatives. Second is writing. Before, during, and after producing a thesis, writing is a key skill for academics and researchers. Finally, think about developing a set of applied skills to use as a toolbox while analyzing questions. The contents of this toolbox might include other languages to facilitate fieldwork abroad. They could include use of statistics and data skills to facilitate quantitative analysis. Or they could include mathematics to use game theoretic models. No matter which tools you emphasize, specialized skills will help you answer research questions, whether as part of the academy or in a private or governmental research organization.

Resources

American Political Science Association. *Earning a PhD in Political Science.* 4th ed. Washington, DC, 2004.
The Chronicle of Higher Education (weekly). Online at chronicle.com/
http://www.apsanet.org
http://www.apsia.org
http://www.isanet.org

13.3 North-South Capital Flows

Outline the ways in which large amounts of debt can hinder the process of economic development for countries of the global South.

Capital from the global North moves to the global South and potentially spurs growth there in several forms—foreign investment, debt, and foreign aid. This section discusses these capital flows from North to South.

13.3.1 Foreign Investment

Poor countries have little money available to invest in new factories, farms, mines, or oil wells. Foreign investment—investment in such capital goods by foreigners (most often MNCs)—is one way to get accumulation started (see Foreign Direct Investment in Chapter 9). Foreign investment has been crucial to the success of China and other developing countries in Asia. Overall, private capital flows to the global South were over $700 billion in 2014—four times the amount given in official development assistance.

Foreigners who invest in a country then own the facilities; the investor, by virtue of its ownership, can control decisions about how many people to employ, whether to expand or shut down, what products to make, and how to market them. Also, the foreign investor can usually take the profits from the operation out of the country (repatriation of profits). However, the host government can share in the wealth by charging fees and taxes, or by leasing land or drilling rights (see Host and Home Government Relations in Chapter 9).

Because of past colonial experiences, many governments in the global South have feared the loss of control that comes with foreign investments by MNCs. Sometimes the presence of MNCs was associated with the painful process of concentrating capital and the sharpening of class disparities in the host state. Although such fears remain, they are counterbalanced by the ability of foreign investors to infuse capital and generate more surplus. By the 1980s and 1990s, as models based on autarky or state ownership were discredited and the NICs gained success, many poor states rushed to embrace foreign investment. China has been the most successful of these by far.

One way in which states have sought to soften the loss of control is through *joint ventures*, companies owned partly by a foreign MNC and partly by a local firm or the host government itself. Sometimes foreign ownership in joint ventures is limited to some percentage (often 49 percent), to ensure that ultimate control rests with the host country. The percentage of ownership is usually proportional to the amount of capital invested; if a host government wants more control, it must put up more of the money. Joint ventures work well for MNCs because they help ensure the host government's cooperation in reducing bureaucratic hassles and ensuring success (by giving the host government a direct stake in the outcome).

MNCs invest in a country because of some advantage of doing business there. In some cases, it is the presence of natural resources. Sometimes it is cheap labor. Sometimes geographical location is a factor. Some states have better *absorptive capacity*—the ability to put investments to productive use—than others

FOREIGN INVESTORS Foreign investment is an important source of capital for economic development in the global South. The relationship of foreign investors and host countries transcends economics and draws in culture, politics, and identity. These Japanese executives visit their Honda factory in India, where Honda has invested $400 million, in 2008.

MANPREET ROMANA/AFP/Getty Images

because of a more highly developed infrastructure and a higher level of skills among workers or managers. These are most often middle-income states, so the funneling of investments to states with high absorptive capacity tends to sharpen disparities *within* the global South. MNCs also look for a favorable *regulatory environment* in which a host state will facilitate, rather than impede, the MNC's business.

MNC decisions about foreign investment also depend on prospects for *financial stability*, especially for low inflation and stable currency exchange rates. If a currency is not convertible, an MNC will not be able to take profits back to its home state or reinvest them elsewhere. Of equal importance in attracting investment is *political stability*. Banks and MNCs conduct *political risk analyses* to assess the risks of political disturbances in states in which they might invest.

Beyond these financial considerations, a foreign investor producing for local markets wants to know that the host country's *economic growth* will sustain demand for the goods being produced. Similarly, whether producing for local consumption or export, the MNC wants the local *labor supply*—whether semiskilled labor or just cheap—to be stable. Foreign investors often look to international financial institutions, such as the World Bank and the IMF, and to private analyses, to judge a state's economic stability before investing in it.

Technology transfer refers to a poor state's acquisition of technology (knowledge, skills, methods, designs, and specialized equipment) from foreign sources, usually in conjunction with foreign direct investment or similar business operations. A developing country may allow an MNC to produce certain goods in the country under favorable conditions, provided the MNC shares knowledge of the technology and design behind the product. The state may try to get its own citizens into the management and professional workforce of factories or facilities created by foreign investment. Not only can physical capital accumulate in the country but so can the related technological base for further development. But MNCs may be reluctant to share proprietary technology.

Most poor states seek to build up an educated elite with knowledge and skills to run the national economy. One way to do so is to send students to industrialized states for higher education. This entails some risks, however. Students may enjoy life in the North and fail to return home. The problem of losing skilled workers to richer countries, called the **brain drain**, has impeded economic development in states such as India, Pakistan, and the Philippines (where more nurses emigrated than graduated nursing school in 2000–2004).

13.3.2 North-South Debt

Borrowing money is an alternative to foreign investment as a way of obtaining funds to prime a cycle of economic accumulation. If accumulation succeeds, it produces enough surplus to repay the loan and still make a profit. Borrowing has several advantages. It keeps control in the hands of the state (or other local borrower) and does not impose painful sacrifices on local citizens, at least in the short term.

Debt has disadvantages too. The borrower must service the debt—making regular payments of interest and repaying the principal according to the terms of the loan. *Debt service* is a constant drain on whatever surplus is generated by investment of the money. With foreign direct investment, a money-losing venture is the problem of the foreign MNC; with debt, it is the problem of the borrowing state, which must find the money elsewhere. Often, a debtor must borrow new funds to service old loans, thus slipping further into debt. Debt service has created a net financial outflow from South to North in recent years, as the South has paid billions more in interest to banks and governments in the North than it has received in foreign investment or development aid.

Failure to make scheduled payments, called a **default**, is considered a drastic action because it destroys lenders' confidence and results in cutoff of future loans. Rather than defaulting, borrowers usually attempt **debt renegotiation**—reworking

technology transfer Third world states' acquisition of technology (knowledge, skills, methods, designs, specialized equipment, etc.) from foreign sources, usually in conjunction with direct foreign investment or similar business operations.

brain drain Poor countries' loss of skilled workers to rich countries.

default Failure to make scheduled debt payments.

debt renegotiation A reworking of the terms on which a loan will be repaid; frequently negotiated by third world debtor governments in order to avoid default.

the terms on which a loan will be repaid. By renegotiating their debts with lenders, borrowers seek a mutually acceptable payment scheme to keep at least some money flowing to the lender. If interest rates have fallen since a loan was first taken out, the borrower can refinance. Borrowers and lenders can also negotiate to restructure a debt by changing the length of the loan (usually to a longer payback period) or the other terms. Occasionally state-to-state loans are written off altogether—forgiven—for political reasons, as happened with U.S. loans to Egypt after the Gulf War.

North-South debt encompasses several types of lending relationships, all of which are influenced by international politics. The *borrower* may be a private firm or bank in a developing country, or it may be the government itself. Loans to the government are somewhat more common because lenders consider the government less likely to default than a private borrower. The *lender* may be a private bank or company, or a state (both are important). Usually banks are more insistent on receiving timely payments and firmer in renegotiating debts than are states. Some state-to-state loans are made on artificially favorable *concessionary* terms, in effect subsidizing economic development in the borrowing state.

Debt renegotiation has become a perennial occupation of the global South. Such renegotiations are complex international bargaining situations, like international trade or arms control negotiations. If a borrowing government accepts terms that are too burdensome, it may lose popularity at home. But if the borrowing state does not give enough to gain the agreement of the lenders, it might have to default.

For lenders, debt renegotiations involve a collective goods problem: All of them have to agree on the conditions of the renegotiation, but each really cares only about getting its own money back. To solve this problem, state creditors meet together periodically as the **Paris Club**, and private creditors as the **London Club**, to work out their terms.

Through such renegotiations and the corresponding write-offs of debts by banks, developing countries have largely avoided defaulting on their debts. However, in 2001, Argentina in effect defaulted. By then, financial institutions had adjusted psychologically to the reality that Argentina could not pay its debt. Indeed, Argentina recovered—its economy growing 9 percent a year since 2001—and in 2005 offered its creditors a take-it-or-leave-it deal for repayment of less than 30 cents on the dollar. Most took it. Still, default is a risky course because of the need for foreign investment and foreign trade to accumulate wealth. Lenders too have generally proven willing to absorb losses rather than push a borrower over the edge and risk financial instability. But in 2008, Ecuador defaulted on its $10 billion in foreign debt, which the leftist president called "immoral and illegitimate."

In the past decade, these debt problems jumped to the global North as the eurozone grappled with the heavy indebtedness of some of its poorer members—especially Greece, as well as Portugal, Spain, and Ireland. In a 2011 bailout agreement, bankers holding Greek debt had to accept 50 cents on the dollar. Even so, Greek voters expressed anger toward budget cuts required to meet conditions for each stage of the bailout. By 2014, fed up with these conditions for the bailout, Greek voters elected a new party to renegotiate the bailout with fewer conditions.

Despite stabilization, developing countries have not yet solved the debt problem. As shown in Table 13.1, the South owes over $6 trillion in foreign debt and pays over $2 trillion a year to service it. The debt service (in hard currency) absorbs over a third of the entire hard-currency export earnings in Latin America—the region most affected. For the entire global South, it is over 35 percent of exports.

In recent years, activists and NGOs have called for extensive debt forgiveness for the poorest countries, most of which are in Africa. Critics say such cancellations just put more money in the hands of corrupt, inept governments. But G7 members in 2005 agreed to eliminate all debts owed by 37 very poor countries to the World Bank and the IMF—cutting almost in half the poorest countries' estimated $200 billion in debt.

Paris Club A group of first world governments that have loaned money to third world governments; it meets periodically to work out terms of debt renegotiations. See also *London Club*.

London Club A group of private creditors that have loaned money to third world governments; it meets periodically to work out terms of debt renegotiations. See also *Paris Club*.

Table 13.1 Debt in the Global South, 2017

Region	Foreign Debt		Annual Debt Service	
	Billion $	% of GDP[a]	Billion $	% of Exports
Latin America	2,000	41%	510	51%
Asia	2,900	18	1,500	43
Africa	480	34	90	30
Middle East	1,000	39	300	29
Total "South"	6,380	33	2,400	38

[a] GDP not calculated at purchasing-power parity.

Source: Based on IMF, World Economic Outlook Database, October 2017.

The first $40 billion, owed by 18 countries, began to be written off in 2006. As of 2017, the IMF had forgiven $76 billion of debt in the poorest 36 countries.

13.3.3 IMF Conditionality

The IMF and the World Bank have a large supply of capital from their member states (see The World Bank and the IMF in Chapter 9). This capital plays an important role in funding early stages of accumulation in developing countries and in helping them get through short periods of great difficulty. As a political entity rather than a bank, the IMF can make funds available on favorable terms.

The IMF scrutinizes developing countries' economic plans and policies, withholding loans until it is satisfied that the right policies are in place. Then it makes loans to help states through the transitional process of implementing the IMF-approved policies. The IMF also sends important signals to private lenders and investors. Its approval of a state's economic plans is a "seal of approval" that bankers and MNCs use to assess the wisdom of investing in that state. Thus, the IMF wields great power to influence the economic policies of developing countries.

An agreement to loan IMF funds on the condition that certain government policies are adopted is called an **IMF conditionality** agreement; implementation of these conditions is referred to as a *structural adjustment program*. Dozens of developing countries have entered into such agreements with the IMF in the past 30 years. The terms insisted on by the IMF are usually painful for the citizens (and hence for national politicians). The IMF demands that inflation be brought under control, which requires reducing state spending and closing budget deficits. These measures often spur unemployment and require that subsidies of food and basic goods be reduced or eliminated. Short-term consumption is curtailed in favor of longer-term investment. Surplus must be concentrated to service debt and invest in new capital accumulation. The IMF wants to ensure that money lent to a country is not spent for politically popular but economically unprofitable purposes (such as subsidizing food). It also wants to ensure that inflation does not eat away all progress and that the economy is stable enough to attract investment. In addition, it demands steps to curtail corruption.

IMF conditionality An agreement to loan IMF funds on the condition that certain government policies are adopted. Dozens of third world states have entered into such agreements with the IMF in the past 30 years. See also *International Monetary Fund (IMF)*.

Because of the pain inflicted by a conditionality agreement—and to some extent by any debt renegotiation agreement—such agreements are often politically unpopular in the global South. On quite a few occasions, a conditionality agreement has brought rioters into the streets demanding the restoration of subsidies for food, gasoline, and other essential goods. Sometimes governments have backed out of the agreement or have broken their promises under such pressure. Occasionally, governments have been toppled.

In Egypt, where the same word is used for bread and for life, cheap bread is vital to political stability, at least in the government's view. An annual subsidy of

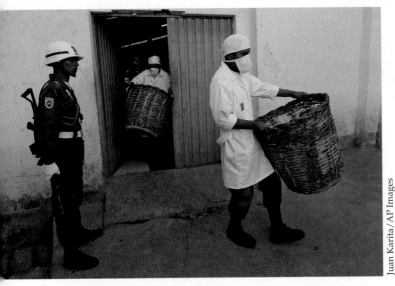

Juan Karita/AP Images

GUARDING THE BREAD IMF conditionality agreements often call for reducing subsidies for food, transportation, and other basic needs. In Bolivia, the government had subsidized imported flour to lower the price of bread. When it ended those subsidies in 2015, bakers in the country went on strike in protest, leaving nearly no bread available in the country. The government then ordered the military to begin making bread to fulfill demand. Here, bread is taken under military guard from military barracks to be delivered to stores.

$3.5 billion provides a supply of bread at one-third its real cost for Egypt's large and poor population. These costs distort the free market, encouraging Egyptians to eat (and waste) more bread than they otherwise would, driving up the need for imported wheat, and offering widespread opportunities for corruption by diverting subsidized flour or bread to black markets. But when the government tried to raise the price of bread in 1977, street riots forced a reversal. Instead, the government has subtly changed the size and composition of loaves, and in 1996 began secretly mixing cheaper corn flour into state-milled wheat flour. Protests also occurred in 2017, when the Egyptian government attempted to revise how bread subsidies were paid, leading to a partial reversal of the policy.

Of course, these IMF conditions have also proved unpopular in developed countries that needed assistance during the 2008–2009 recession. After receiving a $6 billion rescue package from the IMF, Iceland was forced to make fundamental reforms to its banking sector. Greece, which received over $133 billion from the IMF, agreed to eliminate several paid holidays while cutting all wages of all public workers by 3 percent.

13.3.4 The South in International Economic Regimes

Because of the need for capital and the wealth created by international trade, most states of the global South see their future economic development as resting on a close interconnection with the world economy, not on national autarky or regional economic communities. Thus, poor states must play by the rules embedded in international economic regimes (see Chapters 8 and 9).

The WTO trading regime sometimes works against poor states, however, relative to industrialized ones. A free trade regime makes it harder for poor states to protect infant industries in order to build self-sufficient capital accumulation. It forces competition with more technologically advanced states. A poor state can be competitive only in low-wage, low-capital niches—especially those using natural resources that are scarce in the North, such as tropical agriculture, extractive (mining and drilling) industries, and textiles.

Yet just those economic sectors in which poor states have comparative advantages on world markets—agriculture and textiles in particular—were largely excluded from free trade rules for decades (see Chapter 8). Instead, world trade deals concentrated on free trade in manufactured goods, in which states in the North have comparative advantages. As a result, some developing countries had to open their home markets to foreign products, against which home industries were not competitive, yet see their own export products shut out of foreign markets. Current WTO negotiations are attempting to remedy this inequity but so far without success.

Another criticism leveled at the WTO centers on the trade dispute system, in which states may bring complaints of unfair trading practices. Such legal disputes can cost millions of dollars to litigate, requiring expensive lawyers and a large staff at WTO headquarters in Geneva, Switzerland. Few states in the global South can afford this legal process, and therefore few use it to help their own industries knock down unfair barriers to trade. Recall that even if a state wins a WTO dispute, it gains only the right to place tariffs on the offending country's goods in an equal amount. For small states, this retaliation can inflict as much damage on their own economies as on the economies of the offending states.

To compensate for these inequities and to help poor states use trade to boost their economic growth, the WTO has a Generalized System of Preferences (see Chapter 8). These and other measures—such as the Lomé and Cotonou conventions in which EU states relaxed tariffs on goods from the global South—are exceptions to the overall rules of trade and are intended to ensure that participation in world trade advances rather than impedes development. Nonetheless, critics claim that poor states are the losers in the overall world trade regime.

Countries in the South have responded in several ways to these problems with world economic regimes. In the 1970s, the Organization of the Petroleum Exporting Countries (OPEC) shifted the terms of trade for oil—bringing huge amounts of capital into the oil-exporting countries. Some states hoped such successes could be repeated for other commodities, resulting in broad gains for the global South, but this did not occur.

Policy Perspectives
President of Indonesia, Joko Widodo

PROBLEM How do you balance the demands of domestic actors and international financial institutions?

BACKGROUND Imagine that you are the president of Indonesia. Your economy suffered greatly in the 1997 Asian financial crisis, but since then you have experienced solid economic growth, even through the 2008–2009 global financial crisis. Annual GDP growth has hovered around 5 percent since 2003. Exports of raw materials comprise a significant portion of your economy. In general, international organizations have praised your economic success over the last decade.

Yet, one area of your economy has been significantly criticized. That is its level of protection—which entails not only trade protection but also regulation against foreign direct investment (FDI). Indonesia has some of the strongest regulations protecting firms in your country from taking investments from outside your country. Many of these laws were made to protect businesses owned by well-connected families (including those of former presidents). The laws ensured little outside interference in those industries, while guaranteeing profits for the politically powerful.

The IMF and private investment firms heavily criticize these restrictions on FDI. Until 2017, one of the major bond rating firms had refused to raise your bond rating in part because of the restrictions on foreign investment. Once it did raise your rating, portfolio investment (that is, in Indonesian stocks) did increase.

DOMESTIC CONSIDERATIONS You are a popular president and have been successful at undertaking some economic reform—even removing popular programs like fuel subsidies. Yet, the basis of your party support comes from the well-connected families and firms that benefit from investment and trade protection. Thus, your own party is supportive of the investment restrictions.

These investment restrictions are fairly popular among the population as well. In the eyes of the public, the laws prevent "foreign interference" with your economy—either from organizations like the IMF or from outside investors in China and the United States. You will be up for reelection in 2019, so

Mikhail Klimentyev/TASS/Alamy Stock Photo

having popular support for you and your party will become especially important in the near future.

SCENARIO Now imagine that a growing global trade war (that began between the United States and China) creates a significant downturn in your economy. Your economy is struggling and you begin to run significant budget and trade deficits. You turn to the IMF for an emergency loan to help get through the difficult times. The IMF says it is willing to help, but that as a condition of any new loan, you need to repeal regulations on foreign investment. Given that your country is now in need of foreign capital, the IMF will require this change before delivering a significant loan. And because the IMF monitors program commitments for years after a loan is made, any regulatory change will need to remain in place for many years.

CHOOSE YOUR POLICY Do you loosen your investment rules in order to encourage more FDI? Do you risk the domestic political backlash of this move, which would cause key supporters to oppose you? Do you hope that the global economic crisis will soon end and your economy will improve on its own? Do you keep Indonesia isolated from additional capital flows that could help increase economic growth?

Also in the 1970s, many poor and middle-income states tried to form a broad political coalition to push for restructuring the world economy to make North-South economic transactions more favorable to the South. A summit meeting of the non-aligned movement (see Chapter 2) in 1973 first called for a *New International Economic Order* (*NIEO*). Central to the NIEO was a shift in the terms of trade to favor primary commodities relative to manufactured goods. The NIEO proposal also called for the promotion of industrialization in the global South and for increased development assistance from the North. The NIEO never became much more than a rallying cry for the global South, partly because of the South's lack of power and partly because disparities within the South created divergent interests among states there.

Countries in the South continue to pursue proposals to restructure world trade to benefit the South. These efforts now take place mainly through the *UN Conference on Trade and Development* (*UNCTAD*), which meets periodically but lacks power to implement major changes in North-South economic relations. Attempts to promote South-South trade (reducing dependence on the North) have proven largely impractical. China sometimes uses the South-South solidarity argument in wooing new friends in Africa. And efforts continue to boost cooperation and solidarity in the global South through a variety of groups such as the nonaligned movement and the UN. Nonetheless, such efforts have done little to change the South's reliance on the North.

13.4 Foreign Assistance

Describe three reasons why countries might provide foreign aid to countries of the global South.

foreign assistance Money or other aid made available to third world states to help them speed up economic development or meet humanitarian needs. Most foreign assistance is provided by governments and is called official development assistance (ODA). See also *Development Assistance Committee* (*DAC*).

Foreign assistance is money or other aid made available to third world states to help them speed up economic development or meet humanitarian needs. Different kinds of development assistance have different purposes, which often overlap. Some are humanitarian, some are political, and others are intended to create future economic advantages for the giver. The state or organization that gives assistance is called a *donor*; the state or organization receiving the aid is the *recipient*. Foreign assistance creates, or extends, a relationship between donor and recipient that is simultaneously political and cultural as well as economic. Foreign assistance can be a form of power in which the donor seeks to influence the recipient, or it can be a form of interdependence in which the donor and recipient create a mutually beneficial exchange. The remainder of this chapter examines the patterns and types of foreign assistance, the politics involved, and the potential impact of foreign assistance.

13.4.1 Patterns of Foreign Assistance

Development Assistance Committee (DAC) A committee whose members—consisting of states from Western Europe, North America, and East Asia—provide 95 percent of official development assistance to countries of the global South. See also *foreign assistance*.

bilateral aid Government assistance that goes directly to third world governments as state-to-state aid.

multilateral aid Government foreign aid from several states that goes through a third party, such as the UN or another agency.

Large amounts of foreign assistance come from governments in the North. Of the nearly $160 billion in governmental foreign assistance provided in 2016, almost 90 percent came from members of the **Development Assistance Committee (DAC)**, consisting of states from Western Europe, North America, and East Asia. Several oil-exporting Arab countries provide some foreign development assistance, and in 2003, transition economies became a net "exporter" of financial aid. Three-quarters of the DAC countries' government assistance goes directly to governments in the global South as state-to-state **bilateral aid**; the rest goes through the UN or other agencies as **multilateral aid**.

The DAC countries have set themselves a goal to contribute 0.7 percent of their gross national products (GNPs) in foreign aid. But overall, they give less than half this amount. Only Norway, Luxembourg, Sweden, Denmark, the United Kingdom, and Germany meet the target. In fact, as shown in Figure 13.6, aid budgets declined

Figure 13.6 Foreign Assistance as a Percent of Donor's Income, 2016 and 1960–2016

Source: Based on OECD International Development Statistics.

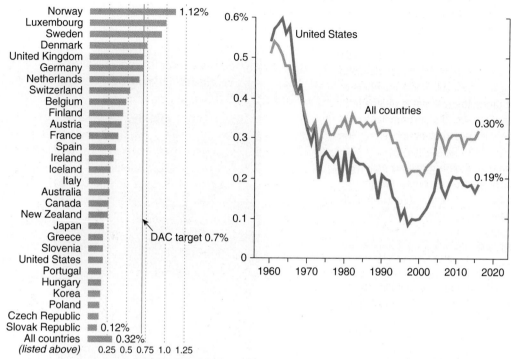

Note: Percent of Gross National Income, which is very close to GDP.

dramatically in the late 1960s and in the 1990s. They have recently returned to the higher levels in the 2000s, but the rise in antiglobalist sentiment of the past two years may erase those gains.

The United States gives one of the lowest percentages of GNP—about two-tenths of 1 percent—of the 30 states of the industrialized West that make up the Organisation for Economic Co-operation and Development (OECD). Yet, in terms of total monies given, the United States contributions are high (just not as a percentage of all U.S. income). In total economic aid given (over $34 billion in 2016), the United States holds a lead over Germany (giving around $25 billion a year) and Britain (which recently increased foreign aid to $18 billion). Japan and France each give $10 billion.

China has become a significant actor in the foreign aid area since 2010. By one estimate, between 2000 and 2014, China had given nearly as much aid ($350 billion) as the United States ($390 billion). Much of this was in the form of loans, with about half of the total amount of aid provided to the continent of Africa.

Another major source of foreign assistance is *UN programs*. The place of these programs in the UN structure is described in Chapter 7. The overall flow of assistance through the UN is coordinated by the **UN Development Program (UNDP)**, which manages 6,000 projects at once around the world (focusing especially on technical development assistance). Other UN programs focus on concentrating capital, transferring technology, and developing workforce skills for manufacturing. The UN Industrial Development Organization (UNIDO) works on industrialization, the UN Institute for Training and Research (UNITAR) on training and research. But most UN programs—such as UNICEF, the UN Population Fund (UNFPA), UNESCO, and the World Health Organization (WHO)—focus on meeting basic needs (see the Seeking the Collective Good box).

UN programs have three advantages in promoting economic development. One is that governments and citizens tend to perceive the UN as a friend of the global South, not an alien force, a threat to sovereignty, or a reminder of colonialism. Second,

UN Development Program (UNDP)
A program that coordinates the flow of multilateral development assistance and manages 6,000 projects at once around the world (focusing especially on technical development assistance).

Seeking the Collective Good
Trick or Treat for UNICEF

COLLECTIVE GOOD: Money to Help Poor Children Around the World

BACKGROUND: The world's children—2 billion people under age 18—have special humanitarian needs. The future depends on them, yet they are among the most vulnerable members of their societies and are most prone to preventable deaths from disease. The great majority of the world's children live in the global South, including large numbers in abject poverty in the poorest countries.

The international community has addressed children's needs through agencies for humanitarian, public health, and economic development assistance—notably through the UN Children's Fund (UNICEF). This benefit is enjoyed by humanity regardless of how much anyone contributes to it. If too many free-ride, however, UNICEF will lack resources and so will needy children.

CHALLENGE: In 2015, the UN adopted the Sustainable Development Goals (SDG) for reducing poverty in the global South. Many of the SDGs affect children, and UNICEF is a core participant. The ambitious goals are supposed to be met by 2030—giving the world 15 years to improve the lives of children in the developing world. And while the last 15 years have seen significant progress is improving the lives of children, more work remains to be done. In the global South, 22 percent of children were underweight, down from 31 percent in the 1990s but still far from meeting the SDG target. In primary-school enrollment, the global South rose from 82 to 91 percent but nearly 60 million children remain out of school.

SOLUTION: The dominance principle does not help the world's children, who occupy the low ranks of the world's hierarchies. Nor does UNICEF have the quality of mutual, reciprocal obligation and monitoring of commitments found in a reciprocity-based organization such as the WTO. Rather, UNICEF relies on voluntary contributions, two-thirds of them from governments and the rest from foundations, NGOs, and individuals. The identity principle works well in this situation because all the world's people were once children and can identify with children.

Pacific Press/Sipa USA/Newscom

Child dressed in UNICEF Trick-or-Treat drive coin box, 2017.

To play up this identity aspect, UNICEF began a campaign in 1950 called "Trick or Treat for UNICEF." As American schoolchildren collect treats on Halloween each year, they also collect contributions for UNICEF in an orange cardboard box. Currently, the campaign raises almost $5 million a year. More important, it has reinforced an identity link of Americans with UNICEF over the decades, helping produce almost $20 million more from U.S. foundations and grants as well as $130 million from the U.S. Congress. The top four donors to UNICEF after the United States are Norway, the Netherlands, Britain, and Sweden—all countries where humanitarian aid is a strong element of national identity.

UN workers may be more likely to make appropriate decisions because of their backgrounds. UN workers who come from the global South or who have worked in other poor countries in a region may be more sensitive to local conditions and to the pitfalls of development assistance than are aid workers from rich countries. Third, the UN can organize its assistance on a global scale, giving priority to projects and avoiding duplication and the reinvention of the wheel in each state.

One major disadvantage faced by UN development programs is that they are funded largely through voluntary contributions by rich states. Each program has to solicit contributions to carry on its activities, so the contributions can be cut off abruptly if the program displeases a donor government. Also, governments that pledge aid may not follow through. For instance, the UN complained in early 2005 that only 5 percent of the $500 million pledged for southern Sudan by the international community five months earlier had actually been paid. A second major disadvantage of UN programs is their reputation for operating in an inefficient, bureaucratic manner, without the cohesion and the resources that governments and MNCs in the North take for granted.

13.4.2 Types of Foreign Assistance

Bilateral aid takes a variety of forms. *Grants* are funds given free to a recipient state, usually for some stated purpose. *Technical cooperation* refers to grants given in the form of expert assistance in some project rather than just money or goods. *Credits* are grants that can be used to buy certain products from the donor state. For instance, the United States regularly gives credits that can be used to purchase U.S. grain. If people in a recipient country become accustomed to products from the donor state, they are likely to buy those same products in the future.

Peace Corps Press Office

HELPING OUT Governments provide around $20 billion annually in foreign assistance and private donors more than $50 billion in additional aid. In the West, the United States gives among the least amount of foreign aid as a percentage of GDP, despite recent increases. Here, a U.S. Peace Corps volunteer works in Panama, 2001.

Loans are funds given to help in economic development and must be repaid in the future out of the surplus generated by the development process (they too are often tied to the purchase of products from the donor state). Unlike commercial loans, government-to-government development loans are often made on concessionary terms, with long repayment times and low interest rates. Although still an obligation for the recipient country, such loans are relatively easy to service.

Loan guarantees, which are used only occasionally, are promises by the donor state to back up commercial loans to the recipient. If the recipient state services such debts and ultimately repays them, there is no cost to the donor. But if the recipient cannot make the payments, the donor has to step in and cover the debts. A loan guarantee allows the recipient state to borrow money at lower interest from commercial banks (because the risk to the bank is much lower).

Military aid is not normally included in development assistance, but in a broad sense it belongs there. It is money that flows from North to South, from government to government, and it does bring a certain amount of value into the economies of the global South. If a country is going to have a certain size army with certain weapons, getting them free from a donor state frees up money that can be used elsewhere in the economy. Of all the forms of development assistance, however, military aid is certainly one of the least efficient and most prone to impede rather than help economic development. It is also geared almost exclusively to political alliances rather than actual development needs.

The main agency dispensing U.S. foreign economic assistance (but not military aid) is the State Department's *Agency for International Development (USAID)*, which works mainly through the U.S. embassy in each recipient country. Major recipients of U.S. foreign aid include Israel, Egypt, and Turkey—all important strategic allies in the volatile Middle East.

The U.S. **Peace Corps** provides U.S. volunteers for technical development assistance in developing countries. They work at the request and under the direction of the host state but are paid an allowance by the U.S. government. Started by President Kennedy in 1961, the Peace Corps now sends over 7,000 volunteers to nearly 70 countries, where they participate in projects affecting about a million people.

Peace Corps An organization started by President John Kennedy in 1961 that provides U.S. volunteers for technical development assistance in third world states.

In foreign aid, the donor must have the permission of the recipient government to operate in the country. This goes back to the principle of national sovereignty and the history of colonialism. National governments have the right to control the distribution of aid and the presence of foreign workers on their soil. Only occasionally is this principle violated, as when the United States and its allies provided assistance to Iraqi Kurds against the wishes of the Iraqi government following the Gulf War. International norms may be starting to change in this regard, with short-term humanitarian assistance beginning to be seen as a human right that should not be subject to government veto.

PRIVATE AID   Private donations provide a smaller amount, although sometimes a significant one. For instance, the Bill and Melinda Gates Foundation contributes more than $4.5 billion annually to various programs, many focused on world health. Private aid is an important source of aid for the global South. By 2016, according to the OECD, private aid flows from DAC countries neared $150 billion. This figure was larger than official development assistance given by state governments.

There are many sources of private aid. Individuals in wealthy states may give as individuals (like Bill Gates or George Soros). Individuals may give to charities that send money or food abroad such as the Red Cross, Doctors without Borders, or their local church. One of the major private charitable groups is **Oxfam America** (one of seven groups worldwide descended from the Oxford Committee for Famine Relief, founded in 1942 in Britain).

Oxfam has developed a unique model of foreign assistance. Originally devoted to short-term aid to famine victims, and still active in that effort, Oxfam America realized that over the longer term, people need not just handouts of food but the means to feed themselves—land, water, seeds, tools, and technical training.

The distinctive aspect of the Oxfam model is that it relies on local communities to determine the needs of their own people and to carry out development projects. Oxfam does not operate projects itself but provides funding to local organizations. Nor does Oxfam call itself a donor and these organizations recipients. Rather, it calls both sides "project partners"—working together to accomplish a task. In this model, a little outside money can go a long way toward building sustained local economic development. Furthermore, projects help participants empower themselves by organizing to meet their own needs.

For example, Oxfam America helped an Ethiopian women's cooperative expand and increase employment. Oxfam did not design or organize the project; women in Addis Ababa did. But when their garment-making workshop became profitable and was ready to expand and employ twice as many women, Oxfam gave the group a $15,000 grant to build a new building.

The relationship between North and South—groups such as Oxfam and their project partners—is likened to a good marriage in which decisions are made jointly and dependency does not develop. In this model, economic development is not charity; it is in the interests of people in the rich countries as well as the poor. A cooperative relationship between North and South is essential for a peaceful and prosperous world. Even in a narrow economic sense, development in the global South creates new markets and new products that will enrich the industrialized countries as well. In economics, the creation of wealth is a positive-sum game.

The Oxfam approach seeks to reconceptualize development assistance to focus on long-term development through a bottom-up basic needs strategy and the political empowerment of poor people. The group's philosophy of a "rights-based approach to development" has drawn praise from human rights NGOs. Because of disappointment with the political uses of foreign aid in the past, Oxfam has tried to minimize the role of governments in its projects in both the North and South. For instance, Oxfam does not accept government funds, nor does it make grants to governments.

Oxfam America A private charitable group that works with local third world communities to determine the needs of their own people and to carry out development projects. Oxfam does not operate the projects but provides funding to local organizations to carry them out.

The general goals of the Oxfam model of foreign aid are consistent with a broader movement in the global South toward grassroots *empowerment*. Efforts such as those of Oxfam partners are organized by poor people to gain some power over their situation and meet their basic needs—not by seizing control of the state in a revolution but by means that are more direct, more local, and less violent. The key to success is getting organized, finding information, gaining self-confidence, and obtaining needed resources to implement action plans.

For example, in India, local women's groups using only the power of persuasion and logic have persuaded some landowners to give them land for cooperative income-generating projects such as vegetable farming and raising silkworms. Elsewhere in India, women working as gatherers of wood and other forest products got organized to win the legal minimum wage for 250,000 female forest workers—three times what they had been paid before. In this case, government action was necessary, but the pressure for such action came from local organizing. The women took their case to the public and the press, staging protest marches and getting an art exhibit relating to their cause displayed in the provincial capital.

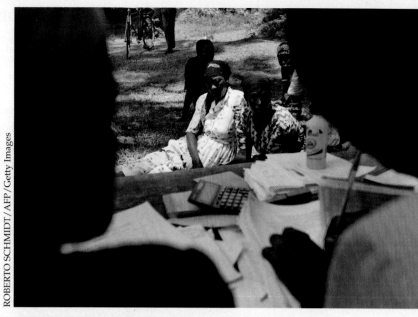

ROBERTO SCHMIDT/AFP/Getty Images

PARTNER IN DEVELOPMENT The Oxfam model of foreign assistance emphasizes support for local groups that can stimulate self-sustaining economic development at a local level. A mutually beneficial North-South partnership is the global goal of such projects. These women meet to discuss business issues with an Oxfam-affiliated group in Kenya, 2007.

Such examples do not mean that national and foreign governments are unimportant. On the contrary, government policies affect millions of people more quickly and more widely than do grassroots efforts. Indeed, grassroots organizing often has as an ultimate goal the restructuring of national political and social life so that policies reflect the needs of poor people. But the successes of grassroots empowerment show that poor communities can be more than victims of poverty waiting to be saved or passive bystanders in North-South relations. Nor do poor people need to place their hopes for change in violent revolutions aimed at toppling national governments—revolutions that lead to greater suffering more often than to stable economic development.

The Oxfam model to date has been tested on only a small scale. Although the model may be effective in the local communities it reaches, it would have to be adopted widely and replicated on a much larger scale in order to influence the overall prospects for development. In the case of assistance to survivors of the 2004 tsunami, Oxfam's $12 million in contributions compares with about 50 times that amount pledged by the U.S. government. It is unclear whether the principles that the model embodies, from a reliance on local community organizers to an avoidance of government involvement, would work on a massive scale. A model that bypasses governments also bypasses the majority of money spent for foreign aid globally.

One advantage of private aid giving, like that of Oxfam, is the flexibility with which it can be given. Private aid organizations may also be more efficient (due to their smaller size) and better able to create partnerships with local recipients. Unfortunately, private aid organizations' lack of size and official government status can also be a disadvantage. They can be barred from entering a country (Zimbabwe banned all private NGOs in 2008; Hungary debated a law to ban NGOs that provided assistance to immigrants in 2018), and they may have difficulty providing large-scale relief in times of crisis. They also may promote development policies that are at odds with government policy, putting them in conflict with other donor governments.

13.4.3 The Politics of Foreign Assistance

Many governments and private organizations provide ongoing development assistance in the form of projects in local communities in the South that are administered by agencies from the North to help meet basic needs. Such charitable programs are a useful means by which people in the North funnel resources to people in the South, but they may create unanticipated problems. For example, the programs do not address the causes of poverty, the position of poor countries in the world economy, or local political conditions such as military rule or corruption. In addition, photos of a hungry child may stare at the reader from a magazine page while the accompanying text notes that a few cents a day can "save" the child, and such approaches may raise awareness in the North of the extent of poverty in the South, but at worst they tend to be exploitive and to reinforce racist and paternalistic stereotypes of the helplessness of people in the global South.

Moreover, although the motivation for foreign aid is to help those who are less fortunate, donor states have discovered that foreign aid is also an important tool of leverage over recipient states. Many donor states thus try to use some types of foreign aid to create economic and political changes in recipient countries.

Like almost all donor states, the United States uses the promise of foreign aid, or the threat of cutting it off, as leverage in political bargaining with recipients. For example, when Pakistan proceeded in the late 1980s with a nuclear weapons program despite U.S. warnings, a sizable flow of U.S. aid was terminated. Then when Pakistan supported U.S. military action in next-door Afghanistan in 2001, U.S. aid was restored.

In 2004, the United States launched the Millennium Challenge Corporation (MCC), which increases U.S. aid but only to governments with certain policies, such as rule of law, control of corruption, investment in education, and sound fiscal management. After potential recipients apply for aid, a board composed of government and private officials reviews the applications. The applicants are then reviewed for their suitability for aid based on a set of criteria established by the MCC. In this way, the United States hopes to reduce the aid lost to corruption and waste.

Of course, foreign assistance is also a complicated domestic political process. Foreign assistance can be unpopular with portions of the public, who feel their tax dollars are going to those abroad rather than those "at home" (see the Public Opinion and International Relations box). This can lead to demands to provide only certain types of aid. For example, in recent years, aid advocates in the United States have fought a U.S. law requiring that food sent to feed the hungry be grown in the United States and shipped in U.S. vessels. Instead of this simple handout system, they proposed using U.S. funds to buy food locally in Africa, which would save a lot of money, get aid to the hungry people months faster, and help African farmers. But the proposal was opposed by the so-called Iron Triangle of food aid—U.S. agribusiness that profits from selling the food to the government, U.S. shipping companies that profit from shipping it, and U.S. charities (including CARE and Catholic Relief Services) that fund a healthy fraction of their budgets by selling in Africa some of the grain they ship from the United States. The charities, by becoming international grain merchants and flooding local markets with cheap food (both sold and given away), compete with local farmers and drive down local prices, harming long-term recovery. Yet because of the Iron Triangle's lobbying power, Congress killed off the proposal to allow purchase of local food in Africa.

The one type of foreign assistance that is the *least* politically motivated is disaster relief. It is the kind of foreign assistance given when poor people are afflicted by famine, drought, earthquakes, flooding, or other such natural disasters. (War is also a disaster and can compound naturally occurring disasters.) When disaster strikes a poor state, many people are left with no means of subsistence and often without their homes. **Disaster relief** is the provision of short-term relief to such people in the form of food, water, shelter, clothing, and other essentials.

disaster relief Provision of short-term relief in the form of food, water, shelter, clothing, and other essentials to people facing natural disasters.

Public Opinion and International Relations
The Politics of Foreign Aid

In the United States, it is possible that no foreign policy topic is debated more than foreign aid. Advocates contend aid is essential to provide basic goods (food and shelter) to poorer countries and is a moral necessity of foreign policy. Detractors suggest that much of the money is wasted by corrupt governments and that the money would be better spent within a donor country's own borders. This debate over aid is, in fact, reflected in the rising and falling levels of foreign aid that the United States has provided over time (see Figure 13.6). Advocates will control Congress, leading to larger budgets, only to be replaced by detractors, who cut aid spending.

Because the subject of foreign aid is so controversial, numerous polls have been conducted asking the American public their views on foreign aid. Figure 13.7 plots survey data asking about levels of foreign aid between 1970 and 2017. These polls ask respondents whether current foreign aid levels are about right, too little, or too much.

Throughout the 1970s and 1980s, the vast majority of Americans believe that foreign aid is too high. The least common answer, by far, is that the United States gives too little aid. This begins to change after 1990, although fairly slowly. Those believing American foreign aid budgets are too high falls more quickly, while those believing the aid budget is just right or too little grows. In recent years, those responding that they believe the United States gives too much foreign aid has reached new lows; yet, still nearly a majority of Americans express this opinion.

What accounts for the negative view of foreign aid levels in American public opinion? The main answer to this question is the public's incorrect beliefs about the size of the foreign aid budgets. When surveyed about how much of the total governmental budget is given to other countries in foreign aid, the average answer is typically 20 percent. In truth, about 1 percent of the budget goes to foreign aid.

What would happen if more Americans knew the true level of foreign aid? In two 2016 public opinion polls, when respondents were informed of the 1 percent figure, those answering "too much" dropped to 26 percent. In other words, it is likely that around one half of people who object to foreign aid might change their minds if they knew the facts surrounding the size of the aid budget.

Indeed, several U.S. secretaries of state note that the U.S. State Department has launched better efforts to educate the public about foreign aid levels. This could account for the decline in the number of Americans responding that "too much" is spent on foreign aid shown in Figure 13.7. No doubt other factors could play a role as well, but there is also little doubt that foreign aid will continue to be a politically divisive part of foreign policy.

Figure 13.7 Views on Foreign Aid Levels in the United States Since 1971

Source: Roper Center for Public Opinion Research, 2017

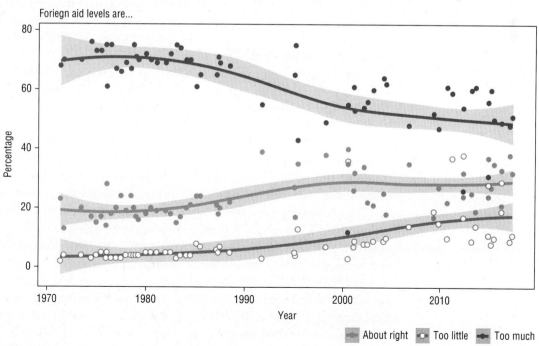

Disaster relief is very important because disasters can wipe out years of progress in economic development in a single blow. Generally, the international community tries to respond with enough assistance to get people back on their feet. The costs of such assistance are relatively modest, the benefits visible and dramatic. Having a system of disaster relief in place provides the global South with a kind of insurance against sudden losses that could otherwise destabilize economic accumulation.

Disasters generally occur quickly and without much warning. Rapid response is difficult to coordinate. International disaster relief has become more organized and better coordinated in the past decades, but it is still a complex process that varies somewhat from one situation to the next. Contributions of governments, private charitable organizations, and other groups and agencies are coordinated through the *UN Office of the Disaster Relief Coordinator (UNDRO)* in Geneva. In 2006, the UN set up a $500 million fund to enable it to respond quickly to disasters without waiting to raise funds first each time disaster strikes. Typically, international contributions make up no more than about one-third of the total relief effort, the remainder coming from local communities and national governments in the affected states.

Disaster relief is something of a collective good because the states of the North do not benefit individually by contributing, yet they benefit in the long run from greater stability in the South. Despite the potential collective action problem with a large number of actors, disaster relief is generally a positive example of international cooperation to get a job done—and an example of the use of the identity principle to solve a collective goods problem. Food donated by the World Council of Churches may be carried to the scene in U.S. military aircraft and then distributed by the *International Committee of the Red Cross (ICRC)*. Embarrassing failures in the past—of underresponse or overresponse, of duplication of efforts, or of agencies working at cross-purposes—became rarer in the 1990s, and in the twenty-first century, groups are coordinating their actions more effectively.

The devastating earthquake in Haiti in 2010 showed the progress and the limitations of international relief efforts. Overnight, millions lost family members, homes, possessions, safe drinking water, and ways of life. With no functioning government or medical care system, initial relief efforts were chaotic and international aid poorly coordinated. Many victims died as planes stacked up over the small airport, unable to deliver supplies. In days, however, U.S. military forces took over the airport, and massive international assistance flowed in. Governments and NGOs pledged billions of dollars to help Haiti get back on its feet under UN guidance.

Both international organizations (IOs) and NGOs quickly mobilized to carry out what has been termed the "largest relief effort in human history." The efforts of these organizations were coordinated through a variety of relief agencies, including the ICRC, the International Organization for Migration, the UN High Commissioner for Refugees (UNHCR), and Oxfam. Initially, it appeared as though the United States would coordinate its own relief efforts apart from the UN, but after reconsideration, the United States ceded the lead role in relief to the UN. This somewhat spontaneous coordination of states, IOs, and NGOs seems contrary to the anarchical international system.

The relationship between disasters and economic development is complex, and appropriate responses vary according to location, type and size of disaster, and phase of recovery. Different resources are needed in the emergency phase (for example, food and medical supplies) than in the reconstruction phase (for example, earthquake-resistant housing designs). Responses that are too small in scale or too short term may fail to meet critical needs, but those that are too large or prolonged can overwhelm the local economy and create dependency (reducing incentives for self-help).

International norms are changing regarding states' legal obligations to assist others in times of natural disaster and to accept such assistance if needed. Some have even suggested extending the idea of the responsibility to protect to the area of disaster relief. This idea became particularly relevant in the wake of Cyclone Nargis, which struck Burma in 2008. An estimated 130,000 people died in that natural disaster, yet the repressive government of Burma delayed or denied efforts of the international community to provide assistance to those affected by the cyclone. While aid did eventually flow into Burma, weeks had been wasted while the government denied the assistance needed for coping with the cyclone.

13.4.4 The Impact of Foreign Assistance

There is a danger in providing foreign assistance—especially in large-scale governmental aid programs—that people from the North may provide assistance inappropriate for a developing country's local conditions and culture. This danger is illustrated by an experience in Kenya in the 1970s. Nomadic herders in the area of Lake Turkana near the Sahara desert—the Turkana tribe—were poor and vulnerable to periodic droughts. Western aid donors and the Kenyan government decided that the herders' traditional way of life was not environmentally sustainable and should be replaced by commercial fishing of the abundant tilapia fish in Lake Turkana. Norway, with its long experience in fishing, was asked to teach fishing and boat-building methods to the Turkana. To create a commercially viable local economy, Norwegian consultants recommended marketing frozen fish fillets to Kenya and the world. Thus, in 1981, Norway finished building a $2 million, state-of-the-art fish-freezing plant on the shores of Lake Turkana and a $20 million road connecting the plant to Kenya's transportation system.

There were only three problems. First, with temperatures of 100 degrees outside (in contrast to Norway!), the cost of operating the freezers exceeded the income from the fillets. So after a few days, the freezers were turned off and the facility became a very expensive dried-fish warehouse. Second, Turkana culture viewed fishing as the lowest-status profession, suitable only for those incompetent at herding. Third, every few decades, Lake Turkana shrinks as drought reduces the inflow of water. Such a drought in 1984–1985 eliminated the gulf where the fishing operations were based. The Norwegians might have foreseen these problems by doing more homework instead of just transplanting what had worked in Norway. When the drought hit, the 20,000 herders who had been brought to the lake to learn fishing were left in an overcrowded, overgrazed environment in which every tree was cut for firewood and most cattle died. Instead of becoming self-sufficient, the Turkana people became totally dependent on outside aid.

In the past decade, many scholars have undertaken research to understand whether foreign aid is effective in creating economic growth and alleviating poverty in the global South. Heated debates now occur among academics and policy makers about whether aid is effective and, therefore, whether more or less should be given. On one side, scholars suggest increasing foreign assistance in order to deal with the crushing inequalities between the global North and the global South. Because the global South cannot reliably sustain capital accumulation, assistance from the North is necessary to jump-start economic growth.

Countering this position, however, is research suggesting that aid does not always help poor countries develop. In particular, unless recipient countries possess institutions that practice good government, aid will largely be wasted or fall into the hands of corrupt leaders. This research has been the inspiration for the United States' MCC policies as well as more IMF conditionality.

U.S Department of Defense

MOUTHWASH FOR MAURITANIA Sometimes foreign assistance contributes goods to third world economies with little understanding of local needs or long-term strategies. Here, free supplies including cartons of mouthwash are delivered by the U.S. ambassador and the captain of a U.S. Navy ship participating in Project Handclasp, 1989.

Other critics of aid suggest that it should be reduced in general. They contend that the flow of aid has allowed leaders in poor states to avoid difficult policy changes that would pave the way for long-term economic growth. They argue that in some African countries, the massive infusion of foreign assistance after decolonization has led to increased poverty and dependence on charity rather than increased wealth and independence.

CONFRONTING THE NORTH-SOUTH GAP   The giving and receiving of foreign assistance is political, even if the motivations for giving it are not. Perhaps most important is that people in the North become aware of the tremendous gap between North and South and try to address the problem. Poverty can seem so overwhelming that citizens in rich countries can easily turn their backs and just try to live their own lives.

But in today's interdependent world, this really is not possible. North-South relations have become part of everyday life. The integrated global economy brings to the North products and people from the South. The information revolution puts images of poverty on TV sets in comfortable living rooms. Security relations and political economy alike have shifted in the post–Cold War era to give new prominence to the global South.

Chapter Review

Summary

- Economic development in the global South has been uneven. In recent years many poor countries, led by China, have grown robustly. Growth in the global South was strong after the 2008–2009 recession but has recently slowed.

- Evidence does not support a strong association of economic growth either with internal equality of wealth distribution or with internal inequality.

- The newly industrializing countries (NICs) in Asia—South Korea, Taiwan, Hong Kong, and Singapore—show that it is possible to rise out of poverty into sustained economic accumulation.

- China has registered strong economic growth since the 1990s after its market-oriented economic reforms. Though still relatively poor on a per capita basis, China is the world's leading success story in economic development.

- Export-led growth has largely replaced import substitution as a development strategy. This reflects the experiences of the NICs and China as well as the theory of comparative advantage.

- The theory that democratization would accompany and strengthen economic development has not been supported by the actual experiences of poor countries. But the opposite theory—that authoritarian government is necessary to maintain control while concentrating capital for industrialization—has also not been supported.

- Government corruption is a major obstacle to development throughout the global South.

- Given the shortage of local capital in most poor states, foreign investment by MNCs can be a means of stimulating economic growth. MNCs look for favorable local conditions, including political and economic stability, in deciding where to invest.

- Debt, resulting largely from overborrowing in the 1970s and early 1980s, is a major problem in the global South. Through renegotiations and other debt management efforts, the North and South have improved the debt situation in recent years. However, the South remains $6 trillion in debt to the North.

- The IMF makes loans to states in the South conditional on economic and governmental reforms. These conditionality agreements often necessitate politically unpopular measures such as cutting food subsidies.

- The WTO trading regime works against the global South by allowing richer nations to protect sectors in which the global South has advantages—notably agriculture and textiles. The Generalized System of Preferences (GSP) tries to compensate by lowering barriers to exports from the global South.

- Foreign assistance, most of it from governments in the North, plays an important part in the economic development plans of the poorer states of the South.

- Only a few states in the North meet the goal of contributing 0.7 percent of their GNPs as foreign assistance to the South.

- Most foreign aid consists of bilateral grants and loans from governments in the North to specific governments in the South. Such aid is often used for political leverage and promotes the export of products from the donor state.

- Donors in the global North use various relief models to distribute aid to the developing world, each with advantages and drawbacks.

Key Terms

economic development   417
newly industrializing countries (NICs)   418
"four tigers"/"four dragons"   418
import substitution   428
export-led growth   428
microcredit   429
technology transfer   433

brain drain   433
default   433
debt renegotiation   433
Paris Club   434
London Club   434
IMF conditionality   435
foreign assistance   438

Development Assistance Committee (DAC)   438
bilateral aid   438
multilateral aid   438
UN Development Program (UNDP)   439
Peace Corps   441
Oxfam America   442
disaster relief   444

Critical Thinking Questions

1. How might the strong economic growth of the Asian NICs and of China affect proposals for an Asian free trade area similar to NAFTA and the EU? What would be the interests and worries of Japan, of China and the NICs, and of the poor states in the region about such an arrangement?

2. Past successes in economic development have depended heavily on developing a manufacturing base, which requires access to scarce capital. Do you think the information revolution and the increasing role of services in the world economy are changing this pattern? What does India's experience say about the feasibility of finding a niche in these growing sectors of the world economy and perhaps bypassing manufacturing?

3. How does the global South's debt problem compare with the U.S. debt, discussed in Chapter 9, in magnitude and effect? Do the two debt problems arise from similar causes? Which problem do you consider more serious, and why?

4. Some scholars criticize the IMF for imposing harsh terms in its conditionality agreements with poor states. Others applaud the IMF for demanding serious reforms before providing financial resources. If you were a leader negotiating with the IMF, what kinds of terms would you be willing to agree to and what terms would you resist? Why?

5. If the states in North America, Western Europe, and East Asia all were to meet the target of providing 0.7 percent of GNP in foreign assistance, what might the effects be? How much additional aid would be made available? To whom would it likely go? What effects might it have on the recipient states and on economic development overall?

Suggested Readings

Acemoglu, Daron, and James Robinson. *Why Nations Fail: The Origins of Power, Prosperity, and Poverty.* Crown Business, 2013.

Banerjee, Abhijit, and Esther Duflo. *Poor Economics: A Radical Rethinking of the Way to Fight Global Poverty.* PublicAffairs, 2012.

Carmody, Padraig. *The New Scramble for Africa.* Polity, 2011.

Chayes, Sarah. *Thieves of State: Why Corruption Threatens Global Security.* Norton, 2015.

Overholt, William H. *China's Crisis of Success.* Cambridge, 2017.

Panagariya, Arvind. *India: The Emerging Giant.* Oxford, 2010.

Let's Debate the Issue

Foreign Aid: A Solution to Development or a Source of Problems?

Overview

Billions of dollars per year in foreign aid flow from developed countries to developing countries. As discussed in this chapter, however, the amount of foreign aid from the Development Assistance Committee (DAC) has fluctuated greatly over time. When measured as a percentage of DAC countries' GDP, the amount of foreign aid has steadily fallen in the past four decades; however, when measured by absolute dollars, the amount has risen. Is the current giving by DAC countries enough?

Non-DAC foreign assistance has increased in absolute dollars. Multilateral agencies (such as investment banks and the UN) give over $40 billion to the global South. Private donors from DAC countries now provide nearly $50 billion in aid flows as well.

Recently, a controversy has emerged regarding the question of how much aid to give. Some prominent economists and political figures have called for large increases in foreign aid given by DAC countries, larger than the increases seen after the 9/11 attacks. There are some who doubt the wisdom of this course of action, however. While these skeptics do not necessarily call for decreasing foreign assistance, they argue that increasing the level of foreign aid would not help to achieve the ultimate goal of much of the aid, which is economic development. Should DAC countries significantly increase their foreign aid budgets? Would this increase in aid be a help or a hindrance to development?

ARGUMENT 1

DAC Countries Should Significantly Increase Foreign Aid

Foreign aid can help solve important problems.
From health care crises, infrastructure maintenance, and literacy programs to food assistance, foreign aid can be essential to help poorer states kick-start the development process. Higher levels of assistance would increase the quality of life for millions of people living in poverty abroad.

Increasing foreign aid will increase goodwill. As the United States and the EU compete for influence with China in places like Africa and Latin America, increasing foreign assistance will create tighter economic, political, and social bonds between DAC countries and recipient states, potentially preventing China from gaining allies in the developing world.

More foreign assistance will increase Western security. By providing money and other resources to stabilize poor countries, DAC countries decrease the chances that disaffected individuals in those countries will blame the West for their problems. This resentment often leads to anti-Western behavior—in the extreme case, support for terrorism.

ARGUMENT 2

DAC Countries Should Not Significantly Increase Foreign Aid

Large amounts of foreign aid are wasted or stolen.
Some economists estimate that, in certain cases, half of aid packages are stolen by corrupt leaders or state officials, while other times, the aid is simply wasted. Increasing foreign assistance will not help developing countries. It is just throwing good money after bad.

Large foreign aid flows will create dependencies.
Developing countries may get used to receiving large amounts of aid and neglect to develop internal programs to provide education, health care, or infrastructure maintenance. This dependency is dangerous for developing countries because it leaves them vulnerable to the policies of aid donors.

Foreign aid can violate recipients' sovereignty.
Most assistance programs come with strings (conditions) attached. Thus, as a condition for receiving aid, developing states must promise to make certain changes or perform specific tasks. This is a particularly egregious violation of sovereignty because it is done under the guise of helping the recipient states.

Questions

- Should DAC countries increase their foreign aid budgets significantly? Will this aid be a hindrance or a help to development?

- Can DAC countries afford to increase foreign aid significantly? What stops DAC countries from giving more foreign aid?

- Private NGOs (churches, the Bill and Melinda Gates Foundation, etc.) also now provide extensive amounts of aid to help developing countries. How should states and NGOs cooperate to maximize their efforts to provide foreign aid? Do you think private NGOs will be better at some tasks, while states will be better at others?

For Further Reading

Easterly, William. *The White Man's Burden: Why the West's Efforts to Aid the Rest Have Done So Much Ill and So Little Good.* Penguin, 2007.

Honig, Dan. *Navigation by Judgment: Why and When Top Down Management of Foreign Aid Doesn't Work.* Oxford, 2018.

Swedlund, Haley J. *The Development Dance: How Donors and Recipients Negotiate the Delivery of Foreign Aid.* Cornell, 2017.

Whitfield, Lindsay. *The Politics of Aid: African Strategies for Dealing with Donors.* Oxford, 2009.

Chapter 14
Postscript

Shen Zhengyi / AP Images

CHILDREN CLIMB A CLIFF LADDER TO ATTEND SCHOOL, CHINA, 2017.

Ultimately the conflicts and dramas of international relations are the problems of human society—struggles for power and wealth, efforts to cooperate despite differences, social dilemmas and collective goods problems, the balance between freedom and order, debates between globalists and nationalists, and trade-offs of equity versus efficiency and of long-term versus short-term outcomes. These themes are inescapable in human society, from the smallest groups to the world community. The subject of international relations is, in this sense, an extension of everyday life and a reflection of the choices of individual human beings. International relations (IR) belongs to all of us—North and South, women and men, citizens and leaders—who live together on this planet.

This book has shown that in IR, more than other social settings, collective goods problems pose formidable challenges to successful cooperation among the large number of independent (state and nonstate) actors. With no central government to enforce order, actors in IR have developed three kinds of solutions to collective goods problems—our three core principles. Countries turn to the dominance principle, especially military force, most often in international security affairs (Chapters 5 and 6). The identity principle matters most in the remarkable process of integration (Chapter 10). Most important, however, is the reciprocity principle, which underlies international treaties; law; and organizations, from the UN to the World Trade Organization (Chapter 7). Characteristic solutions based on the reciprocity principle are complicated, take forever to agree upon, and require extensive monitoring of compliance thereafter. But woven together, these reciprocity-based agreements offer the basis for an international system that has moved over centuries from extreme war-proneness to stronger and stronger peace and prosperity—notwithstanding the world's many serious remaining problems.

One major theme of this book is the nature of the international system as a well-developed set of rules based on state sovereignty, territoriality, and "anarchy"—a lack of central government. Yet the international system is becoming more complex, more nuanced, and more interconnected with other aspects of domestic societies. State sovereignty is now challenged by the principle of self-determination. International norms have begun to limit the right of government to rule a population by force against its will and to violate human rights. Territorial integrity is also problematic because national borders do not stop information, environmental changes, or missiles. Information allows actors—state, substate, and supranational—to know what is going on everywhere in the world and to coordinate actions globally.

Technological development is just one aspect of the profound yet incremental changes taking place in international relations. New actors are gaining power; long-standing principles are becoming less effective; and new challenges are arising for states, groups, and individuals alike. Technology is profoundly changing the utility and role of military force. Technology plays key roles on both sides in counterinsurgency wars and the other 14 active wars in the world.

Nonmilitary forms of leverage, particularly economic rewards, have become much more important power capabilities. The post–Cold War era is a peaceful one, yet the peace is fragile. Will this era, like past postwar eras, lapse slowly into the next prewar era, or will it lead to a robust and lasting "permanent peace" such as Kant imagined?

In international political economy (IPE), we see simultaneous trends toward integration and disintegration among states. People continue to speak their own language, to fly their own flag, and to use their own currency with its pictures and emblems. Nationalism continues to be an important force. At the same time, however, while people identify with their state, they also now hold competing identities based on ethnic ties, gender, and (in the case of Europe) region. In international trade, liberal economics prevails because it works so well. States have learned that to survive, they must act to support the creation of wealth by multinational corporations (MNCs) and other actors.

Environmental damage may become the single greatest obstacle to sustained economic growth in both the North and South. Because of high costs, the large number of actors, and collective goods problems, international bargaining over the environment is difficult.

Meanwhile, North-South relations are moving to the center of world politics. Demographic and economic trends are sharpening the global North-South gap, with the North continuing to accumulate wealth while much of the South lags. Ultimately, the North will bear a high cost for failing to address the economic development of the South. Perhaps, by using computerization and biotechnology innovations, poor states can develop their economies more efficiently and sustainably than did Europe or North America.

The future is unknowable now, but as it unfolds, you can compare it—at mileposts along the way—to the worlds that you desire and expect. For example, you could ask questions such as the following (asking yourself, for each one, why you answer the way you do for your desired future and expected future):

1. Will state sovereignty be eroded by supranational authority?
2. Will nationalism fade out or continue strong?
3. Will norms of human rights and democracy become global?
4. Will the UN evolve into a quasi-government for the world?
5. Will the UN (especially the Security Council) be restructured?
6. Will World Court judgments become enforceable?
7. Will International Criminal Court membership grow or shrink?
8. Will China become democratic?
9. What effects will information technologies have on IR?
10. Will weapons of mass destruction proliferate?
11. Will traditional forms of military leverage become less important?
12. Will disarmament occur?
13. Will women participate more fully in IR? With what effect?
14. Will there be a single world currency?
15. Will there be a global free-trade regime?
16. Will many people develop a global identity?
17. Will world culture become more homogeneous or more pluralistic?
18. Will the European Union (EU) or other regional international organizations (IOs) achieve full political union?
19. Will global environmental destruction be severe? If so, how soon?
20. Will new technologies avert environmental constraints?
21. Will global problems create stronger or weaker world order?
22. Will population growth continue to level out? If so, when and at what level?
23. Will the poorest countries accumulate wealth? If so, how soon and which ones?
24. What role will the North play in the South's development?

The choices you make and actions you take will ultimately affect the world you live in. You cannot opt out of involvement in international relations. You are involved, and year by year, the information revolution and other aspects of interdependence are drawing you more closely into contact with the rest of the world. You can act in many ways to bring the world you expect more into line with the world you desire. You can empower yourself by finding the actions and choices that define your place in international relations.

Now that you have completed the studies covered in this book, don't stop here. Keep learning about the world beyond your country's borders. Keep thinking about the world that might exist. Be part of the changes that will carry this world through the coming decades. It's your world: Study it, care for it, make it your own.

Glossary

acid rain   Rain caused by air pollution that damages trees and often crosses borders. Limiting acid rain (via limiting nitrogen oxide emissions) has been the subject of several regional agreements. (p. 364)

airspace   The space above a state that is considered its territory, in contrast to outer space, which is considered international territory. (p. 165)

alliance cohesion   The ease with which the members hold together an alliance; it tends to be high when national interests converge and when cooperation among allies becomes institutionalized. (p. 58)

Amnesty International   An influential nongovernmental organization (NGO) that operates globally to monitor and try to rectify glaring abuses of political (not economic or social) human rights. (p. 241)

anarchy   In IR theory, a term that implies not complete chaos but the lack of a central government that can enforce rules. (p. 46)

Anti-Ballistic Missile (ABM) Treaty (1972)   A treaty that prohibited either the United States or the Soviet Union from using a ballistic missile defense as a shield, which would have undermined mutually assured destruction and the basis of deterrence. (p. 199) See also *mutually assured destruction (MAD)* and *Strategic Defense Initiative (SDI)*.

arms race   A reciprocal process in which two or more states build up military capabilities in response to each other. (p. 68)

austerity measures   Government policies that severely cut government spending or raise taxes (or both). The policies are adopted to reduce government budget deficits, usually to pay off debt. (p. 300)

autarky   A policy of self-reliance, avoiding or minimizing trade and trying to produce everything one needs (or the most vital things) by oneself. (p. 261)

balance of payments   A summary of all the flows of money into and out of a country. It includes three types of international transactions: the current account (including the merchandise trade balance), flows of capital, and changes in reserves. (p. 298)

balance of power   The general concept of the power of one or more states being used to balance that of another state or group of states. The term can refer to (1) any ratio of power capabilities between states or alliances, (2) a relatively equal ratio, or (3) the process by which counterbalancing coalitions have repeatedly formed to prevent one state from conquering an entire region. (p. 48)

balance of trade   The value of a state's exports relative to its imports. (p. 258)

ballistic missiles   The major strategic delivery vehicle for nuclear weapons; it carries a warhead along a trajectory (typically rising at least 50 miles high) and lets it drop on the target. (p. 191) See also *intercontinental ballistic missiles (ICBMs)*.

basic human needs   The fundamental needs of people for adequate food, shelter, health care, sanitation, and education. Meeting such needs may be thought of as both a moral imperative and a form of investment in "human capital" essential for economic growth. (p. 385)

bilateral aid   Government assistance that goes directly to third world governments as state-to-state aid. (p. 438)

biodiversity   The tremendous diversity of plant and animal species making up the earth's (global, regional, and local) ecosystems. (p. 359)

Biological Weapons Convention (1972)   An agreement that prohibits the development, production, and possession of biological weapons but makes no provision for inspections. (p. 194)

brain drain   Poor countries' loss of skilled workers to rich countries. (p. 433)

Bretton Woods system   A post–World War II arrangement for managing the world economy, established at a meeting in Bretton Woods, New Hampshire, in 1944. Its main institutional components are the World Bank and the International Monetary Fund (IMF). (p. 296)

burden sharing   The distribution of the costs of an alliance among members; the term also refers to the conflicts that may arise over such distribution. (p. 58)

cartel   An association of producers or consumers (or both) of a certain product, formed for the purpose of manipulating its price on the world market. (p. 272)

cash crops   Agricultural goods produced as commodities for export to world markets. (p. 390)

central bank   An institution common in industrialized countries whose major tasks are to maintain the value of the state's currency and to control inflation. (p. 295)

centrally planned economy   An economy in which political authorities set prices and decide on quotas for production and consumption of each commodity according to a long-term plan. (p. 280)

chain of command   A hierarchy of officials (often civilian as well as military) through which states control military forces. (p. 201)

Chemical Weapons Convention (1992)   An agreement that bans the production and possession of chemical weapons and includes strict verification provisions and the threat of sanctions against violators and nonparticipants in the treaty. (p. 194)

Chernobyl   A city in Ukraine that was the site of a 1986 meltdown at a Soviet nuclear power plant. (p. 364)

civil-military relations   The relations between a state's civilian leaders and the military leadership. In most countries, the military takes orders from civilian leaders. In extreme cases, poor civil-military relations can lead to military coups. (p. 202)

civil war   A war between factions within a state trying to create, or prevent, a new government for the entire state or some territorial part of it. (p. 139)

Cold War   The hostile relations—punctuated by occasional periods of improvement, or détente—between the two superpowers, the United States and the Soviet Union, from 1945 to 1990. (p. 25)

collective goods problem   A tangible or intangible good, created by the members of a group, that is available to all group members regardless of their individual contributions; participants can gain by lowering their own contribution to the collective good, yet if too many participants do so, the good cannot be provided. (p. 4)

collective security   The formation of a broad alliance of most major actors in an international system for the purpose of jointly opposing aggression by any actor; sometimes seen as presupposing the existence of a universal organization (such as the United Nations) to which both the aggressor and its opponents belong. (p. 83) See also *League of Nations*.

Common Agricultural Policy (CAP) A European Union policy based on the principle that a subsidy extended to farmers in any member country should be extended to farmers in all member countries. (p. 323)

common market A zone in which labor and capital (as well as goods) flow freely across borders. (p. 323)

comparative advantage The principle that says states should specialize in trading goods that they produce with the greatest relative efficiency and at the lowest relative cost (relative, that is, to other goods produced by the same state). (p. 259)

compellence The threat of force to make another actor take some action (rather than, as in deterrence, refrain from taking an action). (p. 68)

Comprehensive Test Ban Treaty (CTBT) (1996) A treaty that bans all nuclear weapons testing, thereby broadening the ban on atmospheric testing negotiated in 1963. (p. 199)

conditionality See *IMF conditionality*.

conflict A difference in preferred outcomes in a bargaining situation. (p. 141)

conflict and cooperation The types of actions that states take toward each other through time. (p. 10)

conflict resolution The development and implementation of peaceful strategies for settling conflicts. (p. 95)

constructivism A movement in IR theory that examines how changing international norms and actors' identities help shape the content of state interests. (p. 88)

containment A policy adopted in the late 1940s by which the United States sought to halt the global expansion of Soviet influence on several levels—military, political, ideological, and economic. (p. 27)

convertible currency The guarantee that the holder of a particular currency can exchange it for another currency. Some states' currencies are nonconvertible. (p. 289) See also *hard currency*.

cost-benefit analysis A calculation of the costs to be incurred by a possible action and the benefits it is likely to bring. (p. 69)

Council of the European Union A European Union institution in which the relevant ministers (foreign, economic, agriculture, finance, etc.) of each member state meet to enact legislation and reconcile national interests. Formerly known as the Council of Ministers. When the meeting takes place among the state leaders, it is called the "European Council." (p. 324) See also *European Commission*.

counterinsurgency An effort to combat guerrilla armies, often including programs to "win the hearts and minds" of rural populations so that they stop sheltering guerrillas. (p. 176)

coup d'état French for "blow against the state"; a term that refers to the seizure of political power by domestic military forces—that is, a change of political power outside the state's constitutional order. (p. 203)

crimes against humanity A category of legal offenses created at the Nuremberg trials after World War II to encompass genocide and other acts committed by the political and military leaders of the Third Reich (Nazi Germany). (p. 243) See also *dehumanization* and *genocide*.

cruise missile A small winged missile that can navigate across thousands of miles of previously mapped terrain to reach a particular target; it can carry either a nuclear or a conventional warhead. (p. 193)

Cuban Missile Crisis (1962) A superpower crisis, sparked by the Soviet Union's installation of medium-range nuclear missiles in Cuba, that marks the moment when the United States and the Soviet Union came closest to nuclear war. (p. 27)

cultural imperialism A term critical of U.S. dominance of the emerging global culture. (p. 344)

customs union A common external tariff adopted by members of a free trade area; that is, participating states adopt a unified set of tariffs with regard to goods coming in from outside. (p. 323) See also *free trade area*.

cycle theories An effort to explain tendencies toward war in the international system as cyclical, for example, by linking wars with long waves in the world economy (Kondratieff cycles). (p. 143)

debt renegotiation A reworking of the terms on which a loan will be repaid; frequently negotiated by third world debtor governments in order to avoid default. (p. 433)

default Failure to make scheduled debt payments. (p. 433)

dehumanization Stigmatization of enemies as subhuman or nonhuman, leading frequently to widespread violence. (p. 147) See also *crimes against humanity* and *genocide*.

democratic peace The proposition, strongly supported by empirical evidence, that democracies almost never fight wars against each other (although they do fight against authoritarian states). (p. 86)

demographic transition The pattern of falling death rates, followed by falling birthrates, that generally accompanies industrialization and economic development. (p. 371)

dependency theory A Marxist-oriented theory that explains the lack of capital accumulation in the third world as a result of the interplay between domestic class relations and the forces of foreign capital. (p. 408) See also *enclave economy*.

deterrence The threat to punish another actor if it takes a certain negative action (especially attacking one's own state or one's allies). (p. 68) See also *mutually assured destruction (MAD)*.

devaluation A unilateral move to reduce the value of a currency by changing a fixed or official exchange rate. (p. 294) See also *exchange rate*.

developing countries States in the global South, the poorest regions of the world—also called *third world countries, less-developed countries*, or *underdeveloped countries*. (p. 383)

Development Assistance Committee (DAC) A committee whose members—consisting of states from Western Europe, North America, and East Asia—provide 95 percent of official development assistance to countries of the global South. (p. 438) See also *foreign assistance*.

difference feminism A strand of feminism that believes gender differences are not just socially constructed and that views women as inherently less warlike than men (on average). (p. 99)

digital divide The gap in access to information technologies between rich and poor people, and between the global North and the global South. (p. 337)

diplomatic immunity A privilege under which diplomats' activities fall outside the jurisdiction of the host country's national courts. (p. 235)

diplomatic recognition The process by which the status of embassies and that of an ambassador as an official state representative are explicitly defined. (p. 235)

direct foreign investment See *foreign direct investment*.

disaster relief Provision of short-term relief in the form of food, water, shelter, clothing, and other essentials to people facing natural disasters. (p. 444)

discount rate The interest rate charged by governments when they lend money to private banks. The discount rate is set by countries' central banks. (p. 296)

diversionary foreign policy   Foreign policies adopted to distract the public from domestic political problems. (p. 128)

Doha Round   A series of negotiations under the World Trade Organization that began in Doha, Qatar, in 2001. It followed the Uruguay Round and focused on agricultural subsidies, intellectual property, and other issues. (p. 266) See also *Uruguay Round*.

dominance   A principle for solving collective goods problems by imposing solutions hierarchically. (p. 4)

drones   Another term for unmanned aerial vehicles; these small flying vehicles, which can be armed or unarmed, are increasingly used in combat and reconnaissance operations. (p. 181)

dumping   The sale of products in foreign markets at prices below the minimum level necessary to make a profit (or below cost). (p. 263)

economic classes   A categorization of individuals based on economic status. (p. 93)

economic development   The combined processes of capital accumulation, rising per capita incomes (with consequent falling birthrates), increasing of skills in the population, adoption of new technological styles, and other related social and economic changes. (p. 417)

economic liberalism   In the context of international political economy (IPE), an approach that generally shares the assumption of anarchy (the lack of a world government) but does not see this condition as precluding extensive cooperation to realize common gains from economic exchanges. It emphasizes absolute over relative gains and, in practice, a commitment to free trade, free capital flows, and an "open" world economy. (p. 255) See also *mercantilism* and *neoliberal*.

economic surplus   A surplus created by investing money in productive capital rather than using it for consumption. (p. 398)

electronic warfare   Use of the electromagnetic spectrum (radio waves, radar, infrared, etc.) in war, such as employing electromagnetic signals for one's own benefit while denying their use to an enemy. (p. 183)

enclave economy   A historically important form of dependency in which foreign capital is invested in a third world country to extract a particular raw material in a particular place—usually a mine, oil well, or plantation. (p. 409) See also *dependency theory*.

enclosure   The splitting of a common area or good into privately owned pieces, giving individual owners an incentive to manage resources responsibly. (p. 350)

ethnic cleansing   Euphemism for forced displacement of an ethnic group or groups from a territory, accompanied by massacres and other human rights violations; it has occurred after the breakup of multinational states, notably in the former Yugoslavia. (p. 162)

ethnic groups   Large groups of people who share ancestral, language, cultural, or religious ties and a common identity. (p. 145)

ethnocentrism   The tendency to see one's own group (in-group) in favorable terms and an out-group in unfavorable terms. (p. 147)

Euratom   An organization created by the 1957 Treaty of Rome to coordinate nuclear power development by pooling research, investment, and management. (p. 323)

euro   Also called the ECU (European currency unit); a single European currency used by 19 members of the European Union (EU). (p. 327)

European Commission   A European Union body whose members, while appointed by states, are supposed to represent EU interests. Supported by a multinational civil service in Brussels, the commission's role is to identify problems and propose solutions to the Council of the European Union. (p. 324) See also *Council of the European Union*.

European Court of Justice   A judicial arm of the European Union, based in Luxembourg. The court has actively established its jurisdiction and its right to overrule national law when it conflicts with EU law. (p. 326)

European Parliament   A quasi-legislative body of the European Union that operates as a watchdog over the European Commission and has limited legislative power. (p. 325)

European Union (EU)   The official term for the European Community (formerly the European Economic Community) and associated treaty organizations. At the beginning of 2018, the EU has 28 member states, although Great Britain voted in 2016 to exit the EU. (p. 322) See also *Maastricht Treaty*.

exchange rate   The rate at which one state's currency can be exchanged for the currency of another state. Since 1973, the international monetary system has depended mainly on floating rather than fixed exchange rates. (p. 288) See also *convertible currency*; *fixed exchange rates*; and *managed float*.

export-led growth   An economic development strategy that seeks to develop industries capable of competing in specific niches in the world economy. (p. 428)

fiscal policy   A government's decisions about spending and taxation, and one of the two major tools of macroeconomic policy making (the other being monetary policy). (p. 300)

fissionable material   The elements uranium-235 and plutonium, whose atoms split apart and release energy via a chain reaction when an atomic bomb explodes. (p. 189)

fixed exchange rates   The official rates of exchange for currencies set by governments; not a dominant mechanism in the international monetary system since 1973. (p. 290) See also *floating exchange rates*.

floating exchange rates   The rates determined by global currency markets in which private investors and governments alike buy and sell currencies. (p. 290) See also *fixed exchange rates*.

foreign assistance   Money or other aid made available to third world states to help them speed up economic development or meet humanitarian needs. Most foreign assistance is provided by governments and is called official development assistance (ODA). (p. 438) See also *Development Assistance Committee (DAC)*.

foreign direct investment   The acquisition by residents of one country of control over a new or existing business in another country. Also called *direct foreign investment*. (p. 307)

foreign policy process   The process by which foreign policies are arrived at and implemented. (p. 130)

"four tigers"/"four dragons"   The most successful newly industrialized areas of East Asia: South Korea, Taiwan, Hong Kong, and Singapore. (p. 418)

free trade   The flow of goods and services across national boundaries unimpeded by tariffs or other restrictions; in principle (if not always in practice), free trade was a key aspect of Britain's policy after 1846 and of U.S. policy after 1945. (p. 257)

free trade area   A zone in which there are no tariffs or other restrictions on the movement of goods and services across borders. (p. 323) See also *customs union*.

game theory   A branch of mathematics concerned with predicting bargaining outcomes. Games such as Prisoner's Dilemma and Chicken have been used to analyze various sorts of international interactions. (p. 69)

gender gap   Refers to polls showing women lower than men on average in their support for military actions, as well as for various other issues and candidates. (p. 102)

General Agreement on Tariffs and Trade (GATT)   A world organization established in 1947 to work for freer trade on a multilateral basis; the GATT was more of a negotiating framework than an administrative institution. It became the World Trade Organization (WTO) in 1995. (p. 265)

General Assembly   See *UN General Assembly*.

Generalized System of Preferences (GSP)   A mechanism by which some industrialized states began, in the 1970s, to give tariff concessions to third world states on certain imports; an exception to the most-favored nation (MFN) principle. (p. 265) See also *most-favored nation (MFN)*.

genocide   An intentional and systematic attempt to destroy a national, ethnic, racial, or religious group, in whole or in part. It was confirmed as a crime under international law by the UN Genocide Convention (1948). (p. 149) See also *crimes against humanity* and *dehumanization*.

geopolitics   The use of geography as an element of power, and the ideas about it held by political leaders and scholars. (p. 46)

globalization   The increasing integration of the world in terms of communications, culture, and economics; may also refer to changing subjective experiences of space and time accompanying this process. (p. 16)

global warming   A slow, long-term rise in the average world temperature caused by the emission of greenhouse gases produced by burning fossil fuels—oil, coal, and natural gas. (p. 352) See also *greenhouse gases*.

gold standard   A system in international monetary relations, prominent for a century before the 1970s, in which the value of national currencies was pegged to the value of gold or other precious metals. (p. 288)

government bargaining model   A model that sees foreign policy decisions as flowing from a bargaining process among various government agencies that have somewhat divergent interests in the outcome ("where you stand depends on where you sit"). Also called *bureaucratic politics model*. (p. 114)

great powers   Generally, the half dozen or so most powerful states; the great power club was exclusively European until the twentieth century. (p. 50) See also *middle powers*.

greenhouse gases   Carbon dioxide and other gases that, when concentrated in the atmosphere, act like the glass in a greenhouse, holding energy in and leading to global warming. (p. 353)

gross domestic product (GDP)   The size of a state's total annual economic activity. (p. 12)

groupthink   The tendency of groups to validate wrong decisions by becoming overconfident and underestimating risks. (p. 117)

guerrilla war   Warfare without front lines and with irregular forces operating in the midst of, and often hidden or protected by, civilian populations. (p. 140)

hard currency   Money that can be readily converted to leading world currencies. (p. 290) See also *convertible currency*.

hegemonic stability theory   The argument that regimes are most effective when power in the international system is most concentrated. (p. 53) See also *hegemony*.

hegemonic war   War for control of the entire world order—the rules of the international system as a whole. Also called *world war*, *global war*, *general war*, or *systemic war*. (p. 130)

hegemony   The holding by one state of a preponderance of power in the international system so that it can single-handedly dominate the rules and arrangements by which international political and economic relations are conducted. (p. 52) See also *hegemonic stability theory*.

high seas   The portion of the oceans considered common territory, not under any kind of exclusive state jurisdiction. (p. 362) See also *territorial waters*.

home country   The state in which a multinational corporation (MNC) has its headquarters. (p. 309) See also *host country*.

host country   A state in which a foreign multinational corporation (MNC) operates. (p. 309) See also *home country*.

human rights   The rights of all people to be free from abuses such as torture or imprisonment for their political beliefs (political and civil rights) and to enjoy certain minimum economic and social protections (economic and social rights). (p. 238)

hyperinflation   An extremely rapid, uncontrolled rise in prices, such as occurred in Germany in the 1920s and in some third world countries more recently. (p. 289)

idealism   An approach that emphasizes international law, morality, and international organizations, rather than power alone, as key influences on international relations. (p. 41) See also *realism*.

identity   A principle for solving collective goods problems by changing participants' preferences based on their shared sense of belonging to a community. (p. 6)

IMF conditionality   An agreement to loan IMF funds on the condition that certain government policies are adopted. Dozens of third world states have entered into such agreements with the IMF in the past 30 years. (p. 435) See also *International Monetary Fund (IMF)*.

immigration law   National law(s) that establish the conditions under which foreigners may travel and visit within a state's territory, work within the state, and sometimes become citizens of the state (naturalization). (p. 234)

imperialism   The acquisition of colonies by conquest or otherwise. Lenin's theory of imperialism argued that European capitalists were investing in colonies where they could earn big profits and then using part of those profits to buy off portions of the working class at home. (p. 400)

import substitution   A strategy of developing local industries, often conducted behind protectionist barriers, to produce items that a country had been importing. (p. 428)

industrialization   The use of fossil-fuel energy to drive machinery and the accumulation of such machinery along with the products created by it. (p. 278)

industrial policy   The strategies by which a government works actively with industries to promote their growth and tailor trade policy to their needs. (p. 274)

infant mortality rate   The proportion of babies who die within their first year of life. (p. 374)

infantry   Foot soldiers who use assault rifles and other light weapons (mines, machine guns, etc.). (p. 175)

information screens   The subconscious or unconscious filters through which people put the information coming in about the world around them. (p. 115) See also *misperceptions and selective perceptions*.

intellectual property rights   The legal protection of the original works of inventors, authors, creators, and performers under patent, copyright, and trademark law. Such rights became a contentious area of trade negotiations in the 1990s. (p. 275)

intercontinental ballistic missiles (ICBMs)   The longest-range ballistic missiles, able to travel 5,000 miles. (p. 191) See also *ballistic missiles*.

interdependence   A political and economic situation in which two states are simultaneously dependent on each other for their well-being. The degree of interdependence is sometimes designated in terms of "sensitivity" or "vulnerability." (p. 79)

interest groups   Coalitions of people who share a common interest in the outcome of some political issue and who organize themselves to try to influence the outcome. (p. 122)

intergovernmental organization (IGO) An organization (such as the United Nations and its agencies) whose members are state governments. (p. 13)

International Committee of the Red Cross (ICRC) A nongovernmental organization (NGO) that provides practical support, such as medical care, food, and letters from home, to civilians caught in wars and to prisoners of war (POWs). Exchanges of POWs are usually negotiated through the ICRC. (p. 246)

International Court of Justice (ICJ) See *World Court*. (p. 230)

International Criminal Court (ICC) A permanent tribunal for war crimes and crimes against humanity. (p. 244)

international integration The process by which supranational institutions come to replace national ones; the gradual shifting upward of some sovereignty from the state to regional or global structures. (p. 319)

International Monetary Fund (IMF) An intergovernmental organization (IGO) that coordinates international currency exchange, the balance of international payments, and national accounts. Along with the World Bank, it is a pillar of the international financial system. (p. 297) See also *IMF conditionality*.

international norms The expectations held by participants about typical interactions among states. (p. 209)

international organizations (IOs) Intergovernmental organizations (IGOs) such as the UN and nongovernmental organizations (NGOs) such as the International Committee of the Red Cross (ICRC). (p. 210)

international political economy (IPE) The study of the politics of trade, monetary, and other economic relations among nations, and their connection to other transnational forces. (p. 10)

international regime A set of rules, norms, and procedures around which the expectations of actors converge in a certain international issue area (such as oceans or monetary policy). (p. 82)

international relations (IR) The relationships among the world's state governments and the connection of those relationships with other actors (such as the United Nations, multinational corporations, and individuals), with other social relationships (including economics, culture, and domestic politics), and with geographic and historical influences. (p. 2)

international security A subfield of international relations (IR) that focuses on questions of war and peace. (p. 10)

international system The set of relationships among the world's states, structured by certain rules and patterns of interaction. (p. 11)

International Whaling Commission An intergovernmental organization (IGO) that sets quotas for hunting certain whale species; states' participation is voluntary. (p. 359)

irredentism A form of nationalism whose goal is to regain territory lost to another state; it can lead directly to violent interstate conflicts. (p. 160)

Islam A broad and diverse world religion whose divergent populations include Sunni Muslims, Shi'ite Muslims, and many smaller branches and sects from Nigeria to Indonesia, centered in the Middle East and South Asia. (p. 151)

Islamist Describing a political ideology based on instituting Islamic principles and laws in government. A broad range of groups using diverse methods come under this category. (p. 151)

issue areas Distinct spheres of international activity (such as global trade negotiations) within which policy makers of various states face conflicts and sometimes achieve cooperation. (p. 9)

just wars A category in international law and political theory that defines when wars can be justly started (*jus ad bellum*) and how they can be justly fought (*jus in bello*). (p. 237) See also *war crimes*.

Keynesian economics The principles articulated by British economist John Maynard Keynes, used successfully in the Great Depression of the 1930s, including the view that governments should sometimes use deficit spending to stimulate economic growth. (p. 300)

Kyoto Protocol (1997) A major international treaty on global warming, which entered into effect in 2005 and mandated cuts in carbon emissions. Almost all the world's major countries, except the United States, were participants. (p. 354)

landmines Concealed explosive devices, often left behind by irregular armies, that kill or maim civilians after wars end. Such mines number more than 100 million, primarily in Angola, Bosnia, Afghanistan, and Cambodia. A movement to ban landmines is underway; more than 100 states have agreed to do so. (p. 177)

land reform Policies that aim to break up large landholdings and redistribute land to poor peasants for use in subsistence farming. (p. 391)

League of Nations An organization established after World War I and a forerunner of today's United Nations; it achieved certain humanitarian and other successes but was weakened by the absence of U.S. membership and by its own lack of effectiveness in ensuring collective security. (p. 23) See also *collective security*.

less-developed countries (LDCs) The world's poorest regions—the global South—where most people live. Also called *underdeveloped countries* or *developing countries*. (p. 383)

liberal feminism A strand of feminism that emphasizes gender equality and views the "essential" differences in men's and women's abilities or perspectives as trivial or nonexistent. (p. 99)

limited war Military actions that seek objectives short of the surrender and occupation of the enemy. (p. 139)

Lisbon Treaty A European Union agreement that replaces a failed attempt at an EU constitution with a similar set of reforms strengthening central EU authority and modifying voting procedures among the EU's expanded membership. (p. 337)

London Club A group of private creditors that have loaned money to third world governments; it meets periodically to work out terms of debt renegotiations. (p. 434) See also *Paris Club*.

Maastricht Treaty A treaty signed in the Dutch city of Maastricht and ratified in 1992; it commits the European Union to monetary union (a single currency and European Central Bank) and to a common foreign policy. (p. 327) See also *European Union (EU)*.

malnutrition A lack of needed foods including protein and vitamins; about 3 million children die each year from malnutrition-related causes. (p. 388)

managed float A system of occasional multinational government interventions in currency markets to manage otherwise free-floating currency rates. (p. 290)

Marxism A branch of socialism that emphasizes exploitation and class struggle and includes both communism and other approaches. (p. 93)

mediation The use of a third party (or parties) in conflict resolution. (p. 95)

mercantilism An economic theory and a political ideology opposed to free trade; it shares with realism the belief that each state must protect its own interests without seeking mutual gains through international organizations. (p. 255) See also *economic liberalism*.

microcredit The use of very small loans to small groups of individuals, often women, to stimulate economic development. (p. 429)

middle powers States that rank somewhat below the great powers in terms of their influence on world affairs (for example, Brazil and India). (p. 51) See also *great powers*.

migration Movement between states, usually *emigration* from the old state and *immigration* to the new state. (p. 393)

militarism The glorification of war, military force, and violence. (p. 96)

military governments States in which military forces control the government; they are most common in third world countries, where the military may be the only large modern institution. (p. 203)

military-industrial complex A huge interlocking network of governmental agencies, industrial corporations, and research institutes, all working together to promote and benefit from military spending. (p. 124)

misperceptions and selective perceptions The mistaken processing of the available information about a decision; one of several ways—along with affective and cognitive bias—in which individual decision making diverges from the rational model. (p. 115) See also *information screens.*

Missile Technology Control Regime A set of agreements through which industrialized states try to limit the flow of missile-relevant technology to third world states. (p. 193)

mixed economies Economies such as those in the industrialized West that contain both some government control and some private ownership. (p. 280)

monetary policy A government's decisions about printing and circulating money, and one of the two major tools of macroeconomic policy making (the other being fiscal policy). (p. 300)

Montreal Protocol (1987) An agreement on protection of the ozone layer in which states pledged to reduce and then eliminate use of chlorofluorocarbons (CFCs). It is the most successful environmental treaty to date. (p. 357)

most-favored nation (MFN) A principle by which one state, by granting another state MFN status, promises to give it the same treatment given to the first state's most-favored trading partner. (p. 265) See also *Generalized System of Preferences* (*GSP*).

multilateral aid Government foreign aid from several states that goes through a third party, such as the UN or another agency. (p. 438)

multinational corporation (MNC) A company based in one state with affiliated branches or subsidiaries operating in other states. (p. 305) See also *home country* and *host country.*

multipolar system An international system with typically five or six centers of power that are not grouped into alliances. (p. 51)

Munich Agreement A symbol of the failed policy of appeasement, this agreement, signed in 1938, allowed Nazi Germany to occupy a part of Czechoslovakia. Rather than appease German aspirations, it was followed by further German expansions, which triggered World War II. (p. 23)

Muslims See *Islam.* (p. 142)

mutually assured destruction (MAD) The possession of second-strike nuclear capabilities, which ensures that neither of two adversaries could prevent the other from destroying it in an all-out war. (p. 197) See also *deterrence.*

national debt The amount a government owes in debt as a result of deficit spending. (p. 302)

national interest The interests of a state overall (as opposed to particular parties or factions within the state). (p. 69)

nationalism Identification with and devotion to the interests of one's nation. It usually involves a large group of people who share a national identity and often a language, culture, or ancestry. (p. 144)

nation-states States whose populations share a sense of national identity, usually including a language and culture. (p. 11)

neocolonialism The continuation, in a former colony, of colonial exploitation without formal political control. (p. 408)

neofunctionalism A theory that holds that economic integration (functionalism) generates a "spillover" effect, resulting in increased political integration. (p. 320)

neoliberal Shorthand for "neoliberal institutionalism," an approach that stresses the importance of international institutions in reducing the inherent conflict that realists assume in an international system; the reasoning is based on the core liberal idea that seeking long-term mutual gains is often more rational than maximizing individual short-term gains. (p. 80) See also *economic liberalism.*

neorealism A version of realist theory that emphasizes the influence on state behavior of the system's structure, especially the international distribution of power. (p. 51) See also *realism.*

newly industrializing countries (NICs) Third world states that have achieved self-sustaining capital accumulation, with impressive economic growth. The most successful are the "four tigers" or "four dragons" of East Asia: South Korea, Taiwan, Hong Kong, and Singapore. (p. 418)

nonaligned movement A movement of third world states, led by India and Yugoslavia, that attempted to stand apart from the U.S.-Soviet rivalry during the Cold War. (p. 64)

nongovernmental organization (NGO) A transnational group or entity (such as the Catholic Church, Greenpeace, or the International Olympic Committee) that interacts with states, multinational corporations (MNCs), other NGOs, and intergovernmental organizations (IGOs). (p. 13)

Non-Proliferation Treaty (NPT) (1968) A treaty that created a framework for controlling the spread of nuclear materials and expertise, including the International Atomic Energy Agency (IAEA), a UN agency based in Vienna that is charged with inspecting the nuclear power industry in NPT member states to prevent secret military diversions of nuclear materials. (p. 196)

nonstate actors Actors other than state governments that operate either below the level of the state (that is, within states) or across state borders. (p. 13)

nontariff barriers Forms of restricting imports other than tariffs, such as quotas (ceilings on how many goods of a certain kind can be imported). (p. 263)

norms The shared expectations about what behavior is considered proper. (p. 46)

North American Free Trade Agreement (NAFTA) A free trade zone encompassing the United States, Canada, and Mexico since 1994. (p. 269)

North Atlantic Treaty Organization (NATO) A U.S.-led military alliance, formed in 1949 with mainly Western European members, to oppose and deter Soviet power in Europe. It is currently expanding into the former Soviet bloc. (p. 59) See also *Warsaw Pact.*

North-South gap The disparity in resources (income, wealth, and power) between the industrialized, relatively rich countries of the West (and the former East) and the poorer countries of Africa, the Middle East, and much of Asia and Latin America. (p. 18)

optimizing Picking the very best option; contrasts with satisficing, or finding a satisfactory but less than best solution to a problem. The model of "bounded rationality" postulates that decision makers generally "satisfice" rather than optimize. (p. 117)

organizational process model A decision-making model in which policy makers or lower-level officials rely largely on standardized responses or standard operating procedures. (p. 114)

Organization of the Petroleum Exporting Countries (OPEC) The most prominent cartel in the international economy;

its members control about half the world's total oil exports, enough to affect the world price of oil significantly. (p. 272)

Oxfam America   A private charitable group that works with local third world communities to determine the needs of their own people and to carry out development projects. Oxfam does not operate the projects but provides funding to local organizations to carry them out. (p. 442)

ozone layer   The part of the atmosphere that screens out harmful ultraviolet rays from the sun. Certain chemicals used in industrial economies break down the ozone layer. (p. 357)

Paris Climate Agreement   The main international agreement on global warming signed in 2015. Calls for keeping a global temperature rise this century well below 2 degrees Celsius above preindustrial levels. Nearly all countries of the world are participants. (p. 356)

Paris Club   A group of first world governments that have loaned money to third world governments; it meets periodically to work out terms of debt renegotiations. (p. 434) See also *London Club*.

peacebuilding   The use of military peacekeepers, civilian administrators, police trainers, and similar efforts to sustain peace agreements and build stable, democratic governments in societies recovering from civil wars. Since 2005, a UN Peacebuilding Commission has coordinated and supported these activities. (p. 222)

Peace Corps   An organization started by President John Kennedy in 1961 that provides U.S. volunteers for technical development assistance in third world states. (p. 441)

peace movements   Movements against specific wars or against war and militarism in general, usually involving large numbers of people and forms of direct action such as street protests. (p. 97)

positive peace   A peace that resolves the underlying reasons for war; not just a cease-fire but a transformation of relationships, including elimination or reduction of economic exploitation and political oppression. (p. 96)

postmodern feminism   An effort to combine feminist and postmodernist perspectives with the aim of uncovering the hidden influences of gender in IR and showing how arbitrary the construction of gender roles is. (p. 99)

postmodernism   An approach that denies the existence of a single fixed reality and pays special attention to texts and to discourses—that is, to how people talk and write about a subject. (p. 92)

power   The ability or potential to influence others' behavior, as measured by the possession of certain tangible and intangible characteristics. (p. 43)

power projection   The ability to use military force in areas far from a country's region or sphere of influence. (p. 177)

power transition theory   A theory that the largest wars result from challenges to the top position in the status hierarchy, when a rising power is surpassing (or threatening to surpass) the most powerful state. (p. 52)

Prisoner's Dilemma (PD)   A situation modeled by game theory in which rational actors pursuing their individual interests all achieve worse outcomes than they could have by working together. (p. 69)

prisoners of war (POWs)   Soldiers who have surrendered and who thereby receive special status under the laws of war. (p. 246)

proliferation   The spread of weapons of mass destruction (nuclear, chemical, or biological weapons) into the hands of more actors. (p. 195)

pronatalist   Describing government policy that encourages or forces childbearing, and outlaws or limits access to contraception. (p. 373)

prospect theory   A decision-making theory that holds that options are assessed by comparison to a reference point, which is often the status quo but might be some past or expected situation. The model also holds that decision makers fear losses more than they value gains. (p. 117)

protectionism   The protection of domestic industries against international competition, by trade tariffs and other means. (p. 262)

proxy wars   Wars in the third world—often civil wars—in which the United States and the Soviet Union jockeyed for position by supplying and advising opposing factions. (p. 28)

public opinion   In IR, the range of views on foreign policy issues held by the citizens of a state. (p. 124)

"rally 'round the flag" syndrome   The public's increased support for government leaders during wartime, at least in the short term. (p. 128)

rational actors   Actors conceived of as single entities that can "think" about their actions coherently, make choices, identify their interests, and rank the interests in terms of priority. (p. 68)

rational model   A model in which decision makers calculate the costs and benefits of each possible course of action, then choose the one with the highest benefits and lowest costs. (p. 113)

realism   A broad intellectual tradition that explains international relations mainly in terms of power. (p. 41) See also *idealism* and *neorealism*.

reciprocity   A response in kind to another's actions; a strategy of reciprocity uses positive forms of leverage to promise rewards and negative forms of leverage to threaten punishment. (p. 5)

refugees   People fleeing their countries to find refuge from war, natural disaster, or political persecution. International law distinguishes them from migrants. (p. 394)

remittances   Money sent home by migrant workers to individuals (usually relatives) in their country of origin. (p. 396)

reserves   Hard-currency stockpiles kept by states. (p. 290)

resource curse   The difficulties faced by resource-rich developing countries, including dependence on exporting one or a few commodities whose prices fluctuate, as well as potentials for corruption and inequality. (p. 400)

responsibility to protect (R2P)   Principle adopted by world leaders in 2005 holding governments responsible for protecting civilians from genocide and crimes against humanity perpetrated within a sovereign state. (p. 242)

satisficing   The act of finding a satisfactory or "good enough" solution to a problem. (p. 117)

Secretariat   See *UN Secretariat*.

secular   Created apart from religious establishments and in which there is a high degree of separation between religious and political organizations. (p. 151)

security community   A situation in which low expectations of interstate violence permit a high degree of political cooperation—as, for example, among NATO members. (p. 321)

Security Council   See *UN Security Council*.

security dilemma   A situation in which actions that states take to ensure their own security (such as deploying more military forces) are perceived as threats to the security of other states. (p. 48)

service sector   The part of an economy that concerns services (as opposed to the production of tangible goods); the key focus in international trade negotiations is on banking, insurance, and related financial services. (p. 275)

Single European Act (1985)   An act that set a target date of the end of 1992 for the creation of a true common market (free cross-border movement of goods, capital, people, and services) in the European Community (EC). (p. 326)

Sino-Soviet split A rift in the 1960s between the communist powers of the Soviet Union and China, fueled by China's opposition to Soviet moves toward peaceful coexistence with the United States. (p. 27)

sovereignty A state's right, at least in principle, to do whatever it wants within its own territory; traditionally, sovereignty is the most important international norm. (p. 46)

Special Drawing Right (SDR) A world currency created by the International Monetary Fund (IMF) to replace gold as a world standard. Valued by a "basket" of national currencies, the SDR has been called "paper gold." (p. 297)

state An inhabited territorial entity controlled by a government that exercises sovereignty over its territory. (p. 10)

state-owned industries Industries such as oil-production companies and airlines that are owned wholly or partly by the state because they are thought to be vital to the national economy. (p. 280)

state-sponsored terrorism The use of terrorist groups by states, usually under control of a state's intelligence agency, to achieve political aims. (p. 187)

stealth technology The use of special radar-absorbent materials and unusual shapes in the design of aircraft, missiles, and ships to scatter enemy radar. (p. 184)

Strategic Defense Initiative (SDI) A U.S. effort, also known as Star Wars, to develop defenses that could shoot down incoming ballistic missiles, spurred by President Ronald Reagan in 1983. Critics call it an expensive failure that will likely be ineffective. (p. 197) See also *Anti-Ballistic Missile (ABM) Treaty*.

subsistence farming Rural communities growing food mainly for their own consumption rather than for sale in local or world markets. (p. 390)

subtext Meanings that are implicit or hidden in a text rather than explicitly addressed. (p. 92) See also *postmodernism*.

summit meeting A meeting between heads of state, often referring to leaders of great powers, as in the Cold War superpower summits between the United States and the Soviet Union or today's meetings of the Group of Twenty (G20) on economic coordination. (p. 27)

supranational Larger institutions and groupings such as the European Union to which state authority or national identity is subordinated. (p. 319)

Sustainable Development Goals (SDGs) UN targets for basic needs measures such as reducing poverty and hunger, adopted in 2015. (p. 383)

tariff A duty or tax levied on certain types of imports (usually as a percentage of their value) as they enter a country. (p. 263)

technology transfer Third world states' acquisition of technology (knowledge, skills, methods, designs, specialized equipment, etc.) from foreign sources, usually in conjunction with direct foreign investment or similar business operations. (p. 433)

territorial waters The waters near states' shores generally treated as part of national territory. The UN Convention on the Law of the Sea provides for a 12-mile territorial sea (exclusive national jurisdiction over shipping and navigation) and a 200-mile exclusive economic zone (EEZ; covering exclusive fishing and mineral rights but allowing for free navigation by all). (p. 164) See also *high seas* and *UN Convention on the Law of the Sea (UNCLOS)*.

third world countries See *less-developed countries (LDCs)*.

total war Warfare by one state waged to conquer and occupy another; modern total war originated in the Napoleonic Wars, which relied on conscription on a mass scale. (p. 139)

tragedy of the commons A collective goods dilemma that is created when common environmental assets (such as the world's fisheries) are depleted or degraded through the failure of states to cooperate effectively. One solution is to "enclose" the commons (split them into individually owned pieces); international regimes can also be a (partial) solution. (p. 350)

transitional economies Countries in Russia and Eastern Europe that are trying to convert from communism to capitalism, with various degrees of success. (p. 280)

Treaty of Rome (1957) The founding document of the European Economic Community (EEC) or Common Market, now subsumed by the European Union. (p. 323)

truth commissions Governmental bodies established in several countries after internal wars to hear honest testimony and bring to light what really happened during these wars, and in exchange to offer most of the participants asylum from punishment. (p. 141)

UN Charter The founding document of the United Nations; it is based on the principles that states are equal, have sovereignty over their own affairs, enjoy independence and territorial integrity, and must fulfill international obligations. The Charter also lays out the structure and methods of the UN. (p. 212)

UN Conference on Trade and Development (UNCTAD) A structure established in 1964 to promote third world development through various trade proposals. (p. 227)

UN Convention on the Law of the Sea (UNCLOS) A world treaty (1982) governing use of the oceans. The UNCLOS treaty established rules on territorial waters and a 200-mile exclusive economic zone (EEZ). (p. 362) See also *territorial waters*.

UN Development Program (UNDP) A program that coordinates the flow of multilateral development assistance and manages 6,000 projects at once around the world (focusing especially on technical development assistance). (p. 439)

UN Environment Program (UNEP) A program that monitors environmental conditions and, among other activities, works with the World Meteorological Organization to measure changes in global climate. (p. 353)

UN General Assembly A body composed of representatives of all states that allocates UN funds, passes nonbinding resolutions, and coordinates third world development programs and various autonomous agencies through the Economic and Social Council (ECOSOC). (p. 213)

UN Secretariat The UN's executive branch, led by the Secretary General. (p. 213)

UN Security Council A body of five great powers (which can veto resolutions) and ten rotating member states that makes decisions about international peace and security, including the dispatch of UN peacekeeping forces. (p. 213)

U.S.-Japanese Security Treaty A bilateral alliance between the United States and Japan, created in 1951 against the potential Soviet threat to Japan. The United States maintains troops in Japan and is committed to defend Japan if that nation is attacked, and Japan pays the United States to offset about half the cost of maintaining the troops. (p. 62)

Universal Declaration of Human Rights (UDHR) (1948) The core UN document on human rights; although it lacks the force of international law, it sets forth international norms regarding behavior by governments toward their own citizens and foreigners alike. (p. 239)

urbanization A shift of population from the countryside to the cities that typically accompanies economic development and is augmented by displacement of peasants from subsistence farming. (p. 390)

Uruguay Round A series of negotiations under the General Agreement on Tariffs and Trade (GATT) that began in Uruguay in

1986 and concluded in 1994 with agreement to create the World Trade Organization. The Uruguay Round followed earlier GATT negotiations such as the Kennedy Round and the Tokyo Round. (p. 266) See also *World Trade Organization* (*WTO*).

virtual currencies   Currencies created by users as a way to facilitate the exchange of goods and services beyond the control of governments. (p. 342)

war crimes   Violations of the law governing the conduct of warfare, such as mistreatment of prisoners of war or the unnecessary targeting of civilians. (p. 343) See also *just wars*.

Warsaw Pact   A Soviet-led Eastern European military alliance founded in 1955 and disbanded in 1991. It opposed the NATO alliance. (p. 59) See also *North Atlantic Treaty Organization* (*NATO*).

weapons of mass destruction (WMDs)   Nuclear, chemical, and biological weapons, all distinguished from conventional weapons by their enormous potential lethality and their relative lack of discrimination in whom they kill. (p. 189)

World Bank   Formally the International Bank for Reconstruction and Development (IBRD), an organization that was established in 1944 as a source of loans to help reconstruct the European economies. Later, the main borrowers were third world countries and, in the 1990s, Eastern European ones. (p. 296)

World Court   Also called the International Court of Justice (ICJ). The judicial arm of the UN; located in The Hague, it hears only cases between states. (p. 230)

world government   A centralized world governing body with strong enforcement powers. (p. 97)

World Health Organization (WHO)   An organization based in Geneva that provides technical assistance to improve health conditions in the third world and conducts major immunization campaigns. (p. 227)

world-system   A view of the world in terms of regional class divisions, with industrialized countries as the core, poorest countries as the periphery, and other areas (for example, some of the newly industrializing countries) as the semiperiphery. (p. 398)

World Trade Organization (WTO)   An organization begun in 1995 that replaced the GATT and expanded its traditional focus on manufactured goods. The WTO created monitoring and enforcement mechanisms. (p. 265) See also *General Agreement on Tariffs and Trade* (*GATT*) and *Uruguay Round*.

zero-sum games   Situations in which one actor's gain is by definition equal to the other's loss, as opposed to a non-zero-sum game, in which it is possible for both actors to gain (or lose). (p. 69)

Name Index

Subject Index

Note: **Boldface** entries and page numbers indicate key terms. Entries for tables and figures are followed by "*t*" and "*f*", respectively.

Latin America
civilization, 400, 401*f*
economic development in, 426
GDP, 21*t*
inflation rates, 289*t*
Inter-American Court of Human Rights, 241
Marxist countries, 94–95
peace in, 141
as periphery, 399
seat on Security Council, 217–218
U.S. military intervention in, 168
Latvia, 330
Laws of diplomacy, 235–236
League of Nations, **22**
collective security and, 83
UN and, 214, 215
Leaks of information, 126
Lebanon, 221*t*
Legal scholarship, 229
Legislatures
foreign policy process role, 129
military force use and, 129, 134
women in, 104, 110
Legitimacy of international norms, 209
Lender, 434
Lenin's theory of imperialism, 94
Less-developed countries (LDCs), **383**. *See also*
Developing countries
Levels of analysis, 14–16, 15*t*
defined, 14
domestic (*See* Domestic level of analysis)
individual (*See* Individual level of analysis)
systemic (*See* Systemic level of analysis)
Leviathan, 41
Liberal feminism, **99**
difference feminism versus, 105–106
gender differences and, 105–106, 106*f*
postmodern feminism and, 107
realism and, 102–103
Liberal institutionalism, 79–81
Liberalism
bargaining space and, 256
economic, 255–258, 256*f*
foreign direct investment and, 309
as ideology, 256
individual households/firms and, 257
MNCs and, 306–307
shared interests and, 256, 256*f*
Liberal theories
alternatives, 87
collective security, 83–86
cooperative relationships, 79–80
democratic peace, 86–87
foreign policy process and, 120–131
international regimes, 81–83
Kant on peace, 78–79
liberal institutionalism, 79–81
Liberation movements, 406
Liberia, 221*t*, 222, 361
Libya
air defense disablement, 183
ballistic missile capabilities, 192*t*
Mali rebels and, 158
NATO in, 44, 59
no-fly zone in, 215
nuclear weapons, 190
overthrow of Gaddafi, 158
refugees from, 393
state-sponsored terrorism, 187–188
territorial waters, 164–165
Limited Test Ban Treaty, 28
Limited war, **137**–139
Linear long-term change theory of war, 143
Linkage, 96
Lisbon Treaty, **332**–334
Lithuania, 330
Loans, 441

Lobbying, 122–123
Logic of appropriateness, 90
Logic of consequences, 90
London Club, **434**
Long economic waves and war, 143
Long-term power, 44–45
Low-intensity conflicts, 139

M

Maastricht Treaty, **327**–328, 328*f*
Machiavellian, 41
Macroeconomics, 256
MAD (mutually assured destruction), **197**
Malaria, 377
Malaysia, 425
Male archetype, 107
Mali
rebellion, 44, 158
UN peacekeeping, 221, 221*t*
Malnutrition, 385, **388**
Malta, 330
Malthusian, 370
Managed float, **290**, 297
Manhattan Project, 189
Marine Mammal Protection Act, 360
Marines, 178
Market price, 256
Markets
autarky and, 261–262
corruption and, 260
imperfections in, 260
interventions, 290–293
legal framework for, 260–261
political interference in, 260–262
sanctions and, 261, 261*f*
taxation and, 261
Marshall Plan, 27, 278
Marxism, **93**
dependency and, 408
distribution of wealth, 167
international relations and, 123–124
North-South gap and, 410–411
revolutionary movements, 410–411
theory of, 93–95
Masculinity of realism, 100–101
Mass media, 125–126
MCC (Millennium Challenge Corporation), 444
MDGs (Millennium Development Goals), 383
Mediation, **95**
Megaton weapons, 191
Men, 99–101
Mercantilism, **255**
economic conflict and, 166
economics, 258
foreign direct investment and, 309
as ideology, 256
MERCOSUR (Southern Cone Common
Market), 210, 272, 321
Mexico
drug trafficking and, 168
economic development in, 426
oil export, 366, 368
population control, 373
trade agreements, 271
MFN (most-favored nation), **265**
Microcredit, **429**, 429*f*
Microeconomics, 256
Microlending, 429
Middle class, 428
Middle East. *See also specific countries*
alignments, 64–65
civilization, 401*f*, 402
defined, 18
development, 383
GDP, 20*t*
inflation rates, 289*t*
oil export, 366–367

water problems, 369
women in, 391
Middle powers, **51**, 65*f*
Migration, **392**–396
EU integration and, 333
path to citizenship, 414
refugees and, 393–395
remittances and, 395–396, 396*f*
Militarism, **96**
Military aid, 441
Military force
air, 178–180
budget (*See* Military spending)
capabilities, 174*t*
civil military relations, 202–203
configuration of, 201
control of, 201–202
conventional forces, 173–181
coordinating, 180–181
embedded journalists, 126
evolving technologies, 181–185
foreign policy and, 129
great powers, 50–51
interagency tensions, 121
land, 174–177
legislature role in use, 134
leverage, 173*f*
location of, 180*t*
naval, 177–178
short-term power and, 45, 45*f*
space, 180
terrorism and, 185–189
types of, 174
women in, 104–105
Military governments, **203**
Military-industrial complex, **124**
Military industry, 124, 167
Military logistics, 180–181
Military spending
economic health and, 200–201
global, 200
Japan, 126–127
military-industrial complex and, 124
United States, public opinion, 175, 175*f*
Millennium Challenge Corporation (MCC), 444
Millennium Development Goals (MDGs), 383
Minerals, 368–369
Ministries, 11
Mirror image, 116
Misperceptions, **115**
Missiles
ballistic, 180, 191–193, 192*t*
cruise, 193
in Cuban Missile Crisis, 14–15, 27–28, 71
Missile Technology Control Regime, **193**
Mixed economies, **280**
MNCs. *See* Multinational corporations
Monetary policy, **300**, 311
Monopoly, 260
Montreal Protocol, **357**–358
Morality
just-war doctrine and, 237
power and, 45–46, 209–210
realism versus, 41–42
Most-favored nation (MFN), **265**
Mozambique, 222
Multilateral aid, **438**
Multilateralism, 54–55
Multinational corporations (MNCs), **305**
in China, 420
dependency and, 409
financial, 306
foreign direct investment, 307–309
foreign investment, 432–433
globalization and, 38
home government issues, 311–312
host government issues, 309–311

inflation rates, 289t
Internet and, 340
Islamist violence, 159
Marxism in, 93–94
as permanent Security Council member, 217
post Soviet Union, 29–30
ruble devaluation, 294
territorial waters, 165
Ukraine and, 143–144
Ukraine uprising, 30
United States and, 170
Russian Revolution, 94
Rwanda
    genocide, 149
    international war crimes tribunal, 244
    UN peacekeeping, 222
    violence, 30, 32

S

SALT (Strategic Arms Limitation Treaties), 199
Sanctions
    economic, 261, 261f
    as enforcement tool, 230
    military leaders and, 203
    UN Security Council, 196
Satellites, 180
Satisficing, 117
Saudi Arabia
    al Qaeda and, 158
    ballistic missile capabilities, 192t
    competitive advantage, 259
    Iran and, 156
    oil export, 367
    OPEC and, 273
    refusal to accept Security Council seat, 218
Scapegoating, 150
Schengen area, 331
SDGs (Sustainable Development Goals), 383
SDI (Strategic Defense Initiative), 197
SDR (Special Drawing Right), 297
Secession conflicts, 161–162, 161f
Second-strike capabilities, 197
Secular, 151
Security. *See also* International security
    collective, 83–86, 215
Security community, 321
Security dilemma, 48, 58
Security Sector Reform (SSR), 140
Selective perceptions, 115
Selective perceptions in decision makers, 115
Self-determination, 144
Semiperiphery regions, 398, 399
Senegal, 233
Serbia
    Albanians in Kosovo, 146
    Bosnia and, 162
    Britain and, 89
    Croatia and, 162
    ethnic cleansing, 30
    Kosovo, 161, 217
    NATO bombing of, 202
    U.S. bombing, 179
Service sector, 275
    India, 423, 423f
    multinational corporations, 306
    trade issues, 275–276
    Uruguay Round and, 266
Shelter, as basic human need, 387
Shi'ite Muslims, 151, 151f, 154–155
Shining Path, 188
Short-range ballistic missiles (SRBMs), 191–192
Short-term power, 45
Sierra Leone
    human rights, 140
    international war crimes tribunal, 244
    UN peacekeeping, 222
Singapore, 419

Single European Act, 326
Sino-Soviet split, 27
Sleep deprivation, 119
Slovakia
    ballistic missile capabilities, 192t
    in Czechoslovakia breakup, 162
    EU admission, 330
Smoking, 377–378
Smuggling
    drugs, 167–168
    human trafficking, 393f, 396
    nuclear device delivery, 193
    refugees, 393
    in trade, 276
Social media, 340, 341, 420
Social theories, 87–92
Societal level of analysis. *See* Domestic level of
    analysis
Soft power, 43–44
Somalia
    al Shabab fighters, 158
    clan elders, 140
    as failed state, 86
    great powers failure in, 30
    Islamist takeover, 176
    one ethnic group, 147–148
    pirate attacks and, 89, 177, 178f
    UN peacekeeping, 222
    U.S. troops in, 90
SORT (Strategic Offensive Reductions Treaty), 199
South Africa
    economic development, 427
    human rights, 140
    nuclear weapons, 8
    nuclear weapons facility break-in, 195
    transition from colonialism, 410f
South Asia. *See also specific countries*
    defined, 18
    economic development, 417–418
    GDP, 21t
    HIV/AIDS and, 376
Southeast Asia. *See also specific countries*
    defined, 18
Southern Cone Common Market (MERCOSUR),
    210, 272, 321
South (global)
    arms sales, 200–201
    basic human needs and, 384–388
    control of governments, 165
    corruption in, 430–431
    debt in, 433–435, 435t
    defined, 18
    demographic transition and, 372
    economic development, 417
    economic surplus, 94
    education, 384–385
    hunger and, 388–390
    immigration from, 392–393
    income level and growth rate, 384f
    industrialization and, 398
    in international economic regimes, 436–438
    Internet and, 337–338
    Marxism in, 93
    migration and refugees, 392–396
    nonaligned movement, 64
    Paris Climate Agreement, 356–357
    population, 370
    production in, 398f
    proxy wars, 28
    remittances and, 395–396
    rural and urban populations, 390–391
    smoking, 377
    state of, 383–396
    UN and, 216
    undernourishment, 388–389, 388t
    UN programs, 227f
    war in, 387–388

    women in, 391
South Korea
    ballistic missile capabilities, 192t
    economic development, 418–419, 418f
    financial crisis, 304–305
    Korean War, 27
    K-pop, 344
    as NIC, 419
    protectionism, 262
    territorial waters, 165
South Sudan, 221, 221t
Sovereignty, 46
    as central norm, 47f
    individual rights versus, 238–239
    law and, 235–238
    UN Charter principles, 212
Soviet Union. *See also* Cold War
    Afghanistan invasion, 28
    biological weapons program, 194
    Chernobyl, 364–365
    economy successes, 280
    ethnic tensions and, 150
    final collapse of, 29
    glasnost, 29
    human rights, 239
    Hungary uprising and, 27
    nuclear arms race, 29
    peaceful coexistence, 27
    perestroika, 29
    realists and, 92
    Sputnik, 27, 124
    trading bloc, 271
    in World War II, 23–25
Space forces, 180
Spain, 161f, 324, 330
Special Drawing Right (SDR), 297
Species preservation, 359
Spies, 236
Sports, 343f, 344
Spratly Islands, 163–164
Sputnik, 124, 280
SRBMs (short-range ballistic missiles), 191–192
Sri Lanka, 32, 369
SSR (Security Sector Reform), 140
Standard operating procedures, 114
Standing wealth, 299
START (Strategic Arms Reduction Treaty), 199
State actors, 10–13
Statecraft, 65–68
State level of analysis. *See* Domestic level of analysis
State-owned industries, 280, 423
States, 10
    acts of terror, 187
    balance of payments, 298
    bureaucracy, 45
    capabilities of, 46
    disintegration of, 321
    failed, 86
    financial positions, 298–305
    head of, 11
    industry ownership, 280
    information technologies and, 14
    militaries and, 200–203
    military spending, 200–201
    nation, 11
    neutral, 89
    nonmember observer, 13
    population, 12
    power, 38, 44–46
    sovereignty, 11
    territorial integrity, 47, 47f
    UN benefits, 212–213
State-sponsored terrorism, 187–188
Stealth technology, 184
Steel production, 368
Steering in decision making, 113f
Strands of feminist theory, 99

UN Convention of the Law of the Sea (UNCLOS), 164, **362**
UNCTAD (UN Conference on Trade and Development), **227**, 438
Undernourishment, 388–389
UN Development Program (UNDP), 227, **439**
UNDP (UN Development Program), 227, **439**
UN Educational, Scientific, and Cultural Organization (UNESCO), 102, 227–228, 439
UN Environment Program (UNEP), 226, **353**
UNEP (UN Environment Program), 226, **353**
UNESCO (UN Educational, Scientific, and Cultural Organization), 227–228, 439
UN Foundation, 84
UNFPA (UN Population Fund), 439
UN General Assembly, 213
  autonomous agencies, 227–228
  function, 225–226
  gender and, 103
  human rights and, 239
  membership, 225*f*
  UN program coordination, 226–227
UNHCR (Office of the UN High Commissioner for Refugees), 226
UNHCR (UN High Commissioner for Refugees), 446
UN High Commissioner for Refugees (UNHCR), 446
UNICEF (UN Children's Fund)
  bank loans for women's businesses, 391
  displaced children and, 227*f*
  foreign assistance, 439
  health care and, 385–386
  role of, 226
  "Trick or Treat" campaign, 440
UNIDO (UN Industrial Development Organization), 227, 439
Unilateralism, 54–55
UN Industrial Development Organization (UNIDO), 227, 439
UN Institute for Training and Research (UNITAR), 439
Unintended consequences
  individual decision making and, 114–117
  Libyan revolution, 44
  Somali pirates, 177
Union of Banana Exporting Countries (UBEC), 369
Union of South American Nations (UNASUR), 272
Unipolar system. *See* Hegemony
UNITA, 159–160
UNITAR (UN Institute for Training and Research), 439
Unitary actors, 68
United Arab Emirates, 192*t*
United Nations (UN), 212–228
  Arms Trade Treaty, 201
  budget, 84, 213
  gender advisors, 102
  history of, 215–217
  inspections, 194
  nonmember observer states, 13
  observing, 222–224
  powers, 212
  programs, 226–227, 227*f*
  purposes of, 212–213
  in regime survival, 83
  sanctions, 196
  structure of, 213–215, 214*f*
  "three pillars" principle, 216
  United States and, 54–55
  United States public opinion, 85
  universality of membership, 214
  women and, 102
United States
  alignments, 64–65
  ballistic missile capabilities, 192*t*

bombing efforts, 179
Brazil WTO case, 264, 375
carbon dioxide emissions, 356*f*
Christian fundamentalists in, 151
CIA (*See* Central Intelligence Agency)
container security initiative, 193
counterinsurgency campaigns, 176
departments, 11
diplomat prosecution, 235
dollar (*See* U.S. dollar)
drug trafficking and, 168
emissions reduction, 356
environmental rules, 281–282
Federal Reserve, 296
financial position, 301–302, 301*f*
force to combat security threats, 183
foreign aid and politics, 444
foreign assistance, 439, 439*f*
foreign direct investment in, 309
free trade deals, 269
GDP and military expenditures, 50*f*
human rights, 239
human rights report, 242
India agricultural subsidies deal, 268
jurisdiction for international cases, 233
legislature, 129
military officer opinions, 202
national debt, 302
nuclear arms race, 29
peaceful coexistence with China, 74
Pearl Harbor attack, 25
as permanent Security Council member, 217
in pirate eradication, 89
power transition theory and, 52
protectionism, 262–263
public opinion toward NATO, 60
public opinion toward UN, 85
rescue packages, 287
Russia and, 170
subprime mortgage collapse, 280–281, 287
as superpower, 50
trade deficit, 301–302
UN and, 216
UN dues, 84
views of, 49*f*
world order and, 247–248
in World War II, 25
Universal Declaration of Human Rights (UDHR), 239
Universal justification, 245
Universal Postal Union (UPU), 228
UN peacekeeping, 216, 220–224, 221*t*
UN peacemaking, 223
UN Population Fund (UNFPA), 439
UN Relief Works Agency (UNRWA), 226, 393–394
UNRWA (UN Relief Works Agency), 226, 393–394
UN Secretariat, 213, 224–225
UN Secretary General, 213, 224–225
UN Security Council, 213
  China on, 215
  collective security and, 83–84
  divergent interests on, 219*f*
  gender in peacekeeping and reconstruction, 102
  meetings, 218
  nonpermanent members, 217–218
  permanent members, 217
  proposed changes, 219–220
  regional representation on, 218*t*
  resolution vote requirements, 217
  veto power, 5, 8, 215
UN Standby High Readiness Brigade, 223
Urbanization, 390
Uruguay, 232*f*, 338
Uruguay Round, 266

U.S. Agency for International Development (USAID), 441
U.S. dollar
  changes in value of, 293*f*, 297
  China currency pegged to, 292
  euro and, 289
US AID (Agency for International Development), 441
U.S-Japanese Security Treaty, 62–63
Uzbekistan, 365

V

Vaccination programs. *See* Immunization
Venezuela
  currency policy choices, 292
  oil export, 366, 368
  WTO case, 282
Vietnam
  ballistic missile capabilities, 192*t*
  colonialism and, 406
  economic development in, 425
Vietnam syndrome, 116
Vietnam War
  as guerrilla war, 139
  justification of effort, 116
  public opinion and, 126
  U.S. overspending on, 297
  U.S. policy flaw, 28
  war crimes, 247
Violence
  economic conflict and, 166
  Islamic, 154–159
  structural, 97
Virtual currencies
  development, 294, 294*f*
  in global commerce, 342–343, 342*f*
Voice of America (VOA), 339

W

Wahhabism, 157, 158
WAND (Women's Action for Nuclear Disarmament), 102
War. *See also* International conflicts
  battle-related deaths, 77, 78*f*
  changing nature of, 247
  civil, 139
  conflicts of ideas, 143–160
  conflicts of interest, 160–168
  current conflicts, 137, 138*f*
  cyberwar, 183–185
  cycle theories, 143
  domestic level of analysis, 142–143
  drug, 167*f*, 168
  effect of, 4*f*
  electronic, 183–185
  gender in, 101–102
  global South, 387–388
  guerrilla, 139
  hegemonic, 137
  individual level of analysis, 141–142
  just, 237–238
  limited, 137–139
  militarism and, 96
  as morally just, 237
  positive peace and, 96–97
  post-Cold War era, 32–33
  post-modern feminism and, 106
  proxy, 28, 77
  raids, 139
  of secession, 161–162
  shadow of, 96*f*
  systemic level of analysis, 143
  terrorism vs., 187
  theories of causes, 140–143
  total, 137
  types of, 137–140
  waning of, 77–78